W9-DBS-658

340
P27p

91058

DATE DUE			
Dec 18 '74			
Oct 25 '76			
Jan 28 '77			
Nov 13 '77			
Oct 28 79			
Dec 10 '82			
AUG 0 8 1994			

WITHDRAWN

University Textbook Series

Especially Designed for Collateral Reading

HARRY W. JONES
Directing Editor
Professor of Law, Columbia University

ADMIRALTY
Grant Gilmore, Professor of Law, University of Chicago.
Charles L. Black, Jr., Professor of Law, Yale University.

ADMIRALTY AND FEDERALISM
David W. Robertson, Professor of Law, University of Texas.

AGENCY, PRINCIPLES OF
The late Merton L. Ferson, Dean Emeritus, University of Cincinnati College of Law.

COMMERCIAL TRANSACTIONS—Selected Statutes, Fourth Edition
Robert Braucher, Professor of Law, Harvard University.
Arthur E. Sutherland, Jr., Professor of Law, Harvard University.

CONFLICT OF LAWS, Third Edition
The late George W. Stumberg, Professor of Law, University of Texas.

CONFLICT OF LAWS, COMMENTARY ON THE
Russell J. Weintraub, Professor of Law, University of Texas.

CORPORATIONS, Second Edition
Norman D. Lattin, Professor of Law, University of California, Hastings College of the Law.

CRIMINAL LAW, Second Edition
Rollin M. Perkins, Professor of Law, University of California, Hastings College of the Law.

ESTATES IN LAND & FUTURE INTERESTS, PREFACE TO
Thomas F. Bergin, Professor of Law, University of Virginia.
Paul G. Haskell, Professor of Law, Case Western Reserve University.

EVIDENCE: COMMON SENSE AND COMMON LAW
John M. Maguire, Professor of Law, Harvard University.

EVIDENCE, STUDENTS' TEXT ON THE LAW OF
John Henry Wigmore.

JURISPRUDENCE: MEN AND IDEAS OF THE LAW
The late Edwin W. Patterson, Cardozo Professor of Jurisprudence, Columbia University.

LEGAL RESEARCH, FUNDAMENTALS OF, Third Edition, with 1970 Assignments Pamphlet
Ervin H. Pollack, Professor of Law, The Ohio State University.

THE PROFESSION OF LAW
L. Ray Patterson, Professor of Law, Vanderbilt University.
Elliott E. Cheatham, Professor of Law, Vanderbilt University.

PROPERTY
John E. Cribbet, Dean of the Law School, University of Illinois.

THE STUDY OF LAW, INTRODUCTION TO
Bernard C. Gavit, Late Professor of Law, Indiana University.

TORTS
Clarence Morris, Professor of Law, University of Pennsylvania.

TRUSTS, Second Edition
Ralph A. Newman, Professor of Law, University of California, Hastings College of the Law.

THE
PROFESSION OF LAW

By

L. RAY PATTERSON

Professor of Law, Vanderbilt University

ELLIOTT E. CHEATHAM

Research Professor of Law, Vanderbilt University
Charles Evans Hughes Professor Emeritus of Law,
Columbia University

Foreword

WARREN E. BURGER

Chief Justice of the United States

"Lawyers' Standards Are An Integral Part of Law Itself"

Mineola, New York
The Foundation Press, Inc.
1971

CARL A. RUDISILL LIBRARY
LENOIR RHYNE COLLEGE

340
P27p
91058
Dec. 1974

COPYRIGHT © 1971

By

THE FOUNDATION PRESS, INC.

Library of Congress Catalog Card Number: 79-158635

Patterson & Cheatham Prof. of Law UTB

FOREWORD

The American system for the administration of law is structured like a tripod: the process requires three participants, the contending lawyers and the neutral judge or triers. If any of these three supports of the adversary tripod is missing, the process fails. If any "leg" of this tripod is disproportionately weak, the structure as a whole is weakened.

One great weakness, now being corrected, has been the lack of counsel for the large number of people who could not afford the cost of counsel and especially was this true of the accused in criminal cases. The half century of private development of legal aid and public defender programs are a tribute to the legal profession as the trail blazer for the recent developments of the legal right to counsel and of legislative appropriations for legal aid that have done so much to meet this lack. The bar and the courts are now freer to direct their attention to other aspects of the processes of justice. The most recent activities of the organized bar include the ABA criminal justice project to formulate Standards for the Administration of Criminal Justice, the Code of Professional Responsibility, the new Canons of Judicial Ethics, and efforts in many states to improve the methods and the personnel of law administration. A significant and additional set of standards for the function of the trial judge are now being developed by the ABA. A book, searching for the basic responsibilities and standards of the profession, as does this one, comes at a good time. "Lawyers' standards of conduct and performance are," indeed, "an integral part of the law itself."

Our complex governmental structure, with the federal system and the principle of separation of powers, raises difficult questions on "the authoritative sources" of standards. A most important standard is respect for the dignity of the participants and respect for the system; both are essential to the integrity of the process. Chief Justice Hughes and Justice Holmes were agreed that one of the two most important qualities of the lawyer is tact in the performance of his function. Put in another way, manners and decorum, especially in the courtroom, are the indispensable lubricant to the inherently contentious adversary process. At every stage of the administration of justice good manners contribute enormously. As our English friends have shown, the changes in the tone of their courtrooms a century ago from bullying and posturing of both the lawyers and judges, to the now firmly established tradition of courtesy with firmness, improves and speeds up the work of the courts. Civility is not merely a necessity, it is indispensable to the adversary process. It is of utmost importance that the individual dignity of every accused person be respected. If he leaves the court with a realization that he has been accorded fairness, understanding and respect, he will be the better for it, no matter what the outcome.

The whole system of criminal and civil justice needs reexamination at every level. The projects of the great legal associations must be continued and expanded. In criminal justice, especially, there is need to go beyond the conspicuous part of the criminal law process, the trial, to the least seen and most neglected—imprisonment. Over the years I have visited the Scandinavian countries and The Netherlands to observe their correctional methods. We can learn much from them in wisdom as well as compassion in the treatment of prisoners.

"Change places with the judge," was the excellent advice John W. Davis gave to his fellow advocates. "Change places with the prisoner," is a good starting point in considering correctional methods. Let more and more Americans place themselves in the shoes of the prisoners, and come to know the dehumanizing conditions that prevail in most prisons. Let them think in terms of what a man loses when he is confined even under optimum conditions. Then we will sense that loss of liberty alone is a crushing punishment that needs no added burdens to carry its message. Confinement must be only the beginning—the condition—in which we make every effort to improve those who are committed for their crimes.

WARREN E. BURGER

The Supreme Court Building
Washington, D. C.
April, 1971

PREFACE

The American lawyer, with his work and opportunities, and his consequent responsibilities and standards, is the subject of this book.

Law is society's primary method of advancing the common good as well as its principal means of reconciling the competing desires of men. It is a series of processes within the society of which it is a part. Law is not a set of self-sufficient rules, nor is it self-operative. To give it reality there is need for lawyers. They can apply and utilize it in individual matters and they develop it to meet new conditions. The availability in fact of legal services for all is essential to equal justice under law.

The conditions of the lawyer's work are difficult. He is a participant in the adversary system of the administration of law within the larger competitive economic system. He represents private clients in what is essentially the public function of the administration of law. He has competing loyalties to the client, to the opponent, to the unseen persons also affected by his clients' actions, to the court, and to himself. In the United States the lawyer has special complexities as to himself to resolve arising out of our federal system of government, and out of the division of powers among the legislative, the executive, and the judicial branches of government. To add further to the complexities there are changing conditions and rising demands on government and law.

The recurring inquiries in this book are what standards and what organizations will best enable the profession to carry forward its varied responsibilities. Answers in the affirmative are sought. Limitations and restrictions on the lawyer should find their justification as aids to the affirmative.

The line of our discussion is indicated in Chapter I. In the citations preference is given to annotated cases and to decisions of the Supreme Court of the United States: to the former because the annotations open up related topics with which the book in its limited space cannot deal; to the latter because of the increasing importance of federal law as the authoritative source of the standards of the profession.

We are happy to acknowledge our indebtedness to many people: to our collaborators in a casebook on the subject, Dean Samuel D. Thurman and Professor (now President) Ellis L. Phillips, Jr.; to our Vanderbilt colleagues, Dean John W. Wade,

Professor Robert N. Covington, Professor Frank Maloney, and Professor Theodore Smedley; to our colleagues in the subject in other universities, especially Professor John Bradway and Professor Robert Mathews who have often shared their ideas with us; to our students in law schools who have wrestled with us over the problems; to our aid, Mr. Justin P. Wilson of the Tennessee and New York bars who contributed so much toward the end of our work that we greatly regret we did not have his participation earlier; to Messrs. Larry T. Thrailkill and Bland W. Cannon, Jr. who aided us much with their ideas, and with the manuscript.

L. RAY PATTERSON
ELLIOTT E. CHEATHAM

April, 1971

SUMMARY OF CONTENTS

PART V. THE STRUCTURE OF THE PROFESSION

TABLE OF CONTENTS

PART II. THE LAWYER AT WORK

xiii

than victory by defeat as in the trial of a case—are obvious, both for the client and for the administration of law. Standards for compromise will greatly aid the lawyer in using this process more effectively.

The private legal process, the process in which the lawyer counsels and advises and makes private law for his client—and in which he employs compromise to settle disputes—is the least noticed of the legal processes in our society. It may be, however, the most important, for the successful administration of law in the lawyer's office determines in large measure how well the public legal processes function. The lawyer in his office has affirmative standards suited to the private legal process which may not be the same as those applicable to the public legal process in the courtroom.

The legislative process, a superior form of lawmaking, has not received from the legal profession the attention it deserves. But it is a process in which lawyers have a vital and continuing interest, both as lawyers and as citizens. The profession can contribute much to the development of standards for that process, as all legislators are lawmakers, even though they are not all members of the bar.

The administrative process is commonly viewed as a comparatively recent development in law. In fact, of course, the administrative process antedates the common law in England, for the common law courts—King's Bench, Common Pleas, and Exchequer—were in origin administrative agencies of the king. The uses of the modern administrative agencies, however, differ from their antecedents. Today, the administrative process is essentially a process for regulating the use and abuse of power by individuals and groups. The regulation is for the interest of society, rather than to enhance the position of the sovereign. The standards in the administrative process are naturally somewhat different from those in the private legal and the judicial processes.

The lawyer for the government has special roles in the legal profession. His work is similar to that of his private counterpart—both in the courtroom and in the office—but his position gives him broader, if not greater, responsibilities. Consequently, the standards of the private lawyer are not always appropriate for the government lawyer.

The roles of the lawyer in each of the four major legal processes—the judicial, the private, the legislative, and the administrative—all require their own standards, standards which are developed for the particular role as affirmative aids to the lawyer.

Part III. The Judiciary. A look at the work of the American judge reveals how great are his powers. Like his English ances-

tors he continues to create and develop the common law, and beyond his English contemporary he can reshape institutions
through the exercise of constitutional control. In giving meaning to law for individual citizens, "the lowest court" is the highest and most important court. Three standards of every judge
deserve stress—independence, firmness, and consideration toward others. His power to deal with disruptive tactics is now recognized. The appropriate methods for getting the best men on
the bench and keeping them there are a continuing subject of
discussion and of effort, and adequate judicial administration is
now coming in for the attention it long lacked.

Part IV. The Lawyer and the Client. The general nature of
the questions which arise out of the relation of lawyer and client
is ordinarily obvious, though the answer called for by the reconciliation of competing factors in particular cases is often difficult. For the limited purposes of this introductory chapter it is
enough to refer to the detailed table of contents of this Part and
to repeat mention here of only three matters. An American lawyer is free to accept or to reject a case on his own responsibility,
and his responsibility is especially great when he is aiding his
client to work out plans for future relations with others instead
of representing his client as advocate in controversy over a past
occurrence. The increase in specialization of knowledge raises
new questions on the competence of lawyers and on how the needed competence may be obtained for the client by the general
practitioner. There is increasing questioning of the usual practice that each party to litigation bear the fees of his lawyer and
an increasing willingness to have the lawyers' fees come from the
losing adversary or from a fund in court.

Part V. The Structure of the Profession. The structure of
the profession is in rapid change. Four phases are considered:
the constitutent membership; the organizations employed to
make legal services available; the methods of protection of public, private and group interests; and the private and public responsibilities in the lives of the lawyer.

A discussion of constitutent membership begins with admission and discipline. It deals with the requirement of good moral
character, including troubling problems raised by the political
extremists and by political trials. Two fortunate developments
call for special consideration, the increasing breadth of the privilege to practice across state lines in our interstate economy, and
the increasing yet still insufficient participation of the Negro in
the work of the profession. A concluding bow of acknowledgement is owed to those left out and to those ahead.

The forms of organization to be employed in making legal
services available may be looked at from the viewpoint of the

lawyers or the viewpoints of those needing legal services. From the viewpoint of lawyers, it is manifest that the old forms of organization—solo, partnership—have continued, and that there are expanding use of corporate counsel, new approval of professional corporations under appropriate safeguards, and continuing problems as to the publicity appropriate for lawyers. From the clients' viewpoints the major elements are the diversity of clients and the need for a corresponding diversity of methods of organization. Several classes call for special consideration, as the middle classes, the poor, the hated, and personal injury and death claimants. A fact of great significance is the action of the Supreme Court of the United States in striking down professional restrictions which are not in "the public interest," notably as to group practice of law. There is the increasingly urgent question on the position of the expert layman—whether he should be welcomed as a collaborator or as a fellow professional with an expertise of his own, or whether he should be repulsed as a rival and mere intruder.

For the protection of legal interests the availability of counsel is essential. Yet the assurance of the availability of counsel for the individual is not enough. There is need for other methods of protecting individual and social interests. Three sources of interests and also of action are considered: the individual, the group, and the state or the public, each one acting for itself or for one of the others, in the enforcement of legal or social interests. The principal inquiry is who may maintain an action other than the persons in whom the interests are legally vested. The legalistic aspects of the inquiries include such matters as legal personality and standing to sue. The discussion follows the line of the moving parties in the protective proceedings—state proceedings, group action, and individual action. As to each party it illustrates the possible intended beneficiaries—the public, a group, an individual.

The lawyer lives three lives—in private practice, in public responsibilities, and in individual fulfillment. They are not lived at different times, nor are they opposed in their nature. They are lived at the same time and they contribute to one another. Our last chapter submits some comments and questions on each of them for the reader's consideration.

Part I

THE FUNDAMENTALS

Chapter II

LAW AND LAWYERS

SECTION 1. THE ROLES OF LAWYERS

A society organizes itself through government, and government forwards its purposes through law. (A basic purpose is the maintenance of physical order and security. When this is threatened by the revolutionary or by the ruffian there is insistent demand for "law and order.")

A second purpose of law is (the maintenance of legal order and security,)"a government of laws and not of men." This calls for a dependable system of rules of law to apply to the dealings of citizens with one another so each may know the extent of his liabilities and can have protection for his rights. Through the advancement of this purpose the law protects and encourages economic transactions. Nowhere is this purpose clearer than in the United States with its constantly developing economy calling for new yet dependable forms of business arrangements.

A third purpose of law is its use as an (instrument of government in achieving a fuller measure of justice.) It may be justice between man and man. So a Restatement of a private law subject begins with the statement that the validity of its rules "depend . . . upon certain basic assumptions in regard to what is required by justice in the various situations." [1] It may be justice through protection against government, to which our bill of rights is primarily directed. It may be justice through the affirmative action of government, as protective measures for consumers, social security and the aids given to disadvantaged groups.

Law and Order and Justice are subjects of never ending discussion. They are not opposed ideas, as some controversialists would make it appear. They are three interrelated elements of a

---

1. Restatement of Restitution. Introductory Note, Topic 1 at 11 (1937).

6

functioning society. Law and Order and Justice are associated as Means and Conditions and Ends.

Law is organized society's principal means to both order and justice.

Order is an essential condition of justice. In olden books a firm ruler coming after a period of disorders would be praised, "He brought peace to the land;" he brought order and security against marauders.[2]

Justice is the end sought. Justice is also a means. (The use of law for the advancement of justice, with a resultant felt sense of justice by the people, is the strongest support of order under law.[3]) "Equal Justice Under Law" is the ideal inscribed over the building of the Supreme Court of the United States.

The Preamble to the Constitution shows well the interrelationships of law and order and justice. The means which the Constitution provides are "a more perfect union," one more powerful than the weak and inadequate forms of organization which preceded it.

The necessary conditions are made possible through the powers given the central government to "insure domestic tranquillity, provide for the common defense," that is to insure order at home and defense against dangers from abroad.

The ends envisaged include justice between individuals and also for society as a whole: "[to] establish justice, promote the general welfare." They include even more in the final passage of the Preamble, "[to] secure the blessings of Liberty." In the settings of the period, with immediate insistence on an accompanying Bill of Rights, it meant liberty against government with the individual's freedom to live his own life and with assurance of what Justice Brandeis was to characterize, as the most important of all rights, "the right to be left alone."

(The decline of other agencies of social control, as the church and the family, has placed an increasing burden on the law.) Consequent questions over the role which the law or public institutions may and should assume because of altered conditions are illustrated by controversies on church-state relations and by the continuing debate on the role of the criminal law.

Law has different aspects. In one aspect it is a body of precepts ranging from vague ideals to precise directives. The complex precepts receive most of our consideration in practice and

2. Cf. "And I will give peace to the land and ye shall lie down and none shall make you afraid . . . neither shall the sword go through the land." Leviticus 26:6.

3. "[T]he final answer to the problem of law and order lies in the still larger concepts of justice and opportunity." Bundy, Address, 47 F.R.D. 465 (1968).

even in law school. A system of precepts is not enough, for law is not self-applying or self-developing.

Law is most usefully seen as a social process. Like all processes it has its participants with their ends and conditions and means. In this process the lawyer is the principal participant. (Society, government, law, lawyers are a natural sequence.) The lawyer is the medium through which the law is given meaning in the individual case. He applies the law by advising clients on what they may and may not do, or else by his aid as advocate in having the court apply the law to the case before it. He utilizes the law by counseling and forming and drafting for his client in the large areas in which the law leaves to individuals the power to shape their legal relations with one another.

This most influential participant in the application and utilization of the law is usually not an official retained and paid by the state. He is privately retained and owes a special duty of loyalty to his clients, and he makes his living through the fees he earns. (Mr. Justice Harlan has pointed out three aspects of the lawyer's work and loyalties: [4]

> "It is no less true than trite that lawyers must operate in a three-fold capacity, as self-employed businessmen as it were, as trusted agents of their clients, and as assistants to the court in search of a just solution to disputes.")

The three-fold capacity to which Mr. Justice Harlan referred can be seen as three interlocking sets of objectives for the lawyer. They are his individual ambitions, his professional functions, and his social roles. Individual ambitions begin with the immediately personal purpose of making a good living for his family and himself through his earnings in practice. They certainly extend to the desire to live a fully rounded life and, despite the buffets of fate, to be true to himself and his own standards. The individual ambitions look outward beyond merely personal matters to effectiveness in his chosen work as an attorney and to a wider social contribution through leadership, whether in the administration of law or in public or community life.

The professional functions comprehend the functions the lawyer performs for his clients. They can be summed up as individualization of the law. The vivid form is advocacy of the client's case before a tribunal which will apply the law to the facts. Its more usual form is the utilization of the law through counseling and negotiating and then planning and drafting as an "architect of social relation."

Beyond fulfilling his individual ambitions and his professional functions, the lawyer plays an important social role. For the

---

4.   Cohen v. Hurley, 366 U.S. 117, 124 (1961).

American lawyer this role includes public leadership in the administration of the law and in still larger matters. One such matter is the reorganization of our systems of government. Our federal constitution gives as its first purpose "to form a more perfect union." (Lawyers had the major share in the shaping of a system adequate and workable for its time of the 1780's. (They have the opportunity to contribute much to the formation of new forms of government)needed and adequate under the marvelously different conditions now two centuries later. (Lawyers had the greatest share in the shaping of our bill of rights and its English predecessors) They are still indispensable in giving it meaning for the individual threatened or rejected by government.)

For the surer attainment of his objectives the lawyer will recognize that, as every man, he has the defects of his qualities. He is accustomed in practice to deal with the single case and to look to legal precedent and the past for guidance. In these changing times he needs much more. Chief Justice Stone before he went on the bench urged a recognition of "the energizing forces which are producing the technical doctrines of the law." [5] A leader of the corporate bar was scarcely less insistent on the recognition of these forces in his work for his client: [6]

> ("Today the American lawyer deals with the problems of his business clients on a much broader basis, considers substance as more important than form and attempts to relate legal problems to their political, economic and social implications.")

SECTION 2. LAWYERS IN THE UNITED STATES

Lawyers in this country will continue to give aid in the old and continuing problems of human relations. They must deal also with new social problems created by science and technology, as urbanization within the nation, the new closeness of the nations to one another, and the rising expectations of classes. American lawyers have their own very special opportunities.

The political structure of our federal nation makes our legal system correspondingly complex. This political and legal structure is superimposed upon an economy national in character.

---

5. Stone, The Future of Legal Education, 10 A.B.A.J. 233, 234 (1924).

6. Swaine, Impact of Big Business on the Profession: An Answer to Critics of the Modern Bar, 35 A.B. A.J. 89, 171 (1949).

The question, what is the American law on a question, can be answered only by "fifty tongues speaking at once." [1]   The adjustment of the checkerboard legal system to the nationwide economic system and international needs is a continuing problem for American lawyers.

Our political system from the beginning has been "a legal polity" with many political questions given a legal form.   The demands made by the colonists before the Revolution were couched in legal terms, as by James Otis with his denunciation of writs of assistance.   The Declaration of Independence, usually quoted for its ethical and political passages, is in greater part an indictment of King George III for violation of the legal rights of his subjects.   Today the vague words in the Constitution, as "due process of law" and "equal protection of the laws," are a continuing source of power in the courts.   In England it took years of agitation and The Reform Bill to abolish the rotten boroughs. In our country the county unit system in Georgia, the township system in Vermont and unequal political representation throughout the nation were swept away by the implications of a single court decision.[2]   Protection of the individual against government is given by the courts.   The regulation of business, too, is largely determined by the courts in the interpretation of vaguely worded statutes, as the Sherman Act.

Our economic system is complex and malleable.   It delegates to individuals the largest share in determining their mutual relations under law as by contract.   There is need for an adviser to shape the relation to meet the needs in the particular situation and to make the relations firm and dependable under law.   Inventiveness is stimulated by the American lawyer's acceptance of his responsibility to develop needed legal institutions, "creative conformity" as a critic said.[3]   His inventiveness is favored by the social and legal attitude.   In a review by "a [former] German law teacher of a French book dealing with the peculiarly Anglo-American legal concept of trust," the reviewer saw difficulties in the way of the proposal in that book that Continental countries take over and employ the legal instrument of the trust with all its flexibility.[4]

> "Anglo-American countries are the classical territories of the greatest liberty of individuals in shaping their legal relations .   .   .   .   Continental systems on the other hand may be more rigid; .   .   .   but, they are relatively simpler, clearer, and less complicated."

1. J. Wigmore, Treatise on Evidence, Vol. I. xv (3d ed. 1940).

2. Baker v. Carr, 369 U.S. 186 (1962).

3. E. Smigel, The Wall Street Lawyer 344 (1964).

4. Rheinstein, Book Review, 43 Yale L.Rev. 1049, 1052–53 (1934).

In the administration of law in courts under the adversary system the American lawyer is entrusted with exceptional powers.[5] In no other nation does the representative of the public, the judge, have so limited a role and the partisan representatives, the lawyers, so dominant a part.

Beyond the representation of clients there are other responsibilities that the American lawyer continues to carry. He aids in forming and guiding public opinion and thus in shaping the actions and institutions of government. In largest measure he has manned the higher levels of the political institutions he has shaped. Outside government among a people who have achieved so much through private initiative, the lawyer still develops and guides innumerable institutions that in the fullest sense are public though not political in government, as, "a private university in the public service." Through their independence and initiative these institutions, private in government but public and charitable in purpose and function, have provided much of the leadership for the nation in education, the arts and works of benevolence.

The lawyers in the United States will naturally give their best thought to what their exceptional powers and responsibilities call for as to their own profession and the standards of its members. A purpose of this book is to aid in this task.

5. A perceptive book on the profession begins with a view of the work of lawyers and their skills and functions. M. Mayer, The Lawyers (1967).

Chapter III

HISTORY AND FOREGROUND

SECTION 1. INTRODUCTION

We are no less a part of history—"contemporary history,"—than our predecessors. The profession of law was shaped by the set of forces which bore upon it in the past. It is being reshaped today by a combination of forces which are different in degree from those which went before. It is a commonplace that we live in swiftly moving times. The lawyer who would understand his profession and advise his clients wisely needs must take these forces into account.

The breadth of change is indicated by the attitude of two of our presidents who were heads of the same political party toward the breadth of the appropriate activities of government.

"Jefferson carried further than any other person set in an equally responsible place has ever done," wrote Lord Bryce, "in his faith that government is either needless or an evil, and that with enough liberty, everything would go well." [1]

"[I]t is essential that those who enter into a profession, military or civilian," said Professor Franklin D. Roosevelt, in an address to the United States Military Academy, "must eternally keep before their eyes the practical relationship of their own profession to the rights, the hopes and the needs of the whole body of citizens who make up the nation. One of the most difficult tasks of government today is to avoid the aggrandizement of any one group and to keep the main objective of the general good clear and unimpaired." [2]

SECTION 2. THE ENGLISH BACKGROUND

The English legal profession created, defended and developed the common law. Parliament intervened infrequently, and the few statutes were absorbed into the body of the law made by lawyers. The monarch contributed little. So masterful a ruler as

1. J. Bryce, The American Commonwealth, ch. LIII (3rd ed. 1896).   2. N. Y. Times, June 13, 1935, at 15.

12

Cromwell, confessing defeat in his effort to achieve a reform against the opposition of the lawyers, said: "The sons of Zeruiah are too hard for us." Unlike the situation in the continental nations the universities had no share in shaping the law of their country. It was not until 1753 that the first lectures on English law were given in a university, by Sir William Blackstone, and it was over a century later that his example was followed seriously. It is the legal profession, with its organization and its monopoly of legal work which has "mainly determined the mode and character of the development of the common law." [1]

A striking idea given by a reading of the history of the English profession is the recurrence in changing forms of the conflict of order and stability with justice and change. At the beginning of the common law this conflict appears. As Holdsworth says: [2]

> "The thirteenth century had reaped the benefits of a fixed and orderly system of law. The fourteenth and fifteenth centuries paid the penalty. . . . The law may hinder or it may guide the political and social development of the state; it cannot altogether stop it. The want of flexibility in the law prevented a free development of legal doctrine to correspond with changing needs and ideas."

The conflict reappears in the age of reform in the nineteenth century. It has appeared yet again in our time when the view that the holdings of the House of Lords are beyond overruling, has been supplanted by a quiet statement that the House of Lords, too, can respond to new conditions by new decisions. [3]

A most conspicuous characteristic of the English profession is its division into the two branches, barristers and solicitors. [4] The

---

1. II W. Holdsworth, History of English Law (3rd ed. 1923) 484. The most rewarding history of the legal profession is to be found by piecing together passages from different volumes of Holdsworth, History of English Law, which puts the development of the profession in the political and social settings of the times. See especially Vol. II, 311–319, 484–597, and Vol. III, 640–654 (3d ed. 1923); Vol. VI, ch. VIII (1927); Vol. XII, 3–101 (1938); Vol. XV, 223–56 (Goodhart & Hanbury ed. 1965). The account is made vivid at places by a description of the work of leading members of the profession. An outline of the beginnings of the profession is in F. Maitland & F. Montague, A Sketch of English Legal History 92–99, 110–114 (1915). A critical

study directed to the past two centuries is B. Abel-Smith & R. Stevens, Lawyers and the Courts: A Sociological Study of the English Legal System, 1750–1965 (1967).

2. II Holdsworth, supra note 1, at 591–592.

3. Practice Statement (Judicial Precedent) [1966] 1 W.L.R. 1234. See Leach, Revisionism in the House of Lords: The Bastion of Rigid Stare Decisis Falls, 80 Harv.L.Rev. 797 (1967).

4. A careful evaluation of "a split profession" is made in Q. Johnston & D. Hopson, Lawyers and Their Work ch. 11 (1967) with the conclusion that "the fostering of better legal service through specialization

separation makes it necessary for every litigant in a major court to employ two lawyers, a solicitor and a barrister. The client confers first with the solicitor, the solicitor speaks to the barrister, and only the barrister to the court, a situation suggestive of the bit of doggerel on the Lowells and the Cabots. The increased expense doubles the deterrence to litigation by either claimant or defendant. The deterrence to litigation is redoubled by the system of "costs." The losing party pays the expenses of the winner including the fees of the two lawyers on each side.

"Comprehensive orality" is a striking feature of proceedings in an English court, whether original or appellate. "The whole of the case, from beginning to end, is conducted by word of mouth." [5] Printed argument is lacking even in the appellate courts.

The government of one part of the profession, the barristers, goes back in origin to the uncertainties of medieval times. To be a barrister it is essential to become a member of one of the four inns of court which by custom enjoy this privilege for their members—Lincoln's Inn, Gray's Inn, Middle Temple, Inner Temple. The four inns have joined through the General Council of the Bar in stating rules of professional conduct and in providing educational opportunities for the aspirant. The judges of the principal courts who have shaped the common law are all drawn from the ranks of the barristers.

The solicitors have had a less conspicuous history. They have risen in prestige as the importance of office work has increased. They do most of this work and they outnumber the barristers ten to one. Their voluntary organization, the Law Society, has been entrusted by Parliament with many powers as to the profession. One matter is money accounts. The solicitor is, of course, to hold his clients monies separate and to keep adequate books of account. In addition, he must produce an annual certificate by an approved accountant that the requirements have been observed. Another matter administered by the Law Society is the largely state-financed plan of legal aid which now forms a great part of the lawyers' work.[6]

is . . . the strongest rationale for the English solicitor-barrister division."

5. R. Megarry, Lawyer and Litgant in England 167 (1962). " '[T]he bound and rebound of ideas and arguments between the Bench and the Bar' [is] a practice (or should I say a foible) of judges, which I had believed to be pardonable and hoped to be not without its uses." The King v. The Local Government Board, [1914] 1 K.B. 160, 193 (Hamilton, L. J., dissenting).

6. The standards of the two branches are stated in books by the secretaries of the two principal professional bodies. W. Boulton, A Guide to Conduct and Etiquette at the Bar of England and Wales (4th ed. 1965); T. Lund, A Guide to the Professional Conduct and Etiquette of Solicitors (1960).

When an American lawyer looks to the profession in England, he almost always thinks of the barrister rather than the solicitor. This may be due to the more glamorous role of the barrister. It may be due, too, to the fact that the English judges whose opinions he reads are all drawn from the barristers and not from the solicitors. Yet it is the solicitor who deserves the greater attention, for in his work and even in his organization he is closer to the American lawyer than is the barrister.

The barrister is in the enviable position of being chosen by another lawyer, the solicitor, and not by the lay client. It is the solicitor who deals with and is chosen by the layman and on him rests the decision whether to accept an offered case. Again, it is the solicitor who does the office work as client guide and caretaker, and in litigated matters it is he who does most of the preparatory work as gathering the evidence. In lower courts he may appear as advocate. In the matter of professional organization, The Law Society, rather than the Inns of Court, seem closer to the bar associations in the United States. Dean Pound put it succinctly, "The attorney [solicitor] rather than the barrister was the model for the organization of the profession in America." [7]

SECTION 3. AMERICAN DEVELOPMENTS

The legal profession in the United States had the opportunity to develop a system of law suited to new conditions as the English profession had done for its nation. The reception acts of the states provided that the English common law (as of some stated date, e. g., 1607, 1775, 1776) should be followed in so far as it was suited to American conditions. A negative effect of the acts was the rejection of the parts of English law not suited to the new conditions. An affirmative effect of even greater importance was that in so far as English common law was not suited, it should be replaced by a common law made by the American courts. It was implicit in the acts that the English system taken over was not merely a set of rules but the operative common law system. Under that system the American courts, as the English courts before them, could develop a common law suited to new conditions.

The social and economic life of the new country was different from that of the long settled island. The conditions before and after independence were to be wholly different, too, for unfore-

---

7. R. Pound, The Lawyer—From Antiquity to Modern Times 97 (1953).

seeable reasons affecting both peoples alike. The year 1776 saw something even more important than the Declaration of Independence. It was the year of the invention of the first practicable steam engine which, furnishing as it did a wholly new source of energy, was the essential basis of the world wide Industrial Revolution. It saw also the publication of Adam Smith's Wealth of Nations with its reasoned justification of the freedom of the businessman in his activities.

Democracy even in its then limited form gave new character and spirit to government. Federalism spread powers of government widely. The written constitutions gave a seemingly firm base for the transformation of political and even social problems into legal questions. But even the wisest and strongest of our leaders apparently did not comprehend the poison of slavery and failed to deal effectively with it.

The materials which could be drawn on in shaping American law were varied. English law was the most obvious, and it was drawn on in our earliest state papers. The Declaration of Independence in its indictment of George III and also our Bill of Rights used the ideas and even the language of the English Bill of Rights of a century earlier. In private law the reception acts as stated, authorized the use of the appropriate parts of the English common law.

Legal sources beyond the common law were availed of, as illustrated by the two most important private law makers of the formative years, Kent and Story. Influential judges as they were, they may well have contributed more to the law through their treatises than through their opinions, and they were alike in breadth of view.[1] Kent began his Commentaries with "The Law of Nations," a subject soon unfortunately to lose its place with lawyers for a hundred years, and he described the civil law under "The Various Sources of the Municipal Law of the Several States." Story in the preface to the first of his extraordinary series of treatises, on the Law of Bailments, contrasted the indifference of the English common law toward foreign jurisprudence with Chancellor Kent's action in incorporating some of the best principles of the foreign law into our own. He announced his own purpose to give a systematic view of the common law "and to illustrate it by, and throughout to compare it with the civil law, and the modern jurisprudence of some of the principal nations of continental Europe." [2]

---

1. Kent's Commentaries on American Law, the first volume of which was published in 1826, went through 14 editions. Story wrote treatises on Conflict of Laws, Constitution of the United States, Equity Jurisprudence, Equity Pleadings, Agency, Bailments, Bills of Exchange, Partnership and Promissory Notes.

2. J. Story, Commentaries on the Law of Bailments (1832).

The two men were alike, too, in their attitude toward some branches of private law as being international rather than merely municipal law. In beginning Part V of his Commentaries, on "Personal Property," Kent refers to maritime law as "not the law of a particular country, but the general law of nations," supporting his statement by passages from Cicero and Lord Mansfield. Story used the same passages in Swift v. Tyson,[3] which was the foundation of a misnamed "federal common law" lasting for nearly a century.

"Laws" beyond lawyers' law under the common and the civil law systems were recognized sources. "The Laws of Nature and of Nature's God" had been invoked in the first paragraph of the Declaration of Independence, and one method of giving content to these "Laws" was shown at the beginning of the second paragraph, "We hold these truths to be self-evident." The law maker's conception of natural law, often made seeming legalistic by the word "justice," has been an inexhaustible source of law.

The process of formation of an American law out of the varied sources was rapid. Exactly half a century after the beginning of the nation, the "Commentaries on American Law" by Kent were published. With the sources drawn on so varied Justice Jackson could say rightly:[4]

> "It is not without significance that the most constructive was also the least intellectually isolationist period of our legal history."

"The Golden Age of American Law", it has been called.[5]

The changing types of law practice, as Professor Willard Hurst wrote, have closely reflected "the main concerns of the society as of any given time."[6] They moved on from land and commerce to industry and finance. A great increase in personal injury work has been accompanied by a decline in criminal law work for the leaders of the bar. The subjects of practice relating to the government have changed from government bounty to government regulation to the government's own law work. "The most basic change in the nature of lawyers' professional work was the shift in emphasis from advocacy to counseling." Since 1950 there have been continuing social and political changes. They include the increase in administrative regulation at the state and

---

3. 41 U.S. 1 (1842).

4. Jackson, The Genesis of an American Legal Profession: A Review of 150 Years of Change, 38 A.B.A.J. 547, 616 (1952).

5. C. Haar, The Golden Age of American Law (1965).

6. J. Hurst, The Growth of American Law—The Law Makers 295–305 (1950). A thoughtful discussion of the basic views of "the foremost historian of American law," is D. Flaherty, "An Approach to American History: Willard Hurst as Legal Historian" 14 Am.J.Leg.Hist., 222 (1970).

federal level, the recognition of the need for protection and improvement of our physical environment, the rising demands of the disadvantaged, the shrinkage of the continent by aviation which outmatches the earlier shrinkage by rail, the great increase in international business and the shrinkage of the oceans from a month or a week of sailing time to twenty minutes by rocket.

In the late 1900's the profession again has an opportunity not unlike that of the golden age. There are no explicit reception acts. There are new conditions, however, which in their differences from the old parallel the differences between the old and the new countries in the late 1700's. To meet the demands the profession has at hand agencies for the needed development of law.

The legislature with its system of inquiry and study through committees, the executive with the responsibilities implicit under the principle of separation of powers, the administrative commissions with the wide powers entrusted to them in making as well as enforcing the law—all of these are agencies cognizant of their law-making powers and ready to exercise them. The courts, with which the profession has been accustomed to identify itself, have a renewed conception of their power and duty, not merely to find law in the books and apply it as written, but within limits to make law for new conditions. To paraphrase the language of the reception acts, the law makers are to develop a law suited to American conditions of their time. A method which reflects the new conception of the courts' responsibility is prospective overruling of precedents, with the element of stability preserved by the continued application of the old rule in the particular case but with the statement of a new law for future conditions.[7]

Society has been characterized as a moving equilibrium with conditions and demands constantly changing. Law makes its best contribution by continuously reexamining and improving its methods.[8] In this way it can maintain and advance the values entrusted to it throughout social changes. It is through lawyers that law is developed as well as applied and used. To perform this function well, it is useful to perceive the forces which bear on their work and on them.[9]

7. Great No. Ry. v. Sunburst Oil & Ref. Co., 287 U.S. 358 (1932). For a discussion of the problem, see Levy, Realist Jurisprudence and Prospective Overruling, 109 U.Pa.L. Rev. 1 (1960).

8. J. Gardner, Self-Renewal (1964).

9. John Honnold, The Life of the Law (1964) is a perceptive anthology which treats of the English heritage, of law in the new world, of law in other countries, and begins and ends with insights of Justice Holmes. Anton Chroust, The Rise of the Legal Profession in America, has described the early history in detail.

SECTION 4.   FORCES WHICH WILL CONTINUE
TO SHAPE THE PROFESSION

The law and the profession of law are not self-contained. They are instruments of the society of which they are a part. The American profession applied to itself the admonition of the reception acts and, realizing that the divided English system was not suited to American conditions, did not accept the division between barristers and solicitors. It has changed greatly in its work and structure. Beginning with the individual practitioner and moving through the small partnership it has gone on to such varied methods of providing legal services as are considered in Chapter XVII, infra pp. 311 ff.

Throughout these changes the profession has remained primarily conservative in outlook. Stability is one of the needs of a society, and the law contributes much to it. The common law system of precedent is a method of maintaining stability, as it enables a lawyer to plan with assurance for his client. The successful lawyer is successful under the economic and social system of which he is a part, and changes in the system are naturally looked on askance as threatening the position he has attained. Unlike the situation of the physician, new scientific developments have rarely enabled him to serve better the person he represents, and changes in the law call for additional study to acquaint himself with them without any aid to his professional work.

It takes effort to overcome natural yet excessive conservatism. The effort is made, and made successfully, by good lawyers in representing their clients. In paying tribute to a lawyer friend Judge Cardozo called him "a creative agent" in shaping and directing the institutions of the law itself.[1]

Old standards have been set aside and new standards developed when interests of the clients or of the profession demand modification. One illustration is approval of the system of counsel retained by liability insurance companies to represent the insured despite the danger of conflict of interests and the facts of the lay intermediary and solicitation of clients. Another illustration is the recent approval, under safeguards, of the corporation to practice law.

"To-day we study the day before yesterday," wrote the most gifted of English legal historians, "in order that yesterday may

---

1. Cardozo, Memorial Address on John G. Milburn, 1931 Yearbook, N.Y.C.B.A. 440.

not paralyze to-day, and to-day may not paralyze to-morrow." [1.5] Perspective is the title of the first chapter of Professor Willard Hurst's splendid book, "The Growth of American Law: The Law Makers." Now there is unexampled need for change.[2] Forces new in magnitude are changing our society and so the law and the profession. It is not easy to distinguish these forces from one another as they overlap and interact. It is possible to mention several sets of factors and to comment briefly on each of them: intellectual, economic and social, ethical, political, and leadership. Intertwined with them in their effect on the profession are some special qualities of American life and the self-image of the profession.

Intellectual. The physical scientists have been the great revolutionaries. With their aides, the inventors and the engineers, they have enabled man to transform his environment. One illustration is the source of energy. The muscle of man and beast was the prime source of energy at the time of the founding of this nation. In the same year, 1776, there came to achievement the work of a man whom Justice Frankfurter called the greatest law reformer, James Watt, with his invention of the steam engine. Molecular power released in the combustion of fossil fuels and utilized through the steam engine or the internal combustion motor is the basis of the Industrial Revolution with its social and legal changes. An immensely greater source of power, nuclear power from the fission and fusion of the atom, is now at hand with the changes it will bring: muscular, molecular, nuclear power. The biological scientists, to mention another group, have lengthened human life and put increased burden on the food supply. Through the conception of evolution they have altered man's view of his place in the universe and so have laid on law much of the burden of social control formerly borne by religion and custom. The experts in political science, economics, sociology, social psychology, and psychiatry fields close to the lawyer's work may be the lawyer's collaborators or rivals.

The possession of power which intellect creates does not assure its wise use. Our nation is a victim of a prolonged misapplication of our immense technological knowledge, as the environmental revelations of the 1960's made clear. The knowledge has been directed to increased production of physical goods with scant thought to the hazards and injuries to the environment. Now it is imperative that broader considerations be taken into account, with law and lawyers helping to develop appropriate directives and incentives.

1.5 F. Maitland, A Survey of the Century, in Collected Papers (H. Fisher, ed., 1911) v. III, 432, 439.

2. See J. Hurst, The Growth of American Law: The Law Makers (1950).

Economic and Social. Our country and our profession began with little business and small communities. Little business, rarely disturbed by government, had only occasional need for the services of the lawyer. The Industrial Revolution made possible by the new source of power created big business, big labor, and big cities. Big government brought needed controls through law. New means and speed of transportation brought sister states and even nations across the oceans closer in travel time than neighboring county seats had formerly been, with international relations adding a new dimension to the work of the lawyer. New forms of publicity have made vivid for the shanty or ghetto dweller the ease and opulence of others in the suburbs or across the oceans and have pushed upward the rising expectations of peoples.

Ethical. "The man-made factor—technology" is a fundamental factor, yet "men and their thoughts," as Professor Willard Hurst has said, are the moving causes of changes in the law. The sense of justice or as it has been better put "the sense of injustice" is the immediate cause of change. "There ought to be a law" is the homily preliminary to every legal change. "[C]ertain basic assumptions in regard to what is required by justice in the various situations," is the basis of its rules avowed by a Restatement of the American Law Institute.[3] It is so within the profession itself. It is now accepted that every man should have a lawyer when needed. New forms of law administration are created and new forms of legal services are developed to make this possible.

Political. Ethical demands are given effective legal expression through political methods. It is part of the lawyer's work to develop through law new forms of social organization matching the needs of the constantly changing social and economic conditions which the sciences and their related technologies create. One set of ethical-political principles calls for special mention. It concerns the relation of the citizen to the state, of the individual to the community. Three principles are notable:

    (1) the protection of the individual *against* the state;

    (2) the protection of the individual *through* the state;

    (3) the duty of the individual to the state.

The first principle is illustrated by the English bill of rights of the late 1600's, by the Declaration of Independence, and especially by the bills of rights in the Constitutions in this country. The courts and the lawyers have done much to make these rights effective.[4]

3. Restatement of Restitution, Introductory Note, at 11 (1937).

4. The influential French Declaration of the Rights of Man and the Citizen of 1789 is set out and suc-

The growth of big business and the corresponding decline of self-sufficiency of the individual whether on the farm or in industry brought demands for protection of the individual *through* action by the government. Social security is an obvious illustration. These rights are referred to in the greatest of international documents, the United Nations charter; they are given fuller statement in the Universal Declaration of Human Rights of 1948; and they are set out in detailed form in two proposed covenants of 1966, the International Covenant on Civil and Political Rights, and the International Covenant on Economic, Social and Cultural Rights.

The duty of the individual to the state is mentioned in some of these international documents.

The Constitution (Fundamental Law) of the Union of Soviet Socialist Republics, in Chapter X entitled "Fundamental Rights and Duties of Citizen," is explicit in asserting all three of the principles. It affirms the protection of the citizen against organs of the state, whatever may be the fault in execution because of the inadequate independence and standards of the courts as well as of the bar. The Constitution stresses the duties, too, of the citizen.[5]

An American Bar Association Section through its name indicates its work extends to the implementation of all three principles, the Section on Individual Rights and Responsibilities.[6]

Leadership. Social forces are amorphous. They are organized and given direction and expression by leaders. It has been so with our profession in its work. Some names come at once to mind: John Marshall; David Dudley Field; Evarts who led the formation of an effective local bar association at the time of the Tweed scandals; Simeon Baldwin, the moving figure in the organization of the American Bar Association; Christopher Columbus Langdell; Louis D. Brandeis; Charles Evans Hughes. Beyond the profession and its own work lawyers have given leadership to this nation throughout its history. Every reader will lengthen and especially broaden the list in his own way to include men beyond the law, say Darwin, Marx, Freud.

cinctly discussed in 19 Encyclopaedia Britannica 332 (1968). A fuller discussion by Crane Brinton of the origins of the Declaration and its philosophical basis ("[P]olitics without ethics is inconceivable") is in III Encyclopaedia of the Social Sciences 49 (1931).

5. "It is the duty of every citizen . . . to observe the laws, to maintain labour discipline . . . (Art. 130).

"Military service in the Armed Forces of the U.S.S.R. is the honourable duty of citizens of the U.S.S.R. (Art. 132)".

6. The name given to the first volume of the Section's annual publication, Human Rights, appears to exclude from treatment the Section's work directed to Responsibilities.

In a consideration of what these forces call for as to the profession and its work it is useful to keep in mind some characteristics of our society. The ready application of the scientist's knowledge to meet human needs is an American characteristic. This use of knowledge to meet human needs is the source of the continuing research and development by large corporations. The "art of organization" through the mobilization of intelligence and talent, employed to advance not only invention and development but production and marketing, was found by a European observer to lie at the base of American economic achievements.[7] Other characteristics are closely related to one another. Our society is pluralistic, not monolithic. It is egalitarian, not hierarchical. It is mobile, not static. The wise coordination of our diverse society is a continuing task of our law and the lawyer.

"Foresight" is the quality which a great philosopher says is especially needed in these days, with the forces producing change at an unprecedented and accelerating rate.[8] The perception and forecast of changes are important for the lawyer in advising his client on long term matters. They are important no less in helping him to shape both the law and the structure of the profession. The importance of perception and forecast is affected by the duration of the transaction the lawyer is helping to shape. It may be a mere deed which is operative at once. It may be a will with trusts lasting lives in being and twenty one years. It may be an organization of a business which will continue indefinitely. It may be a new form of regional or international government.

The lawyer's conception of his medium and profession and of his own work will do much to determine the nature of his efforts. He might see the law as a set of rules to be found in the books, or else as a social process with ideals and standards, and principles maintained and developed in aid of a changing society.[9] He might view his profession as a guild with inherited rights and privileges; or he may see it as a group who under very difficult

7. J. Servan-Schreiber, The American Challenge (1968).

8. A. Whitehead, Adventures of Ideas, ch. 6 (1933). "There have been two great creative epochs in the history of our civilization: that of ancient Greece and that of today." J. Shotwell, The History of History 246 (1939).

9. Three justices of the Supreme Court of the United States—one living, one dead, one retired—join in urging thoughtful change. In a review of Mr. Justice Douglas's book, Points of Rebellion, Mr. Justice Clark wrote: "Its three chapters put all of dirty linen on the line: the 'whetted appetites' of the poor, the domestic issues that have aroused our people as never before, and the leveling effects of government invasions of privacy. . . . As Justice Holmes used to point out, 'Behind every scheme to make the world over, lies the question, what kind of world do you want?' I believe most of us want a world of equality and peace in truth, not rhetoric." Clark, Book Review, 83 Harv.L.Rev. 1931 (1970).

and rapidly changing conditions have the opportunity to help administer and develop the law. He might view himself and his fellows as mere agents of their clients obeying their directives; or he may see himself and his colleagues as professional men who serve their clients well when they help them to see their true interests and to be their best selves.

> "Mankind is now in one of its rare moods of shifting its outlook. The mere compulsion of tradition has lost its force. It is our business—philosophers, students, and practical men—to re-create and reenact a vision of the world, including those elements of reverence and order without which society lapses into riot, and penetrated through and through with unflinching rationality. Such a vision is the knowledge which Plato identified with virtue. Epochs, for which, within the limits of their development, this vision has been widespread are the epoch unfading in the memory of mankind." [10]

In an address at the opening session of the American Bar Association Convention in 1970 Professor Paul A. Freund sought out a general explanation of the crisis of confidence in our legal system. "I find this above all," he said, "in the gap that exists between the technological capacity and moral promise of our society, on the one one hand, and the actuality of our achievement on the other. For the first time in human history man has the resources and skills to provide a decent life for the inhabitants of the globe, if we have the will, the imagination, and the political wisdom—and these are very big if's—to direct our technology to the most pressing humane ends and to adapt our institutions to the pace of an electronic age. . . . [I]t is the noble aspiration, the overriding charge of our profession, and of our Association," he concluded, "to help us learn to live, and to live harmoniously together, truly as men and women." [11]

---

10. Whitehead, supra note 5.   11. Freund, A Charge for the Profession, 95 Rep.A.B.A. —— (1971).

Chapter IV

STANDARDS, SUPPORTS AND SANCTIONS

SECTION 1. INTRODUCTION

The legal profession, as the law, looks outside itself to perceive the factors which should guide its development. This chapter considers some of the guiding factors. The chapter is directed to the derivation of the standards of the lawyer and to the agencies which may give them expression and efficacy. Later chapters consider the content of the standards in the varied work of the profession.

The nature of professional standards is considered first. The problems of the authoritative sources of standards is next raised, problems deriving in one aspect from our federal system and in another from the constitutional separation of powers. Then four kinds of supports or sanctions are discussed: the state, the profession, the public, and the individual.

SECTION 2. THE NATURE OF STANDARDS AND THEIR FUNDAMENTAL SOURCES *

The standards of a profession are guides to its members in their work. For the profession of law they are especially important because of the difficult and demanding conditions of practice. Unlike the soldier and the physician the lawyer does not fight his country's enemies or the common enemies of mankind. He gives meaning to the law in individual cases between man and man, under our competitive economic system and at times under the stress of the adversary system in the courtroom. He is employed and remunerated by private clients to aid them in their affairs. Inevitably, he is mindful of the fact that clients go to —and go back to—those lawyers who they believe will represent their private interests successfully. In the public interest there is need for standards which match the lawyer's responsibilities and difficulties.

* See also Chapter V, Sections 3, 4, 5,
infra pp. 68ff, ——.

"Sources of standards" is a term of different meanings. In this chapter two kinds of meanings are discussed. The phrase, *"authoritative* sources", connotes bodies politic and their organs which have the final say. They are the subject of Sections 3 and 4. Under our federal system the powers of government are shared by the nation and the several states. Section 3 is concerned with the consequent division of control over the standards of lawyers, and with the effect of international law. Under the principle of separation of powers the powers of government are divided among the legislative, executive and judicial branches, and Section 4 considers this division.

There is a further question which accompanies both authoritative sources. It concerns the content of the standards, that is, what shall they grant to and call for from the lawyer. The present section outlines factors relevant to this question on the fundamental sources. At first glance the phrase may seem high flown and pretentious. It is not so. To go beyond the letter of rules it is necessary always to inquire into their policies and foundations.

The lawyer's standards may be difficult to define because relevant factors are often opposed in indicating what the lawyer should do. Yet opposition of this sort is not confined to the law. It is everywhere through life. The interest in a drama or a novel inheres in the spectacle of the characters drawn and driven by different forces and in their success or failure in wrestling with them. The difficult controversies in life, as an essayist said, are not between right and wrong but between right and right.

In the work of all men of law, legislators and judges [1] and lawyers [2] alike, there are opposing factors. Whether they be called values or responsibilities or policies or loyalties, these

---

1. "[T]here are few areas of the law in black and white. The greys are dominant and even among them the shades are innumerable. For the eternal problem of the law is one of making accommodations between conflicting interests." Mr. Justice Douglas in Estin v. Estin, 334 U.S. 541, 68 S.Ct. 1213 (1948).

Judge Cardozo has described for the judge some of the opposing values and their reconciliation in his notable lectures. B. Cardozo, The Nature of the Judicial Process (1921); B. Cardozo, Paradoxes of Legal Science (1928).

2. "As an officer of the court concerned in the administration of justice, he [counsel] has an overriding duty to the court, to the standards of his profession, and to the public, which may and often does lead to a conflict with the client's wishes or with what the client thinks are his personal interests. . . . At present it can be said with confidence in this country that where there is any doubt the vast majority of counsel put their public duty before the apparent interests of their clients. Otherwise there would not be that implicit trust between the Bench and the Bar which does so much to promote the smooth and speedy conduct of the administration of justice." Lord Reid in Rondel v. Worley (1967) 3 All E.R. 993, 998, 999.

competing factors call for perception and then coordination. In the practice of law they are most usefully thought of as loyalties of the lawyer—the interests which he strives to advance. It is for the standards of the profession to give each its due weight and to coordinate them wisely. The loyalties of the lawyer in about the order in which he would ordinarily place them are loyalties:

1. *To the client.* This calls especially for competence and zeal unimpaired by divergent interests.

2. *To himself.* To his own economic interest, so that through his professional income he may make a good living for himself and his family. This includes fair measures to make his abilities known to potential clients, good office management and reasonable fees. On quite a different level it includes adherence to his own personal standards in his work as well as living the kind of life he wants to live outside the law.

3. *To his associates in practice.* To his associates in practice, his helpers, his juniors, and his seniors, all of whom together form a team and rely on one another.

4. *To the administration of law.* This involves consideration of the other elements in the administration of law: of the judge as a representative of the state; of the other side—whether the opponent or the lawyer or the witnesses—so the administration of law will proceed well; of his profession so that it may achieve its purposes under changing conditions.

5. *To his community great and small.* In his professional work whether in the office or in the court so he may aid in the profession's immediate task of the administration of law, and also beyond the office and the courtroom in giving leadership in public affairs.

In the coordination of loyalties and the derivation of standards one basic factor to be considered is the nature of the particular process of law involved. Another is the role of the lawyer in that process, as counseling contrasted with advocacy. A third is the setting of his work, that is, the conditions under which the work is carried on. Through consideration of such factors as well as perception of the loyalties it may be possible to determine wisely what the standards of the profession should be so as to aid it in the performance of its roles. The standards and guides so derived are not something remote and imposed. They grow out of the lawyer's work and responsibilities and form a reasoned statement of functional ethics.

In formulating the standards it is essential that the vague and general standards be given content and meaning in application to specific situations. It is no less essential that the specific be brought constantly to the test of the fundamental. "General principles do not decide concrete cases", the aphorism of Justice Holmes, has a fuller statement by Alexander Pekelis, "Concrete cases are not decided by general principles or without them." Part Two of the book, "The Lawyer and His Work", deals with the standards of the lawyer in varied roles.

SECTION 3. THE AUTHORITATIVE SOURCE OF THE STANDARDS OF THE LAWYER: THE FEDERAL SYSTEM

A constant preoccupation of the American lawyer has been: What law governs the activities of his clients? A question which is beginning to force itself on his attention is: What law governs his own activities? In law and its administration our federal nation is complex. The nation's laws are supreme when in conflict with the laws of the states. There are the fifty states each with its own legislature and system of courts. There are the federal courts—more than one hundred and fifty in number—and also numerous and powerful administrative agencies. Despite its great legal diversities our nation is essentially an economic unity with clients' transactions ranging over the whole country.

There is need for the privilege and protection of the interstate practitioner whose work may accompany that of his clients across the country.[1] The problem raised here is a related but different one. It involves not the privilege to practice [2] but the authoritative sources of the standards in practice. The term, "authoritative sources" signifies the components of our governmental and legal systems which determine the standards of the lawyer in practice.

The guiding test is the policy which the standard in question is designed to advance and then the determination of the source which is most closely concerned with its advancement or denial.[3]

One policy underlying his standards is that, though the lawyer is partisan in position, he will aid the tribunal in reaching a wise decision on the case before it. This policy calls naturally for the

---

1. See Note, 20 Vand.L.Rev. 1276 (1967).

2. See Chapter XVI infra pp. 280ff. on Membership in the Bar.

3. A helpful discussion of the policy underlying privileged communica-

tions and the consequent conclusions as to the appropriate choice in federal-state and state-state cases is by Professor (now Judge) Weinstein, Recognition in the United States of the Privileges of Another Jurisdiction, 56 Colum.L. Rev. 535 (1956).

application of the standards of the tribunal before which the advocate appears. The Supreme Court of the United States, in reproving vituperative counsel, announced its standards for "arguments in *this Court*." [4] When out of state counsel, granted the privilege of appearance *pro hac vice*, wrote a vehement letter about his case and distributed it in a way which would assure wide publicity, the Supreme Court of New Jersey revoked his privilege. The Court said: [5]

> "There must be a fair trial, both for a defendant and for the State. The conduct here involved invaded that interest. But of even greater moment than the interest of the immediate parties is the interest of the public in the integrity of the judicial process. The antics here involved spill over upon the right of all litigants to expect justice in the courtroom and in accordance with the rules of law."

The Committee on Enrollment and Disbarment of the Patent Office disbarred a lawyer from practice before the office because of the deceptive use of a ghost written article. The Committee stated the special duties of lawyers toward that office in language quoted by the Supreme Court of the United States in upholding the disbarment: [6]

> "By reason of the nature of an application for patent, the relationship of attorneys to the Patent Office requires the highest degree of candor and good faith."

When a claim or defense is based on federal law the lawyer's standards, it may be urged, should be based on federal law. The practice of law is essentially the individualization of law and a state imposed standard might be a restriction on federal law in violation of the supremacy clause. An illustration of this view is a case in which a lawyer who had prepared a federal estate tax return was summoned to testify on the matter before a federal agency. He objected that to testify would be a violation of the attorney-client privilege under state law. The federal court ordered him to appear and testify, stating that a claim of privilege in a federal tax law matter is determined by federal law. [7] In another case a lawyer retained by a seaman filed an action under federal law in a federal court against the seaman's employer. The employer induced the seaman to discharge the lawyer and

---

4. National Surety Co. v. Jarvis, 278 U.S. 610, 611 (1928). (Emphasis added.)

5. State v. Kavanaugh, 52 N.J. 7, 18, 243 A.2d 225, 231, cert. denied 393 U.S. 924 (1968).

6. See Kingsland v. Dorsey, 338 U.S. 318, 319 (1949).

7. United States v. Threlkeld, 241 F.Supp. 324 (W.D.Tenn.1965); see Cheatham, The Reach of Federal Action over the Profession of Law, 18 Stan.L.Rev. 1288 (1966). Contra, Baird v. Koerner, 279 F.2d 623 (9th Cir. 1960).

abandon the claim. The lawyer then brought suit on his behalf against the employer for interferring with the lawyer-client relationship. In holding the employer liable to the lawyer the judge stated that the governing law was to be enunciated on a national basis [8] and quoted Professor Paul Freund: [9]

> "[T]here should be a uniform national rule of law, binding on state and federal courts alike, where the operative legal policies are federal in origin."

In developing the standards of the lawyers in federal law matters it will be kept in mind that there is a true federal common law which it is for the courts to develop. As Justice Jackson said: [10]

> "Federal common law implements the Federal Constitution and statutes, and is conditioned by them. Within these limits federal courts are free to apply the additional common-law technique of decision and to draw upon all the sources of the common law in cases such as the present".

There are few federal statutes on lawyers' standards. The federal law applicable in these matters will ordinarily be federal common law.

A difficulty in determining whether federal standards or state standards should control is that the two kinds of law are often intertwined in the same case. In drawing a will a lawyer will give attention, first, to its validity under state law and, with that assured, go on to avoid federal taxes. State law is so basic that a learned book on the subject could refer to federal law as "interstitial" law.[11] Even when the federal standard is controlling, the content of that standard may be borrowed and taken over from state law.[12]

When the choice is between the laws of two or more states, the guide suggested above as to policy and the state of most concern as to that policy should also apply. To put in compressed form the language of Restatement, Second, Conflict of Laws,[13] it is the state which as to the issue in question has the most significant relationship to the transactions and the parties. Usually, it will

8. Greenberg v. Panama Transport, 185 F.Supp. 320, 324 (D.Mass.1968), rev'd on other grounds, 290 F.2d 125, cert. denied 368 U.S. 891 (1961).

9. Freund, Federal-State Relations in the Opinions of Judge Magruder, 72 Harv.L.Rev. 1204, 1213 (1959).

10. D'Oench, Duhme & Co. v. Federal Deposit Ins. Corp., 315 U.S. 447, 472 (1942) (concurring opinion); see Friendly, In Praise of Erie and of the New Federal Common Law, 19 Record of N.Y.C.B.A. 64 (1964).

11. H. Hart & H. Wechsler, The Federal Courts and The Federal System 435 (1953).

12. See Mishkin, The Variousness of "Federal Law": Competence and Discretion in the Choice of National and State Rules for Decision, 105 U.Pa.L.Rev. 797 (1957).

13. Restatement, Second, Conflict of Laws §§ 6 (P.O.D.1967) & 188 (P.O. D.1968).

be the state in which the lawyer is admitted to practice and in which he renders the services.[14]

Yet another source of difficulties is the system of federal courts. These courts have their own standards of admission and of discipline as well as rules of "procedure". It may be that some or even all phases of the lawyers' standards in practice before these courts might be characterized as "procedure" and so governed by principles moulded by these courts. While the Rules of Civil Procedures of the United States District Court were promulgated pursuant to an enabling act of Congress, the control of the federal courts over their bar may be rested on the more fundamental principle of the inherent power of a court to set standards and impose sanctions for those who practice before it. An illustration is a case to which the substantive law of California applied but which was in a federal court in that state because of diversity of citizenship. The defendant's motion to disqualify counsel for the plaintiff because of earlier representation of conflicting interests was denied by the District Court, apparently in reliance on state law. The Court of Appeals, in reversing the District Court and granting the motion to disqualify, held that the law of the federal courts governed: [15]

> "When an attorney appears before a federal court, he is acting as an officer of that court, and it is that court which must judge his conduct."

The difficulty in determining which standard should be used and which standard was used is illustrated by New York Cent. R. R. Co. v. Johnson.[16] A woman passenger on an interstate train brought action in a federal court in Missouri against the railroad company for alleged injuries suffered through the alleged negligence of the company's employees. In his argument before the jury plaintiff's counsel used inflammatory language repeatedly asserting that the "eastern railroad" was charging the plaintiff with having syphilis. The plaintiff recovered a verdict. On appeal the Circuit Court of Appeals, affirming the decision, merely admonished counsel "that this line of argument was likely to create prejudice".[17] The Supreme Court of the United States granted certiorari "limited to the question whether alleged misconduct of counsel for the plaintiffs in their argument to the jury was so unfairly prejudicial to the defendant as to justify a new trial." The Supreme Court reversed the decisions below because the arguments of plaintiff's counsel "so plainly tended to excite prejudice".

14. Id. § 196, Comment a (P.O.D. 1968).

15. Cord v. Smith, 338 F.2d 516, 524 (9th Cir. 1964).

16. 279 U.S. 310 (1929).

17. New York Cent. R. R. Co. v. Johnson, 27 F.2d 699, 702 (8th Cir. 1928).

In such a case what should be the authoritative source of the professional standard (admonishment) or of the legal standard (judgment reversed) for the actions of the lawyer in appealing to prejudice?

(1) Should it be the standard of the federal courts, in which the action was brought?

(2) Should it be the standard of the state whose substantive law was applicable to the transactions?

(3) Should it be a constitutional standard under the due process clause which would have brought reversal even if the judgment below had been recovered in a state court?

(4) In the Johnson case would the standard have been any different if the action had been brought under federal law (as by an employee against the railroad company under the Federal Employer's Liability Act) instead of an action by a passenger?

The *Johnson* case discussed next above illustrates a further difficulty in this area. The courts are not explicit on the authoritative source of the standard which they are applying. In the federal courts an opinion may be unclear on the question whether it is a special law of the federal courts, or a special law of federal causes of action, or whether it rests on constitutional grounds. The fact that federal law could be extended to a situation is no sufficient reason to conclude that it does apply. Mr. Justice Harlan in his dissent as to group legal services in the *United Mine Workers* case urged that "state courts and legislatures should be left to govern their own Bars". He conceded in language with which there was no disagreement: [18]

> "And, all else failing, the Congress undoubtedly has the power to implement federal programs by establishing overriding rules governing legal representation in connection therewith."

The International System. Public international law is not as such an authoritative source of law, though treaties are authoritative as a part of the supreme law of the land. Public international law, however, is consulted and drawn upon in formulating the rules of municipal law. The needs and practices of the international community and the international sense of justice are also considered in formulating these rules.[1]

18. United Mine Workers of America v. Illinois State Bar Ass'n, 389 U.S. 217, 234 n. 17 (1967) (dissenting opinion).

1. See Cheatham & Maier, The Authoritative Sources of Private International Law, 22 Vand.L.Rev. 27, 33, 39 (1968).

The international sense of justice has come to be expressed with increasing definiteness in such international actions as the Charter of the United Nations; the Universal Declaration of Human Rights; and the European Convention for the Protection of Human Rights and Fundamental Freedoms, the European Commission of Human Rights, and the European Court of Human Rights. The insistence on human right in these documents surely carries with it the right to counsel to present effectively the cases of the complainants.

In the Nuremberg trials, and in the case of Eichmann prosecuted in Israel for the murder of millions of Jews,[2] the accused were given counsel.

In studies and proposals by private non-governmental organizations as by the American Law Institute,[3] there has been insistence on the right to counsel as an element in the international standard of justice. The International Commission of Jurists in its studies of particular conditions and in its Declarations on the Rule of Law has repeatedly emphasized the importance of an independent legal profession as a part of The Rule of Law and Protection of Human Rights.[4]

Taken together these actions in the international field give strong support by analogy to the right to counsel and the freedom of counsel in the field of municipal law.

SECTION 4. THE AUTHORITATIVE SOURCES OF THE
STANDARDS OF THE LAWYER: THE SEPARATION
OF POWERS PRINCIPLE

The courts claim wide control over the legal profession. At times statutes explicitly give this control. Even in the absence of a statute, the control has been inferred from the principle of the separation of powers among the three branches of government. The constitutions of the states, as well as the federal constitution, all provide that the legislative, the executive and the judicial branches shall be separate. But the language of the constitutions is not explicit on the control of the courts over the profession. To determine the extent of this control it is essen-

---

2. Silving, In re Eichmann: A Dilemma of Law and Morality, 55 Am.J.Int'l L. 307, 335 (1961).

3. Restatement of The Foreign Relations Law of the United States § 183 (1962).

4. The principal declarations of the Commission are brought together and restated in The Rule of Law and Human Rights: Principles and Definitions (1966).

tial to resort to the policies supporting the constitutional framework of separation of powers.

The framework had a curious origin in Montesquieu's, The Spirit of the Laws, published in the 1740's. It is an irony of American history that the erroneous speculation of a French political writer on the English constitution came to be accepted as an axiom of government and to be written into all our constitutions.[1] The mistaken origin of the principle is no reason to reject it. It is cause to interpret the principle guardedly as good sense calls for and not to apply it literally as if there were rigid walls separating the departments of government from one another. The purpose of the principle, as the framers of our early constitutions understood, is to safeguard the Republic against tyranny through the vesting of all powers in one body, and it is consistent with "a partial mixture of powers." [2]

In its affirmative aspect the policy is primarily one of political liberty—in the present matter, the independence of the judiciary from undue outside influence in the matters entrusted to it. What does this policy call for as to the power of the judiciary over the bar?

No single answer can be given for all the varied situations in which the question may arise as: (1) The determination of who may become or remain members of the bar, that is admission and disbarment. (2) The control over the conduct of individual members of the bar exercised through contempt or disciplinary proceedings. (3) The consideration and determination of the general standards of conduct of the bar, as through a wide inquiry into their conduct or through the promulgation or approval of canons of professional ethics. (4) The form of general organization of the profession, as the self-governing bar. (5) The scope of the bar's exclusive field of activity, as, what is the unauthorized practice of law. (6) The methods by which the legal services may be rendered, as through group legal services. (7) The inherent power of the courts to determine their rules of procedure and practice.

While no single answer can be given on the variety of situations in which the principle of separation of power has been invoked, some cases give an unfortunate impression. It is that at times the courts, through a letterbound and legalistic reading of the constitutions, draw conclusions on the breadth of their

1. In an introduction to a 1900 republication of the book Justice Holmes stressed that "His [Montesquieu's] England—the England of the threefold division of power into legislative, executive and judicial—was a fiction invented by him, a fiction which misled the makers of our Constitution as it misled Blackstone and Delolme."

2. See The Federalist, Nos. 47–50 (J. Madison & A. Hamilton).

powers quite unwarranted by the basic purpose of the principle of political liberty, as its creator, Montesquieu conceived it [3] and as it was understood by those great contemporaries of the adoption of our constitutions, the authors of The Federalist Papers. This broad scope given by some courts is the more unfortunate because of the accompanying American principle of judicial review under the constitutions. The combination of the two, the principle of the separation of powers and the principle of judicial review, has as a consequence that any decision by a state supreme court in such a matter fixes the law beyond change except by amendment of the state constitution or else overruling under the federal constitution. It was this situation which the Supreme Court of the United States dealt with in a case involving group legal services by a labor union.[4]

A wiser attitude toward the principle of separation of powers and one more consonant with its origin was expressed by the Supreme Court of California when it upheld the statute creating the State Bar of California and its provision on admission to the bar: [5]

> "Our courts .   .   . have and should maintain vigorously all the inherent and implied powers necessary to properly and effectively function as a separate department in the scheme of our state government . . . But this does not mean that the three departments of our government are not in many respects mutually dependent. Of necessity the judicial department as well as the executive must in most matters yield to the power of statutory enactment."

There are still other difficult questions created by the separation of powers. If the judiciary does have power in the areas mentioned and, perhaps, others, what is the degree of its control? Is the power held only at the sufferance of the legislature; or is the court's control shared with the legislature so that legislative provisions which do not unduly hamper the courts in their function are valid; or is the control free of legislative action?

Yet another set of questions concerns the part of the judicial system in which the power is vested. Is it vested wholly or primarily in the highest court of the state? Or is it vested, at least

---

3. "Again, there is no liberty if the judiciary power be not separated from the legislative and executive. Were it joined with the legislative, the life and liberty of the subject would be exposed to arbitrary control; for the judge would then be the legislator. Were it joined to the executive power, the judge might behave with violence and oppressions." 11 J. Montesquieu, The Spirit of the Laws, Ch. V., at 182 (Nugent transl. 1900).

4. See infra p. 320.

5. Brydonajack v. State Bar of California, 208 Cal. 439, 442, 281 P. 1018, 1020, Annot., 66 A.L.R. 1512 (1929).

partially, in each court so that, for example, each court may deal with contemptuous conduct before it?

An Officer of the Court

In support of the inherent power of the courts over the bar, the statement is often made—and as often denied—that the lawyer is "an officer of the court." He does have a privileged and essential part in the operation of the tribunals of law administration. His advice on suit or defense or compromise ordinarily determines whether there shall be litigation, and his standards and practices determine how well the courts function. In his office work he is in fact making law when drafting documents for within the wide range permitted by law the terms of the documents become law for the parties, and in advising clients on the law he is administering the law. As Justice Jackson said: [6]

> "It too often is overlooked that a lawyer and the law office are indispensable parts of the administration of justice."

At times the courts have employed the conception of an officer of the court as the basis of special rights and duties. In holding a lawyer not liable for false imprisonment of his client's adversary the court said: [7]

> "An attorney is an officer of the court . . . He therefore occupies what may be termed a quasi judicial office."

Judge Cardozo referred to the lawyer as: [8]

> "an officer of the court, and, like the court itself, an instrument or agency to advance the ends of justice."

He stated the conclusions that the lawyer is subject to the duty of accepting assignment as counsel for the needy, to summary proceedings, and to discipline. He drew the further conclusion in the particular case that the court had the power to authorize a general inquiry into reported evils in personal injury practice and to require lawyers to testify in the course of the inquiry.

Against this view is the fact that the lawyer is retained and paid by clients to advance their private interests. Even more important is the fact that the lawyer is not under the direction of a judge or subordinate to him in any way. It is his professional duty to challenge the rulings of the court when he believes them erroneous and harmful to his client.

Insistence on the essential independence of lawyers is the basis of the decision in Cammer v. United States.[9] There a federal

---

6. Hickman v. Taylor, 329 U.S. 495, 514–515 (concurring opinion) (1947).

7. Langen v. Borkowski, 188 Wis. 277, 301, 206 N.W. 181, 190, Annot., 43 A.L.R. 639 (1925).

8. People ex rel. Karlin v. Culkin, 248 N.Y. 465, 470–471, 162 N.E. 487, 489, Annot., 60 A.L.R. 860 (1928).

9. 350 U.S. 399 (1956).

statute provided for summary contempt proceedings by a court of the United States for

> "(1) misbehavior of any of its *officers* in their official transactions." (Emphasis added)

A lawyer had sent a letter of inquiry to governmental employees who had been members of a grand jury in the District of Columbia and who returned an indictment charging the lawyer's client with filing a false noncommunist affidavit. The Supreme Court held

> "a lawyer is not the kind of 'officer' who can be summarily tried for contempt."

under the statute, giving as its reason the deep interest of the public in the independence of the bar. So the conclusions from the idea, "officer of the court" are dependent, not on the dictionary but on broad considerations of policy.

Does the view of the lawyer as an "officer of the court" aid in the wise determination of the privileges and duties of the lawyer in a particular case? A criticism of the term "officer of the court" is that it is misleading, because both too broad and too narrow. It is too broad if it implies that the lawyer is subject to direction by the judge as his superior. It is too narrow in its implication that his special responsibilities are concerned only with court work when the fact is that most of the work of most lawyers is done out of court. "Officer of the law" might be a more helpful term but it has been taken over for the police. Professor Willard Hurst has proposed the helpful term "officer of the legal order." [10]

Judgment Reversed

"Judgment reversed" is the principal sanction for misconduct or error by the advocate with the burden cast on the client rather than the lawyer. Even in gross cases the court rarely calls the lawyer himself to account through proceedings for discipline or contempt. The court seemingly did not do so in an early state case in which the lawyer actually changed sides in the same litigation,[11] nor did the Supreme Court of the United States in a criminal case where, as the court found, "in the context of the revolting crime . . . the prosecution deliberately misrepresented the truth." [12] There has been some questioning of the

10. Hurst, The Legal Profession, 1966 Wis.L.Rev. 967, 976.

11. Weidekind v. Tuolumne County Water Co., 74 Cal. 386, 19 P. 173 (1887).

12. Miller v. Pate, 386 U.S. 1, 4, 6 (1967). Because of the charges by the Court, the Grievance Committee of the Illinois State Bar Association made an inquiry with a view to appropriate discipline. In its independent investigation the commit-

justice and even the legality of visiting upon the client the faults of his lawyer. On the denial of the petition for certiorari in a criminal case where the appeal in the state court had been dismissed for failure to prosecute, Mr. Justice Black's dissent indicates the kinds of cases in which, in his view, "vicarious punishment" is appropriate: [13]

> "[T]here is a vast difference between holding the litigant responsible for errors in not objecting to evidence or pleadings, and on the other hand holding the litigant responsible for complete failure to file papers and then without notice to the litigant dismissing his entire case or defense. . . ."

SECTION 5. STATE IMPOSED SANCTIONS

The state may subject the profession of law to reasonable regulations. In this section some of the sanctions will be sketched. In the sections immediately following three agencies important in the development of standards will be considered: the organized bar, the public, and the individual. Now the state imposed sanctions.

Criminal prosecutions. They may be based on wrongs forbidden to laymen and lawyers alike. Occasionally they are based on actions forbidden only to lawyers.[1]

Contempt of court. The lawyer's zeal in contentious proceedings might lead him to acts which would interfere with proper functioning of the court's work and so to a charge of contempt. Yet at times state appellate courts [2] as well as the Supreme Court of the United States [3] have struck down rulings by trial courts holding lawyers in contempt of court, because the appellate courts insisted that "the independence of the bar is almost as important as the independence of the bench." [4]

---

tee found that the Supreme Court of the United States was in error in its findings of fact, and the committee publicly exonerated the prosecuting attorney. See 54 A.B. A.J. 803 (1968).

13. Morris v. Florida, cert. denied, 393 U.S. 850, 851 (1968) (dissenting opinion).

1. Advertising for divorce cases is made criminal in some states. See,

e. g., Ill.Rev.Stat.1969 c. 40, § 22 (Smith-Hurd).

2. E. g., Blankenbaker v. State, 201 Ind. 142, 166 N.E. 265 (1929).

3. Holt v. Virginia, 381 U.S. 131 (1965).

4. Cammer v. United States, 350 U.S. 399 (1956).

Disqualification. A lawyer's appearance in a case may violate the standards of the profession, as when he represents an interest in conflict with one he represented at an earlier stage. He may be barred from participation.[5]

A constructive trust. A constructive trust will be imposed when the lawyer has received property in violation of a professional duty, as when the receipt of the property violated his duty of unimpaired loyalty to the client.[6]

Actions for damages, or proceedings for the denial of fees or liens. When the lawyer does not measure up to a professional standard of competence and care, he as any other professional man may be liable in damages.[7]

Summary proceedings. This is a special remedy against a lawyer. When he has received money which he should turn over to his client, the client can maintain expeditious proceedings against him instead of suffering the delay of the usual calendar congestion.[8]

The declaration of a mistrial or the grant of a new trial. When the acts of the lawyer for one of the parties violate an important standard in the conduct of a trial, the trial may be halted or the judgment set aside. Similarly, when the lawyer fails to comply with a reasonable order of the court in the conduct of a case, the case may be dismissed. In these cases the burden falls more heavily on the client than on the lawyer, and in the last class of cases there has been criticism of action thus penalizing the client.[9]

Disciplinary proceedings. These may lead to censure, suspension or disbarment.

This is a formidable list of court-imposed negative sanctions. More important than any of them or than all of them together in securing adherence to standards is the affirmative support given by the representative of the state, the judge, in his work.[10]

---

5. See T. C. Theatre Corp. v. Warner Bros. Pictures, 113 F.Supp. 265 (S. D.N.Y.1953).

6. See Tracy v. Willys Corp., 45 F.2d 485 (6th Cir. 1930).

7. E. g., Trimboli v. Kinkel, 226 N.Y. 147, 123 N.E. 205 (1919).

8. E. g., Tenn.Code Ann. § 25-320 (1956).

9. See Link v. Wabash Railroad Co., 370 U.S. 626 (1967) (dissenting opinion).

10. Writing at the end of the nineteenth century, an English barrister stated: "Of all the mighty changes that have taken place in the nineteenth century, the greatest change has been in the tone of the administration of both the civil and the criminal law . . . . This is due partly to the improved education of the Bar; partly no doubt to the influences of an omnipresent press; but still more to Her Majesty's judges." W. Odgers, A Century of Law Reform 41–42 (1901).

SECTION 6. THE ORGANIZED PROFESSION

Law is one of the three original learned professions along with medicine and the ministry. Despite occasional objections, law should continue to regard itself as a profession, "a group, possessing a particular skill, which has an enlightened regard for the goals and aggregate consequences of the exercise of that skill." [1]

The characterization is a constant reminder to lawyers and to those with whom they deal that lawyers are a group with special responsibilities and special standards. With their responsibilities great and their setting difficult, lawyers should not surrender the aid that the conception of themselves as professional men may give. The fact that it can give aid is indicated by proposals that other groups with corresponding responsibilities seek this support. Justice Brandeis before he went on the bench urged that business management regard itself as a profession with a heightened sense of responsibility [2] and, as Professor Dodd put it, with the standards of action attaining "the status of a professional code of ethics rather than of a legal rule." [3] The most important function of standards is that they determine what is expected of the lawyer. As with most men, lawyers tend to act as others expect them to act and the level of expectations is a major factor in their conduct. The standards of the profession are the largest element in determining the level of expectations of the lawyer.

Lawyers have formed many associations. Some are based on geography as international, national, state and local bar associations. Others developed from a shared professional desire to improve the law and its administration, as the American Law Institute and the American Judicature Society. Other organizations arise from professional concern in a particular area such as the American Society of International Law. The discussion here will be directed primarily to a description of bar associations and their concern with professional responsibility.

1. McDougal, The Law School of Tomorrow 204 (D. Haber & J. Cohen eds. 1968). An often quoted definition of a profession by Dean Pound is: "The term [a profession] refers to a group of men pursuing a learned art as a common calling in the spirit of a public service—no less a public service because it may incidentally be a means of livelihood." R. Pound, The Lawyer from Antiquity to Modern Times 5 (1953).

2. L. Brandeis, Business—A Profession (1914).

For Mr. Brandeis professional responsibility evidently means the qualities which will lead a man to carry out his professional obligations despite distractions and difficulties in practice.

3. Dodd, Is Effective Enforcement of the Fiduciary Duties of Corporate Managers Practicable, 2 U.Chi. L.Rev. 194, 199 (1935).

The American Bar Association is the national organization of lawyers, to which law students are now eligible for membership. At its founding in 1878 it was scarcely more than a minor social group. It has developed in numbers (in 1970 its membership was over 140,000) and in form of organization so that now it is fairly representative of most of the lawyers of the country. Most of its activities are carried on by committees and sections which range in their fields from general practice to improvement of law administration and world peace through law.[4] The Association publishes its monthly Journal devoted especially to matters of current importance for lawyers, and some of the sections publish yearbooks as The International Lawyer. Some of the Association's committees have come to develop independent lives of their own, as the National Conference of Commissioners on Uniform State Laws and the Association of American Law Schools. The American Bar Association has sponsored several "conference groups" which seek working arrangements on the cooperation with or else the delimitation of the respective fields of activities of lawyers and other specialized groups, as certified public accountants.

At times the Association has been criticized as too conservative. The true mark of the criticism, is not the Association but the bar as most lawyers are conservative. The Association has been ahead of the average of its membership, since many of its officers gain from their position and opportunities a stronger sense of responsibility. The Association has furnished much of the leadership in the development of the law and of legal services.

Fortunately, the Association has given opportunity within itself for expression of essentially opposing attitudes on controversial matters. The Committee on Education against Communism lays the stress wholly differently from the Special Committee on Individual Rights as Affected by National Security, and the Standing Committee on Individual Rights and Responsibilities. The sweeping condemnation of group legal services by the Code of Professional Responsibility[5] adopted at the 1969 meeting finds its refutation in the careful report at the same meeting of the Special Committee on the Availability of Legal Services.[6]

The National Bar Association, wholly or predominately Negro in membership, was organized in 1925 at a time when the Ameri-

4. The annual reports of the Association include reports of its wide-ranging committees and sections and the statement of principles agreed on by the Association with representatives of other specialized groups.

5. A.B.A. Code of Professional Responsibility, DR 2–103.

6. 94 A.B.A.Rep. 223 (1969).

can Bar Association did not cordially welcome Blacks to membership. Its stated purposes, besides more general ones as advancing the science of jurisprudence, stress the protection of the political and economic rights of all citizens. It has continued despite the change in the attitude of the American Bar Association.[7]

The National Lawyers Guild was organized in 1937 with the purpose stated in its constitution of "being a professional organization which shall function as an effective social force in the service of the people to the end that human rights shall be regarded as more sacred than property rights." It quickly ran into difficulties and many of its leaders resigned believing it had been taken over by the Communist Party. In 1970 its membership was about 1300 with also some 500 student members. Its fate is unfortunate. With successful lawyers naturally conservative there is need for effective liberal bar associations.[8]

The state bar associations were all voluntary in membership until 1921.[9] That year there began "the integrated bar" system under which all practicing lawyers are members of the associations of their states. By 1970 over half of the states had the integrated bar. An example of a strong state association which has been notably effective in continuing education is the State Bar of California. There has been disagreement on whether the separation of powers principle permits the state legislature, instead of the supreme court of the state, to create the system. Integration has been achieved in some states by act of the legislature[10] and in others by order of the supreme court of the state[11] with the latter taking at times the form of a temporary or tentative organization for a trial period.[12]

The Supreme Court of the United States upheld the constitutionality of a state court order integrating the bar of the state.[13]

---

7. See Ortique, The National Bar Association—Not Just an Option!, 53 Judicature 390 (1970).

8. The Story of the Guild is sympathetically sketched in V. Countryman & T. Finman, The Lawyer in Modern Society 392–402 (1966).

9. See G. Winters, Bar Association Organization and Activities (1954).

Whether a bar association is entitled to tax exemption depends on the nature of the particular association and the language of the tax statute. A case upholding exemption from the federal estate tax is Dulles v. Johnson, 273 F.2d 362 (2d Cir. 1959), cert. denied 364 U.S. 834 (1960).

10. The State of California is an illustration.

11. The State of Wisconsin is an illustration.

12. In re Unification of the New Hampshire Bar, 109 N.H. 260, 248 A.2d 709 (1968); In re Integration of the Bar, 273 Wis. 281, 77 N.W. 2d 602 (1956).

13. Lathrop v. Donohue, 367 U.S. 820 (1961).

The view has been expressed that it would be unprofessional for a lawyer employed by the federal government or a corporation to join a labor union which includes laymen

The justices, however, were divided in opinion. Three would uphold the order on broad, four on narrow, grounds, and two would strike it down as imposing a "guild system".

Local bar associations are common. What is uncommon is leadership which makes the association count for something. The centennial history of one shows it has had such leadership much of the time, The Association of the Bar of the City of New York.[14] In his review of the history, Anthony Lewis characterized the Association as [15]

> "a body of lawyers that perhaps more than any other has kept faith with its duty to professional conscience and country."

On professional standards the organized bar has laid down general principles and has also acted in individual cases. The basic guide to the standards is "the public interest", as the Supreme Court of the United States held in three cases involving group legal services.[16] The most important statements of general principles are three by the American Bar Association,[17] (1) the Canons of Professional Ethics of 1908 [18] (2) "Professional Responsibility: A Statement" of 1958,[19] and (3) the Code of Professional Responsibility of 1969.* The Canons have been

among its members and officers, since the decisions made for union members by laymen might be inconsistent with the lawyer's professional obligation. A.B.A.Comm. on Professional Ethics, Informal Opinion 917 (1966).

14. G. Martin, Causes and Conflicts: The Centennial History of The Association of the Bar of the City of New York, 1870–1970. (1970).

15. Lewis, Book Review, 56 A.B.A.J. 478 (1970).

16. See Chapter XVII infra.

17. The adoption of standards by the organized bar does not give them the force of law, yet the standards are often referred to by the courts in the development of the law. "The American Bar Association is not a legislative tribunal, and its canons are not of binding obligation and are not enforced as such by the courts, although they constitute a safe guide for professional conduct in the cases to which they apply, and an attorney may be disciplined for not observing them." Hunter

v. Troup, 315 Ill. 293, 302, 146 N.E. 321, 324 (1925).

18. The history of the Canons and the amendments made to them are set out in H. Drinker, Legal Ethics, (1953) at 23–26 & 309–325. An excellent appraisal of the background and range of the Canons is given in J. Hurst, The Growth of American Law—The Law Makers 329–333 (1950).

19. The Statement is published in 44 A.B.A.J. 1159 (1958).

* The Code is superior to the old Canons in many ways. It is so, for example, in Canon 2 which is more explicit on the duty of the profession to make counsel available; in Canon 5 which substitutes for the idea of conflicting interests the broader principle of differing interests and independent judgment; in Canon 6 which recognizes that competent representation may call for the association of professionals in other disciplines; in Canon 7 which mentions the desirability of making clear to the client relevant moral as well as legal considera-

adopted by numerous state bar associations, by some courts and by a few legislatures, and they have been frequently cited by the courts. "Professional Responsibility: A Statement" was prepared by joint committees of the American Bar Association and the Association of American Law Schools. It is the most explicit in its expression of the guiding factors and it is the only one which gives adequate attention to the principal work of the modern lawyer as counsellor and draftsman in his office. The Code of Professional Responsibility, adopted in 1969, has the advantage of precision and detail in statement. The Code states nine brief Canons as "axiomatic norms", and under each Canon gives two sets of principles, "Ethical Considerations" and "Discipli-

tions; in Canon 8 which calls for aid in improving the legal system; and throughout in being more specific in the guidance it gives.

The Drafting Committee recognized that inevitably the Code was imperfect. On the motion of its chairman the Association continued the committee so it could consider and propose changes. At the first meeting following its adoption, the Association did make one substantial amendment. It deleted the provision of the Code (DR 2–108(B)) approving provisions in settlement agreements which would bar lawyers from representation in other matters arising out of the transactions dealt with in the settlements.

Four other changes which it is believed would be helpful will be mentioned. Three of them would be fuller statements of matters perhaps now implicit, and the last one a return to the original view of the Committee.

(1) The fundamental sources of the standards should be made clearer so the fundamental will not be obscured by the detail. "The public interest" is the source on which the Supreme Court of the United States insisted in some cases in which it overrode the views of the organized bar. (See infra pp. 320–24). A clear and insistent statement of these forces is the more important, for lawyers are in danger of using the Code as a set of letter-bound rules and as a ceiling rather than a floor.

(2) Office work and counseling on plans for the future call for much fuller consideration, together with

the lawyer's responsibility for the plans he helps to design and carry through. Here the Code is less helpful than its immediate predecessor, "Professional Responsibility: A Statement." The Code is primarily courtroom-directed, like the original Canons.

(3) Responsibility and participation in public affairs, whether in or out of political office should be stressed. The Code is explicit on the lawyer's duty to aid "in improving the *legal* system." It does not mention expressly the larger social and political systems now in rapid movement and in need of the longer view and the steadying hand of good lawyers. Two lawyers of such differing views as Jefferson and Hamilton contributed much, as all know, to the shaping of our government. In the reshaping now under way their successors have an opportunity and a duty. In this matter the Code lags behind the Association itself. The American Bar Association through its committees considers such public problems as Pollution, Housing and Urban Development, and Individual Rights and Responsibilities.

(4) On group legal services surely the Code must drop the present unseemly provision DR 2–103 (D) 5 under which the statement of professional ethics sinks to the level of constitutional requirement. Opposed to that provision is the preliminary draft of the Code itself as well as the 1969 Report of the Special Committee on the Availability of Legal Services which approved these services under appropriate safeguards.

nary Rules". Their nature is explained in the Preliminary Statement to the Code:

> "The Ethical Considerations are aspirational in character and represent the objectives toward which every member of the profession should strive. They constitute a body of principles upon which the lawyer can rely for guidance in many specific situations.
>
> "The Disciplinary Rules, unlike the Ethical Considerations, are mandatory in character. The Disciplinary Rules state the minimum level of conduct below which no lawyer can fall without being subject to disciplinary action."

On the relation of the Code to the Canons the preface to the code states that all of the Canons that are sound in substance have been brought forward into the Code.[20]

On specific matters of professional conduct, the bar associations' activities are of two kinds, furnishing guidance and also aiding in discipline. "The Committee on Professional Ethics" is the title of the committee of the first nature which answers questions on legal ethics. This kind of committee had its origin in the New York County Lawyers' Association.[21] The American Bar Association's committee is now the most influential one. By 1970 it had published several hundred opinions in one volume and over a thousand "informal opinions" in another volume.

"The Committee on Grievances" is the usual title of the committee of the second kind. It aids the courts by investigating alleged misconduct by lawyers and by presenting to the courts the cases which it believes warrant discipline. It aids lawyers, too, by explaining to clients the misunderstandings out of which most complaints arise and occasionally through public exoneration of the lawyer.[22] The committees of the state and local bar associations are the active agencies in these matters.

The bias of our discussion has manifestly been toward regarding the bar as a profession with the special qualities and consequences which naturally follow. The objection may be made that

---

20. The Code was drafted by a Committee with Mr. Edward L. Wright as Chairman and Professor John F. Sutton, Jr. as Reporter.

21. See Cheatham & Lewis, Committees on Legal Ethics, 24 Calif.L. Rev. 28 (1935).

22. The role of the grievance committee in protecting the reputation of lawyers is strikingly illustrated in an Illinois case. The Supreme Court of the United States set aside a conviction in Illinois on the stated ground that at the trial the prosecutor had "deliberately misrepresented the truth." The Grievance Committee of the State Bar on its own motion commenced an investigation to determine whether disciplinary proceedings against the prosecutor were called for The Committee concluded that the Supreme Court of the United States had misapprehended the facts, Grievance Committee's Findings Re Prosecution of the Miller Murder Case, 54 A.B.A.J. 803 (1968).

there will be increased power over dissident members, and the aggrandizement of the profession and its members at the expense of other groups. It may be urged, further, that it would be better to have lawyers regard themselves merely as ordinary members of society without any peculiar group or professional consciousness and organization.

There are historical and contemporary illustration of group power and narrowness. The guild system of the late Middle Ages, the exclusionary attitude of craft labor unions toward disadvantaged groups, and cartels and trusts are familiar illustrations. Closer home is the action of the organized medical profession in opposing group medical practice. Our profession can scarcely deny the charge of narrowness in the use of its powers, at times under the guise of "professional ethics" or "the unauthorized practice of law." Holdsworth agreed, saying:

> "The selfishness of a group, disguised under the form of group loyalty, will be a danger to other groups and persons and to the state, proportioned to its size and power." [23]

Judge Cardozo expressed the same idea as to our profession: "No doubt the power can be abused, but that is true of power generally." [24]

With our profession, two safeguards will be useful. One is the assurance that the exercise of the power of the organized bar be kept under the control of those who are responsive to the whole community and not merely to the profession. The second is to seek to assure that the leaders of the bar, through education and a sense of responsibility, will use powers reposed in the organized bar for the general good. Then the words of Judge Cardozo in referring to the power entrusted to the courts and to the organized bar over lawyers will be justified.[25]

> "In so holding we place power and responsibility where in reason they should be. . . . In the long run the power now conceded will make for the health and honor of the profession and for the protection of the public. If the house is to be cleaned, it is for those who occupy and govern it, rather than for strangers, to do the noisome work."

The stress laid here on the work of the bar associations in setting and enforcing standards of professional conduct must not obscure the fact that the associations engage in many activities for the improvement of the law and of law administration. Every annual report of the American Bar Association indicates the

---

23. W. Holdsworth, Some Lessons from Our Legal History 150 (1928).

24. People ex rel. Karlin v. Culin, 248 N.Y. 465, 479, 162 N.E. 487, 493 (1928).

25. Id.

wide scope of its activities. "The Survey of the Legal Profession" was authorized by the Association in 1944 as a broad study of the functioning of lawyers in a free society, with first Dean Arthur T. Vanderbilt and then Mr. Reginald Heber Smith as Director.[26] "The Survey" is a generation old as these lines are written. There is need already for another broad study of the profession. This new survey may be aided, as the first one was not, by informed and sympathetic and critical persons outside the profession. Such a study would aid the profession to achieve what Mr. John Gardner reminds us is needed by every institution as well as every individual, "Self-renewal".[27]

The variety in our society may be urged as a reason for a variety of standards of the bar.[28] The variety so urged might concern (1) the classes of work; (2) the classes of clients; (3) the classes of lawyers; (4) the levels of attainment. On differences according to the nature of the work it will readily be agreed, and it will be urged in the chapters ahead, that there should be differences in standards according to the nature of the lawyer's work.[28.5] For example, one kind of work is that of the advocate in a court of law who typically is dealing with a past transaction under a highly structured system which assumes that he will have an opponent ready to challenge him at every step. A very different kind of work is that of the lobbyist or of the office lawyer who is urging or planning for the future, it may be without a present challenger. This difference has not ordinarily received from the organized bar the consideration in difference of standards which its fundamental importance calls for.

It is the opportunity of the office lawyer to help the client to be his best self. It is in this sense that a lawyer could say that at times his advice had "an almost pastoral quality." The fate of the heads of the two largest banks in the country in an earlier era is an illustration of the need for such advice. These men were driven out of business life in the 1930s when there came to

---

26. The essence of the Survey reports are given in A. Blaustein and C. Porter, The American Lawyer. (1954). The reports are listed and cited in an appendix to the book at 342 as well as in a Note, 39 A.B.A.J. 548, 551 (1953).

27. See J. Gardner, Self-Renewal (1964). See also J. Gardner, Excellence (1961).

28. See, e. g., Cohen, Pluralism in the American Legal Profession, 19 Ala.L.Rev. 247 (1968); Shuchman, Ethics and Legal Ethics: The Propriety of the Canons as a Group

Moral Code, 37 Geo.Wash.L.Rev. 244 (1968).

The Code of Professional Responsibility in the Preliminary Statement states: "Within the framework of fair trial, the Disciplinary Rules should be applied to all lawyers, regardless of the nature of their professional activities."

28.5 An excellent illustration of standards developed for specific roles of the lawyer is the American Bar Association's Profect for the Administration of Criminal Justice. See Chapter VI infra at p. 92.

light conduct in the 1920s which was cheap though lawful. Their lawyers could have saved their careers.

On differences in clients, too, it may be agreed that there should be a difference in the methods employed to make counsel available, as discussed below in Chapter XVII. These differences in making counsel available in fact do not call for material differences in the standards of the lawyer in his work once he is retained. He would owe the same basic duties of loyalty and competence and zeal to his client, as well as of candor toward the tribunal and fairness toward the opponent. The disturbing differences between the quality of services now given to the wealthy and to the poor are surely no reason to set different standards. Rather they call for new methods of making counsel available under conditions which would encourage and facilitate adherence to established standards.

On differences between classes of lawyers, say between the lawyers with established clienteles and the beginning lawyers with their future to make, again there can be no differences in standards once the lawyer-client relationship is established. There is an obvious difference in the need to make the lawyers and their abilities known to prospective clients. If there is to be a difference in standards or in permitted practices, it is here. Any differences in practices to make the lawyers known must have as their decisive factors the welfare of the public and the protection of the clients.

A difference between the levels of the morality of aspiration toward which lawyers should strive and the morality of duty enforced by disciplinary proceedings is accepted by the Code of Professional Responsibility.[29] The difference poses difficult problems for the lawyer, who is acting as representative and protector of another and not for himself.[30]

The diversities of clients and lawyers and consequent needed variations in some details must not obscure the essential unity of the bar in its major responsibilities:

> "(W)e now realize that we are all parts of a seamless professional web. . . . We are essentially homogeneous about the major concerns of the Bar, but it would be impossible and undesirable to homogenize us. . . . Such a Bar must be prepared to make the adversary system work for every one, so that every litigant, rich or poor, popular or despised, may be sure to have a spokesman who will say

29. The difference is implicit in the opinion of Circuit Justice Miller in In re Thomas, 36 F. 242 (C.C.Colo. 1888). It is explicit in Professor Lon Fuller's lectures, The Morality of Law (1964).

30. See Thode, The Ethical Standards for the Advocate, 39 Tex.L. Rev. 575 (1961).

for him what can properly be said so that an independent court can decide after fairly hearing both sides." [30.5]

A professional man publicly charged with wrongdoing has the professional duty, even though there be no legal duty,[31] to come forward and give the facts. Senator Joseph McCarthy is an illustration. The Senator failed to appear before a Senate committee which was investigating charges of misconduct, including the diversion to his personal account of funds raised to help in his "anti-communist" activities, and the use of his official position to obtain a fee. The Senate committee of inquiry in its report which recommended censure stated:

> "[W]hen the personal honor and official conduct of a Senator of the United States are in question before a duly constituted committee of the Senate, the Senator owes a duty to himself, his State, and to the Senate, to appear promptly and cooperate fully when called by a Senate committee charged with the responsibility of inquiry.[32] .   .   ."

More important, of course, than all the formal matters sketched above is the informal attitude of lawyers toward one another and toward their work, the self-image of the bar as a sociologist might put it. Rarely has this attitude been exemplified so happily as it was by Mr. Harrison Tweed of the New York bar in his many professional activities out of which he got fun and for which he was honored. Rarely has it been expressed so well as by him in his report as president of his local bar association which he had transformed: [33] "I have a high opinion of lawyers. With all their faults, they stack up well against those in every other occupation or profession. They are better to work with or play with or fight with or drink with than most other varieties of mankind."

SECTION 7. THE PUBLIC

The attitude of the public bears strongly on the legal profession and its work. Three bearings call for mention: (1) the values of the community, (2) the attitude toward the profession generally, (3) the attitude toward a particular client.

30.5 Whitney North Seymour, The Unity of the Bar, 86 Rep.A.B.A. 443, 445–47 (1961).

31. Cf. Spevack v. Klein, 385 U.S. 511 (1966).

32. Senate Select Comm. to Study Censure Charges, Report on Resolution to Censure, S.Rep.No. 2508, 83d Con., 2d Sess. 27 (1954).

33. 1 Rec. of N.Y.C.B.A. 8 (1946).

The Values of the Community

The general values and standards of the community of which the lawyer is a part have naturally a strong effect on him. He is retained by a client to protect and advance the client's interests in the society of which both are members. In advancing these interests he takes into account, and he can not escape, the effect of the values of the larger community. He may identify himself with his clients' particular segment of that community. Yet it is the very nature and use of a profession to instill and develop the qualities needed for the adequate performance of its social function in spite of what may be opposing values in the community it serves. This is at the heart of Judge Cardozo's statement that a fiduciary is held to a standard stricter than that of the morals of the market place.[1] There is a reciprocal relation between the standards of the community and those of the lawyer. In advising the client in a way which takes decent account of the interests of others, the lawyer is aiding the client and also helping to shape the standards of the community. As was said in denying an application for admission to the bar:[2]

> "[H]e has an unparalleled opportunity to fix the code of ethics and to determine the moral tone of the business life of his community."

The Public Image of the Lawyer

To see ourselves as others see us is useful. It is a preliminary to measures to make the others see us at our true worth or else to try to set right what the others see more clearly than we do.

The attitude of the public toward the profession is not friendly; though the attitude of clients toward their own lawyers, it is gratifying to observe, is higher than that toward the profession as a whole.[3]

One harmful result of the low esteem is that it deters those in need of legal services from consulting lawyers, a fact which is at the basis of the development of group legal services vouched for by a trusted intermediary. Another unfortunate result is that it may lead to pressure by clients on lawyers to aid them in questionable plans, a matter noted in studies of the bar in two cities.[4]

1. Meinhard v. Salmon, 249 N.Y. 458, 464, 164 N.E. 545, 546 (1928).

2. In re Farmer, 191 N.C. 235, 239, 131 S.E. 661, 663 (1926).

3. See Drinker, Laymen on the Competency and Integrity of Lawyers, 22 Tenn.Law Rev. 371 (1952); Missouri Bar, Prentice Hall Survey 34, 40, 67 (1963).

4. See J. Carlin, Lawyers' Ethics; A Survey of the New York City Bar (1966); J. Carlin, Lawyers on Their Own (1962).

Some reasons for the dislike are inherent in a system of law, as Dean Pound has pointed out.[5] The law through its generality of statement seeks to eliminate the personal feelings of the judge, to promote equality of treatment of all persons before the court, and to make possible dependable planning of human relations. This generality of statement may lead the layman who is looking for justice as he conceives it in the individual case to view the law as a mass of technicalities.

The cultural lag of law is another ground of criticism. In a democracy law and law making are usually not in the forefront of social change. Except under dictators or rare social leaders, law often delays its advances until public opinion is clear in its judgment. For critics of the social order who are clear in their judgments on the certainly imperfect present—and sure of the future they would quickly bring about—the lag will always be irritating. Through their criticisms and proposals and urgings they can fortunately shorten the lag.

Another reason for the negative attitude is a lack of understanding of law and of lawyers' methods. The public can perceive the law as an instrument of "law and order" in the larger sense. They fail to perceive that it is through the work of lawyers that the law gives structure and firmness to the consensual arrangements which are the fabric of our economic and social life. They are unaware that most of the work of lawyers is devoted to this structuring of private arrangements. It is useful to take note here of some other general criticisms.

One of these is that the lawyer is a mercenary who will defend or advance any cause however questionable for which he is retained. The charge is directed in part at what the bar conceives as its high responsibility and, indeed, duty under the Constitution to provide counsel for every defendant accused of a serious crime. The bar will continue to perform this duty however disagreeable despite public misunderstanding and criticism. Unfortunately, the bar's sense of duty to give representation to one accused of a past crime may be distorted by some of its members into the wholly different role of giving aid and counsel in the planning and execution of shady schemes. A forceful restatement of the bar's own standards so as to make clearer the distinction between representing one accused of a past crime and aiding in the planning of a future dubious scheme would do much to correct the public's misconception.

Another of the criticisms is based on the adversary system of law administration. At times there are inescapable reasons for

5. Pound, The Lay Tradition as to the Lawyer, 12 Mich.L.Rev. 627 (1914).

dislike. One of them is the privilege and duty of the lawyer to present his client's case in the most favorable light as the Code of Professional Ethics states: [6]

> "The advocate may urge any permissible construction of the law favorable to his client, without regard to his professional opinion as to the likelihood that the construction will ultimately prevail."

Another inescapable reason is that when a trial in court is pressed to the end, there is a loser as well as a winner and the loser can scarcely feel kindly toward the aggressive representative of his opponent in a process through which he suffered public defeat. One way, fortunately, of avoiding the impact of this feeling—and lawyers make great use of it—is compromise. Compromise brings peace without defeat which is even more important than peace without complete victory. But when a case is pressed to trial under the adversary system, the party or the witness subjected to a grilling cross-examination has a lasting hatred of the process which humiliated him and the persons who were parties to it. An example is Harold Laski, the English political scientist, who was subjected to such a cross-examination when unwise enough to sue for political libel. He commented that neither he nor any of his friends could recognize the picture portrayed of him in court. Unjustified harshness in this part of the trial process may be reduced by giving to the judge a greater share in the proceedings. This may call for a better method of selection of judges to whom this greater power is entrusted. A recent development which reduces some of the friction in trials is the discovery process. This enables each side to know ahead of time the nature of the evidence to be presented by the other side. Lack of surprise means lessened acrimony.

A common criticism of lawyers is that they represent the well-to-do in oppressing debtors. Shakespeare writing of the 1400's had Dick, the rebel, urge: [7]

> "The first thing we do, let's kill all the lawyers,"

and Jack Cade responded with reasons:

> "Is not this a lamentable thing, that of the skin of an innocent lamb should be made parchment? That parchment, being scribbled o'er should undo a man?"

These rebels of the 1400's had their followers in the Iowa farmers in the great depression of the 1930's who, when their farms were threatened with foreclosure, put the noose around the neck of the chief justice of the supreme court of their state as a warning. This conception of lawyers is linked with a misconception of

---

6. A.B.A. Code of Professional Responsibility, EC 7–4.

7. W. Shakespeare, Henry VI, Part II, act 4, sc. 2.

law itself. As the executive head of the national legal aid organization put it: [8]

> "The law is popularly regarded as a negative and restraining force, something darkly mysterious and forbidding—not a positive and constructive social device for regulating human relations in a way which provides a maximum of opportunity and freedom to the greatest number."

This misconception of law and of lawyers is being corrected by the extension of legal services to all levels of our people to represent them in their public interests as well as their private affairs. Yet debtors will remain with us and in our credit economy their tribe will increase so long as eager merchants urge, "Buy Now, Pay Next Year." And poverty is no assurance of wisdom or of honesty in purchasing or paying. When the lawyer's role is accepted by the poor as well as the rich as that of one who can help to plan wisely, some of the trouble will be removed.

Linked to the misconception above is the fear of the lawyer as one who will overreach his clients in fees and in affairs. Few clients are aware of the nature and extent of the lawyer's work in the preparation of their cases. Even intelligent clients may be aided to an understanding of the lawyer's fees by the time record of the lawyer's work. For the less intelligent and more suspicious other measures are needed. One is the assumption by the grievance committees of the task of conferring with clients who thought they had grievances and of explaining the misunderstandings out of which most complaints arise. As to well-founded grievances there has been suggested the creation of a bar committee which would represent clients in the proceedings against their lawyers for wrongdoing which resulted in loss.[9]

The clients' security fund is maintained by many bar associations. More stringent laws to protect the reputation of the bar by protection of clients against overreaching lawyers may well be useful. The law already puts the burden on the lawyer to show the fairness of his dealings with clients. There is the rare but always much publicized case of the lawyer who is the beneficiary under a will he drew, and the charge made by the client's family of undue influence. It might be a wise rule, which would strike down every gift in a will to the draftsman or his family.

Public Attitude Towards a Particular Client—"Free Press" and "Fair Trial"

These are the catchwords of the controversy over the public attitude toward an accused. Behind the catchwords is the fact that

8. E. Brownell, Legal Aid in the United States 55 (1951).

9. Thatcher, Annual Statement of the President, Yearbook of Ass'n of Bar of N.Y.C. 141 (1935).

when a sensational crime is committed, many local newspapers now publish all the material the reporters can dig up as to the crime and the accused and his background. The publication makes it difficult to get jurymen who can render a verdict only on the facts brought out in court.

"What confounds our problem" as an excellent study of the subject commented, "is, in G. K. Chesterton's phrase, its competition is not between right and wrong but between right and right." [10]

The issue between the press and the bar is usually the narrow one of time. The bar seeks the prevention of publication before trial *only* of material which might substantially affect the jury's action. There is no thought of excluding newsmen from the courtroom, or of halting publication after the verdict of material about the case, or of preventing criticisms however harsh of judges, lawyers, jurymen, witnesses or court procedures after the case is over. There is recognition of the value, even the necessity, of criticism of courts as of other institutions. Newspapers are essential instruments of public scrutiny, and some lawyers have stressed indebtedness to laymen and the press for procedural reform, as with the great English procedural reforms of the 1870's [11] and with the reorganization of the court system of New Jersey in the 1940's.[12]

Justice Holmes put the matter as lawyers see it: [13]

> "When a case is finished, courts are subject to the same criticism as other people, but the propriety and necessity of preventing interference with the course of justice by premature statement, argument or intimidation can hardly be denied."

The standard of the profession in the matter of newspaper publicity is not an isolated thing. It is a part of the measures taken to attain the bar's ideal in a court case of having a dispassionate tribunal reach its result on the consideration of the evidence brought out in court uninfluenced by extraneous factors. In pursuing this ideal, the law requires that an indictment allege specific wrongs and not general undesirability of the accused. Before the trial, it makes available such measures as a change of venue or a continuance and the challenge for cause of the jurymen. During the trial, it excludes irrelevant evidence and permits sequestration of the jury. After the verdict, it makes possible a new trial and the grant of habeas corpus—even by the

---

10. A. Friendly & R. Goldfarb, Crime and Publicity 237 (1967).

11. Sunderland, The Struggle for Procedural Reform, 39 Harv.L.Rev. 725 (1926).

12. A. Vanderbilt, The Challenge of Law Reform 85–86 (1955).

13. Patterson v. Colorado, 205 U.S. 454, 463 (1907).

Supreme Court of the United States[14] for errors seriously impairing a fair trial.

The censensus of recent opinion in the profession is that the essential precautions to prevent harmful publicity are to be taken by the bar and its associates in the administration of justice by drying up the source of information about the cases. The Supreme Court of the United States has referred with approval[15] to the statement by the Supreme Court of New Jersey in its interpretation of the Canons of Professional Ethics[16] that the Canons ban statements to news media by the prosecutors and their staff members of matters harmful to the accused and of statements by defense counsel of exculpatory matters, as well as statements by the police, on pain of discipline by the proper authorities.

An Advisory Committee on Fair Trial and Free Press, created by the American Bar Association, directed its standards primarily to the conduct of lawyers, law enforcement officers and judges. The standards were approved by the Association.[17] The substance of the Advisory Committee's recommendations are included in the Code of Professional Responsibility as to civil and administrative as well as criminal proceedings.[18]

The English practice of holding the publisher of harmful material in contempt of court has not been followed in this country.[19]

On television in the courtroom, two things can be said. One is that most courts now forbid its use.[20] The second is that whether its use is condemned by the Constitution is uncertain. In one case the Supreme Court of the United States reversed a conviction because of television in the courtroom.[21] The five opinions in the case, however, are extraordinarily diverse, ranging from the view that the use of television is inherently unconstitutional to the conclusion that its use was not harmful in the particular

14. See, e. g., Sheppard v. Maxwell, 384 U.S. 333 (1966).

15. Id. at 361.

16. State v. Van Duyne, 43 N.J. 369, 204 A.2d 841 (1964).

17. See A.B.A. Project on Minimum Standards for Criminal Justice, Standards Relating to Fair Trial and Free Press (1968).

18. A.B.A. Code of Professional Responsibility, DR 7–107.

19. An excellent review of the English and American cases is given in A. Friendly & R. Goldfarb, Crime and Publicity 269–314 (1967).

20. Id., Ch. 12. The Supreme Court of Colorado, after a referee found from experiments that the use of the camera, radio and television in the courtroom did not interfere physically with the administration of justice, ordered that their use be left to the discretion of the trial judge. In re Hearings Concerning Canon 35 of the Canons of Judicial Ethics, 132 Colo. 591, 296 P.2d 465 (1956).

21. Estes v. Texas, 381 U.S. 532 (1965).

case and the determination as to limitations on its use should be made later in the light of developments in the industry.[22]

Publicity for Clients

The discussion of publicity for the client has been limited thus far to court cases involving past transactions in which the bar's standards call for decisions reached on the record before the court. Such cases form only a small part of the lawyer's work, and in other areas the standards of the bar are much less clear. In these other situations the public attitude may be the decisive factor which the parties seek. Some illustrations follow.

A large grocery chain was the defendant in an anti-trust action. Its officers, believing the charges harmful to its good will unless publicly denied, decided on a publicity campaign which would include a portrayal of the failure of the government in earlier cases against it. The first law firm which the defendant sought to retain in the case declined the retainer under the circumstances, saying "We try our cases in the courts." Another firm of equal standing took the case.

In the 1920's a few run-away neckwear manufacturers which paid sub-standard wages moved their shops to New Haven to escape from an industry wide agreement made in New York with a labor union. The controversy with its consequent picketing was ignored by the New Haven newspapers. "Our problem, then, became," as the lawyer for the union wrote, "one of attracting the attention of citizens of New Haven to the pivotal labor controversy going on in their midst. . . . Our only chance to win was through the mobilization of public opinion."[23] The lawyer for the union spoke before the Yale Liberal Club. The up-shot was that Yale students distributed leaflets in violation of a city ordinance (later held unconstitutional); nineteen of them were arrested and went on trial. This was news that could not be ignored, and "(t)he conspiracy of silence on the part of the New Haven papers was broken."[24]

Legislation is dependent on public support, and public support is dependent on publicity. The lawyer who represents a client as in legislative matters knows that his client is seeking publicity in various ways to support the measure he desires. Yet this alone is surely no reason for the lawyer to refuse to represent the client.

The stated standards of the profession do not deal directly and clearly with such matters. Some comments will be submitted. One is that the broadly determinative factors should be the na-

22. See note 20 supra.

23. L. Waldman, Labor Lawyer 169–170 (1944).

24. Id. at 172.

ture of the proceedings and the wisdom of permitting or condemning publicity in that kind of proceeding. The standards developed for the highly structured criminal trial, with the jury protected against outside influences, may be unsuited to other proceedings. A second comment is that it would ordinarily be unwise, even when proper, for the lawyer to guide publicity methods if for no other reason than that public relations is not his field. Finally there must be some professional limitations on the lawyer in these matters, even though they are not yet clearly developed. The comment made by one writer, expert in securing publicity, that the only requirement is accuracy must be rejected.[25]

SECTION 8.   THE INDIVIDUAL

The supports mentioned so far—the law, the profession, the public—are all outside the particular lawyer. Is there something individual to him however derived which helps to influence him in his actions.

Inner conviction in private and professional action and social conscience are different things. A supporter of social justice in the large may be a shyster in his practice, and a man honorable in his personal and professional dealings may be callous to injustices in the system of which he is a part. The profession of law needs both qualities, inner conviction and social conscience, in its quest for equal justice under law.[1]

"Knowledge is virtue," said Socrates, and knowledge is also the assurance of virtue for a man will do what he knows he should do. A lawyer who knows the true standards of the profession, the great teacher would have said, needs no further support or sanction in his acts. Regretably, we cannot agree. Knowledge is not enough. The lawyer, "must also possess the resolution necessary to carry into effect what his intellect tells him ought to be done."[2]

25. J. Ehrlich, Controlling Trial Publicity in American Jurisprudence, 1 Trials 303, 310 (1964).

1. Norman Thomas, the Socialist leader, thus characterized a controversial and tragic figure: "No one did more harm to the cause of civil liberties in this country in the last 20 years than did Alger Hiss. He meant well, but by acting on the belief that the moral law could be broken to achieve a proper purpose, he defeated that very purpose." Harvard Law School Record, Nov. 13, 1952, 1, 4.

2. Professional Responsibility: A Statement, 44 A.B.A.J. 1159 (1958).

"Inner disposition," "ethical concern," were found by a law-yer-sociologist to be powerful factors no less influential than external pressure in securing adherence to ethical standards by the individual.[3]

What is this further quality? How can we strengthen it in ourselves? When may we follow its guidance in the representation of clients though it departs from the accepted standards of the bar? These are some of the questions that occur.

At the heart of this inner concern and resolution is a sense of personal and professional values.[4] A passage linking three great judges indicates its nature.[5]

> "We care less for what a man does than for what he is; and what he is depends upon what seems to him good, upon where his treasure lies."

Belonging to and sharing in something beyond ourselves is the great source of strength. Religion is the ultimate source for many, as even an unbeliever will agree. Mr. Justice Brennan joined in the regret of Judge Fahy that a notable work failed to include religion as a source of strength.[6] Association with others who command our respect, as the same Justice points out, may give aid even though the association is only through history and biography.[7] The power to lift ourselves by our efforts and to make us more of what we wish to be is emphasized by a notable lawyer-sociologist:[8]

> "We are only beginning to understand the power of individuals to shape their own character by their selection among models and experiences."

Pride in one's profession can be a great factor. Fortunate is the lawyer who shares such feelings as those of Edouard Clunet, founder of the international law review which informally took his name. In acknowledging a resolution in his honor at a meeting of the International Law Association he said:[9]

3. J. Carlin, Lawyers' Ethics: A Survey of the New York Bar (1966).

4. "For this the lawyer requires a sense of attachment to something larger than himself." Professional Responsibility, 44 A.B.A.J. 1159, 1218 (1958).

5. This passage, from Chief Justice Warren's address at a Special Session of the Court of Appeals of the Second Circuit to Commemorate Fifty Years of Federal Judicial Service by Judge Learned Hand, had been applied by Judge Hand to Justice Brandeis on his 82nd birthday. 264 F.2d 19 (1959).

6. W. Brennan, Charles Fahy, 54 Geo.L.J. 1, 3–4 (1965).

7. W. Brennan, Occasional Pamphlet Number Nine, Harvard Law School (1967).

8. Riesman, The Study of National Character: Some Observations on the American Case, 13 Harv.Lib. Bull. 5, 24 (1951).

9. Bellot, Maitre Clunet, 4 Brit.Y.B. Int'l L. 187, 189 (1923–24). (Transl.)

"You will greatly oblige me if you permit me not to keep these compliments for myself. If I am something here, if I have worked during my life, it is because I have developed at the bar some habits of mind, a discipline, a method, which perhaps have made something of me. . . . So these compliments which you have kindly directed to me, if you will be good enough to permit me, and on this point I expect your unanimous support, it is to the bar of Paris to which we will direct them."

There is a further question. When may a lawyer adhere to his personal standards of conduct, and when must he act in accordance with accepted standards of the bar different from his own? If he is acting without harmful effect on a person for whose welfare he is responsible, he is free to apply his personal standards. So it is when a case is offered and he is determining whether to accept it. In non-adjudicatory matters he has a broad privilege of advice and withdrawal, as the Code of Professional Responsibility EC 7-8 points out:

"In assisting his client to reach a proper decision, it is often desirable for a lawyer to point out those factors which may lead to a decision that is morally just as well as legally permissible . . . In the event that the client in a non-adjudicatory matter insists upon a course of conduct that is contrary to the judgment and advice of the lawyer but not prohibited by Disciplinary Rules, the lawyer may withdraw from the employment."

In a litigated matter the question is more difficult. It has been urged that a lawyer should follow the authoritatively established standard only and should not use his own standard, and the client is entitled to the full protection of the law.[10] Two comments are offered. A lawyer may follow his own judgment over the client's objection as to matters of procedural detail. A lawyer may not surrender any substantial claim or defense without the client's knowledge.

This chapter has raised many questions on the fundamental and the authoritative sources of the standards of the profession and on their supports and sanctions. Here at the end it is manifest that there is no sharp distinction in fundamental sources between the rules of law, the Canons of the profession and the individual's own standards. They have as their common purpose to

---

10. Thode, The Ethical Standard of the Advocate, 39 Tex.L.Rev. 575 (1961); C. Curtis, It's Your Law (1954). An English court held that trustees in making a sale may not apply their personal standards of honesty in carrying out an oral promise within the statute of frauds when before the contract was signed a larger sum was offered by another purchaser. Buttle v. Saunders, [1950] All E.R. 193 (Vol. 2, Ch.Div.).

aid the bar to carry the responsibilities entrusted to it under difficult conditions. They have as a common characteristic that the spirit is more important than the letter of rules. Never has the primacy of the spirit over the letter been more important than in these years of unmatched range and speed of social change.

Part II

THE LAWYER AT WORK

Lawyers are guilty of the law. The greatest of English legal historians, Maitland, made the point. "It is we who are guilty of our own law, for as Hobbes rightly says, 'The legislator is he not by whose authority the laws were first made, but by whose authority they continue to be laws.'"[1] Laws in this country continue to be laws primarily at the sufferance of private lawyers, the principal administrators of law. Holmes' aphorism comes to mind: we need study of the obvious more than investigation into the obscure.

This Part of the book—The Lawyer at Work—is directed to a simple and obvious proposition: The most important part of the lawyer's work is standards.

> "In contemporary juristic thought, if we look the world over, the significant names are those of Jhering, Stammler, Geny, Duguit and Kelsen. . . . Looking back at the work of these five significant jurists, do we find anything in common? For one thing, they all put the problem of values, of a criterion for valuing interests or claims or desires, in the first place as the fundamental problem of jurisprudence."[2]

The importance of "a criterion for valuing interests or claims or desires" for the lawyer means that lawyer's standards are an integral part of law itself. Yet, this obvious idea, the theme of this Part—and indeed of the whole book—seems to have escaped the notice of the profession. Reading the Code of Professional Responsibility, one can hardly avoid the impression that it is regarded as a mere appendix to the law which the lawyer is charged with administering. The hortatory tone of the canons in the Code—A Lawyer Should . . . —belies the importance of standards.

There is another major aspect of standards. As a successor to the Canons of 1908, the Code of Professional Responsibility carries forward the emphasis of the earlier standards on the role of advocate in court with little recognition or discussion of the problems outside the judicial process. And we lawyers our-

1. Maitland, The Law of Real Property, in Collected Papers, vol. 1, 162, 194 (H. Fisher, ed. 1911).

2. Pound, Law and the Science of Law in Recent Theories, 43 Yale L. J. 525, 530, 534 (1934).

selves have been curiously blind to the other processes that make up our legal system. The private legal process, the legislative process, and the administrative process are as important in our society as the public legal process in court.

The roles of the lawyer in these processes differ widely—from that of advocate in the highly structured setting of the common law trial dealing with past events to the lawyer in his office planning the future actions of his client, from that of the lawyer lobbying in the legislature to the lawyer representing a client in an *ex parte* proceeding before an administrative agency. These roles, their settings, and the responsibilities they entail vary. Standards grow out of responsibilities, and they, too, must vary, for the standards of the lawyer are, and must be, functional.

The need for functional standards arises from the two fundamental policies of our legal system—order and stability for society, and justice for the individual—which may, and do, often conflict. The lawyer ordinarily is privately employed to represent one side in a controversy. Yet, he is engaged in what is essentially a public enterprise. The responsibilities which these two roles—private representative of his client and public agent of the social order—impose upon him are present in all the legal processes, and it is these responsibilities which give rise to his three basic standards—loyalty to the client, candor to the tribunal, and fairness to the opponent.

These loyalties, as do the basic policies underlying our legal system, all conflict in some measure. The lawyer needs affirmative guides in the form of standards to aid him in resolving these conflicts. The stated standards create for him a level of expectations, a matter of fundamental importance, for lawyers, as do all men, tend to act as others expect them to act.

These ideas recur throughout this Part in the various chapters, each of which is written to be a self-contained unit. The purpose here is to aid all of us in the law—lawyers, judges, law students, and law teachers—in perceiving the differences in their roles as men of law and the differing standards which these roles require and which arise naturally from the contexts of the various roles. After a discussion of the nature of the lawyer's work, separate chapters deal with the judicial process, the private legal process, the legislative process, and the administrative process as distinct legal processes in our society. Two other chapters treat the role of compromise in our legal system and the special role of the government lawyer.

Chapter V

THE NATURE OF THE LAWYER'S WORK

SECTION 1. INTRODUCTION

The American lawyer exercises great power. In a nation based on the principle that men can best live in harmony under the rule of law, it could not be otherwise. Law is the principal instrument of power in our society, and, since it is not self-applying, the lawyer is the principal participant in its administration. As a social instrument to define the limits of conduct in society, law restrains some actions, encourages some, and permits others. The lawyer is necessary to interpret law to give it meaning for the individual, to apply law to give the individual its benefits, and, often, as when he draws a contract or charters a corporation, to make law to enable the individual to engage in a desired course of conduct. Law is thus both a restraining and an enabling instrument of society.

The restraints which law imposes, however, are more affirmations than limitations. In restraining some, the law gives greater freedom to others, for law is the source of order and through order we have liberty for the individual[1]—ordered liberty in Justice Cardozo's phrase. Even so, despite the fundamental importance of law, the extent of the lawyer's power is seldom recognized or acknowledged, for it is a subtle power of varied forms. It has its intellectual component, the ability to analyze, synthesize and organize raw facts into meaningful patterns and to persuade and influence through the use of ideas. It has its economic component, for the lawyer often has at his disposal economic power, either of his firm or his client, or both. In its most important aspects, it is a legal power, for the lawyer is the only non-governmental employee authorized to administer law and to make law for others. Still, the fact of the lawyer's power often goes unperceived. In part this is because he exercises it not for himself, but for another. His primary task is to individualize the law for his client. He counsels and advises his client on what the law requires, what it permits, and what it prohibits; he gives order to his client's relationships with others through the making

---

1. See R. Hale, Freedom through Law (1952).

63

of private law, as by contract; he resolves conflicts through conciliation, negotiation and compromise, or, that failing, by litigation.

Another factor which helps conceal the lawyer's power is that he exercises it as a participant in the various legal processes— the judicial, the private, the legislative, and the administrative —which make up the American legal system. Attention is directed to the institutions of these various processes—the court, the law office, the legislature, and the administrative agencies— rather than to the lawyer's part in them. The private legal process goes almost unobserved.

Even lawyers themselves, for the most part, are not conscious of their power or of its impact on clients or of its importance to the freedom of our society. The adversary system, perhaps, is the primary reason for this lack of perception, for that system requires that the lawyer deal and work with other lawyers. This lawyer-to-lawyer, rather than the lawyer-to-layman, relationship dispels the impression of power and authority. Yet, while the conduct is that of lawyers, the interests affected are those of clients. Too often the lawyer fails to realize that he does not deal with legal problems so much as he deals with human problems in a legal context.

The lawyer's power carries with it commensurate responsibilities which require appropriate standards. There is here a paradox. No profession has devoted so much attention to standards as the legal profession, and no profession has failed so completely in making its members realize the importance of standards in their work.

> "Lawyers confirm what social scientists studying the profession from the outside have observed: that the bar has long been woefully lax in enforcing its professed ethical standards, especially those which apply to the quality of representation rather than to financial dealings with clients or relations among lawyers. Moreover, the judiciary can make little claim to clarifying or adequately enforcing appropriate standards of professional and ethical conduct. In the last analysis, failure in this area rests broadly upon the bar, but specifically upon judges—and upon trial judges the more so." [2]

This failure results, in part at least, from the failure of lawyers —and of judges—to recognize the lawyer's power. Without an awareness of this fact, neither judges nor lawyers can accept an-

---

2. A.B.A. Project on Standards for Criminal Justice, Standards Relating to the Prosecution Function and the Defense Function 10 (T.D. 1970).

other equally fundamental fact: Lawyers' standards are an integral part of law itself.

The difficult problem for the lawyer in his work is not the technical problem of what can be done or how to do it. It is, rather, what should be done. Yet, it is this problem which is most often ignored. This part of the book—The Lawyer at Work —deals with the problem in different settings. The purpose is to perceive and describe the elements of the lawyer's work and to aid the reader in determining the appropriate standards for the lawyer's different roles.

SECTION 2.   THE CHANGING ROLES OF THE LAWYER

To the common law and the judicial process created for its administration, we owe most of our fundamental ideas of freedom. Chief Justice Coke's idea and insistence in seventeenth century England that the sovereign was subject to law found its fullest fruition in the first eight amendments to the United States Constitution. Yet, the common law system, with its emphasis on the rights of the individual and its reliance on the affirmative action of the individual to protect those rights, has its shortcomings. The aid of lawyers in the private legal process is beyond the reach of many. The judicial process has grave deficiencies as an instrument of government in a modern society. Litigation is time consuming and expensive and it is best suited for the protection of the rights of those who need it least. Too often those who need the protection of law and the aid of lawyers do not have the knowledge, the time or the resources to obtain the benefits of "equal justice under law in an adversary system of law administration." A major reason for the development of the administrative process is the unsuitability of the judicial process for many situations. "The Trade Commission Act," for example, "is one of several in which Congress, to make its policy effective, has relied upon the initiative of administrative officials and the flexibility of the administrative process." [1] But that process, too, is inadequate alone to meet the problems. The next important stage in the development of the legal processes in this country, already begun, will be a further development of the private legal process to insure its availability for all rather than merely for those who can afford it.

1.   United States v. Morton Salt Co., 338 U.S. 632, 640, 70 S.Ct. 357, 363 (1950).

Such is the power of history and tradition, however, that despite the increasing importance of these other legal processes, the lawyer is still most closely identified with the judicial process. The private legal process has never had a clear and separate identification. The lawyer's role in the administrative process has had little effect on either the popular conception of the lawyer or the profession's own view of itself.

The interrelationship of the various legal processes and the dominance of the judicial process have tended to obscure the changing nature of the lawyer's work. Results of both the private legal process (e. g., a contract) and the administrative process (e. g., a rule or order) are subject to judicial review, and the court is viewed as the ultimate arbiter of all disputes. Moreover, the basic skills of the lawyer developed in law school in the study of court cases—analysis, synthesis, organization, and communication—are the same for all the processes. And, finally, the changes have not visibly altered the larger, dual setting of the lawyer's work, the competitive economy of our society and the adversary system of law administration.

Yet, the changing nature of the lawyer's work cannot long remain obscure. As the traditional courtroom setting of the lawyer's work is more and more supplanted by the settings of the office and the administrative agency, the result will be a change in the adversary system itself. That system is not well suited to the responsibilities of the lawyer in his office or before an administrative agency.

Even today the nature of the trial, the mainstay of the adversary system, has already been changed by procedural reforms. The emphasis on form, characteristic of legal systems in their early stages, has given way to emphasis on substance. The pleadings under the Federal Rules of Civil Procedure are limited to three, the complaint, the answer, and, in some instances, a reply. All other pleadings are replaced by motions. The rules for discovery enable each litigant to learn the facts of the case, with a consequent emphasis on candor rather than concealment.

The principal function of the private legal process—the ordering of the client's relationship with others through private law—becomes more important and more complex as the interdependence of our society increases. That process, too, is changing, for "[a]n institutional framework designed for the service of the law's traditional clients, with their ready access to legal services, cannot now satisfy the profession's responsibility to the client born of more recent social upheavals . . . ."[2] There is an

2. Brennan, The Responsibilities of the Legal Profession, 54 A.B.A.J. 121, 122 (1968).

increasing responsibility on lawyers who arrange the private affairs of individuals to be concerned that their clients do not infringe the basic interests of others. A racially restrictive covenant in a deed is no longer legally permissible.

The modern administrative process is not in fact a part of the common law or the adversary system, and the profession owes itself a more careful consideration of the differences between the administrative and judicial processes than it has given. "It must not be forgotten that the administrative process and its agencies are relative newcomers in the field of law and that it has taken and will continue to take experience and trial and error to fit this process into our system of judicature." [3] A major part of this consideration must be the relationship of the courts and the agencies. "Neither body should repeat in this day the mistake made by the courts of the law when equity was struggling for recognition as an ameliorating system of justice . . . ." [4]

There is yet another role of the lawyer, a traditional role, which has not generally been identified as having its own unique characteristics and problems within the adversary system. This is the role of the government lawyer. Yet, it is clear that the government lawyer both in court and in his office must function differently from his private counterpart. In form, his work may be the same, but in purpose and function, it is different, for he represents the interest of the public and not that of an individual client.

The lawyer's increasing roles are interrelated with his increasing responsibilities.

> "Society's overriding concern today is with providing freedom and equality of rights and opportunities, in a realistic and not merely formal sense, to all the people of this nation: justice, equal and practical, to the poor, to the members of minority groups, to the criminally accused, to the displaced persons of the technological revolution, to alienated youth, to the urban masses, to the unrepresented consumers—to all, in short, who do not partake of the abundance of American life." [5]

---

3. United States v. Morton Salt Co., 338 U.S. 632, 642, 70 S.Ct. 357, 364 (1950).

4. United States v. Morgan, 307 U.S. 183, 191, 59 S.Ct. 795, 799–800 (1939).

5. Brennan, supra note 2, at 122.

SECTION 3. THE PROBLEM OF STANDARDS

"[T]he profession of the law, in its nature the noblest and most beneficial to mankind, is in its abuse and abasement the most sordid and pernicious." [1] These words of Lord Bolingbroke indicate the fundamental importance of standards to the lawyer's work, for "The practice of the law is not a business but a profession—a form of public trust . . .." [2] The general standards of society are not always an adequate guide for fulfilling this trust. The work of the lawyer requires a special kind of conduct for special purposes, to give order to individual relationships through the making of private law, to resolve conflicts, and to prosecute or defend a lawsuit.

Standards of the legal profession, being statements of the lawyer's obligations and guides to his conduct in using the law for his client, vary in purpose and function as do rules of law. Stated standards for lawyers, prepared and published by the profession, however, are of recent origin in this country, for the role of standards in the highly structured system of the common law was a limited one. The early common law procedure provided precise and detailed guides to the lawyer's conduct in court.

As the common law system of procedure became more flexible, it became more amenable to the exercise of discretion by the lawyer and the need for stated standards for lawyers became more apparent. Only sixty years after the beginning of procedural reform in this country, with the adoption of the Field Code in New York in 1848, the American Bar Association adopted its first statement of standards by the profession, the Canons of Ethics in 1908. [3] These canons were superseded in 1969 by the Code of Professional Responsibility, only thirty one years after the second major procedural reform in this country, the Federal Rules of Civil Procedure in 1938.

The ABA Canons of 1908 were concerned largely with the role of the lawyer as an advocate in the judicial process in an adversary system. The Code of Professional Responsibility, to a somewhat lesser degree, continues this emphasis on the role of the lawyer in the trial. The Code does make explicit the dis-

---

1. See People ex rel. Bulkley v. Salomon, 184 Ill. 490, 501, 56 N.E. 815, 818–819 (1900). See Chapter IV, Standards, Supports and Sanctions.

2. State v. Horan, 21 Wis.2d 66, 70, 123 N.W.2d 488, 489–90 (1963).

3. Eleven states enacted codes of professional conduct prior to 1908. Report of the Comm. on Code of Professional Ethics, 31 A.B.A.Rep. 676 (1907).

tinction between the lawyer as advocate and as adviser,[4] but while it deals in detail with the standards of the advocate, there is no fullness of treatment for his other roles. The recognition and brief discussion in the Ethical Considerations of the roles of the lawyer in the administrative [5] and legislative [6] processes and of the government lawyer [7] are inadequate, and only the latter is specifically subjected to any Disciplinary Rules.[8]

The Code is subject to the same criticism made of the Canons of Ethics by a great judge, Chief Justice Stone. "Our canons of ethics for the most part are generalizations designed for an earlier era." [9] There is a basis for saying that the Code, as did the Canons of 1908, reflects too much the role of the lawyer as advocate in a trial, and manifests only a minimal regard for the other roles of the lawyer. Yet, two factors in defense and support of the Code must be borne in mind. One is that the criticism is a criticism of the profession and of legal writers, rather than the Code. The standards of any profession are not imposed; they evolve from awareness and concern by the individuals in the profession. The draftsmen of the Code were not legislating; they were drafting a restatement of the profession's standards. The other point is that the Code, as a statement of definitive and fixed standards, may have been drafted at an unfortunate time of rapid change. The awareness and recognition of new and current problems the legal profession must deal with have not been fully developed in the consciousness of the profession.[10] The individual lawyer, however, is not limited to the minimal standards of the Code in his conduct. He need only recognize that standards applicable to the role of the lawyer in the trial of a case are not readily transferrable to his other roles in different settings.

4. "Where the bounds of law are uncertain, the action of a lawyer may depend on whether he is serving as advocate or adviser. A lawyer may serve simultaneously as both advocate and adviser, but the two roles are essentially different. In asserting a position on behalf of his client, an advocate for the most part deals with past conduct and must take the facts as he finds them. By contrast, a lawyer serving as adviser primarily assists his client in determining the course of future conduct and relationships. While serving as advocate, a lawyer should resolve in favor of his client doubts as to the bounds of the law. In serving a client as adviser, a lawyer in appropriate circumstances should give his professional opinion as to what the ultimate decisions of the courts would likely be as to the applicable law." A.B.A. Code of Professional Responsibility, EC 7–3.

5. Id., EC 7–15.

6. Id., EC 7–16.

7. Id., EC 7–13.

8. Id., DR 7–103.

9. Stone, The Public Influence of the Bar, 48 Harv.L.Rev. 1, 10 (1934).

10. See Chapter XVIII, Private, Public and Group Interests and Their Protection.

Trial standards are designed for adversary proceedings, and they relate primarily to the conduct of the lawyer, not to the conduct of the client. The trial is concerned only with a determination of the consequences of the client's past actions, and the lawyer is not free to sit in judgment on those actions. He may, for example, have the duty of defending a confessed murderer, and the standards of the advocate require that he do so to the utmost of his ability, without regard to the heinous nature of the crime.

In the unstructured setting of the private legal and the administrative processes, the conduct of the client is relevant to the lawyer's standards, for the lawyer outside the trial most often looks to the future, not the past. He is not only free to judge his client's proposed actions, it is part of his job to do so. He prepares and submits a prospectus to the Securities and Exchange Commission for approval to make a public offering of securities; he prepares a tax return; he represents a client in an administrative hearing to determine if a drug is safe for the market; he negotiates a contract.

These problems may raise difficult questions for the lawyer as to what he may and may not properly do. To the extent that the requirements of the law are clear, the lawyer has a duty to comply with it and the law requires absolute candor for the prospectus. The law, however, may be clear, but not comprehensive. The tax return must be accurate, but must it be candid? May the lawyer prepare a return with the correct information, but stated in such a way that a questionable deduction is obscured? In the administrative hearing, must the lawyer volunteer information that may prevent approval for the marketing of the drug? Does the lawyer have a duty of fairness to the party with whom he is contracting?

For such problems—which he must resolve for the concrete situation in all its complexities—the lawyer needs the aid of affirmative standards of the profession. He acts not for himself, but for another in a fiduciary capacity. The fiduciary role, however, is a unique one. The lawyer has a duty of loyalty to his client, but he also has a duty of loyalty to himself, to his profession, and to society. The standards which guide him thus must be accepted as an integral part of the law which he is charged with administering.

The issues involved in these problems, and the factors the lawyer may consider in resolving them, come into sharper focus if the lawyer's role is analyzed in terms of the power of his client, that is the authority and ability to achieve a certain result in a given situation. The usual analysis of the lawyer's role is in terms of the rights of his client, and from this view, standards are seen as an aspect of the client's rights. The protection afforded by the attorney-client relationship, for example, is for the benefit of the client, not the lawyer. The client's legal right, however, is in fact often a legal power to create private law which will govern his relationship with another, as the power to enter into a contract or charter a corporation. Whenever he exercises rights for his client, the lawyer exercises this legal power, which may be closely related to economic power. And as the legal system gives individuals the legal power to order their relationships by the making of private law, the great advantage rests with those individuals who have the money. The fair operation of the system depends upon the responsible exercise of power by these individuals in their relationships with others. The lawyer should consider not only his client, but also others with whom he deals on behalf of his client and those with whom the client himself deals.

The primary function of standards, then, is to aid the lawyer in making the rules of law work properly through the proper exercise of power. To the extent the standards fulfill this function, they aid in protecting and preserving the power of individuals to control their own affairs wisely and fairly. To the extent they fail, they may bring about a limitation on this power, for the law, while it applies to all equally, also operates on a compensatory principle. The government acts both in cases and in statutes to redress the balance of abused power. The abuse of power in the individual case may be corrected by the decision, often reached through a process of construction. Adhesion contracts will be construed most strongly against the party who drew the instrument. "Standardized contracts such as insurance policies, drafted by powerful commercial units and put before individuals on the 'accept this or get nothing' basis, are carefully scrutinized by the courts for the purpose of avoiding enforcement of 'unconscionable' clauses. At times this avoidance is effected by a process of pseudo 'interpretation'; at other times by refusing to permit successful 'overreaching.' "[11] The abuse of power which affects a large group is most often corrected by statute. Labor legislation, workmen's compensation acts, the Fair Food and Drug laws, and, more lately, civil rights acts show how the abuse of power by groups may lead to corrective legislation.

When the lawyer's role is viewed in terms of power, it becomes apparent that standards are not so much an aspect of the client's rights as they are an aspect of the client's power. The real issue of standards for lawyers today is his responsible exercise of power rather than the right of the client. The responsible exercise

11. 6A A. Corbin, Contracts, § 1376 (1962).

of power, in turn, depends upon the particular facts of a given situation. A lawyer negotiating a contract for Corporation X with Corporation Y, for example, may not have the same obligation which he has in negotiating a contract with an ignorant laborer. The latter contract will be much more readily overturned for unfairness than the former.

The lawyer, for the most part, exercises the power of his client, but when he advises his client, he also exercises a power of his own. The lawyer's power is more subtle than that of his client, for it is based on his judgment and influence and is derived from the client's reliance on him. Canon 5 of the Code of Professional Responsibility states the matter well: "A Lawyer Should Exercise Independent Professional Judgment on Behalf of a Client." Unfortunately, the statements in the Ethical Considerations and the Disciplinary Rules by-pass the main point. They are concerned, and properly so, with the lawyer's avoiding undue influence and conflicting interests which may affect his representation of a client. They suggest but do not require that a lawyer's duty to exercise independent professional judgment extend as well to the duty of avoiding undue influence by the client, as when the client wishes to engage in an improper course of conduct.

The lawyer's primary concern in the judicial process is to protect the rights of his client in determining the consequences of past actions. His task is broader in the administrative and the private legal processes. In these processes, the question is not what the client did or should have done, but what he should do. What is permissible under the letter of the law is not a satisfactory answer, for the concern must be also the spirit of the law and what is best for the client taking all factors into consideration. A part of the lawyer's task is to protect the reputation of his client and to help him be his best self. Treated as an integral part of law, standards aid the lawyer in helping the client be his best self, for as such, they require the lawyer to utilize law in a manner consistent with its purpose and function.

SECTION 4. THE BASIC STANDARDS

Some standards of the legal profession are much like the standards of any profession. They are statements of the duties of the members to that profession and to society. Duties to maintain "the integrity and competence of the legal profession," [1] to make "legal counsel available," [2] and to assist in

1. A.B.A. Code of Professional Responsibility, Canon 1.   2. Id., Canon 2.

"improving the legal system" [3] are in this category. But no other professional man is in so difficult a position as the lawyer acting for his client, and in his work of representing another, the lawyer's standards differ from those of other professions both in complexity and importance. The physician's patient is rarely in conflict with the patient of another physician, as the lawyer's client most often is with the client of another lawyer. The working standards of the lawyer thus must provide solutions to practical problems of conflict and potential conflict which no other professional man faces as a normal part of his work. As the lawyer's roles change and enlarge, so does the potential for conflict, and so does the need for standards which properly measure his increasing duties.

The answer to this problem of standards is to be found in a better understanding of the basic, rather than in the proliferation of specific, standards. To state specific standards to cover the variety of situations the lawyer encounters is impossible. A lawyer must ultimately in most instances, rely upon his own judgment. The quality of that judgment, however, will depend upon his understanding and appreciation of basic standards, for these standards provide the general ideas from which he derives the solution to his problems in a given situation.

The lawyer's basic standards are only three in number—loyalty to his client, candor to the tribunal, and fairness to the opposing party. These standards are fundamental because they are directed to the problems of conflict that the lawyer encounters in his practice and because any problems of conflict he encounters will involve one or all of them. The duty of competence, for example, is a matter of loyalty to the client. But the duty to maintain the confidence of the client or the measure of zeal in representing the client may involve all three standards: loyalty to the client, candor to the tribunal, and fairness to the opposing party. The problem in applying these standards in fact, most often involves the resolution of a conflict between them. The difficulty is not so much in determining what the standards require, as it is in determining the priority to be given them in the particular situation. This difficulty, in turn, is complicated by the fact that the third of the basic standards, fairness to the opposing party, has not yet been articulated as a generally accepted standard for the legal profession.

The point is illustrated in Spaulding v. Zimmerman [4] in which the Supreme Court of Minnesota overturned a court approved settlement. The plaintiff suffered serious injuries from an automobile accident, including "a severe crushing injury of the

---

3. Id., Canon 8.

4. 263 Minn. 346, 116 N.W.2d 704 (1962).

chest with multiple rib fractures", and had several physical examinations by his own doctors, including one on March 1. Several days earlier, on February 22, he had been examined by a doctor for the defendant, whose report showed " 'that this boy of 20 years of age has an [aorta] aneurysm, which . . . may dilate further and . . . rupture . . . this would cause his death.' " [5] The report further stated that if the aneurysm was not present immediately following the accident, "[W]e could be sure that it came out of the accident." [6] Neither the plaintiff nor his doctors was aware of this dangerous condition. The defendant's lawyer did not reveal it either to them or to the court which approved the settlement.

The problem of what the defendant's lawyer should have done in this case is patently clear to anyone except a lawyer. To him it is not at all clear. The issue was essentially one of priorities as to which of the three basic standards should prevail. But there were only two basic stated standards accepted by the profession to choose from—the duty of loyalty to the client and the duty of candor to the court. The court made this clear in its opinion upholding the lower court in setting aside the settlement. The two bases for the court's action were: the minority of the plaintiff, and the duty of candor *to the court* in seeking approval for the settlement.

The appellate court quoted from the memorandum of the trial court: " 'There is no doubt of the good faith of both defendants' counsel. There is no doubt that during the course of the negotiations, when the parties were in an adversary relationship, no rule required or duty rested upon defendants or their representatives to disclose this knowledge.' " [7] That the higher court approved this reasoning is indicated by its own language: "While no canon of ethics or legal obligation may have required them to inform plaintiff or his counsel with respect thereto, or to advise the court therein, it did become obvious to them at the time, that the settlement then made did not contemplate or take into consideration the disability described." [8]

The layman may be excused if he should characterize this reasoning as barbaric. It seems to say that a lawyer's duty to his client to save him a few dollars may be fulfilled at the risk of another's life. Fortunately, neither court meant what it said, for the fact is they held for the plaintiff. Both the lower and the higher court were engaged in the time honored common law tradition of fiction in relying on the lawyer's duty to the court and the minority of the plaintiff. They were in fact recognizing, if

5. Id. at 349, 116 N.W.2d at 707.

6. Id.

7. 263 Minn. at 352, 116 N.W.2d at 709.

8. Id., at 353–54, 116 N.W.2d at 710.

not saying, that there is a duty of fairness to an opponent in adversary proceedings. The duty clearly exists, but the use of fictions enabled the courts to avoid the onerous task of defining it.

The use of fictions in imposing standards on lawyers is an unsatisfactory practice because it obscures the problem. The lawyers in the *Spaulding* case, acting under the pressure of time and conscious of the duty of loyalty to the client, may well have thought that they would be violating the standards of the profession if they had informed the plaintiff of his condition. Many of their collegues might well agree with them, and the court's treatment of the problem does little to clarify the issues for the future. The case can be distinguished on the ground of the minority of the plaintiff, and the language in the opinion can even be used to argue the absence of a duty of fairness to the opponent. Yet, the sanction of reversal applied to the case was the most effective sanction at the court's disposal. Nor should we overlook a basic fact—the client rather than the lawyer bore the brunt of the lawyer's misconception of his duty.

A standard of fairness to the opponent in an adversary proceeding serves to protect the client and to enable the lawyer to avoid undesirable conduct as to which he may feel he has no choice. Contrary to the common assumption—that it will inhibit the lawyer from doing the best job for his client—a standard of fairness to the opponent is in fact complementary of the duty of loyalty and the duty of candor. The duty of fairness gives the lawyer a sound means of resolving problems of conflict between standards when they do arise.

This duty of fairness is the most difficult of the basic standards to apply. A determination of what is fair is particularly hard, when one is acting for another. The lawyer, however, must remember that he is dealing in terms of what the situation calls for, not in terms of absolute standards. The point most often overlooked is that without a duty of fairness to the opponent, the duty of loyalty to the client tends to become absolute, and as it does, it distorts the operation of the legal system.

SECTION 5. THE STANDARDS IN CONTEXT

The context of the working standards of the lawyer is a competitive system of law administration in a society based on a competitive economy. Competition operates on the principle of self-interest, with the freedom and the right to act in accordance with that interest. Yet, rules of law are designed to restrain and limit the actions of the individual and to require him to act in a manner consistent with the larger interests of society. The paradox is that law provides freedom through order, and, this paradox places the lawyer in an anomalous position. As the representative of his client, he has a duty to serve the interest of that client. Consequently, he often feels, and naturally so, a duty to take advantage of the principle of self-interest implicit in the adversary system to act in a way he would not if he were acting for himself. The point has been succinctly stated. "I don't see why we should not come out roundly and say that one of the functions of a lawyer is to lie for his client; and on rare occasions .   .   . I believe it is." [1] But lying lawyers can no more be approved than lying judges, for as a private administrator of the law, the lawyer has a public responsibility to utilize the law for his client only in a way consistent with the larger purposes and fundamental goals of law.

Standards of the legal profession promote and also limit the lawyer's actions in the selfish interest of his client, the former, for example, by the duty of loyalty, the latter by the duty of candor. The first function promotes the policy of the freedom of the individual to control his own affairs, a fundamental policy in our society. The second requires that the freedom be exercised in a responsible manner. The standards thus serve to coordinate two policies which may tend to conflict in the particular case, as do the fundamental policies of the law itself, order for society and justice for the individual. The wise coordination of the two policies means that the standards must be applied according to the context of the particular problem, as working guides rather than abstract principles.

The lawyer's standards stated in general terms may seem to be no more than mere words. But this is so with all general principles of law, as the standards of due care, the reasonable man, proximate cause, and due process. Lawyers agree that these ideas, general as they are, can be usefully applied in the particular case. The ideas of loyalty, candor and fairness are equally

1. Curtis, The Ethics of Advocacy, 4 Stan.L.Rev. 3, 9 (1951).

useful for their purposes. These standards, too, have little meaning until they are applied to, and defined by, the concrete situation, for the facts are necessary to give them content. Without the goals stated by the standards, however, there would be no principles to which the facts are relevant. Due process, for example, exists as a principle stating a goal. This goal can be achieved only in terms of the facts of a given situation in light of the policy implicit in the principle. The meaning of due process varies with the facts of the particular case.

So it is with the standards of loyalty, of candor and of fairness. These duties are as difficult to define in the abstract as due process, but as long as the situation is a normal one, the lawyer has little problem in fulfilling them. They are based on the assumption of normal and ordinary conditions, and precedent and tradition have defined these conditions. Loyalty to the client clearly demands that the lawyer refuse to represent the adversary of the client. The difficulty arises in the unusual situation. Normally, for example, the defendant's lawyer has no duty to reveal to plaintiff the result of a physical examination of plaintiff. But what of the situation where the defendant's report shows a physical disability endangering the plaintiff's life of which he is unaware, as in the *Spaulding* case? The stated standards did not require the defendant's lawyer to act, but the standards as applicable to the facts of the case obviously did.

Another factor which creates difficulty in the application of the standards is that lawyers face not one, but several, continuing normal situations in the representation of clients. One normal situation, of course is that of the advocate in a trial. Another is that of the office lawyer negotiating a contract, and others are the lawyer before an administrative agency, and the government lawyer in either a criminal or a civil case. Each of these situations has its own characteristics which are normal for it, but different from the others. A major factor in the lawyer's determination of the appropriate conduct necessary to comply with standards, then, is his particular role.

The conduct which fulfills the requirements of loyalty for the advocate in a trial may be completely unacceptable to fulfill the duty of loyalty for the office lawyer negotiating a contract. The advocate, for example, may take advantage of his opponent's ignorance in a trial, as when he fails to prove a part of his case; he may even use surprise tactics, as when defense counsel waives final argument to avoid letting the plaintiff have a closing argument to the jury. In the trial of a case, such tactics are within the permissible limits of zeal, but in negotiations for a contract, they reach the borderline, at least, of fraudulent conduct. Clearly a higher degree of candor is appropriate in a civil case than for a defense lawyer in a criminal case, and the duty of candor by lawyers for the government is higher in both civil and criminal cases than the duty of candor by private lawyers. Just as clearly, an administrative tribunal may require complete candor, while the court does not.

The common failure to make these distinctions results, perhaps, from the importance attached to the duty of loyalty to the client, regardless of the nature of the client's problem. For most lawyers, the most difficult problem in applying professional standards is placing the duty of loyalty to the client in proper relation to the duty of candor to the tribunal and the duty of fairness to the opponent. Partly, this is because the role of the lawyer as advocate has been the most important formative factor in the development of the standards. The conduct necessary to fulfill the advocate's duty of loyalty does go further than the conduct necessary to fulfill this duty for the lawyer in his other roles, for the advocate is always faced with a conflict situation. The advocate's special privilege, however, is derived from his particular role, and not from his status as a lawyer.

Another possible reason for the importance attached by the profession to the duty of loyalty is that the duty has a self-serving aspect. The decision in a given case may, for example, determine the lawyer's fee. The lawyer in acting to benefit his client in a trial most often acts to benefit himself also, if by nothing more than to enhance his reputation by winning. The purpose of this duty, of course, far outweighs the self-serving aspect, for it insures the client the type of representation necessary in an adversary system. The loyalty of the lawyer prevents a conflict of interest and requires him to do his best for the unpopular client. But the self-serving aspect may be one reason the duty is too often used in a narrow sense, meaning to the lawyer that he must protect his client's immediate pecuniary interest. Loyalty exists also in a broader sense, as when the lawyer must act to protect the client's interest in his reputation and good name, qualities considered by most to be more important than the pocketbook.

The problem of standards may be the single most important aspect of the lawyer's work for it is standards which determine the quality of the legal profession. Without them, the profession would tend to take on aspects of an oppressive monopoly designed to serve only the selfish interests of the privileged few. At times in our history, and even today in our society, this has happened and is happening. Fortunately, the times and places of this kind of thing are few, for most lawyers are decent men of good will who wish to serve their profession and their community as well as their clients and themselves.

The errors of the profession have been, for the most part, sins of omission rather than sins of commission, resulting from a lack of sensitivity, a lack of vision, and satisfaction with the status quo, qualities nurtured and enhanced by the weight of history and tradition.

Yet, paradoxically, the profession's standards tend to be too general and they may be too idealistic. At too high a level of abstraction, they serve the pride of the profession more than they aid the individual lawyer in dealing with difficult and complex problems in the context of his daily work. Standards must be directed to achieving the right results.

> While the idealist philosophers have been striving to find some *a priori* principle of ethics, the ordinary people of the world, who have to live, and to live in communities, have been silently developing, all through the ages, their own systems of practical morals. While philosophers have been trying, as it were, to construct the roof first and then hang the house from it, the people have been building, brick by brick, from the foundations up. And the house stands. The philosophy for which we are searching is there all the time—is in practice all around us; only we do not recognize it as a philosophy because it is not dignified by the name. It uses no technical terms; but in effect it abandons the *a priori* and proceeds *a posteriori*. It adopts the simple rule that right is that which leads to good results and wrong that which leads to bad results.[2]

2. H. Samuel, Belief and Action 112–13 (1937).

Chapter VI

THE LAWYER AND THE JUDICIAL PROCESS

SECTION 1. INTRODUCTION

Government in this country is subject to the rule of law. The men who drafted the Constitution made law the instrument to determine the power of the government and the relationship of the government to the people. They also made law the instrument to govern the people in their relationship with each other. In so doing, they made the judicial process the central process in the American legal system. The common law trial became the means to determine what matters come within the language of a rule of law and to give meaning and content to the rule. The courts, as instrumentalities of the judicial process, thus emerged as the final arbiters of the results of the other legal processes which make up our legal system: the legislative, the administrative and the private legal process.

Two obvious, and for this reason little noticed, characteristics of the judicial process in this country aid its effectiveness. One is its simplicity and uniformity. There are many courts and many court systems in the United States with its federal system: there are only two kinds of courts, trial and appellate. There are fifty-one jurisdictions, and in all of them, the trial and the appeal have the same basic structures. The other characteristic is its reliance on the private lawyer. While the private legal process is clearly the domain of the lawyer, the judicial process is the only one of the three public legal processes dominated by private lawyers representing private interests. The lawyer's participation in the legislative and the administrative processes is a subordinate one, for these processes are dominated by officials who serve the public interest, not the interest of the private individual.

There is here an anomaly, for in the judicial process the administration of justice is left for the most part to private initiative. Yet it is this process to which the citizen looks above all for justice. Legislatures, sometimes rightly, sometimes wrongly, are viewed as being controlled by lobbyists and special interest groups. Administrative agencies, too, have been criticized as becoming captives of the industries they regulate, and if not, they may become paralyzed into effectiveness by their own bureaucracy. The judicial process, by comparison, is concerned with the rights of the individual. The courts have continually expanded the first eight and the fourteenth amendments of the Constitution to protect the private citizen, and government officials can be called upon to show the courts that their acts are within the law. "The poorest he in England," it was said in Oliver Cromwell's time, "hath a life to live as the richest he." The judicial process is a means available to the poorest as well as the richest he in this country.

The use of the judicial process as the primary instrument of justice in this country, as all lawyers know, places an unusually heavy burden on the legal profession. The lawyer, although a private representative of his client, is at the same time a public representative of the social order and justice. This dual role creates for him a fundamental problem. How to determine his responsibilities to his client and his responsibility to society as he performs his task of administering the law.

This chapter is directed to the problem of standards of conduct for the advocate. Section two is directed to the nature of the trial as both a rational and an emotional proceeding; section three to the role of the advocate and his three basic standards in the trial: loyalty to the client, candor to the court and fairness to his opponent. Sections four, five, and six deal with the several standards in context. Section four discusses the duty of loyalty to the client, which calls for fidelity to the interests of the client, competence and zeal; zeal involves problems as to conduct in the courtroom, appeal to emotion and prejudice, and reliance on technicalities. Section five treats candor to the court, and its two aspects, candor as to the facts and as to the law. The duty of fairness is the topic of section six, with a discussion of fairness to the opponent and to the client of the opponent. Section seven offers some comments on the lawyer's standards and the adversary system: Standards are an integral part of the administration of justice. The concluding section deals briefly with arbitration, a dispute settling process half-way between litigation and compromise, the subject of the next chapter.

SECTION 2. THE NATURE OF THE TRIAL

The common law trial, as an adversary proceeding, is one in which the court depends upon a partisan presentation of the relevant facts and the applicable law for decision by the trier, whether judge or jury. Throughout the stages of its development— trial by ordeal, by combat, and the long development of trial by jury—it has served the basic purpose of enabling individuals to resolve their disputes in a peaceable manner. The trial, however, is not merely a means of resolving disputes. Accompanying this purpose is a second one of providing a means of applying and enforcing rules of law. But disputes cannot be effectively settled unless there are rules by which they can be resolved, and rules necessary to resolve the particular disputes have not always been provided. So the common law trial fulfills still a third purpose, the development of new rules of law in light of the concrete facts of a given situation, as illustrated by the creation of the common law and the constantly evolving body of case law that is so important a part of our jurisprudence. The trial is thus one of the social processes which provide both stability and change in the law.

These purposes of the trial exist, in varying degrees, in all civilized societies. The factor which distinguishes and has shaped the common law trial is its adversary nature. The adversary trial gives the parties, or rather their lawyers, the primary responsibility for the proceedings. The plaintiff brings the case to the court, and the plaintiff and defendant formulate the issues, gather and present the evidence and argue the case. Consequently, as is generally recognized, the common law trial is not, and was not developed to be, a scientific investigation for truth. It is, and was developed to be, a rational proceeding.

To be rational, a trial must be conducted in accordance with predetermined rules and procedures accepted and understood by all. Trial by ordeal in the context of its times was a rational proceeding, because the participants accepted the validity of the idea of divine retribution for the guilty. Today, a trial to be rational must be a fair proceeding which gives each litigant an opportunity to present his side of the dispute, and the decision must be rendered on the basis of the issues as presented.

The framework of the trial is rational, and although the trial itself is most often viewed as being rational, it can never be wholly so. A trial must also be an emotional proceeding, for emotions as well as reason govern men's actions. Emotion, in fact, is the motivating source for most of our conduct, though the emotional basis is often concealed, even from ourselves. And in a trial, the emotions involved are not only those of the litigants, whose property or liberty may be at stake, but of their lawyers, who bear a heavy responsibility in representing their clients in trouble. The witnesses and jurors, too, are affected by emotion, for people do not lightly assume the burden of giving information and making decisions which affect, and even determine the course of, the lives of others. Witnesses are usually biased in favor of their side, and jurors cannot fail to be moved by the equities and inequities of the case as determined by their own experiences and emotions.

Lawyers and judges, well aware of the emotional nature of the trial, do not often discuss and seldom acknowledge it. The formal standards of the profession ignore it, and even Wigmore, recognizing the role of emotion in argument, still framed his comments in terms of logic.[1] But, "the issue which we typically submit to juries is an issue which the jury cannot decide by the exercise of its reason. The decision of an issue of fact in cases of closely balanced probabilities, therefore, must, in the nature of things, be an emotional rather than a rational act; . . .".[2] The soundness of this point carries over to the conduct of the trial itself, for the common law trial developed so as to take into account and to minimize the emotional aspects of the trial. "The common law system of proof is exacting in its insistence upon the most reliable sources of information."[3] And one of the fundamental lines of impeachment is "showing that the witness is biased, by reason of emotional influences such as kinship for one party or hostility to another, or motives of pecuniary interest, whether legitimate or corrupt."[4] The judge does not submit a case to the jury unless the jurors could reasonably decide either way. Moreover, he has the power, except when the verdict is not guilty in criminal cases, to hold the jurors to a rational decision by granting a new trial or judgment notwithstanding the verdict.

The nature of emotion in a trial has been well stated in an article on the argument of an appeal:

> "An argument of an appeal, like every other form of advocacy, has two related functions. Its first function is to appeal to the emotion of your hearer, to the emotion of the person you are trying to persuade to act in your favor. Its second is to appeal to his intellect.
>
> ". . . By 'emotion' . . . I mean neither more nor less than that part (however defined and wherever located) of the human organism which moves it to act. By way of oversimplification, it might be said that all human beings are moved to act by emotion, and guided in action by intellect. The twin objectives of an appeal, then, is to arouse the emotion of the judge so that he will be moved

1. "Now in this domain of logic it is conceded, the counsel is free from restraint during argument. His desired inferences may be forced, unnatural, and untenable; but as to this the jury are the judge; that is precisely their function." VI Wigmore, Evidence § 1807 (3rd ed. 1940).

2. Michael, The Basic Rules of Pleading, 5 Record of N.Y.C.B.A. 175, 200 (1950).

3. McCormick, Evidence 19 (1954).

4. Id. 62.

to act (if he is not so moved, the judgment will be affirmed without opinion); and to satisfy the intellect so that he will feel it correct to take action favorable to your client." [5]

For the lawyer, the fact that a trial is an emotional proceeding within a rational framework may be its single most important quality. The problem of his standards of conduct can be traced to this characteristic of the trial. If the trial could be a wholly rational proceeding, conducted only in accordance with reason, neither standards nor their implementation would present any serious difficulties.

SECTION 3. THE BASIC STANDARDS OF THE ADVOCATE

The basic standards of the advocate, often lost in detailed statements of standards, are in fact only three in number. An advocate deals with only three people who share with him the responsibility for the disposition of the case: his client, the judge, and the opposing lawyer. To these people he owes a primary duty, and since standards are essentially only statements of obligations to others, it is his relationships with these people which determine the basic standards. These relationships, representative of his client, officer of the court, and opponent of his adversary, give the advocate three basic duties: to represent the interests of his client to the best of his ability; to aid the court in the proper disposition of the case (under the adversary system); and to respect his opponent. These duties give rise to his basic standards—loyalty to the client, candor to the court, and fairness to his opponent—from which all of his other standards are derived.

The critic of the profession may immediately perceive that the standards are all inconsistent in some degree with one another. The advocate represents first and foremost the interests of his client. Regardless of the merits of the client's cause, he is duty bound to present the facts in their most favorable light and to attempt to persuade the trier to render a decision in his favor. Yet, in each case, one side or the other is at fault, or at least, only one side is entitled to a judgment. How can both advocates in the trial be loyal to their clients in presenting the case and be candid to the court at the same time? Moreover, loyalty to the

---

5. Knapp, Why Argue an Appeal? If So, How? 14 Record of N.Y. C.B.A. 415, 416–17 (1959).

client would seem almost automatically to preclude any measurable degree of fairness to the opponent in an adversary trial. The critic is not alone in his perception, for the advocate is continually faced with these problems. The difference is that the advocate must resolve them, while the critic is free to criticize at large.

The difficulty for the advocate is increased by the fact that the common law trial serves different policies—the policy of enabling litigants to resolve their own dispute, the policy of justice for the individual, and the policy of order in the administration of law. The advocate must coordinate these policies. The basic standards thus do not exist separately and independently of each other. They are interrelated as an integral part of a system in which they balance and complement each other. The duty of loyalty to the client limits the duties of candor to the court and fairness to the opponent, and duties of candor and fairness define and modify the duty of loyalty.

The interrelationship of these standards is best seen when they are correlated with the three basic characteristics of the trial which give rise to them: its adversary nature, its concern with resolving disputes based on past events, and its highly structured setting.

The adversary system of trial is an idea so familiar as to lose its impact for lawyers, but it is this quality of the trial that gives rise to the need for standards of loyalty to the client. The client is in conflict with another, and the advocate, as his representative, must assume the responsibility for protecting the client's interests. The client is not always in the right and the advocate's ideas and ideals may not coincide with those of the client. There must be a measure by which the advocate's actions on behalf of the client are accepted as a socially desirable norm. The layman, for example, may overlook the fact that our law is administered through adversary proceedings and that a loyal lawyer on each side is essential. "Angel or devil, a man has a claim to a fair trial, not of his social desirability, but of his guilt of the *specific* offense charged against him. Such is the letter of our law. Such also is our law's spirit." [1]

A trial is directed to the resolution of disputes based on past events. The duty of loyalty demands that the advocate present the facts as to those events in their most favorable light, for the decision in the case will be based not on the events as they occurred, but as they are shown in the record. Yet, the court must be concerned with obtaining the true facts and must rely wholly

1. K. Llewellyn, The Sacco-Vanzetti
Case, Unpublished Manuscript.

upon the advocates and their witnesses for the presentation of these facts. Thus, a recognized duty of candor to the court is necessary to modify and define the duty of loyalty to the client. The advocate must tell the court the truth and nothing but the truth, but he need not tell the whole truth. This latter qualification is the result, not of a right to be dishonest, but of a duty to the client in a system of law which requires that the lawyer respect and maintain the confidences of his client.

Standards of fairness are necessary if the adversary system is to function properly. The structured setting of the trial, with its many and complex rules, gives rise to the need for the basic standard of fairness to the opponent. The rules are necessary to give order to the trial. They are based on the desire to assure fairness to the parties and the presentation of the facts as they occurred. Yet, they become technical and complex as they become specific, and they place a premium on skill and competence which are not shared in equal measure. The superior lawyer may often have the opportunity to take advantage of a lesser opponent. The advocate who files a complaint one day too late will be faced with the statute of limitations as a defense. The layman might well view this as being unfair, but the advocate does not. The duty of loyalty to his client requires the plea, regardless of the merits of the claim. But there is a difference between invoking a clearly applicable rule of law and manipulating rules of procedure for an unfair advantage. The advocate, for example, may not use a discovery deposition to obtain irrelevant information about the indiscretions of the opponent's client to secure a settlement.

The trial is the central feature of the judicial process, and the importance of the lawyer's role as advocate and of his standards in that role extends beyond the courtroom. It is from this role that the lawyer derives his self-image for it is this role with which he most readily identifies. Even while he is engaged in other legal processes, the private, the administrative, and the legislative, the good lawyer is continually conscious of the possibility of litigation. When negotiating a contract, he is concerned not only with the effect of the provisions of the contract if litigation should result, but also of the effect of the rules of evidence. In an administrative proceeding, he is constantly aware of the need for making a record, should resort to the courts be necessary. And even in the legislative process, when he is engaged in lobbying, the possible reaction of the courts is not far from his mind. The role of advocate thus exercises a pervasive influence on the lawyer in all of his work.

The most important effect of this influence has been on the standards of the profession. The trial is the legal process in which the problem of standards has had its most telling effect, and the standards evolved for the trial have been extended to the lawyer's other roles.   The problem which the profession has not faced directly is whether the standards for the role of the advocate in a trial are appropriate also for the lawyer in his other roles.

SECTION 4. STANDARDS OF THE ADVOCATE IN CONTEXT: LOYALTY

The defendant facing the possibility of paying a judgment of fifty or fifty thousand dollars is more likely to be concerned with his pocketbook than his conscience; the plaintiff seeking damages is more likely to be influenced by his injury than by his sense of the right thing to do.   The client, viewing the case in terms of his own plight, expects his lawyer to do the same.   To a large extent, he does so, not only because his income bears a direct relation to the kind of job he does, but because he identifies himself with his client, and loyalty is a natural duty for the advocate.

The pride of the profession in the lawyer's duty of loyalty, however, tends to obscure its appropriate limitations, limitations particularly difficult for the advocate to perceive because his client is in trouble.   Loyalty does not, for example, justify the advocate in resorting to extra legal means to reach the settlement of the case, as by threatening a criminal prosecution.[1]   Nor does it justify him in aiding his client in the commission of a crime, as by advice to dispose of a murder weapon.[2]   And an advocate cannot invoke the attorney-client privilege to enable him to secrete in a safety deposit box the proceeds of a bank robbery and a sawed-off shotgun turned over to him by his client.[3]

The conduct illustrated by these examples has the elements of extortion, aiding and abetting the commission of a crime, and illegal possession of a weapon.   But the lawyers involved probably did not think of their acts as criminal, since they acted in a representative capacity, with the highest duty of loyalty to their clients.   The mistake is in assuming that the loyalty of the advo-

---

1. In re Hyman, 226 App.Div. 468, 235 N.Y.S. 622 (N.Y.Sup.Ct.1929).

2. Clark v. State, 159 Tex.Cr.R. 187, 261 S.W.2d 339 (1953).

3. In re Ryder, 263 F.Supp. 360 (E. D.Va.1967).

cate is a license to engage in illegal conduct, protected by the attorney-client relationship. The scope of loyalty does not extend so far. "A lawyer should never encourage or aid his client to commit criminal acts or counsel his client on how to violate the law and avoid punishment therefor." [4] Regardless of the potential benefit to his client, the advocate may not engage in such activity. " 'An attorney's duty to his client is a solemn obligation, but it has never been held to be greater than the law itself. However just an attorney may believe his client's claim to be, he may not liquidate it by force or arms, by bribery or any other unlawful means.' " [5]

Apart from illegal conduct, the scope of the advocate's loyalty is determined by professional standards. The application of these standards presents much the same problem as the application of ordinary legal standards, as in negligence. Due care for the layman, for example, and loyalty for the advocate may be similarly defined. As due care is that care which the reasonable man exercises under the circumstances, so loyalty is that conduct which the advocate as fiduciary exercises on behalf of his client. Loyalty as a professional standard, however, differs from the standard of due care, for professional standards and legal standards serve two different purposes. The latter is used to determine liability, the former to enable the advocate best to serve his client within the adversary system. The standard of loyalty thus involves three basic duties: fidelity to the interests of the client, competence and zeal.

The duty of fidelity to the interests of the client is the most important of these duties, for it is concerned with the personal relationship of the lawyer and his client. Basically, it requires independent professional judgment on behalf of the client,[6] and an absence of conflict of interest. The Code of Professional Responsibility states the point well.

> "The professional judgment of a lawyer should be exercised, within the bounds of the law, solely for the benefit of his client and free of compromising influences and loyalties. Neither his personal interests, the interests of other clients, nor the desires of third persons should be permitted to dilute his loyalty to his client." [7]

Here, as everywhere in the law, each factual situation is unique, and in the close cases—the only ones which give the lawyer concern—he must use his best judgment. One point, however, is clear: The lawyer has a special duty of candor in dealing

4. A.B.A. Code of Professional Responsibility, EC 7–5.

5. In re O'Keefe, 49 Mont. 369, 377, 142 P. 638, 641 (1914).

6. A.B.A. Code of Professional Responsibility, Canon 5.

7. Id., EC 5–1.

with his client in regard to all matters pertaining to their relationship. "A lawyer should exert his best efforts to insure that decisions of his client are made only after the client has been informed of relevant considerations. A lawyer ought to initiate this decision-making process if the client does not do so." [8] The advocate who is sufficiently confident of his conduct to be completely candid with his client runs little risk of conflict of interest or violation of a confidence. Equally as important is the realization by the client that his lawyer is loyal to his interests.

An important part of the duty of loyalty is the duty of competence, a duty explicitly recognized in the stated standards of the profession.[9] Yet, the difficult problems of incompetence are not those instances where the lawyer is grossly negligent or clearly incompetent. Rather, they are those instances where the lawyer attempts to fulfill his duty, but does so poorly and consequently loses the case for his client. This is the problem of carelessness, inexcusable yet seldom recognized, resulting as it does from lack of preparation. The thorough preparation of his case by the advocate is a duty which is again and again neglected, even in the Supreme Court,[10] to the detriment of the client. One experienced trial judge and former trial lawyer, for example, estimated on the basis of personal experience on the bench that in over eighty per cent of the cases, "The lack of preparation was in my opinion directly responsible for a result unfavorable to the client." [11] Chief Justice Burger, when a judge of the Court of Appeals, expressed a deep concern about poor preparation on the part of trial lawyers. Writing of his personal experiences from more than twenty years of practice and ten years on the bench and personal inquiry of lawyers and judges, he concluded:

> "On the most favorable view expressed, seventy-five percent of the lawyers appearing in the courtroom were deficient by reason of poor preparation, inability to frame questions properly, lack of ability to conduct a proper cross-examination, lack of ability to present expert testimony, lack of ability in the handling and presentation of documents and letters, lack of ability to frame objections adequately, lack of basic analytic ability in the framing of issues and lack of ability to make an adequate argument to a jury." [12]

8. Id., EC 7–8.

9. Id., Canon 6. "Because of his vital role in the legal process, a lawyer should act with competence and proper care in representing clients. He should strive to become and remain proficient in his practice and should accept employment only in matters which he is or intends to become competent to handle." Id., EC 6–1.

10. See Clark, The Decisional Processes of the Supreme Court, 50 Corn.L.Q. 385, 392 (1965).

11. P. McCook, Trials and the Art of Advocacy 8 (1933).

12. Burger, A Sick Profession?, 5 Tulsa L.J. 1, 3 (1968).

A lack of concern best explains this failing, a lack of concern resulting from a failure to recognize that for the advocate competence is as much a duty of conscience as the duty to avoid perjury. Several factors may serve to explain further this blind spot. Since only one of the parties can win a given case, the losing side seldom knows whether the loss was due to the merits of the case or the way in which it was handled. Courts do not often refer to the lawyer's skill or lack of skill in trying a case because it is impossible to know the reasons for the jury's verdict. The sanction for incompetence is imposed directly on the client. It is he who pays the judgment or fails to receive compensation for his injury. The lawyer suffers, too, but the sanction of the loss of a case is not felt so keenly by him as by his client. And, lawyers do not generally recognize that incompetence is a subtle form of fraud. It is fraud because it denies the client what he is entitled to, and it is subtle because most often the denial is unintentional.

Of all the standards of the advocate, the duty of competence is the one least subject to qualification, for it is the only standard not modified by another duty or limited by multiple relationships. The standard which gives rise to the most complex problems for the advocate is zeal. For him, zeal, or the will to win, is as essential as it is desirable.[13] His role is not that of a friend of the court in aiding it to reach the golden mean, a result fair to all parties to the controversy. He is a partisan representative. "He is in no particular a judicial officer if that phrase is given the connotation of one who is called upon to weigh the merits of the proceeding and pass on the rights of the respective litigants. . . . [H]e acts purely and solely as the attorney for the particular person whose interests he is designated to protect."[14]

The advocate usually finds the presence of zeal to be no problem. He wants to win not only for his client, but for himself as well, because his pride, and often his fee, are involved. Judges understand this and tend to give lawyers wide latitude as to their zeal in the courtroom, often treating the pressures of a trial as a mitigating circumstance. In one case, for example, the client testified falsely that he had purchased a bottle of medicine when in fact the attorney had done so and given it to him. The judge in disciplinary proceedings stated that it was the advocate's duty to elicit the correct answer, but his failure to do so did not mean

13. A.B.A. Code of Professional Responsibility, Canon 7. "The duty of a lawyer, both to his client and to the legal system, is to represent his client zealously within the bounds of the law, which includes Disciplinary Rules and enforceable professional regulations." Id., EC 7-1.

14. Matter of Schrier, 157 Misc. 310, 312, 283 N.Y.S. 233, 235 (Sur.Ct. 1935).

a willful disregard of the ethical standards of the profession. "It was in the midst of the trial and respondent doubtless was taken unawares and did not expect or think that his client would make such a statement. Under such circumstances, the wisest most experienced lawyer might hesitate to elicit the real truth for fear of jeopardizing his client's case." [15]

The court's view is sound. Anyone who has felt the pressures of trying a case knows only too well how easy it is to make an error in judgment. The jury must be impressed; a witness may surprise the examiner with his answers; objections must be made quickly; cross-examination is always a risky endeavor; and the arguments must be persuasive. During the trial, the problem is not a lack, but an excess, of zeal. Unlike the duty of competence, zeal must be limited, for while "All advocacy involves conflict and calls for the will to win," [16] the conflict must be resolved in accordance with accepted procedures.

Three aspects of zeal in the courtroom—manners, appeal to emotion and prejudice, and reliance on technicalities—present unusually difficult lines of demarcation between proper and improper conduct.

Manners. "The dignity, decorum and courtesy which have traditionally characterized the courts of civilized nations are not empty formalities. They are essential to an atmosphere in which justice can be done." [17] For the lawyer, there is a very practical consideration involved. "The things jurors seem to find offensive are the bad manners of lawyers who abuse witnesses, lawyers who snarl at each other across the counsel table, lawyers who are discourteous or slovenly in their communication with the judge and jury. The jury surveys confirm . . . that the bad manners of a trial lawyer almost invariably count against his case." [18]

The substantive nature of the amenities in the trial of a case has not often in the past been emphasized. But "[a]nyone who has spent even a part of his years in the courtroom knows that good manners, courtesy and etiquette are more than a matter of form. They are the lubricant which helps prevent a trial from deteriorating into a brawl." [19] Their importance is measured by the malfunctioning of the trial when they are absent, as the Supreme

15. In re Hoover, 46 Ariz. 24, 30–31, 46 P.2d 647, 650 (1935); accord, In re Zanger, 266 N.Y. 165, 194 N.E. 72 (1935).

16. A. Vanderbilt, Forensic Persuasion 13 (1950).

17. American College of Trial Lawyers, Report and Recommendations on Disruption of the Judicial Process 4 (1970).

18. Burger, A Sick Profession? 5 Tulsa L.J. 1, 4 (1968).

19. Id.

Court recognized in Illinois v. Allen, affirming the trial court's action in removing a disruptive defendant from the courtroom.[20] The purpose of the amenities in the trial is not to protect personal feelings but to assure a fair trial. The duty of respect extends to the court, opposing counsel, and to the witnesses, for "Basic to an efficient and fair functioning of our adversary system of justice is that at all times there be an atmosphere manifesting mutual respect by all participants."[21]

Respect for the court is essential in any trial. "During the trial, a lawyer should always display a courteous, dignified and respectful attitude toward the judge presiding, not for the sake of his person, but for the maintenance of respect for and confidence in the judicial office."[22] This does not mean that the advocate may not protect his client's rights, even to the extent of interrupting the court's instructions to the jury, if he does so in a respectful manner. The Supreme Court of California, for example, reversed a contempt conviction of a lawyer who insisted that the trial judge was wrong in interrupting jury deliberations to state his view on the comparative credibility of certain witnesses.[23] But when the bounds of propriety are exceeded, the lawyer may be in contempt. In In re Sacher,[24] the lawyer " 'persistently, in disregard of the repeated warnings and orders of the Court, argued without permission; [and] refused to desist from argument and comment' and . . . made 'insolent, sarcastic, impertinent and disrespectful remarks to the Court and conducted himself in a provocative manner.' "[25] Suspension was affirmed by the Court of Appeals, although the trial judge had found that the conduct was not " 'tainted by venality or lack of fidelity to the interests of his clients . . . . His fault, rather, seems to have stemmed from a temperament which led to such excess of zeal in representing his clients that it obscured his recognition of responsibility as an officer of the court."[26]

Equally as important are the respect and courtesy of lawyers for each other.[27] The Supreme Court insists on this, and has or-

20. 397 U.S. 337, 90 S.Ct. 1057 (1970).

21. American College of Trial Lawyers, Supra note 17, at 5, quoting from proposed A.B.A. Standards for Criminal Justice Relating to the Prosecution and Defense Functions.

22. American College of Trial Lawyers, Code of trial conduct, Rule 18 (a). See A.B.A. Code of Professional Responsibility, EC 7–36.

23. Cooper v. Superior Court, 55 Cal. 2d 291, 10 Cal.Rptr. 842, 359 P.2d 274 (1961).

24. 206 F.2d 358 (2d Cir. 1953).

25. Id. at 360.

26. Id. at 359. The disbarment was reversed by the Supreme Court as unnecessarily severe, in view of the fact that the attorney served a six month prison sentence for contempt of court. Sacher v. Association of the Bar of the City of New York, 347 U.S. 388 (1954).

27. A.B.A. Code of Professional Responsibility, EC 7–37.

dered vituperative briefs stricken from the files.[28]   When a petition for certiorari contained denunciations of opposing counsel, the Court, after issuing a rule to show cause, held the lawyer who filed the petition in contempt of court and punished him through a fine and suspension from its bar.[29]   The standards have been clearly stated:

> "We must insist that arguments in this Court, either oral or written, though often properly in sharp controversy, shall be gracious and respectful to both the Court and opposing counsel, and be in such words as may be properly addressed by one gentleman to another." [30]

Yet, mindful no doubt of the stress at the trial court level and of the importance of not hampering the advocate in the zealous prosecution of his client's case, the Court reversed on constitutional grounds the action of a trial judge in finding exuberant advocates in contempt and imposing petty fines on them.[31]

The concern, of course, is not for the lawyers, but for the right of the clients to a fair trial.   "The objective of such standards is to keep the understandably contentious spirit of the opposing advocates within appropriate bounds and constructive channels so that the issues may be resolved on the merits and the proceedings not be diverted by the intrusion of factors such as personality or acrimonious exchanges between the advocates . . ." [32]

The advocate's treatment of the witness, particularly the hostile witness, provides, perhaps, the severest test of his manners. Conduct relating to witnesses is governed by the rules of evidence, which were not developed for their comfort.   The witness is not, for example, allowed to tell his story in his own words and he is subject to cross-examination and impeachment.   And because the witness is so important, the courts give counsel wide latitude in dealing with him.

A few points are clear.   A lawyer may not express his conviction as to the credibility of witnesses.[33]   He may not use cross-examination as a tactical device to intimidate a witness and ask questions for the sole purpose of prejudicing the jury.[34]   And

---

28. National Sur. Co. v. Jarvis, 278 U.S. 610 (1928); Royal Arcanum v. Green, 237 U.S. 531 (1915).

29. In the Matter of Thomas Marshall, 55 S.Ct. 513 (1935).

30. National Sur. Co. v. Jarvis, 278 U.S. 610, 611 (1928).

31. Holt v. Virginia, 381 U.S. 131 (1965).

32. American College of Trial Lawyers, supra note 17, at 5, quoting from A.B.A. Standards for Criminal Justice Relating to the Prosecution and Defense Functions.

33. Puckett v. State, 168 Tex.Cr. R. 615, 330 S.W.2d 465 (1959), Annot., 81 A.L.R.2d 1237 (1962).

34. Newton v. State, 147 Md. 71, 127 A. 123 (Ct.App.1924).

even violation of the oft-abused rule against leading witnesses may result in reversal.[35]

These limitations do not protect the witness himself against excess zeal of the advocate, and there seems to be no recognized duty of the advocate to the witness as there is to the court or to his client. The Code of Professional Responsibility requires only that a lawyer refrain from asking irrelevant questions to harass a witness.[36] Yet, every trial lawyer knows of instances where witnesses have been needlessly abused and mistreated with impunity. And every trial lawyer knows, too, of persons who, because of mistreatment, will go to great lengths to avoid the ordeal again.

The problem is one which the profession, in its concern for rights of the parties, has virtually ignored. Even so, this is one problem with which professional standards can most effectively deal, for this is one area where the highest standards are always consistent with the client's interest. The basic standard is a simple one—respect for the man, respect for the witness as an individual. This respect is possible even with the most hostile witness and is appropriate for every witness, even the one who can be, and is, impeached. The cost of acting otherwise is the dignity of the judicial process, a high price indeed for a failure to understand human nature.

Appeal to Emotion and Prejudice. The most complex problem for the advocate in determining the appropriate degree of zeal is appeal to emotion and prejudice. Two cases illustrate the point. In an old Tennessee case, Ferguson v. Moore,[37] a suit for seduction and breach of promise to marry, error was alleged because

---

35. Straub v. Reading Co., 220 F.2d 177 (3d Cir. 1955).

36. A.B.A. Code of Professional Responsibility, DR 7–106(c) (2). See Id., EC 7–10; cf. the following from the Tentative Draft of Standards Relating to The Prosecution Function:

5.7 *Examination of witnesses.*

(a) The interrogation of all witnesses should be conducted fairly, objectively and with due regard for the dignity and legitimate privacy of the witness, and without seeking to intimidate or humiliate the witness unnecessarily. Proper cross-examination can be conducted without violating rules of decorum.

(b) The prosecutor's belief that the witness is telling the truth does not necessarily preclude appropriate cross-examination in all circumstances, but may affect the method and scope of cross-examination. He should not misuse the power of cross-examination or impeachment to discredit or undermine a witness if he knows the witness is testifying truthfully.

(c) It is unprofessional conduct for a prosecutor to call a witness who he knows will claim a valid privilege not to testify, for the purpose of impressing upon the jury the fact of the claim of privilege.

(d) It is unprofessional conduct to ask a question which implies the existence of a factual predicate which the examiner cannot support by evidence.

37. 98 Tenn. 342, 39 S.W. 341 (1897).

plaintiff's counsel shed tears in his final argument before the jury. The Supreme Court of Tennessee said that it is not only a privilege for the advocate to cry for his client, it may be his professional duty to do so. "It is certainly, if no more, a matter of the highest personal privilege." [38] In a modern Missouri case, Fitzpatrick v. St. Louis-San Francisco Railway Co.,[39] the plaintiff lost on appeal a judgment in his suit for the loss of an eye because a blind man, a friend of plaintiff's lawyer, came into the courtroom and sat during the latter part of the trial. "Misconduct," said the court, "which is *calculated* to create sympathy or prejudice and *may* have done so justifies the grant of a new trial." [40]

The viewpoints in these two cases may not be as divergent as they first appear. Emotion is a part of life, and the advocate in a trial must not only prove his case, a matter of reason, he must persuade the jury, a matter of emotion. Appeal to emotion by an advocate is inevitable and the problem is not to avoid, but to make a proper appeal to, emotion.

The reports are filled with cases reversed for an appeal to improper emotion. The appeal may take the form of an attack on the integrity of the opposing party and his counsel. "The argument of defendant's counsel presents a studied effort to convey to the jury the idea that plaintiff and her counsel had conspired to present a 'fixed-up' and 'framed-up' case . . . An express and direct charge was made that counsel for plaintiff had attempted to obtain perjured testimony and that they were dishonest and lacking in integrity." [41] Or it may be in the form of a witness' testimony, as where a doctor stated that he preferred not to answer the question as to plaintiff's life expectancy with the wife in the courtroom.[42] Or it may be a seemingly inadvertent remark of counsel. In response to a judge's request for affirmation of his statement to the jury that any traffic citation against defendant was irrelevant, the plaintiff's counsel answered, "Unfortunately yes, Your Honor." [43] Often, of course, the appeal takes place in argument to the jury, for example, with a reference to the wealth of defendant: "Now, my friends, this

---

38. Id. at 351, 39 S.W. at 343. "Indeed, if counsel has them at command, it may be seriously questioned whether it is not his professional duty to shed them whenever the proper occasion arises . . ." Id. at 351–52, 39 S.W. at 343.

39. 327 S.W.2d 801 (Mo.1959).

40. Id. at 808. See Kickham v. Carter, 314 S.W.2d 902, 908 (Mo.1958).

41. Critcher v. Rudy Fick, Inc., 315 S.W.2d 421, 426–427 (Mo.1958). See also Missouri-Kansas-Texas R. R. Co. of Texas v. Ridgway, 191 F.2d 363 (8th Cir. 1951), Annot., 29 A.L. R.2d 984 (1953).

42. Lange v. Coca-Cola Bottling Co. of Chicago, 105 Ill.App.2d 99, 245 N.E.2d 35 (1969).

43. Riedel v. Driscoll, 124 So.2d 42, 47 (Dist.Ct.Fla.App.1960).

young boy does not possess the wealth that the defendants have at their command. . . ." [44]

These cases, all of which were reversed, give a clue to the difference between a proper and an improper appeal to emotion. The basic problem is one of relevancy, for just as there is relevant and irrelevant evidence, there is also relevant and irrelevant emotion.

An item of evidence is relevant if it is a proposition of fact which expresses a condition necessary or appropriate for a decision in the case. If the conclusion is that D negligently injured P in an automobile accident, the fact that D ran a red light is relevant. The fact that he was returning from a meeting of the local Communist Party or from a meeting of Boy Scouts is not. The fact that he is black or white is irrelevant, but not the fact that he was driving while drunk.

In the same way, an appeal to emotion is relevant and may be proper if it is based on and limited to a factor in the case necessary or appropriate to induce conviction in the minds of the jurors for a decision in the case. The advocate must persuade as well as prove. The appeal may be through the presentation of evidence, as the use of photographs, or in argument, where the advocate may rely not only upon the evidence, but also upon all proper inferences to be drawn therefrom. Appeal to emotion, however, must be related to the evidence or an issue in the case. "The comment in argument to the jury that plaintiff nearly had a miscarriage, treated as argument by an advocate, is supported by the record. . . . Comment upon the appearance of one of the defendants as a well-dressed gentleman, wearing a diamond, comes under the same category. The wealth of defendants is a matter to be considered upon the question of punitive and exemplary damages." [45]

The mistake to be avoided is giving the jury the opportunity to base its decision solely on the emotional factors. Relevant evidence which is too inflammatory, as gory pictures of a murder victim, may be excluded as being too prejudicial. But it may be proper, for example, to make the jury aware that the widow is poor or that a beautiful girl is disfigured for life or that the children have been left fatherless, for the amount of damages is an issue in the case. To argue or to give the impression that plaintiff is entitled to a verdict merely because she is a poor widow or because she is a beautiful girl disfigured for life or because the children have been left fatherless is not proper. The

44. Book v. Erskine & Sons, Inc., 154 Ohio St. 391, 394, 96 N.E.2d 289, 291 (1951), Annot., 32 A.L.R.2d 1, 4 (1953).

45. Lamb v. Woodry, 154 Or. 30, 47, 58 P.2d 1257, 1264 (1936).

plaintiff is entitled to verdict only if the defendant was at fault or is legally responsible.

The reason the views as to emotion in the *Ferguson* and in the *Fitzpatrick* cases are not so divergent as may first appear now becomes apparent. The latter may be construed as an attempt to have the jury use emotion, the fact that the plaintiff was blind in one eye, as the basis of their decision. In the former, the lawyer was not asking the jury to render a decision because he was crying, but because the girl had been seduced with false promises.

The other examples above are all subject to the defect of the *Fitzpatrick* case. An appeal for the jury to render a verdict because the plaintiff and his lawyer were dishonest; because the plaintiff would not live long; because the defendant got a traffic citation; because the defendant was rich and the plaintiff poor.

Not everyone will agree with all the decisions, but in each of them, the appeal could be viewed as being directed to matters irrelevant to the issues in the case and thus to the decision. When this judgment is made, appeal to emotion will be viewed as appeal to prejudice. " 'Counsel in argument to the jury should avoid saying anything designed as, or having the effect of, an appeal to the social, class, or sectional prejudices of the jury.' " [46] Such appeals to race, religion, or politics are manifestly improper, not because they are wrong—although they are—but because each litigant has a fundamental right that his case shall be decided on the relevant facts as determined by the issues. Any appeal for a decision or verdict on any other basis comes under the heading of an appeal to prejudice.

Reliance on Technicalities. Every legal system contains rules which are unrelated to the merits of a case, but which may be used on occasion to dispose of the case without regard to the merits. Such are rules as to infancy, the statute of frauds, the dead man's statute, the statute of limitations, and rules as to default judgments. The question is whether the advocate's duty of zeal requires him to take advantage of such rules to the benefit of his client.

One view, the most generally accepted perhaps, is that the advocate does have a duty to do so. "He may do and ought to do whatever the client could lawfully and honestly do for himself, if arguing his own cause. It may not always be honorable to claim the benefit of the Statute of Limitations. It may not always be honorable to take advantage of the defense of infancy. But it is

---

46. Taulbee v. Commonwealth, 438 S.W.2d 777, 779 (Ky.App.1969), (dictum). See 53 Am.Jur.Trial § 499, at 402–03.

the legal right of a party to set up such a shield and, if he desires, it is the legal duty of his lawyer to do it for him." [47]

Another view is implied in Marcus v. Simotone & Combined Sound & Color Films, Inc.[48] concerning a motion to open a default judgment for failure of defendant to answer the case. "With due regard to the zeal which an attorney should properly display in his client's behalf, and quite irrespective of what he believes to be the merits of the pending litigation, ordinary professional courtesy demands that he should not ask for judgment by default against his opponent unless he is satisfied, after communicating with him, that the default is willful or intentional." [49]

The two views, one requiring, the other eschewing, technicalities, are not, in fact, very far apart. The statute of frauds, the statute of limitations and the defense of infancy, for example, are not merely technical rules, they are rules of policy designed for the protection of individuals. Certain kinds of contracts must be in writing, claims must be prosecuted within a reasonable time, and infants are not to be bound by contracts. The rules relate to the conduct of the client rather than the lawyer.

Rules as to default judgments are also based on policy, that of imposing sanctions to compel the defendant to appear and defend his case. Where, however, the defendant is represented by counsel, a new dimension is added to the problem. The issue then is not the conduct of the client, but of his lawyer, and the failure to appear at the proper time is almost invariably the result of a mistake.

Courts clearly have the power to set aside a default judgment under such circumstances, and they frequently do,[50] but the cases seldom reach the two issues involved. One issue is, as Mr. Justice Black stated in Morris v. Florida, that [51] default judgments against a person represented by a lawyer are "a form of vicarious punishment." Speaking against the denial of certiorari in the case, he pointed out that, "there is a vast difference between . . . holding the litigant responsible for errors in not objecting to evidence or pleadings, and . . . holding the litigant responsible for complete failure to file papers and then without notice to the litigant dismissing his entire case or defense." [52] The other issue is a duty of professional courtesy to fellow members of the bar, a courtesy which goes beyond the

47. Baldwin, Legal Ethics, in E. Cheatham, Cases and Materials on the Legal Profession 146–47 (2d ed. 1955).

48. 135 Misc. 228, 237 N.Y.S. 509 (1929).

49. Id. at 228, 237 N.Y.S. at 510 (1929).

50. See Kohlbeck v. Handley, 3 Ariz. App. 469, 415 P.2d 483 (1966), Annot., 21 A.L.R.3d 1248 (1968).

51. 393 U.S. 850 (1968) (denying cert.).

52. Id. at 851.

amenities, for cooperation between members of the profession is essential to the proper functioning of the legal system. Lack of such cooperation can result only in a waste of time, effort, energy and a lack of good will.

The advocate is thus not under a duty to go to the limits of the law for his client in this situation. The purpose of the law of default judgments is not to give the client a judgment, but to protect his right to have the defendant appear in court and defend, to make the legal system work. And taking default judgments when the opposing party is represented by counsel is a perversion which threatens the system itself. Lawyers, as members of a profession, have a duty to make the legal system work, and a part of this duty is cooperation with their fellow members of the bar.

Another aspect of reliance on technicalities is illustrated by Ostendorf v. State,[53] where defense counsel "relied upon a technical defense," objecting to everything that was done. "In some states this practice may be beneficial, but it has directly the opposite effect in this state. If it does not in effect amount to a plea of guilty, it at least shows clearly that counsel was relying alone upon a technical defense . . . . We have time and again condemned such practice. . . . Counsel has nowhere in his brief attempted to show that any alleged error had deprived his client of a single substantive right to his injury." [54]

The proper functioning of the adversary trial requires the advocate to represent his client zealously within the bounds of the law. The bounds of the law, however, are not determined solely by the words of a statute or case. They are determined also by the purpose of the law. The advocate's duty is to consider the purpose of the law as well as the words in which the rule is expressed, for the application of the rules of substantive law is greatly affected by the standards of the lawyer.

Disrespect, discourtesy, and a lack of concern for others in the trial of a case, appeals to improper emotion and prejudice, and reliance on technicalities all constitute obstacles to the administration of justice. When the advocate tends to become overzealous, he would do well to remember: "Every member of the public has an inalienable right that our courts shall be left free to administer justice without obstruction or interference from whatever quarter it may come. Take away that right and freedom of speech together with all the other freedoms would wither and die, for in the long run it is the courts of justice which are the last bastion of individual liberty." [55]

53.   8 Okl.Cr. 360, 128 P. 143 (1912).

54.   Id. at 364, 128 P. at 144.

55.   Morris v. Crown Office, [1970] 2 W.L.R. 792, 800–801 (C.A.)

The duty of loyalty is not only the most fundamental, but also the most complex of the advocate's standards. Consisting as it does of fidelity to the interest of the client, competence, and zeal, the duty is to be ranked as the highest of the advocate's duties. On the personal level, the level of relationship between the client and his lawyer, it is absolute and it is to be maintained at all costs. No lawyer, advocate or otherwise, can gain at the expense of his client. Yet, on another level, the level that involves relationships with other persons, other lawyers and with the court, the duty cannot be absolute, for the interests of the client are not absolute. The client is a member of society and a citizen of the community, he has a reputation and good name as well as physical possessions, and his interest in the former is no less important than his interest in the latter. His interests in the various roles he fills extend also to the proper functioning of the legal system, and there are times when this interest is superior to his immediate self-interest. One of the advocate's most difficult tasks is to determine in the particular case which of these many interests of the client he must serve in dealing with others on behalf of his client.

SECTION 5. THE STANDARDS OF THE ADVOCATE IN CONTEXT: CANDOR

The duty of candor is the most objectionable standard of all for the advocate. Unlike loyalty, which springs naturally and enhances his power, candor may appear to the lawyer an unnatural duty in the adversary system, for it limits his power. The traditional view is that the lawyer should admit nothing, deny everything, and put his adversary to proof. At common law, in fact, the advocate was expected, almost required, not to tell the other side anything that might be helpful to it.

Despite the rejection of common law procedure, the tradition of a lack of candor lingers on and the resistance to explicit recognition of such a duty continues. The Code of Professional Responsibility, for example, contains no use of the term, although it does make clear that a lawyer may not "Conceal or knowingly fail to disclose that which he is required by law to reveal," [1] or "Knowingly use perjured testimony or false evidence," [2] or "Knowingly make a false statement of law or fact." [3]

---

1. A.B.A. Code of Professional Responsibility, DR 7–102(A) (3).

2. Id. at DR 7–102(A) (4).

3. Id. at DR 7–102(A) (5).

Modern procedural reforms have made the absence of a duty of candor an anachronism. A point commonly ignored is that while common law procedure was not directed to candor, it was directed to the ascertainment of truth. The absence of a duty of candor, for example, explains many of the complexities of common law rules of evidence. Rules as to oath, cross-examination, impeachment, best evidence, hearsay, and the incompetency of parties in interest as witnesses all had the common purpose of insuring the reliability of testimony at a time where there was no duty of candor on the part of the advocate. Many of the rules remain, but discovery rules have largely eliminated the surprise element of the trial. And as procedure is further liberalized—the law of evidence, for example—the importance of an affirmative duty of candor will increase.

Yet, the duty of candor for the advocate cannot be an absolute one. The whole truth is neither necessary nor desirable in all situations, and in the trial of a case the duty of candor varies. There is a duty of candor to the opponent and to the court, and a duty of candor as to the facts and the law.

Modern procedure moves forward the advocate's opportunity to learn all the facts by providing methods of discovery for compelling disclosure prior to trial. The discovery devices, however, preserve the adversary posture of the lawyers. They place the duty of disclosure on the parties and the witnesses, when inquiry is made. Discovery is thus a substitute for a duty of candor by the advocate to his opponent. The absence of this duty to the opponent in litigation does not come from a cynical disregard for the truth. The adversary system makes it necessary, for the advocate is a representative of his client. The client must, if the representation is to be effective, be able to communicate freely with his attorney in confidence without fear of having his confidence violated by reason of a legal duty otherwise imposed. The lack of a duty of candor to the opponent, however, must be properly understood and properly limited. The advocate has, and should have, a continuing duty to maintain the confidences of this client. Except for this fundamental limitation, the lack of duty of candor to the adversary is not a duty to conceal, but only a privilege not to exercise initiative in revealing. The lack of a duty of affirmative candor does not imply a privilege to be dishonest. The difference is the same as that between misfeasance and non-feasance. An advocate may not have to reveal the presence in the courtroom of an eyewitness to the incident in dispute of whom his opponent is unaware,[4] but he may not suborn perjury.

4. New York County Lawyers Association Committee, Q. 309.

CARL A. RUDISILL LIBRARY
LENOIR RHYNE COLLEGE

The advocate's relationship to the court is manifestly different from that of his relationship to his adversary, and the privilege of a lack of candor to the opponent does not extend to the court. Except for those matters which are privileged, the advocate has a duty to be candid to the court both as to the facts and the law, a duty which arises from his position as an officer of the court and his role in the administration of law.

The duty of candor as to the facts, however, is limited to facts presented to the court for its action in matters of law, as opposed to facts presented in the court to the jury or to the court as trier of fact without a jury. So long as the facts are being presented to a trier of fact, whether judge or jury, the duty of candor to the court as to the facts does not come into play, for the proof of these facts is the responsibility of the litigants. The judge expects the advocate to present the truth and nothing but the truth. He does not expect the advocate to reveal the whole truth.

When facts are presented to the judge for him to act upon as a matter of law, rather than as a trier of fact, the duty of candor does come into play, and it is more than a duty not to conceal. It is an affirmative duty to reveal. When the advocate presents false facts to the court for action, he is guilty of a fraud on the court.

A clear example of this fraud is in the misrepresentation of the facts in a complaint or petition. Thus in Harkin v. Brundage[5] the appointment of receivers in a state court was delayed until a federal receiver could be appointed. Said the court: "What was done here in delaying the state court and inducing the federal court to act without a full disclosure of what had been done in the state court, was a fraud not only upon the state court but upon the federal court itself . . ."[6] And in In re Backes,[7] disciplinary proceedings against a lawyer for filing a divorce for his client without disclosing the client's second, and bigamous, marriage, the court said: "It is implicit in our scheme of things that the lawyer who endeavors deliberately to prevent the revelation of facts which, revealed, may be destructive of his client's right to secure a divorce under our laws is faithless to his trust as an officer of the court to conserve and protect the state's interest and is deserving of the severest censure."[8]

The duty of candor to the court as to facts exists also during the process of litigation when action by the court is sought on the basis of the facts presented. In In re Carroll,[9] an attorney

5. 276 U.S. 36 (1928).

6. Id. at 56 (1928).

7. 16 N.J. 430, 109 A.2d 273 (1954).

8. Id. at 434, 109 A.2d at 275 (1954).

9. 244 S.W.2d 474 (Ky.Ct.App.1951).

was disciplined because in a hearing on temporary alimony, his client said he owned no property, when in fact his attorney held real estate in his own name in trust for his client. The court concluded that the answer was false and the lawyer knew it to be false. "Under any standard of proper ethical conduct an attorney should not sit by silently and permit his client to commit what may have been perjury, and which certainly would mislead the court and the opposing party on a matter vital to the issue under consideration." [10]

The duty of candor to the court as to the law presents little problem, for the principle is the same as that involved when presenting facts to the court for action. The difference is that whenever law is presented to the court, it is always presented for the court's action. To assume that the advocate has a privilege to mislead the court as to the law to be applied is to strike at the very foundation of our legal system. "Where a lawyer knows of legal authority in the controlling jurisdiction directly adverse to the position of his client, he should inform the tribunal of its existence unless his adversary has done so; but, having made such disclosure, he may challenge its soundness in whole or in part." [11]

The only real question that seems to have arisen in connection with this duty is whether it should be limited to controlling law.[12] To place such a limitation, however, is to assume that the client has a vested right in the ignorance of the judge. The right of the client becomes blurred with the role of the lawyer in the administration of law in the adversary system. The adversary aspects of the system should control the facts and their presentation and the arguments as to what the law is or should be. Extension of a privilege of concealing law that has been developed on the point in issue, controlling or otherwise, is a different matter. "It is only when each branch of the profession performs its functions properly that justice can be administered to the satisfaction of both the litigants and society and a body of decisions developed that will be a credit to the bar, the courts and the state." [13]

On the appellate level, the duty of candor to the court, both as to facts and law, is even more important than at the trial level. Unlike the trial judge, the appellate judge bears full responsibility for the decision and closer cooperation between court and

10. Id.

11. A.B.A. Code of Professional Responsibility, EC 7–23.

12. See Tunstall, Ethics in Citation: A Plea for Re-Interpretation of a Canon, 35 A.B.A.J. 5 (1949).

13. In re Greenberg, 15 N.J. 132, 138, 104 A.2d 46 (1954).

counsel are necessary. Thus, in In re Greenberg,[14] disciplinary proceedings against an attorney for erroneously asserting before the court on appeal, in both his brief and oral argument, a fact as being shown by uncontradicted evidence, the court said: "[I]t is so obvious as not to require citation of authorities that the work of our appellate courts cannot go on satisfactorily if we cannot rely on the representation of counsel to us both as to the facts and as to the law." [15]

The duty of candor is not only the most objectionable standard for the advocate; it is also the most difficult. At the same time, it may also be the most important, for the duty of candor is the very basis of sound and effective law administration in an adversary system. The problem, however, is not one the individual lawyer can solve, for it is not a matter of personal honesty. To be sure, personal honesty is involved, but so is professional integrity. An advocate, merely because of his own personal attitudes, cannot afford to be candid at the expense of his client.

The right to be candid with an adversary on behalf of one's client depends upon the duty of the adversary to be similarly candid on behalf of his client. Candor is thus a reciprocal standard which must be integrated into the adversary system. This means, of course, that the matter is one for the profession. The need is, first, for a recognition of an affirmative, rather than a negative, duty of candor. The need is, secondly, for a careful delineation of the policies which the trial serves, with a statement of principles to guide lawyers in determining the factors to consider in the implementation of the duty of candor. The range of the affirmative duty of candor, for example, may be affected by the human elements present, including the natural attitude of a client toward his lawyer's actions. The client must have absolute assurance that anything he tells his lawyer in confidence will be so treated. The client's belief and trust in his lawyer's loyalty should not be strained by anything the lawyer does. The ordinary client would doubt the lawyer's loyalty if the lawyer revealed to the other side facts that are harmful to the client. But while the client is usually responsible for the facts and may feel a proprietary interest in them, he is in no such position as to the law. The facts apply only to his case, the law applies to all. Thus, disclosure of matters of law may be wisely required without infringing upon the duty of loyalty.

---

14. 15 N.J. 132, 104 A.2d 46 (1954).   15. Id. at 135, 104 A.2d at 48.

SECTION 6. THE STANDARDS OF THE ADVOCATE IN CONTEXT: FAIRNESS

Few advocates think in terms of fairness. The adversary system, with its emphasis on conflict, tends to preclude any concern for the plight of the opponent, and the stated standards of the profession do not explicitly require fairness as an element of the advocate's conduct. Yet, the adversary system of private law administration is not so bankrupt that a concern for fairness is wholly lacking. Judges do not speak in terms of fairness, but their actions carry more force than their words. Two cases illustrate the point.

In the first, Wyman v. Newhouse,[1] plaintiff, fraudulently lured defendant into the jurisdiction to serve him with process; in the other, Halloran v. Blue & White Liberty Cab Co.,[2] defendant defended the action although the defendant as named in the complaint was non-existent.

Relief was granted in both of these cases in the face of important policies in our legal system, the full faith and credit clause in the first and *res judicata* in the second. In the *Wyman* case, a federal court in New York refused to give effect to a Florida default judgment because plaintiff, the defendant's former paramour, lured him to Florida under false pretenses for the purposes of serving him with process.

The *Halloran* case is even more interesting. There, plaintiff sued a non-existent corporation, Blue & White Liberty Cab Co., for injuries received in a collision. The cab involved was in fact owned by an individual doing business as the Blue & White Liberty Cab Co., the rule of law making service of process a basis of jurisdiction. The attorney for the alleged defendant answered, admitting the collision, but denying that the injuries were caused by defendant. The case, which involved only about a thousand dollars, had been in the municipal court of Minneapolis four times and was in the Minnesota Supreme Court for the second time, where the court was faced with a plea of *res judicata*. Despite this plea, the court, treating the conduct in defending the case as constituting a fraud on the court, reversed for a specific finding on this basis. "The principle of *res judicata* may not be invoked to sustain fraud."

There was no mention of a duty of fairness in either case. Yet it is apparent that this was the concern of both courts. In

---

1. 93 F.2d 313 (2d Cir. 1937). 2. 253 Minn. 436, 92 N.W.2d 794 (1958).

the *Wyman* case, the fairness of the service of process on an individual was predicated on the assumption of normal presence in the state. This was made explicit, by the court in another case, Western States Refining Co. v. Berry,[3] in which plaintiff in Utah invited defendant, a citizen of Idaho, to Utah to negotiate a dispute. When negotiations failed, the plaintiff had defendant served with process before he could leave the state. The Utah Supreme Court quashed the service. "It is our opinion that when plaintiff extends an invitation to defendant to enter the jurisdiction for settlement negotiations, equity and good conscience will not permit plaintiff to take sharp advantage of defendant's presence in the jurisdiction so long as defendant is in the jurisdiction for the purpose for which plaintiff invited him." [4]

In the *Halloran* case, the answer to the suit pre-supposed the existence of the party. The fact of non-existence, and the response of defendant as if the defendant did exist, resulted in an undue advantage by the real defendant not contemplated or provided for by the rules.

As these two cases demonstrate, fairness is a part of the adversary system. The fairness, however, is determined by rules of law. There is no explicit duty on the advocate, nor is there a sense of professional responsibility on his part which that duty would carry. The fault, however, is not that of the lawyer, so much as it is of the common law system. The history of the common law, unfortunately, is virtually devoid of any recognition of an advocate's duty of fairness to his opponent, a striking omission for which several explanations may be offered. The most obvious is the adversary system itself. Since the responsibility for resolving the dispute in a trial is on the litigants, the courts have tended to give advocates wide latitude in their conduct. The common law courts, for example, did not prohibit the use of illegally obtained evidence in criminal trials, and there is apparently no prohibition against the use of such evidence in civil trials even today.

Another explanation for the common law's lack of explicit recognition of a duty of fairness may be that fairness is too subjective in that it means different things to different people. Most advocates think of fairness as a matter for the judge in the even handed application of the law, and quite often, when the ruling is against him, the lawyer will consider the judge to have been unfair. Yet, with the responsibility for the trial resting primarily on the advocates, fairness cannot be limited to the actions of the judge. Essentially, fairness is the responsible exercise of power. As the one who exercises most of the power in the trial, the law-

---

3. 6 Utah 2d 336, 313 P.2d 480   **4.** Id. at 337–38, 313 P.2d at 481.
    (1957).

yer is under a duty to use rules of law consistently with their purpose and function. When he does otherwise, when he engages in unfair conduct, he misuses law. From this perspective, fairness ceases to be merely a subjective matter and its relevance to the proper administration of law becomes clear.

Perhaps the best explanation for not placing on the advocate a duty of fairness to the opponent, however, is the very heavy burden the adversary system imposes on him in his dual capacity. He is the representative of his client. Yet, he is expected to serve also the public interest. Thus, as one court stated:

> "The nature of his obligations is both public and private. His public duty consists in his obligation to aid the administration of justice; his private duty, to faithfully, honestly, and conscientiously represent the interests of his client. . . . wherever the duties to his client conflict with those he owes to the public as an officer of the court in the administration of justice, the former must yield to the latter." [5]

The advocate is thus faced with a continuous dilemma in representing his client. The courts, as well as the profession, have been unwilling to add to his burden by imposing upon him an additional duty of fairness to the opponent. Nor would an explicit recognition of a duty of fairness solve the problem. Rather, it would bring a difficult problem out into the open. The dilemma of the advocate in his dual capacity has to be resolved, and it is presently resolved by emphasizing as a professional standard the duty of loyalty to the client. Much conduct that would otherwise be wholly unacceptable is excused because the conception of the duty of loyalty to the client is too broad in scope. There is no counter-balancing standard requiring a duty of fairness to the opponent to aid the advocate in resolving the inevitable dilemma that results from his dual role.

The problem is that the stated standards of the profession are all directed to the proper use of the rules of law by the lawyer. There is no stated standard directed to the use of the standards themselves. A standard of fairness to the opponent would help to cure this defect, for it would aid the advocate when he is faced with a choice of two standards, as, for example, whether to take a default judgment in a case when the defendant is represented by a lawyer.

To be effective, a standard of fairness to the opponent must first be accepted and recognized as a professional duty by all lawyers, and it must be one which is enforced. Lawyers as advocates are not willing to be fair to an opponent unless they can be

5. Langen v. Borkowski, 188 Wis. 277, 301, 206 N.W. 181, 190 (1925), Annot., 43 A.L.R. 639 (1926).

sure that he will be fair in return. The risk to their client's interest is too great and they are justified in not taking it. Judges must be willing to take the lead in being more concerned with the conduct of lawyers in their courts, to exercise a firmer hand in order to insure a higher standard of conduct. Yet the problem is one that can best be dealt with by the development of mutual trust among lawyers themselves.

A troubling aspect of the American legal profession is that advocates in the trial of cases do not trust each other. They do not, because there is no professional responsibility for them to be fair in their relationships. The cost of this lack of trust in terms of time, effort and energy is incalculable, and the cost goes for nothing. Most cases in the courts end in the right result, and most advocates know at the beginning what the right result is and what to expect. What the profession has not yet realized is that a duty of fairness to the opponent will not change the results. Rather, it will make lawyers more efficient and more effective. Honesty, decency, and fairness, contrary to what many may think, are not only consistent with, but essential for, sound advocacy.

Lawyers, like other people, tend to act as those with whom they deal expect them to act. The initial step is to create a new and higher level of expectation in regard to the advocate's duty to his opponent, both before and during the trial. Only the judges can create this higher level of expectation. Despite the difficulties, it can be done, for it has been done as a notable precedent shows.

> Of all the mighty changes that have taken place [in England] in the nineteenth century, the greatest change has been in the tone of the administration of both the civil and the criminal law. The manners of our law courts have marvelously improved. Formerly judges browbeat the prisoners, jeered at their efforts to defend themselves, and censured juries who honestly did their duty. Formerly, too, counsel bullied the witnesses and perverted what they said. Now the attitude and temper of Her Majesty's judges towards parties, witnesses, and prisoners alike has wholly changed, and the Bar too behave like gentlemen. Of course if a witness is deliberately trying to conceal the truth, he must be severely cross-examined; but an honest and innocent witness is now always treated with courtesy by counsel on both sides. The moral tone of the Bar is wholly different from what it was when Bentham wrote: "they no longer seek to obtain a temporary victory by unfair means: they remember that it is their duty to assist the Court in eliciting the truth." This is due partly to the improved education of

the Bar; partly no doubt to the influence of an omnipresent press; but still more to Her Majesty's judges. If counsel for the prosecution presses the case too vehemently against a prisoner; if counsel cross-examining in a civil case pries unnecessarily into the private concerns of the witness; a word, or even a look, from the presiding judge will at once check such indiscretion.[6]

SECTION 7. STANDARDS AND THE ADVERSARY SYSTEM

The major weakness of the common law trial—the placing of the primary responsibility for resolving disputes upon the litigants—is also its greatest strength. The weakness is that it emphasizes self-interest in a situation of stress. The strength is that it gives persons power to seek redress for wrongs without interference from government and thus aids in securing the independence of the individual. The essential feature of the adversary system is not the law which it applies, but the way in which it applies the law. This is the characteristic which gives such great importance to standards. It means that lawyers' standards are an integral part of law itself.

The major defect of the adversary trial at common law was the lack of appropriate standards for the advocate. The complex and cumbersome system of common law procedure obscured the fundamental problem. Lawyers practicing under that procedure apparently gave little thought to standards; the system was so technical and the rules so detailed they did not perceive the need for standards to govern their conduct beyond the many rules.

The legal profession in this country did not give attention to standards until the reform of common law procedure had begun. Indeed, common law procedure had to be changed before the importance of standards became apparent, for the complexities of that procedure made the trial of a case a "battle of wits" and the rules encouraged surprise as a major weapon of the advocate. Individual lawyers representing their clients under the system were powerless to develop the necessary standards, for their primary duty was to their client. The defendant guilty of wrongdoing deserved the loyalty of his lawyer no less than the injured and innocent plaintiff. The rules were applicable to both alike, and they did not include standards relating to the lawyer's conduct.

6. Odgers, A Century of Law Reform
41–42 (1901).

More than coincidence, then, explains the beginning of both procedural reform and the public recognition of the need for standards within the space of a few years in the middle of the nineteenth century. The Field Code of Procedure was adopted in New York in 1848 and only six years later in 1854 Judge Sharswood published his Essay on Professional Ethics.[1]

The correlation between the development of the law of procedure and standards has continued, but the latter continues to lag behind the former. The American Bar Association adopted the Canons of Professional Ethics in 1908, well after code pleading had become accepted and established, and more than a half century after the Field Code. The next major procedural reform, the Federal Rules of Civil Procedure in 1938, was followed by the adoption of the Code of Professional Responsibility in 1969.

The Federal Rules, simple and flexible, reducing the number of pleadings to three—the complaint, the answer, and in some instances, a reply—give increased importance to standards, for they give the advocate greater freedom of action and consequently an increased measure of responsibility for his own conduct. At the same time, the rules make the framework of the adversary system more realistic in terms of the advocate's various loyalties. The rules of discovery, for example, do not impose a duty on the lawyer to reveal information to his opponent; they enable each lawyer by using his own initiative to learn all the facts of the case. The discovery rules thus resolve a basic dilemma for the advocate in regard to evidence created by his duty of loyalty to the client and his duty of candor to the court. But discovery, despite the protective provisions of the rules, is also susceptible to abuse by a lawyer who is not cognizant of his responsibilities in the administration of law. Discovery can be an expensive process and the advantage it can give to the wealthy litigant over his poor opponent is obvious.

Despite the increased importance of standards under the Federal Rules, the standards as stated in the Code of Professional Responsibility do not measure up to the responsibilities of the advocate. The Code, despite its Ethical Considerations, continues to treat standards merely as guides for the lawyer in representing his client, rather than as an integral part of the law itself. It is to standards what code pleading was to procedure—a necessary stage of development.

---

1. "The first code of legal ethics in the United States was adopted by the Alabama Bar Association in 1887. This code was inspired in large part by the Essay on Professional Ethics, published in 1854 by Judge George Sharswood of Philadelphia." E. Cheatham, Cases and Other Materials on The Legal Profession 109 (2d ed. 1955). The draftsmen of the American Bar Association Canons of Professional Ethics, adopted in 1908, relied heavily on The Alabama Code of 1887.

The advocate in the trial of a case is part of "a tripartite entity consisting of the judge (and jury where appropriate)" [2] and counsel for the plaintiff and counsel for the defendant. The successful functioning of the adversary trial depends upon the coordination of these three roles, for if any one of the participants does not do his job properly, the system fails. The tripod theory of the adversary system is for the first time made the basis of standards in the Standards Relating to the Prosecution Function and the Defense Function, a part of the American Bar Association Project on Standards for Criminal Justice. The superiority of these standards over the Code of Professional Responsibility lies in the fact that they treat standards as an integral part of the administration of law, rather than merely as guides for the conduct of the individual lawyer in representing his client.

The Prosecution and Defense Standards may represent a development as significant for standards as the Federal Rules for procedure. They are the best statement of professional standards ever made, and they may well serve as the pattern for future statements of standards. The advantage the draftsmen of those standards had was that they were dealing with two specific roles of the advocate, as prosecutor and as defense counsel in the criminal trial. Consequently, they were able to state standards in relation to the particular role of the lawyer and to make them functional. The duties of the prosecutor and the defense counsel in a criminal case obviously vary from the duties of lawyers for the plaintiff and defendant in a civil case. Even more clearly, the duties of the advocate in court differ from those of the lawyer in his office. The same is true for the lawyer in the administrative and legislative processes. Future statements of standards must be devoted to the particular roles of the lawyer if standards are to become accepted by the practitioner as an integral part of law itself. And if the adversary system is to function at its best, this development is essential. The development is all the more important because the influence of the adversary system is not, as many suppose, limited to the courtroom. It influences and pervades all of the major legal processes in this country—the private, the legislative, and the administrative, as well as the judicial. The wisdom of the caution expressed in the preamble of the Canons of Professional Ethics in 1908 is only now being realized: "No code or set of rules can be framed, which will particularize the duties of the lawyer in the varying phases of litigation or in all the relations of professional life." The need is for several codes.

---

2. ABA Standards Relating to The Prosecution Function and The Defense Function 153 (T.D.1970).

SECTION 8. ARBITRATION

Arbitration, as a means of resolving disputes, is halfway between litigation and compromise, for it is a private judicial process. Parties to arbitration, as in court, submit their dispute to a third party; but they create the tribunal which is to render the decision. This process of litigation before private persons may be based upon an agreement in a contract to arbitrate future disputes (a future disputes clause) or upon a contract to submit an existing dispute (submission clause) to arbitration. In this country arbitration is of two principal types: commercial and industrial.

At common law, agreements to arbitrate were difficult to enforce, for the authority of the arbitrator was based upon the submission. This was a private contract, and could be revoked like powers generally, "unless there was a public policy against it which took it out of the general rule of powers not coupled with an interest." [1] But while the common law courts jealously guarded their jurisdiction as to arbitration, they also made use of one of its principal advantages, experts. "In the Tudor Period, the Privy Council, a major forum for commercial matters, solved its mercantile cases by reference to merchant arbitrators. . . . Chancery referred its mercantile cases to arbitration, while the common law courts seemed to be using merchant juries." [2]

The common law view of arbitration has been rejected in large measure by statutes. The common law held "future disputes" clauses invalid. Modern statutes make them valid, so a party to a contract with such a clause in it who resorts to an action at law to resolve the dispute may have his action enjoined or dismissed. While arbitration "statutes have existed in this country from earliest times." [3] the first of the "modern acts" was passed in New York in 1920. [4] The United States Arbitration Act was

---

1. See Sayre, Development of Commercial Arbitration Law, 37 Yale L.J. 595 (1928). "[B]oth the common and early statutory laws imposed technical requirements which, if not observed, could render the agreement non-enforceable and the award void. For example, failure to file a submission with the court, or to have it made an order of the court, could have this effect. Other requirements, such as that of beginning suit before arbitration, made it necessary for parties in dispute to conform to various court regulations before they could proceed with arbitration." F. Kellor, American Arbitration 5–6 (1948).

2. Mentschikoff, Commercial Arbitration, 61 Colum.L.Rev. 846, 854–55 (1961).

3. Pirsig, Some Comments on Arbitration Legislation and the Uniform Act, 10 Vand.L.Rev. 685, 686 (1957).

4. M. Bernstein, **Private** Dispute Settlement 45 (1968).

enacted in 1947 [5] and a Uniform Arbitration Act was promulgated in 1955.

The modern revival of commercial arbitration as a means of private dispute settlement can be attributed to its advantages, described by a leading expert in the field, Dean Wesley Sturges:

> "Commercial arbitration, . . . contemplates that the parties to a dispute shall choose one or more persons specially qualified to decide their particular case. There are no pleadings. Each party may tell his side of the case and present his testimony and other evidence informally. An arbitral hearing is held in private and at such time and place as meet the convenience of the parties and arbitrators. Experience teaches that an arbitral adjustment of a business dispute leaves the parties susceptible to future business dealings. What is more significant, the use of future-dispute clauses often induces the parties to resolve their own misunderstandings before they require a formal arbitration." [6]

In ordinary business dealings commercial arbitration is primarily a matter of convenience for businessmen. In international commerce, it is a practical necessity. In the other principal area of arbitration in this country, labor-management relations, it is more than a matter of convenience. Labor arbitration represents an effort to enable private parties to settle their disputes in an area vested with a large public interest. The employer and the union are required by law to bargain in good faith, an illustration of the public use of the private legal process.

> "The labor policy of the United States Government is designed to foster and promote free collective bargaining. Voluntary arbitration and factfinding are tools, in appropriate case, of free collective bargaining and may be desirable alternatives to economic strife. The parties assume broad responsibilities for the success of the private judicial system they have chosen. . . ." [7]

Arbitration thus exists as a major means of dispute settlement in our society, but it apparently is not a process with which the legal profession has been primarily concerned. The Code of Professional Responsibility, for example, makes only passing reference to arbitration.[8] In almost all self-contained trade as-

5. Act of July 30, 1947, ch. 392, 61 Stat. 669, 9 U.S.C.A. §§ 1–14.

6. Sturges, Arbitration, I Encyclopedia of Social Sciences 151, 152 (1937).

7. 29 C.F.R. § 1404.1 (Supp.1970).

8. "A lawyer is often asked to serve as an impartial arbitrator or mediator in matters which involve present or former clients. He may

sociations and exchanges . . . lawyer participation in the arbitration proceedings is either forbidden or discouraged, and very few of the arbitrators are lawyers or law-trained." [9] Two reasons are given for this attitude: "(1) lawyers [do] not understand the business usages and practices that [are] typically involved in adjudicating the dispute and [are] therefore not helpful; and (2) lawyers [make] the proceedings unduly technical and [tend] to create unnecessary delays." [10] The first reason is not the fault of the profession. The second is, and it is a cause for some concern, because arbitration will undoubtedly become a process of increasing importance in our society.

The major factor in the undesirability of lawyers as arbitrators is the standards of the profession. Trained as an advocate for the common law trial, the lawyer carries over to arbitration proceedings his attitudes, his habits of thought, and his standards. Yet, one of the reasons for the use and success of arbitration is that it is not a common law trial. Here is an illustration of a basic idea recurring throughout this book: standards of the lawyer must be functional in that they must be suited to the particular role the lawyer is performing and for the setting in which he performs that role.

Reliance on technicalities, procedural delays, and unnecessary objections are bad enough in the trial; in an arbitration proceeding they become intolerable, for simplicity is one of the major virtues of arbitration. The lawyer's view that he is an advocate in an arbitration proceeding as in the courtroom and that loyalty to his client demands that he do everything necessary to protect his client contains a fallacy. Loyalty in an arbitration proceeding does not demand the same conduct as loyalty in the courtroom.

People in dispute, particularly businessmen, who resort to arbitration are not interested in technical procedures. Their desire is to have their dispute settled in a fair and just manner with a minimum of friction and conflict. Thus, arbitration, despite its adversary form, is not a process of conflict so much as it is a process of coordination.

serve in either capacity if he first discloses such present or former relationships. After a lawyer has undertaken to act as an impartial arbitrator or mediator, he should not thereafter represent in the dispute any of the parties involved."

A.B.A. Code of Professional Responsibility EC 5–20.

9. Mantschikoff, Supra note 2, at 859.

10. Id.

Chapter VII

COMPROMISE: ADJUSTMENT WITHOUT LITIGATION

SECTION 1. INTRODUCTION

Compromise is a process of dispute settlement in which the advocacy of the lawyer is directed to the opposing party rather than to a superior tribunal. As a method by which the parties settle their dispute upon their own terms, compromise has many advantages. Each party has an opportunity to express his feelings and to make clear his position and the reasons for it fully without being limited by rules of procedure and evidence. Equally as important, each has the opportunity to understand the other's position and reasoning. Rarely is a dispute so one-sided that there is no middle ground upon which the parties can agree. Face-to-face discussion provides the means for searching out and locating the areas of agreement before positions are hardened and views become fixed. The process of give and take preserves the dignity and protects the pride of the participants, and the conclusion of the process results in a resolution of the dispute by the parties themselves rather than by a court.

The disadvantages of litigation as a means of dispute settlement correspond to the advantages of compromise, for contrary to the legislative process of compromise, litigation is a judicial process of victory or defeat. Litigation sharpens disagreement. The dispute is decided not by the parties, but by a trier who must depend upon the testimony of witnesses for a knowledge of the facts. The result is complete defeat for one of the parties, leaving little or no basis for future cooperation.[1]

The law itself is the result of compromise and conflicting policies. "[T]here are few areas of the law in black and white. The greys are dominant and even among them the shades are innumerable. For the eternal problem of the law is one of making accommodations between conflicting interests."[2] Yet, the judgment in a lawsuit is not sufficiently flexible to accommodate the differing interests of the parties. By its very rigidity, the law

1. Judge Learned Hand acknowledged this when he said, ". . . as a litigant, I should dread a law suit beyond almost anything else short of sickness and of death." J. Frank, Courts on Trial 40 (1949).

2. Mr. Justice Douglas in Estin v. Estin, 334 U.S. 541, 545 (1948).

encourages compromise and settlement, and most disputes, in fact, are settled without litigation and most litigation is settled without trial. One study, for example, has shown that of 193,000 personal injury claims in New York City, only 7,000 reached trial, and only 2,500 of these went all the way to a verdict.[3] It has been estimated that in Chicago, eighty-five percent of all personal injury claims handled by insurors are settled prior to the filing of a suit. Only ten percent of the suits filed are brought to trial.[4] The facts are fortunate for the public as well as for the parties, for if all disputes were turned into lawsuits and all lawsuits into trials, courts would be overwhelmed by the burden.

"Lawyers," said Chief Justice Hughes, "Are the greatest conciliators of mankind." The lawyer prefers that disputes end in compromise through conciliation and negotiation rather than in a judgment through litigation. Compromise not only reduces the number of disputes to a manageable proportion, it results also in a more satisfactory solution to disagreements and enables the lawyer to be affirmative, rather than negative, in his work. To provide the client, or to aid him in providing himself, a basis for compromise that will be fair and acceptable to all is more satisfying than attempting to defeat another in a lawsuit.

This chapter is devoted to the lawyer's role in compromise. Section two discusses the nature of compromise, and section three the processes of compromise, conciliation and negotiation. Section four discusses professional standards for, and the concluding section aids to, compromise.

SECTION 2. THE NATURE OF COMPROMISE

"All government—indeed, every human benefit and enjoyment, every virtue and every prudent act—is founded on compromise and barter," said Edmund Burke.[1] Yet, to most people, compromise implies defeat, for we give attention to agreements as compromise only when they fail. The greatest compromise in our history, the Constitution of the United States, receives no recognition as such.

---

3. Rosenberg & Sovern, Delay and the Dynamics of Personal Injury Litigation, 59 Colum.L.Rev. 1115 (1959).

4. Comment, Settlement of Personal Injury Cases in the Chicago Area, 47 Nw. U.L.Rev. 895, n.5, 902 (1953).

1. Speech on Conciliation with America, March 22, 1775.

Two common errors give the term compromise a bad connotation. One is the treatment of compromise as a result, rather than a process of conciliation of the parties and the adjustment of their differing interests. This error is most common when the process is directed to the settlement of a dispute based on past events. The result is called a compromise. When the process is directed to future arrangements, the process of coordinating differences for a cooperative endeavor, the result is a contract or an agreement or plan. Yet, all collaborative efforts, whether to arrange for the future or to settle disagreements based on a past event, require essentially the same process for a successful conclusion. A better and more accurate term than compromise is coordination.

The other error is equating compromise with conduct in derogation of principles, a by-product, perhaps, of our Judeo-Christian heritage, for all religions tend by nature to be absolute. A public official who has accepted a bribe, we say, has compromised himself. The client is particularly subject to this error, for he tends to think not in terms of the facts, but in terms of his legal claims, and he equates those claims with legal rights.

The lawyer can perceive this fallacy in the client's judgment, but he himself is a victim of the same error in a different way. The obstacle for him is the principle of loyalty to his client. Compromise he thinks of as a yielding, a giving up, a violation of his duty to obtain everything he can for his client. The fault here is the failure to realize the nature of compromise. Compromise is no more than the adjustment of mutual but differing interests by agreement without the intervention of a superior force. Yet, the unfortunate connotation given to compromise obscures the fact that compromise in the adjustment and readjustment of human relations is a part of everyday life. People in close contact are always in conflict in varying degrees, and compromise is the means by which they resolve their differences. The alternative to compromise is increased conflict and victory or defeat, a condition contrary to the principles of sound human relationships as the larger setting of history shows us.

Before the United States entered World War I, President Wilson urged peace without a victor or vanquished in a much derided phrase, "peace without victory." In the British elections immediately after the armistice, Lloyd George swept to triumph on a platform of making the Germans pay "the uttermost farthing." The Treaty of Versaille fulfilled the prime minister's promise, not the president's hope, and fifteen years later Adolph Hitler came to power in Germany. A major factor in his rise was his denunciation of the Versailles Treaty as an instrument dictating humiliation for the German people.

Compromise is the means of victory without defeat for the lawyer and his client. The words of Diderot are well remembered:

"   .   .   .   [O]ur judgments are too much of a single piece; we should learn to bring more freedom into them. We ought to inspire ourselves with more of the clearest result of all the lessons of life, that everything even among the greatest of all the sons of men is incomplete, mixed, relative; everything is possible in the way of contradictions and limits; every virtue neighbours elements of uncongenial alloy, all heroism may hide points of littleness, all genius has its days of shortened vision." [2]

SECTION 3. THE PROCESS OF COMPROMISE: CONCILIATION AND NEGOTIATION

The process of compromise involves two related processes, conciliation and negotiation. Conciliation requires the participation and effort of the parties themselves, and it is the lawyers' role, through the use of tact, good judgment, and human understanding, to get them to participate and make the effort. Negotiation may proceed with or without the parties, for it is essentially a bargaining process. The two processes are thus distinct, but not necessarily separate, for when the parties are in emotional conflict, conciliation and negotiation often occur at the same time.

"Interests always compromise, passions never do," said the French philosopher, Alain, and conciliation is a necessary process in compromise because disputes have an emotional as well as a rational basis. The parties in dispute must come to a recognition of the fact that the settlement of their dispute is to their mutual benefit, and this is the purpose of conciliation. Where the dispute is purely a personal one, as between parties in marital discord, conciliation may effectively resolve it without negotiation. If negotiation is the primary concern, as in the settlement of a personal injury claim or the making of a contract, conciliation still has a vital role, since no agreement can be reached as long as emotion prevails over reason. Even when the negotiations fails, conciliation still has a useful role, for it is important that the parties sever their relationship in an amicable manner, for rational, rather than emotional, reasons.

2. Quoted in J. Morley, On Compromise 144 (The Thinker's Library Ed. 1933).

The importance of the process of conciliation, however, receives little attention. While there are many official aids to litigation in this country, there are few official aids to conciliation. In other countries, conciliation has long been a part of the official machinery,[1] but in the United States, there are only two principal areas where official aids to conciliation have been developed: domestic relations [2] and labor law.[3] This lack of official aid to conciliation means that the process has been left largely to private lawyers. Yet, the lawyer's role as conciliator is overshadowed by his image as a litigious advocate in court, and his lack of identification as a conciliator serves to inhibit his imagination and the use of opportunities to make himself more effective in this role. Conscious as he is of serving his client's best interest, it may at times be difficult for him to realize that as conciliator, he serves his client's best interest, not by extracting concessions, but by aiding him and the other party to recognize that their best interests call for compromise. His task is to perceive the emotional bias involved and to aid the parties to displace emotion with reason.

The process of conciliation is inevitably intertwined with the process of negotiation, that is the process of reaching decisions by coordinating mutual but differing interests where there is no superior authority. The basic elements of this process are preparation and fairness.

Lack of preparation is perhaps the greatest fault of lawyers as negotiators.

> "Since we want to settle the case, since we feel the case ought to be settled, since preparation is such a bore anyhow, since we are always thrifty, since it runs up the overhead, since it is so expensive and since it is going to cut into the fee . . . why not try to settle the case before you prepare it? That is the line of least resistence. That is what we all do and that is the greatest mistake that any of us ever makes." [4]

The necessity of preparation extends, of course, to the law and the facts. The law provides the structure, but the facts are the basis, of the agreement.

1. See, e. g., Smith, The Danish Conciliation System, 11 J.Am.Jud. Soc'y 85 (1927).

2. See Crenshaw, A Blueprint for Marriage: Psychology and the Law Join Forces, 48 A.B.A.J. 125 (1962); Burke, An Instrument of Peace: The Conciliation Court in Los Angeles, 42 A.B.A.J. 621 (1956).

3. 29 U.S.C.A. § 173(a). See Williams, Settlement of Labor Disputes in Industries Affected with a National Interest, 49 A.B.A.J. 862 (1963).

4. Buckner, The Lawyer in Court, 13 Chi.Bar Ass'n Record 100, 102 (1930).

A negotiator who is not sure of his facts is in no position to negotiate, for a knowledge of the facts is essential for the implementation of the second element of negotiation, fair mindedness. If an agreement is to be sound, it must be fair, and to be fair, it must accurately reflect the facts. And the facts upon which the agreement is based must be known and accepted by the parties.

In Modern Trials, the author emphasizes the importance of these two elements, preparation and fair mindedness, in describing the "Brochure Method" of settling a case. The brochure requires investigation and insures careful preparation, and "The brochure should contain all of the facts or none." [5] The reason is simple. "A hopeful reliance upon defendant's inability to discover weaknesses in plaintiff's case is a dependency upon a false premise in modern trial preparation." [6] More important, perhaps, the author states that the brochure method of settlement is based on certain premises. The plaintiff must have a case with merit; he must be willing to settle that case for an adequate award without trial; he must be sincere and above board in all his dealings with the defendant and must be willing to comply with all reasonable demands and concede all facts necessary to settlement, and there must be a reciprocal measure of good faith from the defendant.[7]

What is true of negotiation for the settlement of cases is even more true for negotiations which involve planning for a continuing relationship between the parties. Fair mindedness is important in the negotiation of the settlement of cases because it enables the parties to reach an agreement. It is essential in negotiating a contract, because the parties will have to live with the agreement. A misuse of facts in such negotiations will almost inevitably lead to a rupture of amicable relationships between the parties, and it may also lead to legal liability. In one case,[8] for example, the plaintiff tenant sought damages for deceit against his landlord because in negotiating for the lease the landlord falsely stated that another had offered an annual rental of $10,000, although plaintiff had been paying only $4,500 per year. The Massachusetts Supreme Judicial Court reversed the lower court's decision sustaining a demurrer to the complaint. Said the court:

> "The defendants represented to the plaintiff that they had received a bona fide offer from Levine to take a lease of the premises at an annual rental of $10,000. This was more

5. M. Belli, Modern Trials, vol. I, 704 (1954).

6. Id. at 702.

7. Id. at 710.

8. Kabatchnick v. Hanover-Elm Bldg. Corp., 328 Mass. 341, 103 N.E. 2d 692, (1952), Annot., 30 A.L.R.2d 923 (1953).

than a statement of opinion; it was a representation of an existing fact. Why, on principle, should one making such a representation be immune from liability if it was false, provided the other elements required by the law of deceit are present?" [9]

Conciliation and negotiation both call for advocacy, but advocacy different from that in a trial. The advocate in negotiation presents his facts and arguments to the other party for agreement, rather than to a tribunal for decision. The difference is best perceived in terms of the assumptions that underlie advocacy in the judicial process of litigation and those which underlie the private process of negotiation. Litigation assumes an irreconcilable conflict between the parties, that one party is wholly at fault, that one party must win, and that the end of the dispute is more important than the right decision. Negotiation assumes that the parties desire to reach an agreement, that each is fair minded and willing to be convinced, that each will yield to a more reasonable view advanced by the other, and that the right decision requires a coordination of interests for their mutual benefit.

The lawyer's greatest weakness as a conciliator and negotiator, perhaps, is his lack of attention to principles of human conduct. Lawyers are highly conscious of what constitutes the practice of law from a technical standpoint, but they tend to overlook in their work that the practice of law involves also the practice of human relationships.

"Ideally, every lawyer's education should include at least a grounding in human psychology. He should learn what we know about interviewing skills. What happens when a client sits down with an authority figure such as his lawyer? What are the psychological forces operating between the parties to such a conversation that may obscure issues and produce failures of communication? . . . The answer to such questions is to be found in the substance of the psychological sciences; before long, we should view it as a matter of neglect if they are not included in the routine training of all lawyers." [10]

A knowledge of principles of human conduct is as important for the lawyer as a knowledge of rules of law. Much of this knowledge is gained through observation and experience. Some of the principles are obvious, as the desire of all persons for the respect of others and the importance that emotion, as well as

---

9.   Id. at 345, 103 N.E.2d 694.

10.   Watson, Could the Legal System be More Humane? 14 Law Quad-rangle Notes (The University of Michigan Official Publication) No. 1, 14, 16 (1969).

reason, plays in our thought, particularly in negotiations.[11] A quality of high importance in the negotiator is what Professor Barton Leach has called moral dominance. The quality is one which is found in the masters of the art of negotiating. Two of the masters in this country were Benjamin Franklin and Charles Francis Adams. Franklin's skillful diplomatic missions were vital to the birth of this country. Adams handled the most difficult foreign assignment in our history while he was minister of England during the Civil War. Both had the quality of moral dominance. The quality is as important for the lawyer in negotiating for his client as it is for a diplomat in negotiating for his country. Moral dominance is, as Professor Leach has said, "a product of basic integrity, habits of thorough preparation, and astuteness."[12]

SECTION 4. PROFESSIONAL STANDARDS FOR COMPROMISE

The standards of the lawyer set out in canons and codes are based on his role as advocate in the courtroom. They are not framed in terms of the several different roles of the lawyer. Thus, there are no generally recognized standards for the negotiator as such, and the standards as they apply to the advocate are assumed by the lawyer to apply to the former role as well. But litigation and negotiation are two entirely different processes involving different means as well as different ends. The goal of the advocate is to defeat the opposing party, the goal of the negotiator is to defeat the problem.

The advocate's standards enable a lawyer to represent his client in a court of law. As an advocate, the lawyer may do, and even be required to do, things that would be neither justified nor wise in the process of negotiation and compromise, as the withholding of facts protected by the attorney-client privilege. Unlike the advocate, who emphasizes the rights of his client, the negotiator recognizes and acknowledges the rights of the other party and the duties of his client. In the courtroom, a lawyer may and should attempt to persuade the jury that his client was not

11. One professor who taught a course in negotiating stated that the most important segment of knowledge conveyed to students in his course was "an appreciation for the importance of emotional forces in negotiation." White, The Lawyer as a Negotiator: An Adventure in Understanding and Teaching the Art of Negotiation, 19 J.Legal Ed. 337, 349 (1967).

12. The idea of moral dominance is taken, with permission, from unpublished notes of Professor Barton Leach of Harvard Law School.

negligent. Around the conference table, he may acknowledge and accept the fact of negligence if he is to negotiate a settlement.

The negotiator in the office and the advocate in the courtroom thus have two entirely different functions to perform which call for different standards. The negotiator is dealing with the other party not as a plaintiff or a defendant, but as an individual person whose cooperation is desirable, and perhaps essential, to the best interest of his client. Thus, there is only one basic standard for the lawyer that is particularly applicable to his role as negotiator and that is honesty. In terms of the standards of the profession, honesty is candor, and acceptance of this standard removes the need for a catalogue of subsidiary standards. Candor to the opponent assures the existence of other standards, as loyalty and fairness.

Even so, the negotiator, as is the advocate in court, is in a special situation and the stated standard of candor calls for a brief discussion of the scope of the matters covered. The duty of candor is applicable to the facts upon which the agreement is to be based, and does not encompass such matters as negotiating technique or strategy. One author, for example, has made the following points as to negotiating techniques in the making of concessions. "The final price the client is prepared to pay should not be laid on the table until [e]very effort has been made to secure the bargain at a smaller price, ... Concessions should normally be made only when they are balanced by concessions from the other side." [1]

Candor is not inconsistent with such strategy, nor is it inconsistent with hard bargaining. But negotiation is a matter of persuasion, and the power to persuade another is based on his feeling of confidence in what one has to say. "Candor and sincerity are the most powerful weapons" of the negotiator. "As soon as the adversary understands that he is dealing with a man of integrity, the discussions can proceed with directness, and the time wasted in beating around the bush may be eliminated." [2]

Candor in negotiation will not always result in an agreement. But just as there are many cases which should never be litigated, there are many agreements which should not be negotiated. Agreements which cannot be achieved on the basis of candor as to the facts are in this category.

The view here expressed as to the standard of candor for negotiations is not one which is generally recognized in the stated standards of the profession. The standards of the lawyer are di-

1. Voorhees, Law Office Training: The Art of Negotiation, 13 Prac. Law, No. 4, 61, 65 (1967).

2. Id. at 64.

rected primarily to the public legal process. They have not been directed in adequate measure to the private legal process, of which negotiation is a part. The violation of professional standards not yet clearly stated may lead to harm for the client through the failure of the private legal process and resort to the costly public process. The suit to rescind a contract, or for a breach of warranty, or to overturn a settlement are not always the direct result of a lack of candor in negotiating, but in many cases, candor in the negotiations would have prevented the dispute. The sanctions for candor in negotiations are thus indirect rather than direct. The lawyer himself is not punished for lack of candor, but the result of his efforts is overturned and it is the client who suffers.

The fact that the courts will overturn agreements reached for lack of candor provides the severest test for candor as a standard for negotiations. That test is whether the standard suggested will facilitate the working of the process involved. That candor as to the facts does facilitate negotiations as a practical matter is too plain to be disputed. Negotiations may be part of the private legal process, but they are vested with a large degree of public interest and the efficacy of any agreement arrived at is determined by public, not private, rules of law. A contract is binding not because the parties agree to it, but because the courts will enforce it. The courts will not enforce it if it is achieved by deceit or fraud or dishonesty.

SECTION 5. AIDS TO COMPROMISE

"The policy of the law has always been to promote and sustain the settlement of disputed claims. It loves peace, hates broils and dissensions, and discourages the prolongation of litigation." [1] Yet, compromise has not been accepted for what it is in fact, the primary method of dispute settlement in our legal system. Official aids to compromise exist, for the most part, only as rules or procedures incidental to litigation. The rule that statements made in negotiations for the settlement of a dispute are inadmissible in the trial of a case should the negotiations fail [2] is intended to promote compromise. Discovery procedures are available to eliminate the surprise element, to encourage a realistic assessment of one's position and thereby encourage settlement. The

---

1. In re Nevitt, 117 F. 448, 452 (8th Cir. 1902).

2. Gallagher v. Viking Supply Corp., 3 Ariz.App. 55, 411 P.2d 814 (1966), Annot., 15 A.L.R.3d 13 (1967).

pre-trial conference is a device which may be effective for encouraging settlement by bringing lawyers together. Thus, despite its prevalence, its importance and its desirability, most lawyers continue to view compromise secondary to litigation as a means of dispute settlement.

A major reason for this attitude, of course, is the adversary system. The orientation of that system toward rights rather than duties is a fundamental obstacle to compromise. Trained in that system to obtain every advantage for his client, the lawyer thinks in terms of victory by defeat in court rather than victory without defeat by compromise and settlement. Consequently, compromise remains a part of the private legal process with little official encouragement. Even the individual lawyer who perceives the value of compromise as an aid to his client is limited in what he can do, for compromise is a cooperative and coordinating process. Unless his adversary is of like mind, the probabilities of compromise in a particular case are slight.

To be truly effective, the policy of the law in promoting the settlement of disputed claims should be directed to the two aspects of compromise for the lawyer: the settlement of disputes which have arisen and the prevention of disputes for the future. The first aspect would be aided by integrating the policy of settlement more fully into the public legal process; the second by rules of law to aid the lawyer in his office.

The problem of integrating the process of dispute settlement into the public legal process involves two steps: a rule of law requiring an attempt at settlement before a complaint can be filed in court; some official aid in promoting settlement. The first is relatively simple. The latter is more difficult, and any detailed suggestions for its implementation would be out of place here. There is little reason, however, why lawyers should not have the opportunity to present their case to a commissioner of the court whose specific task would be to promote settlement. The danger, of course, would be that the process would become judicialized, in which event its advantages would be lost. Thus, such a presentation should be without the rules of evidence or witnesses or even the parties, and the recommendation of the commissioner would not be binding, for the purpose would be to provide a service for the lawyer. The only requirement would be that all suits filed must be submitted to the commissioner, although the filing of the suit would not be necessary in order to submit the matter for evaluation and recommendation.

The important aspect of the plan is its service feature, to give lawyers assistance and encouragement in settling cases. It would not be a substitute for, nor would it replace, the trial, but it would avoid the necessity for a trial in many instances. Equally as important, it would provide a public institution to give dignity and status to compromise as a means of dispute settlement.

The suggestion is not without precedent. In this country, there is precedent in the "good faith" bargaining requirement for employees and employers in labor disputes, and the Federal Conciliation and Mediation Service. An even more striking precedent is the wide use of arbitration as a means of dispute settlement by those who feel the need for resolving disputes without resort to the courts and litigation. The growth of arbitration shows a deep seated desire for an independent evaluation of one's dispute without the rigidities and formalities of a common law trial. Yet, the common law has traditionally been hostile to arbitration as a rival means of dispute settlement.

The development in the public legal process of a means to promote compromise and dispute settlement by the parties themselves would fill a great need in our society and would be a service to clients and lawyers alike—if it can be developed without the restrictive and inhibiting aspects of the judicial process.

The second aspect of compromise, prevention of disputes for the future, is a problem for the office lawyer and exists in regard to the principal subject of private law, contracts. Freedom to contract has almost the status of a sacred right in our society. But the responsibility which that freedom entails carries with it has no such status. Thus, while there exists in our law an implied warranty as to the making of contracts—that the facts relied upon by both parties in the making of the contract are true —there is no express warranty required. To turn this implied warranty—shown by the cases which grant rescission of a contract for fraud and deceit—into an express warranty would constitute a recognition of the responsibility that freedom to contract entails. A recognition and realization of this responsibility would not only be an effective aid in preventing disputes, but also an aid in resolving them after they have arisen.

More important, perhaps, such a rule, or principle of law, would aid lawyers in recognizing that a contract is a human as well as legal document, providing, as it does, a blueprint for human relationships. Principles of human conduct are as important in drafting a contract as rules of law. But most lawyers naturally draft contracts to make them legally, rather than psychologically, binding. Yet, in many, indeed in most, instances, the human element is far more important than the legal element. This simple fact has been put to very effective use by the Conciliation Court of the Superior Court of Los Angeles in the widely acclaimed husband-wife agreement.

> "It was perfectly obvious that these contracts, in a very true sense, must be human documents, going far beyond the

technical requirements of the ordinary business contract or partnership agreement. Immediately, therefore, it became necessary to incorporate . . . certain psychological concepts quite apart and beyond any enforceable language having to do with specific acts and rights." [3]

The appropriateness of such provisions for a domestic relations contract is more immediately apparent than for a business contract. But they can be as effectively used in business contracts as in the domestic relations situation. Two provisions which would be of aid are: (1) a statement of the goals of the contracting parties; (2) a statement of their willingness to attempt to adjust any differences arising thereunder in an amicable manner.

Negotiation and compromise as methods of dispute settlement have a much larger role in our legal system than is ordinarily recognized. Lawyers tend to resist official developments in aid of compromise because they constitute threats to their power. History and tradition are on their side, but it is history and tradition of an earlier, simpler era unburdened by modern problems. A sparsely populated, rural society can afford individual conflict and can leave the assertion of their rights to individuals. In a crowded, urban society, individual conflict becomes an ill-considered luxury, and the assertion of rights becomes a matter of public interest. But the assertion of rights must be accompanied by a recognition of duties, and the primary method of resolving disputes should become cooperation through compromise rather than contest by litigation.

3. Crenshaw, A Blueprint for Marriage: Psychology and the Law　　Join Forces, 48 A.B.A.J. 125, 127 (1962).

Chapter VIII

THE LAWYER AND THE PRIVATE LEGAL PROCESS

SECTION 1. INTRODUCTION

Private law—particular rules created for and applied to particular individuals to govern their relationships with each other —is a marked characteristic of our society. People in a nation of free enterprise with a developing, malleable economy must have the freedom and the power to shape their legal relations with one another through the use of rules of law suited to their goals. Most of this law—contracts, wills, trusts—has only temporary effect. The terms are limited, and all of it is for private, rather than public purposes. The limited scope of private laws, however, is not a good measure of their influence. The private legal process as a part of our system of jurisprudence, makes a great contribution to the social life. Many new forms of legal relations trace their origins not to the courts or to the legislature, but to a new kind of instrument first created in the lawyer's office. "It was the lawyer who devised the long-term lease for real estate improvement, and the collateral trust for real estate financing, or for financing new equipment for a mortgaged railroad. And, greatest perhaps of any single line of growth within our law, it was the lawyer who from the outset shaped the thousand uses of the law of trusts. .   .   ." [1]

The private legal process, however, is not limited to the making of private law. The office lawyer must know not only how to do, but what to do as well, for he must give advice and counsel and settle disputes, functions no less important than the drawing of deeds or partnership agreements or trust indentures. Poor advice can be as harmful to the client as a badly drawn contract, and the failure to settle a dispute can be as costly as both. These tasks give the office lawyer three distinct roles—legal adviser and counsellor, private law maker, and private adjudicator. Clearly separate in function, the roles overlap in practice, for most often the purpose of advice is to settle, or avoid, a dispute and reach an agreement to be reduced to writing as a private statute.

The private legal process has no well defined structure as does the judicial process. The lack of such a structure for the

---

1. K. Llewellyn, The Bramble Bush
146 (1951).

work of the office lawyer does not hinder his effectiveness as a private representative of his client, but it does obscure his important role as a representative of the social order. The common core of ideas as to what the lawyer may and may not do for his client and what his client may and may not do, tends to blend and merge these two roles. Most lawyers want to and do aid their clients in a way consistent with the customs, traditions, and requirements of society. In so doing, they fulfill their public role as they work in the office unaware of their contributions to the stability and advancement of the social order. Yet, a greater awareness of their public responsibilities would enable office lawyers better to contribute to the social order and better to serve the individual client.

The emphasis on the public responsibility of the lawyer has been focused on the advocate rather than the office lawyer. Yet, the public responsibilities of one are no less than those of the other, for their roles are complementary. The office lawyer, too, shares with the advocate a fundamental problem: How best to perform his dual role as a private representative of his client and a public representative of the social order?

This chapter is directed to the problem from the viewpoint of the office lawyer and the private legal process. Section two discusses the nature of the private legal process; section three is devoted to the qualities of the office lawyer. The final section deals with a common but overlooked problem for the lawyer in his office, the use and misuse of law.

SECTION 2. THE PRIVATE LEGAL PROCESS

The least noticed, the private legal process is also the most pervasive process of law in our society. Legal authors have devoted their attention to the judicial, the legislative, and the administrative processes. Yet, said one writer, " .   .   .   I suspect the first book has yet to be written about the process whereby a couple of lawyers bring two .   .   .   parties together in an office, adjudicate their disputes, draw a decree or statute called a contract to govern their conduct .   .   .   and thereafter administer the law they have written in a way that will .   .   .   carry out the legislative intent." [1]

1.   Cavers, Legal Education and Law-
   yer-Made Law, 54 W.Va.L.Rev. 177,
   180 (1952).

The process is, perhaps, too seemingly obvious for a book, but it is too important to be ignored. "[I]t too often is overlooked that the lawyer and the law office are indispensable parts of our administration of justice. Law-abiding people can go nowhere else to learn the ever changing and constantly multiplying rules by which they must behave and to obtain redress for their wrongs."[2] The simple fact is that more law is made and administered and more disputes are adjudicated in the private legal process than in the legislature, the administrative agency, and the courts combined.

Unlike the other legal processes, the private legal process has no official institutional setting to give it form and shape. Its setting is the lawyer's office, which functions as a private administrative agency of law for the individual. The analogy to the public administrative agency is striking. The lawyer in his office administers law by interpreting and utilizing it for his client; he exercises quasi-legislative functions in producing rules and regulations for his clients in the form of legal instruments; he exercises quasi-judicial functions in settling disputes through conciliation, negotiation, and compromise; and his advice, opinions, and decisions are subject to judicial review.

The special nature and breadth of the office lawyer's work and his responsibilities are apparent when they are contrasted with those of the advocate. The advocate deals with the past and is subject to safeguards and restraints in the courtroom. He is faced with an expert adversary, a judge, and often a jury as well. He has one basic role to perform in representing his client in court: he is expected to stress the matters most favorable to his side and to do everything he can within the limits of the law to win for his client. The office lawyer is a problem solver who deals with the future and works alone in his office and performs several roles. In these various tasks he must perceive and appreciate the other's viewpoint. He cannot stress only the matters most favorable to his side, for he does not submit a case to a tribunal for decision, he acts alone or deals directly with his opponent. His primary concern is not conflict, but coordination.

These differences come into sharper relief when we consider some of the details of the three basic roles of the office lawyer. The client who brings his problem to the office of the lawyer typically seeks in the first instance advice as to a proposed course of conduct or advice about his rights and duties under a past transaction. To the extent that the lawyer informs his client that the law forbids, compels, or allows certain conduct, he is in-

---

2. Hickman v. Taylor, 329 U.S. 495,
515 (1947) (Jackson, J., concurring).

terpreting and enforcing the law. The interpretation and advice, of course, carry no official power of enforcement. The sanctions are more subtle; they exist in the form of the client's confidence in his lawyer.

The primary role of the lawyer in his office, however, is the affirmative one of helping his client to achieve his objectives by creating legal relationships through the instrument of private law. The law may be unilateral, as in the case of a will; it may be bilateral, as in the case of a contract; or it may be multilateral, as a partnership agreement or a corporate charter.

Conciliation, negotiation, and compromise, too, are a part of the office lawyer's work, for he also serves as a private judge. Adjudication is usually identified with formal litigation, but it is not necessary to invoke the machinery of the state to resolve human conflicts in a rational manner. Indeed, the elements of wise dispute settlement, conciliation, negotiation, and compromise, are better carried on in the lawyer's office around the conference table than in the courtroom. The goal of dispute settlement is not the victory or defeat provided by the judgment at law which may terminate the relationship of the parties. It is the sound reconciliation of the parties' interests for their future relationships.

These functions of the office lawyer give the private legal process a broader scope than the judicial, the administrative or the legislative process, for the private legal process rests on the power of the individual not of the government. This difference often leads the office lawyer to view his activities and the private law he creates as solely a matter of private concern. His client, for example, has a right to insist on any provision in the contract to which the other party will agree, so long as it does not violate the law, no matter how unfair. The view is supported by the idea of freedom of contract. But private law is no less law than a statute. The common law is not so explicit as Code Napoleon in Section 1134—"Agreements legally formed have the force of law over those who are the makers of them."—but its effect is the same. A valid contract determines the rights and duties of the parties as effectively as a statute. Private law is private in only a limited sense—in that it is law made by persons as private individuals for their own benefit—for any law that may be enforced by the courts is vested with a large public interest.

The lawyer's administration of private law is thus no less important than the government's administration of public law. "The most effective realization of the law's aims often takes place in the attorney's office, where litigation is forestalled by anticipating its outcome, where the lawyer's quiet counsel takes the place of public force." [3] The private lawyer, exercising power in our society as important, if not as specialized, as that of the government official, has a responsibility to exercise his power wisely. The unarticulated premise of American jurisprudence is that power, whether it is economic or legal, public or private, shall be exercised responsibly and fairly. "The lawyer as client caretaker provides the dynamics of the principle that in this society all power shall be constitutional power—that all power, not just public but private as well, should be responsible power, exercised subject to the check of someone other than the power holder." [4] The results of the abuse of this power are well illustrated by decisions such as Baker v. Carr,[5] Miranda v. Arizona,[6] and S. E. C. v. Texas Gulf Sulphur Co.[7] The first case imposed a limitation on the power of a state legislature, the second on police officers, and the third on corporate officials. The failure of the Tennessee Legislature to comply with its own constitutional requirements made it necessary for courts to inquire into abuses of the electoral process even down to county school boards, to which the one-man-one-vote rule now applies.[8] The abuses of the rights of accused persons dealt with in *Miranda* have lessened the discretion of police officers. Corporate officials, as a result of the *Texas Gulf Sulfur* case, must develop new policies for releasing information about new developments in their companies and exercise discretion in naming brokers to their boards of directors. A greater sense of responsibility in the exercise of these powers by the persons involved would not have made it necessary for the courts to limit them, especially not to limit them so severely.

The lawyer can easily overlook this point about the exercise of power, for he thinks in terms of legal rights and legal duties. In fact, however, he acts in terms of power, the ability to bring about a desired result. He plans his client's legal relations first in terms of the client's power at his disposal, and after determining what the client has the power to do, he formulates the plan in terms of rights and duties. The greater the power of the client, the greater the probability that the plan will be to the advantage of the client at the expense of another. The corporate counsel who drafts an adhesion contract might load the contract with protective provisions for his client, minimizing the duties and

---

3. Report of the Joint Conference on Professional Responsibility, 1958 A.A.L.S.Pro. 187, 192, 44 A.B.A.J. 1159, 1161 (1958).

4. Hurst, The Lawyer in American Society, 1750–1966, 50 Marq.L.Rev. 594, 599 (1967).

5. 369 U.S. 186 (1962).

6. 384 U.S. 436 (1966).

7. 401 F.2d 833 (2d Cir. 1968), cert. denied 394 U.S. 976 (1969).

8. Delozier v. Tyrone Area School Bd., 247 F.Supp. 30 (W.D.Pa.1965); see also Avery v. Midland County, 390 U.S. 474 (1968).

maximizing the rights. Yet, courts in construing the contract will view not only the terms of the agreement, but the relative bargaining position of the parties as well. The party who drew the contract has a burden of showing, implicitly or explicitly, that the contract is fair. The greater the disparity between the parties, the heavier the burden. Thus, it is in the client's interest for the private legislation to be fair.

The task of the office lawyer, then, is not merely a matter of determining what is right and what is wrong in terms of rules of law. His problem is what is the wisest course of action in terms of social as well as economic implications. The problem is one to which we shall return in the final section of this chapter.

The private legal process presents the office lawyer with a job that is more complex and challenging than that of the advocate in the judicial process. To deal with the future is more difficult than to cope with the results of the past. To prevent litigation is more helpful than to win a lawsuit. To work alone in the office is less dramatic than to work in the structured setting of a trial. But the opportunities for the office lawyer are greater. He receives problems in their most malleable form and he has the opportunity to mold opinions, to shape conduct, and to provide reasoned, intelligent solutions to problems.

SECTION 3. THE QUALITIES OF THE OFFICE LAWYER

The role of the office lawyer, wide in its scope, deep in its implications, and without any clearly defined structure, may be the most important of the lawyer's roles. The influence of the lawyer in his office begins with the client's statement of his difficulties, and it ends when they are resolved. But the effect of the influence may extend beyond the resolution of the specific problem, even to people of whose existence neither the lawyer nor the client will ever be aware. Indeed, so important is the influence of the office lawyer that standards as mere rules of conduct are not sufficient to guide him in his work. Loyalty, candor and fairness are no less important for him than for the advocate, but the office demands more than the courtroom. Personal qualities, qualities such as judgment, tact, and competence are essential for the office lawyer to advise, counsel and devise solutions for his client's problems, for while the advocate specializes in conflict, the office lawyer specializes in cooperation.

This section will discuss the standards of the office lawyer in terms of the necessary personal qualities. The discussion first deals with the duty of fairness, a recurring theme throughout this part, which applies to the lawyer in all of his roles. This subsection is followed by a discussion of the three basic roles of the office lawyer, as counsellor and adviser, as private lawmaker, and as private adjudicator, and the special qualities appropriate to these roles.

a. The Duty of Fairness

The duty of fairness is a fundamental characteristic of our legal system, for a sense of fairness is part of the Anglo-American heritage. The best known manifestations of this duty, perhaps, are the equal protection, the privileges and immunities, and the due process clauses of the fourteenth amendment and the due process clause of the fifth amendment. These provisions of the Constitution were adopted to serve primarily as restraints against the abuse of governmental power. Their reach, however, may extend beyond that of official action to affect private individuals in their legal relationships, as in Shelley v. Kraemer,[1] which held a racially restrictive covenant unenforceable in courts of law. These provisions thus may support the recognition of a duty of fairness between private individuals, and an accompanying duty on the lawyer to aid his client in maintaining fairness toward the other party to a transaction.

As yet, however, for the most part, the duty of fairness has not been explicitly applied to the private legal process, to that large area of law administration which goes on without the direct aid of the state. The major reason for this lack, paradoxically, may be another basic idea of our jurisprudence, that all men are equal before the law. Individuals who make their own private law are presumed to be equal and to have acted voluntarily and without restraint in entering into a contract. Men are recognized as having the responsibility for the conduct of their own affairs, and the law seldom places the relative bargaining position of the parties into the equation of facts unless the result is manifestly unjust. Even when it does so, the result is usually framed in terms of reasoning to fit accepted rules of law, rather than in terms of a duty of fairness. This attitude of the courts contributes much to the *caveat emptor* complex, derived from the competitive system in economic affairs, that is a part of the adversary system. The office lawyer, no less than the advocate, is subject to the allure of the idea that he must get whatever he can in any way he can for his client. Yet, it is clear that, "The reasons that justify and even require partisan advocacy in the trial of a cause do not grant any license to the lawyer to participate as legal adviser in a

---

1.   334 U.S. 1, 68 S.Ct. 836 (1948).

line of conduct that is immoral, unfair, or of doubtful legality." [2] Unlike the advocate, who deals with adjudicative facts, past facts necessary to the decision in the particular case, the office lawyer deals with managerial facts, facts which are malleable and involve future actions and decisions and which may affect not only the parties to the transaction, but others as well.

Some situations are clear. The lawyer who advises his client to sell property to another who is misinformed as to the acreage involved, or who advises his client to proceed with the construction of a building in violation of a contract or building code because the damages he will have to pay will be worth the risk, or to infringe a copyright because the owner will not be in a position to know or to bring suit is being cheap and petty. Decent lawyers avoid such situations. The point is not one which needs elaboration, for when the person with whom the client is dealing proceeds under a misapprehension known to the client, or when the client proceeds without informing his opposite number, any supposed advantage accruing to the client is the result of unethical conduct.

But what of the wealthy client who wishes to back an impecunious, but talented, young man in a business venture by forming a corporation. With the money, the client is in a position to claim as large a share of the company as he desires. The client wishes ninety percent of the stock. Should the lawyer proceed? Or should he attempt to get his client to accept sixty percent of the stock? The Code of Professional Responsibility provides some helpful aids. "Advice of a lawyer to his client need not be confined to purely legal considerations. . . . A lawyer may bring to bear upon the decision-making process the fullness of his experience as well as his objective viewpoint. In assisting his client to reach a proper decision, it is often desirable for a lawyer to point out those factors which may lead to a decision that is morally just as well as legally permissible. . . ." [3]

Many lawyers would see no problem here, for they do not distinguish between their roles as advocates and as office lawyers. The difference is that the lawyer in the courtroom shares no responsibility for the past conduct of his client; the lawyer in his office, by advising his client as to future conduct, has responsibility in fact for the client's actions in accordance with that advice. A part of this responsibility is to help the client be his better self and to perceive his long term as well as his short term self-interest. This responsibility is what the client pays for, and

---

2. Report of the Joint Conference on Professional Responsibility, 1958 A. A.L.S.Pro. 187, 192, 44 A.B.A.J. 1159, 1161 (1958).

3. A.B.A. Code of Professional Responsibility, EC 7–8.

no decent lawyer can afford to abdicate it on the premise that he is merely doing what his client wants to the advantage of the client. "In the event that the client in a non-adjudicatory matter insists upon a course of conduct that is contrary to the judgment and advice of the lawyer but not prohibited by Disciplinary Rules, the lawyer may withdraw from the employment." [4]

The proper measure of fairness is the responsible exercise of power. Most lawyers do act fairly and most judges reach the fair result. Their actions speak louder than their words. They act within a broad framework of fairness, but they seek to express the result in terms of rules of law. These rules are framed neither in terms of fairness nor power, but as statements of legal rights and duties. Even though the definiteness is often illusory, fairness may be usefully viewed in terms of specified rights and duties in the structured setting of the trial. In the unstructured setting of the law office, it should be viewed in broader, more fundamental terms, not only in terms of legal rights and duties, but also in terms of the effect of the exercise of these rights and duties in the particular situation. The lawyer in the private legal process may and should take into account, for example, the relative position of the parties involved. The lawyer representing General Motors Corporation has different obligations from the one representing the poor widow. "The responsibilities of a lawyer may vary according to the intelligence, experience, mental condition or age of a client, the obligation of a public officer, or the nature of a particular proceeding." [5]

Fairness and the responsible exercise of power by the lawyer are important not only for the client, but for the profession as well. An analogy is the most fundamental limitation on the power of government, the due process clause. The purpose of that clause is to restrain government officials in the exercise of their power and to compel them to exercise it in a responsible manner. The office lawyer often exercises power on behalf of his client in much the same way a government official does on behalf of the government. The requirement that he act in accordance with a private due process is appropriate. The client is assuming to exercise a power given him by law. The lawyer is exercising a privilege entrusted to him as a member of the bar. And failure in the making and administration of private law to comply with a standard that measures up to private due process may lead to redress by statute. As the due process clause of the fourteenth amendment was adopted in response to the abuse of governmental power by the states, so the abuse of power by lawyers, or their clients, calls for limitations on the exercise

---

4. Id.   5. A.B.A. Code of Professional Responsibility, EC 7–11.

of power by the individual.   An illustration of this reaction is the Uniform Consumer Credit Code by the National Conference of Commissioners on Uniform State Laws, approved by the American Bar Association at its meeting in August, 1968.   The abuses and unfairness in the use of law in this area are too well known to discuss, and one of the most revealing provisions of the Code is Section 1.107(1) : "Except as otherwise provided in this Act, a buyer, lessee, or debtor may not waive or agree to forego rights or benefits under this Act."   The difference in the public due process and in a private due process is that the former sets only the utmost limits of unfairness the state may not pass.   Private due process has its affirmative measure.   It must accord with what is fair, not merely avoid what is unfair.   The lawyer is administering law and he should administer it justly.

As the Consumer Credit Code demonstrates, the concept of private due process for the lawyer is one of large social implications, for the lawyer must be concerned with social fairness as well as individual fairness.   "The lawyer's function is in the nature of a fiduciary or trustee, and he is answerable as such, not only to the particular person standing in direct relation to him of client, but answerable also to all those, whether it be the public or individuals, to whom the client himself owes an accounting." [6]

Social fairness requires a judgment as to the soundness of the client's proposed conduct in light of its effect on others apart from question as to its legality, and it involves a long range view of the self-interest of the client which he may not perceive.   The problem is one which is particularly applicable to the businessman client, who must act responsibly in terms of the public welfare and be fair with the public upon whom he depends for a profit.   The corporation proposes to establish a manufacturing plant which will pollute a river, or to produce a product for sale which is unsafe, as an automobile, or wants a warranty drafted which will mislead the consumer.   When his client wishes to engage in such conduct, the lawyer can be effective in educating him to the fact that his own self-interest requires a concern for fairness to others and to the public.   A price business pays for not acting responsibly is government control.   One need only view the present day regulation of railroads, of the trucking industry, of airlines, and of the rise of big labor, for example, to see that the story of government regulation of business is the story of the failure of business to act responsibly.   A still more obvious illustration is the failure of manufacturers to be con-

6.   Brown, Some Applications of the Rules of Legal Ethics, 6 Minn.L. Rev. 427, 435 (1922).

cerned for automobile safety, which has resulted in federal standards imposed by Congress.[7]

Viewed from this standpoint, the lawyer's concern for the social fairness of his client's conduct becomes a matter of practical importance, particularly for the large client. Here, too, the responsible exercise of power is the measure by which the fairness of conduct in relation to the public good can be gauged. As the complexity of the problems in modern society increases, the exercise of power by individuals and groups becomes a circumstance of increasing concern. "[T]he business corporations of this country, perhaps as a result of the series of blows that have been rained upon them in the last twenty-odd years, . . . have begun to feel themselves that they ought to look at the whole panorama in charting their courses. Many of them recognize a public responsibility going beyond bare legal rights. As a result their lawyers have been encouraged to give a broad kind of advice." [8]

The above quotation might be misinterpreted. If it meant that lawyers give a broad kind of advice only in response to the wishes of their clients, and not because of their own sense of professional responsibility, it would be an indictment of the profession, for it means that lawyers have failed as counsellors. The point is one which goes to the heart of the office lawyer's guiding role. To what extent should he control, or attempt to control, his client's actions in the interest of fairness and justice to others?

The lawyer whose client insists upon conduct which will be unfair or unjust to others may follow one of three courses of action. He may refuse to do his client's bidding and lose a client. He may do his client's bidding and gain a fee. Or he may attempt to educate his client and persist in his efforts to get his client to act responsibly. To do the first is to abdicate a responsibility by leaving the client free to injure himself or others. To do the second is to fail as a lawyer. To follow the third course is his professional duty. "It is not only the right and privilege, but it is the professional and personal duty of the lawyer . . . to use his utmost endeavor, even to the extent of shrinking or even losing his standing with his client, to keep his client from doing injustice." [9]

b. The Lawyer as Counsellor

The particular duty of the lawyer in advising his client is "to preserve a sufficient detachment from his client's interest so

7. 40 U.S.C.A. §§ 701-03 (1969).

8. W. Seymour, Religion and the Law in Man at Work in God's World 152–53 (1963).

9. Brown, supra note 6, at 435.

that he remains capable of sound and objective appraisal of the propriety of what his client proposes to do." [10]   This duty requires special emphasis on the qualities of competence, judgment, and tact, each of which will be discussed briefly.

The lawyer's professional duty of competence is clear. "If the attorney is not competent to skillfully and properly perform the work, he should not undertake the service." [11]   More than competence in the law, however, is required for the lawyer in advising his client as to a proper course of action. "The client is not merely a point or problem of law. He is a human being who seeks advice and help in meeting a problem with personal as well as legal aspects." [12]   The client who wishes to disinherit his daughter for marrying a man of a different faith would almost surely regret his actions. The issue for the lawyer in such a problem is not the rules of law necessary for the client impulsively to achieve his immediate objective, but the wisdom of the objective.

The competence of the counsellor, in short, calls for his giving weight to the human factors as well as the legal factors involved. Yet, many lawyers are apt to limit their inquiry to facts they deem relevant to the legal issues, facts necessary to make a given plan effective. The genuinely competent lawyer will go further and be concerned as well for the effects of his client's goals, not only on the client, but on those who will be affected by them.

The lawyer is paid for his judgment. "He contributes not only that feeling for relevance which is the essence of his profession, but a sense of priorities, which is the next step up from relevance. . . . [H]e will be able to see in many situations implications that have escaped other people." [13]   The lawyer thus must remain free of emotional entanglement in the client's problem. "A lawyer should not accept proffered employment if his personal interests or desires will . . . affect adversely the advice to be given or services to be rendered the prospective client." [14]   So he must avoid any conflict of interest. "The professional judgment of a lawyer should be exercised . . . solely for the benefit of his client and free of compromising influences and loyalties. Neither his personal interests, the inter-

10. Report of the Joint Conference on Profession Responsibility, 1958 A.A.L.S.Pro. 187, 192, 44 A.B.A.J. 1159, 1161 (1958).

11. Degen v. Steinbrink, 202 App. Div. 477, 481, 195 N.Y.S. 810, 814 (1922), aff'd mem. 236 N.Y. 669, 142 N.E. 328 (1923); A.B.A. Code of Professional Responsibility, Canon 6.

12. Cheatham, The Growing Need for Specialized Legal Services, 16 Vand.L.Rev. 497, 499 (1963).

13. M. Mayer, The Lawyers 307 (1966).

14. A.B.A. Code of Professional Responsibility, EC 5–2.

ests of other clients, nor the desires of third persons should be permitted to dilute his loyalty to his client." [15] Yet, unquestioning adherence to the client's desires can be an inhibiting factor on the lawyer's judgment, for the exercise of sound judgment requires independence of thought. The lawyer in advising his client must not have his perspective foreshortened by the client's eagerness and desires for the present. The problem at hand must be considered not only in light of the client's aims and his immediate goals, but also in the light of wise policies and long effects, for errors of judgment usually occur when only immediate goals are kept in mind. To advise how to make a contract legally binding is one thing; to advise how to make a contract work is another.

Tact is an essential quality of the lawyer. Justice Holmes and Chief Justice Hughes agreed in giving it the high place of one of the two necessary qualities.[16] The lawyer is concerned with establishing relationships of people involving compatible but differing aims. The process is one which inevitably gives rise to friction, suspicion, and disagreement. The basis for dispelling the friction, allaying the suspicion, and resolving the disagreement is tact, for tact rests on an understanding of the other person—put yourself in his place—and consideration in dealing with him. The essence of tact is the ability to respect others, and to convey that respect, even while disagreeing with them.

A knowledge of the facts and an awareness of the human factors for the exercise of competence, perspective for judgment, and respect as a basis of tact are all interrelated qualities which enable the lawyer to work effectively in his role of advising and counselling his clients.

c. The Lawyer as Private Legislator

Private law is especially important in a free and changing society in which technology requires a continual readjustment of human relationships. The swiftly changing conditions of our times call for new arrangements requiring imagination and creativity, but the need for the lawyer to create new law in the form of a wholly new type of legal instrument is the exception rather than the rule. The problem of most clients can be solved through the use of approved, and perhaps standardized, legal conceptions chosen and applied for the particular situation. The primary duty of the lawyer is to effectuate the desires and plans of his clients in ways which will not be challenged because of

15. Id., EC 5–1.

16. See O. Holmes, The Use of Law Schools, in Collected Legal Papers (1920); C. Hughes, Some Observations on Legal Education and Democratic Progress (1920).

their novelty.   Thoroughness, competence, and a good clear head are the qualities required.

Most legal conceptions, however, are flexible, and skill and imagination are also required to shape them to fulfill the unique needs of the client.   To the client, even the application of a standardized rule is significant, and the role of the lawyer in making law for his client goes beyond that of drafting the instrument. He will, of course, be accurate and full in statement and in formalities so as to avoid future controversies as to meaning or validity.   But no less important, he has an early part in his client's affairs and he is a creator and shaper of relations as they are to be.   As a dispassionate yet loyal adviser, he can be more comprehensive in his views of the interests involved and affected, so he can develop plans which are wiser in the long run than those which the client originally had in mind.   To his role as private law maker, the lawyer must also bring perspective and judgment, perspective which takes into account standards of conduct as well as rules of law, judgment as to what serves the best interest of his client.

The responsibility of the lawyer in molding and shaping his client's plans as well as effectuating them depends in large measure upon whether the situation involves a unilateral or a bilateral transaction.   In the former, typified by the making of a will or the drawing up of a trust, the client is interested in controlling his own affairs.   As in every case, the lawyer will describe the problem, clarify the issues, enlighten the client on the factors affecting his choice and aid the client in making his final decisions.   In the unilateral transaction, however, the social factors are minimal.   The client is interested in preventive law, law which in a family settlement, for example, may give security to his heirs through generations.   For the most part, his exercise of power coincides with the public interest for he uses that power to insure orderly relationships.

In the bilateral or multilateral transaction—by far the majority of transactions most lawyers deal with—another factor enters. The client, whether he realizes it or not, is interested in the exercise of power, and power is a very attractive goal for most men. He wants the completed transaction to vest in him the power to achieve his aims.   The other parties involved in the transaction, too, want the same result for themselves.   What is needed in both clients' interest is not merely a legally valid transaction, but one which will work because the parties believe it is fair.

The lawyer realizes, or should realize, what the client may not —he is dealing here with emotions as well as reasoning.   A famous lawyer made the point well.

"Many of our severest battles are with our own clients; anger and vengeance have to be extirpated from their minds and emotions, and a sense of justice instilled. We have to teach them the limits of the law; . . . We learn that all opposing parties are not rogues and liars; that there is much on their side—sometimes too much. We learn that opposing counsel are not only able and alert, but also in most cases, with only tragic exceptions, prove to be honorable gentlemen. We learn that misunderstanding, rather than greed or spite, is at the root of many quarrels." [17]

The final agreement embodied in the document signed by the parties may constitute law, but it is only a means to an end, and it will be workable, only to the extent that it reflects the wishes of both parties. The same point has been stated differently. A contract may be primarily a framework for cooperative effort, without regard to its enforceability or the interpretations a judge would give to it. The lawyer, in preparing it often has to balance two aims: (1) placing his client in a position to win any lawsuit arising out of the contract, and (2) creating an instrument of collaboration that will function effectively without a lawsuit. "If he cannot have both these things, he may properly favor the second at some cost to the first, since his role as practical legislator for the situation may be more important than his role as advocate in a hypothetical future adjudication." [18]

A man does not enter into a contract with one in whom he has no confidence or trust, and a contract is no substitute for these qualities. The function of a contract, to clarify the agreement between the parties, to define their rights and to delineate their duties, is made necessary because of the fallibilities of men—imprecise communication, faulty memories, and the need for guidelines in a complex undertaking. It is given the force of law to make it effective. But the rights defined and the duties delineated are exercised and performed by men and men act as often on the basis of emotion as well as on the basis of reason.

It is important, then, that rights and duties in a bilateral or a multilateral transaction be obtained and imposed fairly. There must be fairness in reaching the agreement and fairness in the agreement itself. Equally important, all parties must feel themselves to have been dealt with fairly. The lawyer knows, and he must make his client know, that law involves not only rules, but also standards of conduct. The client who obtains his wishes at the expense of his reputation and another's pride will have only a Pyrrhic victory.

17. Smith, Inaugural Statement, 1 Personal Finance L.Q.Rep. 1, 6 (1946).

18. Fuller, What the Law Schools Can Contribute to the Making of Lawyers, 1 J.Legal Ed. 189, 195 (1948).

While the lawyer must keep in mind always the interest of his client, he must not overlook the fact that oftentimes his decisions on the client's behalf are of great social importance. When the client is one who has great power at his disposal, his legal decisions will inevitably affect thousands, and perhaps hundreds of thousands of persons, and the private law which the lawyer makes for him takes on aspects of public law. The client's interest requires that both he and his client keep this fact in mind, for if the client is to retain his power, he must exercise it wisely.

The nature of modern society—increased specialization, increased division of labor, and the interlocking nature of so many interests—make the increased use of private law as a means of providing order inevitable. These conditions, together with the changing nature of our society, call for constantly changing legal methods and adaptations in business and otherwise. One of the tasks of the lawyer is to furnish the imagination and judgment for the creation and selection of appropriate and wise new methods as a private lawmaker.

d.   The Lawyer as Private Adjudicator

The process of private adjudication provides the lawyer with an opportunity for perhaps the greatest service to his client. The simplest and most common adjudication by the lawyer occurs when the client alone asks the lawyer about his rights. The answer will usually resolve the issue for the client. In the more complex situation, when the client is in dispute with another, private adjudication prevents litigation and saves the client time, effort, money, and, perhaps, reputation. The disputes the office lawyer settles usually arise as an incident in the negotiating and planning of future relationships and conduct, but they may also arise out of past relationships and conduct. In either event, the principles of private adjudication are the same, for in contrast to the narrow, highly formalized nature of a trial, private adjudication is a broad, malleable process. It has four distinct stages, reconciliation of aims, exploration and explanation, give and take, and agreement, that is conciliation, negotiation, compromise and settlement. Unlike public adjudication, however, private adjudication is not a process structured by rules to cover designated variable situations. It is a process structured by the lawyer in light of the particular situation, and the various stages intermingle and overlap.

In any legal dispute, the emphasis on the three essentials—the factual, the legal, and the human elements—varies as the dispute moves from the process of conciliation to negotiation to compromise and to settlement or litigation. In the beginning, around the conference table, the dominant factor is the human element, followed by emphasis on the facts and then the law; in the court-room, when positions have become fixed and attitudes hardened, the dominant factor is the legal element, with emphasis on rules of law, which determine the emphasis to be given to the facts, and with less emphasis on the human element. The process of dispute settlement thus moves from reliance on the ability of the parties to reach an accommodation of personal wishes, desires, and motivations to reliance on legal rights and legal duties. With a proper beginning, the transition will usually be made smoothly to a decision concluded in the lawyer's office. Without a proper beginning, the transition may be to an exacerbated dis-pute to be concluded in the courtroom or to a rupture in the rela-tionship of the parties.

The lawyer's role as private adjudicator requires that initially he view the dispute in terms of its human elements, not in terms of the facts or law, which he will utilize at a later stage. So to view the dispute is to recognize that conflicts between people do not originate out of rights or duties granted or imposed by law, but out of personal feelings, personal desires, and personal moti-vations. Disputes can be most effectively dealt with when un-derstood in terms of their origin.

The role of private adjudicator requires one quality in partic-ular, that of tact, the ability to respect other people and to con-vey that sense of respect even while disagreeing with them. The desire and the process are face-saving, referred to at times with derogation and moved far to the Orient. But the Orientals may differ from us only in clearer recognition of its importance and fuller efforts to safeguard it. The pervasiveness of human pride makes it essential in settling any dispute. The continuous desire of all men for the respect of others is a fact of life, and in any dispute, this respect is apt to be the first casualty. The as-sembling of a group of people to resolve one's dispute with an-other represents a continuing threat to one's pride, and the es-sence of tact in the dispute settling process is to protect, and if necessary, to repair the pride of the disputants.

Lawyers are prone to underestimate the importance of this quality. Their emphasis on the traditional skills in dealing with facts and law often leads them to ignore the vital human element in any dispute. Their training to deal with matters objectively tends to cause them to be suspicious of treating matters subjec-tively, as the use of tact requires them to do. Lawyers want to deal with reason not emotion, but emotion is a fact of life which cannot be avoided.

The major threat to the process of private adjudication is the adversary system of the common law. Trained in the adversary system of advocacy, the lawyer tends to view a dispute as a contest for advantage, not an opportunity for settlement. The adversary system was not meant to be a means of settling a dispute but a means of presenting it to a formal tribunal. It has little relevance to the process of private dispute settlement, which is based on the premise that people in conflict remain capable of acting responsibly. The lawyer's duty is to implement that premise. To the extent he fails, he diminishes the efficacy of the private dispute settling process. To the extent he succeeds, he strengthens it and enlarges his contribution to the welfare of society.

SECTION 4. THE USE AND MISUSE OF LAW

A client may wish to pursue a course of conduct which is not consistent with or cannot be realized within the limits of established law or precedents. When he is asked to provide such a plan, the lawyer is faced with the difficult task of determining the fine line between avoidance and evasion of the law and of creating new law which will be accepted by the courts as a sound piece of private legislation. He must develop a plan which involves the proper use, rather than a misuse, of law, the problem to which this section is directed.

The problem is not often perceived in these terms for two reasons. The courts are concerned only with the legal effectiveness of a plan and not with the legal or professional quality of the lawyer's work, and they seldom hold him to account for misuse of the law. The lawyer's duty to his client insulates him from criticism by the court, except in cases of the most flagrant abuse. Courts almost always speak in terms of the actions of the parties, not of the lawyers, even though they are responsible for the parties' conduct.

Equally as important—and perhaps the court's attitude is partially responsible—lawyers rarely acknowledge their own responsibility for misusing law. They can too easily rationalize it away, because both the client and the lawyer use law. The client uses it in a beneficial sense, to obtain a benefit, in a particular situation, as when he enters a contract. The lawyer's use is an instrumental one, for he uses it as an instrument to achieve the goals of his client.

The misuse of law is made most apparent by the sanctions which courts impose when it occurs. The most common sanction, of course, is the striking down of the plan by the court, a sanction which penalizes the client. But in some instances, the sanction is imposed directly on the lawyer, as when he is subjected to censure,[1] or when he is suspended from practice or disbarred.[2] In extreme cases, he may be subjected to criminal prosecution [3] or a suit for damages.[4]

A major consideration involved in the use of sanctions against the lawyer is the social desirability that he be free to do the best he can for his client without the threat of personal condemnation or liability. "Whenever the law draws a line there will be cases very near each other on opposite sides." [5] Consequently lawyers must have a substantial measure of freedom in their work. "Infallibility is an attribute of neither lawyer nor judge. . . . It is a silly perversion of the legal fiction that every one is bound to know the law, to insist that, . . . lawyers shall decide all questions in accordance with what the courts may ultimately hold . . . ." [6]

If the lawyer is to be accorded this freedom, he must accept a corresponding responsibility. Courts impose the responsibility by striking down those plans which do not come within the law. The most difficult problem, however, is whether the lawyer is to be condemned for a questionable plan that comes barely within the letter of the law. The answer, thus far given by default, appears to be no, and given the nature of our legal system, the conclusion may not only be necessary but desirable. This answer, however, is not satisfactory for the individual lawyer who imposes on his client a serious risk whenever he devises a questionable plan. For the lawyer, the issue is one of practical rather than theoretical importance, for he cannot know until after the fact whether his plan is within the law. Unfortunately, he often imposes the risk on his client without being aware of the implications of his actions.

Two observations may be useful. Lawyers do have a responsibility—to themselves, to their clients, and to the profession—to exercise their best judgment in providing decent plans not only for the client, but for others who will be affected by them. The failure to recognize this responsibility increases his risk, and it also tends to weaken the moral underpinning so essential to a healthy and dynamic system of law. Secondly, the purpose and the spirit of the law play a major role in the standards the

---

1. In re Gelman, 230 App.Div. 524, 245 N.Y.S. 416 (1930).

2. People v. Macauley, 230 Ill. 208, 82 N.E. 612 (1907).

3. People v. Kresel, 243 App.Div. 137, 277 N.Y.S. 168 (1935).

4. Lucas v. Hamm, 56 Cal.2d 583, 364 P.2d 685 (1961), cert. den. 368 U.S. 987 (1962).

5. United States v. Wurzbach, 280 U.S. 396, 399 (1930) (Holmes, J.)

6. People v. Kresel, 243 App.Div. 137, 142, 277 N.Y.S. 168, 176 (1935).

courts apply in upholding or striking down plans that come close to the line. The importance of these factors, in turn, depends in large measure on the social values involved, for the courts are concerned with fairness and the responsible exercise of power by lawyers and their clients. The rest of this section is devoted to the development of this latter point, which serves to aid the lawyer in evaluating his plans.

The plans which involve misuse of law typically fall into three basic categories: (1) Plans which so clearly violate the law that the courts strike them down without hesitation; (2) plans which seemingly comply with the law, but in fact are inconsistent with its purposes; and (3) plans in which the parties by agreement supplant a general rule of law with a private rule.

An example of the first category is Ostiguy v. A. F. Franke Construction, Inc.,[7] in which the court held a loan usurious because the defendant was compelled to pay plaintiff's attorney $2,000 under a purported retainer agreement for which no services were rendered.

In the second category is Fraw Realty Co. v. Natanson,[8] in which the court denied effect to an ingenious scheme, within the letter of the law, designed to limit very narrowly the liabilities of real estate promoters. Quoting from an earlier decision, the court said: " 'The logical consistency of a juridical conception will be indeed sacrificed at times when the sacrifice is essential to the end that some accepted public policy may be defended or upheld.' " And in the leading case of Gregory v. Helvering,[9] the court overthrew an effort to escape the taxes incident to the normal method of effecting the purpose in mind, even though the unusual method adopted by the taxpayer exactly followed the provisions of the tax statute.

The third category is well illustrated by Reinhardt v. Passaic-Clifton National Bank and Trust Co.,[10] in which a depositor gave a stop-payment order to defendant bank, which negligently paid the check, and defended an action by the depositor on the ground that the order contained a provision exculpating the bank from liability if for any reason the check was paid. The order form was used by the customer, but prepared by the bank. The court, recognizing that other jurisdictions had upheld such provisions, denied its effect on the ground that the defendant gave no consideration to make the agreement binding in that it promised to do only what it was under a legal duty to do. But in contrast to

7. 55 Wash.2d 350, 347 P.2d 1049 (1959), Annot., 81 A.L.R.2d 1271 (1962).

8. 261 N.Y. 396, 185 N.E. 679 (1933).

9. 293 U.S. 465 (1935).

10. 16 N.J.Super. 430, 84 A.2d 741 (1951), aff'd per curiam 9 N.J. 606, 89 A.2d 242 (1952).

this attitude, in Capehart v. Heady,[11] an action by a lessee against a lessor for breach of a lease for a filling station, the court upheld a provision in the lease that any action against the lessor must be brought within three months. Distinguishing an earlier case, the court said: "The limitation clause in the lease . . . was agreed to by plaintiff in entering the lease, and is clear and distinct."

When the above cases are considered together, a pattern emerges. Each of the plans the court struck down was either created by a lawyer acting unilaterally, as in the *Fraw* and *Gregory* cases, or the lawyer's client was in a far superior bargaining position, as in the *Ostiguy* and *Reinhardt* cases. In the *Capehart* case, where the court upheld the plan, two businessmen, presumably in substantially equal bargaining positions, were involved. The judges in these cases faced the same problem they face in all cases, that of reconciling the two basic policies of the law, order for society and justice for the individual. The two policies are directed to the same ends, for without order, justice for the individual is a fortuitous circumstance.

There may be, however, a conflict between these policies, and this conflict lies at the heart of the problem. When will the court sustain a questionable plan in the interest of stability and order on the grounds that " 'contracts, when entered into fairly and voluntarily shall be held sacred, and shall be enforced by Courts of Justice' "?[12] And when will the court sacrifice "the logical consistency of a juridical conception" in the interest of justice for the individual as in the *Fraw* case? Such a conflict can be resolved only by resort to a third policy, the policy of fairness. The ultimate question for the lawyer in evaluating his plan is whether it is fair: Is it fair for the parties, is it fair for society, is it fair in accordance with decent moral standards?

Fairness implies a definite relationship between two parties and the measure of fairness is usually limited to the parties involved in the transaction. The power of individuals, on the other hand, is a product of the law of the society in which they live and as such carries with it a duty to exercise it wisely. This duty naturally extends to persons with whom one is dealing directly, but it also extends to all persons who are affected by the exercise of the power. A contract between a supplier and a utility, for example, may be fair to both, but unfair to the consumers, who are not parties.

To view the duty of the lawyer in the use of law as that of the responsible exercise of power is to provide a basis for resolving

11. 206 Cal.App.2d 386, 23 Cal.Rptr.
    851 (1962).

12. Black & White Taxicab Co. v.
     Brown & Yellow Taxicab Co., 276
     U.S. 518, 528 (1928).

problems of the misuse of law because most of the problems arise out of a misguided sense of loyalty to the client. The duty of the responsible exercise of power serves to bring this duty of loyalty into proper perspective in two ways. First, it serves to make the lawyer aware that part of his duty of loyalty is to enable his client to be his best self. "It is the lawyer's duty to keep the client from putting a black mark on his business record and never to yield, nor to permit his client to yield, to the purpose or intent of following a course of persecution or oppression or of any form of fraud or injustice." [13] Secondly, the duty of the responsible exercise of power by the lawyer gives him a basis for the exercise of independent judgment. The pressure on the lawyer to satisfy his client is enhanced not only by the duty of loyalty, but by his need to make a living. Just as the lawyer needs a basis for acting for his client, the duty of loyalty, he needs also a basis to refuse to act improperly, the duty of the responsible exercise of power.[14]

13. Brown, Some Applications of the Rules of Legal Ethics, 6 Minn.L. Rev. 427, 436 (1922).

14. Cf. L. Brown, Preventive Law (1950).

Chapter IX

THE LAWYER AND THE LEGISLATIVE PROCESS

SECTION 1. INTRODUCTION

The relationship of the lawyer to the legislative process is a natural and desirable one, for legislation is the superior form of law making. A statute can be directed to a perceived need without waiting for a justiciable controversy; it can be drafted with the aid of experts informed on the facts; and it can be shaped to take care of a whole problem instead of being confined to a particular aspect as with a case in courts. The legislature may even create new institutions and not limit itself to the statement of rights and wrongs. The increasing number of statutes makes evident the importance of legislation. In the first three hundred years of the common law, Parliament passed an average of four statutes a year. The 90th Congress passed 1002 statutes, including public and private laws, which covered 2488 pages when compiled in two volumes. No one knows the number of state statutes, and few would hazard a guess as to the mass of ordinances and regulations created by the legislatures' deputies, the municipalities and the administrative commissions.

Yet, the lawyer's participation in the legislative process is more complex than his participation in any of the other legal processes in our society. In the judicial, the private, and the administrative processes, his participation is as a representative of his client. But he participates in the legislative process in four principal ways—as a lobbyist, as attorney for his client before a legislative committee, as an employee of the legislature in a professional capacity, and as a member of the legislature itself. All of these tasks require the skills of the lawyer, but none of them constitutes the practice of law in the formal sense of the word, for their performance does not require membership in the bar. Consequently, there is no formal tie between the legal profession and the legislative process.

A political as well as a legal process, the legislative process is within the primary jurisdiction of the profession of politics and government. The other three legal processes are directed to the administration of law, the application of stated rules to a past or present situation and the rights and duties of the individual. The basic function of the legislature is government. Members of the legislature serve their constituents, conduct investigations,

150

and make law by defining rights and wrongs in terms of the legal rights and duties of the innumerable groups in our society to accord with sound policy. The lack of a formal relationship between the legal profession and the legislative process, however, raises a unique problem for lawyers. To what extent do professional standards apply to the lawyer who actually participates in that process? The question is important because so many lawyers participate in the legislative process and because their roles in that process call for a perspective different from that of the advocate in court or the lawyer in his office concerned with his client's relations with other individuals. A great judge, for example, said privately that a lawyer does no wrong when he argues a bad case before a court, but one who urges and lobbies for a bad law before a legislature is guilty of a mortal sin. The counsel for the legislative committee is not an advocate as in court; he is an official of government interested in obtaining information for legislative purposes. The lawyer who is a legislator, of course, has the most complex and difficult task of all, for he must vote on bills. His duty of loyalty to his constituents is clear. Yet, his constituents have varying and opposing interests. With pressures and counterpressures on him, he can justify his vote to himself and to his constituents only in the light of sound policy.

The natural assumption is that the stated standards of the profession do not apply to the lawyer in the legislative process any more than they would apply to the lawyer engaged in business. The conclusion, however, does not follow. The lawyer as a legislator or legislative committee counsel is performing as a public official essentially the same type functions he performs as a private lawyer. When he acts as a lobbyist or attorney for a client before a legislative committee, he is practicing law, although he is performing functions the layman is legally competent to do.

This chapter is devoted to a discussion of the lawyer's standards in the legislative process. There are two basic premises underlying the discussion: the first is that the lawyer as a professional man does have a duty to adhere to professional standards whenever he works in a professional capacity, whether or not he is engaged in work which a layman may do; the other is that the various roles of the lawyer in the legislative process require special standards, as do his roles in the judicial, the private legal and the administrative processes.

Section two discusses the role of the lawyer as legislative advocate and lobbyist. Section three discusses the legislative committees and their counsel, and section four, the lawyer as legislator.

SECTION 2.   THE LAWYER AS LEGISLATIVE ADVOCATE AND LOBBYIST

"Influence in its broadest sense is integral to representative government. The sensitivity of politicians to factors that affect the outcome of elections is the springhead of responsive and responsible government." [1] The Constitution in its protection of the right of free speech and of the people to petition the government for redress of grievances secures their right to influence and to attempt to influence their representatives. Whether this influence be individual or group, selfish or public spirited, it may be exercised personally or through the employment of a legislative advocate or lobbyist. "In order to facilitate the essential contact between the citizen and his legislative representative, the courts have universally recognized that it is proper to hire an attorney or agent to perform professional services before a legislative body." [2]

Congress utilizes hearings by its committees to give persons an opportunity to be heard. So important are the committee statements and the hearing that it has been said: "[T]he legislative body is not a maker of the rule so much as a sort of court before whom the different interests appear each arguing its own point of view. . . . " [3] The right to be heard is important also when administrative agencies exercise their rulemaking power. A rule laid down by the Federal Communications Commission or the Federal Trade Commission often has as great an impact as a statute passed by Congress, particularly on the industry affected, and the opportunity for the exercise of influence has been formalized in procedures required by law. The Federal Administrative Procedure Act [4] requires formal notice of rulemaking,[5] and provides that "the agency shall afford interested persons an opportunity to participate in the ruling making through submission of written data, views, or arguments with or without opportunity for oral presentation." [6]

Appearances in these hearings and the submission of written data are lobbying, although seldom referred to by that term. The formal nature of the process involved gives these attempts to influence a respectability that is denied informal lobbying,

1. A. Heard, The Costs of Democracy 11 (1960).

2. McDowell, The Legality of "Lobbying Contracts," 41 B.U.L.Rev. 54, 55 (1961).

3. Chamberlain, Book Review, 17 A. B.A.J. 685 (1931).

4. 5 U.S.C.A. §§ 551 et seq.

5. Id. § 553(b).

6. Id. § 553(c).

which involves efforts directed to individual legislators. Yet, the latter form of lobbying is as appropriate, and in most instances, much more effective than the former. Even in the administrative agencies, informal lobbying has an essential role and direct contact with agency officials is not only permissible, it is desirable. The process of making law, whether by the legislature or the administrative agency is too important for those responsible to be denied the opportunity of informal contact with persons who are interested and have something to contribute. Lobbying thus serves two functions—it provides a means for the citizen to exercise influence on the legislative process and it provides the legislator an opportunity to learn and gain insights he would not otherwise have.

Despite its importance, informal lobbying is held in low esteem. The unfortunate history of lobbying in this country has resulted not only in a negative attitude, but also in inadequate regulation by statute. Typically, lobbying statutes are minimal in their provisions, requiring registration showing the interests represented or contributions received in support of a measure. Other regulation is found in corrupt practice acts which do little more than condemn bribery. A third form of regulation is the rule of some courts making contingent fee contracts for lobbying illegal.[7] But whatever form the regulation has taken, it has not succeeded in preventing or eliminating the abuses.[8] The reason is attributable in large measure to the nature of the process. Lobbying, even legitimate lobbying, tends to be covert, and is easily subject to flagrant abuse. More than any other legal process in our society, lobbying depends for its integrity upon the individuals engaged in it.

The negative attitude toward lobbying is understandable, but nevertheless unfortunate, for lobbying is an integral part of the legislative process. Lobbying is legislative advocacy, and as a legal process, its effect on the law may well be more important than judicial advocacy. Yet, relatively few lawyers engage in legislative advocacy as a part of their practice. Two reasons may explain their reluctance to do so. One is that most clients are neither sufficiently interested nor sufficiently wealthy to engage in lobbying. The other is that lobbying is viewed as an activity to serve the selfish interest of the few without regard for the public interest. The purpose of most lobbying is to protect

7. Trist v. Child, 88 U.S. (21 Wall.) 441 (1874).

8. "The practices of lobbyists in the nineteenth and early twentieth centuries provoked periodic scandals. Bribery and blackmail . . . were not uncommon lobbying techniques. The calibre of lobbying activity has generally improved during this century; but abuse is still prevalent, albeit in more sophisticated guises." Note, The Poor and the Political Process: Equal Access to Lobbying, 6 Harv.J.Legis. 369 (1969).

someone's profits or pocketbook, whether it be for the oil deple-tion allowance in the tax law, farm subsidies, import quotas, or larger appropriations for education. Consequently, lobbying is not viewed as a matter of professional concern.

This view is misconceived, and the desirability for more law-yers to engage in lobbying is evident. Legislative advocacy re-quires the knowledge, the skills, and the perspective that legal training provides. The opportunity for the lawyer is not only to serve his client, but to aid in improving the law and governmen-tal processes. The most important process they would improve would be lobbying itself. Lawyers, more than any other profes-sional group, are concerned with standards of conduct, the most important need of the lobbying process. The participation of larger numbers of lawyers in legislative advocacy would almost surely result in improved standards.

Yet, paradoxically, one reason that lawyers shun lobbying may be the absence of standards. Most lobbyists are laymen who, whatever their personal integrity, are not familiar with, or accus-tomed to, professional standards to govern their work. Lawyers, on the other hand, are very conscious of standards, but stated standards specifically for lobbying are not generally recognized. The Code of Professional Responsibility, for example, takes cog-nizance of the lawyer as a lobbyist in the statement of Ethical Considerations, but not in the Disciplinary Rules.[9] The reason may be the difficulty of stating standards for the lobbyist. While lawyers are conscious of standards, they are used to stand-ards in a structured setting, as in a trial. The legislative advo-cate works in an unstructured setting. He is not faced with a formal opponent, and there is no equal representation to present both sides of the issue. Thus the statement of standards for the lobbyist is particularly difficult for standards must be derived from the role and setting to which they are to be applied. As the role and setting of the lobbyist are unstructured, so are his standards.

The basic and fundamental standard of the legislative advo-cate is honesty, both to the legislator and to the client. The duty is so basic and obvious that it has not been recognized as existing in this context, but the necessity for it is clear. Unlike the judicial advocate, the legislative advocate works on the basis of direct personal contact. His task is not only to persuade the

9. "Whenever a lawyer seeks legisla-tive or administrative changes, he should identify the capacity in which he appears, whether on be-half of himself, a client, or the pub-lic. A lawyer may advocate such changes on behalf of a client even though he does not agree with them. But when a lawyer purports to act on behalf of the public, he should espouse only those changes which he conscientiously believes to be in the public interest." A.B.A. Code of Professional Responsibility, EC 8–4. See also Id., EC 8–5.

legislator, but to aid him in understanding the position of the client and the reasons for that position.   More important, he seeks to have the legislator act on the basis of the information and arguments he presents.   No less important, of course, is the duty of the legislative advocate to be honest with the client, both as to his own position and as to what he will do.   These two duties are particularly important in lobbying because of the freedom of action of the lobbyist, which may easily lead the client to expect too much.

The duty of honesty may be specifically applied to several situations the legislative advocate usually faces, as illustrated in the California statute stating the obligations of the legislative advocate.[10]   The greatest temptation of the lobbyist is to try to

---

10.   West's Ann. Cal. Gov't Code § 9910 (West 1966).   The statute reads in full:

§ 9910.   *Obligations of legislative advocate.*   A legislative advocate has the following obligations, violation of which constitutes cause for revocation or suspension of a certificate of registration, but shall not unless otherwise provided by law subject a legislative advocate to any other civil or criminal liability:

1.   Not to engage in any activity as a legislative advocate unless he be registered as a legislative advocate, and not to accept compensation for acting as a legislative advocate except upon condition that he forthwith register as a legislative advocate.

2.   To abstain from doing any act with the express purpose and intent of placing any Member of the Legislature under personal obligation to him or to his employer.

3.   Never to deceive or attempt to deceive any Member of the Legislature of any material fact pertinent to any pending or proposed legislation.

4.   Never to cause or influence the introduction of any bill or amendment thereto for the purpose of thereafter being employed to secure its passage or defeat.

5.   To abstain from soliciting any employment as a legislative advocate except on the basis of his experience, or knowledge of the business or field of activity in which his proposed employer is engaged or is interested.

6.   To abstain from any attempt to create a fictitious appearance of public favor or disfavor of any legislative proposal or to cause any communication to be sent to any Member of the Legislature, the Lieutenant Governor, or the Governor, in the name of any fictitious person or in the name of any real person, except with the consent of such real person.

7.   Not to encourage the activities of or to have any business dealings relating to legislation or the Legislature with any person whose registration to act as a legislative advocate has been suspended or revoked.

8.   Not to represent, either directly or indirectly, through word of mouth or otherwise, that he can control or obtain the vote or action of any Member or committee of the Legislature, or the approval or veto of any legislation by the Governor of California.

9.   Not to represent an interest adverse to his employer nor to represent employers whose interests are known to him to be adverse.

10.   To retain all books, papers, and documents necessary to substantiate the financial reports required to be made under this chapter for a period of two years.

place the legislator under personal obligation to him, conduct which more easily corrupts the legislative process than any other. The most blatant forms of this conduct are bribery and blackmail, but all such attempts require a measure of dishonesty. More usual is the lobbyist's tendency to attempt to deceive the legislator as to material facts pertaining to the legislation in question. Yet, that such conduct is not permissible is a point too clear to require discussion. A common form of this type of dishonesty, for example, is attempts to create fictitious appearances of public favor or disfavor of any legislative proposal.

The duty of honesty to the client is no less important. The lobbyist who seeks the introduction of legislation for the purpose of being employed to secure its passage or defeat is guilty of a form of fraud. One who represents to a client that he can control or obtain the vote or action of any legislator is equally guilty of corrupting the legislative process. And the representation of an interest adverse to the client or the representation of clients whose interests are adverse is a violation of the fundamental duty of loyalty to the client.

These specific examples illustrate the basic importance of the duty of honesty, which is equally necessary for both the lawyer and the lay lobbyist. The duty, however, is minimal and a fundamental question is whether higher standards should be applied to the lawyer than to the lay lobbyist. To make a distinction between the two in this matter would be a mistake, but there are two factors which must be considered. The lawyer is subject to all the standards and discipline of the profession, while the layman is not. To place the lawyer in a position of adhering to higher standards than the layman is to place him at a disadvantage. As a sole consideration, this factor is not very important, except that it is desirable that lawyers take the more active role in lobbying. Because they are better equipped for legislative advocacy than laymen, lawyers can be of more aid to the legislator. Apart from this factor, the process of lobbying is too important a process in our society to be subjected to a double standard. Yet, only the legal profession can take the lead in establishing standards, and the profession has no jurisdiction over laymen.

An obvious solution is the creation of a legislative bar encompassing all lobbyists, lawyers and laymen, with the development of appropriate standards. The point has been well made before, "[L]obbying is not bad— . . . it is a type of advocacy which must assume some of the qualities of judicial advocacy if it is to be effective. . . . This postulate inevitably means the creation of a group or profession peculiarly capable of serving the need of all groups. Is not the method then to encourage those who serve as legislative advocates to assume the responsibilities inherent in their profession and to establish professional standards and professional responsibilities?" [11]

The tasks of a legislative advocate as a specialist would not be limited to lobbying. He would, for example, determine the effectiveness of proposed legislation, draft bills, appear before administrative agencies engaged in rulemaking, advise clients as to their rights and duties before legislative committees, ascertain the meaning of ambiguous language when it is disputed in the courts, and utilize legislative materials in advocacy.[12]

One of the primary goals of a legislative bar would be the creation of uniform standards, and a useful adjunct of the legislative bar would be a Committee on Professional Ethics for Legislative Advocates which would answer questions put to it as do the usual committees on professional ethics. The method of selection of members (say, one by the Governor, and one by the head of each of the legislative bodies and one by the Chief Justice) is not so important. The mere existence of such a committee would add strength to the work of the legislative advocate.

The creation of a legislative bar and the promulgation of uniform standards will not solve the problem of the unscrupulous lobbyist. Expressed and affirmative standards, however, can serve two basic purposes. They can bring lobbying, or legislative advocacy, into the realm of the respected and recognized roles of the lawyer. So long as lobbying remains outside this realm, the lobbyist, lawyer and otherwise, tends not to view it as an activity which carries with it a professional public responsibility. Consequently, he tends to view it as an onerous task rather than as a part of the legislative process which is helpful in resolving the conflicts that are inevitable among the diverse groups in our society.

Secondly, stated standards can provide affirmative guides where none now exist by which the legislative advocate can gauge his own conduct and by which others, too, can gauge it. Because lobbying is an activity dependent for its integrity upon the individual, such guidelines are helpful and important. They are necessary to the development of a tradition of decent and fair conduct for the lobbyist.

A second major purpose of a legislative bar would be to make the process of lobbying available to all persons and groups, not merely to the knowledgeable, the well organized, and the affluent. Lobbying is the essence of representative government in theory, but it tends to be the antithesis of that form of government in practice. The limitation of lobbying to a few, precluding the

11. F. Horack, Cases and Materials on Legislation 1047 (2d ed. 1954).

12. See J. Cohen, Materials and Problems on Legislation v–vi (2d ed. 1967).

poor and the middle class from an effective voice in the legislative process, is a major defect in our society. The problem is one which the organization of a legislative bar would aid in alleviating. Most people do not know of their right to lobby and the creation of awareness and access to respected legislative advocates would provide an opportunity that is now foreclosed to them.

Modern communication has increased the complexities of the legislator's task. People and groups are becoming more cognizant of the rights they do not enjoy and inevitably they will come to recognize lobbying as an effective tool of power. Only in recent years, for example, have the courts recognized the legal right of the poor defendant to be represented by a lawyer in all criminal cases. The right is not yet recognized in civil cases, but this problem is being dealt with through group legal services and offices of legal services for the poor funded largely by the federal government. A similar development in the area of legislative advocacy is inevitable, and it would be well for the profession to prepare for it in a constructive and affirmative way.

SECTION 3. LEGISLATIVE COMMITTEES AND THEIR COUNSEL

Committees are an essential part of the legislature. "Congress," for example, "operates through its committees, and no legislative proposition is in order until it has been considered by the committee having jurisdiction." [1] An aspect of the committee work is hearings, which have become a regular part of the legislative process. Committee findings serve to shape the statute passed by the legislature, and committee reports, particularly in Congress, are important for the courts in interpreting legislation.

The committee process and its functions are usually fair and clear and are not questioned by the legal profession. The ordinary hearing on proposed legislation, for example, usually involves little controversy or concern, except for those persons who may have a special interest in the bill being considered. The same is not true of the investigative hearing. There is in this type of hearing an issue which involves a matter of grave concern not only to the legal profession, but also to the country at large. This is the rights of witnesses summoned before an inves-

1. G. Galloway, The Legislative
Process in Congress 282 (1953).

tigative, as opposed to a legislative, committee. As to the latter, "Congressional tradition exacts courtesy and consideration from committee members." [2] But, "Far different is the role of the witness subpoenaed before an investigating committee. These committees are concerned with facts, rather than opinions about legislation. They are probing bodies, seeking to establish corruption, inefficiency, communist-connection. They do not sit to hear and choose between conflicting opinions. . . . [D]espite constitutional theory they function as legislative courts— trying an individual or group or government agency." [3] The investigative hearing is essentially inquisitorial in nature, and abuses have been frequent enough to make the problem one of serious concern. [4]

The issue of congressional investigations has been a part of our history since 1792, when the House of Representatives authorized the first one. [5] Three aspects of the problem make it particularly complex. First is the desirability, the need, and the power of Congress to investigate, which are not open to question. "It is perhaps also the most necessary of all the powers underlying the legislative function." [6] Second is the fact that the legislative investigation has no established procedural safeguards for the individual which are characteristic of other legal proceedings in our society. Witnesses may be compelled to appear before a committee, but they are dependent upon the rules of the particular committee for fair treatment. "There is, for example, no statutory or common law right for a witness to have advice of counsel; to have witnesses called on his behalf; to cross-examine other witnesses or present preliminary or oral statements to the committee." [7] The fact that in practice some of the procedural privileges may be granted lessens, but does not change, the inquisitorial nature of the proceeding.

The third aspect of the problem results from the separation of powers doctrine. Courts, in dealing with the rights of individuals before congressional committees, are dealing with the powers of an equal branch of government. They, of course have no direct control over congressional committees and deal with the

---

2. Maslow, The Witness Before the Congressional Committee, 13 J. of Soc. Issues, No. 2, 13 (1957).

3. Id.

4. See, e. g., Maslow, Fair Procedure in Congressional Investigations: A Proposed Code, 54 Colum.L.Rev. 839 (1954).

5. 2 Annals of Cong. 490 (1792); Mc-Geary, Congressional Investiga-tions: Historical Development, 18 U.Chi.L.Rev. 425 (1951).

6. Fulbright, Congressional Investigations: Significance for the Legislative Process, 18 U.Chi.L.Rev. 440, 441 (1951).

7. Moreland, Congressional Investigations and Private Persons, 40 So. Cal.L.Rev. 189, 268 (1967).

problem primarily when a person is prosecuted for contempt of Congress and the constituent elements of contempt are in question. While courts may say that the prosecutor must prove the authority of the committee for each investigation, that the refusal to answer was willful and deliberate,[8] and that the subject matter in inquiry was made clear to the witness,[9] they cannot compel the committee to do any of these things.

Underlying these factors is the reluctance of Congress, conscious of the importance of the power to investigate, to inhibit its authority with procedural guarantees of fairness. A senator has made the point well.

"The human shortcomings of congressional investigations lie largely in the abuse or misuse of the investigative power. There is little likelihood that they can ever be eliminated by procedural devices, rules or regulations. The prevention of power abuses is certainly desirable in any situation, governmental or private, but the curtailment of a necessary power is an excessively costly way to curb the abuse. The real hope lies in education, understanding and the development of an ever improving tradition. Above all, it must be realized that there can be no Congress without the free and unrestricted power to investigate." [10]

As the passage implies, the issue of proper congressional investigations is usually viewed as one which requires a choice between the powers of Congress to investigate and the rights of the individual as a witness. To give witnesses extensive procedural rights, of course, may limit the power of Congress, because it gives him an opportunity to obstruct the proceedings. But this does not mean that the persons conducting the proceeding, committee chairmen and committee counsel, should not assume a responsibility for the fair treatment of witnesses.

Their failure to recognize this responsibility and to assume this obligation, however, is not wholly their fault. The legal profession shares the blame for its failure in its ordinary work to develop standards of fairness. The fact is that in no legal proceedings, even in the judicial trial, is there a well developed tradition of respect or duty to the witness by lawyers. The Code of Professional Responsibility makes no mention of a duty of fairness to witness in the trial, although it does counsel as to the duty to treat with consideration all persons involved in the legal process.[11] Even so, while citizens are compelled to testify, they

8. United States v. Lamont, 236 F.2d 312 (2d Cir. 1956).

9. Watkins v. United States, 354 U.S. 178 (1957).

10. Fulbright, supra note 6, at 448.

11. A.B.A. Code of Professional Responsibility, EC 7–10.

have no rights as witnesses—no right to examine or cross-examine other witnesses, no protection in law from slanderous accusations or limitations on questions as to their private affairs relevant to the issues. The legal profession thus must bear a large part of the responsibility for the criticism directed to the treatment of witnesses in congressional investigations, for the profession itself has failed to deal with its own problem. Committee counsel (and often committee chairmen) are lawyers, and in their vigorous pursuit of reluctant witnesses, they are merely following the traditions of their profession.

There is, of course, a difference between the position of a witness before a congressional investigating committee and the position of a witness in a trial. The difference is most apparent in the treatment of witnesses, because the problem arises only in connection with the reluctant witness—the witness whose questionable conduct is under investigation. While he is not a defendant, he is a potential defendant, and he has in fact the status of a quasi-defendant. It is this position of the witness that often gives the congressional investigation the air of a modern Star Chamber proceeding. Yet, the fact that the persons testifying are called witnesses rather than defendants obscures the fact that congressional investigations can, and sometimes do, violate all the traditions and notions of fair play which are a part of the fabric of our society. Those conducting the proceedings tend to view them as an extension of democracy in the form of representative government rather than as an inquisitorial proceeding which may maim reputations and destroy careers. Legislative bodies, highly conscious of the importance of investigative inquiries in their work, have not laid down all the safeguards for the witness or the limitations on inquiry which fair treatment requires. They set the minimum only. Fairness and good sense may call for more. The problem, however, is one which can best be dealt with in terms of standards for the individuals conducting the hearings rather than in terms of the powers of the legislature as an institution. The necessary standards are few. A sense of professional restraint and fairness would be sufficient.

So little is required to alleviate so large a problem that the failure to do so is appalling. The error, perhaps, is the commonly made assumption that what happens to one or a few individuals is not a matter of large social import. The fault is in viewing the problem from the standpoint of the wrong to the individual affected, rather than from the standpoint of who is doing the wrong. The abuse of witnesses is to be regretted not so much because a man's life may be ruined, but because the highest officials of government are guilty of the wrong. The lack of responsibility so manifested is frightening in its implications, as the

McCarthy era of the fifties so clearly demonstrates. Yet, that experience has passed without any preparation to cope with a similar situation in the future by the development of a tradition of fairness and courtesy in legislative investigations.

The abuse of witnesses in any kind of proceeding, particularly legislative investigation, is the result of one or a combination of two factors—malicious intent or ignorance. Most often, perhaps, it is a result of ignorance, a failure to perceive that a good examiner need not resort to unfair methods and that to do so impairs his effectiveness. An insistence on the revelation of relevant facts in a truthful manner may be as effectively made with patient courtesy and an opportunity for the witness to explain as by intimidation. Self-interest and decent conduct are not inconsistent. A lawyer who became a great Chief Justice of the United States, Charles Evans Hughes, provided the example when he was counsel to a legislative committee investigating the insurance business.

> "Because the committee did not allow counsel to appear for witnesses or to cross-examine them, Hughes took special precautions to avoid any unfairness. He encouraged witnesses to explain or defend any conduct that had been brought into question. When the phalanx of lawyers in the front seats suggested questions, he himself would pass them along to the witnesses." [12]

Committee chairmen and committee counsel are not merely legislators or lawyers. They are public servants entrusted with a public trust. Witnesses before congressional committees are a part of the public, and a part of the trust is decency in the conduct of their official duties.

SECTION 4. THE LAWYER AS LEGISLATOR

Many lawyers devote a large part of their careers to public office, and "The more important the office, the higher the percentage of lawyers." [1] On the federal level, "lawyers consistently account for about 60 percent of the Members of Congress." [2] The facts accord with the tradition of public service of the bar. "A part, at least, of today's broad view of the duty of the bar must

12. M. Pusey, Charles Evans Hughes 151 (1951).

1. Cohen, Lawyers and Political Careers, 3 Law & Soc.Rev. 563, 568 (1969).

2. Association of the Bar of the City of New York Special Committee on Congressional Ethics, Congress and the Public Trust 78 (1970). (James C. Kirby, Jr., Executive Director.)

have its roots in the enormous contributions made by the great lawyers who led in the Revolution, and in framing the Declaration and the Constitution." [3]

Despite this tradition, the question whether the standards of the profession impose special obligations on the lawyer as legislator has seldom been raised. Even when dealt with, the problem is treated as one of the legislator as lawyer, directed to restrictions on his practice of law, and not that of the lawyer as legislator. The standards are negative restrictions rather than affirmative aids to guide him in his legislative role. Thus, one professional ethics opinion concluded, "[A]n attorney holding public office should avoid all conduct which might lead the layman to conclude that the attorney is utilizing his public position to further his professional success or personal interests." [4] The Code of Professional Responsibility states, "A lawyer who is a public officer . . . should not engage in activities in which his personal or professional interests are or foreseeably may be in conflict with his official duties." [5] And DR 8–101 implements this prohibition by forbidding a lawyer in public office from using his public position to obtain special advantages for himself or his client contrary to the public interest.

There is a more fundamental point not often discussed. There is a sharp distinction between the legislator-as-lawyer and the lawyer-as-legislator. The legislator-as-lawyer is subject to restrictions on the use of his position as legislator for his aggrandizement as lawyer. The lawyer-as-legislator is in a unique position to fulfill one of the basic obligations of the lawyer—to assist in improving the law. Canon 8 of the Code of Professional Responsibility states this duty,—"A lawyer should assist in improving the legal system"—and the ethical considerations develop the point, both as to procedural and substantive law. EC 8–1 states, "Lawyers are especially qualified to recognize deficiencies in the legal system and to initiate corrective measures therein. Thus they should participate in proposing and supporting legislation and programs to improve the system, without regard to the general interests or desires of clients or former clients." EC 8–2 states, "If a lawyer believes that the existence or absence of a rule of law, substantive or procedural, causes or contributes to an unjust result, he should endeavor by lawful means to obtain appropriate changes in the law. He should encourage the simplification of laws and the repeal or amendment of laws that are outmoded."

3. Seymour, The Obligations of the Lawyer to His Profession, 23 Record of N.Y.C.B.A. 311, 316 (1968).

4. A.B.A.Comm. on Professional Ethics, Opinions, No. 192 (1939).

5. A.B.A. Code of Professional Responsibility, EC 8–8.

The duty of the lawyer to be concerned with the condition of the legal system is thus affirmed. It would be helpful to make clear that this duty is a duty of the lawyer as a member of the legislature as well as the private practitioner. The lack of clarity in the statement of the duty may be because the profession does not consider its jurisdiction to extend to legislators, particularly since many members of the legislature are not lawyers. All members of the legislature, however, both lawyers and laymen, being lawmakers in the most direct form, belong to a specialized branch of the legal profession, whether recognized as such or not. The difference between the lay and the lawyer legislator is that the latter has the training and skills better to perceive the problems and better to exercise leadership in the making of law.

The greatest failing of the lawyer may be in his role as legislator—a surprising failure because the lawyer as a man of law should more than any other recognize the need for just and fair laws. The failure is perhaps made most manifest in such decisions as Baker v. Carr [6] in which it was left to the Supreme Court of the United States to require a state legislature to comply with the constitution of the state in the matter of legislative reapportionment. "We could wish that modern legislatures, often abundantly equipped to carry the main responsibility for law making, would undertake a massive modernization. Instead we must rue with Judge Friendly: The Gap in Lawmaking—Judges Who Can't and Legislators Who Won't. He laments that the legislator has diminished the role of the judge 'by occupying vast fields and then has failed to keep them ploughed.' " [7]

A major reason for this failure on the part of lawyers may be that the lawyer as legislator is not expected to provide the leadership of which he is a capable. There is no recognition of a special duty on his part to use his professional competence to improve the law. All men, particularly in public life, tend to act as they are expected to act. The improvement in the conduct of politicians in this country, for example, is in large measure due to the rise in the level of expectations. Senator Daniel Webster in the 1830's could with impunity write a curt reminder to Nicholas Biddle, President of the Bank of the United States: "If it be wished that my relation to the Bank should be continued, it may be well to send me the usual retainers." [8] No senator today

6. 369 U.S. 186 (1962).

7. Traynor, The Mind Counts, Address delivered at the 47th Annual Meeting of The American Law Institute, May 22, 1970.

8. Letter from Daniel Webster to Nicholas Biddle, December 21, 1833, in McGrane, The Correspondence of Nicholas Biddle 218 (1919).

would consider writing such a note, for the level of expectation precludes such conduct.

It would be most useful to develop a clear and definitive level of affirmative expectation that lawyer legislators will use their professional competence as lawyers in the legislature to provide leadership in recognizing problems and in educating their constituents to the need for resolving them. The blame for the failure here, however, does not rest with the lawyer legislator so much as it does with the legal profession. The expectations of others must come from others, and the bar, is in a position to articulate the appropriate standards for its members. A statement of affirmative standards would yield much, for most politicians, and particularly lawyers, are capable and competent and fair-minded men interested in doing the right thing. What is needed is awareness, and this is what the leaders of the legal profession can provide through an affirmative statement of standards. The profession's insistence on these standards for its own members could be influential throughout our political life and make "politician" a term of esteem.

The question that must inevitably arise in the mind of the lawyer-as-legislator is whether he can rise above his constituency, for he is a politician who desires to be re-elected. The practice of politics as Aristotle conceived it—the highest art—requires that he do so, not in a manner contrary to, but consistent with, the interest of the voters. So long as he does not expect too much, so long as he realizes, as has been said, that politics is the art of the second best—he will not become too discouraged by the difficulty that the correction of most of the deficiencies in the law have no voter appeal. Most voters have no interest in the administration of law; badly drawn and ill considered criminal statutes do not interest them; law which enables the loan shark to bilk the poor do not concern the middle class and affluent voters.

The opportunity and the task of the lawyer legislator are to help guide his constituents. He must coordinate the conflicting interests of the diverse groups in our society, and he must do more. He must make the diverse groups recognize their common interests. The life of the affluent suburbanite is made worse by the slums close by; the denial of civil rights to one individual or group is a denial to all. He may help each of his constituents understand the desires of others by the most effective idea, "put yourself in his place." He may thus give to the more fortunate an understanding of the situations of their less fortunate neighbors so that "the rising expectations of classes" in our country and throughout the world may be realized peacefully. Herein lies the essence of leadership—the ability to perceive the problems and to act with competence, foresight, tact and decisiveness in dealing with them. These are the standards for the lawyer as legislator and these are standards which should be writ large in the Code of Professional Responsibility.

The importance of law to the kind of society this country has and the reliance we place on lawmakers for the coordination of values and desires through legislation make politicians the most important leaders in our society. Politics is not only a part of American society, it is essential to the American way of life. "Any impression that politics can properly be conceived of as simply a 'system of power,' is both naive and wrong. Politics is also a system of obligations and a system of values. . . . [T]he vital stability of a nation, like that of a man, depends upon achieving at least a minimum of reality and consistency in the basic beliefs by which it lives." [9]

9. Subcomm. of the Senate Comm. on Labor and Public Welfare, 82d Cong., 1st Sess., Ethical Standards in Government 608 (1951).

Chapter X

THE LAWYER AND THE ADMINISTRATIVE PROCESS

SECTION 1. INTRODUCTION

"The American administrative process is a figment of the imagination. . . . [I]t does not exist."[1] The point of these statements, of course, is that there is not merely one, but many administrative processes. "What does not exist is any integrated, coherent, unwavering element of government that can be identified as *the* administrative process."[2] Indeed, the fundamental purpose of administrative agencies—to deal with particular, practical problems not easily handled by the regular branches of government[3]—precludes a single basic form or structure such as those which characterize the institutions of the judicial and legislative processes, the courts and the legislatures. The administrative agencies do, and must, utilize elements of both the judicial and legislative processes, as well as elements of the executive process, investigation and enforcement.

The absence of a single structure in the administrative process provides a flexibility necessary to the accomplishment of its varied purposes. It means also that the powers of the agencies are not subjected to the traditional procedural safeguards characteristic of other legal institutions. While courts act only in response to the initiative of the parties after a full and complete hearing, the administrative tribunal often acts on its own initiative to affect an individual, a corporation, or an industry.

Unlike the judicial process, the administrative process contains no structured role for the lawyer, for it is too complicated in both form and function. The county zoning board of three members and the federal regulatory agency in Washington with a staff of hundreds or thousands both come under the same broad heading of administrative agency. Even the number of agencies remains uncertain,[4] and their functions are as varied as their

1. W. Gellhorn and C. Byse, Administrative Law Cases and Comments ix (4th ed. 1960).

2. Id.

3. "The particular, practical problems not easily handled by the regular branches of government have from the beginning been met by reliance on the administrative process." Gardner, The Administrative Process, in Legal Institutions Today and Tomorrow 22 (M. Paulsen ed. 1959).

4. "If anyone knows how many administrative agencies there are in

167

number, including "such diverse tasks as superintending imports and immigration, licensing airlines and attorneys, regulating farm prices and food additives, administering aid to the aged and atomic energy, directing rent control and radio broadcasting, and controlling liquor distribution and labor relations." [5]

The complexity of the administrative process presents no challenge to the lawyer's skills. It does present, however, a challenge to his professional standards, for it is fundamentally different from the judicial process from which his basic standards are derived. The advocate in court, for example, is confident that the decision will be based on the record and has no thought of approaching the judge about the case without the presence of opposing counsel. But much of the work of administrative agencies is done on an *ex parte* basis. "Not only attorneys, but their clients, visit the commissioners in their offices and discuss with them the law and the facts of their cases and frequently learn from them in advance how they stand with respect to the decision of cases . . . ." [6]

Yet, the problem of standards in the administrative process has received little attention. This chapter is directed to two aspects of that problem: differences in the administrative and judicial processes, and the problem of the lawyer's standards in the administrative process. The discussion is less precise than the reader and we might desire, but the purpose is to treat primarily only one aspect of a very complex topic, the problem of standards. "Our discussion will be adequate if it has as much clearness as the subject-matter admits of, for precision is not to be sought for alike in all discussions, any more than in all the products of the crafts . . . . it is the mark of an educated man to look for precision in each class of things just as far as the nature of the subject admits; . . . ." [7]

the government of the United States alone, I have not found that indefatigable and omniscient man." Id. at 22–23.

5. Gellhorn and Byse, supra note 1, at ix.

6. Miller, The Advocate Before Administrative Agencies, 1956 U. of Ill.L.F. 189, 197–98 (1956).

7. Aristotle, Ethics, Book I, ch. B.

SECTION 2. THE JUDICIAL AND ADMINISTRATIVE
PROCESSES

The different functions and processes of the courts and the administrative agencies require different standards for the lawyer, and a comparison of the judicial and administrative processes is useful in determining the standards appropriate for each. The comparison here is limited to the processes employed in carrying out the principal respective functions: the trial of an adversary proceeding in court and the disposition of matters by regulatory actions of a commission.

The two agencies of government, the courts and the administrative agencies, are not sharply separated in the functions assigned to them. The common law trial is the central feature of the judicial process, but the functions assigned to courts also include specialized proceedings. The probate of wills and the administration of estates, juvenile court proceedings and preliminary hearings in criminal cases, as well as the appellate process all differ substantially from the common law trial. Even the trial in equity has important features which distinguish it from its law counterpart.

The central feature of the administrative process is the regulatory process. But a large part of the tasks of administrative agencies is administrative in the strict sense of the word, as the grant of a license or permit upon the fulfillment of formal requirements or the payment of benefits, as social security payments or veterans' benefits. And as some judicial proceedings, for example adoption and the probate of wills, are essentially administrative in nature, so in the same way many administrative proceedings are judicial. A workmen's compensation proceeding is judicial in fact, although it is called administrative.

The judicial and administrative processes thus are distinct and separate processes which tend to merge and become indistinguishable at certain points and in certain types of proceedings, except for the forum. This overlap is historically sound, for the common law courts grew out of the administrative agencies of the king. The Court of Exchequer, for example, was originally the office of the king to collect revenues, and the Court of the Star Chamber remained an administrative agency until it was abolished in 1640.

The processes of the courts and of the administrative agencies differ most widely in the common law trial and in the regulatory functions. The trial is a means of resolving conflicts between individuals, while the regulatory functions are means of regulating the conduct of individuals and groups for the benefit of society. A comparison of these two processes can show why the standards of the advocate are not appropriate for the administrative process, for the professional standards of the lawyer are derived from his role as advocate in the common law trial. The differences can be most usefully viewed in terms of the kinds of law the courts and the administrative tribunals, in their regulatory capacity, administer; the purposes and functions of the respective bodies of law; and the different ways the courts and the agencies administer them and the significance of these differences for the lawyer.

Courts are concerned primarily with private law as related to past transactions, the law of individual relations involving private rights and private duties. The law of contracts, torts, wills and property, typical of the common law curriculum, enables individuals to give order to their relationships and provide guidelines for the peaceful settlement of disputes.

The subject matter of the administrative agencies is public law, that is statutory law which grants rights and imposes duties on individuals in the interest of the welfare of society. A person charging an unfair labor practice, for example, is "vindicating not a private but the public right," [1] and "[t]he Communications Act of 1934 did not create new private rights. The purpose of the Act was to protect the public interest in communications." [2] Thus, the purpose of a large part of administrative law is to regulate conduct through licensing, restraining and prescriptive law. Barbers and lawyers must be licensed; wages must be paid in accordance with the Fair Labor Standards Act and companies must negotiate with unions under the National Labor Relations Act; young men may be drafted and all citizens must pay their taxes. The regulatory aspect of administrative law, however, is most clearly reflected by the law administered by the independent regulatory agencies, as the Interstate Commerce Commission, the Federal Trade Commission, and the Securities and Exchange

1. Teamsters Local 282 v. N.L.R.B., 339 F.2d 795, 799–800 (2d Cir. 1964). Judge Friendly in his opinion discussed the point of public versus private right at some length. "The question whether the National Labor Relations Act gave private rights to the victims of unfair labor practices was authoritatively answered in the negative by Amalgamated Utility Workers v. Consolidated Edison Co., 309 U.S. 261, 60 S.Ct. 561, 85 L.Ed. 738 (1940), only five years after the Act was passed. . . . a unanimous Court, speaking through Chief Justice Hughes, said that in unfair labor practice cases the National Labor Relations Board acts 'on behalf of the public' and 'seeks enforcement as a public agent, not to give effect to a "private administrative remedy,"' and sharply distinguished the position of persons filing charges with the Board from that of complainants as to matters arising under the Interstate Commerce Act and the Railway Labor Act." Id. at 799.

2. Scripps-Howard Radio, Inc. v. F.C.C., 316 U.S. 4, 14 (1942).

Commission. These agencies have two basic functions, the allocation of limited resources, as the awarding of airline routes and television channels, and the establishment and enforcement of minimum standards and rates, as in the case of food and drugs and the sale of securities and transportation.

The regulatory agencies were created because the courts were neither equipped nor designed to deal with the complex problems brought about by the need to require individuals and industries to act responsibly in a highly competitive economy. "To a large degree [administrative agencies] have been a response to the felt need of governmental supervision over economic enterprise —a supervision which could effectively be exercised neither directly through self-executing legislation nor by the judicial process." [3] Laws and legal standards were necessary and agencies to implement and enforce them were inevitable. Thus, while the courts ascertain and determine pre-existing rights and liabilities by fixed and objective standards to serve the ends of order for society and justice for the individual, administrative tribunals have a broader purpose. They implement policy in accordance with guidelines laid down by the legislature.[4] Their concern is social, not individual, justice, and while the judicial process is past oriented, the administrative process is future oriented. The purpose of the regulatory agency is not so much to punish or achieve redress for injury as it is to require the persons under its jurisdiction to act responsibly and with an appropriate regard for the public welfare. Consent decrees and cease and desist orders are common means for achieving this purpose.

These differences in the purposes and functions of the courts and the commissions are most clearly reflected in their different procedures, the most important, and usually the most objectionable, difference for the lawyer. The objections are understandable. A fundamental characteristic of the trial is uniform rules of procedure to which the lawyer is accustomed. Trained for the adversary system, he prefers the clearly structured setting of the trial, uniform, definite rules of procedure, and a disinterested judge, whose duty it is to see that these rules are fairly applied.

3. F.C.C. v. Pottsville Broadcasting Co., 309 U.S. 134, 142 (1940).

4. "Judicial tribunals must treat legal rights and liabilities as pre-existing, because such tribunals declare themselves bound by a fixed objective standard; they profess not to confer rights or impose liabilities themselves, but only to do what is dictated by law. But 'administrative' tribunals, which act upon policy and expediency, themselves dictate what is politic and expedient; they are not concerned with pre-existing rights and liabilities, but themselves create the rights and liabilities they enforce." Gordon, 'Administrative' Tribunals and the Courts, 49 L.Q. Rev. 94, 107-08 (1933).

The situation as to procedure in the administrative process is different. "[A]dministrative agencies 'should be free to fashion their own rules of procedure and to pursue methods of inquiry capable of permitting them to discharge their multitudinous duties.'"[5] Thus, while the commissions have procedural rules, they are not uniform, and for the most part they are created by the commissions themselves, usually consistent with the general requirements of a statute, as the Administrative Procedure Act. "[T]he Administrative Procedure Act . . . is implemented by the various agencies in a manner and to the extent that each agency sees fit. The result is that procedures and practices in administrative law differ substantially in form and quality despite the fact that the same single act gives legal direction for almost all administrative agency type activity."[6]

This situation is not normal for the trial advocate. Procedural rules in the judicial process are for the benefit of the parties, because the trial is for the purpose of enabling the parties to resolve their dispute. They do not always serve this function in the administrative process, for the purpose of the commission is to implement social policy. When compliance with a procedural rule of an agency is called into question, for example, the court may well view the rules as being for the benefit of the agency rather than the individual. "We agree with the [Interstate Commerce] Commission that the rules were promulgated for the purpose of providing the 'necessary information' for the Commission 'to reach an informed and equitable decision,' . . . The rules were not intended primarily to confer important procedural benefits upon individuals in the face of otherwise unfettered discretion . . . ."[7] The commissioner is thus often viewed as both a judge and an adversary. Unlike the trial judge, he is interested in a result in furtherance of the policy he is charged with administering.

The lawyer attaches so much importance to definitive procedural rules in the administrative process because they define and limit the power of the commission to act against the client. The issue is fundamentally the responsible exercise of governmental power, but the lawyer representing a client sees the issue much more narrowly than the agency. The commissioner views his duty of the responsible exercise of power in terms of society at large, the lawyer in terms of his individual client. In litigation, the governmental power, as the service of process and subpoenas,

5. F.C.C. v. Schreiber, 381 U.S. 279, 290 (1965).

6. Deale, A Major Reform Proposed: The Administrative Practice Reorganization Act, 44 A.B.A.J. 133, 133–34 (1958).

7. American Farm Lines v. Black Ball Freight Service, 397 U.S. 532, 538, 90 S.Ct. 1288, 1292 (1970).

is exercised on behalf of the litigants, and, for the most part, it is exercised by the litigants themselves.   The plaintiff with a judgment at law, for example, must act to enforce his judgment, and many judgments, for various reasons, go unsatisfied.   The commissioner acts to affect the individual immediately and directly.

The necessity for the administrative commission to be flexible in its operations is manifest.   Equally clear is the need to protect the individual against the abuses of government.   The problem is neither new nor unique, and the traditional solution sought by lawyers has been to judicialize the administrative process.   Historically in the common law, the exercise of the executive power through administrative agencies tended to become judicialized.   The history of equity, begun in the administrative office of the chancellor, best illustrates this tendency and the dangers of it,[8] with the chancellor, Lord Eldon saying equity was as definite almost as law.   The process of judicialization is facilitated in this country because of the provisions in the Constitution to protect the individual, as the due process clauses of the fifth and fourteenth amendments.

Yet, judicializing the administrative process is not desirable. The very reason for the creation of the administrative commission is the inadequacy of the courts with judicial proceedings to deal adequately with the matters entrusted to the commissions. The problems with which the agencies must deal cannot be dealt with in the manner the judicial process requires.   Nor is judicialization of the process essential to the protection of the parties or the public.   For the problem results not so much from the power of the agencies or commissions or their abuse of powers, as it does from the failure of the legal profession to provide standards for lawyers in their roles in the administrative process.   The lack of these standards has meant the lack of cooperation by members of the bar which the successful operation of the administrative process requires.

SECTION 3.   THE PROBLEM OF STANDARDS OF THE LAWYER IN THE ADMINISTRATIVE PROCESS

The nature of the lawyer's obligations is easier to determine in the judicial and private legal processes than in the administrative process.   Standards in the judicial process are defined and

8.   See Jarndyce v. Jarndyce, reported in full in C. Dickens, Bleak House (1852).

limited in accordance with the structure of the trial, and standards in the private legal process are familiar by reason of history and tradition. The modern administrative process is supported by neither a helpful structure nor a long tradition of standards. The lawyer in the administrative process is naturally inclined to apply the standards with which he is familiar to his role in that process.

The Code of Professional Responsibility, for example, presupposes that the role of the lawyer in the administrative process is that of an advocate. "A lawyer appearing before an administrative agency, regardless of the nature of the proceeding it is conducting, has the continuing duty to advance the cause of his client within the bounds of the law." [1] The statement is not very helpful, nor is the statement following it. "Where the applicable rules of the agency impose specific obligations upon a lawyer, it is his duty to comply therewith, unless the lawyer has a legitimate basis for challenging the validity thereof." [2] The statements, however, do not make clear, for example, that the duty of the lawyer to refrain from attempts to influence administrative officials in quasi-judicial proceedings is as important in the administrative process as in the courtroom. The courts have dealt explicitly with this point.

> " 'From the moment that he ceases to depend upon the justice of his case and seeks discriminatory and favored treatment, he becomes a corrupter of the Government itself and is fortuniate [sic] if he loses no more than the rights he seeks to obtain.' This doctrine applies to the adjudicatory functions of an administrative agency. This is not a mere technicality. Surreptitious efforts to influence an official charged with the duty of deciding contested issues upon an open record in accord with basic principles of our jurisprudence, eat at the very heart of our system of government—due process, fair play, open proceedings, unbiased, uninfluenced decision." [3]

Even more important, perhaps, in the context of the history and tradition of the legal profession, the statements in the standards imply much more than they state, that the administrative process requires a lawyer to be as contentious as an advocate in the judicial process. There is no recognition of a difference between the administrative and judicial processes with consequent differences in the standards of the lawyer. Nor is there

---

1. A.B.A. Code of Professional Responsibility, EC 7–15.

2. Id.

3. WKAT, Inc. v. F.C.C., 296 F.2d 375, 382 (D.C.Cir. 1961), cert. denied 368 U.S. 841 (1961), quoting Root Refining Co. v. Universal Oil Products Co., 169 F.2d 514, 541 (3rd Cir. 1948).

recognition of the fact that there are many different kinds of administrative processes with a need for different standards within the administrative process itself.

The failure of the bar to develop standards for the lawyer in the administrative process has been made easy by several factors. Some administrative proceedings are essentially judicial in character. In them the ordinary standards of the advocate are rightly applied, and the conclusion may be wrongly drawn that these standards are applicable in all kinds of administrative proceedings. The privilege of representing another before an administrative agency may not be limited to lawyers but be extended to any qualified layman, as in the federal administrative agencies, so the use or need for professional standards by the lawyer is obscured. And in most administrative matters, as an application for a permit, the proceedings are so simple they seem scarcely to demand the abilities or the standards of a professional man.

Other administrative processes, however, are sufficiently distinct to require special standards of the lawyer, particularly the regulatory administrative process. The regulatory agencies are charged with the responsibility of regulating industries and groups because of their power and their impact on the public welfare. Transportation, communications and securities, under the jurisdiction of the Interstate Commerce Commission, the Federal Communications Commission, and the Securities and Exchange Commission, are illustrations of industries so highly competitive that the principles of competition supplanted all principles of public responsibility, until restraint and order were imposed by the government. The Federal Trade Commission is directed to businesses in general to prevent them from engaging in unfair or deceptive advertising and unfair competition. The regulatory process, however, is not limited to Washington, for it exists on the state level also, as, for example, a state commission for the regulation of banking and insurance.

Two features of the regulatory process which clearly distinguish it from the judicial process are rulemaking proceedings and the fact that many of its actions are informal. In the former, the lawyer performs the role of a lobbyist or legislative advocate. The first amendment secures the right of the client to be heard and to approach the commission directly, and the Administrative Procedure Act implements this right. And much, even the majority, of administrative actions occur in the informal administrative process. "Just as only a fraction of formal administrative determinations reaches the courts, the vast bulk of administrative decisions is made without resort to formal administrative proceedings." [4] The nature of the administrative process makes it necessary that a lawyer be able to communicate with the agency directly and off the record, for "if the administrative process is to work effectively and as it was intended to work, there must be injected in every possible area a maximum degree of informality in making the process work." [5]

This informality promotes the process of coordination and co-operation, between members of the bar and agency officials. It also increases the importance of standards. In court, professional standards are often merely complementary of procedural rules which state the basic duty. The absence of such definite procedural rules in administrative commissions means that professional standards are the primary, and often the sole, measure of the lawyer's conduct. "[T]here is need for administrative regulations and enforcement of ethical standards. Because so many Washington lawyers are not members of the local bar, the only Grievance Committee to which they are amenable is that of their own bar, which may be remote, uninformed, and even uninterested." [6]

Equally as important as standards for the lawyer, however, are standards for the agency. The major reason for the failure of the profession to develop the necessary standards, perhaps, is the lack of standards for the commissions themselves. There is a "lack of development of adequate standards in various administrative fields. I refer, for example, to the lack of any true standards in the choice . . . between competitors for an airline route. These choices are made and have to be made but the bases upon which they rest are incapable of being accurately briefed." [7]

The problem of standards for the lawyer in the administrative process is thus a twofold problem of standards for the agency and for the lawyer. More attention has been directed to the need for agency standards than to the need for the lawyer's standards. Yet, the problems cannot be solved separately, for the standards of the lawyer are directly related to the standards of the institution he is dealing with, whether it is a court or an administrative agency. The discussion here will deal with two aspects of the standards of the lawyer: the relationship of the lawyer to the agency and the duty of candor.

4. W. Gellhorn & C. Byse, Administrative Law, Cases and Comments 639 (4th ed. 1960).

5. Anderson, Settlement and Compliance Procedures, 14 A.B.A. Antitrust Section 72 (1959).

6. C. Horsky, The Washington Lawyer 154–55 (1952).

7. Landis, The Administrative Process—The Third Decade, 13 Ad.L. Rev. 17, 21 (1960).

The lawyer's relationship to the administrative agency, as does his relationship to the court, determines the kinds of things he may or may not do for his client. As an officer of the court, he has certain duties not only to the court, but to the legal system. He may not, for example, have any contact with the jurors in the case, regardless of how seemingly innocent or how beneficial to his client the contact may be. The lawyer's relationship to the agency, however, is by no means well defined and thus his standards of conduct in proceedings before the agency are not clear.

The lack of clarity here arises because of the lack of clarity as to the nature of the client's relationship to the agency. The lawyer's relationship to the court is so commonly accepted and understood that it is not often realized that this relationship has been determined in large measure by the nature of the client's relationship to the court. The court is a forum for the litigants to resolve their own dispute. The lawyer's duty of loyalty to his client is given priority over his duty of loyalty to the court because the system places the primary responsibility for resolving the dispute on the parties. The relationship of the client to the administrative agency is wholly different. The primary relationship involved is not between two parties, but between the public represented by the agency and the client. Unlike the court, the administrative agency may exercise initiative in bringing the proceedings, may have investigative power, and acts directly upon the client, either in fulfilling a request or issuing an order.

The lawyer in an administrative proceeding serves the role of an intermediary between his client and the agency. His primary duty is to protect and aid his client, but this duty must be defined in terms of the functioning of the agency as well as the rights of his client. The broadest classification of administrative proceedings is between those relating to past and future conduct. Under the former classification are the claim of one private party against another, as in a workmen's compensation proceeding, the claim of an individual against the government, as a claim for welfare payments, and a claim of the government against a private party, as a tax liability. Such proceedings as these are adversary in nature and in them the lawyer's primary duty is to protect the rights of the client. The usual standards of the advocate may be generally appropriate.

The same is not necessarily true of proceedings which are directed to the future. This classification includes, for example, the grant of a monopolistic privilege, as the grant of a permit for a television channel, the grant of a privilege to deal with the public, as the registration and issuance of securities, or a complex regulation for the future, as a rate making proceeding. These proceedings present the most difficult problem of standards for the lawyer. The action involved is usually vested with a large public interest, but the lawyer carrying over his attitude developed in court proceedings is tempted to ignore that interest.

There is here a public-be-damned attitude which is obscured by the emphasis on competition in our society and the adversary system. The legal profession has failed to acknowledge that, at least as to areas in which a special privilege is sought or where special protection for the public is necessary, the lawyer in the administrative process has a more important role and a greater responsibility than the advocate in the courtroom. It is in these areas that the failure of the profession to provide appropriate standards is most telling and most unfortunate.

The most important of the necessary standards is candor. The duty of candor in the administrative process differs from the duty in the judicial process. In court, the lawyer must tell the truth and nothing but the truth, but he need not volunteer the whole truth. But in court, the duty is in relation to his adversary. In the administrative process, the duty of candor is in relation to the tribunal, unless, of course, the administrative proceeding is an adversary one between private parties and is judicial in nature.

The successful functioning of the process in the public interest requires that the parties before it be honest, particularly in regard to future actions. Thus, in some, indeed in most, instances, a standard of absolute candor is not too high. When the Commissioner of Patents barred an attorney from practice before the Patent Office for misconduct, for example, the Supreme Court upheld the action, relying on statements made by the Patent Office Committee which considered the case: " 'By reason of the nature of an application for patent, the relationship of attorneys to the Patent Office requires the highest degree of candor and good faith. In its relations to applicants, the Office . . . must rely upon their integrity and deal with them in a spirit of trust and confidence . . . .' " [8] And a leader of the bar, writing of this same duty, wrote: "The task of the lawyer in connection with the offering of securities is, as it has always been, to endeavor to the best of his ability to see that no essentially important element is concealed from the buying public . . . . A lawyer must insist that all of his questions be answered fully, fairly and frankly and that no avenues of investigation be closed to him. Otherwise the sooner he declines to pass upon the issue, the better." [9]

8. Kingsland v. Dorsey, 338 U.S. 318, 319, 70 S.Ct. 123, 124 (1949).

9. Dean, The Lawyer's Problems in the Registration of Securities, 4 Law & Contemp. Prob. 154, 181 (1937).

One area in which the problem of candor in the administrative process is particularly difficult is that of tax practice, for under our system of self-assessment of income taxes, there is no accepted set of standards. "The question is whether the standards applicable to the conduct of attorneys representing clients before the Bureau of Internal Revenue vary from those which are applicable to attorneys engaged in general practice, and place upon the former a responsibility on certain occasions to put the interest of the Treasury in a position paramount to the interests of their clients." [10]   The lawyer should not set out the facts in a tax return in a way which, though not false, obscures the facts and their probable consequences. But what of facts which, if revealed, will result in a ruling requiring a higher tax, which the lawyer is confident the courts would overturn? The issue is immediately apparent. Does the lawyer have a duty to recommend full and fair disclosure of the facts as to items questionable in law? One leading tax authority has concluded that it is the ethic of the profession that he does not.[11]

The implications of the problem extend far beyond the tax area, for the issue involved is a fundamental one. But it is more difficult in the tax area, because the harm to the public interest, is more difficult to perceive than in the case, for example, of unsafe food and drugs. A few thousand dollars out of a hundred billion is not as significant as a drug taken by pregnant women which might result in deformed children. Between these two extremes are those examples of a manifest public interest, as the granting of an airline route. The action desired may be either harmful or beneficial, but which can neither be determined, nor measured accurately.

The measure of the duty of candor in the administrative process is complex because the administrative process is complex. A simplistic absolute standard of candor could easily prove to be as ineffective as no standard of candor, for lawyers deal with real problems of real people subject to all the ills the flesh is heir to. Precision is not what is needed. Precise minimum standards have a way of becoming maximum standards, and standards do not work because they are precise or general, but because lawyers are aware of the obligations they impose and desire and are willing to comply with them. Moreover, the lack of precision provides a degree of flexibility for a flexible process, but the flexibility does not imply a discretion not to be candid. It implies a limited discretion by the lawyer to use his best judgment and a duty that the judgment be well founded. The need is a workable standard that will serve the best interest of all.

10. Paul, The Lawyer as a Tax Adviser, 25 Rocky Mt.L.Rev. 412, 425 (1953).

11. Id. at 427–31.

The importance of the regulatory administrative process in this country can be measured in part by the discontent expressed with it. A former chairman of the Securities and Exchange Commission has outlined the change in attitude toward the commissions:

> "At one time in the thirties they were treated as the salvation to many government problems, the preserver of our economic liberties. The very structure of an independent agency was thought to provide an independence and an expertise, 'a judgelike wisdom, balance, and insight,' that could not otherwise be achieved. After the euphoria of the New Deal and following World War II, they lost caste and were referred to disparagingly and with suspicion as the fourth branch of government." [12]

The failure of the commissions has been laid to many different reasons and causes. One cause seldom mentioned, however, is the legal profession itself. Lawyers are in large part responsible for the failure because they have continually sought to judicialize, and have failed to develop appropriate standards for, the regulatory process. The tendency to judicialize arises from an unwillingness to accept the regulatory process as a legal system, as it in fact is, distinct and separate from the judicial process. Consequently, the profession has seen little reason to be concerned with standards for the lawyer practicing before a regulatory commission. The problem is further clouded by the fact that the regulatory process is more closely related to the legislative than the judicial process, and the profession has not developed standards for the lawyer's participation in the legislative process.

Contributing to the difficulty is the failure to perceive a basic function of standards in any legal process, with a consequent failure to perceive that only the profession itself can establish effective standards. Standards are measures of conduct accepted and imposed by one's peers. The lawyer, as any professional man, is seldom concerned with the layman's view of his conduct. But he is very much concerned with how his fellow lawyers view his actions. Yet, unless there is an accepted criterion by which to measure the actions, lawyers do not condemn fellow lawyers and are reluctant even to question the propriety of their conduct. The legal profession is in fact the only institution which can provide standards for the lawyer which are so necessary to the successful functioning of the regulatory process.

Much of the malaise in the regulatory process can be traced to the failure of Congress, the commissions, and the legal profes-

12. W. Cary, Politics and the Regulatory Agencies 124–25 (1967).

sion to realize the extent to which the cooperation of lawyers to make the process function successfully is necessary. To make the administrative process work properly, the cooperation of the legal profession is essential. Cooperation alone, however, is not sufficient. The profession must be willing to exercise initiative and take the lead in providing its members affirmative standards to guide them in their conduct in the regulatory administrative process. Standards alone, of course, will not solve the problems of the regulatory commissions, but their problems cannot be effectively resolved without adequate and appropriate standards for the lawyers who practice before them. For this, the profession bears a public responsibility. "The bar . . . has the confidence of our people and in the discharge of that responsibility its talents should be made available to make the administrative process a way of justice, quick, sure and fair." [13]

13. Landis, supra note 7, at 26.

Chapter XI

THE LAWYER FOR THE GOVERNMENT

SECTION 1. INTRODUCTION

Every level of government in this country has its chief legal officer. The federal government and the states have attorneys general and cities and counties have their attorneys, each with its own staff. Most branches or units of government, too, have their own staffs of lawyers: departments of the executive branch, legislatures, congressional committees and administrative agencies, both state and federal. About 40,000 lawyers man these various positions. "They may be thought of as engaged in the practice of public law." [1]

The public practitioner is distinguishable from the private practitioner of law only by his official position. Lawyers share a common core of knowledge and skills that enable them to move back and forth from private to public law practice with ease, and the members of the two groups continually interchange. Many experienced lawyers become prosecuting attorneys for a few years and return to private practice. Others make a career of government service. In some instances, work in the government equips a young lawyer with an expertise that he puts to good use when he goes into private practice. Many lawyers, too, serve a government as a lawyer while remaining in private practice, as, for example, a city or county attorney in small communities.

To change from governmental to private practice is not to surrender public obligations, for most of the work of our free enterprise society is carried on by private organizations. The continuous interchange of private and public lawyers is beneficial both to the government and to the profession. The government obtains highly skilled personnel and the members of the profession obtain an insight into the workings of government that better enables them to serve both their clients and the government in private practice. Yet, there is a major drawback. The ease of transition between the two positions tends to blur the importance of the distinction between the roles of the private and public lawyer. Superficially, the roles may be very similar. The trial lawyer who becomes a prosecutor applies his same skills, and he nat-

---

1. American Bar Foundation, The Legal Profession in the United States 11 (1965).

urally tends to apply also the same standards. But it is obvious that the prosecutor has a different role and a greater responsibility than the defendant's lawyer.

The major difference between the public and private lawyer is not in skills, but in standards and the scope of responsibility. This chapter is directed to this difference and treats four aspects of the problem. Section 2 deals with the unique position of the government lawyer and the reasons for his greater responsibility. Section 3 discusses some problems of the government lawyer in court, both as a prosecuting attorney and as an advocate in a civil case. The subject of Section 4 is the government lawyer when he fulfills the role of an office lawyer. Section 5 deals with problems of conflict of interest which are peculiar to the government, or former government, lawyer.

SECTION 2. THE GOVERNMENT LAWYER: HIS POWERS AND RESPONSIBILITIES

The government is individuals who exercise power by reason of their position, and the government lawyer, as any government official, is the government in the exercise of his powers. The lawyer in government service has greater independence, more discretion in the exercise of his skills as a lawyer, and a broader responsibility than the private lawyer.

He has independence because he is neither aided nor hampered by the wishes of a client, and his duty is only to fulfill the obligations of his office. Even when working under a superior, the government lawyer shares with him the same aims and goals. Unlike the private lawyer who must earn a living and has a duty to serve his clients, the government lawyer is free to use his best judgment as a representative of the people. "The [government] attorney is never the mere hireling of government or of anyone else. He is an independent professional and must stand on what he thinks is right." [1]

An aspect of his independence is his discretion, made necessary by the complexities of his task. The private lawyer is concerned only with the particular situation and the rules applicable to that situation as they affect his client. The government lawyer is concerned not only with the particular situation, but also with all similar situations. His primary concern is policy: the

1. Weinstein, Some Ethical and Political Problems of A Government   Attorney, 18 Maine L.Rev. 155, 162 (1966).

implementation of sound policy for the future and in the interest of all the people. This concern with policy requires that he have discretion in utilizing and applying the many rules that are available for any given situation. "The private lawyer can, within broad limits, attempt to get the best possibile result—from his single client's point of view—letting the adversary system provide the justice." [2]   The government lawyer must be concerned with justice, for the individual with whom he is dealing, as well as for the government.

The broader responsibility of the government lawyer is a necessary aspect of the government's enormous power, and in the exercise of that power, the lawyer has a duty of restraint. Supporting him in this restraint is a fundamental and basic policy of our society, that ours is a government of law and consequently is a government of limited powers. This country had its origins in the abuses of governmental power and has been continually concerned with the problem since 1776. The Declaration of Independence listed the wrongs perpetrated by George III. The Bill of Rights and the Reconstruction Amendments made more explicit the limitations on government, and the recent expansion of governmental activities has been accompanied by an increased emphasis on the civil rights of the citizen in his relations with government and its representatives. The government lawyer thus has a duty to act only in accordance with the law and to see that each person with whom he deals is treated in accordance with due process, for he has a duty to the government that the government remain within the boundaries of law.

The government lawyer's duty, however, is more than to remain within the law. He has a duty to use his best judgment to determine to what extent the resources of the government should be brought to bear on a particular problem. The problem is essentially one of fairness, that is the responsible exercise of power.

The fulfillment of this duty is more difficult than it appears to be, because of the tradition that all men are equal under the law. Paradoxically, the emphasis given to this tradition has made it a substitute for a tradition of fairness on the part of lawyers generally, both for the government and in private practice. But to treat unequals equally is to treat them unequally. The idea that the administration of law requires no more than mere compliance with rules leads to a sterile notion of fairness, for it emphasizes the letter to the detriment of the spirit of the law.

The government lawyer thus must be concerned not only with what action the law requires, but with what action the policy of

2. Id. at 169.

the law calls for in the particular situation. "The bothersome problems of a government attorney are not so much the legal-technical ones of what can be done, or how to do it, but what should be done." [3] He must use sound judgment in weighing and balancing such factors as the effect of the conduct involved on the welfare of society, the status of the parties involved, and the duty of the government to act. The creation of a combination of businesses to monopolize the market in violation of the law obviously calls for vigorous action against the violators to the limit of the law. The problem of the indigent widow seeking to obtain welfare payments is a wholly different one and may require action to aid the claimant against the government, that is against officials who deny the claim on dubious grounds. The denial of a person's civil rights, as for example, the right to vote because of race, may wisely call for a different method of action—persuasion to bring about compliance with the law and respect for the rights of others, before resort to litigation. "One of the most important functions of the government's lawyer is to provide a bridge or neutral meeting ground between opposing forces so that the viable compromises which are the hallmark of a functioning democracy can be developed." [4]

Despite his privileged position, the lawyer for the government often has one disadvantage not suffered by his counterpart in private practice. Many lawyers in government are elected or are appointed through political influence. This is commonly true, for example, of prosecuting attorneys. In many states, the prosecutor must stand for election and even the United States Attorney is a political appointee. The political tradition associated with the prosecutor might be viewed by many as an important element of democratic government.

But law enforcement and law administration are areas of government where the influence of the electorate may be more disadvantageous than otherwise. A prosecutor's office which is also a political office can seldom be run in a professional manner to the best advantage of the people either as taxpayers or as law abiding citizens. Conspicuousness in prosecution may lead to political preferment, and prosecutions in the interest of publicity rather than the interest of justice is a danger few politically minded prosecutors are able to avoid. Justice Frankfurter in a letter to a district attorney of a state expressed the point well: "It has long been my view that one thing, as much as any one thing, to which the serious deficiencies, broadly speaking, of the American system of criminal justice are due is the nonprofessionalism and therefore political embroilment and sensationalism

3. Id. at 158.   4. Id. at 172.

of our agencies of criminal justice." [5]   Chief Justice Stone, many years ago, spoke of the same problem:

> Fundamentally there is no more reason why the office of the public prosecutor should be a political office than that of a Judge of the Federal courts, and yet infinite harm is done to the cause of law enforcement and good government in this country in consequence of the fact that that office is either frankly and avowedly political or in any event is peculiarly subject to untoward political influences. This fact, coupled with our inadequate administrative system or no administrative system at all in the conduct of those offices, is probably more responsible for the lax administration of law than all other causes combined. [6]

A basic reason for the need of such a development, is not often perceived. To fulfill his complex roles, the lawyer for the government, particularly the prosecutor, must have one quality that is not shared by the private practitioner—disinterest in the result. The point is perhaps best illustrated by the inscription in the Department of Justice Building in Washington: "The United States wins its case whenever justice is done one of its citizens in the courts." The quality is an unusual one for the lawyer, used to an adversary system of law administration. It must be cultivated, nurtured and developed as a tradition, for tradition is the mainspring of attitudes. The government lawyer is more than a lawyer. He is a government official who must retain his independence of judgment by being disinterested in all the problems he deals with in that capacity.

SECTION 3.   THE GOVERNMENT LAWYER IN COURT

The government lawyer serves in court in two different capacities, as prosecutor in criminal cases and as advocate in civil cases. The two roles require the same skills, and while each has its special problems, they involve common problems. The basic problem common to both is the psychological dilemma for the government lawyer: He must fight hard, but he must be fair. The common law adversary system was developed for the resolution of disputes between individuals, not between individuals and the government. The advantages of the government in resources, prestige and power are too great for the trial to be con-

---

5. Kuh, Careers in Prosecution Offices, 14 J.Legal Ed. 175 (1961).

6. Stone, Progress in Law Improvement in the United States, 10 A.B. A.J. 633, 636 (1924).

ducted without special responsibilities on the government lawyer. The United States government, for example, can bring witnesses from anywhere and has the resources of the entire Department of Justice, including the investigative resources of the Federal Bureau of Investigation. The government attorney, too, has a special status. By reason of his position, he naturally commands greater respect from the jury and the court than the private lawyer, and he has the responsibility of maintaining the confidence and respect of the people, which would be impaired should he act unfairly.

The restraint his position calls for in the trial is difficult because he is trained in the adversary system which makes no allowance for his special role. His opponent, not under the constraint of representing the government, has a duty of loyalty to his client which requires him to utilize all the advantages that the nature of the system provides. The impact of litigation on the individual is in no way comparable with its impact on the government. For the defendant, it may well mean bankruptcy, the ruin of a career, the destruction of a reputation, or prison and even death. For these same reasons, the government lawyer has a special duty of care in prosecuting a criminal defendant or seeking payment of a claim. As the respresentative of the government, his primary concern is not winning the case, but seeing that justice is done.

The duty of the prosecutor to adhere to higher standards than the private lawyer is recognized: "The public prosecutor cannot take as a guide for the conduct of his office the standards of an attorney appearing on behalf of an individual client."[1] But it may be a duty honored in the breach as much as in the observances. The following discussion is directed to three problems which require the prosecutor to maintain the highest of standards —his decision to prosecute, his acceptance of guilty pleas, and his conduct of the trial. The discussion then deals briefly with the government lawyer in civil cases.

"If every . . . prosecutor . . . performed his . . . responsibility in strict accordance with rules of law, precisely and narrowly laid down, the criminal law would be ordered but intolerable."[2] The decision to prosecute or not to prosecute is thus fundamental and it is a decision which must of necessity be left to the discretion of the prosecutor. "With rare exceptions, legislatures and appellate judges officially approve

1. Report of the Joint Conference on Professional Responsibility, 1958 A.A.L.S.Pro. 187, 201 (1958); 44 A. B.A.J. 1159, 1218 (1958).

2. Breitel, Controls in Criminal Law Enforcement, 27 U.Chi.L.Rev. 427 (1960).

of this allocation of power to prosecutors . . . ."[3] They could hardly do otherwise, for in the application of law, decisions must be made by men, and if the prosecutor is not to be free to make them, another official must. "Even the strongest advocates for the establishing of criteria to control discretion would admit that some considerable amount of judgment must remain, if only because of the variety of situations that arise and the limitations inherent in the use of language."[4]

The reasons for not prosecuting at all or not prosecuting to the fullest extent illustrate the complexity of the task.[5] Apart from belief in the innocence of an accused or the lack of sufficient evidence to proceed, there are any number of reasons for not prosecuting. One is the attitude of the victim. The publicity of a trial may be more humiliating and harmful to the prosecuting witness than to the defendant, particularly in sex crimes.

3. F. Miller, Prosecution, The Decision To Charge A Suspect With A Crime 154 (1969).

4. Id. at 153.

5. See Miller, supra note 3, for an excellent study of the subject. The work is a Report of the American Bar Foundation's Survey of the Administration of Criminal Justice in the United States, Frank J. Remington, Editor.

The Tentative Draft of the ABA Standards Relating to The Prosecution Function deals with this point in some detail:

3.9 *Discretion in the charging decision*

(a) In addressing himself to the decision whether to charge, the prosecutor should first determine whether there is evidence which would support a conviction.

(b) The prosecutor is not obliged to present all charges which the evidence might support. The prosecutor may in some circumstances and for good cause consistent with the public interest decline to prosecute, notwithstanding that evidence exists which would support a conviction. Illustrative of the factors which the prosecutor may properly consider in exercising his discretion are:

 (i) the prosecutor's reasonable doubt that the accused is in fact guilty;

 (ii) the extent of the harm caused by the offense;

 (iii) the disproportion of the authorized punishment in relation to the particular offense or the offender;

 (iv) possible improper motives of a complainant;

 (v) prolonged non-enforcement of a statute, with community acquiescence;

 (vi) reluctance of the victim to testify;

 (vii) cooperation of the accused in the apprehension or conviction of others;

 (viii) availability and likelihood of prosecution by another jurisdiction.

(c) In making the decision to prosecute, the prosecutor should give no weight to the personal or political advantages or disadvantages which might be involved or to a desire to enhance his record of convictions.

(d) In cases which involve a serious threat to the community, the prosecutor should not be deterred from prosecution by the fact that in his jurisdiction juries have tended to acquit persons accused of the particular kind of criminal act in question.

(e) The prosecutor should not bring or seek charges greater in number or degree than he can reasonably support with evidence at trial.

The cost to the system of law enforcement, either monetary or in terms of public support, may be too high. Extradition, for example, may be too expensive, and the prohibition laws could not be effectively enforced because of public opposition. Prosecution for a lesser offense may be as effective as for a graver offense and avoid undue collateral harm to the defendant, as in a close case where the charge is reduced from drunken to reckless driving. Alternatives to criminal prosecution may be available, as the civil commitment of an alcoholic or psychotic person, or the revocation of parole.[6] The defendant may be prosecuted in another jurisdiction, for example, federal rather than state. Often, civil sanctions are more effective than a criminal prosecution, as an injunction to abate a nuisance or the revocation of a license. And many times, a suspect who is willing to cooperate for other enforcement goals will not be prosecuted. The list could be expanded, but unnecessarily, to illustrate the point that the prosecutor's discretion involves too many and complex factors to be the subject of regulation.

Criminal statutes are not enacted with a view to a single policy to be carried out, and they serve too many purposes to be applied without the exercise of sound judgment. As long as these statutes serve such various functions as providing revenue (traffic fines), preserving personal morals (habitual drunkenness) and the regulation of business (antitrust laws), selective law enforcement is not only desirable, it is essential. Yet, most prosecutors tend to assume they have a duty to prosecute all crimes, and that their discretion not to prosecute is the result of impossibility, because resources are limited. The negative approach to the discretionary power prevents the formation of sound principles to guide him in his job. The fact, of course, is that in some instances, the prosecutor has a duty not to prosecute in the interest of fairness and common decency. The youthful offender who has been tried and sentenced in state court for stealing an automobile should not be subjected to a trial in federal court merely because he drove the car across the state line.

When these two factors are considered, along with the quantity of criminal laws and the poor quality of many of the criminal statutes, it becomes obvious that the prosecutor's task is an ex-

---

6. Cf. the following standard in the Tentative Draft of the ABA Standards Relating to The Prosecution Function:

3.8 *Discretion   as   to   non-criminal disposition.*

(a) The prosecutor should explore the availability of non-criminal disposition, including programs of rehabilitation, formal or informal, in decid-ing whether to press criminal charges; especially in the case of a first offender, the nature of the offense may warrant non-criminal disposition.

(b) Prosecutors should be familiar with the resources of social agencies which can assist in the evaluation of cases for diversion from the criminal process.

tremely difficult one. One United States Attorney, for example, lamented that the problem of low level policy decisions, that is decisions directly affecting only one or a few persons, was his biggest problem. There were no affirmative guides to aid him. Conscious of his duty to enforce the law, he was unsure of his right not to make a conscientious effort to enforce all the law for which he was responsible. Experience gradually made him aware of the wisdom of selective law enforcement, not only because of limited resources, but also because no useful purpose would be served by indiscriminate prosecutions. All persons who violate criminal statutes are not criminals.

The prosecutor is not merely one who enforces the law. He administers the law in a broader sense, and as a law administrator, he functions as a surrogate judge. His decisions are policy decisions and he must not only seek to do justice, he must appear to seek to do justice. Two judicial qualities will serve him well in the exercise of his discretion. One essential is impartiality, the absence of personal interest or involvement in the cases on which he rules. The other is decisions on the particular facts of each case in light of the purposes of the law and the purposes to be served by prosecuting.

Closely related to the discretion to prosecute is the problem of guilty pleas. Ninety percent of the convictions obtained in this country are a result of pleas of guilty.[7] The administrative convenience achieved by the process tends to deceive as to its importance. The presumption of guilt that accompanies a confession in court serves to cure whatever defects may have occurred in the plea process. Yet, one experienced trial judge is said to have stated "that the risk of error is likely to be greater in a guilty plea case than in a case which is tried." [8]

The plea process is thus one which deserves, and has received, special attention. The American Bar Association has approved standards relating to pleas of guilty, which were commended and relied upon by the Minnesota Supreme Court in State v. Wolske.[9] The issue in the case was the right of a defendant to withdraw his plea when the prosecutor failed to keep his promise. "The prosecution failed to seek the charge concessions promised, and defendant did not receive the benefits contemplated by the agreement. Not only from a procedural standpoint but also from a correctional point of view, the record establishes that an actual injustice has occurred." [10]

7. D. Newman, Conviction: The Determination of Guilt or Innocence Without Trial 3 (1966).

8. Id. at 9.

9. 280 Minn. 465, 160 N.W.2d 146 (1968).

10. Id. at 474, 160 N.W.2d at 152.

A statement of the affirmative duties of the prosecutor is desirable. Both the case and the standards approved by the ABA are no less interesting for what they do not say than for what they do say. Despite its conclusion in the case, the Minnesota court made no mention of the duty of the prosecutor to keep his promise. Nor do the standards speak of the obligations of the prosecutor in the plea process. In traditional legal fashion, the standards are framed in terms of the rights of defendant and the obligations of the court.[11] Thus, the defendant is to have aid of counsel to be advised by the court, and the court is to determine the voluntariness and the accuracy of the plea. The defendant has a right to withdraw the plea under certain circumstances, e. g., if the prosecutor does not keep his promises. The prosecuting attorney may enter into discussions and make agreements but the trial judge should not participate in plea discussions. The standards fail to state any affirmative obligations of the most important person in the plea process, the prosecutor.[12]

11. ABA Project on Minimum Standards for Criminal Justice, Standards Relating to Pleas of Guilty (1968).

12. The Tentative Draft of the ABA Standards Relating to The Prosecution Function does impose duties on the prosecutor in the plea process:

4.   *Availability for plea discussions.*

(a) The prosecutor should make known a general policy of willingness to consult with defense counsel concerning disposition of charges by plea.

(b) It is unprofessional conduct for a prosecutor to engage in plea discussions directly with an accused who is represented by counsel, except with counsel's approval. If the accused refuses to be represented by counsel, the prosecutor may properly discuss disposition of the charges directly with the accused; the prosecutor would be well advised, however, to request that a lawyer be designated by the court or some appropriate central agency, such as a legal aid or defender office or bar association, to be present at such discussions.

(c) It is unprofessional conduct for a prosecutor knowingly to make false statements or representations in the course of plea discussions with defense counsel or the accused.

4.2 *Plea disposition when accused maintains innocence.*

A prosecutor may not properly participate in a disposition by plea of guilty if he is aware that the accused persists in denying guilt or the fatual basis for the plea, without disclosure to the court.

4.3 *Fulfillment of plea discussions.*

(a) It is unprofessional conduct for a prosecutor to make any promise or commitment concerning the sentence which will be imposed or concerning a suspension of sentence; he may properly advise the defense what position he will take concerning disposition.

(b) A prosecutor should avoid implying a greater power to influence the disposition of a case than he possesses.

(c) If the prosecutor finds he is unable to fulfill an understanding previously agreed upon in plea discussions, he should give notice promptly to the defendant and cooperate in securing leave of the court for the defendant to withdraw any plea and take other steps appropriate to restore the defendant to the position he was in before the understanding was reached or plea made.

4.4 *Record of reasons for nolle prosequi disposition.*

Whenever felony criminal charges are dismissed by way of nolle prosequi (or its equivalent), the prosecutor should make a record of the reasons for the action.

The major factor that is likely to escape the prosecutor in the plea process is the subtle change that occurs in his relationship with the accused when he decides to plead guilty. At this point, the prosecutor assumes the position of a judicial officer, for he effectually becomes a surrogate judge. This is especially true when the defendant waives his right to counsel, and to a lesser extent when counsel is appointed, for appointed counsel will often encourage a plea on the part of his unwanted client. Moreover, it is the prosecutor who controls the bargaining, which is so often a major part of the process.

There are two factors of major concern to the prosecutor in determining to accept a guilty plea: Is the defendant in fact guilty? Is he acting voluntarily? The first factor is important because the prosecutor is likely to assume guilt, since he made the determination to prosecute in the first place. This decision, however, is made on the assumption that defendant will have a trial in which he will have an opportunity to show otherwise. An accused, as psychologists have made clear, may decide to plead guilty for any number of reasons, when in fact he is not. Often, he is a poor person, frightened, insecure, uneducated, with low intelligence, and unaware of the implications of his actions. His first concern is likely to be one of being removed from the miasma of doubt and uncertainty in which he finds himself. The prosecutor thus has a duty to make an independent determination of guilt or innocence on the basis of all the evidence in his possession. Even though the prosecutor is convinced that the accused is guilty, he has a duty to see that any plea is voluntary. Thus, he has a responsibility to see that the defendant is fully informed as to his rights, and a duty to see that the defendant has sufficient time to consider his decision.

The prosecutor's conduct of the trial, subject as it is to public record, has been dealt with more fully by the courts than either the discretion to prosecute or the acceptance of the guilty plea. The duty of the prosecutor is one of fairness, and its basis is the Constitution. Yet, the prosecutor's duty to see that the defendant gets a fair trial has emerged only in the last few decades. As late as 1918, in People v. Mooney,[13] the Supreme Court of California denied relief to Tom Mooney, convicted of murder as the result of the San Francisco bombing in 1916, on the basis of perjured eyewitness testimony of which the prosecutor was aware. The court decided unanimously that Mooney had no remedy:

"The defendant in such case is without remedy.

. . .

" 'Nor can it be said that the duty of a district attorney differs in the trial of criminal actions from that of counsel in

13. 178 Cal. 525, 174 P. 325, cert. denied 248 U.S. 579 (1918).

civil actions. Each has an equal duty imposed upon him by the oath he has taken and by the law of the land to present to the court and to the jury only competent and legitimate evidence from which may be determined the truth of the issues involved. If that obligation be violated and perjured testimony produced or material evidence suppressed by either, as we have seen, in so far as the judgment is concerned, the injured party is without remedy.' " [14]

The Supreme Court of the United States denied certiorari. But this judicial acquiescence is what Professor Edmund Cahn called "official dishonesty" could not survive in a society whose ideals and goals are dependent upon the integrity of its government officials. The Supreme Court did grant certiorari in the *Mooney* case in 1935 and required a hearing to determine the truthfulness of his allegations.[15] The Court dealt with a similar issue again in 1957, in Alcorta v. Texas.[16] Alcorta, convicted of murder for stabbing his wife, relied on a state statute allowing sudden passion for adequate cause to reduce the offense to murder without malice. Another man testified at the trial that Alcorta came upon him and the wife kissing in a car, but denied that there was anything else between them. The witness and the wife, however, had in fact had sexual relations several times and the witness had so informed the prosecutor. The court held that Alcorta had not been accorded due process of law. The Supreme Court went even further in Napue v. Illinois,[17] reversing a conviction because the principal witness against defendant, in response to a question by the prosecutor, denied that he was receiving any consideration for his testimony. The prosecutor who asked the question had agreed to recommend a reduction of the witness' sentence received under a previous conviction. In a similar case, the Court of Appeals of New York, in an opinion by Judge Fuld, reached the same result. "It is of no consequence that the falsehood bore upon the witness' credibility rather than directly upon defendant's guilt. A lie is a lie, no matter what its subject, and, if it is in any way relevant to the case, *the district attorney has the responsibility and duty to correct what he knows to be false and elicit the truth*." [18]

So direct and forthright a statement of the prosecutor's duty is unusual in these cases. The constitutional right is recognized, but the professional duty of the prosecutor is seldom articulated. Yet, there is value in stating the duty explicitly, for the duty of

14. Id. at 530, 174 P. at 327.

15. Mooney v. Holohan, 294 U.S. 103 (1935).

16. 355 U.S. 28 (1957).

17. 360 U.S. 264 (1959).

18. People v. Savvides, 1 N.Y.2d 554, 557, 154 N.Y.S.2d 885, 887 (1956) (emphasis added).

the prosecutor is a correlative of the right of the accused. The defendant not only has a right to the opportunity for, he has a right to, a fair trial in fact. And it is the prosecutor's recognition of this duty that is the most important factor in assuring the defendant a fair trial in fact. In Miller v. Pate, for example,[19] the Supreme Court reversed the conviction of a man for the rape-murder of an eight year old girl, concluding, "The prosecution deliberately misrepresented the truth." [20] The Court made no comment on the conduct of the prosecutor as such. The Grievance Committee of the Illinois State Bar Association investigated the conduct of the prosecutors and determined that, "The opinion of the United States Supreme Court left the impression that a grave injustice had been deliberately perpetrated by a ruthless and unprincipled prosecutor. A thorough and objective investigation of the matter has shown that this impression is unfounded." [21] The report, however, was limited in its concern to the question of deliberate misconduct, and did not treat the problem of the prosecutor's duty to insure a fair trial. On this point, the opinion of the Supreme Court gave no guidance.

The reluctance on the part of the courts to speak directly to this issue is perhaps due in part to the fact that the traditions of the common law adversary system are against it, and due in part to a recognition of the difficult and complex task of the prosecutor. Yet, there are more subtle and more important reasons. To impose a definitive standard upon the prosecutor would be to limit his discretion in presenting the case as well as the discretion of the trial judge in making rulings and the appellate judges in deciding appeals. Prosecutors, as well as judges, are human, and inevitably they are affected in their reactions and reasoning by the nature and gravity of the offense involved. The nature of the crime and the political implications in the *Mooney* case, for example, explain both the court's position and its reasoning.

There is involved here what Professor David Cavers called "affective facts," that is facts which affect and determine the outcome of a case without being recognized as being determinative. This is characteristic of much legal reasoning and is well illustrated in a case in which the prosecutor took the unusual step of stating in his brief on appeal that he was not convinced that "the People have proved the case beyond a reasonable doubt." [22] The Court in its opinion reversed the conviction and

---

19. 386 U.S. 1 (1967).

20. Id. at 6, 87 S.Ct. 788.

21. Grievance Committee's Findings Re Prosecution of the Miller Murder Case, 56 Ill.Bar.J. 955, 958 (1968).

22. People v. Lagani, 159 N.Y.S.2d 447, 448 (Westchester County Ct. 1957).

praised the prosecutor's action as "one of refreshing candor and in the highest tradition of his office and of the bar." [23] The affective fact was the crime involved—indecent exposure. A different crime might have caused a different reaction.

The problem of affective facts in reasoning is not confined to judges and lawyers, for their use involves rationalization, common to all persons. Judges and lawyers will continue to use them, for they are inevitably a part of our reasoning processes. But the integrity of prosecutors is an area where such rationalization has no place, for professional standards are an integral part of the administration of justice. What was said of the United States Attorney in Berger v. United States [24] is true for all prosecutors: "The United States Attorney is the representative not of an ordinary party to a controversy, but of a sovereignty whose obligation to govern impartially is as compelling as its obligation to govern at all; and whose interest, therefore, in a criminal prosecution is not that it shall win a case, but that justice shall be done." [25]

SECTION 4. THE GOVERNMENT LAWYER AS OFFICE LAWYER

The most pervasive role of the government lawyer, as with the private lawyer, is that of office lawyer rather than advocate.

"It should need no emphasis that the lawyer is today, even when not himself a 'maker' of policy, the one indispensable adviser of every responsible policy-maker of our society— whether we speak of the head of a government department or agency, of the executive of a corporation or labor union, of the secretary of a trade or other private association, or even of the humble independent enterpriser or professional man. As such an adviser the lawyer, when informing his policy-maker of what he can or cannot *legally* do, is, as policy-makers often complain, in an unassailably strategic position to influence, if not create, policy." [1]

Even so, the work of the office lawyer receives less attention than that of the advocate, because the lawyer in his office specializes in cooperation and coordination of interests rather than

---

23.   159 N.Y.S.2d 447, 448.

24.   295 U.S. 78 (1935).

25.   Id. at 88.

1.   Lasswell & McDougal, Legal Education and Public Policy: Professional Training in the Public Interest, 52 Yale L.J. 203, 208–9 (1943).

conflict. This is true of the government lawyer no less than the private lawyer and it is in this area that the work of the government lawyer most nearly approximates that of his private counterpart. Both are concerned with the wise administration of law, one in the interest of the individual, the other in the interest of the government. Wise administration, whether of a university, a corporation, or law in the interest of a client or the government is based upon the same basic principles—a complete understanding of the purpose and function of the task at hand, sound judgment in the wise use of limited resources (time, money, energy, manpower), a thorough comprehension of the policies to be implemented, and an ability to appreciate the future consequences of present conduct.

The government lawyer in his office shares with the government advocate certain advantages over the private lawyer. In addition to the absence of the need to please a client and greater resources for his task, he is more apt to be limited to a specialized area of the law in which he can acquire expertise. Whether serving as a legal adviser in the Department of the State, a staff attorney of the Veterans' Administration, or trial attorney in the Department of Justice, he has the opportunity to become expert in his field.

The most obvious characteristic of the government lawyer as an office lawyer is the diversity of his tasks and his levels of responsibility. They are as broad and ranging in scope as the government itself and often the importance of the different levels is misconceived. The usual view is that the higher the position, the more important it is. This view, however, confuses prestige and power with importance. The higher the position, the greater is the influence on policy, and the setting of goals and defining of policy are enormously important functions. But the implementation of the policy is equally important, and it is a mistake to compare the importance of lawyers in different positions, because their functions differ. The lawyers who are high officials in government may be no more important, or less so, than the staff lawyers, for each group has its own tasks which complement each other's roles. The test of policy is not how it is fomulated but how it is carried out, and it is the lawyer at the lower level who carries out the policy.

The staff lawyer in government has not received the attention he deserves. The position is particularly important for two reasons: (1) The lawyer, as a professional man of independent judgment, is a healthy antidote against the stultifying effects of a bureaucracy bound by detailed regulations; (2) The lawyer at the lower level is the one who most often comes into contact with the members of the public.

Whatever the level of the position of the government lawyer, he is a lawyer, and as such he has the duties and obligations of a lawyer, just as a young associate in a large law firm is no less subject to the obligations of a lawyer than the senior partner. For the government lawyer, the most important of these obligations, perhaps, is independence of judgment and critical thought. The importance of this obligation is in the danger of its being lost, for he is part of a bureaucracy, the major characteristics as defined by Max Weber of which are: "[A] division of labor, a defined system of hierarchy of authority, a consistent system of abstract rules, impersonal detachment of the official in interpersonal relationships, hiring and promotion based on technical qualifications." [2] In such a setting, the danger is that the lawyer will come to view "his office as a slot machine handing out opinions and acting with mechanical exactitude; he fails to grasp its more useful, complex and flexible functions in meeting social problems." [3] The problem, however, is not unique to the government lawyer. The issue of conformity versus individualism is pervasive throughout society, and it is much the same for the young associate in the large Wall Street law firm as it is for the staff attorney of an administrative agency. In the setting of the Wall Street law office, it has been dealt with in terms of what is called "creative conformity." Associates are expected to argue with partners if they believe themselves to be correct. "For these elite lawyers then, dispute is not nonconformity but is, rather creative conformity, for it helps the associate keep his professional independence. The partners are able continuously to sharpen their legal minds, and the client receives the benefits of the free give and take." [4]

Perhaps a better term as applied to the government lawyer would be independent conformity, for both independence and conformity are necessary. The government lawyer to be most effective must retain his independence of analysis, thought and opinion. At the same time, he must be willing to conform to and carry out decisions. The issue is essentially one of loyalty, which requires both the willingness to disagree with superiors when they take an unsound position, and the willingness to abide by the decision once it is final.

Closely related to the problem of independence of judgment is the matter of the staff lawyer's dealing with the public. For most individuals who have a problem with the government, the contact is with a lawyer in an agency. This lawyer is the most

---

2. E. Smigel, The Wall Street Lawyer vii (1964).

3. Weinstein, Some Ethical and Political Problems of a Government Attorney, 18 Maine L.Rev. 155, 159 (1966).

4. E. Smigel, supra note 2, at 322.

important person in the government to the citizen, for to him that lawyer is the government. He will have a far greater impact on the life of a poor widow filing a claim for social security benefits than the Secretary of Health, Education and Welfare.

Yet, the problem of the staff attorney's contact with the public is one of the most neglected of the important roles of the government lawyer. Part of this neglect is found in a lamentable lack in the education of lawyers, a lack of training in the knowledge of human behavior. We quote for a second time:

> "Ideally, every lawyer's education should include at least a grounding in human psychology. He should learn what we know about interviewing skills. What happens when a client sits down with an authority figure such as his lawyer? What are the psychological forces operating between the parties to such a conversation that may obscure issues and produce failures of communication? How can a sensitive interviewer avoid these risks or dispel them when they exist? The answer to such questions is to be found in the substance of the psychological sciences; before long, we should view it as a matter of neglect if they are not included in the routine training of all lawyers." [5]

This lack leads lawyers to believe that they deal only with legal problems. In fact, lawyers do not deal with legal problems, but with human problems in legal terms. The private lawyer, able to get to know and identify with his client, is able to overcome this obstacle of legalism, at least in some degree. The government lawyer in dealing with members of the public has no such advantage, and consequently he tends to see the individual's problem only in relation to his own roles in the government.

The problem is one which needs more extended treatment than can be given here. Only two comments will be made. One is that good manners are vitally important. The small effort that good manners require serves effectively to obscure their importance. The point overlooked, of course, is that manners are more than form, they are form which reflect substance. Courteous treatment of an individual is a manifestation of concern for his problem, whether or not one can solve it. More important, it is a manifestation of respect for the individual, who must not only be treated properly, he must feel that he has been treated properly. The second comment is that the lawyer for the government, whatever his position, has a duty always to keep in mind that his purpose is not to serve the government, but to serve the people for the government.

5. Watson, Could the Legal System be more Humane? 14 Law Quadrangle Notes (The University of Michigan Official Publication) No. 1, 14, 16 (1969).

SECTION 5. CONFLICT OF INTEREST

The government lawyer is much like a trustee in that he acts in a purely representative capacity, exercising his power without the restraint of guidance or direction from the grantors or beneficiaries of his power. The problem of conflict of interest for the government lawyer is thus more subtle and more complex than for the private lawyer.

It is more subtle because of the size and nature of government. Unlike the private lawyer, who can identify his duty of loyalty to an individual client, the government lawyer works for an abstraction, the identity of which is so diffused that the duty of loyalty is not only hard to identify, the harm to the government of obtaining a personal benefit is often difficult to perceive. It is more complex because threats to the loyalty of the government lawyer are more certain and they are more pervasive. Generally, they are of three major kinds, appeals to his financial interest, temptations to favor associates, and the misuse of confidential information.

The most obvious conflict of interest situation is the one in which the lawyer receives compensation or some benefit, such as future employment, for aiding another in his dealings with the government. It is this aspect of the problem to which the statutes on conflict of interest are generally directed. These statutes exist on the state, and to a lesser extent, on the municipal level. The ones of widest application, however, are the federal statutes. In 1963, new federal conflict of interest statutes became effective, and of the seven statutes in effect at the time of the new law [1] only one was retained.[2] Provisions of the others were redrafted and incorporated into the new statutes.[3]

These statutes deal with the obvious situations, forbidding representation of another while in government service,[4] participation in matters as a government official in which the official has a direct or indirect financial interest,[5] and receipt of compensation from other sources than the government for government service.[6]

The statutes are complex and they require careful analysis, but they do not, for the most part, deal with the other two major

1. 18 U.S.C.A. §§ 216, 281, 283, 434, 1914, 5 U.S.C.A. § 99.

2. 18 U.S.C.A. § 216.

3. 18 U.S.C.A. §§ 281, 283 remain in effect for certain purposes.

4. 18 U.S.C.A. §§ 203 & 205.

5. Id. § 208.

6. Id. § 209.

kinds of threats to loyalty, temptations to favor associates and the misuse of confidential information. There are very practical reasons for this lack. A statute with severe criminal sanctions is a drastic remedy. It states a rigid rule of general application which, of necessity, must be limited to the obvious situation. Competing policies, too, are involved. Equally as important as maintaining the loyalty and integrity of government employees is the ability of the government to obtain competent and qualified personnel. To surround government employees with detailed statutes regulating moral conduct is to provide a serious obstacle to recruitment policies.

These factors do not mean that conflict of interest problems are limited to financial interest. They mean, rather, that not all types of acts which result in a conflict of interest are readily subject to statutory regulation, or easily detected. There may be conflicts between official duties and religious or family affiliations. A choice favoring former law partners or one seeking to curry favor in hope of future employment is oftentimes easy to rationalize and justify on its merits. The use of confidential information to make a windfall in the stockmarket is a temptation which may be encouraged by lack of visible harm to the government. It is important to realize, then, that the conflict-of-interest statutes provide only limited and minimum standards and not a detailed code of conduct.

More important is the need to realize that the conduct of the government lawyer should comply with the highest standards because his actions, as do those of all government employees, determine the integrity of the government. Without these standards, fundamental policies of our government run the risk of erosion, policies such as increasing government efficiency, maintaining public confidence, preventing the use of public office for private gain, and preserving the integrity of government policy-making institutions.[7] As stated elsewhere, it is too clear for argument that a corrupt government is an inefficient government; that a government which plays favorites among its citizens is objectionable to American conceptions of equality under the law, notions of fair play and the assumptions of free competition; that the open channels for decision-making are frustrated when a government official appears to perform his ordinary role while in fact responding in secret to the demands of special interests. "It is not simply that he or the outside group makes money out of it. They may not. It is that the public processes of government are being subverted while policy is made silently by forces not known or responsive to the electorate." [8]

7. Association of the Bar of the City of New York, Conflict of Interest and Federal Service 6–7 (1960).

8. Id. at 7.

Problems of conflict of interest are not, of course, limited to government lawyers. They apply to all government employees and officials. There is, however, one aspect of the problem with which lawyers are more likely to be concerned than others, the representation of clients after termination of their government service. The new federal statutes referred to above deal with the kinds of situations in which the former government lawyer must disqualify himself.[9] The statute provides for two kinds of disqualification, a permanent disqualification if the former employee participated personally and substantially in the matter in question [10] and a one year disqualification as to a matter which was within the boundaries of his official responsibility during his last year of government service.[11]

The statute, as in the case of those dealing with situations arising during government service, contains severe criminal sanctions, and thus provides only minimal standards of conduct. The lawyer who is faced with this problem must also comply with professional standards of conduct. The close factual situation requires careful consideration, and the appropriate action in such cases is to seek a judicial determination, as was done in the leading case on this point, United States v. Standard Oil Company,[12] which involved the following situation.

In 1949, a young New York lawyer left his law firm and went to work for the United States government in the Paris office of the Economic Cooperation Administration. In 1951, he returned to the law firm and became a partner in 1953. In 1952, the firm was retained by an oil company to defend it in an action by the United States to recover refunds for overcharges in transactions financed by the Economic Cooperation Administration during the time the former government lawyer in the firm worked for the ECA.

The pertinent statute was not applicable to the facts, for the time limitation for disqualification had expired. Even so, the senior partner to whom the case came recognized the potential conflict of interest problem and received assurance from his young associate, later a partner, that he had never been involved in any way with the subject matter of the controversy while in government service. Having thus satisfied himself, the senior partner then filed a motion in court for an order decreeing that

9. 18 U.S.C.A. § 207 (1964).

10. Id. § 207(a).

11. Id. § 207(b).

12. United States v. Standard Oil Co., 136 F.Supp. 345 (S.D.N.Y.1955). See Kaufman, The Former Government Attorney and the Canons of Professional Ethics, 70 Harv.L.Rev. 657 (1957).

the firm might properly represent the defendant, and the government cross moved for an order disqualifying the firm.[13]

The case was decided on the basis of the Canons of Professional Ethics. The government relied primarily on Canon 37, requiring a lawyer to respect the confidences of a client, and also on Canons 6 and 36. In an extended opinion, the court dealt with three inferences arising from the Canons—the inference of access to confidential information, inferences arising from the appearance of evil, and the inference of imputed knowledge. The evidence showed that the lawyer had not in fact had any personal contact with the case while in government service. The answer, therefore, turned on whether knowledge of other employees would be imputed to him. The court dealt with the vertical theory of imputed knowledge, that is the imputation to the head of an office the knowledge of his juniors, and the horizontal imputation of knowledge of another division head of coordinate rank within the same larger agency, in this case between the Washington and Paris offices. The former imputation is automatic, the latter is a matter of particular factual situations and a matter of proof. The motion to disqualify was denied.

The case is more important for what it tells about the problem of conflict of interest than for its decision. Conflict of interest for the government lawyer is not so much a matter of law or rules as it is of attitude. Laws and rules provide guides, and viewed as affirmative aids, they are helpful. Actions involving a conflict of interest, however, are going to be avoided not by the government lawyer who is intimidated by criminal sanctions, but by the lawyer who feels a duty of loyalty to his government, a high regard for his profession, and a sense of respect for himself.

13. When the lawyers for the oil company learned their action was questioned, they sought the opinions on the matter of the committees of professional ethics of their local bar associations before proceeding further.

Part III

THE JUDICIARY

Chapter XII

THE RESPONSIBILITIES, STANDARDS AND SELECTION OF JUDGES

SECTION 1. THE JUDICIAL PROCESS

The judicial process is the individualization of the law through the authoritative decision of particular cases in accordance with general legal principles. In the process the judge is the most conspicuous figure aided as he is by the lawyers and the jury. Accompanying the individualization of the law is the development of the law. The common law was created, defended and developed by the judges in England. The common law system taken over in this country by the reception acts includes the power in the judges to continue to develop the law as suited to new problems, conditions and ideals. In their work the judges are not mere private arbitrators chosen by the parties to settle their controversies. They are representatives of the state in their function of making and applying the law. Their qualities and their actions, as well as the respect accorded them, should match the responsibilities entrusted to them.[1]

The courts vary widely. They may usefully be seen as of three principal kinds. First is the highest court of the jurisdiction which, subject to constitutions and legislation, sets the frame-

[1] Two state judges, Judge Benjamin N. Cardozo and Chief Justice Roger J. Traynor, have described most helpfully the process of appellate decision. Judge Cardozo broke new ground in his Yale lectures, "The Nature of the Judicial Process." Judge Traynor has discussed various aspects of the subject in essays not yet brought together as Law and Social Change in a Democratic Society, [1956] U.

Ill.L.F.; The Well Tempered Judicial Decision, 21 Ark.L.Rev. 287 (1967).

Professor Karl Llewellyn's volume, The Common Law Tradition: Deciding Appeals (1960), is, as Chief Judge Stanley Fuld wrote, "a remarkably perceptive study of the factors which explain . . . how courts decide appeals."

work of the law. In writing of a great predecessor in "the exacting labors of an appellate judge," Chief Justice Stone called it:[2]

> "the golden opportunity for the practice of a creative art— the moulding of our inherited legal doctrine to the needs of an everchanging social order .   ., the progress of the law toward its ideal end as an instrument of social control."

Next in order of importance is the so called lowest court,—the magistrates' court, the municipal court, the juvenile court. This court is closest to the people and has the greatest effect on their lives, as is recognized by their titular superiors. In a proceeding against a municipal court judge for discipline or punishment for contempt of court because of alleged quashing traffic violation charges at the behest of politicians, Chief Justice Weintraub said:[3]

> "In many respects the municipal court is the most important in our entire judicial system.   No other court can match its volume of causes. .   . .   It is there that most citizens have their sole exposure to the judicial process. The respect they have for the judiciary hinges upon that."

Lastly, are the courts of general jurisdiction, as the circuit courts. In their work of handling the bulk of commercial and personal injury cases, the judges have aids which the lowest courts lack—the cooperation of lawyers in the cases, something like adequate physical facilities, and general respect.

The cases, too vary. Some are "petty" to all but the persons involved, as a case of a delinquent child in a juvenile court. Others involve matters of broad concern, say the power of the President of the United States over the steel industry, or the power of the Congress to initiate broad plans of regional development as the Tennessee Valley Authority.

The American judge has a unique source of strength and a unique power. The separation of powers principle written into all our constitutions has as a purpose to assure the appropriate independence of the judiciary.[4] By implication the principle gives to the courts the inherent powers suited to the performance of their functions.

The written constitutions of the nation and the states are given efficacy by the power of judicial review of the actions of the instrumentalities of government. The lowest party in the lowest court may invoke this protection against the highest official. The power of judicial review may be employed to compel the reorganization of the instrumentalities of government, as one il-

2. Stone, Introduction to Book Notices and Uncollected Letters and Papers of Justice Oliver Wendell Holmes XI–XIII (1936).

3. In re Mattera, 34 N.J. 259, 168 A.2d 38 (1961).

4. See Chapter IV § 4 supra.

lustration is enough to show.   Baker v. Carr [5] held reapportionment of legislative representation was required by the equal protection clause of the federal constitution.   This quiet overthrow of a vested interest is a contrast with the violent controversy in England a century and a half earlier over the rotten boroughs and the disorders which preceded passage of The Reform Bill.[6]

SECTION 2.   THE SUPPORTS AND SANCTIONS OF JUDICIAL CONDUCT

The supports and sanctions of judicial conduct come from the law, or public opinion, or the profession, or the individual himself. The law may direct what a judge must or must not do.   Violation of the law may call for sanctions directed to him, as removal from office or criminal liability.   It may be preventive in purpose, as disqualification to sit in a case in which he has an interest that might affect his decision.   The law may make its impact on a party to a case as when the decision in his favor by the judge is overturned.   Public opinion may express itself less precisely but none the less drastically.   In 1969–70 it led to the resignation of one justice of the Supreme Court of the United States and contributed to the refusal by the Senate to confirm two successive nominees to the office.

The supports and sanctions by the profession occasionally take the authoritative form of official rules issued by the supreme court of a state in the exercise of its inherent power over the judiciary.   "The Canons of Judicial Ethics" express the views of thoughtful members of the profession.   They were drawn up by a committee of judges and lawyers under the chairmanship of Chief Justice Taft and were approved by the American Bar Association in 1924.   In 1969 the Association created a committee, with Chief Justice Traynor as chairman and Professor Thode as reporter, to reexamine the Canons and to propose such changes

5.   369 U.S. 186 (1962). The political background of the decision was illustrated early in 1962 at a dinner given by a law faculty to its graduates in a state legislature.   Professor Paul Sanders asked a member from a rural county how he could justify his failure to vote to reapportion the state for legislative representation purposes since the state constitution, which he had taken an oath to uphold, required reapportionment every ten years and there had been no reapportionment since 1900.   The answer was as revealing as it was unresponsive, "We have the power and we intend to keep it."   Two months later Baker v. Carr came down.

6.   In the last paragraph of his book, The Lawyers, Martin Mayer says that laymen put up with the faults of the profession "because we sense, we hope, that the law seeks justice".

as the committee deemed wise. More important than the formal statement of judicial standards is the informal influence on the judge of a sense of participation with his fellows in carrying forward the responsibility entrusted to him:[1]

> "There is a good deal of shallow talk that the judicial robe does not change the man within it. It does. The fact is that on the whole judges do lay aside private views in discharging their judicial functions. This is achieved through training, professional habits, self-discipline and that fortunate alchemy by which men are loyal to the obligation with which they are entrusted."

The individual's own sense of responsibility will inevitably affect the judge, as it does the lawyer in his work.[2]

SECTION 3. THE STANDARDS OF THE JUDGE

The standards of the judge are derived from a consideration of his functions and the setting in which he perofrms them.[1.5] His basic function is the determination of cases before him in accordance with law. He acts in a setting of controversy where one party must lose, and the loser is ready to blame the loss on anyone but himself. He is the representative of the state, and his actions and even demeanor will do much to determine the measure of respect in which the court is held. Three of his standards will be mentioned, independence from distorting influence, firmness, and consideration of others in the conduct of his office.

1. Justice Frankfurter in Public Utilities Commission v. Pollak, 343 U.S. 451, 466, 72 S.Ct. 813, 822 (1952).

2. Cf. supra pp. 57–9.

1.5 One hundred forty-four trial judges gave Professor Maurice Rosenberg their views on the qualities most important in their work. The six leading qualities given are: (1) moral courage, (2) decisiveness, (3) reputation for fairness and uprightness, (4) patience, (5) good health, physical and mental, (6) consideration for others. Rosenberg, The Qualities of Justices— Are They Strainable?, 44 Tex.L.

Rev. 1063 (1966). The controlling role of the trial judge and his needed qualities are discussed in H. Jones, The Courts, the Public and the Law Explosion 130 & 136 (1965).

The drafting of a new code of ethics for judges was entrusted in 1969 by the American Bar Association to a committee of nine lawyers and judges under the chairmanship of Chief Justice Roger J. Traynor of the Supreme Court of California with Professor E. Wayne Thode as Reporter. A companion project to be undertaken by another committee is the reformulation of the Standards of Judicial Administration.

Independence

Independence is the first quality of the judge. He must be free of any influence which might distort his judgment. He should be impartial, free of fear of personal liability for his actions as judge, and free of fear of loss of office.

Independence: Impartiality. Impartiality is for the judge what loyalty is for the lawyer, the essential quality. Partiality might come from personal interest in the subject of the controversy or family relationship to the parties or the attorneys. It might come from bias or prejudice as to the parties or their lawyers or from prior participation in the controversy.[2]

Disqualification for interest is rigorously applied. An Ohio statute which made the income of a petty criminal judge turn on fees from convicted defendants was struck down under the Fourteenth Amendment. In reviewing the law on the subject Chief Justice Taft said:[3]

> "There was at the common law the greatest sensitiveness over the existence of any pecuniary interest, however small or infinitesimal, in the justices of the peace."

A similar sensitiveness has been felt in civil cases. After a verdict was returned for the defendant in an action against a large corporation the judge recalled what he had not been conscious of during the trial, that he owned as trustee a small number of shares of stock in the corporation. When his ownership was brought to his attention, he informed counsel of the fact. The judgment was vacated and a new trial granted.[4] The appellate court emphasized the two purposes supporting the principle of disqualification: to help assure a fair trial, and to protect public confidence in the integrity of the judicial process.[4.5]

The courts have been less strict in applying the principle of disqualification for alleged bias as to the parties or their lawyers. The same appellate court which vacated the judgment because of the interest of the judge through minor stock ownership

---

2. A Federal statute provides:

"Interest of justice or judge. Any justice or judge of the United States shall disqualify himself in any case in which he has a substantial interest, has been of counsel, is or has been a material witness, or is so related to or connected with any party or his attorney as to render it improper, in his opinion, for him to sit on the trial, appeal, or other proceeding therein." 28 U.S.C.A. § 455.

3. Tumey v. Ohio, 273 U.S. 510, 525 (1927).

4. Tatum v. Southern Pacific Co., 250 Cal.App.2d 40, 58 Cal.Rptr. 238 (1967), Annot., 25 A.L.R.3d 1331 (1969).

4.5 The relation of a federal judge to a family foundation dominated by a former client whose actions were under intensive federal investigation was the subject of ABA Informal Opinion Number 1114, 7/24/69. The Committee on Professional Ethics expressed the view that the conduct of the judge was contrary to the Canons of Judicial Ethics.

refused to disqualify itself when the appellant alleged the whole panel was biased against him and his client, the court finding that its members were in no way biased.[5] This less stringent attitude on disqualification for bias has been explained because disqualification on this ground may often be sought as maneuver to take the case from a severe judge to a lenient one.[6] Even so it is better to apply a principle of ready disqualification on this ground, too. A statute which provided for the disqualification of a judge on the mere filing of an affidavit of prejudice by a lawyer has been upheld as not an undue interference with the judicial function.[7] An appellate court which failed to find a judge legally disqualified for bias intimated he should disqualify himself, stating that self-disqualification might be employed when not required.[8]

At common law the relationship of counsel to the judge was not a ground for disqualification.[9] It is wiser to go beyond what the English law required. Mr. Justice Tom Clark resigned from the Supreme Court of the United States when his son, Mr. Ramsey Clark, became Attorney General, and would have to appear before the Court. Conversely when Mr. Charles Evans Hughes became Chief Justice of the United States, his son, Mr. Charles Evans Hughes, Jr., resigned his office as Solicitor General of the United States. This sensitiveness helps to assure the appearance as well as the fact of impartiality.

In the conduct of a case the judge must, of course, be impartial, "a disinterested and objective participant in the proceedings." [10] This does not require that he be silent. In the federal courts,[11]

> "A trial judge is not 'a mere moderator'; his function extends to necessary assistance to 'the inexperienced laymen

5. Shakin v. Board of Medical Examiners, 234 Cal.App.2d 102, 62 Cal. Rptr. 274 (1967), Annot., 23 A.L.R. 3d 1416 (1969), cert. denied 390 U.S. 410 (1968).

6. Wolfson v. Palmieri, 396 F.2d 121 (2d Cir. 1968).

7. U'Ren v. Bagley, 118 Or. 77, 245 P. 1074, Annot., 46 A.L.R. 1173 (1926).

8. "[A] judge may wish to recuse himself although a legally sufficient affidavit of bias and prejudice could not be presented against him." Wolfson v. Palmieri, 396 F. 2d 121, 125 (2d Cir. 1968). It has been held, though the cases are divided, that a judge may be disbarred even during his period of office. In re Stolen, 193 Wis. 602, 214 N.W. 379, 216 N.W. 127 (1927), Annot., 55 A.L.R. 1373 (1928). It has been held further that a judge may not engage in the practice of law because practice is incompatible with his judicial responsibility. Bassi v. Langloss, 22 Ill.2d 190, 174 N.E.2d 682 (1961), Annot., 89 A.L.R. 2d 886 (1963).

9. See Ex parte Clanahan, 261 Ala. 87, 72 So.2d 833, Annot., 50 A.L.R.2d 143 (1954). A careful discussion of the subject in the context of disqualification generally is J. Frank, "Disqualification of Judges," 56 Yale L.J. 605 (1947).

10. United States v. Barbour, 420 F. 2d 1319 (D.C.Cir.1969).

11. Id. at pp. 1320–1321.

> in the [jury] box in finding the truth in the confusing con-
> flicts of contradictory evidence.' "

In the case quoted from the judge's questioning of witnesses was
held proper as it was directed "toward much needed clarification
rather than challenges of the testimony."

The outside income and activities of the judge should be so
limited that he will not be or seem to be affected by them in his
decisions. It has been urged, further, that they should be so limited as not to impair the public image of him as wholly devoted to
his judicial work. For the latter reason there was criticism of the
designation of Justice Jackson as chief prosecutor in the Nuremberg Trial, and even question, too, of the action of Chief Justice
Warren in accepting the chairmanship of the commission of inquiry into the assassination of President Kennedy. There was
criticism of the action of two members of the Supreme Court of
the United States in giving testimony to the good reputation of
the defendant in a conspicuous espionage trial.[12] There is still opportunity, surely, for the cooperation of judges in the improvement of the administration of law.[13]

Bias is to be distinguished from preconceptions. In a case in
which the court refused to disqualify a special master because of
alleged bias Judge Jerome Frank discussed the inevitability of
preconceptions and the accompanying duty of self-scrutiny by
the judge so that he may discount his prejudices.[14]

Independence: Exemption from Personal Liability: The appropriate independence of a judge calls for freedom from fear as
well as from favor. So a judge is given exemption from civil liability for alleged wrongful acts done in his judicial capacity. In
Bradley v. Fisher [1] a lawyer brought an action against a judge
who had disbarred him, "wilfully, maliciously, corruptly, and un-
lawfully." The court held the action would not lie: [2]

> "For it is a general principle of the highest importance to
> the proper administration of justice that a judicial officer,
> in exercising the authority vested in him, shall be free to
> act upon his own convictions, without apprehension of per-
> sonal consequences to himself."

12. See "Report of the Special Committee [of the American Bar Asso-
ciation] on the Propriety of Judges
Appearing as Witnesses," 36
A.B.A.J. 630 (1950). Of course a
judge may not appear as a witness in a trial before him. Brashier
v. State, 197 Miss. 237, 20 So.2d 65,
Annot., 157 A.L.R. 315 (1944).

13. Editorial, "Judges Should Not
Become Monastic," 53 Judicature 50
(1969.)

14. In re J. P. Linahan, Inc., 138
F.2d 650, 653 (2d Cir. 1943).

1. 80 U.S. (13 Wall.) 335 (1871).

2. Id. at 347.

There is no liability even though the act complained of is alleged to have been done corruptly.[3] The troubling and slippery word, "jurisdiction," is at times used as a limitation. A justice of the peace was held liable in false imprisonment to one committed to jail pursuant to a trial held outside the territorial limits of the justice's jurisdiction.[4] In interpreting "jurisdiction" for this purpose, the broad policy of judicial independence should be the principal guide.[5]

The protection given to the independence of the judge is for like reason extended in large measure to the advocate. Judge Learned Hand stated the reasons of policy in a case which granted the full measure of immunity to the United States Attorney General: [6]

> "[A] United States attorney, if not a judicial officer, is at least a quasi-judicial officer, of the government. . . .
> The public interest requires that persons occupying such important positions and so closely identified with the judicial departments of the Government should speak and act freely and fearlessly in the discharge of their important official functions. . . . [O]fficers of the Department of Justice, when engaged in prosecuting private persons enjoy the same absolute privileges as judges."

The Supreme Court of Oregon, by divided vote, held a state prosecuting attorney was immune from liability for malicious prosecution.[7]

The lawyer in private practice has been given protection in lesser measure. He has been held not liable in false imprisonment, provided his actions on behalf of a client which caused the illegal imprisonment were done in good faith.[8] Again the reason given for the protection was that the lawyer is

> "an officer of the court and fearless discharge of his duties as lawyer is in the interest of the administration of justice."

3. Berry v. Smith, 148 Va. 424, 139 S.E. 252 (1927), Annot., 55 A.L.R. 282 (1928).

4. Cox v. Perkins, 299 Ky. 470, 185 S.W.2d 954 (1945), Annot. 173 A.L.R. 802 (1948).

5. Cf. Bradley v. Fisher, supra note 1, at 353.

There is some intimation in the cases that the exemption should be limited to judges of courts of record or of general jurisdiction. This limitation appears clearly un-wise when a consideration of the possible threats to judges of "lower courts" is brought to mind.

6. Gregoire v. Biddle, 177 F.2d 579 (2d Cir. 1949).

7. Watts v. Gerking, 111 Or. 641, 228 P. 135 (1924), Annot., 34 A.L.R. 1504 (1925).

8. Langen v. Borkowski, 188 Wis. 277, 206 N.W. 181 (1925), Annot., 43 A.L.R. 639 (1926).

He has been held entitled to a qualified privilege against liability in defamation for statements made in oral argument[9] or in a brief.[10]

A bar association authorized by law to institute proceedings to halt the unlawful practice of law was held to enjoy immunity for such action, though there was disagreement in the court as to the extent of the immunity.[11]

Firmness

Firmness is essential for the lawyer and for the judge in their respective roles. The lawyer has the privilege and the duty to allege any errors harmful to his client which he believes the judge committed in the conduct of a trial, and he may not be held in contempt of court for protecting the client's rights even when the allegations in his pleadings reflect on the judge.[1] The judge has the privilege and the duty to hold lawyers within the bounds of reasonableness in their cooperative combativeness, through which, under the adversary system, the truth will be brought out. For excessive actions the judge may find the lawyer in contempt of court—a subject so extensive in its ramifications as to be worthy of a book itself.[2] The contempt power of the courts has been limited by the decisions of the Supreme Court of the United States in a desire to assure that lawyers, especially the representatives of the hated, shall not be unduly hampered in their work.[3]

Consideration and Courtesy

"Of all the mighty changes that have taken place in the nineteenth century, the greatest change has been in the tone of the administration of both the civil and the criminal law. The manners of our law courts have marvelously improved. Formerly judges browbeat the prisoners, jeered at their efforts to defend themselves, and censured juries who honestly did their duty. Formerly, too, counsel bullied the witnesses and perverted what they said. Now the attitude and temper of Her Majesty's judges towards the parties, witnesses, and

---

9. Wall v. Blalock, 245 N.C. 232, 95 S.E.2d 450, Annot., 61 A.L.R.2d 1300 (1958).

10. Waldo v. Morrison, 220 La. 1006, 58 So.2d 210 (1952), Annot., 32 A.L.R.2d 423 (1953).

11. Dacey v. New York County Lawyers' Ass'n, 423 F.2d 188 (2d Cir. 1969).

1. Blankenbaker v. State, 201 Ind. 142, 166 N.E. 265 (1929). For a description of Erskine's notable firmness in the Dean of St. Asaph's Case, see 8 Campbell, Lives of the Lord Chancellors, Ch. CLXXVIII (4th ed. 1878).

2. See, e. g., R. Goldfarb, The Contempt Power (1963).

3. Holt v. Virginia, 381 U.S. 131, 85 S.Ct. 375 (1965).

prisoners alike has wholly changed and the Bar too behave like gentlemen. This is due partly to the improved education of the Bar, partly no doubt to an omnipresent press; but still more to Her Majesty's judges." [1]

Thus a barrister described the improvement of the administration of law in England in the 1800s. The manners of American judges and their tone can do no less for the courts in this country.

Consideration and courtesy are due especially to the poor devil with whom fate has dealt harshly. A woman defendant has the constitutional right, so the Supreme Court of the United States held, to be addressed by counsel in the usual courteous form, "Miss." [2] If the poor devil, on interrogation or sentencing were addressed by the judge as "Mr. Smith," not "Jim," he might square back his shoulders and say to himself. "Yes, I am Mr. Smith, not just Jim. From now on, I am going to act accordingly."

Consideration is surely due also to one's associates on the bench in the form in which disagreement is expressed. Dissenting opinions which read like excerpts from personal debate within the court weaken their influence as well as that of the court. The harm they do to the court may be lessened by recalling Lord Bowen's proposed amendment as evidence that judges recognize their failings. On the diamond jubilee of Queen Victoria, Her Majesty's judges drew up a sonorous address, beginning "Conscious as we are of our own shortcomings." Lord Bowen suggested that the beginning be amended to read, "Conscious as we are of one another's shortcomings."

The duties of reciprocal consideration and respect of court and counsel are well stated in the old Canons.

> "A judge should be courteous to counsel, especially to those who are young and inexperienced, and also to all others appearing or concerned in the administration of justice in the court." [3]

> "It is the duty of the lawyer to maintain towards the Courts a respectful attitude . . . ." [4]

Disruptive Tactics*

Our system of administration of law calls for a large measure of cooperation by the participants. The fact that such coopera-

1. W. Odger, In a Century of Law Reform 41–42 (1901).

2. See infra supra pp. 305–6.

3. ABA Canons of Judicial Ethics No. 10.

4. ABA Canons of Professional Ethics No. 1.

* See also Political Trials, infra pp. 296–99.

tion is usually given is attested by the small number of cases in which a lack of cooperation is asserted. When it is refused the judge may take the measures necessary to make the system function. State of Illinois v. Allen,[1] illustrates the judge's powers. A defendant charged with armed robbery declined the court appointed counsel so as to conduct his own defense. He prolonged the voir dire examination, was boisterous and continued

1. 397 U.S. 337 (1970).

An accused conducting his own defense sought to "denounce, insult and slander the judge and to paralyze the trial." After the verdict of guilty was returned and before the sentence was imposed, the trial judge pronounced the defendant guilty of criminal contempt on eleven occasions and sentenced him to imprisonment for from one to two years for each offense. The Supreme Court of the United States vacated the sentences and remanded the case for disposition before another judge. Mr. Justice Douglas, quoting Chief Justice Taft, said:

" '[W]here conditions do not make it impracticable, or where the delay may not injure public or private right, a judge called upon to act in a case of contempt by personal attack upon him, may, without flinching from his duty, properly ask that one of his fellow judges take his place.' " Continuing, Mr. Justice Douglas stated: "[B]y reason of the Due Process Clause of the Fourteenth Amendment a defendant in a criminal contempt proceeding should be given a public trial before a judge other than the one reviled by the contemnor." Mayberry v. State of Pennsylvania, —— U.S. ——, 91 S.Ct. 499, at pp. 504, 505 (January 20, 1971.)

A group of Welsh university students disrupted a trial in London by singing and shouting in Welsh to call attention to their cause,—the preservation of the Welsh language. The trial judge found them in contempt of court and sentenced some to three months in jail. The Court of Appeal gave first priority to the appeal and heard it one week later, for "our law puts the liberty of the subject before all else." The Court affirmed the conviction for contempt, shortened the martyrdom

of imprisonment to the period already served, and bound the appellants over for a year to keep the peace. Lord Denning said: "Let the students demonstrate, if they please, for the causes in which they believe. Let them make their protests as they will, but they must do it by lawful means and not by unlawful. If they strike at the course of justice in this land . . . they strike at the roots of society itself, and they bring down that which protects them. It is only by the maintenance of law and order that they are privileged to be students and to study and live in peace." Morris v. The Crown Office, [1970] 1 All Eng. Rep. 1079, 1081, 1083.

In 1970 the American College of Trial Lawyers issued a Statement of "Principles as to the Disruption of the Judicial Process". It was drafted by a special committee with Mr. Whitney North Seymour as chairman and was approved by the Regents of the College. The twelve principles deal with: (1) Basic considerations, as equal justice and fair trial. (2) The lawyer: his obligations; protection of him through prompt review of a contempt sentence; protection against him as by discipline and by scrutiny of applications to appear pro hac vice. (3) The judge: his obligations and powers; appropriate measures by him; possible disciplinary measures against him. (4) Litigants and spectators.

In 1971 a report on disruption in the courtroom had been submitted for consideration to the Advisory Committee on the Judge's Function of the American Bar Association Project on Standards for Criminal Justice. See the editorial, "The Disruptive Lawyer in the Courtroom", 57 A.B.A.J. 48 (1971).

to talk, saying "There's not going to be no trial." The judge asked the court appointed counsel to protect the defendant's rights and had the defendant physically excluded from the courtroom, informing him that he could return whenever he would behave. The accused remained outside the courtroom during most of the voir dire examination and the prosecution's case, but was in the room during his defense. He was convicted. He sought release from imprisonment on the ground that the right of confrontation under the Sixth and Fourteenth Amendments is absolute and his removal from the courtroom for disruptive tactics invalidated his conviction. The Supreme Court of the United States held that the accused through his conduct had lost his right to be present throughout the trial and that the conviction was valid. Speaking to the power of the judge Mr. Justice Black stated:

> "We believe that trial judges confronted with disruptive, contumacious, stubbornly defiant defendants must be given sufficient discretion to meet the circumstances of each case."

He mentioned three methods which the court might use depending on the circumstances,

> "(1) bind and gag him thereby keeping him present; (2) cite him for contempt; (3) take him out of the courtroom until he promises to conduct himself properly."

In the actual case, the Justice said,

> "The record shows that the Illinois judge at all times conducted himself with that dignity, decorum and patience that befits a judge."

Mr. Justice Brennan concurred specially and, referring to President Lincoln's often quoted question, said our nation could not endure "if we allow our precious heritage of ordered liberty to be ripped apart amid the sound and fury of our time." Mr. Justice Douglas, concurring specially on the ground that the case was stale, would have deferred dealing with the fundamental elements of "the social compact" until one or the other of the troubling cases of our time is presented, either "the political trials" with the prosecution of unpopular minorities, or else another type of case:

> "[T]rials used by minorities to destroy the existing constitutional system and bring on repressive measures. Radicals on the left historically have used those tactics to incite the extreme right . . . The left in that role is the provacateur."

SECTION 4. SELECTION, TENURE AND REMOVAL
OF JUDGES

A personal question is a useful beginning. When the reader is in his forties or fifties and has built up a good practice, some friends ask permission to propose him for judicial office. What form of selection and what measure of tenure would incline him to accept, or else to decline the proposal? He knows that if he goes on the bench, his old clients will retain other lawyers. If he later leaves the bench and resumes practice, he must build up a clientele anew. The question may be put in general instead of personal terms: what form of selection and what measure of tenure are best suited to place and to keep on the bench men with the qualities called for in the public interest?

Controversy over selection and tenure of judges is as old as our nation. The Declaration of Independence gives as a ground of complaint against King George III:

> "He has made judges dependent on his will alone, for the tenure of their offices, and the amount and payment of their salaries."

The complaint and controversy continue today, though not with such bitterness. Our discussion, after describing three methods of selection, will then raise several interrelated subjects, as, the popular election of judges, the role of the bar, and tenure and removal.

Three Methods Mentioned [1]

Appointment by the executive is one method used. A requirement accompanying executive appointment may be approval of the appointment by another body, as approval by the Senate of a nominee to a federal court. A merit of the appointive method is that it vests the power of selection in a person who (unlike a party boss) is identified by and responsible to the electorate and who can inform himself on the qualities of aspirants. It does not remove the selection from politics, for the executive ordinarily keeps in mind the political associations of his appointees. Another method is selection by the legislature, which tends to keep the choice within the circle of present or past members of the legislature. A third method is the career method, with some men of law choosing the judiciary as their field of work and enjoying protection and advancement under a civil service plan.

---

1. On methods used in various countries see E. Haynes, The Selection and Tenure of Judges Ch. V & VI (1944); E. Stason, Judicial Selection Around the World, 41 J. Am. Jud.Soc'y 134 (1958).

The method is employed in countries of continental Europe.[2] It appears not to be used in this country except as to hearing examiners of administrative commissions.

Popular Election. The method of popular election was given its great impetus by Jacksonian Democracy. In his first message to Congress, President Andrew Jackson stated that the citizens of the Republic generally are fitted to hold almost any public office and that tenure of office should be brief. The statement surely does not apply to the functions and qualities of the judge, especially his independence and firmness. These qualities had been stressed in the thoughtful discussion in The Federalist Papers half a century earlier.[3] Jacksonian Democracy meant as to public offices, "To the victor belong the spoils." The spoils system proved so harmful that everywhere it has been supplanted by a system of security in office, say, by a protective civil service, except as to the most important office, that of the judge.

The elective system impairs the independence of the judge. It is sufficient proof of this inferiority of the elective system to observe the contrast between elective judges and appointive judges in protecting the disadvantaged when public passions are aroused against the accused.

Under the elective system the choice is not made in an informed way. Few voters can evaluate judicial candidates. When a judge's name appears on a partisan ballot, he will almost surely share the fate of the generality of his party candidates. In large cities the nomination may be made by the party boss with usefulness to the party, or in the bad old days even outright bribery,[4] as the criterion of choice. When the candidate cannot depend on the political party for needed votes, he may resort to hypocrisy to make himself known to the voters.[5] The Canons of

---

2. See R. Ensor, Courts and Judges in France, Germany and England (1933).

3. See The Federalist, No. 78. On the development of methods in this country see Niles, The Popular Election of Judges in Historical Perspective, 21 Record of N.Y.C.B.A. 523 (1966).

4. The sale of judicial offices by Boss Croker of Tammany Hall is described in G. Martin, Causes and Conflicts: The Centennial History of The Association of the Bar of the City of New York 1870–1970 167–171 (1970). It should not be inferred that this system led to a sale of justice by the judges. The purchase of the office may have

led to a feeling of independence by the judges in the long term of office following. Their sense of independence in the offices they brought is somewhat like the position of a great reformer of English law, Sir Samuel Romilly, who refused the offer of designation to Parliament by a friend, the owner of a rotten borough, and under an evil system bought a seat so as to preserve his independence. An able young head of the Democratic organization in Manhattan has described the present day methods of selection of nominees. E. Costikyan, Behind Closed Doors (1966).

5. A San Francisco judge, as a colleague on the bench wrote, had the practice of attending the funerals

Judicial Ethics have difficulty, indeed, in reconciling judicial independence and freedom from undue obligations incurred in a campaign, with the means used to obtain the needed votes.[6]

A major block in the way of reconsideration of methods of selecting judges is an unexamined belief that the popular election of judges is called for by "democracy" and that elected judges are more "liberal" than appointed ones. "Democracy" is a philosophy of government and not a particular form of government. It leaves room for the form of selection suited to putting into office the men best equipped to carry the burdens of the office. Professor Evan Haynes, writing a generation ago, showed that the vague view that elected judges are more "liberal" than appointed ones is wrong.[7] Later experience has confirmed his conclusion.

Is there, nevertheless, something of substance to the widely held feeling that the people should have a voice in the selection and rejection of judges? Judges do not merely decide controversies. In the process of decision they also make and remake the law. The judges created the common law in England, and American judges continue to define or even recreate our fundamental law when they interpret the Constitution. It may be argued that in a democracy the people should have a voice in the choice of officials with such power. On the other side it can be urged that it was the very purpose of our written constitutions to deny power to the majority when the power is sought to be exercised in a way contrary to constitutional guarantees as determined and applied by independent judges.

The Nonpartisan Court Plan. The criticisms of the different methods of judicial selection bring to mind Winston Churchill's observation: "Democracy is the worst system of government ever devised—except all the others." The "nonpartisan court plan" seeks to give appropriate weight to the relevant factors in the selection of judges and also to give security of tenure. It calls for a three stage process. First, there is created a nominating committee made up of representatives of interested groups, say, the chief justice of the supreme court, two lawyers elected to the committee by the bar, and two laymen appointed by the gov-

---

of complete strangers since his name and presence would come to be known to the mourners. When at lunch with colleagues of another court, a judge happened to drop his wallet on the table and a batch of membership cards in "fraternal" organizations fell out. Flushing a bit, as he valued the esteem of his associates, he said: "These are my social security cards."

6. See ABA Comm. on Professional Ethics, Opinions, No. 312, 50. A.B.A.J. 998 (1964); Anderson, Ethical Problems of Lawyers and Judges in Election Campaigns, 50 A.B.A.J. 819 (1964); Blakslee, Lawyers and Elections, 54 A.B.A.J. 410 (1968).

7. See E. Haynes, supra note 1, Chapter VII.

ernor. Next, the nominating committee designates a panel of three possible nominees for the office and so informs the governor. Finally, the governor chooses and appoints to the office one of the men on the panel. The year following his appointment the judge is voted on by the electorate. He has no named opponent, however, and the question is only, "Shall Judge [John Doe] continue in office." If the vote is in the affirmative, the judge remains in office for the term the law provides. At the end of the term his name again goes on the ballot with a similar question as to him. If the vote of the electorate is against him, he goes out of office, and his successor is chosen in the same way.

The plan, originating in Missouri in 1940, has the support of the American Bar Association and the American Judicature Society. It is the subject of a careful study in the state of origin, which concludes that a majority of lawyers believe it does improve the quality of the bench.[8]

The Role of the Bar in the Selection Process. At first mention it might appear that the bar should have a predominant share in the selection of judges, since lawyers know best the qualities of other lawyers. There is more to it than that. An able federal judge, while agreeing that the bar knows well the legal competence of their members, stated that there is a danger of lawyers "overstressing professionalism, of looking to the head exclusively, and not to the heart," [1]—say they would approve a Taney or a Hughes but never a Warren—and that there would be an overstress on conservatism, too.

The organized bar has made known its opinions on aspirants or nominees in various ways, as by a bar poll [2] or the report of a committee. In recent years the Attorney General has requested the views of the American Bar Association committee on the judiciary on prospective nominees to the federal judiciary.[3]

8. R. Watson & R. Downing, The Politics of the Bench and the Bar: Judicial Selection Under the Missouri Nonpartisan Court Plan (1969). A similar method was used voluntarily by Governor Scranton of Pennsylvania in the appointment of judges. The number of able lawyers willing to accept appointment, however, was disappointingly small. Since the use of the method was the voluntary action of this governor, his appointees would have to stand for reelection against partisan opposition when their terms expired. See Segal, Nonpartisan Selection of Judges: Pennsylvania's Experiment, 50 A.B.A.J. 830 (1964).

1. Clark & Trubek, The Creative Role of the Judge: Restraint and Freedom in the Common Law Tradition, 71 Yale L.J. 255, 272 (1961).

2. It was within the power of an integrated State Bar to poll its membership on whether a nominee for a federal district judgeship within the state was qualified. Axel v. State Bar of Wisconsin, 21 Wis.2d 661 (1963).

3. See J. Grossman, Lawyers and Judges: The ABA and the Politics of Judicial Selection (1965). It has been stated unofficially that the Attorney General has with-

The controversy in 1969–70 over nominees to the Supreme Court of the United States led the American Bar Association committee to review its role and methods. The committee concluded, that its work should continue since the knowledge that an evaluation will be made encourages the selection of professionally better qualified nominees, and that the Attorney General should be requested to give adequate time for committee consideration before nomination. With special reference to reports to the Senate Committee on the Judiciary on nominees to the Supreme Court the bar association committee stated that it should continue to limit its evaluation to professional qualifications ("integrity, judicial temperament and professional competence") and should not extend it to political and idealogical factors.[4]

Tenure and Removal

The tenure of judges is either for a period of years—as low as two years and as long as fourteen—or else during good behaviour or until a stated age is reached. Security of tenure is more important for an independent judiciary than the method of selection. A judge with a short term will, consciously or unconsciously, think of his next election. A judge for an unlimited term is free of this necessity and he can be his best self from the start. The condemnation in the Declaration of Independence quoted above is directed, it will be noted, to the insecurity of the tenure of the royal judges in the colonies and their consequent lack of independence.

Security of tenure is consistent with removal for good cause. In the federal system the only stated method of removal is impeachment. Its cumbersomeness had led to the proposals for simpler methods, which would safeguard the essential independence of the judiciary while making it more practicable to remove judges who misconduct themselves or are mentally or physically incompetent. In 1970 the American Bar Association endorsed such a method.[1] The Department of Justice, after a careful review of the English and American precedents, concluded that

drawn from further consideration about one-fourth of the persons he mentioned to the committee as possible nominees.

4. Walsh, Selection of Supreme Court Justices, 56 A.B.A.J. 555 (1970).

In July, 1970, Attorney General Mitchell informed the officers of the American Bar Association by letter that in making recommendations to the President for appointment to the Supreme Court of the United States he would take into consideration "the professional judgment of a candidate's fellow lawyers, as expressed to the standing committee of the most broadly based organization of the national bar."

1. See Resolution adopted by the House of Delegates, 56 A.B.A.J. 373–74 (1970).

"judicial proceedings may be utilized to determine whether a judge has violated the requirements of good behavior." [2]

Education for Judges

Special opportunities of education for judges were initiated in the 1950s. They began at New York University with a seminar of appellate judges [1] with the aid of Professor Robert Leflar, who had been an appellate judge. In the 1960s the opportunities were much expanded under the sponsorship of the Section of Judicial Administration of the American Bar Association. The opportunities, voluntary by the participants, have been extended to the judges of trial courts and of special courts,[2] and are available prior to or during the period of service on the bench.

2. To a Subcommittee of the Committee on the Judiciary of the United States Senate which was considering the Judicial Reform Act (S. 1506, 91st Congress) Assistant Attorney General William H. Rehnquist stated: "The Department of Justice therefore agrees with the theory underlying Title I of S. 1506, *viz.* that under the Constitution impeachment is not the exclusive method for the removal of judges, and that judicial proceedings may be utilized to determine whether a judge has violated the requirement of good behavior."

The Constitution of Illinois, Article 6, § 18, provides that a judge may be retired, suspended or removed for cause by a commission of five judges after notice and hearing according to rules of procedure established by the State Supreme Court. The Supreme Court provided by rule for the creation and procedure of the Illinois Courts Commission with powers including "the removal for cause" of a judge. Smith-Hurd Ill.Ann.Stat. ch. 110A, § 51. The Illinois Supreme Court has rejected the appeal by a judge from a decision of the Courts Commission which removed him from the Circuit Court Bench for "conduct unbecoming a judge", in part because he invoked the privilege

against self-incrimination before a grand jury. See 54 Judicature 171 (1970). In Napolitano v. Ward, 317 F.Supp. 83, 85 (1970) a federal court declined to grant a preliminary injunction to prevent nomination of judicial candidates to fill the consequent vacancy, saying:

"The spectacle of a judge invoking the Fifth Amendment is not a pretty one, for a judge owes an obligation to cooperate in promoting the enforcement of the law. Unwillingness to fulfill that duty, as shown by reluctance to aid in a grand jury investigation of suspected criminal activity, may properly be considered to be evidence of a disregard of this obligation."

1. The initiation of the programs and their expansion have been described by Chief Justice Burger and by one of the founders, Professor Karlen. See Burger, Schools for Judges, 33 F.R.D. 139 (1963); Karlen, Judicial Education, 52 A.B.A.J. 1049 (1966).

2. The development of the programs and "the unabashed eagerness of American judges to improve their capacities by in-serving learning" are discussed in Rosenberg, "Judging Goes to College," 52 A.B.A.J. 342 (1966).

SECTION 5.   JUDICIAL ADMINISTRATION

"Judicial administration" sounds dry, almost repellant. When changed to its true form, "the administration of justice" its importance is manifest. Its principal bearing is not on the judge. It is on the parties whom the judge exists to serve and who may have justice denied because delayed, and on the jurors and witnesses who may fritter away their time in idleness.

The nature of the problems of judicial administration is well indicated by two addresses to the American Bar Association sixty years apart, one by a young prairie lawyer, the other by the Chief Justice of the United States. In 1906 a younger lawyer from Nebraska, Roscoe Pound, gave an address of long lasting importance on "The Causes of the Popular Dissatisfaction with the Administration of Justice." Dean Pound, as he was to become, stated the broad scope of his inquiry:

> "[T]he causes of dissatisfaction with the administration of justice may be grouped under four main heads: (1) Causes for dissatisfaction with *any* legal system, (2) causes lying in the peculiarities of our Anglo-American legal system, (3) causes lying in our American judicial organization and procedure, and (4) popular impatience of restraint.[1] "

The address was resented at the time by some members of the Association because of its critical tone.[2] This attitude is no longer dominant. The most effective leadership in the improvement of judicial administration is given by the bar, especially through the Section on Judicial Administration of the American Bar Association and the American Judicature Society.

An address by Chief Justice Burger to the American Bar Association in 1970, beginning with a tribute to Dean Pound's address, was a continuation of the subject in more pointed form, directed as its title indicates to "The State of the Judiciary".[3] The Chief Justice, mentioned, first, some of the increasing demands on the federal courts. Social and economic changes have naturally led to new kinds of laws and cases for the courts. The revolution in criminal justice, beginning in the 1930's, brought additional burdens. The trial of a criminal case took twice as long as it did ten years earlier, and the time lag between indictment and sentence had doubled. The combination of two benefi-

1. 29 A.B.A. Rep. pt. 1, at 395 (1906).

2. The address is reprinted and the criticisms described in Wigmore,

Roscoe Pound's Address of 1906, 20 J.Am.Jud.Soc'y 176 (1937).

3. Burger, The State of the Judiciary 1970, 56 A.B.A.J. 929 (1970).

cent developments in the District of Columbia, the liberal release of an accused without bail and the prompt aid of court-appointed counsel, brought unanticipated results. With the accused
free without bail and always pressing his government-paid counsel to postpone trial, the proportion of pleas of guilty had
dropped so much that the judges assigned to the criminal calendar had tripled in number.

As a first step the Chief Justice urged that court administrators be provided who can bring fairness and efficiency in handling the business of the courts. He called for careful studies as
a preliminary to changes in court structure, in the relation of
the federal and state courts, and in criminal procedure. High
on his list, as in his earlier writings,[4] he urged a better chance for
the convicted men:

> "The system of criminal justice must be viewed as a process
> embracing every phase from crime prevention through the
> correctional system. We can no longer limit our responsibil-
> ity to providing defense services in the judicial process, yet
> continue to be miserly with the needs of correctional institu-
> tions and probation and parole services." [5]

In an address while active in the American Bar Association's
Project on the Administration of Criminal Justice Judge Burger
stressed that the constitutional right of an accused to counsel
shows that defense counsel no less than prosecutors are essential
participants in law administration.[6] Defense counsel are members of Uncle Sam's Loyal Opposition, loyal to Uncle Sam as well
as to his own client. This requires, as Chief Justice Burger
again reminds us that:

> "[W]e must now make certain that lawyers are adequately
> trained, and that the representation is on a high profession-
> al basis. It is *professional* representation we promise to
> give—nothing more—and always with accepted standards of
> *conduct.*" [7]

So the standards of the profession are an integral part of the
administration of law under the Constitution.

Court administration deserves special mention because of the
developments under way. It is the business management of the
courts and their work, the analogue for the judiciary of office
management for a law firm. "The clogged calendars of some
courts," a trial judge wrote to the authors, "is due not to any

---

4. Burger, No Man Is An Island, 56
  A.B.A.J. 325 (1970).

5. Burger, supra note 3, at 934.

6. Burger, Counsel for the Prosecu-
  tion and the Defense Under the
  Minimum Standards, 8 Am.Crim.
  L.Q. 2 (1967).

7. Burger, supra note 3 at 934.

failure of judges to work but to the fact they are poor administrators." In state appellate courts poor administration is compounded where the chief justiceship with duties of administration is handed along as a badge of distinction to each member of the court in turn as he becomes the senior. It is worse still where it is passed around each year so that no consecutive system of management is possible.

The need for good court administration and the methods of meeting this need were expressed in a Handbook prepared by the Section of Judicial Administration of the American Bar Association of which Judge Philbrick McCoy was then the chairman:

> "The demands made upon modern courts require that the non-judicial function of the courts be administered by one judge who has power to assign judges within the system. In order to discharge the duties properly the administrative judge must have expert administrative assistance. Administrative personnel must always be subordinate to the judges they serve." [8]

A state with an effective system of management is New Jersey. Mr. Justice Brennan has told of the developments in that state's judiciary of which he was formerly a member.[9] The federal courts have as aids in their work the Administrative Office of the United States Courts and the Federal Judicial Center. Former Justice Tom C. Clark, the Director of the Center, has described the plans and hopes for the Center.[10]

---

8. The Improvement of the Administration of Justice 18 (4th ed. 1961). See also Excerpts from President's Commission [on Law Enforcement and the Administration of Justice] Report Relating to the Courts, 50 Judicature 239–240 (1967).

9. Brennan, The Administrative Judge—The Key to Effective Court Management, 45 J.Am.Jud.Soc'y 272 (1962).

10. Clark, The New Federal Judicial Center, 54 A.B.A.J. 743 (1968).

Part IV

THE LAWYER AND THE CLIENT

Chapter XIII

A CASE OFFERED

SECTION 1. INTRODUCTION

The first step in the establishment of the relation of attorney and client is a call by a layman on the lawyer asking him to take a case. At this stage the lawyer is free to accept or to decline it. The American lawyer is under no professional obligation as is the English barrister to take any case tendered on the payment of a proper fee. He will reject the case or he will take it, as the old Canons put it, "upon his own responsibility." [1]

A common misconception should be cleared away. The English rule calling for the acceptance of every case tendered does not apply to all lawyers. It applies only to the barrister, the advocate in court. It does not extend to the solicitor, the office lawyer,[2] who aids his client in shaping the future of his business and personal affairs, and on whom the client must call first in any litigation. One reason for the difference in the duty of acceptance is that the barrister knows the case has already been weighed and found deserving of court hearing by another lawyer, the solicitor, for the barrister may be retained only through the solicitor and not by the client directly. A more important reason is that the barrister is concerned only with past events and with working out the rights of the parties under law. A related reason is that given so eloquently by Erskine that the services of a barrister are essential to the protection of the rights of a citizen against the Crown and the State.[3]

The misconception in this country arises from the fact that the profession is not divided into the two parts, barristers and solicitors, with their recognized difference in standards as in England. The American lawyer has the full privileges of both

---

1. ABA Canons of Professional Ethics No. 31.

2. Q. Johnstone & Hopson, Lawyers and Their Work (1966) 384.

3. See infra p. 343.

224

advocacy and office work. He tends to think of his professional rights and obligations in terms of the advocate, and he may uncritically carry over to other parts of his work the standards developed and stated as to advocacy.

The discussion will first merely mention some affirmative factors which make for the acceptance of a case. Then it will raise the troubling factor of the injustice of the cause. Lastly, it will deal with a wide ranging factor which requires the rejection of the case, impairment of continuing loyalty.

SECTION 2. AFFIRMATIVE FACTORS

For obvious reasons the lawyer ordinarily accepts the case offered with an appropriate fee. The lawyer is earning his living from the fees of clients and he welcomes a new case. He has a sense of appreciation toward the person who values his services and seeks to retain him. He has the normal instinct of partisanship and he tends to believe and support the person who has sought him out and whom he will represent.

In addition there is a sense of personal and professional obligation toward the unfortunates who are either hated or unable to pay counsel and yet who need legal services. This sense of obligation has moved many lawyers to volunteer their services and readily to accept cases to which they are assigned.[1] To only a few of them do these clients express their esteem as did the Nazi saboteurs of World War II who at the end of their military commission trial and close to death wrote to their counsel:[2]

> "Being charged with serious offenses in war time we have been given a fair trial .　　.　　. Counsel .　　.　　. has represented our case as American officers unbiased, better than we could expect and probably risking the indignation of public opinion. We thank our defense counsel."

This sense of obligation has led lawyers to accept burdensome individual cases and also to aid in the development of various methods discussed later of making legal services available.[3]

---

1. See infra p. 339ff.

2. See Royall, American Freedom and the Law: Fighting the Communist Menace, 40 A.B.A.J. 559, 560, 561 (1954).

3. See Chapter XVII infra p. 311ff, Methods of Making Legal Services Available.

SECTION 3.   INJUSTICE

"A lawyer has no business with the justice or injustice of the cause which he undertakes unless his client asks his opinion, and then he is bound to give it honestly.   The justice or injustice of the cause is to be decided by the judge." [1]

Dr. Johnson in this often quoted statement to the young Scotch advocate, Boswell, had in mind the barrister in a single cause.   He might have been troubled by the case following.

A man indicted for the possession of narcotics retains a lawyer to defend him.   At an early conference the client says he hopes the case can be cleared up quickly for so long as it is pending the police will watch him and hamper his business.   With appropriate epithets he states that what the District Attorney said will come true when the case is won.   "The rats will come out of their holes."   He continues that he has always disliked being prosecuted for it is embarassing to his business and disagreeable to his family, so he wishes the lawyer later to work out plans under which he and his retailers will be within the law; and if that cannot be done then to develop methods which will protect him from detection.

At first the case appeared to be the defense of a man accused of a single crime.   It reveals itself as the defense of a professional criminal whose acquittal will mean certain return to his trade and aid and encouragement to his fellows in their continuing ruin of others.   It turns into desired help in developing plans which will put these activities within the law or else give them better concealment.

When an offered case raises doubts because of injustice the major competing factors are two.   The first, stated on the side of the client, is the right under our political and legal system for every man to have his rights adjudged according to law.   For such a judgment a lawyer is essential.   The second, as to the lawyer, is the responsibility of every individual for his work.   The lawyer, though a representative and not the principal, can no more escape responsibility than any other representative for the results he helps to achieve.

The contrast can be put in the form of questions as to the lawyer's attitude toward the law and his part in it.   Does he see and employ the law as an impersonal set of ideas so that it is no concern of his whether the results are just?   Or does he view the law and his part in it as a process to be judged by its results, as

---

1.   J. Boswell, Tour to the Hebrides
175 (1773).

whether it works individual or social injustice; and if it is the latter, does this affect what the lawyer will do to make his life and work count for something he values?

In considering which of these elements shall have priority, the time of the client's action is of high importance. Is the action completed and past so all that is asked from the lawyer is aid in determining the rights of the parties under the law? Or is it future action which the lawyer gives his aids in shaping, that is in making private law for the parties?

Fortunately the lawyer need not often be troubled by the question whether the tendered case is unjust. Most clients are decent people, most cases have something on each side, and each side deserves to have a lawyer.

> "[T]here are few areas of the law in black and white. The greys are dominant . . . [T]he eternal problem of the law is making accommodations between conflicting interests. This is why most legal problems end as questions of degree." [2]

The standards of the bar in numerous situations are dealt with in the chapters ahead. Here two matters will be mentioned, one on which many laymen are mistaken and the other which lawyers may not clearly perceive.

The Criminal Case

The lawyer's action in defending a man accused of crime troubles the layman. The lawyer sees his action as proper and even essential under our system of law and order. The criminal law is administered through the adversary system with a lawyer on each side, including counsel for the accused. Individual lawyers have prided themselves on their action in representing unpopular defendants. The most responsible bar associations have taken as one of their duties to help assure that counsel are available for hated accused. When popular feeling against Communism was played upon by demagogues, the American Bar Association adopted a resolution which reaffirmed three connected ideas: (1) the right of a defendant to the assistance of counsel; (2) the duty of the bar to provide such counsel for even the most unpopular defendants; and (3) public acceptance of the correlative right of a lawyer to represent these defendants in accordance with the standards of the profession without having his client's acts or character ascribed to him.[3]

Even a guilty man is entitled to this representation, as an Australian case emphasizes. An aborigine was charged with the killing of a constable. During the trial the defendant through

---

2. Mr. Justice Douglas in Estin v. Estin, 334 U.S. 541, 545, Annot., 1 A.L.R.2d 1423 (1948).

3. 78 A.B.A.Rep. 133 (1953).

an interpreter confessed to his counsel that, fearing what the constable would do, he had thrown a spear and killed him. The lawyer for the defendant told the judge of the confession and made it public. The High Court of Australia, knowing that the publicity made a fair trial impossible, directed a judgment of acquittal. In criticizing the lawyer the court said: [4]

> "He [the lawyer] had a plain duty, both to his client and to the Court, to press such rational considerations as the evidence fairly gave rise to in favor of complete acquittal or conviction of manslaughter only."

There are limitations on the privilege to represent an accused. When the lawyer's personal abhorrence is so great as to impair his effective representation he should decline the case.[5] Of course, he may not aid the commission of future crimes through advice, or by the assurance of representation for those prosecuted for the crimes.[6] The representation of the narcotics wholesaler in the hypothetical case above is troubling. He has the right to a lawyer as to past crimes. He has no privilege to counsel for continuing crimes.

The Private Law Maker

The lawyer, with his eye like Dr. Johnson on advocacy, may underrate his role outside the courtroom where he is helping to shape his client's actions and the law for the parties. Three considerations will be mentioned. One is the importance of the policy to which the law gives expression and which the lawyer may be asked to avoid. Another is fairness in dealing with other persons, especially in dealing with those unable to protect themselves. A third is the decency or the cheapness of the plan. Consider the following business case which parallels that of the narcotics wholesaler. A business man has been indicted for fraud in making his tax returns, and he asks you to defend him at the criminal trial. He goes on to say that he will wish your further aid later in planning his business operations so as to reduce taxes as much as possible. Finally, he says he will wish your help in concealing his assets so that the amount of his net worth at the end of the taxable year will be difficult to ascertain.

"Professional Responsibility: A Statement" [7] shows the reasons which justify partisan advocacy in court. In contrast it goes on to warn against "unworthy involvement" in office work stating:

> "[These reasons justifying partisan advocacy] do not grant any license to the lawyer to participate as legal advisor in a

---

4. Tuckiar v. The King, 52 Commw. L.R. 335, 346 (Austl.1934).

5. ABA Code of Professional Responsibility, EC 2–30.

6. In re Davis, 252 App.Div. 591, 299 N.Y.S. 632 (1937).

7. Professional Responsibility: A Statement, 44 A.B.A.J. 1159 (1958).

line of conduct that is immoral, unfair, or of doubtful legality."

The Code of Professional Responsibility in its discussion of the lawyer's zealousness on behalf of his client states the lawyer's fuller part in aiding the client to decide what he will do: [8]

> "Advice of a lawyer to his client need not be confined to purely legal considerations. In assisting his client to reach a proper decision it is often desirable for a lawyer to point out those factors which may lead to a decision that is morally just as well as legally permissible . . . [W]hen an action in the best interest of his client seems to him to be unjust, he may ask his client for permission to forego such action."

SECTION 4. UNIMPAIRED LOYALTY: CONFLICT OF INTERESTS

Loyalty is owed by a fiduciary to his principal. The loyalty might be impaired by representation of another interest, so the duty of loyalty has the corollary principle that a fiduciary must not represent conflicting interests. The principle is preventive in purpose and scope. It condemns situations in which an opposing interest creates a temptation to violate the duty of loyalty, even though the duty was observed in the particular case.

The lawyer is a fiduciary in the highest sense. Whether in or out of court, he represents the interests of his client and must not represent conflicting interests. The principle encourages full disclosure of the facts of a case by a client to his lawyer, it preserves the trust and confidence of the client in the lawyer, and it helps to assure that the client will have the full devotion and zeal of his lawyer.

The usual form of statement of the principle is the condemnation of representing "conflicting interests." The Code of Professional Responsibility gives as the basic duty the exercise by the lawyer of his "independent judgment." In dealing with the "interests of multiple clients," the Code employs the conception, not merely of conflicting interests but a wider one, "differing interests:" [1]

> "Maintaining the independence of professional judgment required of a lawyer precludes his acceptance or continuation

---

8. ABA Code of Professional Responsibility, EC 7–8, 7–9.

1. ABA Code of Professional Responsibility, EC 5–14.

of employment that will adversely affect his judgment on behalf of or dilute his loyalty to a client. This problem arises whenever a lawyer is asked to represent two or more clients who may have differing interests, whether such interests be conflicting, inconsistent, diverse, or otherwise discordant."

The situations to which the principle may apply are very varied. One fourth of the questions put to committees on professional ethics, by lawyers who are sensitive to their obligations, involve problems of this sort. The distinguished of our profession may be most troubled by them.

An outline of embittered litigation in a federal court in California will make concrete the nature of some of the problems. In an action on a contract the defendant sought to have the counsel for the plaintiff disqualified because he had represented the defendant in the making of the contract. In holding the lawyer disqualified the court stated: (1) The basis and range of disqualification are broader than the principle of privileged communications. (2) The lawyer is disqualified if he had any substantial relation to the matter as a representative of the opponent at an earlier stage. (3) The disqualification applies even though the activities of the lawyer might lawfully have been done by a layman. (4) The disqualification extends to any participation in the suit whether as consultant or adviser or in the trial or the appellate court. (5) The assignment of part of the cause of action to the lawyer who by that device seeks to continue in the suit as party plaintiff would not work. (6) The range of disqualification would be determined by the law of the federal courts and not by state law.[2]

The discussion will be directed first to several forms of conflict of interests as conflict between the lawyer and the client, and between contemporaneous clients and successive clients. Then it will raise some general questions, as to the scope of disqualification and the sanctions. Lastly, it will mention areas of practice in which conflict of interest give special difficulties, as liability insurance, insolvent estates, and the government and its representatives.

Lawyer and Client

At the start there may be temptations. A case might come to the lawyer through the good offices of a person who expects special consideration in the handling of the case. It may be so when a trust company recommends a lawyer to a person who wishes a

2. Cord v. Smith, 338 F.2d 516 (9th Cir. 1964); Cord v. Smith, 370 F.2d 418 (9th Cir. 1966). The applicable standards of the profes- sion are helpfully restated by Judge Tate in Brasseaux v. Girouard, 214 So.2d 401 (Ct.La.App. 1968).

will or trust instrument drawn. To reduce the possibility of dilution of the lawyer's independent judgment the statement of general principles adopted by the National Conference Group of lawyers and trust companies urges that a trust company, in recommending lawyers to its customers, shall submit the names of several lawyers and leave it to the client to make the choice.[1]

Similarly during the relation collateral benefits from third parties must not be accepted. If a title company makes a gift to the lawyer of money because of the title work of the client placed by the lawyer with the company, the "kickback" belongs to the client.[2] When the lawyer purchases property which he should have acquired for the client, he holds it on constructive trust for the client.[3] The prohibition against collateral benefits has been applied even when the client itself was not injured. An illustration is the attorney for the trustee of the holders of first mortgage certificates issued on property in liquidation who purchased some of the certificates on the open market. The certificates rose in value. On the final accounting of the trustee the attorneys were held constructive trustees of the profits made through the purchase of the certificates.[4]

In a sordid case of sex or murder the accused's story may be sought by news media. His lawyer can not share in the publication rights for he "may be influenced, consciously or unconsciously, to a course of conduct that will enhance the value of his publication rights to the prejudice of his client." [5]

Professional judgment might be affected by the acquisition of interests not hostile to but identical with those of the client. To preserve objectivity some lawyers have had the policy of avoiding the ownership of equity securities of their corporate clients.[6]

Fixing the amount of fees involves an escapable conflict of interest. The method of reconciliation is considered elsewhere.

Clients at the Same Time

The injunction against a man serving two masters has its most obvious application when a lawyer represents conflicting inter-

1. See Statement, National Conference Group (1951) in 93 A.B.A. Rep. app. 25 (1966). If the trust company's client does not have independent legal advice and things go wrong, the trust company may be liable in damages. Jothann v. Irving Trust Co., 151 Misc. 107, 270 N.Y.S. 721 (1934), aff'd, 243 App. Div. 691, 277 N.Y.S. 955 (1935).

2. ABA Comm. on Professional Ethics, Opinions, No. 304 (1962).

3. Tracy v. Willys Corp., 45 F.2d 485 (6th Cir. 1930).

4. In re Bond & Mortgage Guarantee Co., 303 N.Y. 423, 103 N.E.2d 721 (1952).

5. ABA Code of Professional Responsibility, EC 5-4.

6. See II R. Swaine, The Cravath Firm 9-10 (1948); cf. ABA Code of Professional Responsibility, EC 5-3.

ests in the same litigation. Representation so diluted in loyalty falls below the protection which the Constitution assures to an accused.[1] Representation for and against the same person at the same time even in different cases is condemned.[2]

In office work a lawyer may represent both parties, with their consent, as in drafting a contract.[3] The dual representation might at times have something like the advantages that conciliation and negotiation have over litigation in reaching an agreement. It does face the lawyer with problems, as Professor Wilber Katz pointed out in an unpublished paper, on how far he shall go in raising possible contingencies and dealing with them when the parties are restive and uncertain as to the possibilities the lawyer perceives. Full disclosure by the lawyer to both parties is essential.[4] When it appears that the parties should have independent counsel, as when the lawyer perceives that one side is under an important misapprehension which he is not privileged to clear up, he must insist on independent counsel.

Divorce cases are a hybrid of litigation and office work, of both personal and property relations, of matters of high concerns to the state as well as to the individuals. They give peculiar difficulty because social attitudes have changed faster than legal forms. The formal method of obtaining a divorce in most states is through an action at law with the defendant charged with fault, so the usual prohibition against representing the two parties applies.[5] Often the actual method is going through these forms of law only after the parties have agreed on the terms of separation. An unconventional lawyer friend of the authors said he would never take a divorce case unless he represented both sides. The greatest service to be rendered the two clients whose joint venture had failed, he thought, was to send them apart without acrimony so each could begin a new life without the poison of bitterness and hatred. This identity of personal interests

1. Glasser v. United States, 315 U.S. 60 (1942).

On the representation of criminal co-defendants by the same lawyer, see the opinion of Chief Justice Traynor in People v. Chacon, 69 Cal.2d 765, 447 P.2d 106, Annot., 34 A.L.R. 3d 454 (1968).

2. Grievance Committee v. Rottner, 152 Conn. 59, 203 A.2d 82 (1964).

3. Hobart's Adm'r v. Vail, 80 Vt. 152, 66 A. 820 (1907); ABA Code of Professional Responsibility, EC 5-15.

4. Failure to give adequate advice to a borrower when borrower and lender came to the lawyer led to his discipline. In re Greenberg, 21 N.J. 213, 121 A.2d 520 (1956).

5. McDonald v. Wagner, 5 Mo.App. 56 (1878). For helpful discussions see H. Drinker, Legal Ethics 122 et seq. (1953); Drinker, Problems of Professional Ethics in Matrimonial Litigation, 66 Harv.L.Rev. 443 (1953).

of the two clients in freedom from hatred does not obscure the fact that there is a conflict of interests as to property certainly, and perhaps as to custody of children. If our friend could work out all these disagreements in fairness to all, he would rank high among the peace makers. The standards of the profession have not yet developed to deal with grounds and methods of divorce not based on fault.

Successive Clients

A lawyer is not barred forever from representing an adversary of a former client. There are, however, some enduring limitations. Of course, the lawyer may not change sides in the same lengthy litigation.[1] He may not seek to overthrow his own work, as by urging the invalidity of a document he drew.[2] He may not reveal privileged communication. He may not take a case against a former client if the two matters are substantially related. The last situation is illustrated by a case in which a lawyer had represented a motion picture producer, Universal, as defendant in an anti-trust prosecution. Later he was retained by motion picture exhibitors against producers in an action brought for damages suffered because of substantially the same monopolistic actions, with Universal as one of the defendants. He was held disqualified in the second case so long as Universal was a defendant. The test laid down in determining the range of disqualification was whether the matters embraced in the two suits are "substantially related" and thus naturally "the attorney might have acquired information related to the subject of his subsequent representation."[3] For the purpose of disqualification it was not necessary for the client to show that in the earlier case it had in fact disclosed matters related to the second case.

Different Causes at Different Times

May a lawyer rely in practice on a law which is helpful to his client and later espouse a change in the law which he believes to be in the public interest? Some cases may make the problem clearer.

An English barrister successfully represented a father in a suit over the custody of a child. Recognizing that a mother has the stronger moral claim, he secured later the enactment of a statute which would prevent the repetition of the result he had achieved for his client. This action of the lawyer in improving

1. Weidekind v. Tuolumne County Water Co., 74 Cal. 386, 19 P. 173 (1887).

2. ABA Comm. on Professional Ethics, Opinions, No. 64 (1932).

3. Judge Weinfeld in T. C. & Theatre Corp. v. Warner Bros. Pictures, 113 F.Supp. 265 (S.D.N.Y.1953).

the law was surely beyond cavil.[1] The decree for the father was deemed something like res judicata. What he had achieved for his client would be in no way affected by the statute he supported, and as a barrister he had no such continuing relation with his client as an American lawyer may have.

More troubling is the situation of the lawyer who has noted a loophole in the tax law and has taken advantage of it for his clients. May he—should he—call the attention of the Treasury or the Congress to the loophole, with resultant plugging of the hole. If he were house counsel for the corporation, his client would surely think him disloyal. An able independent tax lawyer urged that in such a matter a lawyer should recognize and carry out his duties to the public interest as well as to his client.[2]

> "I have said that the tax adviser should not mix into his work for his client his own personal views of tax policy. . . . But I hasten to add that the tax adviser should use for his government, as well as for his clients, the special knowledge his education and experience have bestowed upon him. . . . He should use this knowledge actively, affirmatively, and even aggressively. . . . A number of things—speaking, writing, appearing before committees— could be listed. . . . Of one thing I am very sure— that both tax payers and their government need many more of these tax advisers."

Most troubling is the situation of the lawyer who, believing social conditions call for it, supports legislation which is harmful to his former clients and which is contrary to views he once voiced. An example is given by Justice Brandeis, one of the great men of American law. While in practice he represented the United Shoe Machinery Company before the Massachusetts legislature in support of tying clauses. Several years later, having a slight connection with an opposed economic interest but influenced primarily by his views on the public interest, he supported federal legislation which would overthrow the clauses.[3]

1. Professional Responsibility: A Statement, 44 A.B.A.J. 1159 (1958).

2. Paul, The Responsibilities of the Tax Adviser, 63 Harv.L.Rev. 377, 386, 388 (1950).

3. The change in position was one of the grounds of opposition to the confirmation of his appointment to the Supreme Court. At the hearings of the Committee of the Senate an able lawyer ascribed the opposition to more general attitudes of Mr. Brandeis and of his critics: "He is a radical and has spent a large part, not only of his public, but of his professional career in attacking established institutions, and this alone, in my judgment, accounts for a very large part of his unpopularity." The controversy is ably discussed in Frank, The Legal Ethics of Louis D. Brandeis, 17 Stan.L.Rev. 683, 707 (1965).

Consent

Several general aspects of conflict of interest call for mention. The first is disclosure and consent. The lawyer owes the duty of full disclosure to the client, as the old Canons stated, of all circumstances and any interest "which might influence the client in the selection of counsel." [1] When the clients consent to the representation, despite conflicting interests fully revealed, the lawyer may represent them in office matters. This effect of consent has been held not applicable, however, when one of the consenting clients is a governmental body. [2]

The Scope of Disqualification

The scope of disqualification as to the matters involved has been indicated above. It extends to all matters substantially related to the matter wherein the attorney previously represented a client. [1]

The range of disqualification of persons has been put in broad term: [2]

> "[A]ll authorities agree that all members of a partnership are barred from participating in a case from which one partner is disqualified . . . And once a partner is thus vicariously disqualified, the subsequent dissolution of the partnership cannot cure his ineligibility to act as counsel in that case."

The breadth of the disqualification raises serious difficulties when a lawyer or even an associate [3] moves from one firm to another or from the government service into private practice. Limits on disqualification might be set by looking at the substance of the matter in either the second or the first firm. If the second firm takes all steps to insulate the rest of the firm from the matter, disqualification might not be necessary to carry out the purposes of the conflict of interests principle; though this insulation was held insufficient in a case in which the good faith of the parties was in no way impugned. [4]

Conversely, if the first firm was so compartmentalized and its members so insulated that the moving party did not have, and

1. ABA Canons of Professional Ethics No. 6. See ABA Code of Professional Responsibility, EC 5–15.

2. In re A. & B., 44 N.J. 331, 209 A.2d 101 (1965), Anno., 17 A.L.R.3d 835 (1968).

1. Consolidated Theatres, Inc. v. Warner Bros. C. M. Corp., 216 F.2d 920 (2nd Cir. 1954).

2. Clark, C. J., in Laskey Bros. v. Warner Bros. Pictures, Inc., 224 F. 2d 824, 826 (2nd Cir. 1955).

3. The principle of conflict of interests applies when the law clerk of one firm becomes a partner in another firm. N.Y.City Bar Ass'n Comm.Opinion 200 (1921).

4. W. E. Bassett Co. v. H. C. Cook Co., 201 F.Supp. 821 (D.Conn.1962),

could not reasonably have had, any knowledge or responsibility as to the matter in question, the rule might be that the second firm is not disqualified from participation on the other side. This appears to be the basis of the decision in United States v. Standard Oil Co.[5] There the government brought action against the Standard Oil Company for alleged overcharges made to the Department of Treasury under the Marshall Plan. A young lawyer who had worked with the Treasury in Paris on a phase of the Marshall Plan in Europe unconnected with the activities on which the action was based joined the large firm which represented the defendant. The plaintiff let it be known that it would seek to have the firm disqualified. The firm thereupon asked the opinion of the committees on professional ethics in its city and, after obtaining a favorable opinion, filed a motion in the principal action for a declaration that it was not disqualified. In a careful opinion the court granted the motion and permitted the firm to continue in the case.

This may be the basis of the limits set on disqualification, too, in the Federal Conflict of Interests Act of 1962,[6] to matters in which he "participated personally and substantially" and to those "under his official responsibility." It was recognized that the conflict of interests principle should not extend so as to unnecessarily reduce the mobility and availability of competent counsel.[7]

It is not clear whether this test of disqualification used when a lawyer moves from the government service back to private practice will be applied when he moves from one firm to another. When the two firms are small there is good reason to apply the disqualification principle rigidly, since within them the interchange of ideas on pending cases is probable and the suspicion or charge of disloyalty is inevitable.

Sanctions [1]

One sanction is preventive. It is most effective and probably most usual when it is self-imposed by the lawyer, who rejects an offered case. When a lawyer is a wrongful participant in litigation a request to him to withdraw may be enough. If he persists

---

aff'd 302 F.2d 268 (2nd Cir. 1962). The decision is sharply criticized in Note, Unchanging Rules in Changing Times: The Canons of Ethics and Intra-Firm Conflicts of Interests, 73 Yale L.J. 1058 (1964), which outlines the practices of many law firms.

5. 136 F.Supp. 345 (S.D.N.Y.1955).

6. 18 U.S.C.A. § 201 et seq.

7. See B. Manning, Federal Conflict of Interest Law (1964).

1. See Note, Sanctions for Attorney's Representation of Conflicting Interests, 57 Colum.L.Rev. 994 (1957); Wutchumna Water Co. v. Baily, 216 Cal. 564, 15 P.2d 505 (1932).

his participation can be halted by an injunction in a separate proceeding or, as is more usual, by a special motion in the case itself.[2] If the trial court erroneously permits the lawyer to continue, there is the clumsy corrective measure of upsetting the judgment, primarily at the expense of the client. It is so in a criminal case where the conviction will be set aside [3] and in a civil case with a new trial ordered.[4]

Other sanctions fall on the lawyer.[5] There may be a denial of liens or fees.[6] Benefits gained may be taken away by a constructive trust.[7] In gross cases professional discipline might be imposed.

Liability Insurance

Liability insurance involves dual representation by a lawyer. The policy ordinarily provides that the insurance company will hold the insured harmless against liability incurred to third parties within the monetary limits of the policy, that the company will provide a lawyer to represent the insured in claims or actions covered by the policy, and that the insured will cooperate with the insurance company in the defense against the claims or actions. The arrangement violates the usual standards of the profession.

One standard violated is the prohibition against representing conflicting interests. The insured, who is the named defendant in a claim or action and whom the lawyer represents in that matter, desires a settlement of the controversy without liability to him regardless of the cost to the insurance company. The insurance company seeks to make money by paying as little as is practicable in settlement or after trial. A California case is an illustration. A tenant suffered injuries through alleged negligence in the maintenance of a stairway and she and her husband brought an action against the landlord for $400,000. The landlord had a liability insurance policy for $10,000 and a lawyer chosen by the insurance company appeared on behalf of the landlord. At one time the tenant offered to settle for $10,000.

---

2. Consolidated Theatres, Inc. v. Warner Bros. C. M. Corp., 216 F.2d 920 (2nd Cir. 1954).

3. Glasser v. United States, 315 U.S. 60 (1942).

4. Weidekind v. Tuolumne County Water Co., 74 Cal. 386, 19 P. 173 (1887).

5. The lawyer may be liable in damages for the injuries suffered through his malpractice in representing conflicting interests. Lysick v. Walcom, 258 Cal.App.2d 136 (1968). Annot. 28 A.L.R.3d 368 (1969).

6. Chicago & West Towns Rys. v. Friedman, 230 F.2d 364 (7th Cir.), cert. denied, 351 U.S. 943 (1956).

7. Gaffney v. Harmon, 405 Ill. 273, 90 N.E.2d 785 (1950).

The landlord-client of course desired that the offer be accepted, but the insurance company-client rejected its lawyer's recommendation and declined the offer. At the trial the tenant recovered $101,000. The company paid the policy limit of $10,000, and the insured made arrangements to pay the balance of $91,000. The insured then sued the insurance company for its refusal to settle and recovered $91,000. In affirming a recovery by the insured the Supreme Court of California stated: [1]

> "Liability is imposed . . . for failure to meet the duty to accept reasonable settlements, a duty included within the implied covenant of good faith and fair dealing."

Another standard of the profession which is violated is the condemnation of a lay intermediary, that is, a layman or a corporation, which interposes itself between the client and the lawyer. In the case of liability insurance the insurance company is a lay intermediary which furnishes and pays the lawyer for the insured.

Yet liability insurance is a socially useful institution, and the provision of a lawyer by the insurance company for the protection of the insured and the company is an essential element. So the usual professional standards are modified. It is incumbent on lawyers to take account of the difficulties inherent in their dual representation and to consider the resulting duties. A few illustrations of conflicts of interests will be given.[2]

One limitation is the prohibition against changing sides. If a lawyer has investigated a claim at the instance of an insurance company he may not later represent the claimant, whether the investigation was made by him or through a claim agent. A more usual case is that of the lawyer who is generally employed by a particular insurance company in actions against its insured. A case is tendered to the lawyer by an injured person against a defendant who is insured by that insurance company. It is the practice of the bar for a lawyer so situated to refuse the tendered case.

The insurance company is under a duty to give weight to the interests of the insured as well as its own in determining whether to settle. In a case where the business of the insured was swept away on execution under a judgment against the insured after the company had refused to settle the controversy, the court stated:

> "There is now no serious disagreement that when a company assumes control of litigation based on a claim covered by

---

1. Crisci v. Security Insurance Co., 58 Cal.Rptr. 13, 426 P.2d 173, 177 (1967).

2. The subject is helpfully discussed in H. Drinker, Legal Ethics 114–18 (1953): ABA Comm. on Professional Ethics, Opinions, No. 282, 36 A.B.A.J. 733 (1950).

the policy, it cannot in deciding whether settlement is to be made seek only to protect its own interest but must give some consideration to the protection of the insured's interest in the event there is a possibility of a judgment exceeding the policy limits. . . . There is authority to the effect that the insured may give paramount consideration to its interest . . . . Other jurisdictions have said paramount consideration must be given to protect the insured. . . . A third position is that the insurer must give equal thought to the end that both the insured and the insurer shall be protected."

After stating its acceptance of the third position the court continued:

"A violator of this rule of equality of consideration cannot be said to have acted in good faith. . . . The enunciation of the rule is not difficult but its application is troublesome. It is a matter of consideration of comparative hazards."

A more troubling question is the professional duty of the lawyer. If one client, the insurance company, fails to give appropriate consideration to the interest of the other client, the insured, what is the duty of the lawyer? Surely it is the duty of the lawyer to inform the insurance company of its legal duty to the insured in settlement, and also to use his best influence to have the company comply with its duty. The insurance company officials may fail to give the consideration to the interests of the insured that law and fairness require. Ordinarily, a lawyer is controlled by the wishes of his client as to settlement. Here he has two clients, one of whom he may believe is acting unfairly toward the other. To make the question more difficult the unfair client is the one who retained him in the case, who is paying his fee, and who will be a continuing source of legal work unless it becomes dissatisfied with his services or his attitude. The insured is his client in the case only because of the insurance company's choice and is not apt ever to retain the lawyer who, through the company's choice, represented him in this unpleasant incident.[3]

The insured may fail to give the cooperation in the defense that the policy calls for. This failure is usually in an intra-family case, as one in which a father who was the driver of an automobile when his son was injured is sued by the son. The father desires that the son recover a judgment against him, since as the father hopes the judgment will be paid by the insurance company. What are the duties of the lawyer? There may be no legal liability on the insurance company to indemnify the insured or to provide counsel for him when the insured fails to give the

---

3. Farmers Ins. Exch. v. Henderson, 82 Ariz. 335, 313 P.2d 404 (1957).

cooperation called for by the policy. Yet if the insurance company fails to defend the action and a judgment is given for the plaintiff, the company runs the danger of having a court find in a later action that there was no such failure to cooperate as the policy required so the insurance company must indemnify the insured. If the insurance company defends the actions without any sort of disclaimer, it runs another danger of waiving its defense based on the insured's lack of cooperation. Clearly, it is the duty of the lawyer to inform the insurance company on all these matters and to advise it on the appropriate course of action to take.

Similarly, the insured needs advice and counsel on each aspect mentioned. Should the lawyer retained by the insurance company give his advice and counsel? Or must he inform the insured that he needs independent counsel and then withdraw from the case? Withdrawal is a step of some difficulty. If the lawyer for the insurance company has appeared in a legal proceeding as counsel for the insured defendant, he may not withdraw without good cause and without permission granted by the court.[4] In any event a lawyer who has become the attorney for the insured may not withdraw except at a time and under conditions which leave ample opportunity for the insured to retain new counsel to protect his interests.

A related question is, may the lawyer who was counsel of record for the insured be the counsel for the insurance company in an action between the insured and the company over the issue of lack of cooperation by the insured and consequent loss of his right of indemnity? It is unwise for the same lawyer who had appeared for the insured to appear against him in another phase of the same general controversy.

Liquidation and Reorganization

When a person is insolvent there is need for distribution of his assets among the creditors and for a fresh start for him. When a business is temporarily embarrassed through lack of liquid assets, there is opportunity for a reorganization of the business and of a fresh start. This can be accomplished either through the public legal process, as reorganization in receivership or bankruptcy, or else through the private legal process of a creditors' agreement.[1] For the imaginative and resourceful lawyer

---

4. Mere direction by one client, the insurance company, that he withdraw from the case is not adequate reason for the court to permit the lawyer to withdraw from the case as representative of the other client, the insured. Thomas v. Douglas, 2 App.Div.2d 885, 157 N.Y.S.2d 45 (1956).

1. To expedite simple creditor compositions, Congress enacted Chapter XI of the Bankruptcy Act, 11 U.S.C.A. § 701 et seq. See S.Rep. No. 1395, 82d Cong. 2d Sess. (1952).

there is the chance here to save and recreate a business. Nothing said below as to conflicting interests should blind him to the opportunity and the high value of its realization.

A liquidation or reorganization case, whether a petty bankruptcy or a railroad receivership, may involve numerous interests, and so be particularly apt to present conflicting interests.[2] The purposes and steps in such a case will be mentioned as well as the variety of contending groups and the points at which a conflict of interests may work injury to one interest or another. Then some problems of conflicting interests will be mentioned, whether involving the attorney for the liquidator or the attorney for other interests.

In an ordinary liquidation, the major steps after determination of insolvency are: (1) the collection and preservation of the property by the liquidator; (2) the determination of the claims, including their respective priorities; (3) the reduction of the assets to cash; (4) payment. In a reorganization case, steps (1) and (2) are the same as those above. The third step calls for devising a business plan which will make possible the continued operation of the business, ordinarily through reducing or deferring the various claims against the debtor and providing new capital. The last step is the execution of the plan.

The contending groups are in three main classes with subclasses. They are the creditors, including secured creditors, creditors claiming priority, and general creditors. There are the various groups of stockholders. Finally, there are the management groups, which will include the promoters and bankers of the business, the officers and directors of the corporation, and the liquidators and reorganizers with their lawyers and bankers.

A conflict of interests may arise at the inception of the case, which may be instituted in the name of one person though actually at the instigation and for the purposes of another, and it may involve the selection of a forum thought favorable to a particular interest. There is the selection of the personnel for liquidation proceedings, as, the liquidator, the attorney for the liquidator, and the protective committees. During the running of the liquidation, there are various questions, including what claims shall be enforced or resisted. At the sale or reorganization, there is the question of time and method and upset price. Finally, there is the problem of fees: who shall be paid, and for what services.

---

2. The complexity of some reorganizations is fantastic. Some attorneys estimate that the reorganization of the Penn-Central will generate 50 million dollars in fees. Wall Street Journal, July 23, 1970, at 1, col. 1.

Some of the recurring questions involve: the selection of the liquidator; who may be the attorney for the liquidator; and what relation the attorney for the liquidator may have to the attorneys for other interests. There is the question whether the same lawyer may represent different claimants in the same proceeding.

For our purposes it is enough merely to call attention to these complexities and to the attitude of federal law toward resulting conflicts of interests. The Supreme Court of the United States has been rigorous in insisting on unimpaired loyalty. Representatives who put themselves in a double position have been denied compensation [3] and forced even to repay the compensation they received.[4]

> "Only strict adherence to these equitable principles can keep the standard of conduct for fiduciaries at a level higher than that trodden by the crowd." [5]

Government Officials

"Public office is a public trust." This statement is a principle of law, not a mere political exhortation, as two cases are enough to show. An officer bribed by contractors to approve public work under his supervision had to pay to the government the sums received.[1] The holder of an honorary office in a foreign government was promised by a manufacturer a commission for the use of his influence in effecting a sale to his government. The court denied enforcement because the contract was against public policy, adding that the result would be the same even if the contract was valid under the law of the foreign country.[2]

For the lawyer in government service the representation of conflicting interests has the double condemnation of the principle of law as to public officers as well as the standards of the profession. Some of the consequent limitations in the federal legislative and executive services will be briefly indicated by reference to a bar association study and to a recent statute.

For the legislator it is necessary to distinguish two quite different things both of which might loosely be thought of as conflicts of interest. The first, concerned with competing interests

---

3. Woods v. City Nat'l Bank & Trust Co., 312 U.S. 262 (1941).

4. Wolf v. Weinstein, 372 U.S. 633 (1963).

5. Woods v. City Nat'l Bank & Trust, 312 U.S. 262, 269 (1941).

1. "The larger interests of public justice will not tolerate, under any circumstances, that a public official shall retain any profit or advantage which he may realize through the acquirement of an interest in conflict with his fidelity as an agent." Carter v. United States, 217 U.S. 286, 306 (1910).

2. Oscanyan v. Arms Co., 103 U.S. 261, 277 (1880).

and groups, is well described by Senator Wallace Bennett of Utah: [3]

> "The legislator comes to office as the result of a struggle for power between groups of voters whose interests are in conflict, and he is elected because he is the choice of the larger number . . . [Legislation], with its inevitable compromises, is produced by the clash of obviously conflicting interests, and to say that a legislator must avoid conflict of interest is to ask the impossible."

The second matter is the advancement of the individual's own interests through the use of his official position. This is the action condemned. As the Code of Professional Responsibility states, a lawyer in public office "should not engage in activities in which his personal or professional interests are or foreseeably may be in conflict with his official duties." [4]

Conflict of interests in activities by Members of the Congress is the subject of a recent thoughtful bar association study. The measures recommended are avoidance of the conflict where it is avoidable, or else disclosure, or disqualification: [5]

> "The basic thesis of this Report and the opinion of this Committee is that an avoidable conflict of interest should normally be avoided. If not avoided, it should be disclosed to the Member's colleagues and to the public and perhaps should result in disqualification from voting or committee service."

As to lawyers, the study goes further and recommends that a member of the Congress who has established his position in this political office should give up entirely the practice of law.[6]

In the executive branch of the federal government conflict of interests is dealt with broadly by the "Federal Conflict of Interests Act of 1962." [7] The statute has as its basis two policies.

---

3. 113 Cong.Rec. 2976 (1967), quoted in Congress and the Public Trust, infra note 5, at 35.

4. ABA Code of Professional Responsibility, EC 8–8.

5. Association of the Bar of the City of New York, Congress and the Public Trust, 47 (1970). The book is the Report of the Special Committee on Congressional Ethics of The Association of the Bar of the City of New York of which Mr. Louis Loeb was the Chairman and Professor (now Dean) Kirby the Executive Director.

6. Id., Chapter III.

7. 18 U.S.C.A. §§ 201–218. The federal statute is excellently discussed against the background of the earlier federal legislation in B. Manning, Federal Conflict of Interest Law (1964), and Perkins, The New Federal Conflict of Interest Law, 76 Harv.L.Rev. 1113 (1963). Both Dean Manning and Mr. Perkins were active in the preparation of the influential report of The Special Committee on the Federal Conflict of Interest Laws of the Association of the Bar of the City of New York, Conflict of Interest and Federal Service (1960).

First, the federal executive agencies should be above suspicion in their actions. Second, the government should not be hampered in drawing on lawyers and other citizens for temporary service by restrictions which would needlessly obstruct them on return to private life.

For a former government employee, Section 207 of the Act is specific on two things. On matters in which he participated "personally and substantially" an employee is disqualified forever. On matters which were "under his official responsibility . . . at any time within a period of one year prior to the termination of such responsibility," he is disqualified for one year from appearing personally before any federal court or agency. The statute places no bar on appearance as to new matters before any government agency. Nor does the statute deal explicitly with the disqualification of a firm with which the government employee becomes associated.

It has been assumed that the statute does not seek to occupy the whole field and that "major responsibility for regulations and for administrative enforcement of regulations, in the field of conflict of interest is vested in the individual departments and agencies." [8]

The statute might be implemented and filled out by common law principles and professional standards more exacting than the statute alone. The courts might find that the statute, dealing only with specific matters in a limited way, leaves the rest of the field to be developed in accordance with the usual principles that apply to lawyers and to government officials.

The states develop their conflict of interest principles according to their own standards.

8. Manning, supra note 7, at 271. For example on the Patent Office, see Kinglsland v. Dorsey, 338 U.S. 318, 70 S.Ct. 123 (1949). On the Bureau of Internal Revenue, see its elaborate statement of standards for practitioners before it.

Chapter XIV

COMMENCEMENT, PROTECTION AND TERMINATION OF THE RELATIONSHIP OF LAWYER AND CLIENT

Commencement of the Relationship. The employment of an attorney by a client requires no special formalities. The employment can be oral and implied in fact, or it can be express and set down in writing. The advisability of a writing may turn on the nature of the client. If the client is inexperienced, a written contract of employment is desirable to avoid misunderstandings. One useful method is, after the interview and oral retainer, for the lawyer to send to the client a letter in duplicate which states the terms of the retainer and to ask the client if the letter accords with his understanding, for him to keep one copy and to sign and return the other to the lawyer.

There is a rebuttable presumption that a lawyer has authority to represent a person for whom he appears in litigation.[1] A court may at any time require the lawyer to give proof of his retainer.[2] If the adverse party questions the retainer and authority of the lawyer, he may do so by a special motion in the case.[3]

A more usual question is, when does the relationship begin. The stages of the association of the layman and the lawyer may include the receipt of a letter from the layman seeking to retain the lawyer, a conference, the refusal by the lawyer to accept the case or the acceptance of the case either unconditionally or else conditionally, and the performance of the services. The legal questions incident to the relation include the privileged character of the layman's statements, the disqualification of the lawyer to represent the other side, the validity of a contract or conveyance between layman and lawyer, the right to fees. The answer to these different questions as to the relationship may vary with the stage of the association. So the question should be put, not in the rigid form, when did the relation of attorney and client begin, but in the form what rights and duties arise at each stage of the association of the layman and the lawyer.

1. See Delray Beach Aviation Corp. v. Mooney Aircraft, Inc., 217 F. Supp. 255, 259 (W.D.Tex.1963).

2. See Santa Rosa v. Fall, 273 U.S. 315 (1927).

3. In re Retail Chemists Corp., 66 F.2d 605 (2nd Cir. 1933).

At the inception of the contacts between the layman and the lawyer it is essential that the layman feel free of danger in stating the facts of the case to the lawyer whom he consults. Even though the lawyer rejects the case and the relation of attorney and client never arose, the usual duties as to privileged communications and conflicting interests should apply.[4] The general principle of law should be, each duty incident to the attorney-client relationship begins as early as is helpful to the effective working of the relationship.

When the layman attacks a conveyance to or a contract with a lawyer, the success of the attack need not rest on a preliminary determination of when the relationship of attorney and client began. It may rest on the more general principle of confidential relationship. An excessive fee contract between layman and lawyer might be overthrown on the legal grounds of confidential relation. This goes so far as to give rise to a presumptive invalidity of a fee contract made after the relation of attorney and client had been formed.[5]

Protection of the Relationship. The client has some protection against a lawyer's withdrawing from a case by the professional standard described below.[1] Even when he discharges the lawyer, the client has continuing protections through the lawyer's duties not to reveal confidential information and not to represent conflicting interests.

The lawyer has no protection against the client's action in discharging him, except the client's liability in quantum meruit or in damages.[2] The lawyer has a right of action in tort against a third person who wrongfully induces the client to discharge him and so destroys an advantageous relationship.[3] The Canons in terms condemned efforts to encroach upon the professional employment of another lawyer.[4] Acceptance of employment with knowledge that another lawyer had previously been retained, without consultation with the other lawyer, has been treated as one factor warranting disbarment.[5]

---

4. Cf. Taylor v. Sheldon, 172 Ohio St. 118, 173 N.E.2d 892 (1961). The principle applies even though the lawyer has no recollection of the content or even of the fact of the earlier conference. N.Y. County Lawyer's Ass'n Comm. Opinion On Professional Ethics No. 556 (1968).

5. Lawrence v. Tschirgi, 244 Iowa 336, 57 N.W.2d 46 (1953).

1. See infra pp. 247–48.

2. See infra p. 247.

3. Herron v. State Farm Mutual Ins. Co., 14 Cal.Rptr. 294, 363 P.2d 310 (1961); Richette v. Solomon, 410 Pa. 6, 187 A.2d 910 (1963).

4. ABA Canons of Professional Ethics No. 7.

5. State ex rel. Oklahoma Bar Ass'n v. Hatcher, 452 P.2d 150 (Okl. 1969).

Termination by the Client. As between the parties, the client has the power to discharge the lawyer at any time for any reason.[1] A provision of irrevocability in the contract of employment is invalid.[2] The vague statement is often made that when there is "a power coupled with an interest" the lawyer may not be discharged. The statement is of uncertain meaning. The fact that the lawyer's fee is contingent does not bar the client's right to discharge him.[3]

It is wise to let the client have this power to discharge the lawyer. The relation of lawyer and client calls for continuing confidence in the lawyer by the client. If the confidence ends the relation should end.[4] When the representation is in a court case, the discharge may take the form of a motion in the case for the substitution of attorneys.[5]

There is disagreement over the measure of the lawyer's fee when he has been discharged, whether it should be the terms of the contract or quantum meruit. The latter is preferable. The full contract fee rule is a major deterrent to the client's privilege to continue to have a lawyer of his choice.[6] If an injured man retained one lawyer on a contingent fee basis, say, of one third of the recovery and, being dissatisfied with him, retained another lawyer on the same terms to go ahead with the case, the lawyers together would at the end get two thirds of the recovery —a situation bringing to mind the fable of the cat which was asked to decide a dispute and did so by taking everything for itself.

Termination by the Lawyer. The lawyer has no such easy freedom to end the relation. The emphasis here is on the continuing protection of the interests of the client once the lawyer

1. Matter of Krooks, 257 N.Y. 329, 178 N.E. 548 (1931). A defendant in a political trial was denied the power to discharge his lawyer at the end of the testimony because he desired to make a "flaming address" under the guise of an argument to the jury. L. Hand, J. in Dennis v. United States, 183 F. 2d 201 (2nd Cir. 1950).

2. Richette v. Solomon, 410 Pa. 6, 187 A.2d 910 (1963).

3. Dolph v. Speckart, 94 Or. 550, 186 P. 32 (1920).

4. In Udall v. Littell, 366 F.2d 668, 675 (D.C.Cir. 1966), Judge Burger quoted an earlier case with approval: "The relationship of attorney and client is such as to require perfect confidence between the parties, and, of course, would not be continued by a decree in equity against the will of either party."

5. When the lawyer is not a representative in court proceedings, the client needs no permission from a court. See In re Dix's Estate, 144 Misc. 494, 259 N.Y.S. 449 (1932).

6. A court using the quantum meruit rule held that the terms of the contract did not set a limit on the amount of recovery, and the astounded client who had discharged her lawyer had a judgment given against her for twice the fee agreed on. Re Montgomery, 272 N.Y. 323, 6 N.E.2d 40 (1936).

has undertaken to represent him. The standards of the profession are given in the Code of Professional Responsibility : [1]

> "A decision by a lawyer to withdraw should be made only on the basis of compelling circumstances . . . A lawyer should not withdraw without considering carefully and endeavoring to minimize the possible adverse effect on the rights of his client . . . Even when he justifiably withdraws, a lawyer should protect the welfare of his client by giving due notice of his withdrawal, suggesting employment of other counsel . . . and otherwise endeavoring to minimize the possibility of harm."

The privilege of the withdrawal of counsel retained by a liability insurance company to appear for and represent its insured has been presented under various conditions. The mere direction of the insurance company to the lawyer is not adequate reason for the court to permit his withdrawal.[2] The bankruptcy of the insurance company was ground for permitting the lawyer to withdraw but only on giving lengthy notice to the insured for whom he had appeared.[3]

In a criminal case the lawyer for the accused presented a request to withdraw the day before the case was set for trial, on the ground the client had failed to pay the fee agreed on. When the request was denied, the lawyer sought mandamus to compel the lower court to permit his withdrawal. The court declined to grant mandamus giving as reasons that a lawyer owes a duty to the other side and also the duty not to obstruct the working of justice through delay, and that to allow withdrawal would facilitate collusion of lawyer and client.[4]

1. ABA Code of Professional Responsibility, EC 2–32.

2. Thomas v. Douglas, 2 App.Div.2d 885, 157 N.Y.S.2d 45 (1956).

3. Zitomer v. Holdsworth, 200 F. Supp. 490 (E.D.Pa.1961).

4. Linn v. Superior Court, 79 Cal. App. 721, 250 P. 880 (1926).

Chapter XV

CONSEQUENCES OF THE RELATIONSHIP

SECTION 1. COMPETENCE AND CARE

Competence

The lawyer holds himself out as a capable representative of those who employ him. Competence in the work undertaken is a duty. Yet as Lord Tenterden protested, no lawyer can be competent over the whole range of clients' problems.[1] The century and a half since Lord Tenterden's time have brought unmatched complexities in human relations with new and troubling legal problems. In contrast with the English unitary system which troubled Lord Tenterden, the American federal system is "perhaps the most complicated legal structure that has ever been devised and made effective in man's effort to govern himself."[2]

The lawyer who is offered a case he is not competent to handle has three courses open. He might decline the proffered retainer, an action not helpful to the layman or to him. He might accept it with the accompanying determination to make himself competent through study. This course may be unfair to the client or to him, for a lawyer cannot acquire an adequate knowledge of all the subjects coming to him within a time which makes practicable a fee fair to the client and to him. Lastly, he might accept the retainer and, with the consent of the client, associate a specialist in the field.

The last method is the one used in the large law firm. The firm is a continuing association of specialists grouped around generalists, with teams or task forces formed by drawing on the specialized abilities of its members as the clients' cases call for. As Mr. Harrison Tweed said:

> "The reason for the existence of law partnerships is not
> the possession of a big client but the need to bring to-

1. "No attorney is bound to know all the law; God forbid that it should be imagined that an attorney, or a counsel, or even a judge is bound to know all the law." Montriou v. Jefferys, 172 Eng.Rep. 51 (N.P. 1825) (Charles Abbott, Lord Tenterden).

2. E. Griswold, Law and Lawyers in the United States 3, 64 (1964). The extent to which specialization has developed in the profession is shown vividly in Q. Johnstone & D. Hopson, Jr., Lawyers and Their Work (1967).

gether a group of lawyers collectively qualified to do the things that those of the public sought as clients want done and want done well." [3]

The lawyer practicing alone or in a small firm has no such self-sufficient competence. He must go outside if his clients are to be adequately represented. In the public interest, it is not enough for the organized bar to take the negative position of forbidding a lawyer to accept a case in a field in which he is not competent. There is need for standards and methods which will encourage and make feasible the association of generalist and specialist. An arrangement which is, as Dean Joiner put it, a partnership *pro hac vice* may be in the best interest of clients as well as of the lawyers. So far, however, this duty has not been met. The present standards against fee-splitting may actually discourage the use of needed specialists. Several times the American Bar Association has considered how to deal with specialization, but in 1969 left the matter to the state bar associations.[4]

The organized bar has taken two helpful measures. One is the support of "continuing legal education" designed to keep the lawyer competent in his fields of law or to help him develop adequate abilities in new fields. The other measure is acquainting the generalist with those who are actual or asserted specialists. The specialist is permitted to send informational cards to fellow lawyers,[5] and in some states "the experienced lawyer service" gives to the generalist background information about asserted specialists so an informed choice of association may be made.

There are difficulties in doing more. One difficulty is the assumption by the public that every lawyer is competent over the whole field of law. In medicine, patients pay no such compliment to their physicians, and the calling in of specialists will be accepted with gratitude. For the lawyer to associate a specialist may be seen as merely a mark of general incompetence. The public should be made to realize that there is need for the specialist in law as in medicine. With the public attitude as it is, the general practitioner may object to stress on the need for a specialist as a threat to his practice.

A second difficulty is the lack of systems for qualifying and identifying specialists. This may be a much greater obstacle in law than in, say, medicine, where the hospital serves as the center of the needed training. Young lawyers may resent the

---

3. H. Tweed, The Changing Practice of Law 13 (1955), reprinted in 11 Record of the N.Y.C.B.A. 13, 19 (1956).

4. 94 A.B.A.Rep. 129–132 (1969).

5. See, ABA Code of Professional Responsibility, DR 2–105(A) (3).

years of study required for training and certification, and older lawyers may ignore what they regard as mere paper credentials.

Still another difficulty is the appropriate form of coordination of the several interests, as the protection of the client from excessive charges, and the protection of the generalist from excessive claims by the specialist and from having his client taken away.[6]

The stress laid here on the fact of specialization and the need for specialists implies no disparagement of the generalist. There is need for a lawyer who sees the case not as isolated fragments of law, but as a whole, with the wise judgment the overall view may give for the client.[7]

Some questions on the level of competence, and the supports and sanctions, will be raised after a brief discussion of the closely related matter of care.

Care

The lawyer has the accompanying duty to handle a case with the care it calls for. The organized bar has given useful support through its encouragement of better law office management with the consequent reduction in errors caused by oversight.[8] The essential support comes primarily from the lawyer's own sense of responsibility, derived from commingled qualities of pride and duty and a sense of the meaning of the case to the human being involved. It was pride in his ability which led one lawyer to say that competence is the paramount moral obligation of the lawyer and that he should decline to prepare a will if he doubts his ability to produce the best possible one for the client.[9] Justice Holmes put the emphasis much the same way.

"A man's spiritual history is best told in what he does in his chosen line. . . . This sounds a little pompous, but

---

6. See Niles, Ethical Prerequisites to Certification of Special Proficiency, 49 A.B.A.J. 83 (1963). An excellent background discussion of specialization, prepared for the American Bar Foundation, is G. Greenwood & R. Frederickson, Specialization in the Medical and Legal Professions (1964).

7. The general counsel of a large corporation appraised himself this way: "I do not know as much about any part of this company's business as some others on the legal staff. Somehow I seem to be able to listen to them and to come

up with a pretty sensible overall judgment. I had general practice in a small corporate law office for fifteen years before I came with this company. If I had had five years more of general practice, I might be worth more to it."

8. See A.B.A. Comm. on the Economics of Law Practice, The Lawyers Handbook (1962).

9. See Miller, Functions and Ethical Problems of the Lawyer in Drafting a Will, [1950] Ill.L.F. 415, 423 (1950).

it truly expresses my desire and the way I felt when called on perhaps to construe some temporary statutes, so that untying little knots never seems drudgery." [10]

Levels and Sanctions

There are different possible levels of standards of competence and care and different kinds of sanctions for the failure to measure up. The level might be "the best possible," as a specialist insisted.[11] It might be "reasonably competent" [12] with various factors going to determine what is reasonable.

The sanctions for lack of adequate competence or care may fall on the lawyer with differing degrees of severity: there may be professional discipline ranging from admonition to disbarment; there may be forfeiture of fees; there may be personal liability to the client, or perhaps to a third person, for the loss suffered; there might be a finding of contempt of court; and there might be criminal liability. A wholly different kind of sanction throws its burden on the client's adversary. It is the setting aside of a verdict or judgment occasioned by the lawyer's incompetence or negligence and the grant of a new trial.

Inadequacy may occur in office work or in litigation, in civil cases, or in criminal cases of varying severity of punishment. There are different methods of providing counsel, as through the client's own choice or through assignment by the court.[13]

With the situations so varied, no single level or measure of required competence or care may be stated, except that as the gravity of the case entrusted to the lawyer goes up so will the level of professional duty and the professional sanction. Illustrations will be given of the standard called for according to the application of several sanctions or supports: (1) liability of the lawyer in damages; (2) upsetting the judgment in a case because of the fault of the loser's lawyer; (3) professional discipline and personal standards.

Damages. A lawyer is liable to his client for damages suffered due to incompetence or carelessness. The duty arises from the relationship and is not dependent on a contractual provision

10. O. W. Holmes, Jr., Letters to Doctor Wu 15–16 (1947) cited in 52 A.B.A.J. 1035 (1966).

11. See Miller, supra, note 9.

12. See H. Drinker, Legal Ethics 139 (1953). See also ABA Code of Professional Responsibility, Canon 6.

13. "It would be a strange system of law which first assigned inexperienced or negligent counsel in a capital case and then made counsel's neglect a ground for refusing a new trial." Johnson v. United States, 110 F.2d 562, 563 (D.C.Cir. 1940) (Edgerton, J.).

imposing it.   The measure of the duty is the same as that of a member of a profession or skilled trade generally:

> "[T]he skill and knowledge normally possessed by members of that profession or trade in good standing in similar communities".[14]

Two examples taken from office work may suffice.   A lawyer approved the title to a piece of land which was imperfect because in the chain of title there was a deed of exchange from an executor under a will giving only the power to sell.   In holding the lawyer liable to his client, Judge Cardozo said:

> "The law is settled that a power to sell and distribute the proceeds is not a power to exchange . . . .   It is negligence to fail to apply the settled rules of law that should be known to all conveyancers".[15]

In another case lawyers retained to prepare a chattel mortgage failed to inform their clients that acknowledgment and recordation were essential to make the mortgage effective. When the mortgagors went into bankruptcy, the lawyers were held liable for the client's loss.[16]

A higher standard may be imposed on the specialist.[17]   When the aid of professionals, even in other disciplines, is important, it is the professional duty [18] and, it may be, the legal duty, to obtain it.

The decline of privity as an essential of liability has led to the recent development of the liability of a lawyer to a third person injured through his incompetence or negligence.[19]   The range of this liability will probably be confined for the near future, Dean Wade states, "to persons who were in his contemplation at the time he rendered his services, or could at least have been easily foreseen by him to be directly affected by his conduct." [20]

---

14.   Restatement, Second, Torts § 299A. For a general discussion of the subject, see Wade, The Attorney's Liability for Negligence, 12 Vand.L.Rev. 755 (1959). For a detailed treatment of the cases in one state, see Blaustein, Liability of Attorney to Client in New York for Negligence, 19 Brooklyn L.Rev. 233 (1953).

15.   Trimboli v. Kinkel, 226 N.Y. 147, 149, 123 N.E. 205 (1919), Annot., 5 A.L.R. 1389 (1920).

16.   Theobald v. Byers, 193 Cal.App. 2d 147, 13 Cal.Rptr. 864 (1961), Annot., 87 A.L.R.2d 991 (1963).

17.   "If the actor possesses special competence, he must exercise it, not only in his profession, trade, or occupation, but also whenever a reasonable man in his position would realize that its exercise is necessary to the reasonable safety of others." Restatement, Second, Torts § 299, comment f, at 72.

18.   ABA Code of Professional Responsibility, EC 6–3.

19.   Lucas v. Hamm, 56 Cal.2d 583, 364 P.2d 685, 15 Cal.Rptr. 821 (1961), cert. denied 368 U.S. 987 (1962); Biakanja v. Irving, 49 Cal. 2d 647, 320 P.2d 16 (1958), Annot., 65 A.L.R.2d 1363 (1959).

20.   Wade, supra note 14, at 759–60.

In the conduct of litigation, the same general standard of conduct for the lawyer has been laid down as for office work. So a lawyer was held not liable to his client for the loss of claims against foreign insurance companies through faulty service of process, when he followed the methods which lawyers had generally, though erroneously, followed.[21]

When the lawyer's action in the courtroom is in question, the ex-client who lost his case against the original adversary and now seeks to win it against his lawyer has two obstacles to overcome. One is the great difficulty in proving that the advocate's action was negligent. Contrasting the advocate's work with that of the conveyancer, a court said:

> "To some extent litigation is a game of chance. The conduct of a lawsuit involves questions of judgment and discretion, as to which even the most distinguished members of the profession may differ. . . . If in such cases a lawyer errs on a question not elementary or conclusively settled by authority, that error is one of judgment, for which he is not liable." [22]

The other difficulty is causal relationship, proof that the negligence complained of caused the loss of the lawsuit.[23]

Upsetting the Judgment in Civil Cases. The party losing a civil case may seek another chance, urging that the sins of the lawyer should not be visited upon the client. The determination whether the first judgment shall be set aside and a second chance given, presents a conflict of two policies, finality of litigation (res judicata) versus justice in the individual case. In support of each of them, additional considerations may be invoked, some of which are scarcely more than the policies themselves stated in other forms. In support of finality are such matters as the increased burden which lack of finality would thrust on the courts and on the parties as well as the usual rule that a principal is responsible for the defaults of his representative, and the difficulty in determining the kinds of error of counsel which call for this relief. In support of justice in the individual case is the increased weight now given to a party's "right to counsel" in the fullest sense.[1]

21. Hodges v. Carter, 239 N.C. 517, 80 S.E.2d 144 (1954), Annot., 45 A.L. R.2d 5 (1956).

22. Byrnes v. Palmer, 18 App.Div. 1, 4, 45 N.Y.S. 479, 481–82 (1897), aff'd 160 N.Y. 699, 55 N.E. 1093 (1899). The English courts at all three levels held that an advocate, whether barrister or solicitor, is an officer of the court and is immune from liability in negligence to a losing client. Rondel v. Worsley, [1966] 1 All E.R. 467; [1966] 3 All E.R. 657; [1967] All E.R. 993.

23. "[T]his involves a 'suit within a suit,' and the client must show that he would have won the first suit as one step in order to win the second one." Wade, supra note 14, at 769.

1. See infra pp. 324ff.

In civil cases, a sweeping application of the principle of finality was stated by an able writer a century ago: "The neglect of an attorney or agent is uniformly treated as the neglect of the client." [2] Quite to the contrary a careful study of the 1960's could state: "Cases granting relief from default judgments because of attorney neglect have become frequent." [3]

The changed attitude is due, it is believed, to a clearer perception by the courts of the roles of judges and lawyers in applying and developing the law. A judge is not a mere mouthpiece recording the automatic application of rules of law. He has a continuing responsibility in applying and developing the principles of law. So looking at the whole case an appellate court took into account the actions of the defendant as well as of the plaintiff in reversing the dismissal of a complaint for failure to prosecute. [4]

No specific rules have yet been developed and the courts are left to weigh the policies in the particular case, with an inclination ordinarily against upsetting the judgment. Mr. Justice Black dissented from the affirmance of a trial court's dismissal of an old and dubious case for lack of prosecution when the court had given warning to the lawyer but not to his client. [5] Later the Justice sought unsuccessfully to write into the Rules of Court the view in his dissenting opinion that, no party shall have his case dismissed or his right to defend cut off because of the delinquency of counsel until he has been served with notice of counsel's delinquency and until the client himself has done something which justified the court's action. [6]

The state cases assume that the authoritative source of the law in these matters is state law. Mr. Justice Black intimated that to cast the burden of the lawyer's default on the client in such cases might violate the federal constitution. [7]

Criminal Cases. When the defendant in a criminal case attacks his conviction because of the incompetence or mistakes of counsel, there are in conflict the same general policies as in a civil case, finality of result versus justice in the individual case. There are additional factors on the side of the loser. One is the

2. A. Freeman, Judgments § 112 (4th ed. 1873).

3. Mazor, Power and Responsibility in the Attorney-Client Relation, 20 Stan.L.Rev. 1120, 1124 (1968).

4. Rudd v. Rogerson, 152 Colo. 370, 381 P.2d 995 (1963), Annot., 15 A.L. R.3d 674 (1967).

5. Link v. Wabash R. R. Co., 370 U.S. 626, 636, 82 S.Ct. 1386, 1392, 8 L.Ed. 2d 734, 741 (1962).

6. See L. Mazor, supra note 3, at 1127, quoting Justice Black's dissent, from order amending Rules of Civil Procedure, 383 U.S. 1032, 1036 (1966).

7. Link v. Wabash R. R. Co., supra n. 5.

greater severity of the result in the criminal case which may call for greater protection in this phase of the case as it does in the phase of proof,—proof beyond a reasonable doubt. Another factor is that the government is seeking justice, not victory.[1] A third factor is the increasing stress which has come to be laid on "the right to counsel."[2] This right, characterized in terms of jurisdiction, creates the possibility of post-conviction remedies. All these factors put together bring a greater willingness to give a second try to the convicted man.

On one distinction, the courts are in agreement. It is between the competent lawyer who makes mistakes and the incompetent lawyer. The accused is entitled to a lawyer who is competent, not incompetent; he is not entitled to an infallible lawyer.[3] On two fairly narrow matters, the law is clear. If counsel for the accused represented conflictng interests, the accused did not have a fair trial and the conviction will be upset.[4] If counsel for the accused was deterred, by racial prejudice or otherwise, from using vigorous measures, the conviction cannot stand.[5] Beyond these situations, there is no clear rule. The courts often say the conviction will stand unless the lawyer's inadequacy caused the trial to be "a mockery of justice." With the principle so general, there is wide freedom for the courts to place the stress where they believe it should be laid in the particular case, as some illustrations show.

The stress may be placed on the finality of decision because of the strong and uninhibited reason that the prisoner has, with nothing to lose and freedom to gain, to attack his lawyer and his conviction. Mr. Thurman Arnold as a lawyer had represented more than his fair share of indigent defendants.[6] On the bench he could join in a denial of a new trial when the accused charged the counsel with incompetence, saying:

> "The opportunity to try his former lawyer has its undoubted attraction to a disappointed prisoner. . . . Few trials are free from mistake of counsel."[7]

Mr. Justice Douglas, in joining in a decision which upheld the privilege of a jail-house lawyer to aid his fellows, recognized a

---

1. Infra, pp. 324ff.

2. Infra pp. 324ff.

3. See United States ex rel. Darcy v. Handy, 203 F.2d 407 (3d Cir. 1953), aff'd 351 U.S. 454 (1956).

4. Glasser v. United States, 315 U.S. 60, 62 S.Ct. 457, 86 L.Ed. 680 (1942).

5. Powell v. Alabama, 287 U.S. 45, 53 S.Ct. 55 (1932), Annot., 84 A.L.R.

544 (1933); United States ex rel. Goldsby v. Harpole, 263 F.2d 71 (5th Cir.), cert. denied 361 U.S. 838 (1959).

6. See T. Arnold, Fair Fights and Foul (1965).

7. Diggs v. Welch, 148 F.2d 667, 670 (D.C.Cir.), cert. denied 325 U.S. 889 (1945).

source of "these endless petitions" as "a useful form of therapy."[8]

On the other side, the stress may be placed on the inconclusiveness of the evidence,[9] or on the grossness of the errors of counsel.[10] Different views have been indicated on whether the fact that counsel was appointed, not chosen and retained, is material.[11]

For the judge, the decision comes down to where your treasure lies. In a "bold decision," as an author reviewing the cases called it,[12] the Supreme Court of California reversed a conviction for possession of narcotics when because of ignorance of the rules of evidence the defendant's lawyer failed to object to the introduction of the seized drug itself. Mr. Justice Traynor, referring to these rules as matters which should be "commonplace" to any criminal lawyer, said such ignorance reduced the trial "to a farce and a sham." [13]

Discipline. Negligence is a factor taken into account in disciplinary cases. Negligence followed by misrepresentation to the client has led to suspension.[1] Laziness and inattention were held in some cases to be insufficient grounds for disbarment,[2] but negligence has led to censure [3].

SECTION 2.   CONTROL OVER THE CASE

When a lawyer is retained, over what phases of the case does he have control and over which ones does the client retain the power of direction? Only rarely should the question arise. Lawyers ordinarily keep their clients informed and avoid disagreements. Yet lawyers may presume to make decisions better left to clients.

8. Johnson v. Avery, 393 U.S. 483, 89 S.Ct. 747 (1969).

9. People v. Schulman, 299 Ill. 125, 132 N.E. 530 (1921), Annot., 24 A.L.R. 1025 (1923).

10. Lunce v. Overlade, 244 F.2d 108 (7th Cir. 1957), Annot., 74 A.L.R.2d 1390 (1960).

11. Compare Johnson v. United States, 110 F.2d 562 (D.C.Cir. 1940), with Craig v. United States, 217 F. 2d 355 (6th Cir. 1954).

12. Note, The Right to Effective Counsel in Criminal Cases, 18 Vand. L.Rev. 1920, 1931 (1965).

13. People v. Ibarra, 60 Cal.2d 460, 34 Cal.Rptr. 863, 386 P.2d 487 (1963).

1. Rock v. State Bar of California, 57 Cal.2d 639, 21 Cal.Rptr. 572, 371 P.2d 308 (1962), Annot., 96 A.L.R. 2d 823 (1964).

2. Gould v. State, 99 Fla. 662, 127 So. 309, Annot., 69 A.L.R. 705 (1930).

3. See In re Hirsch, 281 App.Div. 603, 121 N.Y.S.2d 816 (1953).

When lawyers lose cases, clients may seek a second chance, and they may even interpose in the operation of the machinery of the law.

The answer to the question of control is proposed at times in terms of substance—procedure; matters of "substance" are within the control of the client, matters of "procedure" are left to the lawyer. This merely restates the question. As Justice Frankfurter said:

> " '[S]ubstance' and 'procedure' are the same key-words to very different problems. . . . Each implies different variables depending upon the particular problem for which it is used." [1]

Meaning can be given to the terms by taking note of the positions and abilities of the two parties and determining what should be dominant in this particular situation. The client is the real party in interest. It is his property or reputation or future which is at stake, and he naturally feels he is entitled to determine whether to give up or to go ahead. The lawyer's situation is more complex. He is an expert representative of his client and much more besides. He is an officer of the legal order entrusted with the operation of the complicated legal system. He is a member of a special group who have developed professional standards appropriate to the operation of the system. Some court opinions explicitly reflect these considerations. In denying to the lay client the power to sign an effective stipulation extending the time to answer, the court said:

> "[I]t is indispensable to the decorum of the court and the due and orderly conduct of a cause that such attorneys shall have the management and control of the action." [2]

By contrast, in holding that the lawyer has no power to enter a consent decree and so reduce a $370,000 claim to a $22,000 judgment, the court stated:

> "[If] the attorney knew that express authority to enter a consent decree was required . . . the dispatch of litigation would suffer little, if any, delay." [3]

The power to end a case on its merits rests with the client, and a provision in the contract of retainer denying the power is against public policy.[4] When the client has abandoned the case,

1. Guaranty Trust Co. v. York, 326 U.S. 99, 108, 65 S.Ct. 1464, 1469 (1945).

2. Bonnifield v. Thorp, 71 F. 924, 929 (D.Alaska 1896), quoting Commissioner v. Younger, 29 Cal. 147 (1865).

3. Dwight v. Hazlett, 107 W.Va. 192, 200, 147 S.E. 877, 880 (1929), Annot., 66 A.L.R. 107 (1930).

4. Andrews v. Haas, 214 N.Y. 255, 108 N.E. 423 (1915), Annot., 3 A.L.R. 458 (1919); Enos v. Keating, 39 Wyo. 217, 271 P. 6 (1928), Annot., 67 A.L.R. 442 (1930).

his attorney on a contingent fee contract may not continue to press the case,[5] but when the client settled the case directly with the defendant the lawyer's charging lien was enforced against the defendant.[6] The lawyer may not dismiss the case,[7] nor may he compromise the claim.[8] The client can, however, ratify the compromise and will do so unless he disaffirms in a reasonable time.[9]

In the details of litigation the client may not act directly. Thus, when the plaintiff personally authorized the opening of a default, the authorization, as mentioned above, was disregarded by the court.[10]

The lawyer has broad powers over litigation from the inception of the case. The opening statement of plaintiff's counsel to the jury outlining the facts which the plaintiff expected to prove was held to be a basis for a directed verdict for the defendant.[11] The lawyer's consent to an adjudication in bankruptcy was held conclusive. Judge Woolsey gave the guiding reason.

> "Considered steps in a litigation by a member of the bar of a court are binding on his client unless fraud be shown. The apparent authority of attorneys in any proceeding before the court is plenary so far as the court and opposing parties are concerned .   .   .   . To be agents with such authority is one of the reasons for the existence of the Bar." [12]

The conclusion of a careful study of the subject, however, is that there is increasing willingness by the courts to relieve the client from the burden cast on him by his counsel;

> "The traditional cry that 'no one is entitled to a trial free from error' increasingly gives way before the more refined sensitivity of our age to injustice." [13]

---

5. Dow Chemical Co. v. Benton, 163 Tex. 477, 357 S.W.2d 565 (1962).

6. Kotsifakis v. A. Lusi, Ltd., 138 F.Supp. 945 (E.D.Va.1955).

7. Virginia Concrete Co. v. Board of Supervisors, 197 Va. 821, 91 S.E. 2d 415 (1956), Annot., 56 A.L.R.2d 1290 (1957).

8. Yarnall v. Yorkshire Worsted Mills, 370 Pa. 93, 87 A.2d 192 (1952), Annot., 30 A.L.R.2d 944 (1953).

9. Id.

10. Bonnifield v. Thorp, 71 F. 924 (D.Alaska 1896).

11. Oscanyan v. Arms Co., 103 U.S. 261 (1880).

12   In re Level Club, Inc., 46 F.2d 1002, 1003–1004 (S.D.N.Y.1931).

13. See Mazor, Power and Responsibility in the Attorney-Client Relation, 20 Stan.L.Rev. 1120, 1139 (1968).

SECTION 3.   CLIENTS' FUNDS

The funds of the clients must be kept separate from the funds of the lawyer.[1]   Methods of safeguarding the clients' funds and of appropriate bookkeeping are described in a volume prepared by the Committee on the Economics of Law Practice of the American Bar Association.[2]   Commingling of funds may lead to personal liability to the client[3] or to discipline when the commingled funds are lost by the failure of a bank.[4]   The client may be allowed to enforce his right against the lawyer in summary proceedings.[5]

A vivid contrast between the American and the English practices in two respects was drawn by the California Court of Appeal in a case in which:

> "[W]e find Blackmon [the client] still struggling in 1969 to obtain an accounting for money turned over to his attorney in 1961."[6]

The Law Society requires a solicitor to have his accounts audited every year by a qualified accountant.   A similar requirement would be useful in this country.   The knowledge of the periodical requirement and of the power to call for interim audits might have saved some careless lawyers from acts leading to disbarment.   It would aid many lawyers through self-improvement of their systems of office management.

Furthermore, there is in England, as the California court stated:

> "[A] fund for the compensation of loss to third persons due to the dishonesty of a solicitor   .   .   .   and to date all established claims of solicitor dishonesty have been paid in full."[7]

This English precedent has already been followed in half the states.   The funds created by state or local bar associations through annual contributions by members indemnify clients in some measure for losses from the defalcations of lawyers.[8]

---

1.   ABA Code of Professional Responsibility.   DR 9–102.

2.   ABA Comm. on the Economics of Law Practice, The Lawyers' Handbook 175–182 (1962).

3.   Naltner v. Dolan, 108 Ind. 500, 8 N.E. 289 (1886).

4.   Re Dahl, 159 Minn. 481, 199 N.W. 429 (1924).

5.   Cf. Re Long, 287 N.Y. 449, 40 N.E. 2d 247 (1942).

6.   Blackmon v. Hale, 78 Cal.Rptr. 569, 580 (1969), vacated, 1 Cal.3d 548, 83 Cal.Rptr. 194, 463 P.2d 418 (1970).

7.   Id. at 581.

8.   The Supreme Court of Delaware held it had the power, and exer-

SECTION 4. FINANCIAL TRANSACTIONS

The duty of fairness of a fiduciary to his principal applies with special force to the lawyer toward his client. It is so as to gifts to the lawyer by the client whether in life or by will and to business transactions of all kinds between them. The guiding policies and then some illustrative cases will be considered.

One policy, in support of upholding a transaction between them, is the general one of enabling a man to deal with his property as he desires. An opposing policy, condemning such a transaction, is the protection of the client from the selfish action of a fiduciary on whom he would naturally rely. Another policy, supporting the second, is the protection of the reputation of the profession against suspicion of misuse of power at the expense of clients, a matter of great importance in making laymen willing to consult lawyers and to obtain the legal services they need.[1]

The law gives greater weight to the last two policies. It implements them by the legal principle that financial transactions between lawyer and client will be carefully scrutinized. One matter to which scrutiny is directed is full understanding of the transaction by the client. Independent legal advice is often mentioned as an appropriate or essential safeguard. An illustration is a case in which a client desired that her lawyer have her real property at her death. To avoid the danger of a will contest, the lawyer suggested that the client make a deed to him reserving a life estate in herself. Such a deed was drawn by another lawyer who, however, handled the matter in a routine way with little explanation to the client who executed it. Some years later the client became dissatisfied with the arrangement and sought to have the

---

cised it, to establish a clients' security fund to which all lawyers must contribute. In re Reed, —— Del. ——, 257 A.2d 382 (1969). The Supreme Court of Oregon upheld the validity of such a fund based on enabling legislation. Bennett v. Oregon State Bar, —— Or. ——, 470 P.2d 945 (1970).

1. The opposing policies are well set out in a case involving the testamentary gift of a large part of an estate to the lawyer-draftsman who was the testator's closest and long time associate. In his opinion upholding the gift Justice Weaver stated:

"We start with the rule . . . that: The right of testamentary

disposition . . . is by law made absolute [subject to the principle of undue influence]." Re Estate of Smith, 68 Wash.2d 145, 152, 411 P.2d 879, 882 (1966), Annot., 19 A.L.R.3d 575 (1968).

In dissent Chief Justice Rosellini wrote:

"[P]ublic policy should dictate that an attorney not be permitted to take a substantial legacy under a will which he has drawn unless the testator was advised by a disinterested attorney. . . . This court is responsible for the ethics of the legal profession . . . and the image of the profession." Id. at 161, 411 P.2d at 888.

deed set aside. The appellate court, while saying there was no taint of fraud or chicanery, upheld a decree voiding the deed because the lawyer "should have used active diligence to see that the client was fully informed of the nature and effect of the transaction proposed. . . . the significance of her proposed act." [2]

In business transactions the additional requirement has been laid down in some cases that the transaction be fair under the circumstances. It is especially so when the client is inexperienced or necessitous. A lawyer employed in the settlement of a small decedent's estate purchased from one of the distributees, then unemployed, his share in the estate for $2,500 which some years later came to about $8,000. The trial court's action in refusing to set aside the sale was reversed by the appellate court, with the statement that on the second trial the issue would be:

> "[W]hether the attorney has adequately demonstrated that the purchase was for a full and complete consideration and free of all the advantages which an attorney ordinarily has. . . ." [3]

The burden of proof in these matters is on the lawyer. This appears neatly in a case in which a client sued to annul a contract made with her lawyer. Both parties died before the trial and the case was continued by their personal representatives. At the trial the plaintiff offered evidence of the lawyer-client relation and of the client's action without independent advice and then rested, on the view the burden was on the lawyer. The defendant presented no evidence. Judgment was entered against the lawyer's estate, as the burden was on the lawyer to go forward and show that "all was fair, open, voluntary and well understood by the client." [4]

When a client wishes to make a testamentary gift to his lawyer, at least the will should be drawn by another and fully independent lawyer.[5] It might satisfy this admonition for the lawyer-beneficiary to draw the will omitting any gift to himself, and for an independent lawyer to draft a codicil with the gift in it.

There is an unfortunate amount of litigation or of publicity at least over cases of this sort. For the protection of clients and the reputation of the bar, the time may be at hand when the courts will hold any gift from client to lawyer invalid, except

2. Webster v. Kelly, 274 Mass. 564, 571, 175 N.E. 69, 71 (1931).

Another case which upset an inter vivos gift is McDonald v. Hewlett, 102 Cal.App.2d 680, 228 P.2d 83 (1951), Annot., 24 A.L.R.2d 1288 (1952).

3. Deal v. Migoski, 122 So.2d 415, 418 (Fla.Ct.App.1960).

4. Frost v. Bachman, 283 N.Y. 744, 28 N.E.2d 969 (1940).

5. ABA Code of Professional Responsibility, EC 5–5.

when the lawyer is a natural object of the donor's bounty. The Supreme Court of Wisconsin formally reprimanded a lawyer for drawing a will under which he was a beneficiary, stating:

> "The attorney's duty of fidelity to his client involves more than refraining from exercising undue influence." [6]

Two justices in a case already cited stated:

> "I would go further and say the presumption [of undue influence] is all but irrebutable." [7]

SECTION 5.   COMPENSATION

Introduction. The methods of financing legal services greatly affect their availability and quality. The sources of fees will first be raised; then the amount, the control, and the protection of fees; and finally the special problems of division of fees and contingent fees.

Sources of Fees. The possible sources of fees include (1) the client himself, (2) the opponent or the subject matter of the litigation, (3) an organization of which the client is a party and (4) the government and private charity. The first two will be considered here.

a.   The Client

Fees from clients are the principal method of financing legal services in the private sector of our economy. The general principle applies that a person who employs another is under an obligation to pay the reasonable value of the services. In one aspect, the lawyer is, as Mr. Justice Harlan said, "a self-employed business man." [1] Through the Committee on the Economics of Law Practice the American Bar Association has done much to improve the organization and administration of law offices.[2] There is nothing left of the pose that the lawyer receives only an honorarium slipped into the hind pocket of his gown out of the

---

6. State v. Horan, 21 Wis.2d 66, 72, 123 N.W.2d 488 (1963), Annot., 98 A.L.R.2d 1234 (1964). The same court held that a similar presumption arises where there is a gift to a member of a lawyer's family. Re Estate of Perssion, 20 Wis.2d 532, 123 N.W.2d 465 (1963), Annot., 13 A.L.R.3d 381 (1967). On the English rule, see Cordery's Law Relating to Solicitors 130 (6th Ed. 1968).

7. Re Estate of Smith, 68 Wash.2d 145, 163, 411 P.2d 879, 889 (1966), Annot., 19 A.L.R.3d 575 (1968).

1. Link v. Wabash R. R. Co., 370 U.S. 626, 82 S.Ct. 1386 (1962).

2. See ABA Comm. on the Economics of Law Practice, The Lawyer's Handbook (1962).

gratitude of the client. Yet controversies over fees are most distasteful to lawyers and as Canon 14 stated, "lawsuits with clients should be resorted to only to prevent injustice, imposition or fraud." The position of a lawyer as a professional man engaged in the administration of the law may in appropriate cases cause the denial of fees altogether.[3]

b. The Adversary or a Fund in Court

"Attorneys' Fees: Where Shall the Ultimate Burden Lie?"[1] In the United States the general rule is that each litigant pays his own lawyer only. The loser has no duty to reimburse the winner for his legal fees. A man who recovers, say, for injuries suffered in an automobile accident has his physician's bills included as part of his damages but not his lawyer's fees. In England the loser reimburses the winner for his legal fees subject to a determination of their reasonableness by a taxing master.[2]

At times the usual American rule is set aside. The change may come through agreement of the parties, from legislative directives, or through the power of the court.

The parties to a contract, as a promissory note, might provide that if the contract is not performed at maturity and suit has to be brought on it, an additional stated sum shall be paid by the debtor as attorneys' fees.[3] Such provisions have been upheld when reasonable in amount, as 10% of the sum sued for. In some states, however, legislation makes these provisions invalid.

Statutes provide explicitly for the recovery of attorneys' fees in some matters. The typical situation is that in which the defendant has the superior position and could by extended litigation force an unfair settlement, as actions against insurance companies and common carriers, and actions by employees for wages or workmen's compensation.[4] Federal law gives attorneys' fees in some fields where private rights of action are relied on as an additional sanction of public duty, as under the securities acts and the antitrust laws.[5]

3. When an estranged wife became reconciled with her husband the husband was not liable for the fees of counsel employed by the wife in divorce proceedings. In Re De Pass, 231 S.C. 134, 97 S.E.2d 505 (1957).

1. This is the title of a helpful discussion of the subject. Cheek, Note, 20 Van.L.Rev. 1216 (1967).

2. Goodhart, Costs, 38 Yale L.J. 849 (1929).

3. A summary of the practices in the matter is given in ABA Comm. on Professional Ethics, Opinions, No. 157, 22 A.B.A.J. 503 (1936).

4. The constitutionality of a statute authorizing the award of counsel's fees to a successful claimant in an action for wages was upheld in Hunter v. Flowers, 43 So.2d 435 (Fla.1949), Annot., 14 A.L.R.2d 452 (1950).

5. Kahan v. Rosenstiel, 424 F.2d 161 (3d Cir. 1970), cert. denied, 398 U.S. 950, 90 S.Ct. 1970 (1970).

In other matters the courts may find an implicit grant of power as a means of effectuating the legislative policy. This was so in Mills v. The Electric Auto-Lite Co.,[6] where petitioners attacked a corporate merger accomplished through a misleading proxy statement. Mr. Justice Harlan stated that the successful petitioners were entitled "to an interim award of litigation expenses and reasonable attorneys' fees." He based the decision on the ground that "to provide such remedies are necessary to make effective the congressional purpose."

A few other illustrations will be given. In divorce proceedings a wife in financial need has the right to recover attorneys' fees from the husband.[7] If an unfounded claim or defense is asserted for oppressive reasons, a court might award attorneys' fees.[8] When a seaman is denied his right to maintenance and cure, he is entitled to attorneys' fees as "damages." [9]

The American rule, denying reimbursement, has come under increased questioning for a variety of reasons. One set of reasons involves the injustice to the individual litigant and the social harm. It is a manifest injustice, it is said, to subject the winner in a law suit to the payment of his lawyer's fees when the result shows the other party was in the wrong, and reimbursement of attorneys' fees is essential to make him whole. The point is somewhat blunted by recognition of the fact that most legal controversies do not involve clear cut differences between right and wrong, and it might be an injustice to throw on one party the whole burden of the litigation when there was something on his side.

A social harm of the American system is the encouragement of litigation. Litigation with its stirring up of anger and hostility is not the best method to settle most controversies.[10] The American system gives a claimant a double encouragement to sue. He is free of the burden of having to reimburse his adversary for lawyers' fees. With the contingent fee system he will not have to pay even his own lawyer unless he wins. With a contingent fee contract of one third to the lawyer the claimant has two thirds of the recovery to win and nothing to lose, a sort of speculation without putting up a margin.

Another basis for questioning the American rule is the harm it might do in deterring the assertion of a just claim or defense.

6. 396 U.S. 375, 90 S.Ct. 616 (1970).

7. Wallman v. Wallman, 48 Nev. 239, 229 P. 1 (1924), Annot., 35 A.L.R. 1099 (1925).

8. See Fed.R.Civ.P., rules 54(d), 56 (g); Guardian Trust Co. v. Kansas City S. Ry., 28 F.2d 233 (8th Cir. 1928).

9. Vaughan v. Atkinson, 369 U.S. 527, 82 S.Ct. 997 (1962).

10. See supra pp. 115ff.

Professor Ehrenzweig has told how in his time of need he suffered a loss then grievous to him because of the cost litigation would impose on him even though he won.[11] There is the opposing attitude expressed by Justice Goldberg, quoting Justice Clark, that "our conviction that it [the costs system] 'favored the wealthy and unduly penalized the losing party.' "[12]

The desirability of making claimants' litigation free of burdens may depend, it has been suggested, on the nature of the society. A stable society may discourage controversy and litigation. A society conscious of change may wish to make litigation easy as a measure of social change and to use private litigation as a means of enforcing governmental policy.

There is something of value in all of the opinions expressed. Their variety show that what is desirable is not a single method throughout all legal proceedings, but a wise choice of method for the particular kind of controversy involved. The choice should be made, by the court or by the legislature, unhampered by such phrases as "the American system," "the English system," and "the sporting theory of justice." Mr. Justice Harlan so intimated in speaking for an almost unanimous court in the *Mills* case:

> "While the general American rule is that attorneys' fees are not ordinarily recoverable as costs, both the courts and Congress have developed exceptions to this rule for situations in which overriding considerations indicate the need for such a recovery."[13]

He added in a footnote:

> "Many commentators [whom he cited] have argued for a more thoroughgoing abandonment of the rule."

An area which invites a broad use of the power to impose reimbursement of expenses is the personal injury field. Two proposals to this effect were made by a judge who conducted an inquiry into the area.[14] One proposal was that the losing party in a law

11. Ehrenzweig, Reimbursement of Counsel Fees and the Great Society, 54 Cal.L.Rev. 792 (1966). "The present American system says to a man with a small case, 'Regardless of the merits of your cause you cannot have justice because your case is not worth it.' A system allowing recovery of attorneys' fees would say: 'If you really believe in your cause—enough to assume the risk of paying your opponent's attorney's fees if you lose—then you can have justice regardless of how small your case is.' The latter seems vastly superior." B. Christensen, Lawyers for People of Moderate Means: Some Problems of Availability of Legal Services 63 (1970).

12. See Justice Goldberg concurring in Farmer v. Arabian American Oil Co., 379 U.S. 227, 239, 85 S.Ct. 411, 418 (1964).

13. 396 U.S. 375, 391–92, 90 S.Ct. 616, 625 (1970).

14. Wasservogel, Report in the Matter of the Investigation Ordered by the Appellate Division of the Supreme Court in and for the First Judicial Department for an Inquiry

suit which goes to trial pay the reasonable expenses of the winner. The second was that when either side offered to settle at a stated figure and the verdict was for a greater or lesser figure, the amount of the recovery should be increased or decreased by an appropriate percentage of the amount of the verdict at the expense of the party who had refused to settle. A time factor might be included with the extent of the modification of the amount of the verdict affected somewhat by the length of the period elapsing between the offer of settlement and the date of the judgment. This would discourage the use of delay as a weapon against necessitous claimants. Unreasonable clients would be dismayed at having the amount of the verdict moved up or down at their expense. A few such examples would clear the court dockets.

The trial judges are understandably reluctant to extend the reimbursement system widely because of the administrative burdens entailed. There are no taxing masters to take over the task, the quality of lawyers' services and their schedules of charges vary widely, and it would be a heavy additional burden on the judge to have to determine in every case the worth of the services of the winning lawyer and how much of these charges should be reimbursed by the loser. An illustration of the detail involved is a case in which on remand the lawyers claimed a fee of from $12,000 to $17,000. The judge after a review of the briefs and the facts—including mention that as to one matter it was he and not counsel who had to find the law—awarded something less than $3,000.[15] These objections do not apply to the methods proposed for personal injury cases, for the computation would be made by the clerk of court with only rare need for review by the judge.

A wholly different situation from the allowance of fees against the adversary is that in which fees are allowed out of a fund in court, as "where a plaintiff traced or treated a common fund for the benefit of others as well as himself." Here attorneys' fees are generally allowed.[16] The situation includes cases in which "the *stare decisis* effect of the judgment obtained by the plain-

---

by the Court into Certain Abuses and Illegal and Improper Practices Alleged in the Petition (Commonly Referred to as Ambulance Chasing), 14 Mass.L.Q. 1 (1928). See also Lumbard, Can We Save the Trial Bar?, 45 J.Am.Jud.Soc'y 12, 16–17 (1961); Note, Use of Taxable Costs to Regulate the Conduct of Litigation, 53 Colum.L.Rev. 78 (1953).

15. Vaughan v. Atkinson, 206 F. Supp. 575 (E.D.Va.1962).

16. See Sprague v. Ticonic National Bank, 307 U.S. 161, 59 S.Ct. 777 (1939). A review of the kinds of cases in which there is allowance of "costs between solicitor and client" is given in Judge Booth's opinion in Guardian Trust Co. v. Kansas City So. Ry. Co., 28 F.2d 233 (8th Cir. 1928), rev'd on other grounds, 281 U.S. 1, 50 S.Ct. 194 (1930). See also Wallace v. Fiske, 80 F.2d 897 (8th Cir. 1936), Annot. 107 A.L.R. 749 (1937).

tiff established as a matter of law the right of a discernible class of persons to collect upon similar claims." [17]

Occasionally the lawyer for the contestants of a will making a charitable bequest might claim a fee for "having brought the fund into court." It would be a perversion of the principle to award the fee, and it would be unprofessional for the lawyer to receive the fee.[18] The lawyer, seeking to defeat the testator's plan, would be in the rare position of being paid for his efforts or lack of them whichever way the decision went.

A question that has been most manifest in the federal courts concerns the origin and scope of the power, specifically should the use of the power be limited to cases in equity. The Supreme Court of the United States has in some of its opinions emphasized the power in the English court of chancery.[19] A Court of Appeals based its denial of costs to the defendant in a long and vexatious libel action in part on the ground that it could find no precedent for allowing costs in an action at law.[20] By contrast Mr. Justice Harlan based his decision in the *Mills* case on the policy of the statute. In his reference to a possibly wider use of the power to tax costs he gave no hint of limiting the power to proceedings in equity. In these days when law and equity are merged it would be most unfortunate to define the power along the lines drawn centuries ago for wholly different purposes between Lord Coke and Lord Ellesmere. As Professor Moore has said:

> "And we suggest that equitable growth warrants an exercise of the power in all civil actions, and certainly, at a minimum, in court actions." [21]

The authoritative source of the law on fees under our federal system [22] has not often come in question. When the cause of an action is based on federal law and is sued on in a state or a federal court, it is clear that a mandatory federal law, "the Supreme Law of the Land," will govern. When the cause of action is based on state law and is sued on in a federal court, there are in competition the two policies made concrete in the decision of Erie R. R. Co. v. Tompkins [23] and the Federal Rules of Civil Procedure,

17. See Warren, C. J., in Fleischmann Distilling Corp. v. Maier Brewing Co., 386 U.S. 714, 719, 87 S.Ct. 1404, 1407 (1967).

18. ABA Code of Professional Responsibility, Canons 5 & 7.

19. See Sprague v. Ticonic National Bank, 307 U.S. 161, 59 S.Ct. 777 (1939); Fleischmann Distilling Corp. v. Maier Brewing Co., 386 U. S. 714, 87 S.Ct. 1404 (1967).

20. Smoot v. Fox, 353 F.2d 830 (6th Cir. 1965), cert. denied, 334 U.S. 909 (1966).

21. 6 Moore's Federal Practice ¶ 54.77 [2] (2d ed. 1966).

22. For a discussion of "the authoritative sources", see supra pp. 28ff.

23. 304 U.S. 64, 58 S.Ct. 817 (1938).

sometimes expressed in the terms of "substance" and "procedure." The greater weight of the argument is on the side of the application of state law, it is believed, so that the result as to this important aspect will not change materially because of the court in which the action is brought.[24]

c. The Amount and Control of Fees

In fixing the amount of fees there is an inescapable conflict of interest between lawyer and client. The safeguards needed may come from the individual lawyer, the organized profession, the legislature, or the courts.

The Lawyer. Ordinarily the fee is agreed on with the client at the time the lawyer is retained.[1] When uncertainties make it impossible then to fix the fee the lawyer may give the client and himself assurance against excessive charges as a leader of the bar said he did:

> "I cannot now tell you. I can tell you that we keep careful records, these you can see, we have a cost system, when the work is done we will submit a bill we believe fair. You must feel free to discuss this with us if you want. . . . [O]ur rule is that you yourself have the right to fix the bill."[2]

If the fee is fixed during the performance of the lawyer's work when the client is especially dependent there is a heavy burden on the lawyer to show it is reasonable.[3] In most cases the individual lawyer's sense of fairness will be decisive. Studies of personal injury litigation show that most lawyers charge somewhat less than their contracts and the law allow.[4]

The Profession. The organized profession states in general form the factors to be taken into account in setting fees.[5] Its

24. Cf. Cohen v. Beneficial Indus. Loan Corp., 170 F.2d 44 (1948), aff'd 337 U.S. 541 (1949).

1. A good discussion of fixing fees is in ABA Comm. on Economics of Law Practice The Lawyers' Handbook 279 et seq. (1962).

2. Smith, Law Office Organization, 26 A.B.A.J. 494, 496 (1940).

3. Stern v. Hyman, 182 N.C. 422, 109 S.E. 79 (1921), Annot., 19 A.L.R. 847 (1922); Bounougias v. Peters, 49 Ill.App.2d 138, 198 N.E.2d 142 (1964), Annot., 13 A.L.R.3d 701 (1967).

4. Franklin, Chanin & Irving, Accidents, Money and the Law: A Study of the Economics of Personal Injury Litigation, 61 Colum.L.Rev. 1, 20–30 (1961); Law Ass'n of Philadelphia, Report of the Committee of Censors in Re Contingent Fee Accident Litigation, 14 Mass. L.Q. 24 (Supp. Nov. 1928).

5. ABA Code of Professional Responsibility:

EC 2–17 The determination of a proper fee requires consideration of the interests of both client and lawyer. A lawyer should not charge more than a reasonable fee, for excessive cost of legal service would deter laymen from utilizing the legal system in protection of their rights. Furthermore, an excessive charge abuses the professional relationship between lawyer and client. On the other hand, adequate compensation is necessary in order to enable the

statement is a composite of the relevant factors seen from the viewpoints of the client and the lawyer. A factor of almost universal use is the time record of work done. Yet records of office work may not reflect the amount or the value of the work. The lawyer's best thoughts may come, as a New York judge said, "while away from his office, at home, or elsewhere." [6] The profession condemns fees which are either too high or too low. "[C]learly excessive fees" call for discipline.[7] Conversely, many local bar associations publish "Suggested Minimum Fee Schedules." The principal purpose of the schedules is to state a level of fees which is fair to both client and lawyer and which can serve as a guide to lawyers in their work. The American Bar Association Committee approved the preparation of such schedules because:

> "When members of the Bar are induced to render legal services for inadequate compensation, as a consequence the quality of the services rendered may be lowered, the welfare of the profession injured and the administration of justice made less efficient." [8]

The Committee stated further that while the schedules are not binding, the habitual charging of lesser fees might be evidence of unethical conduct.[9] One criticism of the schedules is that they are "tailored to the demands of the higher priced lawyers of the community" and should not be imposed upon other lawyers or their clients.[10] An accompanying criticism is that the schedules violate the anti-trust statutes or at least their policy.[11]

lawyer to serve his client effectively and to preserve the integrity and independence of the profession.

EC 2–18 The determination of the reasonableness of a fee requires consideration of all relevant circumstances, including those stated in the Disciplinary Rules. The fees of a lawyer will vary according to many factors, including the time required, his experience, ability, and reputation, the nature of the employment, the responsibility involved, and the results obtained. Suggested fee schedules and economic reports of state and local bar associations provide some guidance on the subject of reasonable fees. It is a commendable and long-standing tradition of the bar that special consideration is given in the fixing of any fee for services rendered a brother lawyer or a member of his immediate family.

6. In re Pott's, Estate, 213 App.Div. 59, 62, 209 N.Y.S. 655, 658 (1925).

7. ABA Code of Professional Responsibility DR 2–106.

8. ABA Comm. on Professional Ethics, Opinions, No. 302 (1961), reported in 48 A.B.A.J. 159 (1962).

9. A similar view has been expressed by some state bar associations. See Opinion 194 of the Committee on Professional Ethics of the Illinois State Bar Association (1960), reported in 48 Ill.B.J. 790–91 (1960).

10. See Letter, 48 A.B.A.J. 516 (1962).

11. The establishment of such a fee schedule was referred to without condemnation in Lathrop v. Donohue, 367 U.S. 820, 842, 81 S.Ct. 1826, 1837 (1961).

The Legislature. The legislature or the administrative commission may set maximum fees for services to persons who, as a group, are disadvantaged or inexperienced and especially deserving of protection. Employees with claims under workmen's compensation laws [12] and veterans of military service with claims to pensions are illustrations. The courts have applied the legislative limitations strictly. In a workmen's compensation case a lawyer had made a collateral agreement with a brother of the claimant for fifty per cent of the award. In condemning the scheme, the court said it would regard as deserving of disciplinary action "the use of any means which the wit of man may devise" to avoid the limitation.[13] At times the limitation is grievously unfair to the lawyer, as in case in which the lawyer obtained for a disabled veteran an award of $5,000 and $50 a month for life, with his fee limited to $10.[14] The limitations may work harm to claimants with difficult claims, for lawyers, as others, may be unwilling to work for a pittance. And the claimants may have difficulty in obtaining legal services.

The Court. The court may pass on fees in various situations. The client may have retained the lawyer without specifying the fee and the court is asked to make it definite. Or the court itself has to fix or to supervise the fees to be allowed, as the allowance of fees out of a fund in court. Or the fee has been fixed by the parties but it is under review as excessive. The same factors, it is believed, go to determine what is a reasonable fee in all these situations.

Two cases illustrate the relevant factors. In one a lawyer was discharged by the client after years of work on a case. The Supreme Court of Wisconsin raised the fee from $18,000 set by the trial court to $28,000. In an opinion by Mr. Justice Currie the court took into account the time spent on the case as shown by detailed sheets; the minimum fee schedule of the State Bar; the importance of the case and the high quality of the services rendered; and the testimony of experienced lawyers. It took judicial notice that the lawyer's working year has about 250 days and the earnings day about five or six earning hours, and that office overhead consumes about 40 per cent of the gross income of a law office.[15] The same court, however, upheld the action of the trial court in reducing the fee of assigned counsel in a murder trial for more than five weeks from $17,000 claimed to $6,600 be-

---

12. An excellent discussion of limitations on fees is given in 3 A. Larsen, The Law of Workmen's Compensation §§ 83.00–83.30 (1970).

13. In re Fisch, 188 App.Div. 525, 177 N.Y.S. 338 (1919).

14. In re Shinberg's Estate, 238 App. Div. 74, 263 N.Y.S. 354 (1933).

15. Touchett v. E Z Paintr Corp., 14 Wis.2d 479, 111 N.W.2d 419 (1961).

cause counsel, despite the admonitions of the judge, had excessively prolonged the trial.[16]

At times the fee is attacked by the client as excessive. The court has inherent power over the subject, though usually reluctant to exercise it. Judge Washington said:

> "In a very real sense attorneys are officers of the courts in which they practice; and clients are wards of the court in regard to their relationship with their attorneys. . . .
>
> Fee contracts between attorney and client are a subject of special interest and concern to the courts. They are not to be enforced upon the same basis as ordinary commercial contracts." [17]

In the case last cited the court denied recovery on a note given by the client to the lawyer for his fee, and in doing so it subordinated the principle of res judicata to the requirement of fairness between client and lawyer. In cases of gross excessiveness the lawyer may be disciplined.[18]

d. The Protection of Fees

Clients are not always appreciative or honest. The courts and the legislature have invented devices "for the protection of attorneys against the knavery of their clients."

The lawyer may have two kinds of liens to protect his fee.[1] One is a retaining lien which attaches to all papers, securities or moneys belonging to the client and coming into the lawyer's possession by reason of his employment. It protects all fees owed by the client to the lawyer. It has the great disadvantage and even incongruous aspect between persons in fiduciary relationship that its value consists in the inconvenience the principal suffers from the action of his former fiduciary. As the Supreme Court of New Jersey said:

> "the effectiveness of the lien is proportionate to the inconvenience of the client in being denied access to his property." [2]

The second kind is a charging lien against the client's interest in the subject which the lawyer is seeking to enforce for him. It protects only the lawyer's fee in the particular matter involved.

---

16. Conway v. Sauk County, 19 Wis. 2d 599, 120 N.W.2d 671 (1963).

17. Spilker v. Hankin, 188 F.2d 35, 37–39 (D.C.Cir. 1951).

18. ABA Code of Professional Responsibility, EC 2–18; DR 2–106. Re Louis Goldstone, 214 Cal. 490, 6 P.2d 513 (1931), Annot., 80 A.L.R. 706 (1932).

1. The two liens are described by Judge Cardozo in In re Heinsheimer, 214 N.Y. 361, 108 N.E. 636 (1915).

2. Haneman, J., in Brauer v. Hotel Associates, Inc., 40 N.J. 415, 422, 192 A.2d 831, 835 (1963).

The state statutes vary widely in the terms of the lien they provide. The lien may attach at once to the claim the lawyer is retained to enforce, or to the cause of action after suit is filed, or only to the judgment.[3] The law of the state where the action was brought and not the law of the state where the lawyer was retained, so it has been held, determines the lien.[4]

When the client has stepped out of the case, the courts have been disinclined to permit the lawyer retained in the case on a contingent fee to press the case as a means of protecting his fee. It was so when the client had been induced to dismiss the action,[5] and also when the case was dismissed on the motion of the defendant because of the plaintiff's failure to appear for the taking of depositions.[6] The use of a confession of judgment for the amount of the fee agreed on was condemned by a bar association committee, at least when the client was inexperienced and the amount of the judgment included 20 per cent. for "costs of collection." [7]

e. Contingent Fees

A contingent fee is one conditioned on success in the controversy, that is, a percentage of the amount awarded to a claimant in settlement or litigation. In practice it is closely connected with matters considered elsewhere, solicitation of practice and personal injury and death claims.[1] In most countries, as in England, such a fee is unlawful.[2]

The prohibition of the contingent fee in England is associated with "a number of long-standing legal doctrines designed to limit a lawsuit to those immediately affected by it."

> "In Anglo-American law these concepts have taken the following form: [1] the prohibition of assistance to a litigant by one not directly interested in the suit—the doctrine of

---

3. It was held that the lien attached to continuing payments due from an insurer to the successful plaintiff, Blazek v. North American Life & Casualty Co., 265 Minn. 236, 121 N.W.2d 339 (1963), Annot. 99 A.L.R. 2d 451 (1965); but not to the property involved in the litigation against a successful defendant. Wessinger v. Sturkie, 77 F.2d 751 (4th Cir. 1935).

4. Peresipka v. Elgin, Joliet & Eastern Ry. Co., 231 F.2d 268 (7th Cir. 1956), Annot. 59 A.L.R.2d 564 (1958).

5. Enos v. Keating, 39 Wyo. 217, 271 P. 6 (1928), Annot. 67 A.L.R. 442 (1930).

6. Dow Chemical Co. v. Benton, 163 Tex. 477, 357 S.W.2d 565 (1962).

7. Ass'n Bar City N.Y., Op. 839 (1959).

1. See infra pp. 345ff.

2. A court in Germany enforced a contingent fee contract which was governed by American law. It held that though such a contract was unlawful in Germany, it was not so strongly against its country's public policy as to be denied enforcement. See 52 Am.J.Int'l L. 798 (1958).

maintenance; [2] the prohibition of agreements to share in the subject matter of the suit, if successful, in return for assistance in litigation—the doctrine of champerty; [3] the disapproval of the purchase or sale of part or all of an interest which is under litigation—the doctrine of the non-assignability of a cause action; and [4] the disapproval of those who stir up and stimulate litigation—the doctrine of barratry." [3]

The suitability of these doctrines to American conditions will be raised here in almost reverse order.

To stir up and stimulate litigation designed to achieve socially desirable ends is at times taken as a positive good, even protected by the Constitution.[4] If carried on merely to harm another —that would be another matter.

The non-assignability of a cause of action is so unsuited to our conditions that mention is enough to cause rejection.

Assistance to a litigant, "maintenance," may turn for its legality on factors similar to those mentioned above as to barratry.

Agreements to share in the process of the suit, "champerty," is the principal problem.

The validity of such fees as well as the desirable safeguards should be determined by weighing their advantages and disadvantages.

The great advantage of such a fee is that it enables a poor man with a meritorious claim to retain a lawyer to enforce it for its real worth when otherwise he would have to give it up for little or nothing. Another advantage even for a client able to pay a fee is that it meets the ordinary man's view of a sensible basis of charges for intangible services as those of the lawyer, quantum meruit as measured by the result. Yet another advantage urged for it is that this system of compensation does much to support a set of independent lawyers who are ready to challenge injustices done to their clients from any source, whether government or business or labor.

The harms from the method may bear on the client or on the adversary or on the public. As to the client the principal danger is that of overreaching in the fee charged. There have been limitations set by the legislature or by the court.[5] There has also been avowed "strained construction" of an unfair fee contract, as in a case in which the lawyer receiving his fee on win-

---

3. F. Mackinnon, Contingent Fees for Legal Services: A Study of Professional Economics and Responsibilities, 35–36 (1964). See also Radin, Contingent Fees in California, 28 Cal.L.Rev. 587 (1940).

4. N.A.A.C.P. v. Button, 371 U.S. 415, 83 S.Ct. 328 (1963).

5. See infra pp. 352–55.

ning a case in the trial court sought to keep it despite reversal of the judgment on appeal.[6]

For the adversary there is the danger of the vexatious suit filed for nuisance value. Many a claimant would not bring suit if he had first to pay his lawyer. Freed of the burden of paying his own lawyer unless he wins, and freed, too, of the threat of having to pay the fees of his opponent if he loses, the client can sue without risk. There is, further, the encouragement of inflated claims and of excessive measures as the amount of the lawyer's fee turns on the amount of the recovery.

As to the public there is the result of clogging of the courts whose calendars are made up principally of personal injury cases handled on a contingent fee basis. There may be the more serious harm of impairment of a sense of professional obligation on the part of many of the bar, and at least the public's belief in this impairment as voiced by the sneer, "ambulance chaser."

In the United States, as all know, the contingent fee is for the most part lawful. It is prohibited or limited or safeguarded where special conditions call for such restrictions.

In matters in which litigation is especially discouraged, the contingent fee may be forbidden. An example is the suit for divorce where the fee is contingent on the success in the case or on the amount of alimony, since it is the policy of the law to encourage reconciliation.[7] When the divorce has been granted and the husband is in default in the payment of alimony, the opinion has been expressed that a lawyer may take a retainer contingent on the collection of the alimony due.[8]

Where great harm would result from the use of extreme measures to achieve success, again the contingent fee is unlawful. An example is a retainer to help secure the passage of a legislative measure.[9]

As to personal injury and death claims, the principal need is for protection of the clients. Protective measures are discussed elsewhere.[10]

f. Division of Fees

The division of fees between lawyers is condemned by the Code of Professional Responsibility unless the client consents, the

6. Pocius v. Halvorsen, 30 Ill.2d 73, 195 N.E.2d 137 (1963), Annot., 13 A.L.R.3d 672 (1967).

7. Re Sylvester, 195 Iowa 1329, 192 N.W. 442 (1923), Annot., 30 A.L.R. 188 (1924); McCarthy v. Santangello, 137 Conn. 410, 78 A.2d 240 (1951); ABA Code of Professional Responsibility, EC 2–20.

8. N.Y. County Lawyer's Ass'n, Comm. on Professional Ethics, Op. 533 (1964).

9. See Trist v. Child, 88 U.S. (21 Wall.) 441 (1874); 6A Corbin, Contracts § 1447 (1962).

10. See infra pp. 354–55.

whole fee is reasonable, and the division is in proportion to the services performed and the responsibilities assumed.[1] Division of fees with a layman is forbidden outright.[2] The evils guarded against include excessive charges to the client and deception of the court,[3] and the use of laymen as solicitors of practice.[4] The courts have refused to enforce agreements between lawyers for the division of fees when one lawyer did no more than procure the case for the other.[5] Two lawyers call for special attention, the forwarder and the specialist.

When a case is sent to a firm in another city, it is common for the forwarder to share in the fee. In commercial collections the practice has been approved by a rule of the Commercial Law League which is probably known and assented to by the clients.[6] In less routine matters the forwarder usually continues as an active participant in the preparation of evidence, the consideration of compromise offers, and in keeping the client informed, and he may fairly share in the fee.

The association of the specialist with the generalist should be encouraged. About half of the bar are solo practitioners and many cases coming to them call for specialized assistance. The client will be best served by the association of the appropriate specialist, and the Canon should not become a deterrent. The solo practitioner can scarcely be expected to associate the needed specialist if it means the loss of the whole fee and, perhaps, of the client. When the lawyer first retained remains in the case even in a lesser role, he should share in the fee. Lawyers in large firms may naturally minimize the importance of the outside expert or the danger in the loss of the fee or the client. Their partners and office associates provide the expertise needed and the Code of Professional Responsibility, recognizing the need, explicitly approves the division of a fee with "a partner in or associate of his law firm or law office." [7] The solo lawyer may find the specialist in another discipline to be the most helpful as-

1. ABA Code of Professional Responsibility, EC 2–22; DR 2–107. The fee will be evenly divided when there has been no agreement of the lawyers on the terms of the division. Carson v. McMahan, 215 Or. 38, 332 P.2d 84 (1958), Annot. 73 A.L.R.2d 991 (1960).

2. ABA Code of Professional Responsibility, DR 3–102.

3. Weil v. Neary, 278 U.S. 160, 49 S.Ct. 144 (1929).

4. In a gross case the lawyer explained his large fee splits in workmen's compensation cases as neces-

sary "to be competitive in the market place." Columbus Bar Ass'n v. Agee, 175 Ohio St. 443, 196 N.E. 2d 98 (1964), Annot. 6 A.L.R.3d 1446 (1966), cert. den. 379 U.S. 7, 85 S.Ct. 70 (1964).

5. Weil v. Neary, 278 U.S. 160, 49 S.Ct. 144 (1929); McFarland v. George, 316 S.W.2d 662 (Mo.Ct.App. 1958); Silver v. Paulsen, 285 App. Div. 1059, 139 N.Y.S.2d 456 (1955).

6. But see H. Drinker, Legal Ethics, 186–188 (1953).

7. ABA Code of Professional Responsibility, DR 2–107.

sociate and the one who poses the least threat to the loss of the client. When the fellow professional in another discipline has standards paralleling those of the bar, the association and sharing of fees should be approved.[8]

SECTION 6. CONFIDENCES

A rule of law protects communications between attorney and client from disclosure in court. Even more important is a professional standard which requires the attorney to protect the confidences and the secrets of his client everywhere. A professional standard of respect for inviolate personality is an additional safeguard of communications between attorney and client. These three matters will be briefly discussed.

A client will obtain the best advice and action by his lawyer only when the lawyer is fully informed on the client's affairs including the unpleasant aspects, but he will give full information to his lawyer only if he believes the information will not be divulged. To encourage fullness of communication, there is the principle of attorney-client privilege as to testimony in court.

> "The social good derived from the proper functions of lawyers acting for their clients is believed to outweigh the harm that may come from the suppression of the evidence in specific cases." [1]

The principal elements of the privilege are illustrated in a single case, under the anti-trust laws when the defendant objected to the introduction of exhibits on the ground they fell within the attorney-client-privilege.[2] As to the kind of legal expert to whom the privilege extended Judge Wyzanski held it includes independent lawyers consulted by the defendant and also its house

8. Cf. Blumenberg v. Neubecker, 12 N.Y.2d 456, 191 N.E.2d 269 (1963). The court upheld a contract under which a lawyer and an accountant were retained by the client to work together for a contingent fee on an income tax case: "An arrangement such as was here arrived at assures the sort of co-operative effort whereby the expertise of both lawyer and accountant in their respective fields may be availed of and is designed to achieve for the client who retained them the best possible result." Id. at 460, 191 N.E.2d 271.

1. ALI Model Code of Evidence, Rule 210, Comment.

The grant of the privilege not to testify is unrelated to the usual purposes of the rules of evidence, to obtain better answers to questions of fact. Weinstein, Recognition in the United States of the Privileges of Another Jurisdiction, 56 Colum.L.Rev. 535 (1956).

2. Wyzanski, J., in United States v. United Shoe Mach. Corp., 89 F. Supp. 357 (1950).

counsel, but not lay solicitors of patents. On the subject matter
of the communications protected, the judge took account of the
fact that lawyers advise clients on their affairs as a whole and do
not give merely dry legal opinions so

> "[T]he privilege of nondisclosure is not lost merely because
> relevant nonlegal considerations are expressly stated in a
> communication which also includes legal advice." [3]

The court outlined the elements of the privilege succinctly:

> "The privilege applies only if (1) the asserted holder of the
> privilege is or sought to become a client; (2) the person to
> whom the communication was made (a) is a member of the
> bar of a court, or his subordinate and (b) in connection with
> this communication is acting as a lawyer; (3) the communi-
> cation relates to a fact of which the attorney was informed
> (a) by his client (b) without the presence of strangers (c)
> for the purpose of securing primarily either (i) an opinion
> on law or (ii) legal services or (iii) assistance in some legal
> proceeding and not (d) for the purpose of committing a
> crime or tort; and (4) the privilege has been (a) claimed
> and not (b) waived by the client." [4]

Beyond the legal privilege of non-disclosure in court proceedings there is the professional duty of the lawyer to preserve the
secrets of a client everywhere. "A lawyer should preserve the
confidences and secrets of his clients", is the broad injunction of
Canon 4 of the Code of Professional Responsibility. "This ethical precept, unlike the evidentiary privilege," as the Code of
Professional Responsibility states, "exists without regard to the
nature or source of information or the fact that others share the
knowledge." [5]

The moral principle of "inviolate personality" is, it is believed,
an additional safeguard supporting the standards of the profession. This principle was urged in the creative article on the
right to privacy as underlying most of the groping for principle
which the article describes.[6] A similar moral right mentioned in
the article, "the right to be let alone", was found by Dean Prosser as supporting much law on the right of privacy.[7] "[R]espect
for the dignity of man" is a duty laid upon the physician in the

3. Id. at 359.

4. Id., at 358–359. The attorney-
client privilege in court proceedings
is considered at length in C. Mc-
Cormick, Law of Evidence ch. 10
(1954); 8 Wigmore, Evidence ch.
82 (McNaughton rev. ed. 1961).

5. ABA Code of Professional Responsibility EC 4–4.

6. Warren & Brandeis, The Right to
Privacy, 4 Harv.L.Rev. 193, 205
(1890).

7. W. Prosser, Law of Torts 832 (3d
ed. 1964).

first sentence of the Principles of Medical Ethics.[8] Surely from no one more than from his lawyer to whom he has entrusted his secrets and his affairs may a man expect observance of these related duties of respect for the principle of inviolate personality, for the right to be let alone, and for the dignity of man. Preservation of a client's confidences and secrets are a part of these wider duties.

8. "Section 1. The principal objective of the medical profession is to render service to humanity with full respect for the dignity of man."

Principles of Medical Ethics, adopted by American Medical Association, June 1956.

Part V

THE STRUCTURE OF THE PROFESSION

Chapter XVI

MEMBERSHIP IN THE BAR

SECTION 1. INTRODUCTION

The American lawyer gives reality to the law for his clients and for their opponents as well. More than any other man he develops, too, the law that he applies and employs. These powers and responsibilities should be entrusted only to those fitted to bear them, and to those so fitted without discrimination. The determination of membership in the bar is guided by these considerations.

In this chapter, admission to the bar and the discipline of lawyers with the respective elements and procedures will first be outlined. Then the most troubling element in either proceeding, the question of character, will be raised. In that connection, some attention will be given to the extreme political dissenter in the aspects both of his membership in the bar and of his conduct of trials. Lastly, mention will be made of the scope of practice of the admitted lawyer, especially as it is affected by our complex federal system.

SECTION 2. ADMISSION TO THE BAR *

A state can impose standards for admission to the bar which "have a rational connection with the applicant's fitness or capacity to practice law." [1] The view emanating from Jacksonian democracy that every person has the right to practice law has

---

* See The Bar Examiner's Handbook (National Conference of Bar Examiners 1968).

1. Mr. Justice Black in Schware v. Board of Bar Examiners, 353 U.S. 232, 239 (1957).

disappeared.[2]   But the assertion that a state has complete freedom in the matter because entry into the profession is not a
"right" but a "privilege" must also be rejected, for at least there
is a "claim of right" entitled to the protection of procedural due
process.[3]

The courts, under the separation of powers principle, hold that
admission to the bar is a judicial function, though they may accept and apply statutory provisions in aid of their function.[4]
Three usual sets of requirements for admission are directed to
intellectual attainments, moral character, and practical experience.   The requirements as to intellectual attainments are of two
kinds.   One is a prescribed period of college work followed by a
period of law school study.   Through the leadership given by the
American Bar Association's Section on Legal Education and Admission to the Bar and by the Association of American Law
Schools the prescribed period of university study in "approved"
schools has been steadily lengthened until now the minimum period recommended by the associations is six university years.[5]

The educational requirements are laid down in general terms
and not as detailed guidelines.   The resultant freedom for legal
education is fortunate.   Unfettered by the state or by the organized profession, the university law schools have had the opportunity to experiment with and develop new methods.   The revolutionary development of a century ago, the case method, has been
resilient enough to adapt to new conceptions of law foreign to
those of its creators [6] and to continue along side other methods
of study and teaching.   Most fortunate of all is the freedom of

2. An old provision of the Constitution of the State of Indiana which
gave the privilege to all persons of
good moral character is quoted in
In re Leach, 134 Ind. 665, 34 N.E.
641 (1893).

3. Hallinan v. Committee of Bar Examiners, 65 Cal.2d 447, 55 Cal.Rptr.
228, 421 P.2d 76 (1966). See Van Al-
styne, The Demise of the Right-
Privilege Distinction in Constitutional Law, 81 Harv.L.Rev. 1439
(1968).

4. State ex rel. Ralston v. Turner,
141 Neb. 556, 4 N.W.2d 302 (1942),
Annot., 144 A.L.R. 138 (1943).

Some states place hampering difficulties in the way of qualified applicants for admission to the bar. A
requirement of twelve months residence in the state prior to taking
its bar examination has been held
unconstitutional. Keenan v. Board

of Law Examinations of the State
of North Carolina, 317 F.Supp. 1350
(1970).

5. The development of legal education is outlined in A. Harno, Legal
Education in the United States
(1953).   The educational requirement of graduation from an accredited law school, defined as one
approved by the American Bar Association, is valid. Hackin v. Lockwood, 361 F.2d 499 (9th Cir. 1966),
cert. denied 385 U.S. 960 (1966).
The privilege to take the bar examination after study in a law
office instead of in a law school is
so little used that it is of no substantial significance.

6. See Patterson, The Case Method
in American Legal Education: Its
Origins and Objectives, 4 J.Leg.
Educ. 1 (1951).

action given the younger faculty members. The strong law school faculties do not encourage intellectual discipleship. They give to their most junior members full freedom to develop and treat their subjects as they believe best.

Following law study there comes the bar examination. There is the continuing question which Chief Justice Traynor has repeated in Chief Justice Vanderbilt's terms:

> "   .   .   .   whether the law schools have not erred in letting the legal profession, through the boards of bar examiners, shape the curriculum, just as our business civilization has in turn too largely dictated the standards of the profession." [7]

Certainly the bar examiners do exercise much indirect control over legal education through setting the subjects on which they will examine and the qualities they seek to test. The state boards of bar examiners have joined in the National Conference of Bar Examiners which has adopted a "Code of Recommended Standards." [8] The Code, recommending that the major part of the examination consist of hypothetical questions which call for essay answers, states:

> "16. *Purpose of Examination*: The bar examination should test the applicant's ability to reason logically, to analyze accurately the problems presented to him, and to demonstrate a thorough knowledge of the fundamental principles of law and their application. The examination should not be designed primarily for the purpose of testing information, memory or experience."

On the requirements of good moral character, ordinarily the first stage of inquiry is by a bar committee empowered by the court, which submits its conclusion with the evidence to the court. In the hearing before the committee the applicant has the right of confrontation of critics or objectors. [9] The burden of coming forward with the evidence is rightly placed on the applicant, who is of course in the best position to know the facts about himself. Inquiries by the committee through interview or questionnaire or both may be made by the committee into matters relevant to admission. An applicant who refuses to answer relevant questions may be denied admission because of the refusal to cooperate with the committee in its professional task. [10] The committee

7. Traynor, Who Should Be a Lawyer, But Why? 13 J.Leg.Ed. 157 (1960).

8. The Code is included in the Bar Examiners' Handbook (1968) prepared and annotated under the sponsorship of the Conference by Mr. Robert A. Sprecher of the Chicago Bar.

9. Willner v. Committee on Character and Fitness, 373 U.S. 96, 83 S.Ct. 1175, 10 L.Ed.2d 224 (1963).

10. Konigsberg v. State Bar of California, 366 U.S. 36; In re Anastoplo, 366 U.S. 82, 81 (1961). It does not appear yet to have been claimed that an applicant has the privilege to refuse to answer on the ground

submits its conclusion with the evidence to the court. The scope of review given by the court varies in the states. In some states the case is considered de novo by the court on the record before the committee.

It is not entirely clear who has the burden of proof. There is the formal factor that the candidate is a petitioner, and in a legal proceeding ordinarily a petitioner has the burden. There are the substantial factors of the importance of the decision to the public, and of its importance to the applicant who has spent years of his life in preparation for the bar. It has been said that reasonable doubts should be resolved in favor of the applicant.[11]

In a few states there is the requirement of a brief clerkship in a law office. More significant than this formal element is the clinical experience many schools are seeking to develop, so as to enable their students to deal with actual persons and situations.[12] There is the accompanying realization that other disciplines may contribute in the law school years to learning how to deal effectively with people. The Code of Professional Responsibility makes the similar point that "[p]roper preparation and representation may require the association by the lawyer of professionals in other disciplines." [13]

Legal Education *

"The case method is the best method ever devised to enable a poor teacher to give an interesting course," said a critic. The praise is deserved. The cases, with their concreteness and reality, have much the same superiority in interest over the lecture or the textbook that the drama or the novel has over history or philosophy. They are instances of individuals in conflict and the students can identify themselves with the parties or their lawyers. The method has a further advantage that it makes the students active participants in considering the casebook cases and host of other problems brought up by students or by faculty in class discussion. Even in a large class it encourages active

---

the answers might tend to incriminate him. Cf. p. 287 infra.

11. See Hallinan v. Committee of Bar Examiners, 65 Cal.2d 447, 55 Cal.Rptr. 228, 421 P.2d 76 (1966).

12. In a number of states there are statutes or rules of court which permit third year law students, under the general supervision of a lawyer admitted to practice, to participate actively in legal aid work. A firm's training program for associates is helpfully described in a series of articles in The Practical Lawyer now brought together in book form. T. Voorhees, "The Practical Lawyer's Manual of Law Office Training For Associates" (1970).

13. ABA Code of Professional Responsibility, EC 6–3.

* For a history of American legal education, see A. Harno, Legal Education in the United States (1953). See also Education in the Professional Responsibilities of the Lawyer (Weckstein ed. 1970).

intellectual participation by each student so as to hold himself in readiness to ask, or to answer questions as they are put. The case method won on a long trial on the merits. At the end of the first twenty years it had but one adherent besides its creator, the Harvard Law School. After the second twenty years it had been accepted by nearly all university law schools.[1]

The method uses court cases as the staple and focus of class discussion, "the Socratic method," not as illustrations of principles laid down in lecture or text. The principal contribution is the development of the students' powers of analysis. "Lawyers are artists in relevance" said Justice Frankfurter. "I spend two years," said another, "in teaching them to throw out the irrelevant."

Appellate cases are used for the most part. The statement of facts in the opinions is a distillate of the raw facts which the lawyers sought for and dealt with. The contrast of the tidy statement of the facts which are given to the reader of the judicial opinion with the raw and uncertain facts which confront a lawyer when he takes a case has led Chief Justice Burger to protest against the use of the term "case method" as gravely misleading. The appropriate name is, he would say, "the appellate opinion method." Some developments in legal education will be sketched, and a question raised on the law and the structure of university education.

No sooner had the case method won its sweeping victory than there came under attack a conception of the nature of law which accompanied it. It was the view of its creator, Langdell: "First, that law is a science; secondly, that all the available materials of that science are contained in printed books."[2] Justice Holmes had rejected this limiting view of law in a passage long ignored.[3] Chief Justice Stone, while a law school dean, had protested against this confining conception and urged that the law should be brought closer to "the energizing forces" which are constantly remaking it.[4]

1. The origin of the case system is excellently described in The Centennial History of the Harvard Law School, 1817–1917, 34–47 (1918); A. Sutherland, The Law at Harvard 162-225 (1967).

2. The passage is quoted in Patterson, The Case Method in American Legal Education: Its Origins and Methods, 4 J.Legal Ed. 13 (1951). See also Morgan, The Case Method, 4 J.Legal Ed. 379 (1952).

3. "The life of the law has not been logic; it has been experience. The felt necessities of the time, the prevalent moral and political theories, intuitions of public policy, avowed or unconscious, even the prejudices which judges share with their fellow men, have had a good deal more to do than the syllogism in determining the rules by which men should be governed." O. Holmes, The Common Law 1 (1881).

4. See Stone, The Future of Legal Education, 10 A.B.A.J. 233, 234 (1924).

In the 1920s several law schools (as Chicago, Columbia, Yale) began to make fuller use in law of relevant information and insights which the social studies had to offer. The course books, so broadened, came to be called "Cases and Materials." Some law faculties appointed to their membership men from other disciplines. Everywhere the old narrowness has been broken. There are varied methods in seeking to make use of the other disciplines. The social disciplines do not have the precision to offer to the lawyer which the natural sciences give to the physician. In law there is always the troubling question of the values to be preferred, a kind of question on which other disciplines may offer enlightenment but give no firm answer.

The extent of the break with the old case method can be illustrated by a foreword and a preface. Professor Harrop Freeman of Cornell, recognizing that cases concern people and not rules of law, prepared a law school book with judges left out. The book contains actual cases handled by lawyers and members of other professions, but no appellate opinions. Dean Erwin Griswold in a foreword said that Professor Freeman's book might come to rank almost as much a pioneer as was Dean Langdell's Cases on Contracts.[5] In another law school book the preface states its purpose as:

> "the study of law as an on-going, functioning purposive process and, in particular, with the study of the various institutions, both official and private, through which the process is carried on." [6]

The student rebellions of the 1960s were felt in the law schools. One demand was for a share in the government of the institution which has the students as its reason for being. The demand, though not pressed far, has the support of an illustrious precedent. It is the great law school of the Middle Ages whose influence was felt throughout Western Europe, the University of Bologna. That law school was essentially a guild of law students, with the students hiring and firing and fining the faculty members.[7]

Another fortunate demand by students was that the schools give more attention to the bearing of the law on the underprivileged. The Director of the American Bar Foundation, sharing some of their uncertainties, said:

> "If we were more frankly concerned with morality, of course without being moralistic in the prudish sense, we could deal

5. H. Freeman, Legal Interviewing and Counseling (1964).

6. H. Hart & A. Sack, The Legal Process: Basic Problems in the Making and Application of Law (1958).

7. L. Cowen, Student Participation in Law School Administration, 13 J.Legal Ed. 214 (1960).

more effectively with questions that really interest students, and ought to interest them. . . . Possibly the greatest challenge for legal education, therefore, is that it undertake to be rather more intensely concerned with political and social morality than it has been in times more assured, and perhaps more innocent." [8]

The structure of American universities is a by-product of American history. Unlike the situation in their great predecessors, the continental universities, the college took firm shape as the only form of higher education before professional studies sought to enter the universities. With the college in its unyielding place, professional studies had to come after the four years of college, as with medicine and theology and law, or else to create a structure of their own paralleling the college work, as with engineering. It is time to re-examine this unplanned structure.

The subjects with which the college years deal, as, philosophy, ethics, literature, history—the liberal arts—call for more maturity of understanding than does the first half of the present law school period with its emphasis on the development of the art of the relevant in terms of the law itself. The present university structure brings to mind Alfred North Whitehead's comment in The Aims of Education:

> "Necessary technical excellence can only be acquired by habits of study which are apt to damage those energies of mind which should guide the technical skill."

The usual three years of law school with their close devotion to technical excellence are certainly apt to damage those energies of mind and spirit which it was the purpose of the four years of college to develop. Given the needed freedom from vested interests—an uncertain gift even in universities—the universities could develop a more effective structure for creating necessary technical excellence, and also for developing, preserving and putting to use the guiding energies of mind and of spirit.

SECTION 3.   DISCIPLINE OF LAWYERS *

The discipline of lawyers has as its purpose the protection of the public from those unworthy of trust in the practice of law.

---

8.   Hazard, Challenges to Legal Education, in The Path of the Law from 1968, 193–94, Proceedings and Papers at the Harvard Law School Convocation on the 150th Anniversary of Its Founding (1968).

* Discipline is the subject of the report of an American Bar Association committee made in 1970 under the chairmanship of retired Justice Tom C. Clark. ("Problems and Recommendations in Disciplinary

It may take the form of censure or of suspension or of disbarment. It has the same purpose, Judge Cardozo said, as the denial of an application for admission.

> "To strike the unworthy lawyer from the roll is not to add to the pains and penalties of crime. The examination into character is renewed; and the test of fitness is no longer satisfied. For these reasons courts have repeatedly said that disbarment is not punishment." [1]

Occasionally a judge will himself prefer charges against the lawyer for acts that occurred before him. Most charges of unprofessional conduct are preferred informally by outsiders. The facilitation of charges is, it has been said, "a safety valve for the public," [2] making the public realize that the bar is not seeking to protect its unfaithful members or to punish a member of the public who makes mistaken or unfounded charges.

Ordinarily, there is a screening stage at which the charges are referred by the court to, say, a bar association committee on grievances which considers them. Most complaints arise out of misunderstandings, and they can be dismissed by the committee with explanation to the complainants and, it may be, without the lawyer being even informed of the matter. If there appears to be substance in the charges, the committee will inform the lawyer and give him an opportunity to explain, and, if the explanation is not satisfactory, give him a hearing before the committee. When the committee finds against the lawyer, it makes an appropriate recommendation to the court.[3]

The court will hear the charges. The lawyer is entitled to procedural due process throughout. This requires, that the lawyer be informed of the nature of the charges at the commencement of the proceedings, and that he may not be disbarred on the ba-

---

Enforcement.") The report finds discipline in a lamentable condition in many states. It recommends that disciplinary powers be recognized as vested in the highest court of the state. On procedure it recommends the stages of investigation and inquiry, formal hearings and review, and a final decision by the highest court on the basis of the record at the formal hearings.

1. In re Rouss, 221 N.Y. 81, 85, 116 N.E. 782, 783 (1917).

2. Chronicle Publishing Co. v. Superior Court, 54 Cal.2d 548, 7 Cal. Rptr. 109, 354 P.2d 637 (1960). Public policy requires that filing of a complaint with a grievance committee be privileged so as to preclude an action for malicious prosecution. Toft v. Ketchum, 18 N.J. 280, 113 A.2d 671, 114 A.2d 863 (1955), Annot., 52 A.L.R.2d 1208 (1957).

3. There is no right to a jury trial in a disciplinary proceeding. The authorities are reviewed at length in Ex parte Thompson, 228 Ala. 113, 152 So. 229, (1933), Annot., 107 A.L.R. 682 (1937). A committee of the American Bar Association under the chairmanship of former Justice Tom C. Clark is engaged in drafting a proposed model code of disciplinary proceedings.

sis of facts and charges developed from testimony by the lawyer during the progress of the hearing, so it has been held, even though he was given an opportunity to answer them.[4] The bar committees and the courts have been careful to protect the lawyer's reputation from unfounded charges. A court refused to repeat in its opinion the charges it found groundless because the public statement of them in the court's opinion would help to serve the accuser's malicious purpose.[5] The measure of proof essential to a finding against the lawyer has been variously stated; as one court put it, it is something more than the preponderance of the evidence and less than proof beyond a reasonable doubt.[6]

The Supreme Court of the United States has wavered on the question whether a lawyer may be disciplined for his refusal, before a committee of inquiry to answer questions as to his professional conduct on the ground the answers might tend to incriminate him. The latest case, with the Court closely divided, held the lawyer does have a constitutional privilege not to answer, and a state may not discipline him for asserting it.[7] The decision is wrong, we believe. In the balancing of interests the weight appears clearly to be on the side of frankness and the duty should be felt and expressed by the bar no less than it has been as to political and labor union leaders and the judiciary.[8]

4. In re Ruffalo, 390 U.S. 544, 88 S.Ct. 1222, 20 L.Ed.2d 117 (1968).

5. In re Stern, 137 App.Div. 909, 121 N.Y.S. 948 (1910).

6. State ex rel. Nebraska State Bar Ass'n v. Nielssen, 179 Neb. 55, 136 N.W.2d 355 (1965), cert. denied, 383 U.S. 105.

7. Spevack v. Klein, 385 U.S. 511 (1967).

8. Senator Joseph McCarthy is an illustration of one such political leader. When there were open rumors of embezzlement by him of funds contributed to his "anti-communism campaign," a special committee of the Senate was named to inquire into the matter. He knew of the creation of the committee yet he failed to appear before it. Another committee was created to inquire more broadly into the senator's actions, and it censured him. The first ground of censure was failure to appear before the special committee, for
"[W]hen the personal honor and official conduct of a Senator are in question before a duly constituted committee of the Senate, the Senator involved owes a duty to himself, his state and to the Senate to appear promptly and cooperate fully . . . When persons in high places fail to set and meet high standards, the people lose faith."
(Report of the Select Committee to Study Censure Charges, United States Senate, 83d Congress, 2d Session Report No. 2508, p. 27.) The action of the Select Committee is described by its chairman, Senator Arthur V. Watkins in his book, A. Watkins, Enough Rope (1969).

The action of the Executive Council of the AFL–CIO was prompted by the refusal of the head of the Teamsters Union to answer questions about racketeering in unions. See N. Y. Times, Jan. 29, 1957, at 18.

As to the judiciary see supra pp. 219–20.

The decision in the *Spevack* case is criticized in an article by a Justice of the Supreme Court of Illinois. Underwood, The Fifth Amendment and the Lawyer, 62 N.W.L.Rev. 129

The measure of discipline depends on the gravity of the charges established. Other relevant factors include frankness of the lawyer in the disciplinary proceedings,[9] reparation for injured clients, action in other matters, and reputation in the community.

Reinstatement of a disbarred lawyer is possible. It is achieved through an order of court entered after an appropriate petition and evidence convincing the tribunal of the present fitness of the applicant. So a man disbarred for violation of the tax laws was reinstated.[10] No further order of reinstatement is necessary when the discipline was suspension for a stated period which has expired.[11] By the great weight of authority, however, a pardon for the offense for which the lawyer was disbarred does not restore to him the privilege of practice. A lawyer may resign from the bar with approval of the court and the resignation ends his privilege to practice.[12]

Disciplinary Proceedings and the Interstate System

A state has power over the members of its bar in disciplinary proceedings without the necessity of any special basis of jurisdiction. In individual controversy, the requirement as to bases of jurisdiction, such as domicile or presence, assures that the determination will be made by a court at a "reasonable" place.[1] Disciplinary proceedings concern, not individual controvery, but the suitability of a lawyer to continue to carry the responsibilities which he asked the state to entrust to him. Notice to the lawyer and full opportunity to be heard are essential. When they were lacking, the decree of discipline is invalid in the state where it was rendered and it can be of no effect elsewhere. The place

(1967). It is explained, perhaps, because of the subject inquired into, the solicitation of personal injury cases, on which some of the justices do not feel strongly. Pretty surely the decision would not carry over to a situation of alleged bribery or misappropriation of funds. In such a case there would prevail the duty of a person in a position of responsibility to tell the facts, as the Senate committee stated, when the trustworthiness of a Senator and his group are in question.

9. In determining not to discipline two lawyers charged with an effort to tamper with a witness, Circuit Justice Miller said:
"Mr. Thomas very manfully takes the whole of this matter upon himself. . . . [H]e swears with a great deal of apparent candor, with none of the usual efforts to evade, and not to recollect, and get round things; and it is favorable to him. I think, that he states the case just as he understood it, and tells the truth." In re Thomas, 36 F. 242, 243–44 (D.Colo.1888).

10. Re Daniel, 315 P.2d 789 (Okl. 1959), Annot., 70 A.L.R.2d 269 (1960).

11. Friday v. State Bar, 23 Cal.2d 501, 144 P.2d 564 (1943).

12. Application of Harper, 84 So.2d 700 (Fla.1956), Annot., 54 A.L.R.2d 1280 (1957). The privileges in legal matters of a disbarred or suspended lawyer are helpfully discussed in H. Drinker, Legal Ethics 51–55 (1953).

1. See Restatement, Second, Conflict of Laws § 24.

where the alleged offending act was committed is immaterial.[2] The standard of responsibility is that of the state of the forum since the inquiry concerns privileges which that state granted.

A decree of discipline in one state does not of itself affect the lawyer's standing in a second state. When a proceeding for discipline is brought in a second state for the same misconduct, the cases hold that some effect will be given to the first state's decree.[3] The basis and nature of the effect are not clearly established. "Full faith and credit" is the term used in some cases, indicating a constitutional requirement. "Comity" is the expression employed in other cases, implying the second state's own rule of conflict of laws. The Supreme Court of the United States, it appears, has not passed on the matter. The Supreme Court of Florida held that the first state's decree would be conclusive as to the facts alleged and found by the first state. Recognizing that the states may differ in the standards of conduct they impose on their lawyers, it held that it is for the second state to "determine what discipline should be awarded . . . on an independent appraisal of the acts of misconduct." [4]

SECTION 4. "GOOD MORAL CHARACTER":—
"MORAL TURPITUDE"

Character is an element in the determination of membership in the bar. For admission the requirement is usually stated as "good moral character." "Moral turpitude" is a common form for statement of ground of discipline.

The substance of the requirement is that the lawyer have the qualities fitting him to carry out his obligations under the difficult conditions of practice. The qualities are the same whether the question comes up on proceedings for admission or for discipline.[1] The test to be employed is functional. Usually it involves the function of the individual lawyer in his work, as trustworthiness by the client and trustworthiness by the court or other agencies of administration of law.

Wrongs to clients may be a basis for discipline. Misappropriation of clients' funds is a ground,[2] as is the neglect of

---

2. See Selling v. Radford, 243 U.S. 46 (1917).

3. Copren v. State Bar of Nevada, 64 Nev. 364, 183 P.2d 833 (1947), Annot., 173 A.L.R. 284 (1948).

4. The Florida Bar v. Wilkes, 179 So.2d 193 (Fla.1965).

1. In re Hallinan, 43 Cal.2d 243, 272 P.2d 768 (1954).

2. Re Dahl, 159 Minn. 481, 199 N.W. 429 (1924), Annot., 43 A.L.R. 52 (1926) (failure to remit funds collected).

clients' cases especially when accompanied by misrepresentation to the clients.[3]

Overreaching the client may be ground for discipline, as in the matter of fees. But in refusing to discipline a lawyer because of a controversy over fees Chief Justice Weintraub said:

> "The intangibles which bear upon the fairness of a fee defy translation into simple mathematics. . . . The touchstone is moral turpitude. . . . It is therefore not enough [to justify discipline] that a charge is excessive or unreasonable; rather it must be such to a degree which compels a finding that the attorney intended to overreach." [4]

Wrongs to adversaries have resulted in discipline. The court disbarred a lawyer who bought notes and small claims of debtors living at a distance and obtained jurisdiction over them through sham endorsements, stating that professional obligations extend to the adverse party, his counsel and to the court, as well as to the lawyer's client.[5]

Chief Justice Vanderbilt made explicit the reliance of court on counsel, saying

> "[T]he work of our appellate counsel cannot go on satisfactorily if we cannot rely on the representations of counsel to us both as to the facts and the law." [6]

Personal dishonesty of some kind is the basis of most disciplinary proceedings. The acts may be unrelated to clients. For example, in a disciplinary proceeding against a lawyer charged with making false income tax returns Justice (later Chief Justice) Traynor stated:

> "Although the problem of defining moral turpitude is not without difficulty, . . . it is settled that whatever else it may mean, it includes fraud and that a crime in which an intent to defraud is an essential element is a crime involving moral turpitude. . . . It is also settled that the related group of offenses involving intentional dishonesty for purposes of personal gain are crimes involving moral turpitude. . . . We see no difference between defrauding an individual and defrauding the government." [7]

In that case, however, the court held that violation of the federal income tax laws did not necessarily involve moral turpitude and the matter was remitted to the bar committee for a further

3. Rock v. State Bar, 57 Cal.2d 639, 21 Cal.Rptr. 572, 371 P.2d 308 (1962), Annot., 96 A.L.R.2d 820 (1964).

4. In re Quinn, 25 N.J. 284, 289, 135 A.2d 869, 872 (1957), Annot., 70 A.L. R.2d 962 (1960).

5. Wernimont v. State, 101 Ark. 210, 142 S.W. 194 (1911).

6. In re Greenberg, 15 N.J. 132, 135, 104 A.2d 46, 47 (1954).

7. In re Hallinan, 43 Cal.2d 243, 247–48, 272 P.2d 768, 771 (1954).

hearing on the subject. The violation of the state or federal securities act may constitute moral turpitude.[8]

A quite different basis of discipline is conduct which brings disrepute on the bar.[9] Its use has been questioned since the conduct may have no relation to professional effectiveness. Its use may be justified because of the importance of the general reputation of the profession. The impairment of public trust impairs the performance of the bar's function, since it discourages laymen from seeking the legal services they need. The Code of Professional Responsibility EC 9–6, states, "Every lawyer owes a solemn duty . . . to conduct himself so as to reflect credit on the legal profession and to inspire the confidence, respect and trust of his clients and of the public."

One extreme illustration was disbarment from the federal court for participation in a lynching.[10] Another extreme illustration is that of a lawyer who owned and operated a night club. The night club caught fire and, because of lack of suitable exits, four hundred patrons lost their lives. At the time of the fire the lawyer-owner was away in hospital. He was convicted of involuntary manslaughter for "wanton and reckless conduct" causing the deaths, and sentenced to a term of from twelve to fifteen years in prison. On those facts the lawyer was disbarred, the court saying:

> "Discredit may be cast upon the honorable profession of law by conduct outside the profession which reveals unfitness to remain in it." [11]

In less spectacular cases, involuntary manslaughter resulting from driving while intoxicated,[12] or with defective vision,[13] has been ground for discipline. In these manslaughter cases, there

---

8. Re Clark, 63 Cal.2d 610, 47 Cal. Rptr. 681, 407 P.2d 943 (1965), Annot., 18 A.L.R.3d 1408 (1968). An analogous inquiry concerns the use of prior convictions to impeach a defendant's testimony. On their admissibility Judge (now Chief Justice) Burger stated: "In common human experience acts of deceit, fraud, cheating, or stealing, for example, are universally regarded as conduct which reflects adversely on a man's honesty and integrity. Acts of violence, on the other hand, which may result from a short temper, a combative nature, extreme provocation, or other cause, have little or no direct bearing on honesty and veracity." Gordon v. United States, 383 F.2d 936, 940 (D.C.Cir. 1967), cert. denied 390 U. S. 1029 (1968).

9. "The seriousness of a violation of that standard should be expressed not primarily in terms of the moral code, nor the inherent quality of the act, but in the extent to which, in the minds of those competent to judge, the act has lowered the prestige of the legal profession and rendered less efficient the administration of justice." Bradway, Moral Turpitude as the Criterion of Offenses that Justify Disbarment, 24 Cal.L.Rev. 9, 23 (1935).

10. Ex parte Wall, 107 U.S. 265, 2 S.Ct. 569 (1882).

11. In re Welansky, 319 Mass. 205, 209, 65 N.E.2d 202, 204 (1946).

12. Re Morris, 74 N.M. 679, 397 P.2d 475 (1964), Annot. 17 A.L.R.3d 692 (1968).

were elements of negligence which fell below the profession's standard of care in its own work.

Sexual immorality is generally not deemed ground for discipline.[14] And "[m]ere belief in an unorthodox philosophy does not in itself make one unfit to practice law." [15]

The Political Extremists

The political extremists of contemporary causes, such as Communists who urge overthrow of the government or proponents of civil rights who urge violation of the law as a means of achieving social change, raise problems as to their membership in the bar and their conduct of cases. In the middle of the 1900's, the exclusion of Communists from the bar was demanded by some bar associations on the ground their activities were inconsistent with the lawyer's oath to support the Constitution and showed the person was not of good moral character. The demand was supported by the argument that in our country lawyers are relied on as political leaders, and that those disloyal to the country should not be permitted to hold such positions of leadership. The demand presents a conflict between two basic political rights, the individual's right of criticism and dissent protected by the First Amendment, and the purpose of government as stated in the Preamble to the Constitution to "insure domestic Tranquility, [and] provide for the common defense." [1]

The effectiveness of the anti-Communists efforts has been quite limited. After World War I, there were a few isolated cases of exclusion from the bar. The Hitler-Stalin pact as the prelude to World War II and later actions of the Soviet Union almost destroyed the attractiveness of that nation. After the war there appears to be no reported case of final exclusion or ouster from the bar because of Communist membership. The result can be ascribed in large measure to the stress laid by the Supreme Court of the United States on the constitutional rights of freedom of thought and association. In a unanimous decision, the Court held that past membership cannot be made a ground of exclusion from the bar.[2]

---

13. Re Alkow, 64 Cal.2d 838, 51 Cal. Rptr. 912, 415 P.2d 800 (1966), Annot., 21 A.L.R.3d 886 (1968).

14. People ex rel. Black v. Smith, 290 Ill. 241, 124 N.E. 807 (1919), Annot., 9 A.L.R. 183 (1920).

15. Florida Bar v. Wilkes, 179 So.2d 193, 201 (Fla.1965), cert. denied 390 U.S. 983 (1968).

1. The controversies as to lawyers are a part of broader civil rights cases. The broad subject is dealt with in T. Emerson, D. Haber and N. Dorsen, Political and Civil Rights in the United States (3d ed. 1967). The topic of the legal profession in both admission and disciplinary proceedings is treated Id., Vol. 1, at 262-85.

2. Schware v. Board of Bar Examiners, 353 U.S. 232 (1957), Annot.

The efforts at exclusion are unwise. With most applicants in their middle twenties, a generation gap exists between them and the examiners. There is, also, the continuing effort of youth to make over our imperfect world, and Communism has its appeal as an instant method of righting social wrongs. In our times of rapid change there is need for dissent and criticism, and the duty of the bar must be to protect them.[3] To regard the few who flirt with Communism as traitorous only serves the purpose of the false conservatives.[4] It is to repeat the errors of nearly two hundred years ago at the time of the French revolution when as a great English lawyer, Sir Samuel Romilly said, every effort at reform was defeated by the charge it was "Republican" or "Jacobin."[5] Besides the idealists, there are always the lunatic fringes of the left and the right who vent their frustrations on existing institutions, as one who claimed to be an anarchist, syndicalist and communist all in one. There are spies and revolutionaries, who would serve the Soviet Union despite the burdens and dangers it has created for this country and the world. They can be handled by expert federal authorities and not through sporadic actions of inexpert bar committees.[6]

The political extremist, however, must comply with the usual requirements for admission to the bar. He must answer questions put by the bar examiners which are relevant to the subject of admission.[7] His refusal to answer may be a ground for denial

64 A.L.R.2d 288 (1959). A statute of the 1860's which in effect denied to ex-Confederates the privilege to practice in the federal courts was held unconstitutional. Ex parte Garland, 71 U.S. (4 Wall.) 333 (1867).

3. Cf. pp. 339ff. infra on the duty of the bar to provide counsel for the Hated.

4. The nature of the Communist threat and the appropriate counter measures to preserve liberty as well as security are discussed in the Report of the Special Comm. of the Ass'n of the Bar of the City of New York on the Federal Loyalty-Security Program 43 (1956) under the chairmanship of Mr. (now Judge) Dudley Bonsal: "[I]n planning for national security, it is not enough to consider security alone. . . . [T]he very purpose of national security is to preserve our independence and liberty."
he "anti-communist" work of Senator Joseph McCarthy was charac-

terized by the conservative chairman of the committee of the United States Senate which censured him: "[T]he apprehensions raised by Senator McCarthy were largely destructive and in only a small way useful." A. Watkins, Enough Rope at x (1969).

5. See P. Medd, A Life of Sir Samuel Romilly, Lawyer and Reformer (1968).

6. Sedition has been dealt with broadly by Congress in the Smith Act. So a state anti-sedition statute and its application to a leader of the Communist Party was held unconstitutional as an intrusion into a field which is of special national importance and which the national government has taken over. Pennsylvania v. Nelson, 350 U.S. 497 (1956). The same conclusion might carry over to the occasional efforts to discipline seditious lawyers.

7. The scope of permissible questions to applicants on their subversive

of admission.[8] His answers must, of course, be truthful, and falsehood in his answers may justify the denial of admission.[9]

The civil rights movement, too, has the special support of the youth. The factors involved in planned violation of the law as a means of advancing civil rights and their effect on membership in the bar are illustrated in Hallinan v. Committee of Bar Examiners.[10] An applicant for admission to the bar had engaged in numerous peaceful but unlawful demonstrations. The Committee of Bar Examiners, relying on the statutory requirement of good moral character, denied him admission. In its review of the Committee's action the Supreme Court of California took into account the broad background facts as to the Negro and recognized that demonstration in support of political and social movements are protected by the Constitution. The Court overruled the Committee's conclusion and ordered the applicant admitted. The grounds of the Court's action and the range of its decision are not entirely clear. At one place the opinion stresses the peaceable character of the acts and the applicant's repudiation of violent civil demonstration. At another place it reserves wide discretion stating:

> "Whether these activities involve moral turpitude is dependent upon the issues involved and the motivation of the violator." [11]

views and associations continues to trouble the Supreme Court of the United States. Three 5–4 decisions on the subject were handed down by the Court on February 23, 1971, the month before this book went to press. In Law Students Civil Rights Council, Inc. v. Wadmond, the Court held valid a questionnaire employed in New York state as pruned in scope by a careful and considerate opinion of a three judge federal court. See Case Comment, 23 Vand L.Rev. 131 (1970). However, in the Matter of the Application of Stolar and in Baird v. State Bar of Arizona, the Court sustained the refusal of applicants for admission to the bars of Ohio and Arizona to reply to such questions by the bar admission authorities. Four of the justices would condemn the questions in all three cases because of their "chilling" effect on freedom of speech and association. One other justice cast the swing vote in the last two cases since one question asked concerned past membership in any subversive organization, though the Court had already held that past membership is no ground for denial of admission to the bar.

8. Konigsberg v. State Bar, 366 U.S. 36 (1961); In re Anastoplo, 366 U.S. 82 (1961). In the Anastoplo proceedings, the preferable opinion, is that of the dissenting justices in the Supreme Court of Illinois. 18 Ill.2d 182, 163 N.E.2d 429 (1959), which stated that the applicant's good moral character was so clearly established that he should be admitted despite his refusal on libertarian grounds to answer committee questions; that is, justice in the individual case overrode a valid general rule.

9. Application of Patterson, 213 Or. 398, 318 P.2d 907 (1957); cert. denied 356 U.S. 947 (1958). An illustration of an ex-Communist who testified frankly as to his connections and who was held entitled to admission is the Schware case, supra note 2.

10. 65 Cal.2d 447, 55 Cal.Rptr. 228, 421 P.2d 76 (1966).

11. Id. at 461, 55 Cal.Rptr. at 239, 421 P.2d at 87.

At yet another place it stresses the desirability of leaving disobedience of the law to the criminal courts and of confining the process of bar admission to the determination of suitability for the practice of law.

Political Trials *

Another question concerns the political extremist's conduct as an advocate, especially in representing an accused whose revolutionary views he shares. The lawyer and the client may agree in rejecting our political and legal systems, and the client may be on trial for an act done in rejecting them. The two may wish to use the trial to discredit the systems and to subordinate the defendant's fate to the cause they share, content in the knowledge that the blood of the martyrs is the seed of the church. To take an extreme case, Lenin insisted that in the defense of such a case it must be for the client, not the lawyer, to determine how the case shall be conducted so as to contribute to the larger cause.[1]

The accused on his own motion or at the covert suggestion of his lawyer might refuse the cooperation ordinarily given in a trial and seek to disrupt it by interruptions or violence. Or he might seek to speak over the heads of the twelve jury men to millions of newspaper readers. How can our law deal with a party whose starting point is a rejection of the ordinary purposes of a trial and of the system of which the court is a part? A partial answer was given in the case of the prosecution of Communist leaders when one of the accused sought, at the end of a nine-month trial, to substitute himself for his able counsel in addressing the jury. In affirming the trial court's denial of the request Judge Learned Hand said: "it is difficult to assign any other motive for his request than that he wished to make a flaming address to the jury which would have reverberations not only inside but outside the court room."[2]

Here we are concerned with the lawyer. Again, two of our political ideals are in conflict. We seek, on the one hand, to protect the political process including the individual's right to free expression; on the other hand, to protect the process of law administration against distortion or misuse. A disagreement over the conflict and its resolution, whether to treat one ideal as absolute

---

The part of the lawyer in civil disobedience matters—whether as counselor or advocate or public official or citizen—is helpfully discussed in Cowen, The Lawyer's Role in Civil Disobedience, 47 N.C. L.Rev. 587 (1969).

* See also Disruptive Tactics supra pp. 212–14.

1. See O. Kircheimer, Political Justice 242–46 (1961).

2. United States v. Dennis, 183 F.2d 201, 233 (2d Cir. 1950), aff'd, 341 U.S. 494 (1951).

or to determine which is the weightier in the particular case, appears in dissenting opinions of two justices of the Supreme Court of the United States. Mr. Justice Black urged that the guarantees of the First Amendment are absolutes and that the "balancing" of other values against them is intolerable, for "to 'balance' an interest in individual liberty means almost inevitably to destroy that liberty." [3]   Earlier, Justice Frankfurter had given his reply:

> "But the two great Justices to whom we mostly owe the shaping of the constitutional protection of freedom of speech, Mr. Justice Holmes and Mr. Justice Brandeis, did not erect freedom of speech into a dogma of absolute validity nor enforce it to doctrinaire limits. Time, place and circumstances determine the constitutional protection of utterance." [4]

As to the prosecution, the law is clear. The prosecutor cannot denounce a hated cause and tie the accused to it. An example is the prosecution of a supposed enemy sympathizer during World War II. The Supreme Court reversed the conviction because of the prosecutor's inflammatory argument "at a time when passion and prejudice are heightened by emotions stirred by our participation in a great war." [5]

The lawyer for the defendant, as every lawyer, owes two loyalties. He owes a duty of zeal to his client.[6] If he were guilty of disloyalty to his client by subordinating his fate to the advancement of a larger political cause, he would violate our basic professional standards. A perceptive judge was willing to put aside a lesser professional standard against the solicitation of practice by a Communist lawyer who actively sought representation of disadvantaged defendants; but he insisted that if the lawyer was guilty of disloyalty to his client because of loyalty to a larger cause he should be disciplined.[7]

The lawyer owes also a duty of loyalty to the system of law administration of which he is a part. He is a member of the government's "Loyal Opposition," loyal to the system though opposing the government in the particular case. Occasionally, extreme obstructive tactics make manifest how large a measure of

3. In re Anastoplo, 366 U.S. 82 (1961).

4. In re Sawyer, 360 U.S. 622 (1959).

5. Viereck v. United States, 318 U.S. 236 (1943).

6. See pp. 87ff. supra.

7. In re Ades, 6 F.Supp. 467, 477 (Md.1934). Contrast O. Kircheimer,

Political Justice, 246 (1961): "At the opposite end of the spectrum is the attitude of a conscientious and punctilious member of the bar who looks at his job through shriveled up professional spectacles. One case is like another, in the sense that his job always remains the same: to create maximal conditions for a favorable outcome for his client."

acceptance and cooperation by the participants our system of law administration assumes. Two cases involving prosecution of the opposite ends of the political spectrum illustrate the need for this loyalty.

During World War II several alleged heads of extreme right wing organizations were indicted for conspiracy and tried together. The trial was disorderly. After eight months the judge died under the strain, and a mistrial was declared. Somewhat later the indictment was dismissed for lack of prosecution.[8]

Shortly after the end of the war several Communist leaders were indicted as subversives under the Smith Act. The case and its incidents went through the three levels of the federal courts three times—the prosecution and conviction itself,[9] the punishment of the lawyers for contempt,[10] and proceedings against the lawyers for unprofessional conduct.[11] The trial lasting nine months was turbulent with repeated disregard by counsel of the court's orders. After the jury returned its verdict the trial judge punished the counsel of the defendants for contempt of court, sentencing them to imprisonment for terms up to six months in length. The punishment was upheld by the Supreme Court of the United States because as Justice Jackson stated:

> "The overriding consideration is the integrity and efficiency of the trial process. . . . [I]t (the Supreme Court) will also protect the processes of orderly trial, which is the supreme object of the lawyer's calling." [12]

In the last stage of the controversy the Supreme Court held an order of permanent disbarment of principal counsel for the defense was "unnecessarily severe" and remanded the case for further consideration.[13] Throughout all the opinions in the controversy there is manifest the desire of the judges to do nothing

---

8.   United States v. McWilliams, 163 F.2d 695 (D.C.Cir. 1947). The case is described in a book by a defendant and a defendant's lawyer. M. St. George & L. Dennis, A Trial on Trial: The Great Sedition Trial of 1944 (1945).

The firmness of the trial judge in dealing with the disruptive methods of an ordinary accused, going so far as to exclude him from the court room for a time, has been upheld. Illinois v. Allen, 397 U.S. 337 (1970).

9.   Dennis v. United States, 341 U.S. 494 (1951).

10.   Sacher v. United States, 343 U. S. 1 (1952).

11.   Sacher v. The Association of the Bar, 347 U.S. 388 (1954).

12.   Sacher v. United States, 343 U.S. 1 (1952). On the requirement of due process that after a disorderly trial criminal contempt proceedings be heard before a judge other than the one reviled by the contemnor because "the marks of the unseemly conduct have left personal stings", see Mayberry v. State of Pennsylvania, —— U.S. ——, 91 S.Ct. 499 Jan. 20, 1971.)

13.   See Sacher v. Association of the Bar, 347 U.S. 388 (1954).

that would discourage in the slightest the representation of unpopular defendants and zealous defense in their behalf.

Our political and professional ideals strive to make it impossible to punish a person merely because he is unpopular or espouses unpopular causes. They do so by seeking to reduce each case to its legal issue and confining the controvery and its participants to those issues. In a most controversial case Justice Holmes stated: [14]

> "I do not consider that I am at liberty to deal with this case any differently from the way in which I would treat one that excited no public interest and that was less powerfully presented."

The effort to eliminate the political and social factors from the legal issues into which the controversies have been transformed can never quite succeed, as shown by the history of the case in which the great justice wrote.[15] Yet the constant effort to do so, with the large measure of success attained, is at the heart of our system of government under law. It is our method of replacing force with law and of substituting for revolution peaceful and continuing change.

The claim is at times asserted on behalf of obstructive lawyers and clients that they are doing no more than their greatest predecessors whose memories we venerate. The claim is wrong. Socrates, though urging acquittal on his own terms, accepted condemnation quietly and refused to flee lest he violate the laws of the Athenian state. Jesus, as an ancient tradition of sacrifice has it, was fated to die here so men might live hereafter. He rebuked a disciple who would have used violence to save him. He did not seek to escape his fate at the hands of Pilate, "the local commander of the military government of a foreign occupation power." The claim is wrong, too, as to the greatest of counsel. Erskine employed his eloquence to obtain the acquittal of his clients, and also to protect the processes of the law and of the state of which he recognized himself a part. He opened his successful defense of a man who had tried to assassinate the King with words which associated his task with the nation and its system of administration of justice.

> "Gentlemen of the jury, the scene in which we are engaged, and the duty which I am not merely privileged but appointed by the court to perform, exhibits to the whole civilized world a perpetual monument of the national justice."

14. Memorandum of Mr. Justice Holmes in the Sacco-Vanzetti Case 5515–17 (1929); J. Michael and H. Wechsler, Criminal Law and Its Administration 1230 (1940).

15. See G. Joughin & E. Morgan, The Legacy of Sacco and Vanzetti (1948).

SECTION 5. THE FEDERAL SYSTEM AND THE BREADTH OF THE PRIVILEGE TO PRACTICE

In a legal sense, the United States is a highly diverse federal nation. Each of the fifty states has its own bar admission system, as well as its own law and procedures which control in matters to which they apply. For economic and social purposes, however, our country is a unitary nation with people and goods moving across the country almost without regard to state lines. Even in a legal sense, it is increasingly a unitary nation as the range of federal law ("the supreme Law of the Land") expands, and federal law governs the coordination of the laws of the fifty states with one another and with federal law. Clients need lawyers who can guide and represent them in transactions as a whole and not as cut up in pieces by the lines of the states. To serve their clients well, lawyers need a corresponding breath of privilege in their work. In considering the effect of the two sets of factors—the local factors and the national factors—on the scope of the privilege to practice, there will be sketched, in turn, practice within a state, in the federal courts, and in interstate matters.

Within the State

Every state has its own requirements and procedures for admission to its bar.[1] Membership in the bar carries with it the privilege to practice law broadly, including office work as well as advocacy. Passing the examination and meeting the character requirements may make the lawyer eligible to appear before the tribunals of first instance only. For appearance before appellate tribunals an additional admission proceeding without separate examination may be required. Admission to the bar carries with it, ordinarily, the privilege of practice before state administrative tribunals.

The Federal Tribunals

Admission to the bar of a state does not carry with it the right to practice in the federal courts. Admission is granted by each court in each of the levels of the federal judicial system separately.[2] A common requirement is membership in the bar of the highest court of a state in which the federal court sits. Nor does admission to one federal court carry with it the right to

1. The variety in the methods of dealing with out-of-state lawyers and in the federal courts is described in a summary of studies made for The Survey of the Legal Profession. See A. Blaustein and C. Porter, The American Lawyer 231–39 (1954).

2. Id.

practice before another federal court, unless the rules of the latter so provide. The ending of the membership in a state bar on which the membership of a state bar was predicated does not require, the termination of the membership in the federal court bar. In a case in which the Supreme Court of Louisiana disbarred a man for acts done nearly twenty years earlier while he was deranged, the Supreme Court of the United States held that the federal court should make an independent inquiry and disposition under its rules, saying: [3]

> "While a lawyer is admitted into a federal court by way of a state court, he is not automatically sent out of the federal court by the same route. . . . The two judicial systems of courts . . . have autonomous control over the conduct of their officers."

Membership in the bar of the highest court of state carries with it, so a federal statute provides, the right to be a representative before any federal administrative agency except the Patent office.[4] The statute disclaims the authorization or limitation by it, of the power of discipline, including disbarment of representatives, by the agencies. The agencies do have their sets of standards as illustrated by the detailed standards of the Bureau of Internal Revenue.

Interstate Problems

A lawyer who moves to another state may ordinarily become a member of the bar of the second state without taking the bar examination of that state. Admission by reciprocity is the term used, since reciprocity between the states is a usual practice. The conditions the lawyer must meet, such as a certain period of active practice in the first state, are determined by the law of the second state.[5] There appears to be no constitutional duty on the second state to admit sister state lawyers to its bar.

A lawyer desiring to appear as advocate in another state in a particular case—*pro hac vice*—is ordinarily given permission to do so. The requirement of association of a local lawyer is a common one.[6] The lawyer must abide by the professional standards of the second state. When a lawyer who received the privilege to appear as counsel in a New Jersey case gave out an inflammatory statement which he knew would get wide publicity, the supreme

3. Theard v. United States, 354 U.S. 278, 281 (1957).

4. 5 U.S.C.A. § 500.

5. In re Harvey, 309 N.Y. 46, 127 N.E.2d 801 (1955), Annot., 51 A.L.R. 2d 1196 (1957).

6. See Martin v. Walton, 368 U.S. 25 (1961).

court of the state ordered the privilege revoked, with ample time allowed for the client to obtain other counsel.[7]

The broad power of a court to impose conditions on the appearance of out-of-state counsel *pro hac vice* may be overriden by more basic considerations. It is so when the vindication of civil rights is involved and there is difficulty in obtaining local counsel because of racial differences. A rule of a federal court which imposed hampering restrictions on the privilege of out-of-state counsel was held invalid.

> "Any rule, whatever its source, that unnecessarily restricts a litigant's choice of counsel in civil rights litigation cannot be sustained." [8]

The privilege to appear as advocate *pro hac vice*, even though readily granted, does not meet the broad needs of clients or of lawyers in interstate practice. Most work of most lawyers is office work to which the extension of the privilege to practice *pro hac vice* does not apply except in so far as the office work is concerned with the preparation of a court case. Two recent decisions may mark the beginning of a wide extension of the right to practice in interstate matters.

In Appell v. Reiner [9] a New York lawyer was retained by a New Jersey client who was in financial difficulties, with his largest creditor in New York and others in New Jersey. The lawyer obtained extensions of time and compromises from creditors in the two states. The client refused to pay the lawyer's fee on the ground the New York lawyer's services constituted the practice of law in New Jersey without a license and this illegality tainted the whole intertwined transactions. The Supreme Court of New Jersey held the lawyer could recover his fees. Judge Haneman in his opinion recognized the general rule that out-of-state lawyers may not practice within the state but he stated "the public interest" calls for some exceptions to the rule and this was such a case. He referred to "the numerous multistate transactions arising in modern times," and the greater efficiency and the lesser costs of services rendered by a single lawyer in such a case as this one. In this creative development of the common law of the state, the court did not cite a single precedent but relied on "the public interest".

In Spanos v. Skouras Theatres Corporation [10] a young California lawyer was retained by the defendant as one of its lawyers in

---

7. "It is not easy for us to oust counsel of a client's choice. But the misbehavior here is so great that we cannot risk more of it." State v. Kavanaugh, 52 N.J. 7, 243 A.2d 225 (1968).

8. Sanders v. Russell, 401 F.2d 241, 246 (5th Cir. 1968).

9. Appell v. Reiner, 43 N.J. 313, 204 A.2d 146 (1964).

10. 364 F.2d 161 (2d Cir.), cert. denied, 385 U.S. 987 (1966).

anti-trust litigation under federal statutes in a federal court in New York. After working for years on the preparation of the case he was dismissed by the client. When he brought the present action for additional fees he was met by the defense of illegality because as a California lawyer, he had been practicing law in New York in violation of the state law. In the district court, Judge Wyatt upheld the plaintiff's right to recover on the ground that he would readily have been admitted to the bar of the federal court in New York if application had been made and the court would treat the matter as though this detail had been carried out.[11] The Court of Appeals, *in banc,* affirmed on the ground given in the District Court, admission *pro hac vice nunc pro tunc.* Because of "the importance of the problem and the desirability of furnishing guidance to the bar" the court considered other grounds urged by the plaintiff. In a careful opinion by Judge Friendly it held that:

> "[U]nder the privileges and immunities clause of the constitution no state can prohibit a citizen with [1] a *federal* claim or defense from engaging an out-of-state lawyer [2] to *collaborate* with an in-state lawyer and give legal advice concerning it within the state." [12]

Several bar associations had filed briefs amici curiae. Some urged the extension more broadly of the privileges of the out-of-state lawyer making unnecessary the elements marked by the numerals added to the quoted passage above. The learned judge said these were "questions better left to another day." The privilege protected, it will be observed, is the privilege of the client rather than the lawyer, and the lawyer's right is a derivative from his client's privilege

The result in the two cases was based on the needs of clients and the effectiveness of lawyers in our nationwide system. Taken together, this fundamental policy gives content to three different authoritative sources of law.[13] State common law was the authoritative source in the *Appell* case. Federal courts law, a special body of law for those courts, was the source used in the *Spanos* case by the District Court and the Court of Appeals. Federal (National) law was an additional source of law used in Judge Friendly's opinion in the Court of Appeals.[14]

The lawyer in international practice has no established right. A foreign lawyer who maintained an office in New York and ad-

11. 235 F.Supp. 1 (S.D.N.Y.1964).

12. 364 F.2d 161, 168 (2d Cir. 1966).

13. On the authoritative sources of law see supra pp. 28ff.

14. The privileges of the interstate practitioner are discussed in Note, Attorneys: Interstate and Federal Practice, 80 Harv.L.Rev. 1711 (1967); Note, The Practice of Law by Out-of-State Attorneys, 20 Vand. L.Rev. 1276 (1967).

vised on foreign legal proceeding was enjoined from such conduct.[15] Other nations accord wide freedom to laymen, including foreigners, in giving legal advice, and American law firms exercise the freedom by having offices in some of these nations. These nations, however, may deny the right of foreign lawyers to appear as advocates. The Supreme Court of the United States under its rules may accord the right of a foreign lawyer to appear *pro hac vice* when associated with an American lawyer.

SECTION 6. THE NEGRO AND THE PROFESSION OF LAW

The Negro in American life is a striking illustration of the strength and weakness of the American legal system. For too long, law was used as an instrument to deny equality of rights to the Negro; today, it is the instrument used to insure equality of rights. No part of our history better illustrates the nature of law as a process for adjusting human relations, and none better illustrates the importance of the attitudes of men who make and administer law. Were this section concerned with race relations generally, it would consider the importance and the difficulties in directing the leveling process upward, not downward.[1] Our discussion is limited to what the profession can do to set its own house in order.

"Change places with the judge",[2] is the first of the ten commandments given to advocates by one of the greatest of their number. Restated it is:

> "If the places were reversed and you sat where they do, think what it is that you would want first to know about the case." [3]

"Put yourself in his place" is at the base of all good human relationships. Especially it is so for the white man and the Negro. For the Negro a large part of that place is emphasized history: two centuries of slavery with its precursor, the slave trade; a civil war; a century of discrimination under law. Now there is a

---

15. In re Roel, 3 App.Div.2d 742, 160 N.Y.S. 982 (1957).

1. The difficulties are indicated by the comment of a lawyer in Washington. He put his older daughter in the public schools for a year and then sent her to a private school, explaining: "I decided she had suffered enough for my principles."

2. Davis, The Advocate on Appeal, 26 A.B.A.J. 895, 986 (1940).

3. Id.

new period with discriminations under law struck down, and with opportunity for him to achieve his rightful place. At least three forms of that place are offered to him by leaders. One is integration into our national society to which he will make his own contribution. A second is maintenance of his separateness and the creation of black nationalism in some undefined form,—a Balkanization of the country along racial lines. Another is revolution and the destruction of present society, to be succeeded by an imagined new society.

On a symposium of over 150 law students, lawyers and judges at the Harvard Law School in 1870 a reporter wrote:

> "Their main themes seem to be 'Look how far we have come', and particularly emphasized by the younger students 'Look how far we have to go.' . . . [B]lacks constitute only one percent of the nation's lawyers, while they are about twelve per cent of the general population." [4]

Besides understanding given by, "put yourself in his place", three things which our profession can contribute to the wise developments out of a long-continuing situation call for mention. They are respect, participation and steadiness.

Respect. Fundamental to good social relations are self-respect of the individual, and the fostering of it through respect accorded by others. Many recent decisions of the Supreme Court of the United States seek to assure equality in governmental privileges. More important than any of them is Hamilton v. Alabama [5] which requires respect and courtesy. A Negro woman was a witness in court in her own behalf.

The cross-examination began:

> "Q. What is your name, please?
> A. Miss Mary Hamilton.
> Q. Mary, I believe—you were arrested.
> A. My name is Miss Hamilton. Please address me correctly.
> Q. Who were you arrested by, Mary?
> A. I will not answer . . . your question until I am addressed correctly.
> The Court: Answer the Question.
> The Witness: I will not answer them unless I am addressed correctly. . . .

4. 51 Harv.L.Record, No. 3, 1.

5. 376 U.S. 650, 84 S.Ct. 982 (1964), rev'g Ex parte Mary Hamilton, 275 Ala. 574, 156 So.2d 926 (1963). The case in both courts is reported at length in 9 Race Rel.L.Rep. 56, 336

(1964). The case is discussed in an address by Chief Justice Warren, "Unfulfilled Ideals", republished in 1 Human Rights 24, 28 (1970), the Journal of the Section of Individual Rights and Responsibilities of the American Bar Association.

> The Court: You are in contempt of this court, and you
> are sentenced to five days in jail and a fifty dollar
> fine."

The Supreme Court of the United States in a per curiam decision reversed the decision of the state court. The Court perceived, as had the witness, that the form of address, "Mary", was a slight to which a white woman would not have been subjected, and the Court invoked the Constitution to assure equality of respect. The decision struck down annoying indignities. The natural reaction to indignities has been the slogan, "I Am A Man", and the assertiveness implicit in Black Pride, Black Power, Black Nationalism, Black Panthers.

One thing that white lawyers and the organized bar can do is to feel and to accord full respect to the Negro. The long unhappy past may make him sense disrespect when not intended.

Participation. Participation by the Negro in the making and administration of laws is called for by justice. It helps contribute to a sense of self-respect and of respect for the laws in which he now shares. Two aspects only will be mentioned, legal education and bar associations.

The number of Negro lawyers is small. The law schools are now reaching out to increase the number of not merely those admitted to the bar but of well trained lawyers. The law schools can see to it that the education given is of a kind effective with a group long culturally deprived. To treat unequals equally is a denial of equality. Dean Tollett of Texas Southern University has wisely recognized the special needs of many of his students:

> "Although it is unpleasant and a little embarrassing to talk
> about the deprivation of some black students in terms of
> preparation for law, it is a fact. It is a fact explained by
> over two hundred years of slavery and one hundred years of
> segregation and second class citizenship." [6]

He added that some of his students are free of the false pride which would lead them to refuse the special training which their disadvantaged position calls for:

> "Many of our students desire special attention in a tutorial
> like situation. . . . Our young people deserve special
> compensation . . . through an opportunity to get a
> professional education in circumstances suited for realizing
> their abilities."

The long disinclination of the American Bar Association to admit Negro lawyers to membership has ended. It would be most helpful for local bar associations, too, to reach out as the

6. Tollett, Making It Together, 53
Judicature 366, 369 (1970).

law schools have done to include Negroes in their membership and on their committees. Their number, as said, is disturbingly small. Yet their participation in the work of the bar associations would add a breadth of understanding by both white and black which may be out of all relation to the numbers engaged in the work.

Steadiness. In classical antiquity when a Greek was owned by a Roman the master knew that in matters which counted most the slave might well be his superior. Even if the slave was a barbarian from Gaul or England the master would know that the descendants of the slave would in a generation be indistinguishable from his own. Slavery was then very different in its immediate relationships and also in the quick disappearance of distinguishing marks from slavery of modern times when men of one continent seized or bought men of another continent and transported them to a third. Frederick Douglass emphasized the continuing mark and difficulties of color in a passage quoted by Mr. Justice Douglas.

> "They carry in front the evidence which marks them for persecution. They stand at the extreme point of difference from the Caucasian race, and their African origin can be instantly recognized though they may be several removes from the typical African race." [7]

It is heartening in a way to reread two books, Gilbert Stephenson's careful study of 1910, "Race Distinctions in American Law" and Gunnar Myrdahl's great work of 1945, "The American Dilemma". The reading makes clear the great gains in this century. The subject of the first has been swept away. No longer can there be race distinctions in American law. The grossest of the injustices portrayed in the second have been undone. It would be agreeable to be as the Fabians, the comfortable and talented English group around the turn of the century who could support socialism, content in the belief of "the inevitability of gradualness." It could scarcely have been in their thoughts that their objectives would be taken over by men in a hurry in their own country who would insist on "Socialism in our lifetime", and certainly not that in another country men of a moderate brand of socialism who had overthrown the Czar would in their turn be overthrown in the name of socialism.

In race relations, too, the old belief in slow self-healing can not stand. A wrestler who has his shoulders pinned to the mat may cease to struggle. When he gets half way up he strives to go the whole way. So it is with the Negro. In this likeness to the wres-

---

7. See Douglas, J., concurring in
Jones v. Alfred H. Mayer Co., 392
U.S. 409, 446 (1968).

tler the Negro is not peculiar. Professor Harry Jones, condemning racial discrimination, warned against the dangerous oversimplification of believing that civil disorders will decrease in proportion to the decrease in racial inequality.[8] He quoted Robert MacIver:

> "One thing that struck me was a direct relation between the degree of liberation of groups and peoples from powerlessness or sheer subjection and the amount of social violence and civil commotion. In other words, liberty in this context brought forth not peace but the sword."

In this difficult setting the legal profession's part is a compound of understanding and action and steadiness. The profession understands and will help make others understand the Negro's sense of frustrations from hopes long deferred, and the inevitability of demagogues. In its associations and its schools it will set its own house in order. Seeing things steadily, it will not be dismayed by the inevitable jolts which accompany great social readjustments. Seeing them whole, the profession will preserve and protect against misuse or overthrow the institutions of law and justice entrusted to it. It will know that in this way the American lawyer will be true to himself as Gunnar Myrdal portrayed him:

> "[A]merica, relative to all the other branches of Western civilization, is moralistic and 'moral-conscious'. . . . We recognize the American, wherever we meet him, as a practical idealist. Compared with members of other nations of Western civilization, the ordinary American is a rationalistic being, and there are close relations between his moralism and his rationalism. . . . This moralism and rationalism are to many of us—among them, the author of this book—the glory of the nation, its youthful strength, perhaps the salvation of mankind." [9]

SECTION 7. TO THOSE LEFT OUT AND TO THOSE AHEAD

To Those Left Out. This book concerns the profession of law and the standards which will aid its members in carrying out their roles in the law. The profession does not work alone. We wish at least to express our acknowledgement to some of our associates.

8. H. Jones, The Efficacy of Law 88–89 (1969).

9. G. Myrdal, An American Dilemma at xlvi (1944).

To the members of the police force and other agencies of law enforcement ("officers of the law," as they are known) who have the primary task in enforcing our criminal laws;

To the jurymen and arbitrators who have the final word in the cases before them;

To court administrators who can do so much to assure that justice is prompt;

To prison administrators, who strive to make imprisonment a stage on the way to rehabilitation, not degeneration.*

To the social workers who do so much to aid the underprivileged to be their best selves.

To the ordinary citizens whose law abiding habits do the most to keep our society a working whole.

To Those Ahead. The framework within which we write may become outmoded. Our social and political ideals and the derivative legal institutions are changing with unmatched speed. Some institutions which the reception acts took over and which the Constitution safeguards may become as unsuited to this country as they have been found in their old home. The structure of the "more perfect union" of 1787, created when Europe was a month away by sailing time, may need to be supplanted by a still more perfect union now that Europe is hours away by plane and minutes by rocket.

We extend our best wishes to those who keeping within the framework of our political and social systems would carry out the injunction laid upon them by the Code of Professional Responsibility, "A Lawyer Should Aid in Improving the Legal System." They will reexamine fundamentally our system of law administration in places become lethargic. They may take note of the questions whether legal protections wise in origin have turned into obstructions of justice, and whether elaborate legal remedies delaying the fate of a man for years have transformed protection into injury, for him and for society.

We extend our best wishes as well to those who will seek to improve our political and social system. Without them society stands still. They need must keep their efforts within the framework of order without which society turns into riot. When they threaten an orderly society they elevate their enemies to pow-

---

* See Burger, No Man is an Island, 56 A.B.A.J. 325 (1970).

In a class action it was held that imprisonment in the Arkansas Penitentiary System of prison farms was cruel and unusual punishment. Holt v. Sarver, 309 F.Supp. 362 (1970). "Noteworthy" improvements detailed in a Report of Progress by the Commissioner of Corrections, a respondent in the action, are outlined in a Case Comment, 84 Harv.L.Rev. 456, 462, n. 36 (1970).

er. The Emperor Napoleon, the young officer who had cleared the streets of Paris with a "whiff of grapeshot," was the child of the French Revolution. Stalin, the dictator, was the natural heir of Lenin, the revolutionary.

For institutions as well as for men, we have been reminded, there is need for self-renewal "Institutions that cannot bend, break." Stability and change through law is our society's means of self-renewal.

Chapter XVII

THE METHODS OF PROVIDING LEGAL SERVICES

SECTION 1. INTRODUCTION

Lawyers are essential in the administration and development of law. "A basic tenent of the professional responsibility of lawyers is that every person in our society should have ready access to the independent professional services of a lawyer of competence and integrity." [1]

The bar has shown initiative in developing new methods of providing better services for good clients and in overriding professional standards which might stand in the way of these new methods. The mention of two examples of creativity will suffice. To serve well its corporate clients the bar has moved far from its old ideal of the lawyer working alone and has developed the large corporate law firm. And in response to the public need for protection from the burden of damages in personal injury cases, the profession has accepted the liability insurance company and its counsel chosen by the company to represent the insured; though in this situation there is manifest violation of the usual standards of the bar against the lay intermediary, against the solicitation of practice, and against the representation of conflicting interests. There is need for similar creativity as to methods of providing legal services throughout our varied society.

Some professional attitudes support the present system with little or no change. These attitudes range from inertia and conservatism on to the conviction that proposed changes would impair the independence of the bar or its income. Yet there are powerful factors which support substantial change, as increased sensitivity to the needs of the disadvantaged and the realization that under the present system legal services do not reach many who need them.

Clients are diverse and this calls for corresponding diversity of methods in providing legal services.[2] The chapter deals first

1. ABA Code of Professional Responsibility, EC 1–1.

2. A thoughtful analysis and discussion of the subject of this chapter, prepared for the American Bar Foundation, is the book, B. Christensen, Lawyers for People of Moderate Means: Some Problems of Availability of Legal Services (1970). An early and provocative discussion is Llewellyn, The Bar Specializes—With What Results?, 167 Annals 177 (1933).

with the usual method of providing counsel through lawyers in private practice who render services to clients coming to them. Next it takes up the situations of several classes of prospective clients and special methods employed or proposed for rendering services to them, the middle classes, the poor, the hated, and personal injury and death claimants. Lastly it considers more general problems concerning publicity and solicitation by lawyers, and the roles of laymen in rendering legal services.

SECTION 2. ORGANIZATIONS OF LAWYERS TO RENDER SERVICES

The forms of organization to render legal services include the lone practitioner, the partnership, the corporation, and the salaried lawyer whether as associate of a law firm or corporate counsel or government employee.

The Lone Practitioner and the Partnership

The majority of American lawyers practice alone.[1] Many of them share offices with other lawyers and have something like a partnership in office expenses but not in fees. Numerous lawyers practice in partnerships, which vary from the informal partnership of two men to the metropolitan offices with a score of partners and many more associates. There have been critical comparisons of lawyers practicing alone—solo as the term goes —and of partnerships. On behalf of the solo lawyer it is pointed out that his situation fosters direct relationship of lawyer and client as well as independence of thought and action and responsibility. In support of the partnership it is urged that there are greater expertness and efficiency, ready interchange of views on a case, a no less effective relation of lawyer and client, the greater possibility for public service by men whose practice is carried on in their absence, and an *esprit de corps* of the firm.[2]

---

1. The 1967 Lawyer Statistical Report of the American Bar Foundation gives the number of lawyers in the United States in 1966 as 316,000 with 212,000 in the "private sector" of whom 113,000 were individual practitioners.

2. The cases for the partnership and for the individual practitioner are set out in H. Tweed, The Changing Practice of Law (1955); Gerhart, Practicing Law: The Case for the Individual Practitioner, 43 A.B.A.J. 793 (1957). Studies show that lawyers practicing in partnerships have larger incomes than those practicing alone and the income of each partner goes up with the size of the firm. Certainly, this is not because the partnership form assures a larger income. Lawyers with prosperous clients find the partnership form effective or even essential in meeting their clients' needs.

The standards of lawyers in practice apply to solo practitioners and to partnership members alike. In the matter of conflicting interests the courts and the bar committees have been strict, holding a whole firm disqualified if an incoming member however junior has had any relation to the other side of the matter in question. In one case a lawyer joining a new firm which had been on one side in a case took every precaution that honesty would dictate to assure that he would neither acquire nor misuse information in continuing to represent the other side. Yet the court held he was disqualified.[3] It has been questioned whether the sweeping condemnation is wise in office matters as to large firms, when there is no misuse of information and there is full disclosure to both clients. A study revealed that many firms act according to their own standards of honesty and fairness in such matters.[4]

The increase of practice across state lines has led to the approval in firm membership of lawyers admitted in different states at least when approved by local custom, though care should be taken as through appropriate notation on the firm letterhead to show the limited nature of the privilege of practice of out-of-state lawyers.[5] The desire to encourage the participation of lawyers in public life has led a committee to approve the continuation in firm membership of men holding legislative or executive office.[6] As to public officials, the principle against the representation of conflicting interest is rigorously applied.[7] The standards of the profession provide that a lawyer may not have a layman as a partner in practice.[8] A stated ground for the prohibition is that a layman cannot be held up to the standards of the legal profession. An unstated ground is the fear that a firm which combines within it two fields of expertness may have an advantage over the general practitioner in the view of clients. The increasing importance in legal matters of the use of tested experts in other fields and the development of ethical standards in those fields, of which the certified accountant is an illustration, may lead to a modification of this professional standard.

---

3. W. E. Bassett Co. v. H. C. Cook Co., 201 F.Supp. 821 (D.Conn.) aff'd per curiam 302 F.2d 268 (2nd Cir. 1962).

4. Note, Unchanging Rules in Changing Times: The Canons of Ethics and Intra-firm Conflicts of Interest, 73 Yale L.J. 1058 (1964).

5. ABA Comm. on Professional Ethics, Opinions, No. 256, (1943) An extensive review of the subjects of firm membership and firm names is given in ABA Comm. on Professional Ethics, Opinions, Nos. 316 & 318, 53 A.B.A.J. 353, 838 (1967). On the status of foreign lawyers, see ABA Comm. on Professional Ethics, Opinions, No. 263 (1944).

6. ABA Comm. on Professional Ethics, Opinions, No. 192 (1939).

7. Id.

8. ABA Canons of Professional Ethics No. 33.

The firm name, of course, should not be misleading. The practice in large cities of continuing the use of the name of a deceased partner has irked and been challenged by many solo or small firm practitioners. The practice has been approved by the courts and the bar committees, when the name is used to identify a continuing partnership of which the dead man was a member and not to give false lustre to a new partnership.[9] The use of the name makes clear that the firm is a continuing organization rather than merely a group of identified individuals. The good will attached to the firm name was built up by all the partners, and the loss of identification and good will with changes in firm membership would be harmful to the remaining partners without public gain. The American practice, however, has not gone so far as the English usage which seemingly permits the use of "and Company" at the end of the name of a firm of solicitors.

The relationship of the partners among themselves is fixed in large measure by the terms of the partnership agreement.[10] It is proper for the agreement to provide that on the death of a partner, the partnership pay to designated persons for a fixed period a sum based on his average earnings prior to his death.[11] The agreement may also set the terms for withdrawal or for ouster.[12] A partner who through his special work carries to completion a case pending when he withdraws is not entitled to an addition to his share of the fee. This was so held because all members are equally obligated in firm cases.[13] As to new cases it has been ruled that a restrictive covenant prohibiting a lawyer employee from practicing in the vicinity for a stated period is improper.[14] The professional and personal problems which arise when some partners withdraw and take clients of the old firm with them have not been dealt with by the authorities.

9. Mendelson v. Equitable Life Assurance Soc'y, 178 Misc. 152, 33 N.Y.S.2d 733 (1942); ABA Code of Professional Responsibility, EC 2–11.

10. Basic forms of agreements for the small and the large partnerships and for lawyers non-partnership arrangements are given in The Lawyers Handbook Part V, 1962), prepared by the Committee on the Economics of Law Practice of the American Bar Association.

11. ABA Comm. on Professional Ethics, Opinions, No. 308 (1963).

12. A reserved power of ouster, it is believed, should be limited by public policy. A situation in which there may have been such a limitation was the reported ouster of a member of a Birmingham firm because at the request of the Attorney General of the United States, he had accepted an unpopular case tinged with racial discrimination. See the N. Y. Times, May 30, 1965.

13. Frates v. Nichols, 140 So.2d 321 (Fla.Dist.Ct.App.1962); Platt v. Henderson, 227 Or. 212, 361 P.2d 73 (1961).

14. ABA Comm. on Professional Ethics, Opinions, No. 300 (1961).

The Corporation

The use of the general incorporation laws as a basis for the formation of a corporation for profit to render legal services through lawyers is condemned.[15] The condemnation is justified because the business motives of the corporate stockholders and executives may be inconsistent with the socially desirable standards of the lawyers whom the corporation employs and directs. In recent years some states have by new statutes authorized the creation of "professional corporations" because of supposed federal tax advantages of the corporate form. A common requirement is that all members of the corporation be members of the profession and so subject to its standards. Two principal questions about such a corporation are whether it satisfies the meaning of a "corporation" for federal income tax purposes, and whether the standards of the profession are violated by the use of the corporate form. The corporate form of organization has been approved by the ABA Committee "provided appropriate safeguards are observed." [16] The Supreme Court of Florida, stating "[w]e are pioneering in a new field of professional relationships", ruled that when the corporate form is used the personal obligation of the lawyer to his client must in no way be affected and the corporate entity itself would come under the court's disciplinary power.[17]

The Salaried Lawyer

Employment on a salary is common. This is the usual method for large law firms in associating young lawyers with them. The method looks ordinarily to its termination by the associate becoming a member of the firm or else withdrawing for other opportunities. In recent years there has been a marked increase of salaried lawyers retained by large business organizations to look after most of their legal work. Corporate counsel, as they are sometimes called, have the advantage of continuing knowl-

15. Matter of Cooperative Law Co., 198 N.Y. 479, 92 N.E. 15 (1910); People v. People's Stock Yards State Bank, 344 Ill. 462, 176 N.E. 901 (1931).

16. ABA Comm. on Professional Ethics, Opinions, No. 303 (1961).

In several cases the United States Court of Appeals held a professional corporation was a corporation for federal income tax purposes. The Solicitor General determined, with the concurrence of the Chief Counsel of the Internal Revenue Service, not to apply for certiorari in two key cases. The Internal Revenue Service then announced that "it is conceding that organizations of doctors, lawyers and other professional people organized under state professional acts will, generally, be treated as corporations for tax purposes" with the reservation of the right "to conclude differently in any case that reflects special circumstances." Internal Revenue Service Technical Information Release 1019, (Aug. 8, 1969). See What's New in the Law, 55 A.B.A.J. 992 (1969).

17. In re The Florida Bar, 133 So.2d 554, 557 (Fla.1961).

edge and insight into the activities of the business, ready availability, and the opportunity to observe and counsel early against illegal or harmful activities. Their professional standards in practice are the same as those of other lawyers.[18]

This sketch of the forms of organization of lawyers to render legal services may well end with the findings of sociologists as to the work of lawyers at the opposite ends of the clients' financial scale. Professor Smigel's study concludes that the Wall Street firm serves its clients well in giving dependable independent advice.[19] The quality of the advice is strengthened by the expectation that even the most junior associate will give to his seniors his independent views on the problems involved at least within the range of the client's interests, a kind of independence which the author calls "creative conformity" or conforming creativity. The author questions the social desirability of having so much of the nation's best legal talent concentrated in the service of one segment of society. Two studies of lawyers serving other classes in Chicago and New York City reveal a wholly different situation.[20] The poorer and less stable the clientele, the less ethical is the lawyer, his insecurity leading him at times to disregard common honesty. The lawyers for the lower income groups are less prosperous, less effective, and less ethical. Other forms of organization are needed to provide services to these groups.

SECTION 3. THE MIDDLE CLASSES

Recent social changes have greatly affected the need and the availability in fact of legal services for the middle classes. The productivity of our economic system has resulted in the leveling up of income in "the affluent society", so an increasing proportion of our people have the problems which wealth brings as well as the continuing personal difficulties which lawyers may help to settle. Urbanization has as a consequence the decline of personal and neighborhood knowledge of whom to retain as a professional man. A third change is the reliance of individuals on group organizations, as labor unions, for the protection of their interests. A result of the first two changes is that there is a

---

18. In re O'Neil, 228 App.Div. 129, 239 N.Y.S. 297 (1930).

19. E. Smigel, The Wall Street Lawyer (1964).

20. J. Carlin, Lawyers on Their Own (1962); J. Carlin, Lawyers Ethics (1966).

large unsatisfied need of legal services by persons who can pay at least something for them.[1]

The middle classes have as common elements their unfamiliarity with lawyers and their services, reluctance to consult lawyers until emergency is compelling, and ignorance of whom to choose as a lawyer. Their attitudes, unfortunately, stand in the way of obtaining the legal services they need. One set of attitudes is based on ignorance—ignorance of the legal problem, ignorance of the aid a lawyer could give, ignorance of where to find a lawyer and of whom to choose. Another set rests on fear—fear of overreaching and overcharging by lawyers and fear of the law's processes and delays.

On the side of the bar, too, there are obstacles in the way of rendition of the services needed. They include undiscrimiating application of the bar's standards, especially the standards which forbid publicity, the representation of conflicting interests, and lay intermediaries standing between lawyer and client. Each standard has a substantial basis which needs no statement here. In other situations than that of the middle classes they have been subordinated to public needs, as with the liability insurance company and the legal aid society. Another obstacle on the side of the bar is inertia and fear of change. Successful lawyers are successful and effective under the system as it is and they are content with it. Inertia may have the active support of fear—fear of lowered standards of the bar and fear of loss of practice under changed conditions.

Lawyers and their standards do not exist, of course, for their own sake. When old methods and standards block the rendition of the services which lawyers alone have the privilege to perform, the standards must be modified and new methods created. A variety of methods have been proposed and call for mention below. The primary emphasis of the methods has been laid on making the lawyer known and accessible or on making the fee bearable or on assurance of availability and dependability through choice by a trusted organization.

Lawyer Referral Service

"Lawyer Referral Service" is a plan administered by local bar associations through which a person needing legal services can on inquiry be referred to a lawyer with whom he may consult for

---

1. There has been a shortage of dependable studies of the extent and areas of needed legal services for the middle classes. Among the pioneer studies are Clark and Corstvet, The Lawyer and the Public, 47 Yale L.J. 1272 (1938). Judge Albert Conway of the Court of Appeals of New York, venturing an estimate urged "a fresh and adequate approach . . . to the subject of legal aid for the hundred or more millions of Americans who have no access to any form of organized legal aid". 70 N.Y.S.B.A. Rep. 314, 318 (1947).

a low initial fee. If the case warrants, it will proceed on terms the client and the lawyer agree on.[2] An element of the plan is a panel of lawyers who have agreed to let these clients consult them. The plan has withstood attacks on ethical and legal grounds.[3] The usefulness of the plan, as pointed out by one most conversant with it, depends on public awareness of the service and an effective method of bringing the lawyer and the client together.[4] It has not yet had the strong and continuing support of the local bar associations which would make it an adequate method of making legal services available in fact.

Neighborhood Law Office

A "neighborhood law office" plan has been developed in Philadelphia. It is approved and in a measure supervised by the local bar association. The law offices are opened at places convenient to low income clients and they are identified by signs conspicuous according to usual standards, at times by neon lights. They are independent law offices marked only by their accessibility and by their agreement to follow some bar association guide lines. "Over the years 82 per cent of those who have come have stated that they never before had consulted a lawyer."[5] The Philadelphia example has not been followed widely.[6]

Legal Services Insurance

A study of the feasibility of legal services insurance was made for the American Bar Foundation. The excellent report finds that such a plan is an actuarially feasible way of financing legal services for persons of modest means and need not be too costly to be sold.[7] Its primary value would be the encouragement of preventive law services. In comparison with another system the conclusion is:

> "For selected groups, legal insurance would be more attractive than group legal services, but, in general, legal insur-

2. The plan is the subject of a symposium by Messrs. Carrington, Gallantz, Madden and Meyer in 45 J.Am.Jud.Soc'y 306 (1962).

3. The Jacksonville Bar Association v. Wilson, 102 So.2d 292 (1958); ABA Comm. on Professional Ethics, Opinions, No. 291 (1956).

4. Christensen, Lawyer Referral Service: An Alternative to Lay-Group Legal Services, 12 U.C.L.A. L.Rev. 341 (1965). Mr. Christensen has prepared for the American Bar Association and for the American Bar Foundation a helpful manual on Lawyer Referral Services Offices and a monograph appraising their achievement. The American Bar Association Committee on Lawyer Referral has sponsored and, doubtless, will continue to sponsor a workshop for the exchange of ideas on the subject.

5. Abrahams, The Neighborhood Law Office Plan, 1949 Wis.L.Rev. 634.

6. The use of such offices widely is urged in R. Smith, Legal Service Offices for Persons of Moderate Means, 31 J.Am.Jud.Soc'y 37 (1947).

7. Stolz, Insurance for Legal Services: A Preliminary Study of Feasibility, 35 U.Chi.L.Rev. 417 (1968).

ance cannot achieve the economies of scale possible through group legal services." [8]

Group Legal Services [9]

Group legal services calls for extended discussion, first of the opposition of the bar and the state courts, then path-breaking decisions by the Supreme Court of the United States, and lastly some unresolved questions.   The Committee on Unauthorized Practice of Law of the American Bar Association has ruled that the furnishing of legal services as fringe benefits constitutes the unlawful practice of law whether furnished by a labor union to its member or by a corporation to its employees.[10]   The attitude of the state courts generally is illustrated by three decisions of one state court condemning indiscriminately as lay intermediaries a bank which carried on trust and estate practice through its legal staff, a non-profit corporation of taxpayers attacking through counsel the validity of tax assessments, and a labor union which furnished a lawyer to its members in workmen's compensation cases.[11]

These state court decisions did more, it will be noted, than merely to condemn group legal services.   They wrote that condemnation into the state constitution, for under the separation of powers principle the same court had held it had the last word on what constitutes the unlawful practice of law.   So the decisions blocked all efforts by the organized bar or by the legislature to develop such forms of group practice unless either the state constitution was amended or else the Supreme Court of the United States stepped in.

8.   In a few cities lawyers have developed with banks a legal fee finance plan, under which a client with credit standing may borrow from a bank the amount of the lawyer's fee. The lawyer receives his fee at once and the client pays the bank over the period of the loan. The American Bar Association committee, recognizing that some local committees were of a different view, has ruled that the plan is not necessarily unprofessional. ABA Comm. on Professional Ethics, Opinions, No. 320, 54 A.B.A.J. 476 (1968). The plan has limited usefulness in making legal services available. It is assurance for the lawyer rather than insurance for the hard pressed client.

9.   An excellent volume on the subject of this section, prepared for the American Bar Foundation, is B. Christensen, Lawyers for People of Moderate Means: Some Problems on Availability of Legal Services (1970). In Chapter VII, Mr. Christensen deals with Group Legal Services.

10.   Informative Opinion of the Committee on Unauthorized Practice of Law, 36 A.B.A.J. 677 (1950). The validity of the opinion was questioned by Mr. Henry Drinker, long the chairman of the Committee on Professional Ethics. See H. Drinker, Legal Ethics 161–168 (1953).

11.   People v. People's Stock Yards State Bank, 344 Ill. 462, 176 N.E. 901 (1931); People v. Association of Real Estate Tax-Payers of Illinois, 354 Ill. 102, 187 N.E. 823 (1933); Illinois State Bar Ass'n v. United Mine Workers of America, District 12, 35 Ill.2d 112, 219 N.E.2d 503 (1966).

Three recent decisions of the Supreme Court of the United States reveal the opposition of the majority of the members of the Court to this attitude. The first case, National Association for the Advancement of Colored People v. Button,[12] involved a statute of Virginia which would have condemned the NAACP for soliciting and conducting litigation directed at racial segregation in schools. The counsel for Virginia based the support of the statute on the professional standard condemning a lay intermediary which stands between the lawyer and the clients. The majority of the Court upheld the action of the NAACP under the constitutional protection to "right of association". The opinion mentioned several state decisions condemning lay intermediaries, thus implying questions as to their constitutional validity. Brotherhood of Railroad Trainmen v. Virginia [13] concerned a plan of a national union to aid its members and their families in retaining lawyers in case of accidents during employment. The Brotherhood's officers designated lawyers in sixteen districts over the country who agreed to take cases on a contingent fee of twenty per cent and whom Brotherhood members would promptly recommend when a member was injured or killed, with the resultant channeling of cases to these firms. The majority of the Court, relying on the constitutional guarantees of free speech, petition and assembly, upheld the plan against condemnation by the common law, the statutes of the state, and the Canons of Ethics adopted as part of the rules of the state court. United Mine Workers of America v. Illinois State Bar Association [14] is the third state case mentioned above. The union employed a lawyer on a salary to represent its members who had claims under the workmen's compensation act and who wished his services. The letter of employment stated the lawyer would receive no further instructions from the union and his obligations would be to the union members directly. When an injury happened a claim file was prepared by secretaries of the union office. From that file the lawyer sought to reach an agreement with the employer, which the union member was free to reject. If the employee rejected the tentative agreement, the lawyer would present the claim before the commission. The full amount of the settlement or award was paid to the union member. At the suit of the state bar association the trial court enjoined the union from proceeding with the plan, and the state supreme court affirmed the decision. Again the Supreme Court of the United States reversed the state court's decision and held that the plan for providing counsel was protected by the Constitution.

"We hold that the freedom of speech, assembly, and petition guaranteed by the First and Fourteenth Amendments gives

12. 371 U.S. 415 (1963).   14. 389 U.S. 219 (1967).

13. 377 U.S. 1 (1964).

petitioner the right to hire attorneys on a salary basis to assist its members in the assertion of their legal rights.[15]

Two conclusions are manifest from these cases.   One is that the basic reason for the decisions was the deep dissatisfaction of the majority of the justices with the lack of vision and creativity of the bar and the bench in developing or even approving methods for making legal services available in fact to the middle groups of our people.   The dissatisfaction with the undiscriminating application of old standards was so great that it made the majority of the justices willing to employ the national Constitution in an area long reserved to the States.   Another conclusion is that while the three decisions protect the plans against prohibition, they clearly intimate that the plans can be subjected to appropriate regulation.   In the last case the Court emphasized that "the States have broad power to regulate the practice of law".

Accepting the decisions the bar and the state courts have the opportunity to help develop group legal services in a way which will make them most effective.   The common idea which ties together the opinions of the Supreme Court of the United States is "the public interest", or, to put it concretely, there was no showing in those cases that the limitations questioned were in the public interest.   Accepting this as the basic guide there are several factors to be taken into account in the development of such plans in the future.

The first and most important is the moral duty on the Bar, to whom alone are entrusted the privilege to practice law, to make legal services available in fact to those who need them.   The statement of Justice Traynor, involving the *Brotherhood of Railroad Trainmen* plan, deserves repetition:

> "Given the primary duty of the legal profession to serve the public, the rules it establishes to govern its professional ethics must be directed at the performance of that duty." [16]

A second set of factors concerns the assurance of the essential qualities of the lawyer, under a group service plan.   Of course he must be free from any supervision or control in his work for his clients and free as well from conflicting interests, with no connection that might impair his zeal.   A third factor of great importance is an appropriate system of authorization and supervision of group legal services, whether it be by the court or a commission.   An unsupervised system would give large opportunities for sharpers posing as benefactors.

---

15.   Id. at 221–22.

16.   Hildebrand v. State Bar, 36 Cal. 2d 504, 522, 225 P.2d 508, 519 (1950) (dissenting opinion).

The three cases mentioned suggest further comments and questions. All of the cases involved the middle or disadvantaged classes, they concerned persons with a common relationship, and they were confined to controversies arising out of this relationship. Are all of these elements essential to the constitutional protection of the plan? The questions can be made specific. Would the constitutional protection extend to the converse of the situation in the *United Mine Workers* case, that is an association of self-insured employers who band together to retain counsel to represent them individually in workmen's compensation cases? [17] Does it include representation of the members of the union in all their ordinary legal matters as buying and selling homes, or is it confined to representation in workmen's compensation cases? Would the constitutional protection extend to a cooperative association the members of which had no other common interest and which would provide legal services to its members along with other benefits?

So far the discussion has been in terms of the constitutional requirements. Obviously it would be most unwise as well as unfair for the bar to deal with the broad problem merely in terms of the minimum that the Constitution permits or requires. "The public interest" calls for what is wise when all factors are taken into consideration. A troubling element, to mention but one, is raised in Mr. Justice Harlan's dissent in the *United Mine Workers* case. During the period that plan had been in operation some three hundred appeals had been taken in workmen's compensation cases in Illinois, but only one of them on behalf of a mine worker and none for over twenty years past. The figures raise the questions whether the union lawyer, representing the miners on a fixed salary and also maintaining a private practice, had the zeal required of a lawyer. The figures suggest the broad question, what should be the terms of employment of a group service lawyer so as to assure or at least encourage those essential qualities of a lawyer, zeal and loyalty, as well as competence?

Two more aspects of group legal service will be mentioned. This system should give to the lawyers employed a financial security the lack of which has pulled down the standards of many lawyers now representing the lower middle classes and would raise the quality of services rendered. The spread of group practice would not mean the end of the bar as in independent profession. It is true that continued representation of one class intensifies the sympathy with that class. Yet the wide extension of group practice, bringing adequate legal services to those who now do not receive them, will not eliminate the independent lawyer

17.   See Copaken, Group Legal Services for Trade Associations, 66 Mich.L.Rev. 1211 (1968).

ready to challenge abuses from whatever side they come. "Of all men", as John W. Davis said, "lawyers are the least promising material for the drill-master." [18]

Our discussion of group legal services began with an opinion of a bar association committee which condemned group legal services broadly. It must end for the time being with a statement of opposing views within the American Bar Association. The Code of Professional Responsibility, in its final form unlike the preliminary draft, condemns group legal services in extraordinary language. After first giving its approval to legal services furnished through such methods as legal aid, lawyer referral, and a bar association, it deals with "any other non-profit organization that recommends, furnishes or pays for legal services to its members." As to the latter it gives approval on stated conditions, the principal one of which is:

> "only in those instances and to the extent that controlling constitutional interpretation at the time of the rendition of the services requires the allowance of such legal service activities." [19]

In short, group legal services are condemned except as they are protected by the constitution. This is a challenge to the state supreme courts and the Supreme Court of the United States to give broad constitutional protection.

Elsewhere the Code itself takes a wholly different attitude. It gives broad recognition to the duty of the bar to make legal services available and to develop new methods as new conditions call for them.[20]

Several years earlier the American Bar Association created a Special Committee on Availability of Legal Services under the chairmanship of Mr. F. William McAlpin of St. Louis. The Special Committee's report to the 1969 meeting proposed broad approval to the rendition of legal services "to individual members of a group identifiable in terms of some substantial common interest." The report also recommended several safeguards to prevent the misuse of group legal services. The report was not accepted.[21]

---

18. The monograph cited earlier concludes: "The profession's interest in preserving the lawyer as an effective element in society—as well as the public's interest—would therefore seem to be best served by extending and expanding the ability of lawyers to serve the public and thus increasing the public's utilization of lawyers." Christensen, supra, note 9, at 73.

19. ABA Code of Professional Responsibility, DR 2–103(D) (5).

20. Id., EC 2–1 & 2–7.

21. In 1970, the Supreme Court of California, in accordance with the recommendations made by the State Bar after public hearings, adopted Rules of Professional Conduct which approve group legal services under safeguards similar to those

The controversy over group legal services will continue within and beyond the Association.[22]

SECTION 4. THE POOR

Introduction *

In the midst of our affluent society there are many millions unable to pay for legal services they need.[1] This society, democratic in ideals as well as prodigious in production, has come to accept the duty to assure protection for the legal interests of the poor—Thou shalt not ration justice, as Judge Learned Hand put it. One line of effort in giving protection is to make the lawyer unnecessary through active efforts of administrative bodies in the investigation of cases before them, as by workmen's compensation commissions; but bureaucracy may harden and come to deny the rights it was created to protect. Another method is to supplant the lawyer through simplifying court procedures so that a layman can handle his own case. The method may have quite a different result from that hoped for by its founders, as when in a small claims court a tongue-tied debtor is pitted against the fluent small business man, with a disparity that can be righted only by counsel for the poor.

"The right to counsel" has several meanings. The basic meaning, from which the other meanings are derived, is a moral right. With the administration of law a public function and with lawyers essential to it there is a moral right that every person who needs a lawyer shall have one. The recognition of this moral right and the transformation of it into a legal right or, even more broadly, into public acceptance of new methods of provid-

proposed by the American Bar Association Special Committee.

22. See Voorhees, Group Legal Services, 55 A.B.A.J. 532 (1969).

* The opportunities as well as the frustrations of "The Lawyer Among the Poor" are vividly portrayed by Professor Robert E. Mathews in his volume, Problems Illustrative of the Responsibilities of the Legal Profession (5th Printing 1970), Ch. 14, The Lawyer Among the Poor.

"The general conclusion emerging from the study is that the problem of providing legal services is not

only the amount of help resources to be made available . . . The assumption that merely making legal services available is all that needs to be done to guarantee that people will seek counsel is naive. The problem is primarily one of education and the communication of information." F. Levine and E. Preston, "Community Resource Orientation Among Low Income Groups", 1970 Wis.L.Rev. 80, 112.

1. The legal aid clientele was estimated as compromising nearly thirty million in 1951. E. Brownell, Legal Aid in the United States (1951).

ing counsel beyond the legal right, comes from a revulsion at the thought of convicting an innocent man and an aroused sensitivity toward the poor.   It is a part of broader movements, as the protection of civil rights and the efforts to secure a larger measure of social justice.

A second meaning of the right to counsel beyond the moral right is the legal right of a person to employ and have the aid of counsel.   At the time of the American Revolution the English law denied this limited right to one accused of felony.[2]   There is no trace of this denial in American law except as to tribunals to which the adversary process may not be suited.[3]   As the leading constitutional case put it, "a defendant should be afforded a fair opportunity to secure counsel of his own choice." [4]   Closely associated with this last meaning is the obligation on the bar to develop forms of organization and standards of the profession which will make it practicable for a prospective client to obtain the services of a lawyer.

A third meaning is the legal right of an accused to have counsel provided for him when he cannot obtain counsel himself.   A basis for the right is set out in the American Bar Association's Standards Relating to Providing Defense Service:

> "[S]ociety has deliberately chosen the adversary system—a vigorous clash of opposing sides—as the mechanism for trying criminal cases.   .   .   .   Because society—not the defendant—has selected the adversary system as its choice of mechanism, our deliberate choice of that kind of system, rather than some notion of benevolence or gratuity to the poor, requires that both sides have professional spokesmen who know the rules, i. e., that they be trained lawyers."

The transformation of the moral attitude into a legal right and into availability of counsel in fact is a process which is continuing and developing on many fronts.   The legal right to counsel will first be outlined.   Then the methods of making counsel available in fact, in civil and in criminal matters, will be taken up.

The Legal Right to Have Counsel Provided

The discussion of this legal right will be confined to criminal cases for there appears to be no clear legal duty as yet on the state to furnish counsel in civil matters.[1]   It will be divided ac-

2.   See Powell v. Alabama, 287 U.S. 45 (1932).

3.   Even in some stages of a juvenile court proceeding the constitutional right to have counsel has been affirmed.   Re Gault, 387 U.S. 1 (1967).

4.   Powell v. Alabama, 287 U.S. 45, 53 (1932).

1.   The cases on the subject of the legal right are numerous and the commentaries voluminous.   An early helpful discussion is Beaney, The

cording to the nature of the tribunal, whether state or federal court, and of the legal source of the requirement, state or federal law.

Federal Court and Federal Law. The Sixth Amendment to the United States Constitution provides "In all criminal prosecutions, the accused shall enjoy the right . . . to have the Assistance of Counsel for his defense." Considered in the light of the English law of its time which denied the privilege to employ counsel in certain criminal cases, the provision might have been interpreted to do no more than to grant this privilege. In a prosecution in a federal court, the Supreme Court of the United States held that the Amendment does much more and requires that counsel be provided for an accused unable himself to retain counsel.[2] It held further that federal law, not the law of the state in which the federal court sat, was determinative. Most importantly it put the effect of lack of counsel in the strong terms of lack of "jurisdiction," thus opening the way to later attack on a conviction through the writ of habeas corpus:

> "If this requirement of the Sixth Amendment is not complied with, the court no longer has jurisdiction to proceed."[3]

The extent of this right in the federal courts under the Sixth Amendment is certainly no less than that in the state courts under the Fourteenth Amendment dealt with below.

State Courts and State Law. The states by their own laws have long required that counsel be provided for indigents accused of serious crimes. The variety in state requirements, the problems common to all the states, and the methods employed by each state are set out in a three volume study prepared for the American Bar Foundation by a national reporter and a state reporter in each state.[4] The fortunate attitude of cooperation, not opposition, of state and federal authorities in the requirement of counsel is illustrated in the decisive federal case of Gideon v. Wainwright.[5] There protection under federal law in a state case was urged in a brief filed *amici curiae* on behalf of twenty three state governments with only two in opposition. Most criminal cases are state cases and the first source to look to is state law and practice. State prosecutors recognize, as a Kansas county attorney put it, "Prosecutors are supposed to protect the inno-

Right to Counsel in American Courts (1955). The discussion here will be restricted to the policies and to a few leading cases. On the right to counsel in civil cases see Douglas, J., dissenting in Hackin v. Arizona, 389 U.S. 143 (1967).

2. Johnson v. Zerbst, 304 U.S. 458 (1938).

3. Id. at 468.

4. L. Silverstein, Defense of the Poor in Criminal Cases in American State Courts (1965).

5. 372 U.S. 335 (1963).

cent as well as prosecute the guilty." [6]   The state requirements may go beyond the federal constitutional requirements discussed below.   The particular method for the appointment of counsel will be set by state law.   A state court may well prefer to rest its decision on state law rather than federal law. [7]

State Courts and the Federal Constitution.   The first leading case, Powell v. State of Alabama, [8] is one in which relief was manifestly demanded.   In a small Alabama community several young Negroes were charged with rape of two white girls.   They were quickly indicted and brought to trial with public feeling so aroused that National Guardsmen were called out.   The judge assigned as their counsel all members of the small local bar but their representation at the trial was a sham.

The Supreme Court of the United States in reversing the conviction, found a constitutional right to counsel, at least in so serious a case as this one.

For twenty years there was uncertainty as to the kind of case in which the right existed, whether it was confined to extraordinary cases or whether it extends to ordinary cases.   The second leading case, Gideon v. Wainwright, [9] was the ordinary case.   Gideon was charged with a minor felony.   He was experienced enough with criminal courts to ask the judge to appoint counsel to represent him. [10]   When the judge denied the request, saying he had no such right under state law, Gideon replied: "The United States Supreme Court say I am entitled to be represented by Counsel."   Without the assistance of counsel he was convicted and sentenced to five years in prison.   In setting aside the conviction the Court rested its judgment on the importance, even the necessity, of having a lawyer if justice is to be done.   Quoting the earlier case Mr. Justice Black said:

> " 'The right to be heard would be, in many cases, of little avail if it did not comprehend the right to be heard by counsel.' " [11]

6. Silverstein, supra, note 3, Vol. 1, at 12.

7. An illustration is Johnson v. Tennessee, 213 Tenn. 55, 372 S.W. 2d 192 (1963).

8. 287 U.S. 45 (1932). The case is a vivid illustration of the old maxim, "The law arises out of the facts." The first half of defendant's brief in the Supreme Court of the United States gave a well organized, low key statement of the facts of the case, which made manifest the trial was unfair. The last half of the brief set out three possible constitutional grounds for relief.   The court drawing largely in its opinion on the statement of facts, chose the second ground, the right to counsel.

9. 372 U.S. 335 (1963).

10. Gideon's Trumpet, by Anthony Lewis, vividly describes the case from the start through Gideon's acquittal on a new trial when he was represented by counsel.

11. 372 U.S. at 344–45.

The Qualities of the Lawyer and His Actions. To meet the constitutional requirement the accused's counsel must measure up to the standards of the lawyer. One element is loyalty. The vague appointment of a group of lawyers as counsel does not suffice for no one would have "that individual sense of duty", "that clear appreciation of responsibility or impressed with that individual sense of duty." [12] The designation of a lawyer who represents conflicting interests is not enough,[13] nor is the appointment of a lawyer who was so intimidated by racial prejudice as to refrain from the obvious action of seeking a continuance or else a change of venue [14] or from challenging the practice of systematic exclusion of Negroes from the jury.[15] Counsel must function in the active role of an advocate and not as amicus curiae.[16] The emphasis in the decisions has been on the qualities of counsel and not on the wisdom or effectiveness of their actions at the trial. The accused is entitled not to errorless counsel or to counsel judged ineffective by hindsight but to counsel rendering reasonably effective assistance.[17] The qualities of counsel and of their actions may be affected more by professional action than by court decisions. The American Bar Association carried forward in the 1960s a "Project on Minimum Standards of Criminal Justice". Local bar associations have supported continuing legal education programs for education in criminal law practice of lawyers untrained in that field who wish to devote some of their time to making real the right to counsel.

The Nature of the Case and the Stage of the Proceedings. The nature of the case in which there is the right to counsel is determined by the severity of the sanction or the importance of the question involved and not by its classification for other purposes. In a case of seemingly hasty and inconsiderate action of a juvenile court in finding a fifteen year old boy "delinquent" with consequent commitment to a state institution possibly until his majority, the denial of the right to counsel vitiated the decree; though as the Court said it might not be so as to the whole range of action by such a court.[18] In a hearing on contempt of

---

12. Powell v. State of Alabama, 287 U.S. 45 (1932).

13. Glasser v. United States, 315 U.S. 60 (1942).

14. Downer v. Dunaway, 53 F.2d 586 (5th Cir. 1931).

15. United States ex rel. Goldsby v. Harpole, 263 F.2d 71 (5th Cir. 1959); United States ex rel. Seals v. Wiman, 304 F.2d 53 (5th Cir. 1962).

16. Anders v. California, 386 U.S. 738, reh. denied 388 U.S. 924 (1967).

17. MacKenna v. Ellis, 280 F.2d 592 (5th Cir. 1960); Johnston v. United States, 110 F.2d 562 (D.C.Cir. 1940).

18. Re Gault, 387 U.S. 1 (1967).

In the *Gault* case the author of the opinion, Justice Fortas, while in practice, had been the assigned counsel in the *Gideon* case, the climatic case on the right to counsel

court charges against a lawyer resulting in a fifty dollar fine the accused was held entitled to be represented by counsel, apparently because of the importance of protecting the independence of the bar.[19]

The early cases involved the right to counsel during trial. Later cases have pressed the question, how early and how late is an accused entitled to the right. It has been said he is entitled to counsel at all "critical" stages. At the early stages the question is associated with other civil rights, as, the privilege against self-incrimination with its accompanying safeguards.[20] After conviction he is entitled to counsel on his first appeal[21] and also in proceedings for the revocation of probation and the imposition of a deferred sentence.[22]

Methods of Waiver and of Assertion of Right. The right can be waived. The requirements of an effective waiver are stringent. They are not met by a failure to make a request nor by the knowledge of the right. Explicit explanation to the accused of the right and of his privilege to have a lawyer appointed to aid him are prerequisites.[23]

Review of a federal or state court conviction may be sought in direct appellate provisions. Most attacks have been "collateral". The methods of assertion of the right in the state courts are governed by the laws of the states. In the federal courts the principal remedy is the writ of habeas corpus.[24]

There are other privileges which the law gives to the poor in its effort to have him stand as an equal with the rich before it. They include the waiver of court costs, the provision of a copy of

in criminal cases. Naturally he retained as justice the sense of unquestioned primacy of values he had successfully espoused as advocate. Chief Justice Burger, in a case involving the proof of fault in a juvenile court, brought into consideration an additional set of values beyond those to which the justices had become accustomed to give priority automatically. In a case holding that in a juvenile court proof of guilt must be beyond a reasonable doubt the Chief Justice in dissent protested against "the trappings of legal procedure and judicial formalism" in the juvenile court system and the "trauma of exposing youthful offenders to a traditional criminal court." In re Winship, 397 U.S. 358 (1970).

19. Holt v. Virginia, 381 U.S. 131 (1965).

20. Escobedo v. Illinois, 378 U.S. 478 (1964); Miranda v. Arizona, 384 U.S. 436 (1966).

21. Swenson v. Bosler, 386 U.S. 258 (1967).

The duties of counsel when he believes the appeal frivolous are stated in Anders v. California, 386 U.S. 738, reh. denied 388 U.S. 924 (1967).

22. Mempa v. Rhay, 389 U.S. 128 (1967).

23. See Miranda v. Arizona, 384 U.S. 436 (1966).

24. The requirements of federal law for an attack on a state court's determination are set out in 28 U.S.C.A. §§ 2241–2254, as amended, 28 U.S.C.A. §§ 2241(d), 2244.

the record, and the payment of witness fees. They rest on the same policy as the right to counsel.

Retroactivity. The recent decisions affirming broader civil rights for an accused have raised the question whether their principle is to be applied retroactively, so that a prisoner convicted without compliance with a right later established may rely on the violation in habeas corpus proceedings.[25] On the same day the Supreme Court had before it two cases without counsel for the accused at opposite ends of the trial court process. One involved the use at the trial of a confession made at a preliminary hearing,[26] the other concerned the revocation of probation.[27] In both cases the right to counsel was applied retroactively because, as the Court said:

> "The right to counsel at the trial . . . on appeal and at the other 'critical states' of the criminal proceedings . . . have all been made retroactive, since the 'denial of the right must almost invariably deny a fair trial.' " [28]

The Methods of Making Counsel Available. Throughout a consideration of adequate legal services for the poor there run several interrelated factors, as the breadth of the services, whether to help the individual client or to alter laws which are unfair to the poor; the source and adequacy of the financial support; and the control over policies and administration. This discussion follows the lines of the last two factors. It considers the profession and its members, private charity, and the state whether acting through the courts or the legislature. Civil as well as criminal cases are included, though the two are not identical in the provisions made for them.

The Profession of Law. Lawyers individually render much service to the poor without fees. This sort of service, haphazard as to both clients and lawyers and with the burden cast on the young or else the charitably disposed of the profession, is unsatisfactory and unfair.

"Assigned counsel" has come to have two meanings. One is the old system under which the trial judge, when an accused was brought into court without a lawyer, assigned counsel somewhat at random to accept and carry forward the defense with little or no fee. It has been said there is a professional duty on the lawyer to accept such a case.[1] There have been notable illustrations

---

25. For a discussion of the problem of retroactivity, see Johnson v. New Jersey, 384 U.S. 719 (1966).

26. Arsenault v. Massachusetts, 393 U.S. 5 (1968).

27. McConnell v. Rhay, 393 U.S. 2 (1968).

28. Arsenault v. Massachusetts, 393 U.S. 5, 6 (1968).

1. See Cardozo, J., in People ex rel. Karlin v. Kulkin, 248 N.Y. 465, 162 N.E. 487 (1928). The Supreme court of New Jersey, speaking through Chief Justice Weintraub, held it had the power to require

of assigned counsel performing their duty, though it was the practice of many judges to assign young lawyers who gained courtroom experience at the cost of their clients' fate. The unsatisfactory character of the method will readily be perceived by the reader if he puts himself in the position of the lawyer, or worse still, the client in such a case. Even with an experienced lawyer the system no longer meets the constitutional minimum in serious cases, since the appointment when the defendant is in court comes too late. Another meaning of "assigned counsel", discussed below, refers to a system under which a member of a panel of lawyers in private practice is named as counsel for the accused.

The organized profession and its leading members have done a good deal in legal aid matters. The old standards of the bar which condemn publicity and which might stand in the way have been modified.[2] Every Chief Justice of the United States beginning with Chief Justice Taft has given the prestige of his office by accepting the post of Honorary President of the National Legal Aid and Defender Association. A few corporate firms have lent the services of younger members in this work, and post-admission training has been developed for able lawyers who wish to serve but who are unaccustomed to the criminal courts. Many law schools have legal aid clinics through which students gain both understanding and a sensitiveness to the plight of the underprivileged as well as some experience in practicing law and in dealing with human beings under stress. There have been successive proposals of improved methods by such bodies as the National Conference of Commissioners on Uniform State Laws in the Model Defense of Needy Persons Act, by the National Legal Aid and Defender Association, and by the American Bar Association. One is the Standards Relating to Providing Defense Services of the American Bar Association Project on Minimum Standards for Criminal Justice. The Introduction states:

> "The fundamental premise of these standards is that representation by counsel is desirable in criminal cases both from the viewpoint of the defendant and of society. To achieve this goal, it is not necessary that any particular formula be followed, but it is essential that the problem be attacked systematically, through adoption of a plan suited to local conditions [employing a defender or assigned counsel system or a combination of these]. Whatever system for providing counsel is employed, it must guarantee the freedom of defense counsel to act for their defendant-clients with all the

counties to compensate counsel appointed to defend indigent defendants. New Jersey v. Rush, 46 N.J. 399, 217 A.2d 441 (1966).

2. See infra p. 360.

independence traditional to the professional role of the defense lawyer. For the representation provided to be effective, defense counsel must be provided with adequate resources for investigation and the employment of experts to assist in preparation of the case." [3]

The American Bar Association has continued its support in various ways as through the Project mentioned and through committees on legal aid, and other committees charged with reexamination of methods of making legal services available, and of the Canons of Professional Ethics.

Charity. The history of legal aid up to 1918 has been told in a pioneer book by the man who for a long and lean generation was the leader of the movement, Mr. Reginald Heber Smith. [4] The movement began independently in New York and Chicago in the 1870s and the 1880s through societies formed to protect immigrants from exploitation. The stage it had reached in the 1950s was described by the Executive Director of the National Legal Aid Association, Mr. Emery Brownell. [5] Passages from these books show well enough why, because of the nature of legal services and the difficulty in financing them, private charity is not enough.

On the nature of the work Mr. Smith wrote: [6]

> "The directors of legal aid societies and the attorneys in charge have nearly all, through their closer contact with the work, come to an appreciation of the fact that they are engaged in essentially a public undertaking, and that they have a part in the administration of justice."

And again:

> "[I]t was not so much giving anything to the poor as it was obtaining for them their just dues; that it was not dispensing charity, but was securing justice."

Mr. Brownell wrote of the major difficulty in the way. [7]

> "By far the most serious obstacle confronting organized Legal Aid work on both the civil and the criminal side is financial."

3. ABA Project on Minimum Standards for Criminal Justice, Standards Relating to Defense Services 3 (T.D.1967).

4. R. Smith, Justice and the Poor (1924).

5. E. Brownell, Legal Aid in the United States (1951).

A vivid portrayal of varied difficulties of the poverty lawyer, caused by the client or his creditors or the profession, is given in R. Mathews, Problems Illustrative of the Responsibilities of Members of the Legal Profession (5th Printing, 1970), Chap. XIV, "The Lawyer Among the Poor".

6. Smith, supra note 4, at 149.

7. Brownell, supra note 5, at 243.

He quoted the conclusions of two Justices of the Supreme Court of the United States a generation apart. Chief Justice Taft wrote in 1926:

> "I think we shall have to come and ought to come to the creation in every criminal court of the office of public defender and that he should be paid out of the treasury of the county or state."

Writing of legal aid more broadly Justice Jackson said:

> "Legal aid in obtaining justice seems so obviously a community concern that its slow progress is hard to understand."

Legal aid societies at first emphasized civil cases but in recent years they have extended their services to criminal cases as well, a change marked by a broadened name for the national body, "National Legal Aid and Defender Association".

The Courts. The old practice of the trial judge of assigning counsel for indigent defendants brought before him has been mentioned. When the Supreme Court of the United States grants certiorari to an indigent petitioner in a habeas corpus proceeding, it appoints an able lawyer to represent him, an appointment accepted as an honor. The court has affirmed the constitutional right to counsel of the accused in criminal cases and, no less important, it has struck down old self-imposed limitations on the bar in making its services available in civil cases to those who need them. It is for the bar and the legislature to determine the particular measures which will carry forward the policies on which the Court's decisions rest.

The Legislature. The essential in action by the state is the provision of adequate funds to make counsel available. The methods of representation and of administration may vary even under the same legislation. The Criminal Justice Act of 1964,[8] dealing with the provision of counsel for the indigent in federal criminal cases, provides for a decentralized system. Each District Court has the power to choose the method for its district, subject to the limitations of the statute and the approval of the Judicial Conference of its circuit.

The methods employed in providing counsel are in general three. One is representation by a salaried employee of the government; a second is representation by an assigned lawyer in private practice whose fee is paid by the state; the other is a public-private system, with the government providing all or part of the funds and entrusting the administration to a private organization.

---

8.   78 Stat. 552 (1964), 18 U.S.C.A. § 3006A.

Representation by lawyers employed by the government is wide spread. Wage claims and cases involving men in the military service are illustrations. "The public defender" is the best known illustration. Originating in Los Angeles,[9] the system varies widely in the scope of representation and the methods of selection of the official from state to state. The loyalty and effectiveness of the public defender have been attested to by the courts as well as by students of the subject.[10]

The second method is the use of private counsel employed on a case by case basis and compensated by the state, of which the modern "assigned counsel" system is illustrative. The principal illustration is the system for civil cases established in England in the 1940s.[11] The English system is based on three principles, involving the clients, the government, and the lawyers. The client has available to him the services which a reasonable man would provide for himself had he sufficient means to do so. The government pays the costs of the services beyond what the client can pay, but the government has no part in the administration of the plan. The organized legal profession administers the plan, the services are rendered by lawyers in private practice whom the client chooses from those electing to come on the panel under the system (nearly all have done so), and the fees are reduced slightly below ordinary charges.

Under the older system of assigned counsel it appears to have been assumed that the assigned lawyer was entitled to no compensation and served as a matter of professional duty. The extension of the right to counsel in criminal cases and the consequent increase of demands on lawyers made evident the unfairness of making lawyers bear the whole financial burden. The modern statutes provide modest compensation for the assigned lawyer.

The mixed public-private system, with the government providing the funds and a private body administering the services, had a slow beginning in this country with a few cities appropriating funds for support of their local legal aid societies. It has grown greatly through the use of federal funds under the Legal Services Program, which is a turning point in the whole subject.

In 1964 the Congress passed the Economic Opportunity Act as a part of the "War on Poverty." [12] The Act made possible the

9. M. Goldman, The Public Defender 81–82 (1919). Apparently the first state wide plan originated in Connecticut in 1917. See State v. Reid, 146 Conn. 227, 149 A.2d 698, 701 (1959).

10. See, e. g., People v. Adamson, 34 Cal.2d 320, 210 P.2d 13 (1949); State v. Reid, 146 Conn. 227, 146 A.

2d 698 (1959); Report, Att'y Gen. Comm. on Poverty & the Ad. of Crim. Justice (1963); Comm. of N.Y.C.B.A. & Nat'l Legal Aid & Def. Ass'n, Report, Equal Justice for the Accused (1959).

11. See supra p. 12.

12. 78 Stat. 508 (1964).

use of federal funds in support of legal services for the poor, as perceptive officials noted, and the "Legal Services Program" was established to forward this purpose.[13]   Several aspects of the Program call for stress.   (1) For the first time something like adequate funds for legal services for the poor in civil and criminal cases are made available.   (2) Variety in methods is permitted ranging from support for the established legal aid society in a city on to the testing in a rural environment of "Judicare", a system of employment of private counsel chosen from a panel. (3) Federal standards are established and enforced.   (4) There is greater combination in use of legal and social services.   (5) Most important of all is a broadened conception of the nature of the legal services to be rendered.   These services include the accustomed services to the individual clients in their controversies. They extend as well to efforts to improve the law which bears unfairly on the poor, by test cases and by legislation.

The Department of Health, Education and Welfare has a program of legal services for public welfare clients.   The principles of the program call for close coordination and complementary relationships with the Legal Services Program of the Office of Economic Opportunity and other community legal assistance services.

Comparison.   Several thoughtful comparisons of the plans have been published,[14] some elements to be taken into account in a comparison will be mentioned.

One element is compatability with our political system and ideals.   At the time our government was formed the dominant political conception was that government should restrict its activities narrowly, and our Bill of Rights was planned as a protection against government.   The changes time has brought is made evident by the range of activities our government now undertakes. It is expressed in general terms by the Universal Declaration of Human Rights of the United Nations which embodies, not so much the negative conception of restraints on government as the affirmative duties of government to advance the welfare of the peoples.   Most American lawyers adhere to the older attitude especially when their own work is concerned, an attitude strengthened by the views of some that newer methods of providing legal service would reduce their practice.   Yet governmental regulation and aid to individuals and corporations have become commonplace, and the wisdom of a proposed action of government must be measured by its consequences, and not by preconception.

---

13. An influential article is Cahn and Cahn, The War on Poverty; A Civilian Perspective, 73 Yale L.J. 1317 (1964).

14. See 1 L. Silverstein, Defense of the Poor (1965) (especially Chs. 2, 3, 4, 10).   See also Reports, supra note 10.

Another political ideal is the independence of the lawyer from the court and from government. This conception has increasing force, it will be agreed, as the activities of government which the lawyer may have to challenge continue to expand. In the words of the Supreme Court of the United States quoting from a Congressional report, "The public have almost as deep an interest in the independence of the bar as of the bench." [15] Any system adopted must preserve this independence.

A third political ideal is equality before the law. Lawyers know well that equality before the law means counsel on each side. Whatever system is proposed must meet the test of availability in fact of counsel for those who need them.

Close to these political ideals is the quality of the lawyer made available. He must be adequate, zealous and loyal. Another factor is cost. The method adopted should be as economical as is consistent with effectiveness. An unpublished study dealt with that aspect. A statute of New York provided that legal counsel should be provided at public expense for the indigent in all criminal cases except minor traffic violations and left to the counties and cities the option of providing counsel through a public defender, a private legal aid society, a private assigned counsel system, or any combination of them. If private counsel were assigned the compensation was $15 per hour for in-court time and $10 per hour for out-of-court time. Most indigent defendants in New York City for whom there were court-assigned counsel had been represented by The Legal Aid Society, to which the City contributed $400,000 out of a Society budget of about $1,300,000. The Society employed full-time attorneys of specialized experience stationed regularly in the courthouse. The Institute of Judicial Administration of New York University was requested to study the comparative costs of representation by private assigned counsel and by The Legal Aid Society. Professor Delmar Karlen, Director of the Institute, in his unpublished report to the mayor of the city stated:

> "It is evident that the cost of representing indigent defendants through a system of assigned counsel would be vastly greater than the cost of having them represented by the Legal Aid Society. According to the minimum estimate given above, the cost would be more than four times as great; and according to the maximum estimate, it might be 30 times as great. According to our most moderate estimate and best judgment, the cost would be approximately 10 times as great."

15. Cammer v. United States, 350 U.S. 399 (1956).

The conclusion Professor Karlen reached, as he indicated, might well not be applicable under other conditions, as a rural community.

The attitude fostered in the clients is an important consideration. Publicly supported legal aid has the advantage that it makes some clients feel they are obtaining their rights under the law of the land and spares them the humiliation of being aided by private charity.

Finally, there is the kind of work to be undertaken by legal aid. The rendition of aid case by case by private lawyers on a panel, as under the English system, does not stimulate a perception of the underlying causes and problems of which the individual cases are illustrations. Continuing participation in the legal difficulties of the poor, as by a legal aid society, encourages observation of the sources of the problems. This may lead, in turn, to a willingness and determination to attack the problems wholesale at the sources instead of merely aiding individuals one by one when they are in difficulty. The histories of The Legal Aid Society of New York City by Professor John M. Maguire and Mr. Harrison Tweed illustrate this advantage.[16] The Society carried on continuing legal actions against the more flagrant oppressors, as in the old days against impressment of seamen, bucket shops, and installment frauds. The Society's work expanded to include sponsorship and support of legislation which attacked the causes of the need for legal aid.

The Legal Services Program of the Office of Economic Opportunity has undertaken affirmative measures on a vastly increased scale. The leaders of the program have perceived that many of the repeated economic troubles of the poor come from laws which are unfair to them as in the areas of housing, consumer purchasing, and collections with their accompaniment of garnishment. To defend the individuals in such matters would exceed the available time of the personnel of the Program. So the Program has encouraged attacks on the unfair law themselves through test cases and new legislation. "Law in Action", the monthly periodical of the Program, gives vivid illustrations.

"People's Counsel" in Administrative Rule Making Proceedings. The Administrative Conference of the United States made an interim report in January, 1969, published in the Annual Report of the Conference for 1969. The Conference recommended

---

16. J. Maguire, The Lance of Justice (1928); H. Tweed, The Legal Aid Society, New York City, 1876–1951 (1954). A useful discussion of the subject in modern dress, considering claims against governmental agencies and test cases, is Robb, Controversial Cases and the Legal Services Program, 56 A.B.A.J. 329 (1970).

by divided vote the creation of "People's Counsel". The recommendation, in part, follows:

> "4.   (a) An organization should be authorized by statute to employ a staff to act as 'People's Counsel'. The People's Counsel should represent the interests of the poor in all Federal administrative rule-making substantially affecting the poor.   .   .   .
>
> "5.   (a) Congress should provide for an appropriate body to perform the functions outlined in Section 4.
> .   .   .
>
> "6.   .   .   .   [A]ny special provision therefor should be so structured as to take maximum advantage of the capabilities in this field of non-governmental organizations, and of other public bodies, including notably the Office of Economic Opportunity."

The Stages in the Development of the Availability of Counsel. The measures for making counsel available for the disadvantaged and the poor came in several stages.   At the first there were a lack of awareness of the problem and the assumption that the need for counsel as other needs would be met through the individual's own efforts.

The second stage was marked by an awareness of the problem by a few leaders of the bar and primarily by private efforts. Illustrations are the legal aid societies, the lawyer referral plans, and the proposal more than the actuality of the neighborhood law office.

The third stage was characterized by the action of the Supreme Court of the United States.   It began with the Court's requirement of the right to counsel as an essential part of a fair criminal trial.   It moved on to the recognition of the right to counsel as a part of the protection of civil rights, again especially in criminal cases.   Turning to the area of civil litigation, the Court struck down professional standards and legal rules which unduly restrict the availability in fact of legal services.   The third stage has included efforts by the states to develop methods for providing counsel in criminal cases.   Not yet have there been similar efforts by the states or by the organized bar to take advantage of the opportunities opened up by the Court in civil matters.

The fourth stage is a part of the general movement to upgrade the poor thoroughly relieving them from unfair laws and "to break the cycle of poverty" by helping the poor to help themselves.   It includes the cooperation of social service workers with lawyers in aiding individual clients.   It coincides with the demands of the lesser privileged and disadvantaged ethnic groups for equality of respect no less than equality of opportunity.

This sketch of developments will end with a question: Do the poor have the constitutional right to counsel in civil cases as in criminal cases? Certainly, there is no lack for a textual basis of such a right in the Constitution. "Property" is listed along side "life and liberty" in the Bill of Rights. The failure of the Supreme Court of the United States to affirm the right must have other reasons.

One factor is the validity of the contingent fee which enables anyone with a substantial claim for damages against a solvent defendant to retain private counsel. On the side of a defendant his indigency makes a claim against him not worth pressing, so it may appear he does not need counsel. These reasons alone are inadequate, as the calendars of the legal aid societies show. A large part of their work involves family problems as to which the poor may be as sensitive as the rich. The court cases against the indigent are often very harsh, as dispossessory proceedings brought against a tenant or enforcement of claims against an over-sold purchaser on the installment plan, with its accompaniment of repossession or else of garnishment of wages.

There are stronger reasons. Civil matters are more varied in nature as well as in substantiality than criminal matters, including as they do office advice and drafting as well as litigation. The poor are as contentious as others and some would enjoy litigating indefinitely at government expense. The legislature is far better suited than the courts to determine the appropriate extent of the right as well as the methods of satisfying it. The strongest reason of all is the fact we have seen in this chapter, that society through its various agencies is providing counsel widely. When these other agencies are dealing fairly well with the social problem, it might be thought wise to leave the matter to them and not to invoke the broad and imprecise provisions of the Constitution.

SECTION 5. THE HATED

Violent public hatred is at times directed at an accused. The hatred may come from the atrociousness of the crime charged. Often its strongest element is a group loyalty and a correlative animosity based on race, religion, language, class, or even political views. One example is the Communist who, sharing the views of a foreign revolutionary power, betrays his country or only urges a new and revolutionary form of government. Many people have an inherent dislike and even hatred for political extremists. Yet normal society has its lunatic fringe of the left as well as of the right. Our American principles given legal force in the bill of rights require that these critics shall not be penalized for their views, and when on trial shall have the full measure of due process.

Another example comes from those who have suffered long from slavery and its aftermath. The ruling white leaders may seek through various stratagems, as the denial in fact of counsel, to prolong their advantages through suppression of efforts at change. Through civil disobedience the Negroes may seek to redress at once the results of centuries of exploitation, efforts which can lead to wild disorders and then frustration. It is the part of wisdom as well as of fairness to see to it that counsel are provided for the accused. The work of the Legal Services Program in furnishing counsel promptly for urban rioters has been an aid to the reestablishment of order.

Hatred toward a litigant endangers his right to a fair trial and threatens the operation of our legal and political system. A major element of hatred is fear. When the hatred comes from the atrocity of the crime, it is personal fear. When the hatred comes from cultural differences, it is fear of change. A book which traces through the centuries the difficulties of a fair trial identifies fear of change as the moving source of hatred.[1]

> "But—and it is one of the chief lessons to be derived from these studies—fear brings back the primitive conception of the function of courts; not necessarily, or indeed often, personal fear, but fear of changes; fear on the part of the upholders of the old order; fear of the effects of the discoveries of new truths; fear of emerging into the full light. Where such fear is justice cannot be; a court becomes an instrument of power; judges are soldiers putting down rebellion."

The fear of change resulting in hatred of individuals or of groups is often played upon. Usually the demagogue exploits this fear indirectly through appeal to the emotion of loyalty. Loyalty may effectively generate, as well as disguise, anger and fear and hate. The opportunities for the demagogue so to play on human emotions are particularly great in our country of immigration which is a great nation, but not yet a people. Although the appeal to hatred may be self-defeating eventually, its end often comes too late to repair the harm done to individuals.

The bar is concerned with the hated client because of his right to a fair trial. It is concerned, too, because the fulfillment of the lawyer's duty to help assure a fair trial may be impeded by visiting the hatred of the accused upon his lawyer. The identifi-

1. J. Macdonel, Historical Trials 86 (1927).

cation of lawyer with client is the readier in this country where the lawyer does not merely present the case at trial, as the English barrister, but represents his client from preparation for trial through post-conviction remedies. The identification of lawyer with client in the public mind is at its strongest in a small town, which lacks the diversity of a city.[2]

The identification of lawyer and client may cause loss or destruction of the lawyer's practice because the clients share the fear and hatred or because they believe the lawyer has lost his influence and usefulness. Wherever the group from which a lawyer draws his clientele shares the fear and hatred, he risks his professional future by doing what our system of justice calls for —giving fair representation in a court of law to every man.[3] Several aspects of fair representation are specified in an American Bar Association Resolution:

> "Resolved: (1) That the American Bar Association reaffirms the principles that [1] the right of defendants to the benefit of assistance of counsel and [2] the duty of the bar to provide such aid even to the most unpopular defendants involves [3] public acceptance of the correlative right of a lawyer to represent and defend in accordance with the standards of the legal profession, any client without being penalized by having imputed to him his client's reputation, views or character.[4] "

This discussion will treat briefly some factors which affect fair representation, that is the public, the law, the court, the organized bar whether national or local, and the individual lawyer.

> On the attitude of the public the same resolution stated: "That the Association will continue to educate the profession and the public on the rights and duties of a lawyer in representing any client, regardless of the unpopularity of either the client or his cause."

The resolution rightly assumes the continuing misunderstanding by the public of the adversary system and of the lawyer's role. The "education" it refers to may be a general and continuing one or it might well include specific efforts in particular cases. Specific efforts repeated in spectacular cases would do much to impress the average man with the necessity for fair representa-

2. An illustration is the case in which the constitutional right to have counsel provided was first established. Powell v. Alabama, 287 U.S. 45 (1932).

of Sacco and Vanzetti 319–320 (1948); C. Morgan, A Time to Speak (1964). See Zeisler, "Reminiscences of the Anarchist Case," 21 Ill.L.Rev. 224 (1926).

3. A few illustrations are given in L. Joughin & E. Morgan, The Legacy

4. 78 ABA Rep. 133 (1953).

tion as a part of a fair trial when, perhaps, that man himself gets into trouble with the law.

The law has done a good deal. Every accused is now constitutionally guaranteed the right to counsel.[5] The requirement of loyal counsel is enforced by the sanction of habeas corpus.[6] The constitutional right of out-of-state-counsel to be permitted to represent accused who are so hated that local lawyers refuse to represent them has been indicated.[7] Where there is no general public defender, there might usefully be a limited system of public defender for such defendants when local counsel would not come forward. Yet there is no effective substitute for the local lawyer with his knowledge of local people and prejudices, as illustrated on the second trial of Gideon.[8]

The judge may designate counsel in a way which disarms the haters. He may designate a lawyer of standing who is beyond suspicion. He may also appoint several counsel. Mr. Peter Holme has described a case in Denver in which at the instance of a judge, he asked several firms to contribute the services of one member of each in the defense of persons accused of unlawful Communist activities.[9] Going beyond the designation of counsel, the judge may subordinate the usual standards of the profession when they come into conflict with the more fundamental matter of need for zealous counsel.[10] But the judge might be an elective official whose unfortunate system of tenure makes him subject to the same sort of hatred as counsel, if he carried out his duty.

The American Bar Association's general resolution, adopted at a time when hatred of Communists impaired the retention of counsel has already been quoted and the Association, alone or in conjunction with other bodies, has continued to affirm this view. Because of the structure of this national body, it has not been for it but for state and local associations affiliated with it to act in specific cases. The American Civil Liberties Union has as a chief purpose to see that counsel are provided in unpopular cases, and the National Lawyers Guild for years has devoted its principal efforts to the protection of civil rights.

Ultimately the decision and the burden fall on the individual lawyer. It may be his good fortune to convince the jury and the

5. Gideon v. Wainwright, 372 U.S. 335, 83 S.Ct. 792 (1963).

6. See supra p. 329.

7. See Lefton v. City of Hattiesburg, Mississippi, 333 F.2d 280 (5th Cir. 1964).

8. A. Lewis, Gideon's Trumpet (1964).

9. See J. Stone, Legal Education and Public Responsibility, 151–152 (1959).

10. In re Ades, 6 F.Supp. 467 (D.Md. 1934).

public of the necessity of the lawyer in the administration of justice. Thomas Erskine did more than any other man to establish the rights of the accused and the privilege of the lawyer, first in his cases involving alleged revolutionaries in England when Revolution was near its peak in France, and then in a successful defense of a deranged man who had attempted to murder the King. Erskine, assigned by the court to represent the latter accused, began his statement to the jury:

> "Gentlemen of the jury, the scene in which we are engaged, and the duty which I am not merely privileged but appointed by the court to perform, exhibits to the whole civilized world a perpetual monument of our national justice." [11]

Counsel's lot may be quite otherwise. So it was for a young lawyer who has told the story of his actions and the consequent destruction of his practice and life's hopes.[12] There must be many another lawyer unknown to us who suffered the consequences of doing what our profession tells him to do.

Representation of the unpopular is called for by our political as well as our professional ideals. We are not a monolithic people in a static society but a people holding and urging as of right a variety of views in a rapidly changing society. Inevitably, there are strident apostles of the right and of the left, the ones who would have us stand still in the perfect present and the others who would at once smash and make over our imperfect system. Most of us will adhere to the counsels of moderation without which a society cannot long hold together; yet we will accept and give a fair hearing to critics as instruments of change through law. The lawyer's work in defending the unpopular may not only support change. It may support stability in showing that criticism and change are possible under law.[13]

The availability of lawyers for the unpopular is important, of course, outside criminal law and even before charges are filed. An illustration of the wider importance is the federal loyalty-security program, under which an unfavorable finding might disqualify a person for employment in many areas of government

---

11. L. Stryker, For the Defense 372, 374 (1947).

12. C. Morgan, A Time to Speak (1964), (especially 74–76).

13. The historian, Trevelyan, wrote of the broader effects of Erskine's successful defense of petty subversives: "Thanks to Erskine's persuasive eloquence, twelve Tory jurymen acquitted Huntley and his fellow prisoners on the capital charge, and reminded the government that the methods of Robespierre were not wanted over here . . . . This timely check saved England from a reign of terror and perhaps ultimately from a retributive revolution." Trevelyan, History of England, bk. V, ch. 4 (1926, 1952). In this country there has been testimony of the helpfulness of the Legal Services Program in dampening ghetto riots of the 1960s.

service and of industry. A bar association committee would apply to this field the conclusions of the American Bar Association report in making provisions for adequate representation of employees at the early screening stage with cleared employees reimbursed for their reasonable attorneys' fees.[14]

It is gratifying to remember that our professional tradition of effective representation of the hated is even older than our nation. In colonial times the Philadelphia lawyer, Andrew Hamilton, made an effective defense of a publisher in New York. And a young Massachusetts lawyer, John Adams, successfully defended British soldiers accused in the Boston Massacre.

Inside the universities there is the fact of student dissent. Some inescapable facts making for dissent are the generation gap, the fortunately recurring student perception of present wrongs and the determination to set them right, and as a college dean put it a normal student body is not made up entirely of normal students. In the universities of all places dissent should be encouraged, and yet prevented from turning into hatred. One measure is for the older university members to take the always wise step in cases of disagreement—to put themselves in the place of the other person. So they will consider complaints, say, as to "relevance" from the point of view of the students whose interests lie in the present and the future rather than in the study of the past. Another measure is to defuse "non-negotiable demands" by raising and canvassing their subjects ahead of time. For those who might present such demands it is useful to remember that nothing is easier than to create an ideal society out of whole cloth. Rousseau did it with The Noble Savage, say, of the Natchez Tribe of Mississippi. What is difficult is to make work pretty well our society of fallible, disparate, and envious human beings. Rousseau's creation, as we know, helped to lead to the French Revolution, to the rise of the young military officer who cleared the streets of Paris with "a whiff of grapeshot", and some years later to his acceptance as Napoleon, the Emperor, in the name of law and order.

When dissent on the campus turns into violence, discipline may follow. In a serious disciplinary proceeding there may be the right to counsel.[15] An American Bar Association committee gave its categorical view on the right stating:

> "A student should have the right to be represented at the hearing by any person selected by him, such as a fellow stu-

14. Ass'n of the Bar of the City of N. Y. Spec. Comm. on Fed. Loyalty-Sec. Program, 15, 180–185 (1956).

15. An excellent discussion of the subject in broad context is the Oli-

ver Wendell Holmes, Jr., Lecture by Professor Charles Alan Wright, The Constitution on the Campus, 22 Vand.L.Rev. 1027, 1075–1076 (1969).

dent, a faculty member, a lawyer, or by a friend from outside the university community." [16]

In this way the individual student's rights can be best safeguarded and the institution's reputation for fairness be protected. The Committee's general conclusion stated:

> "The challenge to the university community is one of self-evaluation and self-reform. . . . The process of self-evaluation and self-reform can only be accomplished within a climate of freedom of dissent and freedom from disorder."

When student violence brings prosecution by the state, there is the usual problem of providing counsel for the accused considered in this chapter. The Report quoted from rejects the claim of some students that they are uniquely above the law, saying "A citizen is not immunized from the law by virtue of his status as a student." [17]

SECTION 6. PERSONAL INJURY AND DEATH CLAIMS

The expansion of industry in the last century brought a vast increase of industrial accidents. The injured workers could recover from their employers only in tort when they proved fault by the employers and they were gravely limited by the principles of law as to fellow servant, assumption of risk and contributory negligence. The plight of many workers unable to recover led first to the mitigation of the harsh tort rules by the abolition of the fellow servant and assumption of risk principles. Under public pressure it led much farther, to the abolition of tort law as to the basis of recovery in most industries and to the adoption of workmen's compensation laws now in force in all the states. Workmen's compensation substitutes the employee's work connection for the employer's fault as the basis of recovery, covering as it does injuries "arising out of and in the course of employment." [1] The employer covers his liability by industrial

---

16. Report of the American Bar Association Commission on Campus Government and Student Dissent 24 (William T. Gossett, Chairman 1970) p. 24.

17. Id. at 216. For a consideration of "the fundamental rights of the individual in modern society", see I. Emerson, D. Haber & N. Dorsen, Political and Civil Rights in the United States (3d ed. 1967).

1. The nature and development of workmen's compensation is excellently described in A. Larsen, The Law of Workmen's Compensation Chs. I & II (1968). The personal and social, as well as legal, problems under the system are vividly discussed in Gellhorn and Lauer, Administration of the New York Workmen's Compensation Law, 37 N.Y.U.L.Rev. 3 (1962).

insurance and passes the cost of the insurance on to the purchases of his product. The amount of recovery is usually based on the employee's wages with maximum limits set. In most states workmen's compensation is administered by a commission which is active in obtaining the facts and which disposes of ninety per cent of the claims without further controversy, though the claimants may retain lawyers. There is a natural disagreement on the worth of the lawyers' services, with the lawyers thinking of the controversial cases in which they are retained and the commissioners considering the bulk of the cases handled by the commission alone. The amount of the lawyers' fees is either limited by statute or else subject to the supervision of the commission.[2] There are continuing criticisms of the workmen's compensation system, especially on the ground of inadequacy of the awards permitted. For the present purposes it is enough to say that there is no serious proposal for returning industrial accidents to the old system of tort liability based on fault.

Automobile accidents now hold the unfortunate preeminence which industrial accidents once had. Since 1910 twice as many Americans have been killed in automobile accidents, it has been said, as have died in battle in all our history.[3] Every resident of California, statistics indicate, has a fifty per cent chance of being either killed or seriously injured in such an accident.[4] The reduction of the number of accidents is of first importance. This discussion, is confined to the narrower subject of the work of the profession in dealing with accidents after they have occurred.

In a simpler society torts were almost on a man to man basis between persons who knew each other, as assault and battery and trespass. In our complex and urban-centered society it is no longer so, and the tortfeasor may not even know the person he harms. In earlier days deterrence of conduct harmful to others was an important purpose. For a man who would commit a trespass the threat of a civil judgment may well have been as powerful a deterrent as a threat of a fine of that amount. It may have been even more powerful for there is usually no limitation of the amount of civil liability as there is on criminal fines. Liability insurance has changed this, as it protects the careless driver from the consequences of civil liability for negligence.[5]

2. The limitations on lawyers' fees and the harm the limitations may bring are discussed in Larsen, supra note 1, §§ 83.10–83.19.

3. Two reports of studies of the subject are A. Conard, J. Morgan, R. Pratt, C. Voltz, R. Bombaugh, Automobile Accidents Costs and Payments (1964); Franklin, Chanin, Mark, Accidents, Money, and the Law, 61 Colum.L.Rev. 1 (1961).

4. Weigel, Preliminary Report on Plans for Inquiry into a California Automobile Accident Commission, 34 Cal.St.B.J. 393, 407 (1959).

5. See A. Conard, supra note 3, at 88–92.

When a person is injured by another, he may be able to shift the financial burden of his loss on the other through an action in tort. The method of administration of the tort claim is an action at law in the ordinary courts at law which are passive even if notified of an accident. There is need for lawyers on each side to prepare the cases and to settle them at a fair figure or else to try them.

The injured person is ordinarily dependent on his earnings for support and under consequent pressure to obtain money through a settlement. He has had little or no experience or even acquaintance with lawyers. When this case ends he will rarely return to the lawyer for further services. He cannot prepare or evaluate his claim. The actual defendant is usually a liability insurance which is in the business of conducting defenses and is of course under no pressure to settle.

There are many lawyers who welcome tort claims, ranging from the beginner to the expert. There is also the lay intruder who may obtain from the injured man a written retainer with the lawyer's name in blank and who will turn the case over to the lawyer promising him the largest share of the recovery. On the other side the insurance company has a staff of claim agents ready to go to the scene of the accident to obtain evidence and to effectuate a favorable settlement. It is represented by experienced lawyers chosen ahead of time.

On the surface the two sets of lawyers appear as mortal enemies. In a particular case, it is true, each lawyer does his best for his side. At times a claim agent may seek to use the machinery of professional discipline to hold within bounds the more vigorous of his opponents. In fact the two groups of lawyers are complementary with each dependent upon the other for existence, symbiosis as a biologist might put it. If there were no claimants and claimants' lawyers, there would be no defendants and no defendants' lawyers. Neither group would survive if the tort basis of liability was abolished. The nature of the relation is made obvious in the encyclopedia, Trials, devoted primarily to personal injury cases. Volume I of the set opens with not merely one foreword but two, "Plaintiff's Foreword" and "Defense Foreword". They are alike in urging the continuance of the basic elements of the present system—tort law, liability based on fault, jury trials—and in denouncing those who would do away with them.

This situation of necessitous and inexperienced persons dealing with eager professionals calls for scrutiny and, perhaps, special protective measures. The claimant needs early representation to prepare his case and protection against the defendant's representative who seeks a low settlement. He may need protection, too, against overreaching by his own lawyer. Yet some obstacles stand in the way of the needed consideration by the profession. One is the natural objection by lawyers, as by all of us, to legal restraints. Whether it be big business or big labor or big profession, every group insists on freedom of action for itself and its members. Another obstacle is a feeling which, again, affects all of us, self-interest. Many lawyers have a strong financial interest in the maintenance of the present system. The informed estimate has been made that over 60 per cent of the bar, including claimants' lawyers and defendants' lawyers, would have their income substantially affected by abolition of the present system. In the circuit courts 80 to 90 per cent of the cases tried are personal injury cases. All together the lawyers concerned form the largest vested interests in the profession and seek to continue the system as it is.

It will be useful to observe the common characteristics of this field of practice, to take note of the strengths and the weaknesses of the present system, and then to mention some proposals for change. Personal injury practice, at least on the claimants' side, has been looked upon askance by many conservative lawyers as violating the standards of the profession. Three features of it are the contingent fee which is almost universal, solicitation of practice which is common, and advancement of court costs and living expenses to clients which it seems is not unusual.

Contingent Fees

In most countries the contingent fee is forbidden on the ground it makes the lawyer a party to the case and may lead to evil measures to achieve success. Such a fee does give to the lawyer a share of the claim in fact and makes him a party to the case. Yet in this country no one seriously urges the prohibition of the contingent fee except in special areas where the encouragement of controversy and litigation are felt to be harmful, as divorce cases. Such a fee makes possible the enforcement of many claims which otherwise would have to be abandoned. It is not inherently unfair, and excesses can be prevented by law.

Solicitation

Personal injury and death claims are the principal kind of cases in which solicitation of practice is denounced. Solicitation of practice has been assumed to be in violation of the standards of the profession [6] and also of the law. The sanctions have in-

---

6. ABA Code of Professional Responsibility, EC 2–3, DR 2–103. For a humorous defense of solicitation, see "A Letter to a Member of a Grievance Committee" in Ass'n of Am. Law Schools, Selected Readings on the Legal Profession 130 (1962).

cluded criminal liability,[7] the loss of some legal rights,[8] and professional discipline.[9]

Professional discipline by the courts has ranged from mild censure to disbarment, with severe discipline caused by other misconduct beyond solicitation alone. Mitigating circumstances leading to mildness of discipline include such matters as candor of the attorney in the disciplinary proceedings, the absence of other misconduct, cessation of the activities when the proceedings were begun, and the fact that the disciplinary proceedings were instigated by defendants' attorneys or claim agents. The mildness of action in many cases may indicate the judges do not view the practice as peculiarly heinous.[10]

The claimant needs prompt and experienced representation. This representation will help to make certain that the evidence is gathered and that no hasty settlement is made. If it could be assured that there was no pressure on the claimant and that the lawyer for whom the claim was solicited was competent and dependable, solicitation would have much to be said for it. In two of the three cases in which the Supreme Court of the United States upheld the group practice of law there was manifest solicitation under exactly those conditions. The lawyer on whose behalf there was solicitation was an experienced practitioner in the field who was chosen ahead of time by an intermediary in which the claimant would naturally have confidence, his labor union. Our discussion is directed to the typical parties and their lawyers, to some characteristics of the present system of dealing with accidents, and with changes which have been proposed.

Maintenance

Maintenance or the officious intermeddling in legal proceedings was condemned in the Middle Ages, as the perversion of justice by the rich and powerful.[1] In England today the principal application is the unjustified agreement to bear or share the heavy burden of "costs". The English courts have had difficul-

---

7. The imposition of criminal liability has been upheld. McCloskey v. Tobin, 252 U.S. 107 (1920); Kelley v. Boyne, 239 Mich. 204, 214 N.W. 316 (1927) Anno., 53 A.L.R. 279 (1928).

8. The right to a fee was denied in Hightower v. Detroit Edison Co., 262 Mich. 1, 247 N.W. 97, 86 A.L.R. 517 (1933). The prosecution of cases in a seriously inconvenient forum has been enjoined. Atchison, T. & S. F. Ry. Co. v. Andrews, 338 Ill.App. 552, 88 N.E.2d 364 (1949), Anno., 14 A.L.R.2d 740 (1950).

9. See In re Heirich, 10 Ill.2d 357, 140 N.E.2d 825 (1959). The annotation to the case shows the factors which the courts have weighed in determining the severity of discipline. 67 A.L.R.2d 859 (1959).

10. E. g., In re Heirich, supra, n. 9.

1. See 3 W. Holdsworth, History of English Law 394–400 (3d ed. 1922); F. MacKinnon, Contingent Fees for Legal Services 35–37 (1964).

ty in giving the term a meaning and scope appropriate to modern times.[2] In the United States the condemnation has been confined in fact to the advancements by lawyers with a personal injury practice on a contingent fee basis. The advancements are at times made to cover the court costs and also the living expenses of poor clients during the period, often long because of calendar congestion, before the case can be brought to trial. These payments are, apparently condemned by the stated standards of the profession,[3] at least unless there is an unconditional agreement for repayment, which is meaningless because of the clients' poverty. The principal considerations in support of these advancements are that the payments are not within the evil condemned as maintenance under common law, and the advancement may enable an impoverished claimant to enforce a claim which otherwise he would have to surrender or else to compromise for an inadequate sum.[4] Yet the validation of the practice would give lawyers an increased and still more strongly felt stake in their clients' cases, with the consequent temptation to use excessive measures to insure reimbursement as well as fees. It might also tend to have the personal injury practice concentrated in a few firms which were wealthy enough to meet their clients' needs. The attitude of the courts is not clear.[5]

Strengths of the System

One strength of the present system is that often it gives to the injured party a more adequate award, that is, a substantially larger sum than, say, workmen's compensation. The success of the efforts of the claimants' lawyers to secure an adequate award are indicated by a several volume work devoted to this subject.[1]

A factor beyond the interests of the immediate claimants which has been urged in support of the system is its importance

2. Martell v. Crossett Iron Co., Ltd., [1955] Ch. 363. Two of the justices in the Court of Appeal mention poverty as a possible justification.

3. ABA Canons of Professional Ethics No. 42.

4. See 1 M. Belli, Modern Trials 39–40 (1954); Note, "Loans to Clients for Living Expenses, 55 Calif. L.Rev. 1419 (1967).

5. A Cleveland lawyer who had made advances to client was the object of decisions in four courts. The Supreme Court of Ohio suspended him from practice indefinitely. Mahoning County Bar Ass'n v. Ruffalo, 176 Ohio St. 263, 199 N.E.2d 396,

cert. denied 379 U.S. 931 (1964), Anno., 8 A.L.R.3d 1155 (1966). On the same record the United States Court of Appeals by a divided vote suspended him indefinitely. In re Ruffalo, 370 F.2d 447 (6th Cir. 1966). The United States District Court declined to discipline the lawyer. In re Ruffalo, 249 F.Supp. 432 (N.D.Ohio 1965). The Supreme Court of the United States reversed the decision of the Court of Appeals on the ground of lack of adequate notice in the Ohio disciplinary proceedings. In re Ruffalo, 390 U.S. 544 (1968).

1. See M. Belli, Modern Damages (1959).

in furnishing economic support of an independent bar who will resist the pressures of the large interests in our society. Such a bar is of great social and political importance as our society coalesces into larger units—big business, big labor, big government—and there is increasing need for a lawyer who will say for the little man, "You cannot do that to my client."

A related factor is the value of the system of tort liability and the personal injury bar in the enforcement of private sanctions of governmental policy. Most tort cases involving automobile accidents are seemingly petty controversies between the owners or drivers of different cars. Yet many potential cases involve the fault of the manufacturer. In the late 1960s the manufacturers "recalled" several millions of its cars for the correction of defects, which might lead to serious accidents. The recall of the cars was due in large measure, without doubt, to the knowledge of the manufacturer that accidents caused by the defects would lead to suits brought by the personal injury bar. The broad public policy protected by the threat of private actions was stated by Justice Traynor:

> "[P]ublic policy demands that responsibility be fixed wherever it will most effectively reduce the hazards of life and health inherent in defective products that reach the market." [2]

Any proposal for change from the present system of liability based on fault should take into account the usefulness of the system of tort liability as a private method for the protection of the public.

Some supporters of the present system have urged reasons which are so manifestly bad as almost to make one believe the supporters feel the system is beyond defense. One reason given is "freedom of contract" between the lawyer and client. The hollowness of this argument is demonstrated in every session when a legislature enacts measures to limit freedom of contract because the legislature believes the public good calls for limitation. Another reason urged is even the support of the Deity. The Insurance, Negligence and Compensation Law Section of the American Bar Association recommended the maintenance of the adversary-jury system of reparation for automobile accidents and in doing so it stated that "the principle of liability for fault is derived from the religious belief that each of us is responsible to God for his own conduct." [3]

---

2. Escola v. Coca-Cola Bottling Co., 24 Cal.2d 453, 462, 150 P.2d 436, 440 (1944) (concurring opinion).

3. 93 Rep.A.B.A. 285, 287 (1969).

Weaknesses and Dangers

A weakness in the system on which its supporters agree is its uncertainty. In the Introduction to Mr. Melvin Belli's "Modern Damages" Professor Fowler Harper wrote:

> "The results are appalling, if for no other reason than for inconsistency. Persons maimed for life by the legal fault of the defendant have recovered nothing or next to nothing upwards to what most reasonable people would regard as an adequate award." [4]

The author of the same book has told that when a prospective juror in Las Vegas gave his occupation as "gambler", Mr. Belli commented "I, too, am a gambler every time I go before a jury." These hazards and uncertainties are inescapable under the present system. In this field, with the support of the claimant and his family involved, it is important that there be prompt and reasonable recovery.

Another weakness close to the shortcoming of uncertainty is unfairness to both claimant and defendant in letting liability and recovery turn on factors the existence of which it is impossible to ascertain with accuracy, as Judge Jerome Frank so well showed. [5] Even if it is known that the defendant was negligent, this has little to do with the fairness of the result. Everyone who has driven a car knows that he has often been negligent and it is the barest hazard whether he was negligent at the particular instant. It is scarcely fair to the defendant to impose liability because of negligence at the particular time, nor is it fair to the claimant to let his recovery turn on it.

A third continuing weakness is delay in recovery when the claim is brought to suit. The cases which clog the calendars of the courts are for the most part personal injury cases. Increases in the number of judges are marked in most places by a corresponding increase in the number of cases. The delay in trial is an element taken into account by the defendants in offers of settlement.

The system does not measure up to the principal support urged for it, the assurance of competent counsel for impoverished claimants. A leading personal injury lawyer related to Mr. John Frank the factors which, naturally enough, go into the determination whether to accept a tendered automobile injury case. [6] They are the probability of liability, the severity of inju-

---

4. Belli, Modern Damages vol. I, p. vi (1959).

5. See J. Frank, Courts on Trial (1950) (especially Ch. III, Facts Are Guesses).

6. J. Frank, American Law: The Case for Radical Reform 76–77 (1969).

ry, and unmentioned but obvious the ability of the defendant to respond in damages. The firm's method rates liability in five classes from "excellent" down to "slim." As the prospect of liability goes down the severity of the injury must go up to induce acceptance of the case. The "excellent liability" case may be accepted with "estimated value" as low as $1,500 since it can probably be settled without much work. The "slim liability" case would invariably be rejected unless it had a value of at least $10,000. It is a rare lawyer who, disagreeing with a decision of his state supreme court which had denied recovery to one like the present would-be client, will accept the claimant's case, carry it with assured defeat through the state courts, and at last have the Supreme Court of the United States vindicate the lawyer's view.[7]

The present system has been challenged because of its wastefulness as well as because of its delays and uncertainties. Professor Conard has reminded us that there are several other measures of injury reparation besides tort actions, as social security, public aid, private insurance, and workmen's compensation.[8] The administrative expenses of the several systems listed are only 3 per cent, 5 per cent, 20 per cent, and 45 per cent respectively, as contrasted with the tort system under which only "about 44 per cent of the total social costs end up as net benefits to injury victims." [9]

One criticism often made of the tort system is that the claimant who recovers a large award, inexperienced and incapable of handling such a sum, as he usually is, will not deal with it well. It would be practicable for the verdict to call for installment payments, as demonstrated by a case in which the verdict was for $36,000 with the provision, "To be paid at $150 per month for 20 years". Pretty surely this novel form of verdict was the creative work of an intelligent layman, the foreman of the jury. The judges did not like it. The trial court struck out the proviso. The appellate court reinstated it only because of the technicality that the trial judge had no power to alter the verdict after the jury was discharged.[10]

Besides the general strengths and weaknesses of the fault system there are complaints directed to the actions of the representatives of each side. There are complaints of the actions of the defendant's representative in settling the case either too

---

7. Such a lawyer was the third one retained, as described in Matter of Uravic, 142 Misc. 775, 255 N.Y.S. 638 (1932). The surrogate, in approving a fee of fifty per cent of the sum received in settlement commented on the action of the lawyer "in thus championing an apparently hopeless cause."

8. Conard, Live and Let Live: Justice in Injury Reparation, 52 J.Am. Jud.Soc'y 105 (1968).

9. Id.

10. M.&P. Stores v. Taylor, 326 P. 2d 804 (Okl.1958).

soon or too late. The complainants are frequent that the claim agents put pressure on necessitous claimants to settle quickly for inadequate sums at a time when they cannot know either their rights or the extent of the injuries. This harmful tactic of quick settlement might be met by a rule of law that a settlement within, say, two weeks of the injury would not be valid unless the claimant had a lawyer. There is the companion objection that settlement is offered too late. With the court calendars clogged there is pressure on a necessitous claimant to accept an inadequate award. The law could provide a stimulus to prompt and fair settlement. An analogy is the statutes in some states which call for a percentage increase of the amount of a verdict awarded against an insurance company when the claim goes to trial. A similar penalty could be related to offers of settlement with a percentage increase or decrease depending on the variation of the verdict from the offer of settlement.

The claimant may need protection against his own lawyer. One thing he is certainly entitled to is to have his claim handled on its individual merits. There must be no en bloc settlement of a batch of claims.[11] A more troubling aspect is the excessiveness of the fee. Varied protective actions have been taken by, for example, the Appellate Division of the Supreme Court, First Department, in New York. Pursuant to an order of the court there was an investigation of excesses by claimants' lawyers as well as by claim agents of the insurance companies. The judge who conducted the investigation concluded that [12]

> "most personal injury claimants are in the same position as infant claimants when it comes to dealing with attorneys, and require the same protection from the courts."

This New York court has taken three measures.[13] Its first action called for the filing of copies of all such contingent fee contracts. A second required a detailed "closing statement". The third set in effect limitations in all but exceptional cases on the amount of the fee, with the fee permitted being either one-third of the net recovery or else one determined by a sliding scale with the percentage permitted declining with the amount of the recovery.[14] The last action of the Appellate Division was upheld

---

11. The settlement of a bunch of personal injury cases on a lump sum basis was condemned. In re Glucksman, 230 App.Div. 185, 243 N.Y.S. 1 (1930).

12. The report is reprinted in 14 Mass.L.Q. 1 (1928).

13. The formal action of the court was preceded by a case in which two lawyers were litigating over

the division of a fifty per cent fee. Judge Peck expressed the court's disapproval at such a fee as a usual charge and its hope that the bar would take appropriate limiting measures. Buckley v. Surface Transp. Corp., 277 App.Div. 224, 98 N.Y.S.2d 576 (1950).

14. The rule of court is set out in 204 N.Y.S.2d at xliii et seq. (1960) and in F. MacKinnon, Contingent

by the Court of Appeals of the state.[15]   Other states have employed a different method of limitation, which correlates the increase in fees with the stage of the case, running from settlement before suit to recovery after appeal.[16]   Self limitation by lawyers in setting fees is still an important factor. Most lawyers in New York City charge somewhat less than the fees permitted by law.[17]

The defendant insurance companies may need no special measures for their protection against fictitious or inflated claims. The rules of law now condemn fraudulent claims. There are companion matters, small and large, which are subjects of complaint. It does appear demonstrated that small claims get better treatment than large ones because of their nuisance cost. Then there is the large verdict, grossly excessive as the insurance companies contend.

The complaints against the present system have led to a number of studies with resultant proposals.[18]   One proposal is to speed up the settlement of claims. This might be done through incentives to settle or else through simplification of the tribunal, as the use of a commission. Another is to change the measure of recovery. If the conditions of recovery are broadened the measure of recovery may have to go down so as to make the burden of payment bearable by whomever it is cast on. To this end a common proposal is the elimination of the right to recover for pain and suffering.

The most radical proposal calls for the source of reparation to be the injured party's own insurance company.[19]   An obvious possible source is the government, whether state or federal, under a system of social insurance. The claimants' lawyers have their own proposals for the expansion of the rights of their clients as the abolition of the defense of contributory negligence.[20]   The present system of reparation under a system

Fees for Legal Services 221–229 (1964).

15. Gair v. Peck, 6 N.Y.2d 97, 160 N.E.2d 43 (1959); Anno., 77 A.L.R. 2d 411 (1961).

16. See F. MacKinnon, Contingent Fees for Legal Services 184–185 (1964). This sort of limitation according to the fact and stage of litigation has manifest disadvantages. It encourages litigation instead of settlement, and it disregards the fact that settlements as well as litigation are won primarily by hard preparatory work which is much the same whether a case is filed or tried.

17. Id. at 187–188.

18. See Conard, Live and Let Live: Justice in Injury Reparation, 52 Judicature 105 (1968); Walter E. Meyer Research Institute of Law, Dollars, Delay and the Automobile Victim (1968).

19. R. Keeton & J. O'Connell, Basic Protection for the Traffic Victim, (1965).

20. Fuchsberg, A Lawyer Looks at Proposed Changes, 51 Judicature 158 (1967).

Counsel for claimants have their association originally known as Na-

of tort law administered by the courts needs fundamental re-examination.[21]

SECTION 7.   PUBLICITY AND SOLICITATION

Most legal services are rendered by lawyers in private practice who are chosen and retained by the clients. For prospective clients some publicity of the lawyer is essential. The client must know the whereabouts of the lawyer and have at least a pretty good opinion of his ability if he is to retain him. For the lawyers, too, publicity is essential. It is only when a prospective client knows of the lawyer and his office and his qualities that the client will retain him.[1]

The Code of Professional Responsibility wisely deals with publicity in Canon 2 in the context of the duty of the profession to make legal counsel available. The first factor mentioned under the Ethical Considerations concerns the prospective clients and their needs.

> "EC 2–1.   The needs of members of the public for legal services is met only if they recognize their legal problems, appreciate the importance of seeking assistance, and are able to obtain the services of acceptable legal counsel."

The Canon recognizes the difficulties in the selection of a lawyer created by new social conditions, stating, "Changed conditions, however, have seriously restricted the effectiveness of the traditional selection process."   EC 2–7.

From the fact that some publicity by lawyers is proper and essential it has been urged that any and all publicity is proper.[2] and even that it is protected by the free speech provision of the

---

tional Association of Claimants' Compensation Attorneys (NACCA) and the periodical NACCA Law Journal. The names have been changed to American Trial Lawyers Association and the periodical to Trials.

21. The report of an American Bar Association committee which recommended the retention of the system of liability based on fault and the objection to its hasty consideration by the Association is outlined in 55 A.B.A.J. 374 (1969).

1. A thoughtful discussion of the problems of this section is B. Christensen, Lawyers for People of Moderate Fortune: Some Problems of Availability of Legal Services, Ch. IV, (Bringing Lawyers and Clients Together) (1970).

2. See argument in Barton v. The State Bar of California, 209 Cal. 677, 289 P. 818 (1930).

Constitution.[3] The further fact is urged in support of this view that much indirect publicity is tolerated and approved. The best publicity, it is said, is a satisfied client who tells his friends of his lawyer's ability. Some lawyers select their friends and social acquaintances and even religious activities with an eye to professional advancement. When such actions are tolerated, then why condemn the direct approach by a lawyer who frankly tells of his record and achievements in the law and asks for a retainer? We may agree that the candid approach is more honorable. Yet this is not all. The failure to condemn the cheapness of some indirect methods comes from the inevitable limitations on the effectiveness of professional standards. The choice of friends and churches cannot be dealt with by professional restrictions and must be left to personal decisions.

Rules of law and standards of the profession do set limits on publicity. There are statutes of varying breadth of prohibition. The Code of Professional Responsibility is more guarded than its predecessor, the Canons, in the limits it sets on publicity. Some court opinions refer to the condemnation of barratry, champerty and maintenance as though these common law principles are carried over without change and applied in this country. This is not so as the validity of the contingent fee alone is enough to show.[4] Such a "speculative" fee is forbidden to the English solicitor and the barrister while it is accepted throughout our country. "The public interest", as the Supreme Court of the United States put it, is the determinant of the legal limits on publicity.[5] What limits should be set may be determined best by perceiving the policies involved and the particular nature and conditions of the publicity in question.

There are three major policies condemning publicity. One is indicated by the term "stirring up litigation", another is directed to the wise selection of counsel, and the third with the public image of the bar. There is an almost universal feeling that litigation is an evil when compared with the peaceful settlement of differences. Litigation stirs the animosities of the parties and is both costly and uncertain for them. On the other side it may be said that the prohibition of solicitation is an indirect way of protecting the status quo which perhaps can be challenged best by a law suit. Litigation is often the only way of en-

---

3. See argument in In re Jones, 431 S.W.2d 809 (Mo.1966).

4. "The common law of champerty and maintenance has never been adopted in this state or applied in civil actions, and the true and exclusive inquiry and test of the right of these plaintiffs to seek relief from a court of equity is whether the transaction upon which they rely is opposed to public policy." Rulnick v. Schulman, 106 Conn. 66, 136 A. 865 (1927).

5. See cases supra pp. 319ff., (the group practice cases).

forcing one's rights and solicitation is a useful way of informing a person of his rights. Certainly the policy against solicitation would be overmatched when the suit was used to protect the rights of a disadvantaged group. That policy has no application to office counseling or to the representation of a defendant in an action already begun.

Another reason for limitations on publicity is that extravagant publicity by lawyers more adept in obtaining than in representing clients would mislead the uninformed layman in his choice of a lawyer. This is especially so when the publicity is accompanied by pressure to sign at once a contract of retainer. Assurances held out in getting clients would increase the temptations on the lawyer to achieve success by any means. The inevitable disappointment of expectations of many clients would lead to lack of trust of the profession as a whole, a trust which is so important to the willingness of the inexperienced layman to seek counsel when needed. The harm done by gross publicity would be all the greater since the public despite, or even because of, the immense volume of advertising by business, still entertains the image of a dependable professional man as one of dignity and restraint.

The guiding question and answer are what forms of publicity are socially useful and should be protected and encouraged, and what forms are apt to lead to social and professional evils and can be dealt with effectively by the courts and the profession. In answering the question the nature of the parties, the kind of work involved, and the character of the publicity are all relevant. Laymen vary widely in their knowledge of lawyers and even in their willingness to retain them. Other sections deal with special kinds of clients and the measures their particular needs require. For ordinary cases, too, it is important to consider the nature of the prospective clients. If the person approached is accustomed to dealing with lawyers and can choose wisely in an unhurried way, direct publicity may be appropriate. When the lawyer and the layman have had earlier dealings which would naturally lead the layman to rely on the lawyer as to the matter in question, again direct publicity may be proper and wise. If the client's interests would be forwarded by publicity of the lawyer and his representation of the client, the publicity of the lawyer by the client may be appropriate.

Litigation may be treated differently from office counseling and some kinds of litigation which society seeks to discourage, as for divorce, may call for special condemnation. The nature of the publicity and its surroundings are factors. When it is informational in character and can be acted on after reflection, it may be useful and approved. When the publicity is flamboyant and especially when it is accompanied by pressure on the layman for immediate retainer, there is good reason to condemn.

"[R]elatively few cases concerning the canons reach the courts, first, because the canons are clear, and, secondly, because the bar in general respects them." [6] The relationship of the standards set out by lawyers in their canons and the principles of law enunciated by the judges is one of mutual influence of the two branches of the profession. The profession accepts, of course, the applicable rules of law. The rules of law are much influenced by the professional standards. In nearly all court cases on professional discipline there has already been professional condemnation, for disciplinary proceedings are rarely instituted until there has been a hearing and recommendation by a bar association committee.

It will be useful to take note, first, of some of the kinds of publicity which the professional committees and the courts have deemed appropriate despite the broad language of the Canons and then to mention practices condemned.

A sharp distinction is drawn between publicity directed to other lawyers, who of course are able to evaluate claims made, and publicity directed to laymen. A lawyer may apply directly for a place as associate in a law office whether by letter or by personal interview. As the "Positions wanted" of the American Bar Association illustrates, he may insert in a lawyers' journal a blind advertisement which gives his background. He may seek employment with a governmental agency. Similarly he may seek the position of house counsel of a corporation.[7] He may publish in legal periodicals a notice of specialized legal service to be rendered to lawyers as Canon 46 explicitly authorizes. A lawyer entering or returning to private practice after government service may include in an announcement card a reference to his position with the government immediately prior to the entry or return.[8] If the listing of the directors of a bank shows the occupation of directors, a lawyer-director may be identified as such.[9]

When the publicity is for the good of the client it may be permitted. So a lawyer may inform a client of a change in the law which might affect the consequences of a document which the lawyer drew; though the communication should leave it open to the client to consult another lawyer.[10] An underwriter of municipal securities may publish the name of the lawyer who approved their legality.[11]

6. Vanderbilt, C. J., in In re Rothman, 12 N.J. 528, 547, 97 A.2d 621, 631 (1953).

7. ABA Comm. on Professional Ethics, Opinions, Nos. 197, 244.

8. Id., Opinion, No. 301.

9. Id., Informal Opinion, No. 645.

10. Id., Opinions, Nos. 210, 213.

11. Id., Opinion, No. 290.

When there is public interest in providing legal services which otherwise might not be available, direct institutional publicity is appropriate. This is the case as to legal aid and as to lawyer referral services, as well as to a bar association's services in protecting the victims of loan sharks.[12] These rulings are manifestly wise, for the publicity aids in providing services without pressure to those who otherwise would not obtain them. It is so as to bar association actions encouraging the public to obtain needed legal services [13] and as to the annual legal checkup.[14] The situation when a client is one of a group with common interests which would be forwarded by common legal representation, as holders of the securities of a corporation in liquidation, has not been dealt with uniformly. At least a client may solicit retainer by others of the lawyer he has employed.[15]

The "professional card" may mean any one of at least three things, the identifying card which a man may carry in his card case as a means of introducing himself; the card sent by mail announcing such developments as the opening of an office or a change in a firm; or the published announcement of a firm. The card of introduction is appropriate. The card of announcement of the formation of a firm and of the admission of new members and similar matters may be sent to lawyers and also to laymen when "warranted by personal relations".[16] Two New York City committees, emphasizing the difference that professional announcements have on lawyers and on laymen, ruled that a lawyer retiring from a government position could send to lawyers both known and unknown to him an announcement which includes a statement of his intention to specialize in a particular branch of law." [17] Similarly he may publish such an announcement in a legal periodical together with brief biographical and informative data.[18] May a firm include in its announcements sent to lawyers and appropriate laymen the names of associates as well as of partners? It is common practice to include these

12. Gunnels v. Atlanta Bar Ass'n, 191 Ga. 366, 12 S.E.2d 602 (1940).

13. ABA Comm. on Professional Ethics, Opinion, No. 179.

14. Id., Opinion, No. 307.

15. ABA Comm. on Professional Ethics, Opinion, No. 111. N. Y. City Lawyer's Ass'n Comm. on Professional Ethics Opinion No. 717 would go further and permit the lawyer to participate in the solicitation. See also People ex rel. Chicago Bar Ass'n v. Ashton, 347 Ill. 570, 180 N.E. 440 (1932).

16. ABA Canons of Professional Ethics No. 27. But a lawyer may not send out Christmas cards except to those with whom a personal relationship exists. ABA Comm. on Professional Ethics, Opinion, No. 309.

17. Joint Opinion No. 375 (N.Y.C.B.A. & N.Y.County Lawyer's Ass'n; cf. ABA Canons of Professional Ethics No. 46.

18. See ABA Canons of Professional Ethics No. 43; H. Drinker, Legal Ethics 265 et seq. (1953).

names in a firm's announcement in a law list. In the authors' opinion, it is appropriate to include them in a card of announcement sent by mail. It is helpful to the associates and useful to their prospective clients, and it is free of pressure. The practice appears to vary with the size of the city. In a small city it would be useful, but useless in the metropolis. The publication of a card of announcement in a newspaper of general circulation is now prohibited.[19] Again, metropolitan conditions may have prevailed over a practice useful and free of abuse in a small town.

Common and indispensable forms of publicity are the lawyer's letterhead and the listing of his office in the telephone directory. The bar's unwillingness to recognize professional fields of specialization of which the public may be informed (except the traditional ones of patent, trademark and admiralty) makes it inappropriate for a lawyer to list a speciality on his letterhead or to include it in the telephone directory.[20]

Self-laudation is condemned by the Canons and the Code. For newspaper articles describing the work of lawyers and prepared with their aid, a New York case censured a small corporate firm but the Florida court refused to condemn a conspicuous personal injury lawyer.[21]

The few court cases on the subject assume that direct publicity is condemned by the law unless justified by special conditions. The court's disciplinary action has ranged from censure to disbarment depending on whether there were "aggravating circumstances." The decisions have involved newspaper advertising,[22] the gift of a laudatory diary,[23] and advertising by mail.[24] They have involved some indirect methods, as pamphlets designed to attract divorce cases[25] and particiption in a "feeder business" which would naturally lead the patrons of the business to employ the lawyer.[26]

19. ABA Comm. on Professional Ethics, Unrep. Opinions, Nos. 140, 142.

20. Id., Opinions, No. 284; cf. ABA Canons of Professional Ethics No. 27.

21. In re Connelly, 18 App.Div.2d 466, 240 N.Y.S.2d 126 (1967); State ex rel. Florida Bar v. Nichols, 151 So.2d 257 (Fla.1963).

22. Barton v. State Bar of California, 209 Cal. 677, 289 P. 818 (1930); In re Cohen, 261 Mass. 484, 159 N.E. 495, Anno., 55 A.L.R. 1313 (1928).

23. People v. Berezniak, 292 Ill. 305, 127 N.E. 36 (1920).

24. Matter of Schwarz, 175 App.Div. 335, 161 N.Y.S. 1079 (1916).

25. In re Donovan, 49 S.D. 95, 178 N.W. 143, Anno., 9 A.L.R. 1500 (1920).

26. In re Rothman, 12 N.J. 528, 97 A.2d 621 (1953). The last case is especially interesting for Mr. Justice Brennan dissented. After his appointment to the Supreme Court of the United States he wrote the prevailing opinion in the first case giving constitutional protection to

The organized bar's ideal has been the lawyer with an established clientele and the satisfied client with a lawyer already chosen. For them it is enough that the publicity of the lawyer extends only to information on where the client can find the lawyer. Publicity, so it has been put, should be intended to enable a person looking for a lawyer already selected to find him and not to attract the attention of persons looking for a lawyer.

This ideal does not match the conditions of many lawyers. It does not meet the situation of young lawyers unless they go with established firms. So the present standards of the bar have been questioned on the ground they favor the established lawyer at the expense of the little fellow and the beginner.[27] What is worse it does not meet the needs of many clients. The difficulties of a new client in making a wise selection of a lawyer are compounded by the changes of our people from a stationary and rural society to a mobile and urban society and by the increasing complexity of the law with many lawyers incompetent to handle the work of many clients who may come to them.

To be kept in mind is the fact that publicity is a necessary step in bringing client and lawyer together. "The Services of a Lawyer Are Within Your Means", together with an identifying address, is an advertisement which the English legal assistance plan employs.

What should be the methods used here? Few can look with equanimity on the prospect of unlimited advertising by lawyers with some of it reading "like the advance bills of the late P. T. Barnum in heralding the approach of the Greatest Show on Earth." [28] Perhaps, approval might be given to individual publicity that is brief and informational in character and free of pressure, as that in a law list. Certainly, there must be fuller support by the bar for lawyer referral services with accompanying publicity.

The manifest uncertainty of our discussion in this section is caused in part by the varied and changing conditions of clients. The uncertainty is increased by the decisions of the Supreme Court of the United States on group legal services with attendant solicitation, discussed above.[29] No less important than the

---

the group legal services there involved, NAACP v. Button, discussed supra pp. 320 ff. It is not clear to what extent the considerations set out by the justice in his dissent in the New Jersey case would be applied by him in a case involving constitutional protection.

27. Shuchman, Ethics and Legal Ethics: The Propriety of the Canons as a Group Moral Code, 37 Geo.Wash.L.Rev. 244 (1968); Note,

a Critical Analysis of Rules Against Solicitation by Lawyers, 25 U.Chi.L.Rev. 674 (1958).

28. See Matter of Schwarz, 175 App. Div. 335, 161 N.Y.S. 1079 (1916).

29. Supra pp. 319 ff.

decisions themselves is a change in the considerations underlying the Court's decisions on the constitutional protection of solicitation of practice. In 1920 there had come before the Court a prosecution under a Texas statute which "defined, with much detail, the offense of barratry", and which applied to lawyers as well as to laymen. A layman prosecuted under the statute for seeking to obtain employment to collect two claims, urged the statute violated the Fourteenth Amendment. Mr. Justice Brandeis, speaking for a unanimous court in upholding the statute, relied on history and on the standards of the profession, saying:

> "The evil against which the regulation is directed is one from which the English law has long sought to protect the community through proceedings for barratry and champerty. . . . Regulation which aims to bring the conduct of the business into harmony with ethical practice of the legal profession, to which it is necessarily related, is obviously reasonable." [30]

In the 1960s the Court used the Constitution to protect group legal services against condemnation by state law.[31] In all three of the cases active solicitation of practice was involved. The Court explicitly refused to be bound by history or by legal ethics in determining the validity of the state's condemnation. The test it employed was "the public interest", with the burden cast on the state and the bar to show that the public interest supported the limitation.

The decisions certainly do not mean that all solicitation is protected. In the first of them Mr. Justice Brennan gives illustrative cases in which, evidently, solicitation may be condemned.

> "Hostility still exists to stirring up private litigation where it promotes the use of legal machinery to oppress: as, for example, to sow discord in a family; to expose infirmities in land titles, as by hunting up claims of adverse possession; to harass large companies through a multiplicity of small claims; or to oppress debtors by seeking out unsatisfied judgments."

No more definite test can be formulated than that set by the Court, "the public's interest".

---

30. McCloskey v. Tobin, 252 U.S. 107, 108 (1920).

31. Supra pp. 319 ff.

SECTION 8. THE EXPERT LAYMAN: COLLABORATOR OR RIVAL OR INTRUDER *

Introduction

The lawyer is a generalist. Until recently he was almost the only expert in the adjustment of human relations, though aided somewhat by the physician and the clergyman. As a generalist he draws on other bodies of knowledge and gives the client a whole answer to his problem, not a fragmentary one to a part. A lawyer's communications with his client do not cease to be privileged because his recommendation at times deals with economic or policy aspects in addition to the legal factors.[1] The position of the lawyer as the generalist may be challenged at times by, say, the business manager or the family counselor or the social worker who claims this right for himself and would treat the lawyer as a mere technician to carry out the specialized legal details of the plan drawn up by a man of wider vision; or, worse still, as an unauthorized practitioner when he presumes to give advice within the other fields.

The lawyer is also a specialist, an expert to whom the state has entrusted the sole privilege in the practice of law and who has developed standards appropriate for the protection of clients and the administration of law. One of his standards calls for the exclusion of trespassers from his domain. Always there have been petty poachers, as, the J.P. who draws bad wills for small fees. In recent years the problem of encroachment has changed its character.

The twentieth century brought an enormous extension of knowledge. The developments in the social sciences, though not so great or precise as those in the natural sciences which have transformed our sister profession, medicine, have brought the economist, the sociologist and the political scientist out of the universities into businesses and into government bureaus form-

---

* The material on the subject is extensive. An early probing symposium is The Unauthorized Practice of Law Controversy, 5 Law & Contemp. Prob. 1 (1938). The fullest source is Unauthorized Practice News of the Committee on Unauthorized Practice of Law of the American Bar Association which includes unpublished decisions, sidelights unavailable elsewhere, and at times thorough discussions of particular subjects, as two articles on title insurance by Professor John C. Payne vol. 35, pp. 1 and 36 (1969).

A useful guide to the material is S. Bass, Unauthorized Practice Source Book (1965).

1. "And it is in the public interest that the lawyer should regard himself as more than predictor of legal consequences. His duty to society as well as to his client involves many relevant social, economic, political and philosophical considerations", Wyzanski, J., in United States v. United Shoe Mach. Corp., 89 F.Supp. 357, 359 (D.Mass 1950).

erly dominated by lawyers. The desire to understand human action and to aid twisted or disadvantaged persons has produced the psychologist, the psychiatrist, the criminologist and the social worker. Increased efforts in the clarification of business conditions have created the accountant and the statistician. Following close behind the extension of knowledge by the scientists came the development of new groups whose members apply this knowledge to human affairs, as the accountant, the rate expert, the social service worker. They call themselves professions since it is of the essence of a profession to apply accumulated knowledge to the cases of individual clients. Two other factors deserve mention. One is the passion for large-scale methods with consequent economy and lower charges leading to the creation of the title company, the trust company and the collection agency. Another factor is the ingenuity of laymen in offering to the public many of the services which in the past were rendered by the lawyer.

The measures which the bar has taken in dealing with the new conditions are of three kinds, affirmative, cooperative and prohibitive. The affirmative measures have several immediate purposes. One is to make the lawyer's services more readily available in fact so there is no need to rely on others. Illustrations discussed elsewhere are the lawyer reference service, expanded legal aid for the poor, and group legal services. Another affirmative measure is strengthening the dependability of the lawyer's work. An illustration is the lawyer's title guaranty funds created in some states which would give to the clients of individual lawyers the same or a fuller measure of protection than that offered by the title companies.[2] A third affirmative measure is to help assure that the client obtains the services of the bar's co-professionals needed by him. Here the bar has lagged badly. The Canons prohibit partnerships with laymen. There is little indication of the participation of experts with the ordinary lawyer.[3] The bar associations have been loath to recognize specialization within the bar itself, and they may be even more reluctant to accept the needs by a client of specialized services rendered by other professions. In this matter the poor may be best off. The social service worker will call on a variety of professionals and disciplines to help her clients, while the lawyer for the well-to-do continues to think of himself as still the omni-competent man.

---

2. In 1968 the American Bar Association proposed the creation of a bar-related title insurance corporation which would issue real estate title insurance to the public only through lawyers. See 93 ABA Rep. 499, 504 (1968).

3. In large anti-trust cases, however, the participation of the economist is a matter of course.

Cooperation of a sort by the lawyer with his rivals has developed on the national level through agreements of the American Bar Association with representatives of other groups on the nature of the work appropriate to each. The agreements are directed to drawing the line marking off the fields of activity of each of the groups.[4] They do little to advance the cooperation of the members of the bar with members of other professions in the representation of clients.

The third set of measures is prohibitive and protective in purpose. They seek to protect the lawyer's field from encroachments by others, that is from "the unauthorized practice of law." The sanctions employed are varied. One kind is preventive in form, as an injunction or a quo warranto proceeding to oust the layman from the field. A second set is punitive in character, as criminal prosecution; or proceedings for contempt of court in assuming to act as a lawyer without a license; or disciplinary proceedings against a lawyer who participates in the unauthorized practice by a layman. Yet another is indirect in its nature, as the denial of fees to the unauthorized practitioner[5], or the dismissal of court proceedings instituted by him. The organized bar has been most active in pressing the third set of measures. The American Bar Association has long had the Committee on the Unauthorized Practice which publishes the informative quarterly, Unauthorized Practice News, and state and local associations have similar committees. The discussion will deal first with the authoritative sources of law on the subject; next with the fundamental factors which it is believed should guide the bar and the courts; then court decisions on types of practices; and lastly with joint practice.

The Authoritative Sources

The problem of authoritative sources, already mentioned, arises from two aspects of our government. The first is its federal nature which creates the question whether state law or federal law in any of its numerous forms is the determining authority. The second is the principle of separation of powers which, as embodied in the federal and the state constitutions, divides the powers of government among the three branches of government, the legislative, the executive, and the judicial.

The federal government has the power to prescribe who may practice before the federal courts [6] and also before its agencies

---

4. The agreements are published in III Martindale-Hubbell Law Directory 263A (1970).

5. The courts have held a will not invalid merely because drawn by a layman in violation of law. Peter-

son v. Hovland, 230 Minn. 478, 42 N.W.2d 59 (1950) Annot., 18 A.L.R. 2d 918 (1951).

6. Theard v. United States, 354 U.S. 278 (1957).

in Washington. The power extends as well to authorize lay practitioners of federal agencies to carry on their work not merely in Washington but within the states, so it was held as to a patent agent.[7] After consideration of that decision a state court, withdrawing an earlier judgment, held that a lay Interstate Commerce Commission practitioner could appear before the Commission's hearings in the state and also give his clients his opinion on Commission matters.[8] The federal power discussed so far rests on the nature of a tribunal as federal. If not the tribunal but the applicable law is federal, does this aspect enable the federal government to determine who may be the practitioner? The fact that the practice of law is essentially the individualization of law suggests a federal standard might apply. The Supreme Court of the United States does not appear to have spoken categorically on the matter.[9] It may be reluctant to take over the field since practitioners admitted by the states are ordinarily adequate in the enforcement of federal law claims or defenses. Another reason for reluctance is that federal law and state law are often intertwined. It may be enough to assert the federal power over the right to practice in the rare cases in which state practitioners are unavailable in fact for the protection of federal law rights.[10]

  Federal law may take the form, not of prescribing who may practice, but of striking down state limitations. The most important illustration is the set of cases discussed above which struck down state laws against lay intermediaries.[11] These decisions were placed by the Supreme Court of the United States on the constitutional right of association. Other provisions of the Constitution, as the equal protection and due process clauses, might be invoked by those who assert they are as fully equipped as the lawyer to represent the client. So far these constitutional provisions have not had substantial application.[12]

7. Sperry v. Florida ex rel. Florida Bar, 373 U.S. 379 (1963).

8. State Bar of Wisconsin v. Keller, 21 Wis.2d 100, 123 N.W.2d 905 (1963).

9. In a passage in a dissenting opinion Mr. Justice Harlan wrote, without disagreement: "[T]he Congress undoubtedly has the power to implement federal programs by establishing overriding rules governing legal representation in connection therewith." United Mine Workers v. Illinois State Bar Ass'n, 389 U.S. 217, 234 n. 17 (1967).

10. See Sanders v. Russell, 401 F.2d 241 (5th Cir. 1968), cf. Note, 20 Vand.L.Rev. 1276 (1967).

11. Supra pp. 319 ff.

12. A state statute which forbade the carrying on of the business of debt adjustment except as an incident to the practice of law was upheld despite the contention it violated the due process and equal protection clauses of the constitution. In upholding the exception as to lawyers Mr. Justice Black mentioned the "relationship of trust", the need for legal advice, and the similarity to a proceeding

The question as to which of the three branches of government has power to determine who may be practitioners has not been answered uniformly. It would appear that the legislature has the power to determine who shall appear before its committees; though the right of free speech and of assembly might be invoked to strike down any limitation which interfered seriously with the power of the people to express themselves to their representatives. The executive acts through various officials and doubtless, it has the power to determine who shall practice before it.[13]

The courts, so it has been held, have the inherent power of control over the bar as essential aids to the court in the administration of law. From this control over the bar it has been inferred the courts have the ultimate power under the respective state constitutions to determine what is the practice of law and to oust or to punish unauthorized practitioners;[14] though statutes on the subject have often been accepted as legislative support to the courts in the performance of their function.[15] This view, however, is not unanimous, and in some cases it has been held or assumed that the legislature's power extends over the subject. There is a strong consideration against the view that the ultimate power rests in the courts. Judges are lawyers and in these situations in which there is a contest between lawyers and their competitors they are in the most uncomfortable of situations— judges in their own case, with inevitable excessive appreciation and emphasis on the values and claims of their profession.[16] A man may be better able to perceive and to put aside an interest personal to him than to resist the subtler assumptions taken for granted by his whole profession. Lawyers would feel outraged if title company executives or accountants claimed the constitutional power of decision in controversies with lawyers, and they are unwise to claim the privilege for themselves. There is an inescapable burden on judges in construing statutes and in developing the common law on the subject of the coordination of the work of lawyers with that of other disciplines. This is enough without claiming the final decision under the constitution beyond the power of the legislature to alter.

in bankruptcy. Ferguson v. Skrupa, 372 U.S. 726 (1963). See also State Bar of Wisconsin v. Keller, 21 Wis. 2d 100, 123 N.W.2d 905 (1963).

13. Cf. Sperry v. Florida ex rel. Florida Bar, 373 U.S. 379 (1963); State Bar of Wisconsin v. Keller, 21 Wis. 2d 100, 123 N.W.2d 905 (1963).

14. Re Opinion of the Justices, 289 Mass. 607, 194 N.E. 313 (1935).

15. Id.

16. See Merrick v. American Sec. & Trust Co., 107 F.2d 271, 272 (D.C. Cir. 1939), cert. denied 308 U.S. 625 (1940).

The Fundamental Factors

In the development of all law the law-making body draws on factors outside the law itself—ideals, policies, objectives, practicalities. So it is in delimiting "the practice of law", and it is these ever-present elements which are here called "the fundamental factors". At times the court has looked solely to history and custom. In an Arizona case the court said baldly: [17]

> "We believe it sufficient to state that those acts, whether performed in court or in the law office, which lawyers customarily have carried on from day to day through the centuries must constitute 'the practice of law.' "

This test seems clearly wrong, for at least two reasons. One is that in rapidly changing times it is most unwise to look for guidance wholly to the past. The test is somewhat like the claim of the carpenters' union in jurisdictional disputes with other labor unions, that whatever was once made of wood still belongs to the carpenters though the material used may be metal and the skills needed wholly new ones.

The other reason, even more important, is that the test directs its attention to lawyers and their activities when the focus should be shifted to clients and how their needs for legal services can best be met. The shift in focus from lawyer to client may be even a constitutional requirement. It was so in the three Supreme Court of the United States decisions on lay intermediaries already discussed.[18] The organized bar had there sought to condemn the activities involved as "the unauthorized practice of law". The court, however, upheld them and in doing so applied throughout the test of "the public interest". These cases as well as fairness on the part of the bar call for a shift of the general question from, "what is the unauthorized practice of law" to the much more complex one, "how and through whom shall services calling for legal ability be made available to those who need them?"

The courts are accustomed to dealing with such problems in the development of the law, especially difficult though this one may be. In dealing with such a problem there are at least three elements which may usefully be distinguished from one another. One is an understanding of the policies to be advanced; a second is the social facts which bear on the advancement of the policies and their attainment; the third is the weighing of the relevant factors and the determination of how the scales tip.

The most important social fact is the nature of the prospective clients served by the bar and its rivals. Two very large classes

---

17. State Bar of Arizona v. Arizona Land Title & Trust Co., 90 Ariz. 76, 87, 366 P.2d 1, 9 (1961).

18. Supra pp. 319 ff.

of these clients have already been discussed, the middle class with their reluctance to employ lawyers unless the lawyers are made available by trusted intermediaries, and the poor, especially the gravely disadvantaged and socially incompetent. These two classes cannot be treated alike nor like the well to do. Yet all of them are equally entitled to legal services by some means. As Cromwell and his officers proclaimed in council three centuries ago, "The poorest he in England hath a life to live as the richest he." [19]

Some of the relevant policies will be mentioned beginning with those in favor of the claimed privilege of the bar. So far as service to the client is concerned the claim of the lawyer can be summed up as his superior competence, dependability, and breadth of view. The individual client will be better served by the lawyer's greater competence, because of his knowledge of the principles of law and their utilization and because of the lawyer's ability to see and deal with a situation as a whole and not a mere specialized part of it. The client will be better protected also by the higher sense of obligation which the bar seeks to instill and enforce in its members. Despite depreciation lawyers have better organizations and better methods for holding its members up to standards of fairness than most lay groups. The lawyer rarely accepts a conflicting interest case while the layman often does; as the real estate broker who is interested in making the sale, not primarily in protecting the interests of either party. Finally, there is the breadth of view so well expressed by a leader of the bar:

> "[H]e knows that the wise client today looks to him not only for technical skill in advice but for that broader wisdom, bred of a need for clients to act compatibly with their public images and responsibilities, which require an almost pastoral quality in the proper formulation of professional advice." [20]

There are other policies involved beyond the protection of the individual client. The administration of the law is improved when lawyers are the representatives of clients, whether the administration be through the giving of advice, the preparation of documents, or service as advocates. There is a still larger social interest in the preservation of a strong and independent bar. In the past it provided much of the leadership of the nation. Such a bar is needed even more in these days when big government with its officialdom require lawyers who will challenge it no less

---

19. Westwood, A Stir in the Land, 50 J.Am.Jud.Soc'y 158, 162 (1967).

20. Seymour, The Obligations of the Lawyer to His Profession, 23 Record of N.Y.C.B.A. 311, 321 (1968). See ABA Code of Professional Responsibility, Canon 3 Ethical Considerations.

than those who will serve it. This kind of bar will not be maintained if most of its field of work is taken over by others.

Before dealing with the opposing considerations it is well to take note of the nature of some of the bar's rivals and their work. They include co-professional men, who are trained in universities and licensed by the state as certified public accountants and social workers; men engaged in other activities in which legal knowledge and advice are helpful to the conduct of the work itself, as salesmen of life insurance and real estate; corporations which through lawyers in their employ carry on work in competition with lawyers, as title companies, or which need constant legal advice in their work, as trust companies; non-profit corporations which serve as lay intermediaries for clients unaccustomed to employ lawyers; planners of complex business transactions in which legal knowledge is essential, as the architects; or the merely aggressive laymen. The work undertaken varies as the lawyer's does from advising and planning and drafting; or the assertion of claims or defenses and the consequent settlement without suit, as by the collection agency or the insurance claim agent and adjuster; or litigation in court or before governmental agencies. The work varies, too, in complexity and in the measure of usefulness in it of other skills along with those of the lawyer.

In support of the privilege of laymen there are several substantial factors the importance or even presence of which vary with the situation. One is the readier access to laymen. This may be because of physical isolation, as the remoteness of a mountain town. The more common cause comes from the client's attitude toward lawyers and their services. So a workman may be unwilling to use the services of a lawyer unless vouched and paid for by the organization he trusts. A disadvantaged person in a ghetto may not bestir herself to go to a legal aid office, unless the first measures are taken by a social worker. And there is the unwillingness of the most disadvantaged of all, a man in prison, to assert his rights unless aided by one of his peers who is trusted, the jail-house lawyer. A second factor is the equal or superior value to the client of the layman's kind of expertness, as that of the rate expert or the accountant. A third factor is economy and lower charges. This may come from large scale operations, as those of a title company. Yet another factor is speed in business transactions. The real estate salesman who claims the right to draw up or fill out the legal instruments necessary in the purchase and sale of land would be badly hampered if both vendor and purchaser had to consult their lawyers. Lastly is the individualistic American spirit which asserts the right of every man to act in his own case, whether it be the drawing of a will or the trying of a case.

With services, conditions and policies so varied what is called for is not an all-inclusive definition of "practice of law", but rather a basic guide. The guide, to repeat, is the public interest. The lawyer may fairly assert an exclusive privilege only when the skill possessed by the trained lawyer or the higher standard of personal responsibility of the lawyer outweighs the other advantages which the laymen may possess. The Code of Professional Responsibility, EC 3–5, uses this test of the public interest and relates it to the functions of the lawyer:

> "Functionally, the practice of law relates to the rendition of services for others that call for the professional judgment of a lawyer. The essence of the professional judgment of the lawyer is his educated ability to relate the general body and philosophy of law to a specific legal problem of a client."

Court Proceedings

Representation in court is the privilege of the lawyer alone, justified as this is by the complexities of procedure and the importance that proceedings move smoothly and without delay. The only fully recognized exception is the privilege of the party to the action to represent himself. This exception, it has been held, does not extend to the corporation which is denied the privilege to appear for itself through a lay officer.[21]

Giving Advice and Drafting Documents

Legal relations are also human relations, whether the relations concern the family or business or the citizen and his government. It would be intolerable if in the formation of every relation lawyers alone had the privilege to advise on its creation and to supervise its formation. The mention of a few examples will suffice: marriage; the purchase of groceries; a small loan made by a bank; enlistment in the military service; enrollment in law school.

Yet advice on the creation of legal relations and the embodiment of the relations in clear and dependable form make up most of the practice of law. Ordinarily lawyers have superior ability in advising on their clients' actions and certainly greatly superior ability in putting the plans agreed on in a form which is both clear and dependable. What is the test of the areas reserved to the lawyer and, conversely, of the areas shared with others? The test is the public interest, that is the superiority for the public good of the employment of the lawyer's qualities over other considerations.[22] No more specific test can be the general one. There are various elements entering into its appli-

21. Oliner v. Midtown Promoters, Inc., 2 N.Y.2d 63, 138 N.E.2d 217 (1956).

22. Nelson v. Smith, 107 Utah 382, 154 P.2d 634 (1944), Annot., 157 A.L.R. 522 (1945).

cation in support of the layman's action and some of them will be stated.

The interest in the transaction of the party drawing the instrument and the relation of the legal work as incidental to the principal work are important factors, as when a legal instrument is prepared as an incident to the business of the party,[23] though this factor alone has been rejected as inadequate by some courts. The nature of the transaction or instrument, as easy or complex, is a factor. No one would suggest that when a bank makes a loan of $100 to a workman, and has him sign a note which the teller fills in, both the bank and the borrower must employ lawyers to represent them; though if the same company sought to draw a living trust through the same teller, it might well be halted.[24] The certified ability of the lay specialist should certainly be a factor in rendering services, as the certified public accountant. This may become increasingly so with the development of new co-professional groups; but the factor has been rejected as itself a test because of the broader perspective of the lawyer.[25] The accessibility and dependability of legal services in fact were major factors in the decisions upholding group legal services. At times the courts have mentioned the lack of compensation and the occasional nature of the work done as tending to show the alleged offender is not engaged in the practice of law.[26] Economy through large scale work and consequent economy in charges are a factor which, though not mentioned, pretty surely influences decisions as to title companies and trust companies.

Administrative Proceedings

The administrative commissions create a special problem, possessing as they often do powers which appear to be both legislative and judicial as well as even executive in their nature and exercise. Two aspects of practice before them will be mentioned. There is no agreement on the source of the power to determine who may appear before them. A striking contrast is given in the Keller litigation cited above,[27] in which the Wisconsin court held it was within the power of the court to determine who could

23. Merrick v. American Sec. & Trust Co., 107 F.2d 271 (1939) cert. denied 308 U.S. 625 (1940); Ingham County Bar Ass'n v. Walter Neller Co., 342 Mich. 214, 69 N.W.2d 713, Annot., 53 A.L.R.2d 713 (1955).

24. Lowell Bar Ass'n v. Loeb, 315 Mass. 176, 186, 52 N.E.2d 27, 34 (1943). But cf. "The most complex are simple to the skilled, and the simplest often trouble the inex-perienced." People v. Title Guarantee & Trust Co., 227 N.Y. 366, 379, 125 N.E. 666, 670 (1919) (concurring opinion).

25. Gardner v. Conway, 234 Minn. 468, 48 N.W.2d 788 (1951).

26. Opinion of the Justices, 279 Mass. 607, 194 N.E. 313 (1935).

27. Supra n. 8.

practice before the state public service commission while the Supreme Court of the United States assumed it was within the power of the Interstate Commerce Commission to determine who could practice in matters within that commission's jurisdiction. As to a public service commission a Colorado court let the determination turn on the nature of the problem and the work; insofar as the proceeding involved the resolution of "disputes of adjudicative facts" the practitioner was engaged in the practice of law, but not so when engaged in the "[r]epresentation of another in a hearing relating to the making or revision of [future] rates." On the latter, the practitioner was within the control of the commission of the legislature.[28] This accords with the language of the separation of powers provisions of the constitution yet it is scarcely fortunate. In a single proceeding before a railroad commission, for example, the shipper may claim a return of charges already paid as excessive and also seek a corresponding reduction in the rates for the future, with the two claims turning on much the same factors and their presentation calling for identical competence. It would be unwise to deny to the lay practitioner the privilege of representation as to the second claim while granting it as to the first. The classification by the courts of a power as legislative or judicial in earlier cases may have been made for quite other purposes and issues and the classification cannot be transferred uncritically to the new purpose. To do this is to look at language and not substance.

The federal law is more favorable to qualified lay practitioners before its commissions than is state law. Some examples of federal liberality are the Internal Revenue Service, the National Labor Relations Board, the Interstate Commerce Commission, and the Commissioner of Patents. The state law is rather unfriendly. The privilege of representation before a workmen's compensation commission was rejected in a case in which the Supreme Court of the United States denied certiorari.[29] The contrast of action in the representation of trucking lines before the state commission and the federal commission has been described.[30] Nor have accountants fared well before state tribunals.

Lawyers and Laymen Jointly

There are several forms of joint work of lawyers and laymen. The laymen may be associate professionals in law; or lay intermediaries; or co-professionals. Every large law office has lay-

28. Denver Bar Ass'n v. Public Util. Comm., 154 Colo. 273, 391 P.2d 467 (1964). Annot. 13 A.L.R.3d 799 (1967).

29. Re Unauthorized Practice of Law, 175 Ohio St. 149, 192 N.E.2d 54 (1963), cert. denied 376 U.S. 970, (1964), Annot. 2 A.L.R.3d 712 (1965).

30. State Bar of Wisconsin v. Keller, 21 Wis.2d 100, 123 N.W.2d 905 (1963).

men who have become expert in less demanding assignments or who are students of law not yet admitted to practice. May they bear part of the work of the lawyer? In medicine these associate professionals are a recognized, even an essential, part of the profession's work. Hospitals could not get along without their host of medical technicians and trained nurses. In our profession there are only the beginnings of this kind of recognition, as the privilege of a law clerk to appear in court to respond to the call of the calendar.[31] This privilege, which is highly useful to a lawyer with several cases approaching trial in different divisions of the court, is helpful to the clients and is in accord with a policy urged of employing low-cost personnel as far as possible so as to keep down the level of legal expenses.[32] There has been a great extension of the privilege of third year law students to appear in legal aid cases.

The co-professionals who make available to clients another kind of expertness than law might have anyone of several kinds of relationships to the lawyer which are best illustrated by the certified public accountant.[33] The accountant may be employed by the lawyer on a salary, an arrangement to which there is no objection so far as the standards of the bar are concerned. Conversely, the accountant may employ the lawyer on a salary. The employment is not in itself unlawful or improper, though the lawyer in his work must adhere to the standards of his own profession, as house counsel must do. The two professional men, conceivably, might form a partnership. This arrangement, specifically condemned by the Code of Professional Responsibility, DR 3–103, does not appear to have been passed on by the courts.

Lay intermediaries, as corporations which retain lawyers to render services to those served by the intermediary, have been mentioned earlier. In some forms of group legal service, they enjoy constitutional protection. The development of standards which will help to assure the quality of the services rendered without hampering their rendition is now a major concern of the bar.

Dual Expertness

May a lawyer who is also a licensed expert in another field practice in both fields? The question has arisen as to the lawyer-accountant, a group numbering it is estimated two or three

---

31. People v. Alexander, 53 Ill.App. 2d 299, 202 N.E.2d 841 (1964). Annot. 13 A.L.R.3d 1132 (1967).

32. See Q. Johnstone & D. Hopson, Lawyers and Their Work, 163–197, 549–550 (1967); ABA Code of Professional Responsibility, EC–7.

33. The relations of the lawyer and the accountant are considered in ABA Comm. on Professional Ethics, Opinion, No. 297, 47 A.B.A.J. 527 (1961); Id., Opinion, No. 305, 48 A.B.A.J. 473 (1962).

thousand with its own national organization.[34]   There appears to
be no law condemning the practice, and it has been vigorously
urged that such a prohibition would be a violation of the
Constitution.[35]   The Committee of Professional Ethics of the
American Bar Association has condemned the practice as
unethical.[36]   The reasons given were the impracticability of
keeping adequately informed in both fields, the difference in ethical standards with the work of one a feeder to the other, and the
contrast of duties of loyalty and advocacy of the lawyer with the
impartiality and independence required of the accountant.   It
will be remembered the accountant has two quite different functions.   In his work as auditor he makes investigations and reports which are independent and impartial.   In other work, as income tax matters, he is an adviser or advocate no less than the
lawyer.   The answer to the question may depend on the nature of
the accountant's work.   If he limits himself to such work as income tax matters, his position and continuing proficiency as accountant are not incompatible with but strengthen his work as a
lawyer.   A troubling problem may be presented by different
standards, say as to the privilege not to testify in court.   If the
accountant does not possess this privilege, the client may be the
loser through the dual position.   A minor aspect involves publicity of the dual expertness, as on the professional card or on the
office door.   The general practitioner who can claim no such expertness is annoyed, for a prospective client may well be made to
feel he can get both kinds of expertness for a single fee—something which he may be entitled to know if it be true.

Conclusion

   There has been a fortunate shift in the emphasis of the bar
associations' attitude in this field.   At first they devoted most of
their time to proceedings against members of other groups who
crossed the boundary lines.   Later they gave attention to reaching agreements with representatives of other groups on where
the boundary lines are.   Now there is urgent need for another
set of major changes which shifts the focus of inquiry from the
lawyer's privileges to the client's needs, including needs for
methods of employing the knowledge of professionals in other social disciplines to aid the client.   Here, too, the bar's actions will
be client—centered, not profession—centered.

34.   The name of the association is
    American Association of Attorney-
    Certified Public Accountants, Inc.

35.   Mintz, Accountancy and Law:
    Should Dual Practice be Pro-
    scribed?, 53 A.B.A.J. 225 (1967).

But see Levy & Sprague, Accounting and Law: Is Dual Practice in
the Public Interest?, 52 A.B.A.J.
1110 (1966).

36.   See note 33 supra.

Chapter XVIII

PRIVATE, PUBLIC AND GROUP INTERESTS AND THEIR PROTECTION

SECTION 1. INTRODUCTION

Legal relationships are an affirmation and expression of social interests worthy of protection by law. Our society has been individualistic rather than collectivist in nature with individuals given a large share in determining their relations with one another. Most legal relations with which lawyers have been concerned run between individuals, say, as a right-duty relation between Smith and Jones. Our system of law administration, too, has been individualistic as well as adversary in character. It is essential that a person who wishes effectively to assert his legal rights have a lawyer to aid him. Chapter XVII immediately preceding deals with methods of making legal services readily available for those who need them.

Under our individualistic and adversary system a private action at law is the method used ordinarily for the protection of individual interests. It is a medium, also, for the development of the law. The English courts created the common law in such actions. In such actions, the American courts have developed the law in this country even in matters of the greatest public import. The scope of the admiralty jurisdiction was determined in a case over a minor maritime collision; the validity of the old federal income tax was denied in a class action brought by a petty stockholder against a corporation; and the Dred Scott case with its contribution to secession and the Civil War was on its face an action for trespass.

Our society has now moved so far from what it was when our government first took shape that a learned observer characterized it as "The New Feudalism." [1] The terms, "Big Business," "Big Labor," "Big Government," are not epithets. They are indications that the individual may be dependent on the state or his group, and that the old methods of individuals dealing with

1. Pound, The New Feudalism, 16 A.B.A.J. 553 (1930). The process of our society, it has been suggested, may now be the reverse of Maine's famous generalization a century ago of movement from status to contract. H. Laski, The Pluralistic State, in The Foundations of Sovereignty and Other Essays 240 (1921).

one another under laissez faire economic and legal systems may be no longer just or workable. The availability of counsel to individuals is not enough. There is need for other forms of protection and advancement of social and individual interests. This chapter calls attention to and sketches some of them.

The nature of our economic and political and social systems makes it important for the public good that there be varied methods of law administration so that the courts may the more readily have brought before them the protection and reconciliation of the several interests. In the economic area our system is a compound of private striving and state interposition.[2] The public value in the maintenance of private initiative and striving needs no discussion with lawyers who have long protected it under such principles as "freedom of contract." The need for state interposition is indicated well enough by the trilogy above, "Big." The concentration of power in large units involves more than the possible conflict of the large unit with the public welfare. It involves as well a possible conflict of interests of the managers with those whom they are chosen to serve. The conflict of interests of some corrupt labor union leaders with the interests of the union members was stressed by Senator Kennedy before he became president.[3] The leaders of big business have subtler temptations. They naturally seek to continue themselves in power. They, too, may use their power for personal ends through voting for themselves excessive salaries and retirement allowances. Each corporation seeks to justify with stockholders such payment to officers by pleading this is necessary—as it may well be under the present system—to draw or even to hold essential and able executives. A corporation or a single group of stockholders alone can rarely overcome the force of this argument. It can be met only by measures, applicable to all corporations alike, a subject outside our discussion.

The dispersion of public officials accentuates the problem. Each one is elected by and attempts to satisfy his particular constituency even to the injury of others. An illustration is the Attorney General of Tennessee, who sought to uphold the action of the Tennessee Legislature in failing to reapportion the state for purposes of voting in face of an explicit direction in the Con-

---

2. The term, "the public," means the generality of the people instead of an individual or a special interest group. In that sense it is used here in referring to the intended beneficiaries of litigation, despite the unceasing debate among politicians and social scientists over what is the public interest.

The public is not a legal person and it acts at law through its organized form, the state. "The state" means here the participant in a legal proceeding.

3. Kennedy, Union Racketeering: The Responsibility of the Bar, 44 A.B.A.J. 437 (1958).

stitution of the State [4], and of what was held to be an implicit requirement of the national constitution.

One change in our society making for new protective measures is the development of a stronger sense of the injustices under which the disadvantaged suffer as the poor, the consumer, and the ethnic minorities. On their side there is the rising expectations of peoples. There are also newly stressed social interests. They range from the evils of pollution and of urban congestion on to the values of recreation and of beauty. These social interests may well need other methods of legal protection and advancement through law than is given by the traditional one-to-one legal relationship between individuals.[5]

Three sources of interest and methods of action are sketched here—the individual, the group, and the state, each one acting either for itself or for one of the other two. Some preliminary illustrations make clear the interaction of the three methods. A minority stockholders' derivative suit is individual action to protect the interests of the individual and also of the group of shareholders. An action for threefold damages under the antitrust law is individual action to protect the individual and also to protect the public interest against monopoly. A workmen's compensation claim illustrates several possible methods together of protection of the individual. The worker may follow the old method of protection and retain his own lawyer to press the claim; the compensation commission, a state body, has the duty to investigate and enforce the individual's claim; and the worker's group, the labor union, may employ a lawyer who would press his claim.[6]

History shows a variety of methods. To mention a few, private action to enforce public interest against monopolies was authorized by the Monopolies Act of 1623 which gave threefold damages to the injured party and, to encourage his counsel, double costs as well.[7] Public action to protect the individual was an original purpose of the Star Chamber and is so of the regulatory commissions today. Group action to protect public interest against subversion was a basis of the grant of special privileges to the Stationers' Guild.[8] The importance now attached to group protection of the individual's claim is made manifest by the decisions of the Supreme Court of the United States which upheld group practice of law.[9]

4. Baker v. Carr, 369 U.S. 186 (1962).

5. See Chapter XVII supra.

6. United Mine Workers of America v. Illinois State Bar Ass'n, 389 U.S. 217 (1967).

7. 23 Jac. I, c. 3.

8. L. Patterson, Copyright in Historical Perspective, ch. 3 (1968).

9. Supra pp. 319 ff.

The groups for which protection is claimed are varied. They may be narrow groups, as a class of stockholders of a particular corporation. They may be broad economic groups, as the railroads, the textile industry, the consumers. Or, they may be identified on religious or racial lines.

Ordinarily a party may assert at law only interests which run to him and not to another. This requirement is expressed by the principle of standing to sue. In our complex society the satisfaction of "standing" is increasingly broadened. The state may protect private interests; a private person may protect public interests; and a group may protect either. In determining whether the ordinary practice shall be departed from and there shall be cross-enforcement of legal or social interests, the guiding considerations are the same as those controling the development of the law generally as: how important are the interests involved; do they need this off-type method of enforcement for their protection; will the new method be effective; will the harmful side-effects outweigh the value of improved protection.

The consideration of the subject is directed in some books to a particular social interest, as conservation, or else civil and political rights, and the variety of protective measures available for that kind of interests.[10] This book, dealing as it does with the profession of law generally and its activities, is not restricted to a particular kind of social interest. It is limited, however, to protective measures by lawyers.[11] It inquires into who may maintain action to protect varied social interests, other than the persons in whom the interests are legally vested.

The treatment will be brief and merely illustrative. Supplementing the chapter immediately preceding, this chapter is a reminder and suggestion that for the protection of the interests of a person affected other methods may be available besides providing counsel to represent him. The discussion follows the line of the moving parties in the protective proceedings, state proceedings, group action, and individual action. As to each moving party it illustrates the parties who may be benefitted—the public, a group, an individual.

10. An excellent example is T. Emerson, D. Haber & N. Dorsen, Political and Civil Rights in the United States (3d ed. 1967).

11. For a consideration of the advancement of group interests by other means, see J. Skolnick, The Politics of Protest (1969).

SECTION 2. STATE ACTION

Proceedings at law by the state may be for the protection of the general public, or of a group, or of individuals.

State Proceedings for Public Protection. State proceedings for the benefit of the public is obvious. The usual work of lawyers for the government consists of the enforcement of the regulatory and the criminal laws and the protection of government property. The Attorney General of the United States is given the privilege to appear in any suit in which the constitutionality of an Act of Congress affecting the public interest is drawn in question even though the United States is not a party.[1] The attorney general of a state may maintain an action to enforce a charitable trust.[2]

A lawyer for the state may be allowed to appear as amicus curiae in a case of public importance. A notable illustration is the *Gideon* case which involved the constitutional right to counsel in serious criminal cases and in which the attorneys general of more than twenty states appeared in support of the right and two attorneys general in opposition.[3] The Attorney General of the United States is at times invited by the Supreme Court of the United States to appear in cases of importance.

The administrative commissions are agencies for the protection of the public. To help assure observance of the law they may impose the requirement of publicity through reports by the regulated organizations. For the information of the public they may require publicity as to the nature of the goods sold or as to acts done through descriptive labels or financial statements.

In private law making there is often complete disregard of the public interest. Freedom of contract or freedom of controversy may be broadly justified when the parties to it are equals and they alone are affected. When the controversy or the agreement would injure others, they, too, should be heard and considered in private law making as in public law making. Illustrations are labor-management controversies and agreements and the lack of public participation or consideration in them. A useful beginning in public representation of the public interest in such mat-

---

1. 28 U.S.C.A. § 2403.

For a discussion of what constitutes the "public interest," see 13 International Encyclopedia of the Social Sciences 170 (1968). See also Note, "The New Public Interest Lawyers" 79 Yale L.J. 1069 (1970).

2. Brown v. Memorial Nat'l Home Foundation, 162 Cal.App.2d 513, 329 P.2d 118 (1958), Anno., 75 A.L.R. 2d 449 (1961), cert. denied 358 U.S. 943 (1959). See A. Scott, The Law of Trusts § 391 (3d ed. 1967).

3. Gideon v. Wainwright, 372 U.S. 335 (1963).

ters would be the requirement of the presence of a representative of the public as witness and reporter of the negotiations and the background facts from the beginning without waiting, as now, until the negotiations are about to break down. To make public the demands and the relevant facts would do much to create a public opinion compelling an agreement fair to both sides as well as to the public, which bears the ultimate costs through higher prices or interrupted services or bad working and living conditions.

State Proceedings for Group Protection. State proceedings may be taken as to disadvantaged groups whose wrongs would probably go unrighted unless the government steps in. A group which has been the object of special protection is the Negroes suffering disfranchisement. The Civil Rights Act of 1964 empowered the Attorney General to maintain a civil suit for preventive relief.[4]

In economic matters one form of protection is a suit for an injunction against harmful acts accompanied by a prayer for restitution of money wrongly received. An illustration is Porter v. Warner Holding Co.[5] Under a federal statute which set limits on rents the public administrator brought suit to enjoin a landlord from exceeding the rent ceiling, as the statute authorized him to do. He sought also a return for the tenants of the excess rents received. Though the statute did not so provide, the court held the administrator was entitled to the decree of restitution as well as to an injunction. The grounds stated were that "the statutory policy of preventing inflation is plainly advanced" by such a decree and the grant of the decree of restitution came within the general "equitable powers of the District Court." The decision is all the broader in implication because, as the dissenting justices pointed out, the scheme of enforcement specified in the statute was exceptionally complete and detailed.

The decision was followed and its grounds reiterated in a case involving the discharge of employees under the Fair Labor Standards Act, which empowered the Secretary of Labor to maintain actions to restrain violations of the Act.[6] In such an action, as Mr. Justice Harlan stated, the court had accompanying jurisdiction to order an employer to reimburse its employees for wages lost through violation of the Act. Again the decision was based on the policy of the statute, on the general power of a court of equity, and on the practical necessity for the employees of this sort of enforcement.

The principle of these cases could bring broad protection to the disadvantaged against their exploiters. The decisive matter

4.   42 U.S.C.A. § 2000a.

5.   328 U.S. 395 (1946).

6.   Mitchell v. Robert DeMario Jewelry, Inc., 361 U.S. 288 (1960).

may be the government's standing to sue. In the two cases the language of the statute authorized the government to maintain suit to enjoin the wrongdoings. The opinions emphasize not only the language of the statute but the policy of the statutes and the inadequacy in fact of the individual rights of action. Similarly in determining whether the attorney general may sue in other cases of exploitation of the disadvantaged, stress might be laid on the basic policies of equity, that it will take jurisdiction when there is no adequate remedy at law and it will not suffer a wrong to go without a remedy. The right to sue would arise in the public authority whose law was violated to enjoin the violation and there would be the accompanying equitable right to recover the money wrongly withheld from the individuals. The power of the state as *parens patriae* as well as the recognized power of the state to sue to enjoin a public nuisance have been suggested by a careful study as supports of the right to sue.[7] In California it has been said broadly that the state's attorney general has the powers to sue when he deems it necessary in the enforcement of the laws of the state.[8]

Public Protection of Individual Interests. State proceedings may protect disadvantaged individuals through enforcement of their claims against others, as claims for wages or for workmen's compensation.

The Uniform Consumer Credit Code provides a variety of protections. One method is an order by the Administrator himself after notice and hearing.[9] Another method is a civil action for an injunction and for a refund of the amount of the excess charges.[10] State proceedings may protect against the government itself, as through the public defender for indigent accused [11], and the ombudsman who inquires into the complaints of the citizen against government officials.[12]

7. J. Wade & R. Kamenshine, Restitution for Defrauded Consumers: Making the Remedy Effective Through Suit by Governmental Agency, 37 Geo.Wash.L.Rev. 1031, 1064 (1969).

The government may have standing to sue to enjoin illegal business practices which injure the poor. In one case the State of Wisconsin obtained an injunction against the alleged usurious use of revolving charge accounts of customers. State v. J. C. Penney Co., 48 Wis.2d 125, 179 N.W.2d 641 (1970). In another case the United States secured an injunction to halt the practice of obtaining default judg-

ments based on false returns by process servers. United States v. Brand Jewelers, Inc., 318 F.Supp. 1293 (1970).

8. Pierce v. Superior Court, 1 Cal. 2d 759, 37 P.2d 453 (1934).

9. Uniform Consumer Credit Code, § 6.108.

10. Id. §§ 6.110, 6.111, 6.113.

11. Supra p. 333.

12. See W. Gellhorn, Ombudsmen and Others (1966).

The interest of the state in the protection of children has often been asserted. So strong is this interest that it has been said to override the policy of the interstate system and to make the full faith and credit clause of the Constitution inapplicable in custody proceedings.[13]

SECTION 3. GROUP ACTION

Americans have the ability and the inclination, as De Tocqueville observed long ago, to form groups for needed tasks. The variety of group interests is heightened by the diversity in our country of immigation—a great nation but scarcely yet a people. There can be agreement on the desirability of organizations to express group interests and their coordination under law without acceptance of the political theory of plural sovereignty and the consequent lasting Balkanization of the country. The basis of formation of groups may be economic, or racial, or religious, or geographical, or social. Any one basis, as economic, may include within it such various kinds as the United States Chamber of Commerce, the textile industry, a local labor union, or a class of shareholders of a corporation in reorganization.

In the matter of benefits it is difficult, as the reader will perceive from the cases, to distinguish a "group" and its interests from the public and its interests on the one side, and on the other side from individuals and their several interests. Group benefits shade at one end into public benefits and at the other into private benefits. Our concern is primarily with the problems of action by the group rather than with the resulting benefits.

A common problem as to all group actions at law is legal personality: is the group a legal person which can sue and be sued at law? In most cases the difficulty is met by the incorporation of some members of the group; in others it is dealt with by the principle of the class action. An accompanying question concerns standing to sue—does the group have such an interest in the subject matter of the action as enables it to assert or defend against the claim in question? Our brief mention of group actions will follow the same lines as our discussion of state action: protection of the interests of the public, of the group, and of the individual.

Group Action for Public Protection. Many groups have special concern with a particular public interest which they seek to

---

13. See Bachman v. Mejias, 1 N.Y.
2d 575, 136 N.E.2d 866 (1956).

guard in court. The protection of civil liberties is the purpose of the American Civil Liberties Union. Conservation of natural resources, and separation of church and state are the concern of others. Flast v. Cohen [1] will do as an illustration of group action for public protection. The case involved a broad public question on the standing of a taxpayer to challenge the constitutionality of a federal appropriation, and a further question on the validity of a congressional appropriation part of which went to church schools. Ten different groups, moved by their interest in one or the other of the questions, appeared through counsel as amici curiae in the case.

Group Action for Group Protection. A few illustrations will be enough to show the variety of such organizations and their purposes. There may be a protective committee for a particular class of stockholders of a corporation which is in reorganization. The assertion of a common interest may be thrust upon the members of a group by a few assuming to act for all. This is so in a class action. In such an action one or more members of a group may sue or be sued as representative parties on behalf of all when the group is so large as to make joinder of all impracticable; there are common questions of fact or of law; the particular members are typical of the class as a whole; and the representative parties will fairly protect the interests of all. The Federal Rules of Civil Procedure deal with the matter in Rules concerning "Class Actions" generally, and two special kinds of such actions, "Derivative Actions by Shareholders" and "Actions Relating to Unincorporated Associations." [2]

Before the legislatures the labor unions and the employers' organizations seek legislation which they believe to be in the interest of their members. Every industry naturally has its eye on tariffs or regulations which may affect it. Proposed legislation to make possible class actions by "consumers" has the support of the National Legal Aid and Defender Association.[3] The National Association for the Advancement of Colored Peoples is an example of an organization formed primarily to safeguard the interests of a disadvantaged race. The National Bar Association combines professional, racial, and public purposes in the statement of its principles.

A labor union serves the interests of both the members as a group and of the individual members. When making a contract

---

1. 392 U.S. 83 (1968).

2. Fed.R.Civ.P., 23, 23.1, 23.2, 28 U.S.C.A.

3. "[C]lass actions will enhance the forensic opportunities of hitherto powerless groups and too often,

consumers' rights are not protected or enforced only because it is too cumbersome and costly to bring individual suits." Toll Testifies in Support of Consumer Class Action Bill, Legal Aid Briefcase, Oct. 1969, 23, 25.

with management it aids the group as a whole. When a member complains that management has violated the agreement to his injury, the union will aid him in grievance procedures before a labor arbitrator. In determining what shall be the wages of the several classes of its members under the labor contract, it is acting in somewhat the same role as an arbitrator between the classes.

As to corporations contests for control between the management and insurgents is usually carried on by a stockholders' committee with each side holding out the prospect of better conditions for the company and of the stockholders as a group.[4]

Group Action for Individual Protection. The legal aid associations have thus far sought primarily to protect the legal interests of the poor. Some labor unions seek to protect not only the group interests of their members but the interests of individual members under a union contract or workmen's compensation.

SECTION 4. INDIVIDUAL ACTION

Individual Action and Public Interests—In a consideration of individual action and public interests three situations call for mention. One is an individual legal right and action with incidental public effect; another is an individual right and action when both individual and public interests are directly involved; a third is an action by an individual when the public interest, but no special individual interest, is involved.

Most trials involve individuals protecting their individual interests. A sympathetic observer lauded the system under which matters of public moment may arise and be decided in private litigation.[1] Yet it may be wise to have a representative of the public heard in such a case. It may be helpful, as a great judge suggested, to enable the court to draw on aid beyond the briefs of the private parties in making the law for the public as well as deciding the individual controversy.[2]

The second situation mentioned, individual action where there are both private and public interests and legal rights, is illus-

---

4. See E. Aranow & H. Einhorn, Proxy Contests for Corporate Control 17 (2d ed. 1968).

1. J. Bryce, The American Commonwealth, Ch. XXIII (1893).

2. Traynor, Badlands in an Appellate Judge's Realm of Reason, 7 Utah L.Rev. 157, 170 (1960).

trated by the federal antitrust laws. There is the public interest forbidding monopoly. There is the private interest against suffering injury from monopoly. The antitrust laws give encouragement to the private person injured to sue by the three-fold damages provision. In suing under these laws, the injured private party is, as often said, a "private attorney general," whose suit and recovery give protection to the public interest against monopoly as well as protection to his own interest.

Another illustration is an action arising from air pollution when one person suffers special damage and there is also general harm to the public. A careful article shows that the party suffering special injury may maintain his action, as for abatement of a nuisance.[3]

A third illustration is a case with a notably fine opinion by Judge Tamm.[4] The second lowest bidder for a government contract sued to have the award to the successful bidder declared void because made in violation of administrative regulations. Although there was no right in the second lowest bidder to have the contract then awarded to it, the court found the losing bidder had a right to sue under Section 10 of the Administrative Procedure Act which provides that:

> "A person suffering legal wrong because of agency action, or adversely affected or aggrieved by agency action within the meaning of a relevant statute, is entitled to judicial review thereof." [5]

Continuing Judge Tamm emphasized the nature of the plaintiff's case:

> "[T]he essential thrust of appellant's claim on the merits is to satisfy the public interest in having agencies follow the regulations which control government contracting. The public interest in preventing the granting of contracts through arbitrary or capricious action can properly be vindicated through a suit brought by one who suffers injury as a result of the illegal activity, but the suit itself is brought in the public interest by one acting essentially as a 'private attorney-general'." [6]

Two situations have been discussed. One is the private action at law for the protection of the individual interest; the other is the private action when there are both private and public interests. Beyond these situations, there is the third, an action main-

---

3. Juergensmeyer, Control of Air Pollution Through the Assertion of Private Rights, 1967 Duke L.J. 1126.

4. Scanwell Laboratories, Inc. v. Shaffer, 424 F.2d 859 (D.C.Cir. 1970).

5. 5 U.S.C.A. § 702.

6. 424 F.2d 859, 864.

tained by private persons, not for the protection of their special interests or legal rights, but for the benefit of the public. "[T]he distinction [is] between the personal and proprietary interests of the traditional plaintiff," as Mr. Justice Harlan put it, "and the representative and public interests of the plaintiff in a public action." [7]

To illustrate the situations there will be stated two discordant decisions in attacks on federal appropriations and also three recent cases of attacks on administrative action. Then some factors will be outlined which bear on the wisdom of the creation of rights of action in private attorneys general.

Frothingham v. Mellon [8] was a challenge by a taxpayer to the constitutionality of a federal appropriation under the Maternity Act. The Supreme Court of the United States, though recognizing that state courts have entertained suits which attack the validity of state and municipal appropriations, dismissed the action without reaching the merits. Speaking for a unanimous court, Justice Sutherland rested the decision on several interlocking grounds. One set included the separation of powers principle, the refusal to entertain a political as distinguished from a legal question, lack of justiciability of the question, and lack of plaintiff's standing to sue. Another set included the "attendant inconvenience" if such a suit were permitted and the principle of *de minimis* as to the plaintiff's interest.

Flast v. Cohen,[9] arising a whole new court later, undertook
"a fresh examination of the limitations upon standing to sue in a federal court and the application of those limitations to taxpayer suits." [10]

The case was an attack by taxpayers on a federal appropriation, part of which might go to church schools, on the ground it violated the first amendment prohibition against the establishment of religion. The court held the plaintiffs had "standing to invoke a federal court's jurisdiction for an adjudication of the merits." The justices varied widely in opinion. One justice would recognize standing to sue whenever it was charged an appropriation violated the Constitution; two would do so only when the appropriation violated the establishment of religion prohibition; the majority would do so only when there was a certain nexus of the

---

7. See Flast v. Cohen, 392 U.S. 83, 119 n. 5 (1968). Informer statutes of a state and of the federal government have been upheld. Marvin v. Trout, 199 U.S. 212 (1905); United States ex rel. Marcus v. Hess, 317 U.S. 537 (1943).

8. 262 U.S. 447 (1923).

9. 392 U.S. 83 (1968).

10. Id. at 94.

plaintiff with the legislation attacked; and yet another, dissenting, would allow the action only when authorized by Congress.

The first of the three cases attacking administrative action is Gould v. Greylock Reservation Commission.[11]   This was an action brought in a Massachusetts state court by five citizens against a public commission to protect an unspoiled natural forest from conversion into a ski resort.   Without even pausing to discuss plaintiffs' standing the court, speaking through Mr. Justice Cutter, granted the relief sought.

Citizens Committee for the Hudson Valley v. Volpe,[12] another conservation case, was a suit in a federal court brought against state and federal officials to halt plans to fill in a portion of the Hudson River and form an expressway.   The petitioners included a citizens committee and the Sierra Club, a national organization.   On the issue of standing to sue Judge Moore, speaking for the Second Circuit, stated that the plaintiffs, although not claiming any individual or economic harm, were persons "aggrieved" by agency action and could maintain the suit.   Continuing the court said:

> "We hold, therefore, that the public interest in environmental resources—an interest created by statutes affecting the issuance of this permit—is a legally protected interest affording these plaintiffs, as responsible representatives of the public, standing to obtain judicial review of agency action alleged to be in contravention of that public interest." [13]

Association of Data Processing Service Organizations, Inc. v. Camp,[14] was an action brought by an organization of data processing companies.   The petitioner sought a review of a ruling of the Comptroller of the Currency that national banks could make data processing service available to other banks and to their customers.   The controversy involved the private interests of the plaintiff as well as the interests of the public, a subject discussed above, and as in other such cases the plaintiff's interest as a competitor was found to give it standing to sue.

The opinions in this case and in its companion, Barlow v. Collins [15], are of especial interest.   On the vexed question of the individual's "standing to sue" to challenge administrative action there were two opinions.   Prefacing his discussion with the comment, "Generalizations about standing to sue are largely worth-

---

11. 350 Mass. 410, 215 N.E.2d 114 (1966).

12. 425 F.2d 97 (2d Cir. 1970), cert. den. — U.S. —, 91 S.Ct. 237 (1970).

13. Id. at 105.

14. 397 U.S. 150 (1970).

15. 397 U.S. 159 (1970).

less as such," Mr. Justice Douglas insisted on one "necessary" generalization,

> "[T]he question of standing in the federal courts is to be considered in the framework of Article III which restricts judicial power to 'cases' and 'controversies'." [16]

He stated that there are two components of standing.

> "The first question is whether the plaintiff alleges that the challenged action has caused him injury in fact, economic or otherwise." [17]

> "[T]he [second] question [is] whether the interest sought to be protected by the complainant is arguably within the zone of interests to be protected or regulated by the statute or constitutional guarantee in question." [18]

Mr. Justice Brennan disagreed with the reasons given, stating:

> "My view is that the inquiry in the Court's first step is the only one which need be made to determine standing." [19]

Mr. Justice Brennan would distinguish "standing" sharply from two other questions. One is "Reviewability", that is, whether

> "Congress has stripped the judiciary of authority to review agency action." [20]

A third distinct question, Mr. Justice Brennan insisted, is the merits.

> "[W]hether the specific legal interest claimed by the plaintiff is protected by the statute and . . . whether the protested agency action invaded that interest." [21]

For a reason besides the discussion of standing Mr. Justice Douglas's opinion is of special interest. With obvious deliberateness the opinion goes much beyond the facts of the case in stating the breadth of interests for which a plaintiff may obtain protection under the Administrative Procedure Act or under the Constitution:

> "That interest, at times, may reflect 'aesthetic, conservational, and recreational' as well as economic values . . . . A person or a family may have a spiritual stake in First Amendment values sufficient to give him standing to raise issues concerning the Establishment Clause and the Free Exercise Clause . . . . We men-

---

16. 397 U.S. 150, 151.

17. Id. at 152.

18. Id. at 153.

19. Barlow v. Collins, 397 U.S. 159, 168 (1970). The same view is given

in a thorough discussion of "Standing" in 3 K. Davis, Administrative Law Treatise § 22.18 (1958).

20. 397 U.S. 159, 173.

21. Id. at 175.

tion these noneconomic values to emphasize that standing may stem from them as well as from the economic injury on which petitioner relies here. Certainly, he who is 'likely to be financially' injured . . . may be a reliable private attorney general to litigate the issues of the public interest in the present case.[22]

The opinion continued with a statement of the Court's general attitude toward judicial review:

"There is no presumption against judicial review and in favor of administrative absolutism . . . unless that purpose is fairly discernible in the statutory scheme." [23]

This review of a few illustrative cases shows that several factors are relevant in determining whether individual action shall be allowed for the protection of the public interest. One is the form of state action which is attacked. Naturally the courts are less willing to entertain an attack on a statute of the legislature on constitutional grounds than an attack on an order of an administrative commission for failure to observe a statutory directive. Another factor is the importance of the particular public interest. Two of the justices in the Flast case found this decisive, and they would allow an attack on a Congressional appropriation only if it violated the fundamental prohibition against aiding the establishment of religion. The wisdom of substituting the judgment of a court for the determination of another organ of government, whether legislature or executive or commission, is an obvious consideration. Its force may be affected by the court's view on whether through our political processes the public interests can obtain protection in other ways [24] and, as to actions by commissions, on whether the regulatory body is lethargic or has been captured intellectually and sympathetically by the interests which it was established to regulate.

The attitude toward litigation as something to be encouraged or discouraged is an important factor, even when unstated. Plaintiffs' counsel in these actions have the triple attraction of personal publicity, public interest, and fees. The nature of the particular plaintiff, as a "responsible body," in contrast with a person bringing a strike suit, has been referred to.[25] Rarely

---

22. 397 U.S. 150, 154.

23. Id. at 157.

24. This element is illustrated by the unresponsive but revealing answer given to a question put to a Tennessee legislator when litigation on the legal duty to reapportion was pending. Professor Paul Sanders asked how the legislator,

a leader of the rural bloc, could justify his vote against reapportionment for electoral purposes as the Constitution of the state required it and he had taken an oath to uphold the Constitution. The answer was: "We have the power and we intend to keep it."

25. See supra p. 392.

mentioned but important is the burden cast on the public official or body which is attacked, in justifying its action. Mr. Justice Harlan put the matter in summary form:

> "This and other federal courts have repeatedly held that individual litigants, acting as private attorneys-general, may have standing as 'representatives of the public interest.' . . . The problem ultimately presented by this case is . . . to determine in what circumstances, consonant with the character and proper functioning of the federal courts, such suits should be permitted." [26]

Individual Action and Group Interests.—To illustrate actions by individuals to protect group interests it is enough to mention two purposes, one economic and the other social.

The minority shareholder's suit is brought to protect the economic interest of the petitioner and of his group. The requirements in the federal courts for class actions of this sort have already been mentioned.[27] To discourage the harassment of management by holders of a petty number of shares, some states have enacted statutes which call for the petitioner to satisfy requirements of substantial stock ownership. A state requirement of this sort has been held applicable to a suit brought in a federal court in the state.[28] A case which goes as far as any in allowing a class action for economic purposes is one brought against the Yellow Cab Company of San Francisco for overcharging its passengers, both those who used scrip and those who paid in cash.[29] Despite the looseness of the class, the action was a pretty effective sanction in a business in which petty overcharging is common.

The private suit brought for the social purpose of protecting a disadvantaged group is described in the *Button* case. The NAACP solicited and financed law suits brought by Negroes to achieve school desegregation. As Mr. Justice Brennan said:

> "In the context of NAACP objectives, litigation is not a technique of resolving private differences; it is a means for achieving the lawful objectives of equality of treatment . . . for the members of the Negro community in this country." [30]

---

26. Flast v. Cohen, 392 U.S. 83, 120 (1968) (dissenting opinion). See Davis, The Liberalized Law of Standing, 37 U.Chi.L.Rev. 450 (1970); 3 K. Davis, Administrative Law Treatise § 22.10.

27. See Fed.R.Civ.P., Rules 23, 23.1, 23.2.

28. Cohen v. Beneficial Indus. Loan Corp., 337 U.S. 541 (1949).

29. Daar v. Yellow Cab Co., 67 Cal. 2d 695, 63 Cal.Rptr. 724, 433 P.2d 732 (1967).

30. National Ass'n for the Advancement of Colored People v. Button, 371 U.S. 415, 429 (1963).

The court protected the plan and the participants against condemnation by state law.

Conclusion. With science, technology and industry bringing men closer together and, in the process, polluting the environment of all, there is increasing importance of action by the group and the state to protect the individual. There is increasing importance, too, of the subject which the chapter has barely sketched, the interplay of actions at law by one of the three to safeguard the interests of another. New opportunities are opening up for courts and lawyers.

The courts should not repeat the sort of mistake made by the English courts centuries ago when they confined themselves narrowly within the system of the established writs. They should not allow themselves to be held back by such negative and legalistic conceptions as those employed in the *Frothingham* case. In the development of the law some courts may be aided by fictions, as by the use of the idea of "trust." It would be better to face new situations squarely and to meet new problems with new solutions, as Dean Prosser says they have done in his field and created "new *and nameless* torts".[31] The guide is "the public interest" in the largest sense.

This chapter discusses actions in court only. It may be that the public interest can be served in better ways as by legislative direction or the creation of administrative bodies with wide powers.

In Tijerina v. Henry, 48 F.R.D. 274 (D.N.M.1969), a class action was brought by two men with the Legal Aid Society as counsel. The suit represented a class designated as Indo-Hispano also called Mexican, Mexican-American and Spanish American, and also on behalf of "the poor" as those who qualify for free legal process under the law of the state. The suit sought equal educational opportunities. The District Court dismissed the action because of the indefiniteness of the alleged class. The Supreme Court dismissed the appeal, Mr. Justice Douglas dissenting, in an opinion. 396 U.S. 922, 90 S.Ct. 1718 (1970).

31. W. Prosser, Handbook of the Law of Torts 3 (3d ed. 1964) (emphasis added).

Chapter XIX

THE LIVES OF THE LAWYER

SECTION 1. INTRODUCTION

"The law is a jealous mistress." If this old saying means the lawyer's work is hard, it is true. If it is taken to mean that the good lawyer need devote his whole time to the study of the rules of law, it is wrong.

The lawyer does not deal with law alone. He is concerned with the activities of men in the context of law. A justice of the Supreme Court of the United States, when asked whether non-legal studies should be a part of the law school curriculum, replied that he knew of no such thing as non-legal studies, since all studies concern themselves with human activity and understanding. A federal district judge, ruling on the scope of the attorney-client privilege, stated as a guiding consideration:

> "The modern lawyer almost invariably advises his client upon not only what is permissible but also what is desirable. And it is in the public interest that the lawyer should regard himself as more than predicter of legal consequences. His duty to society as well as to his client involves many relevant social, economic, political and philosophical considerations." [1]

The lawyer lives three lives—in private practice, in public activities, and as an individual. They are not lived in different periods. Nor are they opposed in their nature. They are lived at the same time and they contribute to one another. They have the common quality of being lived in swiftly changing times with consequent need in the lawyer for repeated self-renewal:

> "During all human history until this century, the rate of social change has been very slow. So slow that it would pass unnoticed in one person's lifetime. That is no longer so. The rate of change has increased so much that our imagination can't keep up." [2]

1. Wyzanski, J., in United States v. United Shoe Mach. Corp., 89 F. Supp. 357, 359 (D.Mass.1950).

2. C. Snow, The Two Cultures and a Second Look 42–43 (1963).

SECTION 2.   PRIVATE PRACTICE

Private practice consists of the individualization of law through applying and utilizing the law for clients. The opportunities and responsibilities are discussed earlier in the book, and the discussion will not be repeated. Two aspects of it will be mentioned, the usefulness of the lawyer and the intellectual apparatus he employs.

Usefulness. The usefulness of the lawyer in court is obvious. Our adversary system of administration of law calls for expert representatives. The usefulness of the lawyer, even his necessity, in representing an accused is the basis of the constitutional right to counsel in criminal cases. In civil matters the advocate is worthy of his hire. The personal injury claimant has a better chance of recovery, as well as a chance of a higher net recovery, when represented by a lawyer.[1] Even in the Small Claims Court, supposed as it is to do away with the need for lawyers, a judge, "very sensitive to the rights of the *pro se* party," regretfully found that in nearly all cases he was compelled to find for the side represented by counsel because of "the facts and law developed by counsel's superior skill." [2]

On "ordinary" office work, a conference statement is enough to remind us of its importance:

> A lawyer like other men, is engaged most of the time on what might be termed small individual matters. Perhaps it may be the drafting of a will, the drawing of a contract for a merchant, the examination of a real estate title . . . . There is a temptation to think of these matters as trivial, even inconsequential. Yet each is important and, it may be, vital to the client. What is more, they are all part of the larger things. They are the very embodiment of such fundamentals as private property, the distribution of goods, and equal protection of the laws. These fundamental ideas and institutions find their expression and meaning in their application to individual matters . . . . [E]ach individual matter is a part of the larger institutions whose policies and needs will shape the application and growth of the law.[3]

1. See F. Mackinnon, Contingent Fees for Legal Services 168–170 (1964).

2. T. Murphy, "D. C. Small Claims Court—The Forgotten Court," 34 D.C.B.J. 14, 16 (1967).

3. J. Stone, Legal Education and Public Responsibility 356–357 (1959).

In the representation of large units which dominate the economy, lawyers have responsibilities as well as powers which the clear sighted perceive. A leader of the insurance industry attributed to the over-zealousness of its counsel the spate of harsh decisions which followed.[4] A leader of the Wall Street bar drew the general conclusion of restraint in advice and action.

> "[I]t behooves all of us who render 'specialized service to business and finance' to seek such solutions of the legal problems of our clients as are compatible with changing social concepts and as will avoid the abuses of economic power to which our profession too often contributed in past decades." [5]

Whether this be only intelligent self-interest of the lawyers for their clients scarcely matters. The important thing is that these lawyers, and their clients too, have come to perceive, and to contribute to, the responsible exercise of power by big business.

For still larger purposes lawyers are useful. They are essential to our "legal polity," our system of government under law. The meanest citizen may call the government to account and require the government to accord him respect in even small matters.[6]

Intellectual Method. The intellectual method employed by lawyers is well described by an English writer in a paraphrase of the German jurist, Jhering.

> "What the lawyer does, he says in effect, when he takes over the management of a department of social life, whether it be the feudal system, or the custom of merchants, or the relations created by marriage and the family, is to dissect certain things out of, or to read certain things into, the unanalysed medley presented to him by popular custom, the policy of rulers, and the current precepts of religion and morality. These things which the lawyer reads into, or makes definite in his material, are technical concepts, such as things, persons, rights, obligations, ownership, possession, conditions, estates, contract, conveyance, fault, negligence, estoppel, and a hundred more. Borne along by the institutional sense, and by the impulse to give ideas the clear contours of things, the lawyer invests these concepts with a species of independent life, and planting them in a soil rich in dialectic and logical consistency, exposing them to the fertilizing influence of ever-diversified circumstance, he fosters their

4. Parkinson & McComb, Are the Law Schools Adequately Training for the Public Service? 8 Am.L. School Rev. 291, 294 (1935).

5. Swaine, Impact of Big Business on the Profession: An Answer to Critics of the Modern Bar, 35 A.B.A.J. 89, 171 (1949).

6. See supra p. 21.

growth, like a gardener, until from such simple seedlings as the notions of pledge or of seisin he produces such blooms as the floating charge or trustees to preserve contingent remainders.　.　.　.

"The dialectical method of the lawyer is everywhere the same in its general character, isolating, emphasizing, and cultivating abstract technical ideas, under which particular concrete cases are subsumed, and thus conferring upon the practical conclusions reached the socially desirable characters of neutrality, generality, and logical necessity—in short, of justice."[7]

This is a useful warning to us lawyers not to be deceived into confusing our technical constructs and apparatus with the underlying reality.　We will be on our guard against the reification of our concepts, against giving them as Professor Amos says "a species of independent life."

SECTION 3.　PUBLIC RESPONSIBILITIES

"A Lawyer Should Assist in Improving the Legal System."[1] This brief Canon 8 of the Code of Professional Responsibility is given breadth of meaning by the accompanying Ethical Considerations.　"Changes in human affairs and imperfections in human institutions," EC 8–1 states, "makes necessary constant efforts to maintain and improve our legal system."　Rules of law are deficient if they are not just, understandable and," EC 8–2 adds, "responsive to the needs of society."

The Code calls for much more than improvement in the methods of law administration.　It affirms the duty of lawyers to help develop a legal system which is "just, understandable, and responsive to the needs of society."　The background against which the Code asserts this broad professional responsibility for social change through law was indicated by Justice Stone:

"No tradition of our profession is more cherished by lawyers than that of its leadership in public affairs.　.　.　. The great figures of the law stir the imagination and inspire our reverence according as they have used their special training and gifts for the advancement of the public interest."[2]

---

7. Amos, The Legal Mind, 49 L.Q. Rev. 27, 37, 40 (1933).

1. The Canon is discussed in J. Frank, Canon 8 and a Rising Aspiration, 48 Tex.L.Rev. 380 (1970).

2. Stone, The Public Influence of the Bar, 48 Harv.L.Rev. 1, 2 (1934).

Our democracy carries on public activities in different ways all of which draw on law-trained men. The two major classes are governmental and non-governmental activities. The first class includes the three stated arms of government. Lawyers have had a large share in the legislative branch.[3] They have a major share in the second branch, the executive; almost the whole of the third branch, the judiciary; and a great share in what has come to be almost a fourth branch, the administrative commissions. This has come about, so it is suggested, because "the skills which the lawyer develops in interpersonal mediation, conciliation and verbal persuasion are directly applicable to the political process."[4]

The non-governmental class include representation of the major economic units, as Big Business and Big Labor, which, with the aid of science and technology, have created the affluent society. With new international opportunities, with federal income taxes taking half its net income, and with increasing regulation by law of its practices and products, Big Business needs legal advisors at every turn. The lawyers and the clients, fortunately, have an increasing sense of the responsibilities which their positions bring.

A marked characteristic of our society is the ability to carry forward public work, especially of a path-breaking nature, outside government:

> "A century and a quarter ago, Alexis de Tocqueville marvelled at the private initiative of Americans. They walked across the street, he reported, formed a committee, and handled the matter without a by-your-leave to any bureaucrat. They are still doing it. Through foundations, institutes, corporations, unions, schools, churches, associations, leagues, movements, drives, and sundry other forms of private cooperative action, Americans meet and deal successfully with a multitude of intrinsically public concerns."[5]

These activities by their freedom from political direction make possible public service outside government and increase initia-

---

3. Thirty-one of the fifty members of the Continental Congress were lawyers. Continuing the preponderance of lawyers in the legislative bodies at the highest levels, "[i]n the seventy-first through the seventy-fifth Congress, from 61 to 76 per cent members of the Senate and from 56 to 65 per cent of the members of the House of Representatives belonged to the legal profession." H. Eulau & J. Sprague, Lawyers in Politics 12 (1964).

4. Barber, Some Problems in the Sociology of the Professions, in The Professions in America 30 (K. Lynn & Eds. of Daedalus 1965). The preponderance of lawyers in public activities and the reason for it are discussed in A. Blaustein & C. Porter, The American Lawyer 97–100 (1954).

5. A. Heard, The Costs of Democracy 454–455 (1960).

tive in our pluralistic society. Here lawyers who do not desire political office or who would be unacceptable to the electorate contribute much to public life.

The formation and guidance of public opinion is fundamental to our democracy. Holders of political office are rarely leaders on controversial matters, rather they are mediators and followers of public opinion so they may continue in office. Lawyers outside political office can do much to lead and shape public opinion. An illustrative area is racial adjustment. "The Special Committee on Civil Rights and Racial Unrest" appointed in 1963 at the request of President Kennedy began its report with the statement, "Civilization cannot exist without order, and order cannot be maintained without law". The Committee called upon the individual lawyer

> "to assist to the fullest extent of his capabilities in procuring communication and understanding between the races
> .   .   .   to help develop and support needed affirmative legislation or programs   .   .   .   ." [6]

Other disadvantaged groups, too, have had rising expectations. In the first decade of the century Mr. Louis D. Brandeis, later Mr. Justice Brandeis, spoke of the labor movement. He speculated on the way in which the movement would go forward, either "wisely and temperately or wildly and intemperately," and he told his audience, "Nothing can better fit you for taking part in the solution of this problem than the study and preeminently the practice of law." [7]

In shaping public opinion the lawyer has the duty to be competent, that is to assure so far as he can that his own opinions are informed and wise. Writing on responsibility in shaping public opinion Dean Wade asked each lawyer to be careful to consider both sides and, more difficult, to identify and discount his own prejudices before making a determination:

> "Let me remind you of Oliver Cromwell's statement to the Scots just before the battle of Dunbar: 'I beseech ye in the bowels of Christ, bethink ye that ye may be mistaken.' " [8]

From the foundation of a feeling of competence, the lawyer may move on to influence the opinions and actions of others.

Naturally, a lawyer will choose his areas of public participation so his efforts may count for most. There are so many things beckoning that there is the temptation to emulate the fabled rid-

---

6. 88 A.B.A.Rep. 614, 615 (1963).

7. Brandeis, The Opportunity in the Law (1905), reprinted in L. Brandeis, Business—A Profession (1925).

8. Wade, Public Responsibilities of the Learned Professions, 21 La.L. Rev. 130, 137 (1960).

er who, leaving a tavern after a few drinks too many, jumped on his horse and rode off in all directions.

Some young lawyers might put aside and delay these opportunities and duties at a stage when immediate necessities loom so large, as making a living for their families and themselves. It would be most unfortunate if they yielded to such feelings. Unused interests and talents shrivel. The young lawyer has much to contribute in his own time.

There is an area of special responsibility and opportunity for lawyers, law administration. The system of law administration is entrusted to lawyers. They can know whether the existing system is working well and what changes are needed. To make this determination, however, lawyers need to look up from the sort of daily routine in which we are all engaged and to view the system in the light of its purpose. Inertia and habit make this difficult.

Two members of the Supreme Court of the United States have warned us against taking the accustomed as the necessary or the best. Justice Jackson, in his preliminary report on the methods of the Nuremberg trial wrote:

> "Members of the legal profession acquire a rather emotional attachment to forms and customs to which they are accustomed and frequently entertain a passionate conviction that no unfamiliar procedure can be morally right." [9]

Chief Justice Warren on the eve of his retirement attacked the overly contentiousness of our system of administration of law which he said was "at the heart of the malfunctioning of our urban courts." [10] He quoted from Dean Pound's St. Paul address of 1906 in condemning "our American exaggerations of the common law contentious procedure, [t]he sporting theory of justice." [11]

An English parallel, described by Professor Sunderland, is a useful warning.[12] Beginning in the early 1800's there was an attack by lay critics on the English system of procedure. The violence of the attack is illustrated by a passage on "Pleading" in the usually restrained Encyclopedia Britannica:

> "This mischievous mess, which exists in defiance and mockery of reason, English lawyers inform us, is a strict, and

---

9. Report (to the Secretary of State) of Robert H. Jackson, United States Representative to the International Conference on Military Trials vi & x (1945).

10. Warren, Observation: The Advocate and the Administration of Justice in an Urban Society, 47 Tex.L. Rev. 615, 619 (1969).

11. Pound, The Causes of Popular Dissatisfaction with the Administration of Justice, 29 A.B.A.Rep. 395 (1906).

12. Sunderland, The English Struggle for Procedural Reform, 39 Harv. L.Rev. 725 (1926).

pure, and beautiful exemplication of the rules of logic.
.   .   .   All that they see in the system of pleading is
the mode of performing it." [13]

The exemplar of the bar was Lord Eldon, "devoting all the resources of a powerful and technical mind to the preservation of
the current practices of his day." Criticisms were rejected as
"such ribaldry" that there was "no manner of reply which well-
bred persons can employ". The profession did little to change its
ways. The upshot was that the reform of procedure came about
through the leadership of laymen.

For this reason, perhaps, the Chairman of the present Law
Commission with its broad assignment began a discussion of the
Commission and its role by drawing a parallel between the gener-
als and the lawyers:

> "You will all remember the famous saying that war is too se-
> rious a matter to be left to generals. We in England think
> that it is possibly also true that law reform is far too seri-
> ous a matter to be left to the legal profession." [14]

Stating his belief that society "should continue to recognize law
as 'the premier profession'," he suggested as the real test for law
reform

> "[W]hether we as professional men are prepared to lay our
> hands to the reform of questions of law which profoundly af-
> fect interests of great importance to society." [15]

To return to Professor Sunderland's article, he found the
court system of his day grossly inadequate. It was his hope that
the needed changes would be the result of "a broadened and so-
cialized legal education." Could Professor Sunderland write today, almost surely he would place his hope and reliance on bar
associations and some of their leaders who are the kind of men
he envisaged. Not all bar associations, certainly, and not all association members. But the number is large who give much of
their time and thought to the improvement of law administration, broadly conceived, and their labors are manifold.[16] The
achievements in some areas make manifest opportunities in still
other areas, as illustrated by Chief Justice Burger's insistence
that we move from improved methods for defense of the accused

---

13. Id. at 733, quoting Mill, Juris-
     prudence, in Encyclopedia Britan-
     nica (Supp.1828).

14. Scarman, The Role of the Legal
     Profession in Law Reform, 21 Rec-
     ord of N.Y.C.B.A. 11, 12 (1966).

15. Id. at 16.

16. At the cost of seeming to slight
     many others who deserve our grati-
     tude, mention should be made of
     Chief Justice Arthur T. Vanderbilt
     of New Jersey a sketch of whose
     amazing career in law administra-
     tion by his effective co-worker,
     Judge Charles E. Clark, is a fore-
     word to 1 Selected Writings of Ar-
     thur T. Vanderbilt xvii (J. Klien &
     J. Lee 1965).

on to improved methods of correction and treatment of the convicted.[17]

This emphasis on law administration must not obscure for an instant the wider roles the lawyer has in public life. Ours is a *"legal polity"* is a characterization quoted earlier. It is not only our polity, but much of our economy and our social institutions as well that are shaped and reshaped by law. There is no lack of public opportunity for the lawyer. As Mr. Justice Brennan wrote the legalistic nature of our society

> "has caused the society to frame urgent social, economic and political questions in legal terms—to place great problems of social order in the hands of lawyers for their definition, and in the hands of judges for their ultimate resolution.
>
> "Today, the lawyer is still the indispensable middleman of our social progress. . . . In truth, I think the lawyer's role is more important today than ever." [18]

SECTION 4.   THE INDIVIDUAL

> "The makers of our Constitution undertook to secure conditions favorable to the pursuit of happiness. They recognized the significance of man's spiritual nature, of his feelings and of his intellect. They knew that only a part of the pain, pleasure and satisfactions of life are to be found in material things. They sought to protect Americans in their beliefs, their thoughts, their emotions and their sensations. They conferred, as against the Government, the right to be let alone—the most comprehensive of rights and the right most valued by civilized men." [1]

What can one man say to another on matters so individual and personal that the most important aspect is "the right to be let alone"? Possibly, it may be useful to mention some things which

---

17. Burger, A Proposal: A National Conference on Correctional Problems, in Monograph No. 3, Section of Individual Rights and Responsibilities, Am.B.Ass'n. at 1 (1969).

18. Brennan, The Responsibilities of the Legal Profession, 54 A.B.A.J. 121 (1968).

1. Mr. Justice Brandeis dissenting in Olmstead v. United States, 277 U.S. 438, 478 (1928). Mr. Justice Holmes and Mr. Justice Stone concurred in the dissent.

for others have been sources of strength, of re-creation, of self-renewal.

Family, religion.[2]

Gardening, yachting.

Painting, music, poetry, drama, philosophy.

Group discussion, solitude.

History. The understanding this may give a man of movements and developments in his own time, and the sense of being a part of something immensely greater than himself.

Studies of society and of the individual. These subjects basic to law do not as yet have the definiteness of conclusions to offer to the lawyer that the natural sciences give to the physician. They are gaining in methods and in dependability of findings.

The perception of another culture with understanding and sympathy. It may be a culture of his own time and place, whether the intellectual culture of the natural sciences of which the lawyer with his literary culture may be only dimly aware;[3] or the social culture of his neighbors, the disadvantaged, out of which they seek to lift themselves. It may be the culture of another place, of which an intellectual leader of the United Nations spoke in urging us to break out of our professional grooves:[4]

> "[T]he deeply divided, diversified world with its enormous barriers to understanding. For this, we need something more than methodology or history. We are in the realm of the intangibles, sympathy, identification, heroism, tragedy, pride. These are the factors best perceived through literary and humanistic studies but surely they are not entirely foreign to law school studies."

Literature. Law calls for an understanding of our fellow humans. In our daily life we can know only a few people well. Through literature we can observe and know many more, and we may come to sympathize with them or at least to understand their emotions and actions.[5]

A stirring or at least satisfying conception of his profession, and its work. It may be of the profession in idealized form as by Maitre Clunet,[6] or of the work of the lawyer in defending the

---

2. See J. Pike, Beyond the Law (1963).

3. See C. Snow, The Two Cultures and a Second Look (1963).

4. Schachter, Remarks, in II Proceedings, Ass'n Am.L.Schools 157, 161 (1966).

5. A Chicago lawyer has told how Balzac was his guide in prolonged and successful litigation with a miser. Loesch, The Acquisition and Retention of a Clientage, 1 Ill.L. Rev. 455, 465–467 (1907).

6. Supra pp. 58–59.

hated,[7] or the devotions of time to continuing visits to prisons and the uplift this gives to men who feel themselves forgotten.

The law schools require a period of college education before the study of law begins. The requirement is imposed to encourage the development of breadth of interest and understanding, not to assure a period of aging in ivy. The cultural interests developed in college should not be smothered and destroyed in the years of study and practice of law. It is for each man to choose from the many opportunities before him some of which have been mentioned. He may find a more satisfying life in the law through leading a fuller one beyond it.

Can a man lift himself by his bootstraps? Yes, probably. "We are only beginning to understand," a noted lawyer-sociologist wrote, "the power of individuals to shape their own character by the selection among models and experiences." [8] The association of young lawyers, with older men, whether living or dead, whom they admire, was urged by Mr. Justice Brennan.[9] The reading of Pusey's biography of Hughes changed his life, a student said for it made him perceive what great things can be done by a man of law.

The three lives of the lawyer contribute to one another as said by one who lived them all:

> "I am convinced that what leads the lawyer to give of his talents, beyond what has been called 'client serving,' to some form of work of value to the community is a search for variety and a spirit of adventure more than it is a sense of duty or a desire to perform professional or public obligations. To put it in another way, the impulse does not come from the conscience of lawyers as much as from their common sense. It is not a compulsion to do good in the interest of others, but rather to live one's own life to the full." [10]

7. Supra p. 343.

8. Riesman, The Study of National Character: Some Observations on the American Case, 13 Harv.Lib. Bull. 5, 24 (1959).

9. "I include in apprenticeship a dedication to the life or the works or both, of a figure who commands respect and admiration, whether a living figure or a figure understood through history."   W. Brennan, Occas.Pamph. No. 9, Harv.L.Sch. (1967).

10. Harrison Tweed, One Lawyer's Life, in Listen to Leaders in Law, 303, 324 (A. Love & J. Childers eds. 1963).

APPENDIX

CODE OF PROFESSIONAL RESPONSIBILITY *

Table of Contents

* Adopted by the American Bar Association at annual meeting in Dallas, Texas, on Aug. 12, 1969. Copyrighted by American Bar Association. Published with permission.

CODE OF PROFESSIONAL RESPONSIBILITY

*

CODE OF PROFESSIONAL RESPONSIBILITY

With amendments to February 24, 1970

Preamble [1]

The continued existence of a free and democratic society depends upon recognition of the concept that justice is based upon the rule of law grounded in respect for the dignity of the individual and his capacity through reason for enlightened self-government.[2] Law so grounded makes justice possible, for only through such law does the dignity of the individual attain respect and protection. Without it, individual rights become subject to unrestrained power, respect for law is destroyed, and rational self-government is impossible.

Lawyers, as guardians of the law, play a vital role in the preservation of society. The fulfillment of this role requires an understanding by lawyers of their relationship with and function in our legal system.[3] A consequent obligation of lawyers is to maintain the highest standards of ethical conduct.

In fulfilling his professional responsibilities, a lawyer necessarily assumes various roles that require the performance of many difficult tasks. Not every situation which he may encounter can be foreseen,[4] but fundamental ethical principles are always present to guide him. Within the framework of these principles, a lawyer must with courage and foresight be able and ready to shape

the body of the law to the ever-changing relationships of society.[5]

The Code of Professional Responsibility points the way to the aspiring and provides standards by which to judge the transgressor. Each lawyer must find within his own conscience the touchstone against which to test the extent to which his actions should rise above minimum standards. But in the last analysis it is the desire for the respect and confidence of the members of his profession and of the society which he serves that should provide to a lawyer the incentive for the highest possible degree of ethical conduct. The possible loss of that respect and confidence is the ultimate sanction. So long as its practitioners are guided by these principles, the law will continue to be a noble profession. This is its greatness and its strength, which permit of no compromise.

Preliminary Statement

In furtherance of the principles stated in the Preamble, the American Bar Association has promulgated this Code of Professional Responsibility, consisting of three separate but interrelated parts: Canons, Ethical Considerations, and Disciplinary Rules.[6] The Code is designed to be adopted by appropriate agencies both as an inspirational guide to the members of the profession and as a basis for disciplinary action when the conduct of a lawyer falls below the required minimum standards stated in the Disciplinary Rules.

Obviously the Canons, Ethical Considerations, and Disciplinary Rules cannot apply to non-lawyers; however, they do define the type of ethical conduct that the public has a right to expect not

---

[1] The footnotes are intended merely to enable the reader to relate the provisions of this Code to the ABA Canons of Professional Ethics adopted in 1908, as amended, the Opinions of the ABA Committee on Professional Ethics, and a limited number of other sources; they are not intended to be an annotation of the views taken by the ABA Special Committee on Evaluation of Ethical Standards. Footnotes citing ABA Canons refer to the ABA Canons of Professional Ethics, adopted in 1908, as amended.

[2] Cf. ABA Canons, Preamble.

[3] "[T]he lawyer stands today in special need of a clear understanding of his obligations and of the vital connection between those obligations and the role his profession plays in society." Professional Responsibility: Report of the Joint Conference, 44 A.B.A.J. 1159, 1160 (1958).

[4] "No general statement of the responsibilities of the legal profession can encompass all the situations in which the lawyer may be placed. Each position held by him makes its own peculiar demands. These demands the lawyer must clarify for himself in the light of the particular role in which he serves." Professional Responsibility: Report of the Joint Conference, 44 A.B.A.J. 1159, 1218 (1958).

[5] "The law and its institutions change as social conditions change. They must change if they are to preserve, much less advance, the political and social values from which they derive their purposes and their life. This is true of the most important of legal institutions, the profession of law. The profession, too, must change when conditions change in order to preserve and advance the social values that are its reasons for being." Cheatham, Availability of Legal Services: The Responsibility of the Individual Lawyer and the Organized Bar, 12 U.C.L.A.L. Rev. 438, 440 (1965).

[6] The Supreme Court of Wisconsin adopted a Code of Judicial Ethics in 1967. "The code is divided into standards and rules, the standards being statements of what the general desirable level of conduct should be, the rules being particular canons, the violation of which shall subject an individual judge to sanctions." In re Promulgation of a Code of Judicial Ethics, 36 Wis.2d 252, 255, 153 N.W. 2d 873, 874 (1967).

The portion of the Wisconsin Code of Judicial Ethics entitled "Standards" states that "[t]he following standards set forth the significant qualities of the ideal judge . . . ." Id., 36 Wis.2d at 256, 153 N.W.2d at 875. The portion entitled "Rules" states that "[t]he court promulgates the following rules because the requirements of judi-

only of lawyers but also of their non-professional employees and associates in all matters pertaining to professional employment. A lawyer should ultimately be responsible for the conduct of his employees and associates in the course of the professional representation of the client.

The Canons are statements of axiomatic norms, expressing in general terms the standards of professional conduct expected of lawyers in their relationships with the public, with the legal system, and with the legal profession. They embody the general concepts from which the Ethical Considerations and the Disciplinary Rules are derived.

The Ethical Considerations are aspirational in character and represent the objectives toward which every member of the profession should strive. They constitute a body of principles upon which the lawyer can rely for guidance in many specific situations.[7]

The Disciplinary Rules, unlike the Ethical Considerations, are mandatory in character. The Disciplinary Rules state the minimum level of conduct below which no lawyer can fall without being subject to disciplinary action. Within the framework of fair trial,[8] the Disciplinary Rules should

---

cial conduct embodied therein are of sufficient gravity to warrant sanctions if they are not obeyed . . . ." *Id.,* 36 Wis.2d at 259, 153 N.W.2d at 876.

[7] "Under the conditions of modern practice it is peculiarly necessary that the lawyer should understand, not merely the established standards of professional conduct, but the reasons underlying these standards. Today the lawyer plays a changing and increasingly varied role. In many developing fields the precise contribution of the legal profession is as yet undefined." *Professional Responsibility: Report of the Joint Conference,* 44 A.B.A.J. 1159 (1958).

"A true sense of professional responsibility must derive from an understanding of the reasons that lie back of specific restraints, such as those embodied in the Canons. The grounds for the lawyer's peculiar obligations are to be found in the nature of his calling. The lawyer who seeks a clear understanding of his duties will be led to reflect on the special services his profession renders to society and the services it might render if its full capacities were realized. When the lawyer fully understands the nature of his office, he will then discern what restraints are necessary to keep that office wholesome and effective." *Id.*

[8] "Disbarment, designed to protect the public, is a punishment or penalty imposed on the lawyer. . . . He is accordingly entitled to procedural due process, which includes fair notice of the charge." In re Ruffalo, 390 U.S. 544, 550, 20 L.Ed.2d 117, 122, 88 S.Ct. 1222, 1226 (1968), *rehearing denied,* 391 U.S. 961, 20 L.Ed.2d 874, 88 S.Ct. 1833 (1968).

"A State cannot exclude a person from the practice of law or from any other occupation in a manner or for reasons that contravene the Due Process or Equal Protection Clause of the Fourteenth Amendment. . . . A State can require high standards of qualification . . . but any qualification must have a rational connection with the applicant's fitness or capacity to practice law." Schware v. Bd. of Bar Examiners, 353 U.S. 232, 239, 1 L.Ed.2d 796, 801–02, 77 S.Ct. 752, 756 (1957).

"[A]n accused lawyer may expect that he will not be condemned out of a capricious self-righteousness or denied the essentials of a fair hearing." Kingsland v. Dorsey, 338 U.S. 318, 320, 94 L.Ed. 123, 126, 70 S.Ct. 123, 124–25 (1949).

"The attorney and counsellor being, by the solemn judicial act of the court, clothed with his office, does not hold

---

be uniformly applied to all lawyers,[9] regardless of the nature of their professional activities.[10] The Code makes no attempt to prescribe either disciplinary procedures or penalties [11] for violation of a Disciplinary Rule,[12] nor does it undertake to define standards for civil liability of lawyers for professional conduct. The severity of judgment against one found guilty of violating a Disciplinary Rule should be determined by the character of the offense and the attendant circumstances.[13] An enforcing agency, in applying the Disciplinary Rules, may find interpretive guidance in the basic principles embodied in the Canons and in the objectives reflected in the Ethical Considerations.

---

it as a matter of grace and favor. The right which it confers upon him to appear for suitors, and to argue causes, is something more than a mere indulgence, revocable at the pleasure of the court, or at the command of the legislature. It is a right of which he can only be deprived by the judgment of the court, for moral or professional delinquency." Ex parte Garland, 71 U.S. (4 Wall.) 333, 378–79, 18 L.Ed. 366, 370 (1866).

See generally Comment, *Procedural Due Process and Character Hearings for Bar Applicants,* 15 Stan.L.Rev. 500 (1963).

[9] "The canons of professional ethics must be enforced by the Courts and must be respected by members of the Bar if we are to maintain public confidence in the integrity and impartiality of the administration of justice." In re Meeker, 76 N.M. 354, 357, 414 P.2d 862, 864 (1966), *appeal dismissed,* 385 U.S. 449 (1967).

[10] *See* ABA Canon 45.
"The Canons of this Association govern all its members, irrespective of the nature of their practice, and the application of the Canons is not affected by statutes or regulations governing certain activities of lawyers which may prescribe less stringent standards." ABA Comm. on Professional Ethics, *OPINIONS,* No. 203 (1940) [hereinafter each Opinion is cited as *"ABA Opinion"*].

Cf. ABA Opinion 152 (1936).

[11] "There is generally no prescribed discipline for any particular type of improper conduct. The disciplinary measures taken are discretionary with the courts, which may disbar, suspend, or merely censure the attorney as the nature of the offense and past indicia of character may warrant." Note, 43 Cornell L.Q. 489, 495 (1958).

[12] The Code seeks only to specify conduct for which a lawyer should be disciplined. Recommendations as to the procedures to be used in disciplinary actions and the gravity of disciplinary measures appropriate for violations of the Code are within the jurisdiction of the American Bar Association Special Committee on Evaluation of Disciplinary Enforcement.

[13] "The severity of the judgment of this court should be in proportion to the gravity of the offenses, the moral turpitude involved, and the extent that the defendant's acts and conduct affect his professional qualifications to practice law." Louisiana State Bar Ass'n v. Steiner, 204 La. 1073, 1092–93, 16 So.2d 843, 850 (1944) (Higgins, J., concurring in decree).

"Certainly an erring lawyer who has been disciplined and who having paid the penalty has given satisfactory evidence of repentance and has been rehabilitated and restored to his place at the bar by the court which knows him best ought not to have what amounts to an order of permanent disbarment entered against him by a federal court solely on the basis of an earlier criminal record and without regard to his subsequent rehabilitation and present good character . . . . We think, therefore, that the district court should reconsider the appellant's appli-

CODE OF PROFESSIONAL RESPONSIBILITY

CANON 1

A Lawyer Should Assist in Maintaining the Integrity and Competence of the Legal Profession

ETHICAL CONSIDERATIONS

EC 1-1 A basic tenet of the professional responsibility of lawyers is that every person in our society should have ready access to the independent professional services of a lawyer of integrity and competence. Maintaining the integrity and improving the competence of the bar to meet the highest standards is the ethical responsibility of every lawyer.

EC 1-2 The public should be protected from those who are not qualified to be lawyers by reason of a deficiency in education [1] or moral standards [2] or of other relevant factors [3] but who nevertheless

seek to practice law. To assure the maintenance of high moral and educational standards of the legal profession, lawyers should affirmatively assist courts and other appropriate bodies in promulgating, enforcing, and improving requirements for admission to the bar.[4] In like manner, the bar has a positive obligation to aid in the continued improvement of all phases of pre-admission and post-admission legal education.

EC 1-3 Before recommending an applicant for admission, a lawyer should satisfy himself that the applicant is of good moral character. Although a lawyer should not become a self-appointed investigator or judge of applicants for admission, he should report to proper officials all unfavorable information he possesses relating to the character or other qualifications of an applicant.[5]

EC 1-4 The integrity of the profession can be maintained only if conduct of lawyers in violation of the Disciplinary Rules is brought to the attention of the proper officials. A lawyer should reveal voluntarily to those officials all unprivileged knowledge of conduct of lawyers which he believes clearly to be in violation of the Disciplinary Rules.[6] A lawyer should, upon request, serve on and assist committees and boards having responsibility for the administration of the Disciplinary Rules.[7]

EC 1-5 A lawyer should maintain high standards of professional conduct and should encourage fellow lawyers to do likewise. He should be temperate and dignified, and he should refrain from all

---

cation for admission and grant it unless the court finds it to be a fact that the appellant is not presently of good moral or professional character." In re Dreier, 258 F.2d 68, 69–70 (3d Cir. 1958).

[1] "[W]e cannot conclude that all educational restrictions [on bar admission] are unlawful. We assume that few would deny that a grammar school education requirement, before taking the bar examination, was reasonable. Or that an applicant had to be able to read or write. Once we conclude that *some* restriction is proper, then it becomes a matter of degree—the problem of drawing the line.

. . . . .

"We conclude the fundamental question here is whether Rule IV, Section 6 of the Rules Pertaining to Admission of Applicants to the State Bar of Arizona is 'arbitrary, capricious and unreasonable.' We conclude an educational requirement of graduation from an accredited law school is not." Hackin v. Lockwood, 361 F.2d 499, 503–04 (9th Cir. 1966), *cert. denied*, 385 U.S. 960, 17 L.Ed.2d 305, 87 S.Ct. 396 (1966).

[2] "Every state in the United States, as a prerequisite for admission to the practice of law, requires that applicants possess 'good moral character.' Although the requirement is of judicial origin, it is now embodied in legislation in most states." Comment, *Procedural Due Process and Character Hearings for Bar Applicants*, 15 Stan.L.Rev. 500 (1963).

"Good character in the members of the bar is essential to the preservation of the integrity of the courts. The duty and power of the court to guard its portals against intrusion by men and women who are mentally and morally dishonest, unfit because of bad character, evidenced by their course of conduct, to participate in the administrative law, would seem to be unquestioned in the matter of preservation of judicial dignity and integrity." In re Monaghan, 126 Vt. 53, 222 A.2d 665, 670 (1966).

"Fundamentally, the question involved in both situations [*i.e.* admission and disciplinary proceedings] is the same—is the applicant for admission or the attorney sought to be disciplined a fit and proper person to be permitted to practice law, and that usually turns upon whether he has committed or is likely to continue to commit acts of moral turpitude. At the time of oral argument the attorney for respondent frankly conceded that the test for admission and for discipline is and should be the same. We agree with this concession." Hallinan v. Comm. of Bar Examiners, 65 Cal.2d 447, 453, 421 P.2d 76, 81, 55 Cal. Rptr. 228, 233 (1966).

[3] "Proceedings to gain admission to the bar are for the purpose of protecting the public and the courts from the ministrations of persons unfit to practice the profession. Attorneys are officers of the court appointed to assist the

court in the administration of justice. Into their hands are committed the property, the liberty and sometimes the lives of their clients. This commitment demands a high degree of intelligence, knowledge of the law, respect for its function in society, sound and faithful judgment and, above all else, integrity of character in private and professional conduct." In re Monaghan, 126 Vt. 53, 222 A.2d 665, 676 (1966) (Holden, C. J., dissenting).

[4] "A bar composed of lawyers of good moral character is a worthy objective but it is unnecessary to sacrifice vital freedoms in order to obtain that goal. It is also important both to society and the bar itself that lawyers be unintimidated—free to think, speak, and act as members of an Independent Bar." Konigsberg v. State Bar, 353 U.S. 252, 273, 1 L.Ed.2d 810, 825, 77 S.Ct. 722, 733 (1957).

[5] *See* ABA Canon 29.

[6] ABA Canon 28 designates certain conduct as unprofessional and then states that: "A duty to the public and to the profession devolves upon every member of the Bar having knowledge of such practices upon the part of any practitioner immediately to inform thereof, to the end that the offender may be disbarred." ABA Canon 29 states a broader admonition: "Lawyers should expose without fear or favor before the proper tribunals corrupt or dishonest conduct in the profession."

[7] "It is the obligation of the organized Bar and the individual lawyer to give unstinted cooperation and assistance to the highest court of the state in discharging its function and duty with respect to discipline and in purging the profession of the unworthy." *Report of the Special Committee on Disciplinary Procedures*, 80 A.B.A.Rep. 463, 470 (1955).

illegal and morally reprehensible conduct.[8] Because of his position in society, even minor violations of law by a lawyer may tend to lessen public confidence in the legal profession. Obedience to law exemplifies respect for law. To lawyers especially, respect for the law should be more than a platitude.

EC 1-6 An applicant for admission to the bar or a lawyer may be unqualified, temporarily or permanently, for other than moral and educational reasons, such as mental or emotional instability. Lawyers should be diligent in taking steps to see that during a period of disqualification such person is not granted a license or, if licensed, is not permitted to practice.[9] In like manner, when the disqualification has terminated, members of the bar should assist such person in being licensed, or, if licensed, in being restored to his full right to practice.

DISCIPLINARY RULES

DR 1-101   Maintaining Integrity and Competence of the Legal Profession.

(A)   A lawyer is subject to discipline if he has made a materially false statement in, or if he has deliberately failed to disclose a material fact requested in connection with, his application for admission to the bar.[10]

---

[8] *Cf.* ABA Canon 32.

[9] "We decline, on the present record, to disbar Mr. Sherman or to reprimand him—not because we condone his actions, but because, as heretofore indicated, we are concerned with whether he is mentally responsible for what he has done.

"The logic of the situation would seem to dictate the conclusion that, if he was mentally responsible for the conduct we have outlined, he should be disbarred; and, if he was not mentally responsible, he should not be permitted to practice law.

"However, the flaw in the logic is that he may have been mentally irresponsible [at the time of his offensive conduct] . . ., and, yet, have sufficiently improved in the almost two and one-half years intervening to be able to capably and competently represent his clients. . . .
. . . .

"We would make clear that we are satisfied that a case has been made against Mr. Sherman, warranting a refusal to permit him to further practice law in this state unless he can establish his mental irresponsibility at the time of the offenses charged. The burden of proof is upon him.

"If he establishes such mental irresponsibility, the burden is then upon him to establish his present capability to practice law."   In re Sherman, 58 Wash.2d 1, 6–7, 354 P.2d 888, 890 (1960), *cert. denied.* 371 U.S. 951, 9 L.Ed.2d 499, 83 S.Ct. 506 (1963).

[10] "This Court has the inherent power to revoke a license to practice law in this State, where such license was issued by this Court, and its issuance was procured by the fraudulent concealment, or by the false and fraudulent representation by the applicant of a fact which was manifestly material to the issuance of the license."   North Carolina ex rel. Attorney General v. Gorson, 209 N.C. 320, 326, 183 S.E. 392, 395 (1936), *cert. denied,* 298 U.S. 662, 80 L.Ed. 1387, 56 S.Ct. 752 (1936).

See also Application of Patterson, 318 P.2d 907, 913 (Or. 1957), *cert. denied,* 356 U.S. 947, 2 L.Ed.2d 822, 78 S.Ct. 795 (1958).

(B)   A lawyer shall not further the application for admission to the bar of another person known by him to be unqualified in respect to character, education, or other relevant attribute.[11]

DR 1-102   Misconduct.

(A)   A lawyer shall not:

(1)   Violate a Disciplinary Rule.

(2)   Circumvent a Disciplinary Rule through actions of another.[12]

(3)   Engage in illegal conduct involving moral turpitude.[13]

---

[11] *See* ABA Canon 29.

[12] In *ABA Opinion 95* (1933), which held that a municipal attorney could not permit police officers to interview persons with claims against the municipality when the attorney knew the claimants to be represented by counsel, the Committee on Professional Ethics said:

"The law officer is, of course, responsible for the acts of those in his department who are under his supervision and control." *Opinion 85.* In re Robinson, 136 N.Y.S. 548 (affirmed 209 N.Y. 354–1912) held that it was a matter of disbarment for an attorney to adopt a general course of approving the unethical conduct of employees of his client, even though he did not actively participate therein.

". . . . 'The attorney should not advise or sanction acts by his client which he himself should not do.' *Opinion 75.*"

[13] "The most obvious non-professional ground for disbarment is conviction for a felony. Most states make conviction for a felony grounds for automatic disbarment. Some of these states, including New York, make disbarment mandatory upon conviction for *any* felony, while others require disbarment only for those felonies which involve moral turpitude. There are strong arguments that some felonies, such as involuntary manslaughter, reflect neither on an attorney's fitness, trustworthiness, nor competence and, therefore, should not be grounds for disbarment, but most states tend to disregard these arguments and, following the common law rule, make disbarment mandatory on conviction for any felony." Note, 43 Cornell L.Q. 489, 490 (1958).

"Some states treat conviction for misdemeanors as grounds for automatic disbarment . . . . However, the vast majority, accepting the common law rule, require that the misdemeanor involve moral turpitude. While the definition of moral turpitude may prove difficult, it seems only proper that those minor offenses which do not affect the attorney's fitness to continue in the profession should not be grounds for disbarment. A good example is an assault and battery conviction which would not involve moral turpitude unless done with malice and deliberation." *Id. at 491.*

"The term 'moral turpitude' has been used in the law for centuries. It has been the subject of many decisions by the courts but has never been clearly defined because of the nature of the term. Perhaps the best general definition of the term 'moral turpitude' is that it imports an act of baseness, vileness or depravity in the duties which one person owes to another or to society in general, which is contrary to the usual, accepted and customary rule of right and duty which a person should follow. 58 C.J.S. at page 1201. Although offenses against revenue laws have been held to be crimes of moral turpitude, it has also been held that the attempt to evade the payment of taxes due to the government or any subdivision thereof, while wrong and unlawful, does not involve moral turpitude. 58 C.J.S. at page 1205." Comm. on Legal Ethics v. Scheer, 149 W.Va. 721, 726–27, 143 S.E.2d 141, 145 (1965).

CODE OF PROFESSIONAL RESPONSIBILITY

(4) **Engage in conduct involving dishonesty, fraud, deceit, or misrepresentation.**

(5) **Engage in conduct that is prejudicial to the administration of justice.**

(6) **Engage in any other conduct that adversely reflects on his fitness to practice law.**[14]

DR 1-103 Disclosure of Information to Authorities.

(A) **A lawyer possessing unprivileged knowledge of a violation of DR 1-102 shall report such knowledge to a tribunal or other authority empowered to investigate or act upon such violation.**[15]

(B) **A lawyer possessing unprivileged knowledge or evidence concerning another lawyer or a judge shall reveal fully such knowledge or evidence upon proper request of a tribunal or other authority empowered to investigate or act upon the conduct of lawyers or judges.**[16]

CANON 2

A Lawyer Should Assist the Legal Profession in Fulfilling Its Duty to Make Legal Counsel Available

ETHICAL CONSIDERATIONS

EC 2-1 The need of members of the public for legal services [1] is met only if they recognize their

legal problems, appreciate the importance of seeking assistance,[2] and are able to obtain the services of acceptable legal counsel.[3] Hence, important functions of the legal profession are to educate laymen to recognize their legal problems, to facilitate the process of intelligent selection of lawyers, and to assist in making legal services fully available.[4]

Recognition of Legal Problems

EC 2-2 The legal profession should assist laymen to recognize legal problems because such problems may not be self-revealing and often are not

---

"The right and power to discipline an attorney, as one of its officers, is inherent in the court. . . . This power is not limited to those instances of misconduct wherein he has been employed, or has acted, in a professional capacity; but, on the contrary, this power may be exercised where his misconduct outside the scope of his professional relations shows him to be an unfit person to practice law." In re Wilson, 391 S.W.2d 914, 917-18 (Mo. 1965).

14 "It is a fair characterization of the lawyer's responsibility in our society that he stands 'as a shield,' to quote Devlin, J., in defense of right and to ward off wrong. From a profession charged with these responsibilities there must be exacted those qualities of truth-speaking, of a high sense of honor, of granite discretion, of the strictest observance of fiduciary responsibility, that have, throughout the centuries, been compendiously described as 'moral character' ". Schware v. Bd. of Bar Examiners, 353 U.S. 232, 247 L.Ed.2d 796, 806, 77 S.Ct. 752, 761 (1957) (Frankfurter, J., concurring).

"Particularly applicable here is Rule 4.47 providing that 'A lawyer should always maintain his integrity; and shall not willfully commit any act against the interest of the public; nor shall he violate his duty to the courts or his clients; *nor shall he, by any misconduct, commit any offense against the laws of Missouri or the United States of America, which amounts to a crime involving acts done by him contrary to justice, honesty, modesty or good morals*; nor shall he be guilty of any other misconduct whereby, for the protection of the public and those charged with the administration of justice, he should no longer be entrusted with the duties and responsibilities belonging to the office of an attorney.' " In re Wilson, 391 S.W.2d 914, 917 (Mo. 1965).

15 *See* ABA Canon 29; *cf.* ABA Canon 28.

16 *Cf.* ABA Canons 28 and 29.

1 "Men have need for more than a system of law; they have need for a system of law which functions, and that

means they have need for lawyers." Cheatham, *The Lawyer's Role and Surroundings*, 25 Rocky Mt.L.Rev. 405 (1953).

2 "Law is not self-applying; men must apply and utilize it in concrete cases. But the ordinary man is incapable. He cannot know the principles of law or the rules guiding the machinery of law administration; he does not know how to formulate his desires with precision and to put them into writing; he is ineffective in the presentation of his claims." Cheatham, *The Lawyer's Role and Surroundings*, 25 Rocky Mt.L.Rev. 405 (1953).

3 "This need [to provide legal services] was recognized by . . . Mr. [Lewis F.] Powell [Jr., President, American Bar Association, 1963-64], who said: 'Looking at contemporary America realistically, we must admit that despite all our efforts to date (and these have not been insignificant), far too many persons are not able to obtain equal justice under law. This usually results because their poverty or their ignorance has prevented them from obtaining legal counsel.' " Address by E. Clinton Bamberger, Association of American Law Schools 1965 Annual Meeting, Dec. 28, 1965, in Proceedings, Part II, 1965, 61, 63-64 (1965).

"A wide gap separates the need for legal services and its satisfaction, as numerous studies reveal. Looked at from the side of the layman, one reason for the gap is poverty and the consequent inability to pay legal fees. Another set of reasons is ignorance of the need for and the value of legal services, and ignorance of where to find a dependable lawyer. There is fear of the mysterious processes and delays of the law, and there is fear of overreaching and overcharging by lawyers, a fear stimulated by the occasional exposure of shysters." Cheatham, *Availability of Legal Services: The Responsibility of the Individual Lawyer and of the Organized Bar*, 12 U.C.L.A.L. Rev. 438 (1965).

4 "It is not only the right but the duty of the profession as a whole to utilize such methods as may be developed to bring the services of its members to those who need them, so long as this can be done ethically and with dignity." *ABA Opinion* 320 (1968).

"[T]here is a responsibility on the bar to make legal services available to those who need them. The maxim, 'privilege brings responsibilities,' can be expanded to read, exclusive privilege to render public service brings responsibility to assure that the service is available to those in need of it." Cheatham, *Availability of Legal Services: The Responsibility of the Individual Lawyer and of the Organized Bar*, 12 U.C.L.A.L.Rev. 438, 443 (1965).

"The obligation to provide legal services for those actually caught up in litigation carries with it the obligation to make preventive legal advice accessible to all. It is among those unaccustomed to business affairs and fearful of the ways of the law that such advice is often most needed. If it is not received in time, the most valiant and skillful representation in court may come too late." *Professional Responsibility: Report of the Joint Conference*, 44 A.B.A.J. 1159, 1216 (1958).

timely noticed.[5] Therefore, lawyers acting under proper auspices should encourage and participate in educational and public relations programs concerning our legal system with particular reference to legal problems that frequently arise. Such educational programs should be motivated by a desire to benefit the public rather than to obtain publicity or employment for particular lawyers.[6] Examples of permissible activities include preparation of institutional advertisements [7] and professional articles for lay publications [8] and participation in

seminars, lectures, and civic programs. But a lawyer who participates in such activities should shun personal publicity.[9]

EC 2–3 Whether a lawyer acts properly in volunteering advice to a layman to seek legal services depends upon the circumstances.[10] The giving of advice that one should take legal action could well be in fulfillment of the duty of the legal profession to assist laymen in recognizing legal problems.[11] The advice is proper only if motivated by a desire to protect one who does not recognize that he may have legal problems or who is ignorant of his legal rights or obligations. Hence, the advice is improper if motivated by a desire to obtain personal benefit,[12] secure personal publicity, or cause litigation to be brought merely to harass or injure another. Obviously, a lawyer should not contact

---

[5] "Over a period of years institutional advertising of programs for the benefit of the public have been approved by this and other Ethics Committees as well as by the courts. . . .

"To the same effect are opinions of this Committee: *Opinion 179* dealing with radio programs presenting a situation in which legal advice is suggested in connection with a drafting of a will; *Opinions 205* and *227* permitting institutional advertising of lawyer referral plans; *Opinion 191* holding that advertising by lawyer members of a non-bar associated sponsored plan violated *Canon 27*. The Illinois Ethics Committee, in its *Opinion 201*, sustained bar association institutional advertising of a check-up plan . . . .

"This Committee has passed squarely on the question of the propriety of institutional advertising in connection with a legal check-up plan. Informal Decision C–171 quotes with express approval the Michigan Ethics Committee as follows:

As a public service, the bar has in the past addressed the public as to the importance of making wills, consulting counsel in connection with real estate transactions, etc. In the same way, the bar, as such, may recommend this program, provided always that it does it in such a way that there is no suggestion of solicitation on behalf of any individual lawyer."
ABA Opinion 307 (1962).

[6] "We recognize a distinction between teaching the lay public the importance of securing legal services preventive in character and the solicitation of professional employment by or for a particular lawyer. The former tends to promote the public interest and enhance the public estimation of the profession. The latter is calculated to injure the public and degrade the profession.

. . . . .

"Advertising which is calculated to teach the layman the benefits and advantages of preventive legal services will benefit the lay public and enable the lawyer to render a more desirable and beneficial professional service. . . . ." *ABA Opinion 179 (1938).*

[7] "[A bar association] may engage in a dignified institutional educational campaign so long as it does not involve the identification of a particular lawyer with the check-up program. Such educational material may point out the value of the annual check-up and may be printed in newspapers, magazines, pamphlets, and brochures, or produced by means of films, radio, television or other media. The printed materials may be distributed in a dignified way through the offices of persons having close dealings with lawyers as, for example, banks, real estate agents, insurance agents and others. They may be available in lawyers' offices. The bar association may prepare and distribute to lawyers materials and forms for use in the annual legal check-up." *ABA Opinion 307 (1962).*

[8] "A lawyer may with propriety write articles for publications in which he gives information upon the law . . . .." ABA Canon 40.

"The newsletters, by means of which respondents are alleged to have advertised their wares, were sent to the officers of union clients represented by their firm. . . .

They contain no reference to any cases handled by the respondents. Their contents are confined to rulings of boards, commissions and courts on problems of interest to labor union, together with proposed and completed legislation important to the Brotherhood, and other items which might affect unions and their members. The respondents cite Opinion 213 of the Committee on Professional Ethics and Grievances as permitting such practice. After studying this opinion, we agree that sending of newsletters of the above type to regular clients does not offend Canon 27." In re Ratner, 194 Kan. 362, 371, 399 P.2d 865, 872–73 (1965).

Cf. ABA Opinion 92 (1933).

[9] *Cf. ABA Opinions* 307 (1962) and 179 (1938).
"There is no ethical or other valid reason why an attorney may not write articles on legal subjects for magazines and newspapers. The fact that the publication is a trade journal or magazine, makes no difference as to the ethical question involved. On the other hand, it would be unethical and contrary to the precepts of the Canons for the attorney to allow his name to be carried in the magazine or other publication . . . . as a free legal adviser for the subscribers to the publication. Such would be contrary to *Canons 27* and *35* and Opinions heretofore announced by the Committee on Professional Ethics and Grievances. (See *Opinions 31, 41, 42,* and *56*)." *ABA Opinion 162 (1936).*

[10] *See* ABA Canon 28.

[11] This question can assume constitutional dimensions: "We meet at the outset the contention that 'solicitation' is wholly outside the area of freedoms protected by the First Amendment. To this contention there are two answers. The first is that a State cannot foreclose the exercise of constitutional rights by mere labels. The second is that abstract discussion is not the only species of communication which the Constitution protects; the First Amendment also protects vigorous advocacy, certainly of lawful ends, against governmental intrusion. . . .

. . . . .

"However valid may be Virginia's interest in regulating the traditionally illegal practice of barratry, maintenance and champerty, that interest does not justify the prohibition of the NAACP activities disclosed by this record. Malicious intent was of the essence of the common-law offenses of fomenting or stirring up litigation. And whatever may be or may have been true of suits against governments in other countries, the exercise in our own, as in this case of First Amendment rights to enforce Constitutional rights through litigation, as a matter of law, cannot be deemed malicious." NAACP v. Button, 371 U.S. 415, 429, 439–40, 9 L.Ed.2d 405, 415–16, 422, 83 S.Ct. 328, 336, 341 (1963).

[12] *See* ABA Canon 27.

a non-client, directly or indirectly, for the purpose of being retained to represent him for compensation.

EC 2-4 Since motivation is subjective and often difficult to judge, the motives of a lawyer who volunteers advice likely to produce legal controversy may well be suspect if he receives professional employment or other benefits as a result.[13] A lawyer who volunteers advice that one should obtain the services of a lawyer generally should not himself accept employment, compensation, or other benefit in connection with that matter. However, it is not improper for a lawyer to volunteer such advice and render resulting legal services to close friends, relatives, former clients (in regard to matters germane to former employment), and regular clients.[14]

EC 2-5 A lawyer who writes or speaks for the purpose of educating members of the public to recognize their legal problems should carefully refrain from giving or appearing to give a general solution applicable to all apparently similar individual problems,[15] since slight changes in fact situations may require a material variance in the applicable advice; otherwise, the public may be misled and misadvised. Talks and writings by lawyers for laymen should caution them not to attempt to solve individual problems upon the basis of the information contained therein.[16]

---

[13] "The Canons of Professional Ethics of the American Bar Association and the decisions of the courts quite generally prohibit the direct solicitation of business for gain by an attorney either through advertisement or personal communication; and also condemn the procuring of business by indirection through touters of any kind. It is disreputable for an attorney to breed litigation by seeking out those who have claims for personal injuries or other grounds of action in order to secure them as clients, or to employ agents or runners, or to reward those who bring or influence the bringing of business to his office. . . . Moreover, it tends quite easily to the institution of baseless litigation and the manufacture of perjured testimony. From early times, this danger has been recognized in the law by the condemnation of the crime of common barratry, or the stirring up of suits or quarrels between individuals at law or otherwise." In re Ades, 6 F.Supp. 467, 474–75 (D. Mary. 1934).

[14] "*Rule 2.*

"§a. . . .

"[A] member of the State Bar shall not solicit professional employment by

"(1) Volunteering counsel or advice except where ties of blood relationship or trust make it appropriate." Cal. Business and Professions Code § 6076 (West 1962).

[15] "*Rule 18* . . . A member of the State Bar shall not advise inquirers or render opinions to them through or in connection with a newspaper, radio or other publicity medium of any kind in respect to their specific legal problems, whether or not such attorney shall be compensated for his services." Cal.Business and Professions Code § 6076 (West 1962).

[16] "In any case where a member might well apply the advice given in the opinion to his individual affairs, the lawyer rendering the opinion [concerning problems common to members of an association and distributed to the members through a periodic bulletin] should specifically state that this opinion should not be relied on by any

Selection of a Lawyer: Generally

EC 2-6 Formerly a potential client usually knew the reputations of local lawyers for competency and integrity and therefore could select a practitioner in whom he had confidence. This traditional selection process worked well because it was initiated by the client and the choice was an informed one.

EC 2-7 Changed conditions, however, have seriously restricted the effectiveness of the traditional selection process. Often the reputations of lawyers are not sufficiently known to enable laymen to make intelligent choices.[17] The law has become increasingly complex and specialized. Few lawyers are willing and competent to deal with every kind of legal matter, and many laymen have difficulty in determining the competence of lawyers to render different types of legal services. The selection of legal counsel is particularly difficult for transients, persons moving into new areas, persons of limited education or means, and others who have little or no contact with lawyers.[18]

EC 2-8 Selection of a lawyer by a layman often is the result of the advice and recommendation of third parties—relatives, friends, acquaintances, business associates, or other lawyers. A layman is best served if the recommendation is disinterested and informed. In order that the recommendation be disinterested, a lawyer should not seek to influence another to recommend his employment.[19] A lawyer should not compensate another person for recommending him, for influencing a prospective client to employ him, or to encourage future recommendations.[20]

Selection of a Lawyer: Professional Notices and Listings

EC 2-9 The traditional ban against advertising by lawyers, which is subject to certain limited exceptions, is rooted in the public interest. Competitive advertising would encourage extravagant, artful, self-laudatory [21] brashness in seeking business and

---

member as a basis for handling his individual affairs, but that in every case he should consult his counsel. In the publication of the opinion the association should make a similar statement." *ABA Opinion* 273 (1946).

[17] "A group of recent interrelated changes bears directly on the availability of legal services. . . . [One] change is the constantly accelerating urbanization of the country and the decline of personal and neighborhood knowledge of whom to retain as a professional man." Cheatham, *Availability of Legal Services: The Responsibility of the Individual Lawyer and of the Organized Bar*, 12 U.C.L.A.L. Rev. 438, 440 (1965).

[18] *Cf.* Cheatham, *A Lawyer When Needed: Legal Services for the Middle Classes*, 63 Colum.L.Rev. 973, 974 (1963).

[19] *See* ABA Canon 27.

[20] *See* ABA Canon 28.

[21] " 'Self-laudation' is a very flexible concept; Canon 27 does not define it, so what course of conduct would be said to constitute it under a given state of facts would no doubt vary as the opinions of men vary. As a famous English judge said, it would vary as the length of the chancellor's foot. It must be in words and tone that will 'offend the traditions and lower the tone of our profession.' When it

thus could mislead the layman.[22] Furthermore, it would inevitably produce unrealistic expectations in particular cases and bring about distrust of the law and lawyers.[23] Thus, public confidence in our legal system would be impaired by such advertisements of professional services. The attorney-client relationship is personal and unique and should not be established as the result of pressures and deceptions.[24] History has demonstrated that public confidence in the legal system is best preserved by strict, self-imposed controls over, rather than by unlimited, advertising.

---

does this, it is 'reprehensible.' This seems to be the test by which 'self-laudation' is measured." State v. Nichols, 151 So.2d 257, 259 (Fla. 1963).

[22] "Were it not for the prohibitions of . . . [Canon 27] lawyers could, and no doubt would be forced to, engage competitively in advertising of all kinds in which each would seek to explain to the public why he could serve better and accomplish more than his brothers at the Bar.

"Susceptible as we are to advertising the public would then be encouraged to choose an attorney on the basis of which had the better, more attractive advertising program rather than on his reputation for professional ability.

"This would certainly maim, if not destroy, the dignity and professional status of the Bar of this State." State v. Nichols, 151 So.2d 257, 268 (Fla. 1963) (O'Connell, J., concurring in part and dissenting in part).

[23] Cf. ABA Canon 8.

[24] "The prohibition of advertising by lawyers deserves some examination. All agree that advertising by an individual lawyer, if permitted, will detract from the dignity of the profession, but the matter goes deeper than this. Perhaps the most understandable and acceptable additional reasons we have found are stated by one commentator as follows:

" '1. That advertisements, unless kept within narrow limits, like any other form of solicitation, tend to stir up litigation, and such tendency is against the public interest.

" '2. That if there were no restrictions on advertisements, the least capable and least honorable lawyers would be apt to publish the most extravagant and alluring material about themselves, and that the harm which would result would, in large measure, fall on the ignorant and on those least able to afford it.

" '3. That the temptation would be strong to hold out as inducements for employment, assurances of success or of satisfaction to the client, which assurances could not be realized, and that the giving of such assurances would materially increase the temptation to use ill means to secure the end desired by the client.

" 'In other words, the reasons for the rule, and for the conclusion that it is desirable to prohibit advertising entirely, or to limit it within such narrow bounds that it will not admit of abuse, are based on the possibility and probability that this means of publicity, if permitted, will be abused.' Harrison Hewitt in a comment at 15 A.B.A.J. 116 (1929) reproduced in Cheatham, Cases and Materials on the Legal Profession (2d Ed., 1955), p. 525.

"Of course, competition is at the root of the abuses in advertising. If the individual lawyer were permitted to compete with his fellows in publicity through advertising, we have no doubt that Mr. Hewitt's three points, quoted above, would accurately forecast the result." Jacksonville Bar Ass'n v. Wilson, 102 So.2d 292, 294-95 (Fla. 1958).

EC 2-10 Methods of advertising that are subject to the objections stated above [25] should be and are prohibited.[26] However, the Disciplinary Rules recognize the value of giving assistance in the selection process through forms of advertising that furnish identification of a lawyer while avoiding such objections. For example, a lawyer may be identified in the classified section of the telephone directory,[27] in the office building directory, and on his letterhead and professional card.[28] But at all times the permitted notices should be dignified and accurate.

EC 2-11 The name under which a lawyer conducts his practice may be a factor in the selection process.[29] The use of a trade name or an assumed name could mislead laymen concerning the identity, responsibility, and status of those practicing thereunder.[30] Accordingly, a lawyer in private practice should practice only under his own name, the name of a lawyer employing him, a partnership name composed of the name of one or more of the lawyers practicing in a partnership, or, if permitted by law, in the name of a professional legal corporation, which should be clearly designated as such. For many years some law firms have used a firm name retaining one or more names of deceased or retired partners and such practice is not improper if the firm is a bona fide successor of a firm in which the deceased or retired person was a member, if the use of the name is authorized by law or by contract, and if the public is not misled thereby.[31] However, the name of a partner

---

[25] See ABA Canon 27.

[26] Cf. ABA Opinions 309 (1963) and 284 (1951).

[27] Cf. ABA Opinions 313 (1964) and 284 (1951).

[28] See ABA Canon 27.

[29] Cf. ABA Opinion 303 (1961).

[30] See ABA Canon 33.

[31] Id.

"The continued use of a firm name by one or more surviving partners after the death of a member of the firm whose name is in the firm title is expressly permitted by the Canons of Ethics. The reason for this is that all of the partners have by their joint and several efforts over a period of years contributed to the good will attached to the firm name. In the case of a firm having widespread connections, this good will is disturbed by a change in firm name every time a name partner dies, and that reflects a loss in some degree of the good will to the building up of which the surviving partners have contributed their time, skill and labor through a period of years. To avoid this loss the firm name is continued, and to meet the requirements of the Canon the individuals constituting the firm from time to time are listed." ABA Opinion 267 (1945).

"Accepted local custom in New York recognizes that the name of a law firm does not necessarily identify the individual members of the firm, and hence the continued use of a firm name after the death of one or more partners is not a deception and is permissible. . . . The continued use of a deceased partner's name in the firm title is not affected by the fact that another partner withdraws from the firm and his name is dropped, or the name of the new partner is added to the firm name." Opinion No. 45, Committee on Professional Ethics, New York State Bar Ass'n, 39 N.Y.St.B.J. 455 (1967).

Cf. ABA Opinion 258 (1943).

CODE OF PROFESSIONAL RESPONSIBILITY

who withdraws from a firm but continues to practice law should be omitted from the firm name in order to avoid misleading the public.

EC 2–12 A lawyer occupying a judicial, legislative, or public executive or administrative position who has the right to practice law concurrently may allow his name to remain in the name of the firm if he actively continues to practice law as a member thereof. Otherwise, his name should be removed from the firm name,[32] and he should not be identified as a past or present member of the firm; and he should not hold himself out as being a practicing lawyer.

EC 2–13 In order to avoid the possibility of misleading persons with whom he deals, a lawyer should be scrupulous in the representation of his professional status.[33] He should not hold himself out as being a partner or associate of a law firm if he is not one in fact,[34] and thus should not hold himself out as a partner or associate if he only shares offices with another lawyer.[35]

EC 2–14 In some instances a lawyer confines his practice to a particular field of law.[36] In the absence of state controls to insure the existence of special competence, a lawyer should not be permitted to hold himself out as a specialist [37] or as having special training or ability, other than in the historically excepted fields of admiralty, trademark, and patent law.[38]

---

[32] Cf. ABA Canon 33 and *ABA Opinion* 315 (1965).

[33] Cf. *ABA Opinions* 283 (1950) and 81 (1932).

[34] See *ABA Opinion* 316 (1967).

[35] "The word 'associates' has a variety of meanings. Principally through custom the word when used on the letterheads of law firms has come to be regarded as describing those who are employees of the firm. Because the word has acquired this special significance in connection with the practice of the law the use of the word to describe lawyer relationships other than employer-employee is likely to be misleading." In re Sussman and Tanner, 241 Ore. 246, 248, 405 P.2d 355, 356 (1965).

According to *ABA Opinion* 310 (1963), use of the term "associates" would be misleading in two situations: (1) where two lawyers are partners and they share both responsibility and liability for the partnership; and (2) where two lawyers practice separately, sharing no responsibility or liability, and only share a suite of offices and some costs.

[36] "For a long time, many lawyers have, of necessity, limited their practice to certain branches of law. The increasing complexity of the law and the demand of the public for more expertness on the part of the lawyer has, in the past few years—particularly in the last ten years—brought about specialization on an increasing scale." *Report of the Special Committee on Specialization and Specialized Legal Services*, 79 A.B.A.Rep. 582, 584 (1954).

[37] "In varying degrees specialization has become the *modus operandi* throughout the legal profession. . . . American society is specialization conscious. The present Canons, however, do not allow lawyers to make known to the lay public the fact that they engage in the practice of a specialty. . . ." Tucker, *The Large Law Firm: Considerations Concerning the Modernization of the Canons of Professional Ethics*, 1965 Wis.L.Rev. 344, 348–49 (1965).

[38] See ABA Canon 27.

EC 2–15 The legal profession has developed lawyer referral systems designed to aid individuals who are able to pay fees but need assistance in locating lawyers competent to handle their particular problems. Use of a lawyer referral system enables a layman to avoid an uninformed selection of a lawyer because such a system makes possible the employment of competent lawyers who have indicated an interest in the subject matter involved. Lawyers should support the principle of lawyer referral systems and should encourage the evolution of other ethical plans which aid in the selection of qualified counsel.

Financial Ability to Employ Counsel: Generally

EC 2–16 The legal profession cannot remain a viable force in fulfilling its role in our society unless its members receive adequate compensation for services rendered, and reasonable fees [39] should be charged in appropriate cases to clients able to pay them. Nevertheless, persons unable to pay all or a portion of a reasonable fee should be able to obtain necessary legal services,[40] and lawyers should support and participate in ethical activities designed to achieve that objective.[41]

Financial Ability to Employ Counsel: Persons Able to Pay Reasonable Fees

EC 2–17 The determination of a proper fee requires consideration of the interests of both client and lawyers.[42] A lawyer should not charge more than a reasonable fee,[43] for excessive cost of legal service would deter laymen from utilizing the legal system in protection of their rights. Furthermore, an excessive charge abuses the professional relationship between lawyer and client. On the other hand, adequate compensation is necessary in order to enable the lawyer to serve his client effectively and to preserve the integrity and independence of the profession.[44]

EC 2–18 The determination of the reasonableness of a fee requires consideration of all relevant circumstances,[45] including those stated in the Disciplinary Rules. The fees of a lawyer will vary according to many factors, including the time required, his experience, ability, and reputation, the

---

[39] See ABA Canon 12.

[40] Cf. ABA Canon 12.

[41] "If there is any fundamental proposition of government on which all would agree, it is that one of the highest goals of society must be to achieve and maintain equality before the law. Yet this ideal remains an empty form of words unless the legal profession is ready to provide adequate representation for those unable to pay the usual fees." *Professional Representation: Report of the Joint Conference*, 44 A.B.A.J. 1159, 1216 (1958).

[42] See ABA Canon 12.

[43] Cf. ABA Canon 12.

[44] "When members of the Bar are induced to render legal services for inadequate compensation, as a consequence the quality of the service rendered may be lowered, the welfare of the profession injured and the administration of justice made less efficient." *ABA Opinion* 302 (1961). Cf. *ABA Opinion* 307 (1962).

[45] See ABA Canon 12.

nature of the employment, the responsibility involved, and the results obtained. Suggested fee schedules and economic reports of state and local bar associations provide some guidance on the subject of reasonable fees.[46] It is a commendable and long-standing tradition of the bar that special consideration is given in the fixing of any fee for services rendered a brother lawyer or a member of his immediate family.

EC 2-19   As soon as feasible after a lawyer has been employed, it is desirable that he reach a clear agreement with his client as to the basis of the fee charges to be made. Such a course will not only prevent later misunderstanding but will also work for good relations between the lawyer and the client. It is usually beneficial to reduce to writing the understanding of the parties regarding the fee, particularly when it is contingent. A lawyer should be mindful that many persons who desire to employ him may have had little or no experience with fee charges of lawyers, and for this reason he should explain fully to such persons the reasons for the particular fee arrangement he proposes.

EC 2-20   Contingent fee arrangements[47] in civil cases have long been commonly accepted in the United States in proceedings to enforce claims. The historical bases of their acceptance are that (1) they often, and in a variety of circumstances, provide the only practical means by which one having a claim against another can economically afford, finance, and obtain the services of a competent lawyer to prosecute his claim, and (2) a successful prosecution of the claim produces a *res* out of which the fee can be paid.[48] Although a lawyer generally should decline to accept employment on a contingent fee basis by one who is able to pay a reasonable fixed fee, it is not necessarily improper for a lawyer, where justified by the particular circumstances of a case, to enter into a contingent fee contract in a civil case with any client who, after being fully informed of all relevant factors, desires that arrangement. Because of the

human relationships involved and the unique character of the proceedings, contingent fee arrangements in domestic relation cases are rarely justified. In administrative agency proceedings contingent fee contracts should be governed by the same considerations as in other civil cases. Public policy properly condemns contingent fee arrangements in criminal cases, largely on the ground that legal services in criminal cases do not produce a *res* with which to pay the fee.

EC 2-21   A lawyer should not accept compensation or any thing of value incident to his employment or services from one other than his client without the knowledge and consent of his client after full disclosure.[49]

EC 2-22   Without the consent of his client, a lawyer should not associate in a particular matter another lawyer outside his firm. A fee may properly be divided between lawyers[50] properly associated if the division is in proportion to the services performed and the responsibility assumed by each lawyer[51] and if the total fee is reasonable.

EC 2-23   A lawyer should be zealous in his efforts to avoid controversies over fees with clients[52] and should attempt to resolve amicably any differences on the subject.[53] He should not sue a client for a fee unless necessary to prevent fraud or gross imposition by the client.[54]

---

[46] *Id.*
"[U]nder . . . [*Canon 12*], this Committee has consistently held that minimum fee schedules can only be suggested or recommended and cannot be made obligatory . . . ." *ABA Opinion* 302 (1961).

"[A] compulsory minimum fee schedule is contrary to *Canon 12* and repeated pronouncements of this committee." *ABA Opinion* 190 (1939).

Cf. ABA Opinions 171 (1937) and 28 (1930).

[47] *See* ABA Canon 13; *see also* Mackinnon, Contingent Fees for Legal Services (1964) (A report of the American Bar Foundation).

"A contract for a reasonable contingent fee where sanctioned by law is permitted by *Canon 13*, but the client must remain responsible to the lawyer for expenses advanced by the latter. 'There is to be no barter of the privilege of prosecuting a cause for gain in exchange for the promise of the attorney to prosecute at his own expense.' (Cardozo, C. J. in Matter of Gilman, 251 N.Y. 265, 270–271.)" *ABA Opinion* 246 (1942).

[48] *See* Comment, *Providing Legal Services for the Middle Class in Civil Matters: The Problem, the Duty and a Solution,* 26 U.Pitt.L.Rev. 811, 829 (1965).

[49] *See* ABA Canon 38.
"Of course, as . . . [Informal Opinion 679] points out, there must be full disclosure of the arrangement [that an entity other than the client pays the attorney's fee] by the attorney to the client . . . ." *ABA Opinion* 320 (1968).

[50] "Only lawyers may share in . . . a division of fees, but . . . it is not necessary that both lawyers be admitted to practice in the same state, so long as the division was based on the division of services or responsibility." *ABA Opinion* 316 (1967).

[51] *See* ABA Canon 34.
"We adhere to our previous rulings that where a lawyer merely brings about the employment of another lawyer *but renders no service and assumes no responsibility in the matter,* a division of the latter's fee is improper. (*Opinions* 18 and 153).

"It is assumed that the bar, generally, understands what acts or conduct of a lawyer may constitute 'services' to a client within the intendment of *Canon 12*. Such acts or conduct invariably, if not always, involve 'responsibility' on the part of the lawyer, whether the word 'responsibility' be construed to denote the possible resultant legal or moral liability on the part of the lawyer to the client or to others, or the onus of deciding what should or should not be done in behalf of the client. The word 'services' in *Canon 12* must be construed in this broad sense and may apply to the selection and retainer of associate counsel as well as to other acts or conduct in the client's behalf." *ABA Opinion* 204 (1940).

[52] *See* ABA Canon 14.

[53] *Cf. ABA Opinion* 320 (1968).

[54] *See* ABA Canon 14.
"Ours is a learned profession, not a mere money-getting trade. . . . Suits to collect fees should be avoided. Only where the circumstances imperatively require, should resort be had to a suit to compel payment. And where a lawyer does resort to a suit to enforce payment of fees

Financial Ability to Employ Counsel: Persons Unable to Pay Reasonable Fees

EC 2-24 A layman whose financial ability is not sufficient to permit payment of any fee cannot obtain legal services, other than in cases where a contingent fee is appropriate, unless the services are provided for him. Even a person of moderate means may be unable to pay a reasonable fee which is large because of the complexity, novelty, or difficulty of the problem or similar factors.[55]

EC 2-25 Historically, the need for legal services of those unable to pay reasonable fees has been met in part by lawyers who donated their services or accepted court appointments on behalf of such individuals. The basic responsibility for providing legal services for those unable to pay ultimately rests upon the individual lawyer, and personal involvement in the problems of the disadvantaged can be one of the most rewarding experiences in the life of a lawyer. Every lawyer, regardless of professional prominence or professional workload, should find time to participate in serving the disadvantaged. The rendition of free legal services to those unable to pay reasonable fees continues to be an obligation of each lawyer, but the efforts of individual lawyers are often not enough to meet the need.[56] Thus it has been necessary for the

profession to institute additional programs to provide legal services.[57] Accordingly, legal aid offices,[58] lawyer referral services,[59] and other related programs have been developed, and others will be developed, by the profession.[60] Every lawyer should support all proper efforts to meet this need for legal services.[61]

---

which involves a disclosure, he should carefully avoid any disclosure not clearly necessary to obtaining or defending his rights." *ABA Opinion* 250 (1943).

But *cf. ABA Opinion* 320 (1968).

[55] "As a society increases in size, sophistication and technology, the body of laws which is required to control that society also increases in size, scope and complexity. With this growth, the law directly affects more and more facets of individual behavior, creating an expanding need for legal services on the part of the individual members of the society. . . . As legal guidance in social and commercial behavior increasingly becomes necessary, there will come a concurrent demand from the layman that such guidance be made available to him. This demand will not come from those who are able to employ the best of legal talent, nor from those who can obtain legal assistance at little or no cost. It will come from the large 'forgotten middle income class,' who can neither afford to pay proportionately large fees nor qualify for ultra-low-cost services. The legal profession must recognize this inevitable demand and consider methods whereby it can be satisfied. If the profession fails to provide such methods, the laity will." Comment, *Providing Legal Services for the Middle Class in Civil Matters: The Problem, the Duty and a Solution,* 26 U.Pitt.L.Rev. 811, 811–12 (1965).

"The issue is not whether we shall do something or do nothing. The demand for ordinary everyday legal justice is so great and the moral nature of the demand is so strong that the issue has become whether we devise, maintain, and support suitable agencies able to satisfy the demand or, by our own default, force the government to take over the job, supplant us, and ultimately dominate us." Smith, *Legal Service Offices for Persons of Moderate Means,* 1949 Wis.L.Rev. 416, 418 (1949).

[56] "Lawyers have peculiar responsibilities for the just administration of the law, and these responsibilities include providing advice and representation for needy persons. To a degree not always appreciated by the public at large, the bar has performed these obligations with zeal and devotion. The Committee is persuaded, however, that a system of justice that attempts, in mid-twentieth century America, to meet the needs of the financially incapacitated accused

through primary or exclusive reliance on the uncompensated services of counsel will prove unsuccessful and inadequate. . . . A system of adequate representation, therefore, should be structured and financed in a manner reflecting its public importance. . . . We believe that fees for private appointed counsel should be set by the court within maximum limits established by the statute." Report of the Att'y Gen's Comm. on Poverty and the Administration of Criminal Justice 41–43 (1963).

[57] "At present this representation [of those unable to pay usual fees] is being supplied in some measure through the spontaneous generosity of individual lawyers, through legal aid societies, and—increasingly—through the organized efforts of the Bar. If those who stand in need of this service know of its availability and their need is in fact adequately met, the precise mechanism by which this service is provided becomes of secondary importance. It is of great importance, however, that both the impulse to render this service, and the plan for making that impulse effective, should arise within the legal profession itself." *Professional Responsibility: Report of the Joint Conference,* 44 A.B.A.J. 1159, 1216 (1958).

[58] "Free legal clinics carried on by the organized bar are not ethically objectionable. On the contrary, they serve a very worthwhile purpose and should be encouraged." *ABA Opinion* 191 (1939).

[59] "We are of the opinion that the [lawyer referral] plan here presented does not fall within the inhibition of the Canon. No solicitation for a particular lawyer is involved. The dominant purpose of the plan is to provide as an obligation of the profession competent legal services to persons in low-income groups at fees within their ability to pay. The plan is to be supervised and directed by the local Bar Association. There is to be no advertisement of the names of the lawyers constituting the panel. The general method and purpose of the plan only is to be advertised. Persons seeking the legal services will be directed to members of the panel by the Bar Association. Aside from the filing of the panel with the Bar Association, there is to be no advertisement of the names of the lawyers constituting the panel. If these limitations are observed, we think there is no solicitation of business by or for particular lawyers and no violation of the inhibition af Canon 27." *ABA Opinion* 205 (1940).

[60] "Whereas the American Bar Association believes that it is a fundamental duty of the bar to see to it that all persons requiring legal advice be able to attain it, irrespective of their economic status . . . .

"Resolved, that the Association approves and sponsors the setting up by state and local bar associations of lawyer referral plans and low-cost legal service methods for the purpose of dealing with cases of persons who might not otherwise have the benefit of legal advice . . . .." *Proceedings of the House of Delegates of the American Bar Association,* Oct. 30, 1946, 71 A.B.A.Rep. 103, 109–10 (1946).

[61] "The defense of indigent citizens, without compensation, is carried on throughout the country by lawyers representing legal aid societies, not only with the approval, but with the commendation of those acquainted with the work. Not infrequently services are rendered out of sympathy or for other philanthropic reasons, by individual lawyers who do not represent legal aid societies. There is nothing whatever in the Canons to prevent a lawyer

CODE OF PROFESSIONAL RESPONSIBILITY

Acceptance and Retention of Employment

EC 2-26 A lawyer is under no obligation to act as adviser or advocate for every person who may wish to become his client; but in furtherance of the objective of the bar to make legal services fully available, a lawyer should not lightly decline proffered employment. The fulfillment of this objective requires acceptance by a lawyer of his share of tendered employment which may be unattractive both to him and the bar generally.[62]

EC 2-27 History is replete with instances of distinguished and sacrificial services by lawyers who have represented unpopular clients and causes. Regardless of his personal feelings, a lawyer should not decline representation because a client or a cause is unpopular or community reaction is adverse.[63]

EC 2-28 The personal preference of a lawyer to avoid adversary alignment against judges, other lawyers,[64] public officials, or influential members of the community does not justify his rejection of tendered employment.

EC 2-29 When a lawyer is appointed by a court or requested by a bar association to undertake representation of a person unable to obtain counsel, whether for financial or other reasons, he should not seek to be excused from undertaking

the representation except for compelling reasons.[65] Compelling reasons do not include such factors as the repugnance of the subject matter of the proceeding, the identity[66] or position of a person involved in the case, the belief of the lawyer that the defendant in a criminal proceeding is guilty,[67] or the belief of the lawyer regarding the merits of the civil case.[68]

EC 2-30 Employment should not be accepted by a lawyer when he is unable to render competent service[69] or when he knows or it is obvious that the person seeking to employ him desires to institute or maintain an action merely for the purpose of harassing or maliciously injuring another.[70] Likewise, a lawyer should decline employment if the intensity of his personal feeling, as distinguished from a community attitude, may impair his effective representation of a prospective client. If a lawyer knows a client has previously obtained counsel, he should not accept employment in the matter unless the other counsel approves[71] or withdraws, or the client terminates the prior employment.[72]

EC 2-31 Full availability of legal counsel requires both that persons be able to obtain counsel and that lawyers who undertake representation complete the work involved. Trial counsel for a convicted defendant should continue to represent his client by advising whether to take an appeal and, if the appeal is prosecuted, by representing him through the appeal unless new counsel is substituted or withdrawal is permitted by the appropriate court.

---

from performing such an act, nor should there be." *ABA Opinion* 148 (1935).

[62] *But cf.* ABA Canon 31.

[63] "One of the highest services the lawyer can render to society is to appear in court on behalf of clients whose causes are in disfavor with the general public." *Professional Responsibility: Report of the Joint Conference,* 44 A.B.A.J. 1159, 1216 (1958).

One author proposes the following proposition to be included in "A Proper Oath for Advocates": "I recognize that it is sometimes difficult for clients with unpopular causes to obtain proper legal representation. I will do all that I can to assure that the client with the unpopular cause is properly represented, and that the lawyer representing such a client receives credit from and support of the bar for handling such a matter." Thode, *The Ethical Standard for the Advocate,* 39 Texas L.Rev. 575, 592 (1961). "§ 6068. . . . It is the duty of an attorney:
. . . .

"(h) Never to reject, for any consideration personal to himself, the cause of the defenseless or the oppressed." Cal.Business and Professions Code § 6068 (West 1962). Virtually the same language is found in the Oregon statutes at Ore.Rev.Stats. Ch. 9 § 9.460(8).
See Rostow, *The Lawyer and His Client,* 48 A.B.A.J. 25 and 146 (1962).

[64] *See* ABA Canons 7 and 29.
"We are of the opinion that it is not professionally improper for a lawyer to accept employment to compel another lawyer to honor the just claim of a layman. On the contrary, it is highly proper that he do so. Unfortunately, there appears to be a widespread feeling among laymen that it is difficult, if not impossible, to obtain justice when they have claims against members of the Bar because other lawyers will not accept employment to proceed against them. The honor of the profession, whose members proudly style themselves officers of the court, must surely be sullied if its members bind themselves by custom to refrain from enforcing just claims of laymen against lawyers." *ABA Opinion* 144 (1935).

[65] ABA Canon 4 uses a slightly different test, saying, "A lawyer assigned as counsel for an indigent prisoner ought not to ask to be excused for any trivial reason . . . ."

[66] *Cf.* ABA Canon 7.

[67] *See* ABA Canon 5.

[68] Dr. Johnson's reply to Boswell upon being asked what he thought of "supporting a cause which you know to be bad" was: "Sir, you do not know it to be good or bad till the Judge determines it. I have said that you are to state facts fairly; so that your thinking, or what you call knowing, a cause to be bad, must be from reasoning, must be from supposing your arguments to be weak and inconclusive. But, Sir, that is not enough. An argument which does not convince yourself, may convince the Judge to whom you urge it: and if it does convince him, why, then, Sir, you are wrong, and he is right." 2 Boswell, The Life of Johnson 47–48 (Hill ed. 1887).

[69] "The lawyer deciding whether to undertake a case must be able to judge objectively whether he is capable of handling it and whether he can assume its burdens without prejudice to previous commitments. . . ." *Professional Responsibility: Report of the Joint Conference,* 44 A.B.A.J. 1158, 1218 (1958).

[70] "The lawyer must decline to conduct a civil cause or to make a defense when convinced that it is intended merely to harass or to injure the opposite party or to work oppression or wrong." ABA Canon 30.

[71] *See* ABA Canon 7.

[72] *Id.*
"From the facts stated we assume that the client has discharged the first attorney and given notice of the discharge. Such being the case, the second attorney may properly accept employment. *Canon 7; Opinions 10, 130, 149.*" ABA Opinion 209 (1941).

420

EC 2-32 A decision by a lawyer to withdraw should be made only on the basis of compelling circumstances [73], and in a matter pending before a tribunal he must comply with the rules of the tribunal regarding withdrawal. A lawyer should not withdraw without considering carefully and endeavoring to minimize the possible adverse effect on the rights of his client and the possibility of prejudice to his client [74] as a result of his withdrawal. Even when he justifiably withdraws, a lawyer should protect the welfare of his client by giving due notice of his withdrawal,[75] suggesting employment of other counsel, delivering to the client all papers and property to which the client is entitled, cooperating with counsel subsequently employed, and otherwise endeavoring to minimize the possibility of harm. Further, he should refund to the client any compensation not earned during the employment.[76]

DISCIPLINARY RULES

DR 2-101 Publicity in General.[77]

(A) A lawyer shall not prepare, cause to be prepared, use, or participate in the use of, any form of public communication that contains professionally self-laudatory statements calculated to attract lay clients; as used herein, "public communication" includes, but is not limited to, communication by means of television, radio, motion picture, newspaper, magazine, or book.

(B) A lawyer shall not publicize himself, his partner, or associate as a lawyer through newspaper or magazine advertisements, radio or television announcements, display advertisements in city or telephone directories, or other means of commercial publicity,[78] nor shall he authorize or permit others to do so in his behalf [79] except as permitted under DR 2-103.

This does not prohibit limited and dignified identification of a lawyer as a lawyer as well as by name [80]:

(1) In political advertisements when his professional status is germane to the political campaign or to a political issue.

(2) In public notices when the name and profession of a lawyer are required or authorized by law or are reasonably pertinent for a purpose other than the attraction of potential clients.[81]

(3) In routine reports and announcements of a bona fide business, civic, professional, or political organization in which he serves as a director or officer.

(4) In and on legal documents prepared by him.

(5) In and on legal textbooks, treatises, and other legal publications, and in dignified advertisements thereof.

(C) A lawyer shall not compensate or give any thing of value to representatives of the press, radio, television, or other communication medium in anticipation of or in return for professional publicity in a news item.[82]

DR 2-102 Professional Notices, Letterheads, Offices, and Law Lists.

(A) A lawyer or law firm shall not use professional cards, professional announcement cards,

---

[73] *See* ABA Canon 44.
"I will carefully consider, before taking a case, whether it appears that I can fully represent the client within the framework of law. If the decision is in the affirmative, then it will take extreme circumstances to cause me to decide later that I cannot so represent him." Thode, *The Ethical Standard for the Advocate*, 39 Texas L.Rev. 575, 592 (1961) (from "A Proper Oath for Advocates").

[74] *ABA Opinion* 314 (1965) held that a lawyer should not disassociate himself from a cause when "it is obvious that the very act of disassociation would have the effect of violating *Canon 37.*"

[75] ABA Canon 44 enumerates instances in which ". . . the lawyer may be warranted in withdrawing on due notice to the client, allowing him time to employ another lawyer."

[76] *See* ABA Canon 44.

[77] *Cf.* ABA Canon 27; *see generally* ABA *Opinion* 293 (1957).

[78] *Cf.* ABA *Opinions* 133 (1935), 116 (1934), 107 (1934), 73 (1932), 59 (1931), and 43 (1931).

[79] "There can be no justification for the participation and acquiescence by an attorney in the development and publication of an article which, on its face, plainly amounts to a self-interest and unethical presentation of his achieve-

ments and capabilities." Matter of Connelly, 18 App.Div. 2d 466, 478, 240 N.Y.S.2d 126, 138 (1963).
"An announcement of the fact that the lawyer had resigned and the name of the person to succeed him, or take over his work, would not be objectionable, either as an official communication to those employed by or connected with the administrative agency or instrumentality [that had employed him], or as a news release.
"But to include therein a statement of the lawyer's experience in and acquaintance with the various departments and agencies of the government, and a laudation of his legal ability, either generally or in a special branch of the law, is not only bad taste but ethically improper.
"It can have but one primary purpose or object: to aid the lawyer in securing professional employment in private practice by advertising his professional experience, attainments and ability." *ABA Opinion* 184 (1938).
Cf. ABA Opinions 285 (1951) and 140 (1935).

[80] "The question is always . . . whether under the circumstance the furtherance of the professional employment of the lawyer is the primary purpose of the advertisement, or is merely a necessary incident of a proper and legitimate objective of the client which does not have the effect of unduly advertising him." *ABA Opinion* 290 (1956).
See ABA Opinion 285 (1951).

[81] *See ABA Opinions* 299 (1961), 290 (1956), 158 (1936), and 100 (1933); *cf. ABA Opinion* 80 (1932).

[82] "Rule 2.

. . . .

"[A] member of the State Bar shall not solicit professional employment by . . . .

"(4) The making of gifts to representatives of the press, radio, television or any medium of communication in anticipation of or in return for publicity." Cal.Business and Professions Code § 6076 (West 1962).

office signs, letterheads, telephone directory listings, law lists, legal directory listings, or similar professional notices or devices,[83] except that the following may be used if they are in dignified form:

(1) A professional card of a lawyer identifying him by name and as a lawyer, and giving his addresses, telephone numbers, the name of his law firm, and any information permitted under DR 2-105. A professional card of a law firm may also give the names of members and associates. Such cards may be used for identification [84] but may not be published in periodicals, magazines, newspapers,[85] or other media.[86]

(2) A brief professional announcement card stating new or changed associations or addresses, change of firm name, or similar matters pertaining to the professional office of a lawyer or law firm, which may be mailed to lawyers, clients, former clients, personal friends, and relatives.[87] It shall not state biographical data except to the extent reasonably necessary to identify the lawyer or to explain the change in his association, but it may state the immediate past position of the lawyer.[88] It may give the names and dates of predecessor firms in a continuing line of succession. It shall not state the nature of the practice except as permitted under DR 2-105.[89]

(3) A sign on or near the door of the office and in the building directory identifying the law office. The sign shall not state the nature of the practice, except as permitted under DR 2-105.

(4) A letterhead of a lawyer identifying him by name and as a lawyer, and giving his addresses, telephone numbers, the name of his law firm, associates, and any information permitted under DR 2-105. A letterhead of a law firm may also give the names of members and associates,[90] and names and dates relating to deceased and retired members.[91] A lawyer may be designated "Of Counsel" on a letterhead if he has a continuing relationship with a lawyer or law firm, other than as a partner or associate. A lawyer or law firm may be designated as "General Counsel" or by similar professional reference on stationery of a client if he or the firm devotes a substantial amount of professional time in the representation of that client.[92] The letterhead of a law firm may give the names and dates of predecessor firms in a continuing line of succession.

(5) A listing of the office of a lawyer or law firm in the alphabetical and classified sections of the telephone directory or directories for the geographical area or areas in which the lawyer resides or maintains offices or in which a significant part of his clientele resides [93] and in the city directory of the city in which his or the firm's office is located; [94] but the listing may give only the name of the lawyer or law firm, the fact he is a lawyer, addresses, and telephone numbers.[95] The listing shall not be in distinctive form [96] or type.[97] A law firm may have a listing in the firm name separate from that of its members and associates.[98] The listing in the classified section shall not be under a heading or classification other than "Attorneys" or "Lawyers",[99]

---

[83] Cf. ABA Opinions 233 (1941) and 114 (1934).

[84] See ABA Opinion 175 (1938).

[85] See ABA Opinions 260 (1944) and 182 (1938).

[86] But cf. ABA Opinions 276 (1947) and 256 (1943).

[87] See ABA Opinion 301 (1961).

[88] "[I]t has become commonplace for many lawyers to participate in government service; to deny them the right, upon their return to private practice, to refer to their prior employment in a brief and dignified manner, would place an undue limitation upon a large element of our profession. It is entirely proper for a member of the profession to explain his absence from private practice, where such is the primary purpose of the announcement, by a brief and dignified reference to the prior employment.

". . . [A]ny such announcement should be limited to the immediate past connection of the lawyer with the government, made upon his leaving that position to enter private practice." ABA Opinion 301 (1961).

[89] See ABA Opinion 251 (1943).

[90] "Those lawyers who are working for an individual lawyer or a law firm may be designated on the letterhead and in other appropriate places as 'associates'." ABA Opinion 310 (1963).

[91] See ABA Canon 33.

[92] But see ABA Opinion 285 (1951).

[93] See ABA Opinion 295 (1959).

[94] But see ABA Opinion 313 (1964) which says the Committee "approves a listing in the classified section of the city directory for lawyers only when the listing includes all lawyers residing in the community and when no charge is made therefor."

[95] "The listing should consist only of the lawyer's name, address and telephone number." ABA Opinion 313 (1964).

[96] "[A]dding to the regular classified listing a 'second line' in which a lawyer claims that he is engaged in a 'specialty' is an undue attempt to make his name distinctive." ABA Opinion 284 (1951).

[97] "[Opinion 284] held that a lawyer could not with propriety have his name listed in distinctive type in a telephone directory or city directory. We affirm that opinion." ABA Opinion 313 (1964).
See ABA Opinions 123 (1934) and 53 (1931).

[98] "[I]f a lawyer is a member of a law firm, both the firm, and the individual lawyer may be listed separately." ABA Opinion 313 (1964).

[99] See ABA Opinion 284 (1951).

except that additional headings or classifications descriptive of the types of practice referred to in DR 2-105 are permitted.[100]

(6) A listing in a reputable law list [101] or legal directory giving brief biographical and other informative data. A law list or directory is not reputable if its management or contents are likely to be misleading or injurious to the public or to the profession.[102] A law list is conclusively established to be reputable if it is certified by the American Bar Association as being in compliance with its rules and standards. The published data may include only the following: name, including name of law firm and names of professional associates; addresses [103] and telephone numbers; one or more fields of law in which the lawyer or law firm concentrates; [104] a statement that practice is limited to one or more fields of law; a statement that the lawyer or law firm specializes in a particular field of law or law practice but only if authorized under DR 2-105 (A)(4); [105] date and place of birth; date and place of admission to the bar of state and federal courts; schools attended, with dates of graduation, degrees, and other scholastic distinctions; public or quasi-public offices; military service; posts of honor; legal authorships; legal teaching positions; memberships, offices, committee assignments, and section memberships in bar associations; memberships and offices in legal fraternities and legal societies; technical and professional associations and societies; foreign language ability; names and addresses of references,[106] and, with their consent, names of clients regularly represented.[107]

(B) A lawyer in private practice shall not practice under a trade name, a name that is misleading as to the identity of the lawyer or lawyers practicing under such name, or a firm name containing names other than those of one or more of the lawyers in the firm, except that the name of a professional corporation or professional association may contain "P.C." or "P.A." or similar symbols indicating the nature of the organization, and if otherwise lawful a firm may use as, or continue to include in, its name, the name or names of one or more deceased or retired members of the firm or of a predecessor firm in a continuing line of succession.[108] A lawyer who assumes a judicial, legislative, or public executive or administrative post or office shall not permit his name to remain in the name of a law firm or to be used in professional notices of the firm during any significant period in which he is not actively and regularly practicing law as a member of the firm,[109] and during such period other members of the firm shall not use his name in the firm name or in professional notices of the firm.[110]

---

[100] See Silverman v. State Bar of Texas, 405 F.2d 410, (5th Cir. 1968); but see ABA Opinion 286 (1952).

[101] Cf. ABA Canon 43.

[102] Cf. ABA Opinion 255 (1943).

[103] "We are asked to define the word 'addresses' appearing in the second paragraph of Canon 27 . . . .
"It is our opinion that an address (other than a cable address) within the intendment of the canon is that of the lawyer's office or of his residence. Neither address should be misleading. If, for example, an office address is given, it must be that of a bona fide office. The residence address, if given, should be identified as such if the city or other place of residence is not the same as that in which the law office is located." ABA Opinion 249 (1942).

[104] "[T]oday in various parts of the country Committees on Professional Ethics of local and state bar associations are authorizing lawyers to describe themselves in announcements to the Bar and in notices in legal periodicals and approved law lists as specialists in a great variety of things. Thus in the approved law lists or professional announcements there appear, in connection with the names of individual practitioners or firms, such designations as 'International Law, Public and Private'; 'Trial Preparation in Personal Injury and Negligence Actions'; 'Philippine War Damage Claims'; 'Anti-Trust'; 'Domestic Relations'; 'Tax Law'; 'Negligence Law'. It would seem that the ABA has given at least its tacit approval to this sort of announcement.

"It is important that this sort of description is not, in New York at least, permitted on letterheads or shingles or elsewhere in communications to laymen. This is subject to the single exception that such announcement to laymen is permitted in the four traditional specialties, Admiralty, Patent, Copyright and Trade-mark." Report of the Special Committee on Specialization and Specialized Legal Education, 79 A.B.A.Rep. 582, 586 (1954).

[105] This provision is included to conform to action taken by the ABA House of Delegates at the Mid-Winter Meeting, January, 1969.

[106] See ABA Canon 43 and ABA Opinion 119 (1934); but see ABA Opinion 236 (1941).

[107] See ABA Canon 27.

[108] See ABA Canon 33; cf. ABA Opinions 318 (1967), 267 (1945), 219 (1941), 208 (1940), 192 (1939), 97 (1933), and 6 (1925).

[109] ABA Opinion 318 (1967) held, "anything to the contrary in Formal Opinion 315 or in the other opinions cited notwithstanding" that: "Where a partner whose name appears in the name of a law firm is elected or appointed to high local, state or federal office, which office he intends to occupy only temporarily, at the end of which time he intends to return to his position with the firm, and provided that he is not precluded by holding such office from engaging in the practice of law and does not in fact sever his relationship with the firm but only takes a leave of absence, and provided that there is no local law, statute or custom to the contrary, his name may be retained in the firm name during his term or terms of office, but only if proper precautions are taken not to mislead the public as to his degree of participation in the firm's affairs."

Cf. ABA Opinion 143 (1935), New York County Opinion 67, and New York City Opinions 36 and 798; but cf. ABA Opinion 192 (1939) and Michigan Opinion 164.

[110] Cf. ABA Canon 33.

(C) A lawyer shall not hold himself out as having a partnership with one or more other lawyers unless they are in fact partners.[111]

(D) A partnership shall not be formed or continued between or among lawyers licensed in different jurisdictions unless all enumerations of the members and associates of the firm on its letterhead and in other permissible listings make clear the jurisdictional limitations on those members and associates of the firm not licensed to practice in all listed jurisdictions; [112] however, the same firm name may be used in each jurisdiction.

(E) A lawyer who is engaged both in the practice of law and another profession or business shall not so indicate on his letterhead, office sign, or professional card, nor shall he identify himself as a lawyer in any publication in connection with his other profession or business.

(F) Nothing contained herein shall prohibit a lawyer from using or permitting the use, in connection with his name, of an earned degree or title derived therefrom indicating his training in the law.

DR 2-103 Recommendation of Professional Employment.[113]

(A) A lawyer shall not recommend employment, as a private practitioner,[114] of himself, his partner, or associate to a non-lawyer who has not sought his advice regarding employment of a lawyer.[115]

(B) Except as permitted under DR 2-103(C), a lawyer shall not compensate or give anything of value to a person or organization to recommend or secure his employment [116] by a client, or as a reward for having made a recommendation resulting in his employment [117] by a client.

(C) A lawyer shall not request a person or organization to recommend employment, as a private practitioner, of himself, his partner, or associate,[118] except that he may request referrals from a lawyer referral service operated, sponsored, or approved by a bar association representative of the general bar of the geographical area in which the association exists and may pay its fees incident thereto.[119]

(D) A lawyer shall not knowingly assist a person or organization that recommends, furnishes, or pays for legal services to promote the use of his services or those of his partners or associates. However, he may cooperate in a dignified manner with the legal service activities of any of the following, provided that his independent professional judgment is exercised in behalf of his client without interference or control by any organization or other person:

   (1) A legal aid office or public defender office:

      (a) Operated or sponsored by a duly accredited law school.

      (b) Operated or sponsored by a bona fide non-profit community organization.

      (c) Operated or sponsored by a governmental agency.

      (d) Operated, sponsored, or approved by a bar association representative of the general bar of the geographical area in which the association exists.[120]

   (2) A military legal assistance office.

   (3) A lawyer referral service operated, sponsored, or approved by a bar association representative of the general bar of the geographical area in which the association exists.[121]

   (4) A bar association representative of the general bar of the geographical area in which the association exists.[122]

---

[111] See ABA Opinion 277 (1948); cf. ABA Canon 33 and ABA Opinions 318 (1967), 126 (1935), 115 (1934), and 106 (1934).

[112] See ABA Opinions 318 (1967) and 316 (1967); cf. ABA Canon 33.

[113] Cf. ABA Canons 27 and 28.

[114] "We think it clear that a lawyer's seeking employment in an ordinary law office, or appointment to a civil service position, is not prohibited by . . . [Canon 27]." ABA Opinion 197 (1939).

[115] "[A] lawyer may not seek from persons not his clients the opportunity to perform . . . a [legal] check-up." ABA Opinion 307 (1962).

[116] Cf. ABA Opinion 78 (1932).

[117] " 'No financial connection of any kind between the Brotherhood and any lawyer is permissible. No lawyer can properly pay any amount whatsoever to the Brotherhood or any of its departments, officers or members as compensation, reimbursement of expenses or gratuity in connection with the procurement of a case.' " In re Brotherhood of R. R. Trainmen, 13 Ill.2d 391, 398, 150 N.E. 2d 163, 167 (1958), quoted in In re Ratner, 194 Kan 362, 372, 399 P.2d 865, 873 (1965).

See ABA Opinion 147 (1935).

[118] "This Court has condemned the practice of ambulance chasing through the media of runners and touters. In similar fashion we have with equal emphasis condemned the practice of direct solicitation by a lawyer. We have classified both offenses as serious breaches of the Canons of Ethics demanding severe treatment of the offending lawyer." State v. Dawson, 111 So.2d 427, 431 (Fla. 1959).

[119] "Registrants [of a lawyer referral plan] may be required to contribute to the expense of operating it by a reasonable registration charge or by a reasonable percentage of fees collected by them." ABA Opinion 291 (1956).

Cf. ABA Opinion 227 (1941).

[120] Cf. ABA Opinion 148 (1935).

[121] Cf. ABA Opinion 227 (1941).

[122] "If a bar association has embarked on a program of institutional advertising for an annual legal check-up and provides brochures and reprints, it is not improper to have these available in the lawyer's office for persons to read and take." ABA Opinion 307 (1962).

Cf. ABA Opinion 121 (1934).

(5) Any other non-profit organization that recommends, furnishes, or pays for legal services to its members or beneficiaries, but only in those instances and to the extent that controlling constitutional interpretation at the time of the rendition of the services requires the allowance of such legal service activities,[123] and only if the following conditions, unless prohibited by such interpretation, are met:

(a) The primary purposes of such organization do not include the rendition of legal services.

(b) The recommending, furnishing, or paying for legal services to its members is incidental and reasonably related to the primary purposes of such organization.

(c) Such organization does not derive a financial benefit from the rendition of legal services by the lawyer.

(d) The member or beneficiary for whom the legal services are rendered, and not such organization, is recognized as the client of the lawyer in that matter.

(E) A lawyer shall not accept employment when he knows or it is obvious that the person who seeks his services does so as a result of conduct prohibited under this Disciplinary Rule.

DR 2-104 Suggestion of Need of Legal Services.[124]

(A) A lawyer who has given unsolicited advice to a layman that he should obtain counsel or take legal action shall not accept employment resulting from that advice,[125] except that:

(1) A lawyer may accept employment by a close friend, relative, former client (if the advice is germane to the former employment), or one whom the lawyer reasonably believes to be a client.[126]

(2) A lawyer may accept employment that results from his participation in activities designed to educate laymen to recognize legal problems, to make intelligent selection of counsel, or to utilize available legal services if such activities are conducted or sponsored by any of the offices or organizations enumerated in DR 2-103(D)(1) through (5), to the extent and under the conditions prescribed therein.

(3) A lawyer who is furnished or paid by any of the offices or organizations enumerated in DR 2-103(D)(1), (2), or (5) may represent a member or beneficiary thereof, to the extent and under the conditions prescribed therein.

(4) Without affecting his right to accept employment, a lawyer may speak publicly or write for publication on legal topics[127] so long as he does not emphasize his own professional experience or reputation and does not undertake to give individual advice.

(5) If success in asserting rights or defenses of his client in litigation in the nature of a class action is dependent upon the joinder of others, a lawyer may accept, but shall not seek, employment from those contacted for the purpose of obtaining their joinder.[128]

DR 2-105 Limitation of Practice.[129]

(A) A lawyer shall not hold himself out publicly as a specialist[130] or as limiting his practice,[131] except as permitted under DR 2-102(A)(6) or as follows:

(1) A lawyer admitted to practice before the United States Patent Office may use the designation "Patents," "Patent Attorney," or "Patent Lawyer," or any combination of those terms, on his letterhead and office sign. A lawyer engaged in the trademark practice may use the designation "Trademarks," "Trademark Attorney," or "Trademark Lawyer," or any combination of those terms, on his letterhead and office sign, and a lawyer engaged in the admiralty practice may use the designation "Admiralty," "Proctor in Admiralty," or "Admiralty Lawyer," or any combination of those terms, on his letterhead and office sign.[132]

---

[123] United Mine Workers v. Ill. State Bar Ass'n, 389 U.S. 217, 19 L.Ed.2d 426, 88 S.Ct. 353 (1967); Brotherhood of R.R. Trainmen v. Virginia, 371 U.S. 1, 12 L.Ed.2d 89, 84 S.Ct. 1113 (1964); NAACP v. Button, 371 U.S. 415, 9 L. Ed.2d 405, 83 S.Ct. 328 (1963).

[124] ABA Canon 28.

[125] Cf. ABA Opinions 229 (1941) and 173 (1937).

[126] "It certainly is not improper for a lawyer to advise his regular clients of new statutes, court decisions, and administrative rulings, which may affect the client's interests, provided the communication is strictly limited to such information. . . .

"When such communications go to concerns or individuals other than regular clients of the lawyer, they are thinly disguised advertisements for professional employment, and are obviously improper." ABA Opinion 213 (1941).

"It is our opinion that where the lawyer has no reason to believe that he has been supplanted by another lawyer, it is not only his right, but it might even be his duty to advise his client of any change of fact or law which might defeat the client's testamentary purpose as expressed in the will.

"Periodic notices might be sent to the client for whom a lawyer has drawn a will, suggesting that it might be wise for the client to reexamine his will to determine whether or not there has been any change in his situation requiring a modification of his will." ABA Opinion 210 (1941). Cf. ABA Canon 28.

[127] Cf. ABA Opinion 168 (1937).

[128] But cf. ABA Opinion 111 (1934).

[129] See ABA Canon 45; cf. ABA Canons 27, 43, and 46.

[130] Cf. ABA Opinions 228 (1941) and 194 (1939).

[131] See ABA Opinions 251 (1943) and 175 (1938).

[132] See ABA Canon 27; cf. ABA Opinion 286 (1952).

(2) A lawyer may permit his name to be listed in lawyer referral service offices according to the fields of law in which he will accept referrals.

(3) A lawyer available to act as a consultant to or as an associate of other lawyers in a particular branch of law or legal service may distribute to other lawyers and publish in legal journals a dignified announcement of such availability,[133] but the announcement shall not contain a representation of special competence or experience.[134] The announcement shall not be distributed to lawyers more frequently than once in a calendar year, but it may be published periodically in legal journals.

(4) A lawyer who is certified as a specialist in a particular field of law or law practice by the authority having jurisdiction under state law over the subject of specialization by lawyers may hold himself out as such specialist but only in accordance with the rules prescribed by that authority.[135]

DR 2-106 Fees for Legal Services.[136]

(A) A lawyer shall not enter into an agreement for, charge, or collect an illegal or clearly excessive fee.[137]

(B) A fee is clearly excessive when, after a review of the facts, a lawyer of ordinary prudence would be left with a definite and firm conviction that the fee is in excess of a reasonable fee. Factors to be considered as guides in determining the reasonableness of a fee include the following:

(1) The time and labor required, the novelty and difficulty of the questions involved, and the skill requisite to perform the legal service properly.

(2) The likelihood, if apparent to the client, that the acceptance of the particular employment will preclude other employment by the lawyer.

(3) The fee customarily charged in the locality for similar legal services.

(4) The amount involved and the results obtained.

(5) The time limitations imposed by the client or by the circumstances.

(6) The nature and length of the professional relationship with the client.

(7) The experience, reputation, and ability of the lawyer or lawyers performing the services.

(8) Whether the fee is fixed or contingent.[138]

(C) A lawyer shall not enter into an arrangement for, charge, or collect a contingent fee for representing a defendant in a criminal case.[139]

DR 2-107 Division of Fees Among Lawyers.

(A) A lawyer shall not divide a fee for legal services with another lawyer who is not a partner in or associate of his law firm or law office, unless:

(1) The client consents to employment of the other lawyer after a full disclosure that a division of fees will be made.

(2) The division is made in proportion to the services performed and responsibility assumed by each.[140]

(3) The total fee of the lawyers does not clearly exceed reasonable compensation for all legal services they rendered the client.[141]

---

[138] *Cf.* ABA Canon 13; *see generally* MacKinnon, Contingent Fees for Legal Services (1964) (A Report of the American Bar Foundation).

[139] "Contingent fees, whether in civil or criminal cases, are a special concern of the law. . . .

"In criminal cases, the rule is stricter because of the danger of corrupting justice. The second part of Section 542 of the Restatement [of Contracts] reads: 'A bargain to conduct a criminal case . . . in consideration of a promise of a fee contingent on success is illegal. . . .' " Peyton v. Margiotti, 398 Pa. 86, 156 A.2d 865, 967 (1959).

"The third area of practice in which the use of the contingent fee is generally considered to be prohibited is the prosecution and defense of criminal cases. However, there are so few cases, and these are predominantly old, that it is doubtful that there can be said to be any current law on the subject. . . . In the absence of cases on the validity of contingent fees for defense attorneys, it is necessary to rely on the consensus among commentators that such a fee is void as against public policy. The nature of criminal practice itself makes unlikely the use of contingent fee contracts." MacKinnon, Contingent Fees for Legal Services 52 (1964) (A Report of the American Bar Foundation).

[140] *See* ABA Canon 34 and *ABA Opinions* 316 (1967) and 294 (1958); *see generally ABA Opinions* 265 (1945), 204 (1940), 190 (1939), 171 (1937), 153 (1936), 97 (1933), 63 (1932), 28 (1930), 27 (1930), and 18 (1930).

[141] "*Canon 12* contemplates that a lawyer's fee should not exceed *the value of the services* rendered. . . .
. . . .

"*Canon 12* applies, whether joint or separate fees are charged [by associate attorneys] . . . ." *ABA Opinion* 204 (1940).

---

[133] *Cf. ABA Opinion* 194 (1939).

[134] *See* ABA Canon 46.

[135] This provision is included to conform to action taken by the ABA House of Delegates at the Mid-Winter Meeting, January, 1969.

[136] *See* ABA Canon 12.

[137] The charging of a "clearly excessive fee" is a ground for discipline. State ex rel. Nebraska State Bar Ass'n. v. Richards, 165 Neb. 80, 90, 84 N.W.2d 136, 143 (1957).

"An attorney has the right to contract for any fee he chooses so long as it is not excessive (see Opinion 190), and this Committee is not concerned with the amount of such fees unless so excessive as to constitute a misappropriation of the client's funds (see Opinion 27)." *ABA Opinion* 320 (1968).

Cf. ABA Opinions 209 (1940), 190 (1939), and 27 (1930) and State ex rel. Lee v. Buchanan, 191 So.2d 33 (Fla. 1966).

(B) This Disciplinary Rule does not prohibit payment to a former partner or associate pursuant to a separation or retirement agreement.

DR 2-108 Agreements Restricting the Practice of a Lawyer.

(A) A lawyer shall not be a party to or participate in a partnership or employment agreement with another lawyer that restricts the right of a lawyer to practice law after the termination of a relationship created by the agreement, except as a condition to payment of retirement benefits.[142]

(B) In connection with the settlement of a controversy or suit, a lawyer shall not enter into an agreement that restricts his right to practice law.

DR 2-109 Acceptance of Employment.

(A) A lawyer shall not accept employment on behalf of a person if he knows or it is obvious that such person wishes to:

    (1) Bring a legal action, conduct a defense, or assert a position in litigation, or otherwise have steps taken for him, merely for the purpose of harassing or maliciously injuring any person.[143]

    (2) Present a claim or defense in litigation that is not warranted under existing law, unless it can be supported by good faith argument for an extension, modification, or reversal of existing law.

DR 2-110 Withdrawal from Employment.[144]

(A) In General.

    (1) If permission for withdrawal from employment is required by the rules of a tribunal, a lawyer shall not withdraw from employment in a proceeding before that tribunal without its permission.

    (2) In any event, a lawyer shall not withdraw from employment until he has taken reasonable steps to avoid foreseeable prejudice to the rights of his client, including giving due notice to his client, allowing time for employment of other counsel, delivering to the client all papers and property to which the client is entitled, and complying with applicable laws and rules.

    (3) A lawyer who withdraws from employment shall refund promptly any part of a fee paid in advance that has not been earned.

(B) Mandatory withdrawal.

A lawyer representing a client before a tribunal, with its permission if required by its rules, shall withdraw from employment, and a lawyer representing a client in other matters shall withdraw from employment, if:

    (1) He knows or it is obvious that his client is bringing the legal action, conducting the defense, or asserting a position in the litigation, or is otherwise having steps taken for him, merely for the purpose of harassing or maliciously injuring any person.

    (2) He knows or it is obvious that his continued employment will result in violation of a Disciplinary Rule.[145]

    (3) His mental or physical condition renders it unreasonably difficult for him to carry out the employment effectively.

    (4) He is discharged by his client.

(C) Permissive withdrawal.[146]

If DR 2-110(B) is not applicable, a lawyer may not request permission to withdraw in matters pending before a tribunal, and may not withdraw in other matters, unless such request or such withdrawal is because:

    (1) His client:

        (a) Insists upon presenting a claim or defense that is not warranted under existing law and cannot be supported by good faith argument for an extension, modification, or reversal of existing law.[147]

        (b) Personally seeks to pursue an illegal course of conduct.

        (c) Insists that the lawyer pursue a course of conduct that is illegal or that is prohibited under the Disciplinary Rules.

        (d) By other conduct renders it unreasonably difficult for the law-

---

[142] "[A] general covenant restricting an employed lawyer, after leaving the employment, from practicing in the community for a stated period, appears to this Committee to be an unwarranted restriction on the right of a lawyer to choose where he will practice and inconsistent with our professional status. Accordingly, the Committee is of the opinion it would be improper for the employing lawyer to require the covenant and likewise for the employed lawyer to agree to it." *ABA Opinion* 300 (1961).

[143] *See* ABA Canon 30.
"*Rule 13.* . . . . A member of the State Bar shall not accept employment to prosecute or defend a case solely out of spite, or solely for the purpose of harassing or delaying another . . .." Cal.Business and Professions Code § 6067 (West 1962).

[144] *Cf.* ABA Canon 44.

[145] *See also* Code of Professional Responsibility, DR 5-102 and DR 5-105.

[146] *Cf.* ABA Canon 4.

[147] *Cf.* Anders v. California, 386 U.S. 738, 18 L.Ed.2d 493, 87 S.Ct. 1396 (1967), *rehearing denied*, 388 U.S. 924, 18 L.Ed.2d 1377, 87 S.Ct. 2094 (1967).

yer to carry out his employment effectively.

   (e) **Insists, in a matter not pending before a tribunal, that the lawyer engage in conduct that is contrary to the judgment and advice of the lawyer but not prohibited under the Disciplinary Rules.**

   (f) **Deliberately disregards an agreement or obligation to the lawyer as to expenses or fees.**

(2) **His continued employment is likely to result in a violation of a Disciplinary Rule.**

(3) **His inability to work with co-counsel indicates that the best interests of the client likely will be served by withdrawal.**

(4) **His mental or physical condition renders it difficult for him to carry out the employment effectively.**

(5) **His client knowingly and freely assents to termination of his employment.**

(6) **He believes in good faith, in a proceeding pending before a tribunal, that the tribunal will find the existence of other good cause for withdrawal.**

CANON 3

A Lawyer Should Assist in Preventing the Unauthorized Practice of Law

ETHICAL CONSIDERATIONS

EC 3-1 The prohibition against the practice of law by a layman is grounded in the need of the public for integrity and competence of those who undertake to render legal services. Because of the fiduciary and personal character of the lawyer-client relationship and the inherently complex nature of our legal system, the public can better be assured of the requisite responsibility and competence if the practice of law is confined to those who are subject to the requirements and regulations imposed upon members of the legal profession.

EC 3-2 The sensitive variations in the considerations that bear on legal determinations often make it difficult even for a lawyer to exercise appropriate professional judgment, and it is therefore essential that the personal nature of the relationship of client and lawyer be preserved. Competent professional judgment is the product of a trained familiarity with law and legal processes, a disciplined, analytical approach to legal problems, and a firm ethical commitment.

EC 3-3 A non-lawyer who undertakes to handle legal matters is not governed as to integrity or legal competence by the same rules that govern the conduct of a lawyer. A lawyer is not only subject to that regulation but also is committed to high standards of ethical conduct. The public interest is best served in legal matters by a regulated

profession committed to such standards.[1] The Disciplinary Rules protect the public in that they prohibit a lawyer from seeking employment by improper overtures, from acting in cases of divided loyalties, and from submitting to the control of others in the exercise of his judgment. Moreover, a person who entrusts legal matters to a lawyer is protected by the attorney-client privilege and by the duty of the lawyer to hold inviolate the confidences and secrets of his client.

EC 3-4 A layman who seeks legal services often is not in a position to judge whether he will receive proper professional attention. The entrustment of a legal matter may well involve the confidences, the reputation, the property, the freedom, or even the life of the client. Proper protection of members of the public demands that no person be permitted to act in the confidential and demanding capacity of a lawyer unless he is subject to the regulations of the legal profession.

EC 3-5 It is neither necessary nor desirable to attempt the formulation of a single, specific definition of what constitutes the practice of law.[2] Functionally, the practice of law relates to the rendition of services for others that call for the professional judgment of a lawyer. The essence of the professional judgment of the lawyer is his educated ability to relate the general body and philosophy of law to a specific legal problem of a client; and thus, the public interest will be better served if only lawyers are permitted to act in matters involving professional judgment. Where this professional judgment is not involved, non-lawyers, such as court clerks, police officers, abstracters, and many governmental employees, may engage in occupations that require a special knowledge of law in certain areas. But the services of a lawyer are essential in the public interest whenever the exercise of professional legal judgment is required.

EC 3-6 A lawyer often delegates tasks to clerks, secretaries, and other lay persons. Such delegation is proper if the lawyer maintains a direct relationship with his client, supervises the delegated work, and has complete professional responsibility for the work product.[3] This delegation enables a law-

---

[1] "The condemnation of the unauthorized practice of law is designed to protect the public from legal services by persons unskilled in the law. The prohibition of lay intermediaries is intended to insure the loyalty of the lawyer to the client unimpaired by intervening and possibly conflicting interests." Cheatham, *Availability of Legal Services: The Responsibility of the Individual Lawyer and of the Organized Bar,* 12 U.C.L.A.L.Rev. 438, 439 (1965).

[2] "What constitutes unauthorized practice of the law in a particular jurisdiction is a matter for determination by the courts of that jurisdiction." *ABA Opinion* 198 (1939).

"In the light of the historical development of the lawyer's functions, it is impossible to lay down an exhaustive definition of 'the practice of law' by attempting to enumerate every conceivable act performed by lawyers in the normal course of their work." State Bar of Arizona v. Arizona Land Title & Trust Co., 90 Ariz. 76, 87, 366 P.2d 1, 8–9 (1961), *modified,* 91 Ariz. 293, 371 P.2d 1020 (1962).

[3] "A lawyer can employ lay secretaries, lay investigators, lay detectives, lay researchers, accountants, lay scriveners,

yer to render legal service more economically and efficiently.

EC 3–7 The prohibition against a non-lawyer practicing law does not prevent a layman from representing himself, for then he is ordinarily exposing only himself to possible injury. The purpose of the legal profession is to make educated legal representation available to the public; but anyone who does not wish to avail himself of such representation is not required to do so. Even so, the legal profession should help members of the public to recognize legal problems and to understand why it may be unwise for them to act for themselves in matters having legal consequences.

EC 3–8 Since a lawyer should not aid or encourage a layman to practice law, he should not practice law in association with a layman or otherwise share legal fees with a layman.[4] This does not mean, however, that the pecuniary value of the interest of a deceased lawyer in his firm or practice may not be paid to his estate or specified persons such as his widow or heirs.[5] In like manner,

profit-sharing retirement plans of a lawyer or law firm which include non-lawyer office employees are not improper.[6] These limited exceptions to the rule against sharing legal fees with laymen are permissible since they do not aid or encourage laymen to practice law.

EC 3–9 Regulation of the practice of law is accomplished principally by the respective states.[7] Authority to engage in the practice of law conferred in any jurisdiction is not per se a grant of the right to practice elsewhere, and it is improper for a lawyer to engage in practice where he is not permitted by law or by court order to do so. However, the demands of business and the mobility of our society pose distinct problems in the regulation of the practice of law by the states.[8] In furtherance of the public interest, the legal profession should discourage regulation that unreasonably imposes territorial limitations upon the right of a lawyer to handle the legal affairs of his client or upon the opportunity of a client to obtain the services of a lawyer of his choice in all matters including the presentation of a contested matter in a tribunal before which the lawyer is not permanently admitted to practice.[9]

---

nonlawyer draftsmen or nonlawyer researchers. In fact, he may employ nonlawyers to do any task for him except counsel clients about law matters, engage directly in the practice of law, appear in court or appear in formal proceedings a part of the judicial process, so long as it is he who takes the work and vouches for it to the client and becomes responsible to the client." *ABA Opinion* 316 (1967).

ABA Opinion 316 (1967) also stated that if a lawyer practices law as part of a law firm which includes lawyers from several states, he may delegate tasks to firm members in other states so long as he "is the person who, on behalf of the firm, vouched for the work of all of the others and, with the client and in the courts, did the legal acts defined by that state as the practice of law."

"A lawyer cannot delegate his professional responsibility to a law student employed in his office. He may avail himself of the assistance of the student in many of the fields of the lawyer's work, such as examination of case law, finding and interviewing witnesses, making collections of claims, examining court records, delivering papers, conveying important messages, and other similar matters. But the student is not permitted, until he is admitted to the Bar, to perform the professional functions of a lawyer, such as conducting court trials, giving professional advice to clients or drawing legal documents for them. The student in all his work must act as agent for the lawyer employing him, who must supervise his work and be responsible for his good conduct." *ABA Opinion* 85 (1932).

[4] "No division of fees for legal services is proper, except with another lawyer . . . ." ABA Canon 34. Otherwise, according to *ABA Opinion* 316 (1967), "[t]he Canons of Ethics do not examine into the method by which such persons are remunerated by the lawyer. . . . They may be paid a salary, a per diem charge, a flat fee, a contract price, etc."

See ABA Canons 33 and 47.

[5] "Many partnership agreements provide that the active partners, on the death of any one of them, are to make payments to the estate or to the nominee of a deceased partner on a pre-determined formula. It is only where the effect of such an arrangement is to make the estate or nominee a member of the partnership along with the surviving partners that it is prohibited by *Canon 34*. Where the payments are made in accordance with a pre-existing agreement entered into by the deceased partner during his lifetime and providing for a fixed method for determining

their amount based upon the value of services rendered during the partner's lifetime and providing for a fixed period over which the payments are to be made, this is not the case. Under these circumstances, whether the payments are considered to be delayed payment of compensation earned but withheld during the partner's lifetime, or whether they are considered to be an approximation of his interest in matters pending at the time of his death, is immaterial. In either event, as Henry S. Drinker says in his book, Legal Ethics, at page 189: 'It would seem, however, that a reasonable agreement to pay the estate a proportion of the receipts for a reasonable period is a proper practical settlement for the lawyer's services to his retirement or death.' " *ABA Opinion* 308 (1963).

[6] *Cf. ABA Opinion* 311 (1964).

[7] "That the States have broad power to regulate the practice of law is, of course, beyond question." United Mine Workers v. Ill. State Bar Ass'n, 389 U.S. 217, 222 (1967).

"It is a matter of law, not of ethics, as to where an individual may practice law. Each state has its own rules." *ABA Opinion* 316 (1967).

[8] "Much of clients' business crosses state lines. People are mobile, moving from state to state. Many metropolitan areas cross state lines. It is common today to have a single economic and social community involving more than one state. The business of a single client may involve legal problems in several states." *ABA Opinion* 316 (1967).

[9] "[W]e reaffirmed the general principle that legal services to New Jersey residents with respect to New Jersey matters may ordinarily be furnished only by New Jersey counsel; but we pointed out that there may be multistate transactions where strict adherence to this thesis would not be in the public interest and that, under the circumstances, it would have been not only more costly to the client but also 'grossly impractical and inefficient' to have had the settlement negotiations conducted by separate lawyers from different states." In re Estate of Waring, 47 N.J. 367, 376, 221 A.2d 193, 197 (1966).

Cf. ABA Opinion 316 (1967).

DISCIPLINARY RULES

DR 3-101   Aiding Unauthorized Practice of Law.[10]

(A) A lawyer shall not aid a non-lawyer in the unauthorized practice of law.[11]

(B) A lawyer shall not practice law in a jurisdiction where to do so would be in violation of regulations of the profession in that jurisdiction.[12]

DR 3-102   Dividing Legal Fees with a Non-Lawyer.

(A) A lawyer or law firm shall not share legal fees with a non-lawyer,[13] except that:

    (1) An agreement by a lawyer with his firm, partner, or associate may provide for the payment of money, over a reasonable period of time after his death, to his estate or to one or more specified persons.[14]

    (2) A lawyer who undertakes to complete unfinished legal business of a deceased lawyer may pay to the estate of the deceased lawyer that proportion of the total compensation which fairly represents the services rendered by the deceased lawyer.

    (3) A lawyer or law firm may include non-lawyer employees in a retirement plan, even though the plan is based in whole or in part on a profit-sharing arrangement.[15]

DR 3-103   Forming a Partnership with a Non-Lawyer.

(A) A lawyer shall not form a partnership with a non-lawyer if any of the activities of the partnership consist of the practice of law.[16]

---

[10] Conduct permitted by the Disciplinary Rules of Canons 2 and 5 does not violate DR 3-101.

[11] See ABA Canon 47.

[12] It should be noted, however, that a lawyer may engage in conduct, otherwise prohibited by this Disciplinary Rule, where such conduct is authorized by preemptive federal legislation. See Sperry v. Florida, 373 U.S. 379, 10 L.Ed.2d 428, 83 S.Ct. 1322 (1963).

[13] See ABA Canon 34 and ABA Opinions 316 (1967), 180 (1938), and 48 (1931).

"The receiving attorney shall not under any guise or form share his fee for legal services with a lay agency, personal or corporate, without prejudice, however, to the right of the lay forwarder to charge and collect from the creditor proper compensation for non-legal services rendered by the law [sic] forwarder which are separate and apart from the services performed by the receiving attorney." ABA Opinion 294 (1958).

[14] See ABA Opinions 309 (1963) and 266 (1945).

[15] Cf. ABA Opinion 311 (1964).

[16] See ABA Canon 33; cf. ABA Opinions 239 (1942) and 201 (1940).

ABA Opinion 316 (1967) states that lawyers licensed in different jurisdictions may, under certain conditions, enter "into an arrangement for the practice of law" and that a lawyer licensed in State A is not, for such purpose, a layman in State B.

CANON 4

A Lawyer Should Preserve the Confidences and Secrets of a Client

ETHICAL CONSIDERATIONS

EC 4-1   Both the fiduciary relationship existing between lawyer and client and the proper functioning of the legal system require the preservation by the lawyer of confidences and secrets of one who has employed or sought to employ him.[1]   A client must feel free to discuss whatever he wishes with his lawyer and a lawyer must be equally free to obtain information beyond that volunteered by his client.[2]   A lawyer should be fully informed of all the facts of the matter he is handling in order for his client to obtain the full advantage of our legal system.   It is for the lawyer in the exercise of his independent professional judgment to separate the relevant and important from the irrelevant and unimportant.   The observance of the ethical obligation of a lawyer to hold inviolate the confidences and secrets of his client not only facilitates the full development of facts essential to proper representation of the client but also encourages laymen to seek early legal assistance.

EC 4-2   The obligation to protect confidences and secrets obviously does not preclude a lawyer from revealing information when his client consents

---

[1] See ABA Canons 6 and 37 and ABA Opinion 287 (1953).

"The reason underlying the rule with respect to confidential communications between attorney and client is well stated in Mecham on Agency, 2d Ed., Vol. 2, § 2297, as follows: 'The purposes and necessities of the relation between a client and his attorney require, in many cases, on the part of the client, the fullest and freest disclosures to the attorney of the client's objects, motives and acts. This disclosure is made in the strictest confidence, relying upon the attorney's honor and fidelity.   To permit the attorney to reveal to others what is so disclosed, would be not only a gross violation of a sacred trust upon his part, but it would utterly destroy and prevent the usefulness and benefits to be derived from professional assistance.   Based upon considerations of public policy, therefore, the law wisely declares that all confidential communications and disclosures, made by a client to his legal adviser for the purpose of obtaining his professional aid or advice, shall be strictly privileged;—that the attorney shall not be permitted, without the consent of his client,— and much less will he be compelled—to reveal or disclose communications made to him under such circumstances.' " ABA Opinion 250 (1943).

"While it is true that complete revelation of relevant facts should be encouraged for trial purposes, nevertheless an attorney's dealings with his client, if both are sincere, and if the dealings involve more than mere technical matters, should be immune to discovery proceedings. There must be freedom from fear of revealment of matters disclosed to an attorney because of the peculiarly intimate relationship existing." Ellis-Foster Co. v. Union Carbide & Carbon Corp., 159 F.Supp. 917, 919 (D.N.J. 1958).

Cf. ABA Opinions 314 (1965), 274 (1946) and 268 (1945).

[2] "While it is the great purpose of law to ascertain the truth, there is the countervailing necessity of insuring the right of every person to freely and fully confer and confide in one having knowledge of the law, and skilled in its practice, in order that the former may have adequate advice and a proper defense.   This assistance can be made safely and readily available only when the client is free

after full disclosure,[3] when necessary to perform his professional employment, when permitted by a Disciplinary Rule, or when required by law. Unless the client otherwise directs, a lawyer may disclose the affairs of his client to partners or associates of his firm. It is a matter of common knowledge that the normal operation of a law office exposes confidential professional information to nonlawyer employees of the office, particularly secretaries and those having access to the files; and this obligates a lawyer to exercise care in selecting and training his employees so that the sanctity of all confidences and secrets of his clients may be preserved. If the obligation extends to two or more clients as to the same information, a lawyer should obtain the permission of all before revealing the information. A lawyer must always be sensitive to the rights and wishes of his client and act scrupulously in the making of decisions which may involve the disclosure of information obtained in his professional relationship.[4] Thus, in the absence of consent of his client after full disclosure, a lawyer should not associate another lawyer in the handling of a matter; nor should he, in the absence of consent, seek counsel from another lawyer if there is a reasonable possibility that the identity of the client or his confidences or secrets would be revealed to such lawyer. Both social amenities and professional duty should cause a lawyer to shun indiscreet conversations concerning his clients.

EC 4-3 Unless the client otherwise directs, it is not improper for a lawyer to give limited information from his files to an outside agency necessary for statistical, bookkeeping, accounting, data processing, banking, printing, or other legitimate purposes, provided he exercises due care in the selection of the agency and warns the agency that the information must be kept confidential.

EC 4-4 The attorney-client privilege is more limited than the ethical obligation of a lawyer to guard the confidences and secrets of his client. This ethical precept, unlike the evidentiary privilege, exists without regard to the nature or source of information or the fact that others share the knowledge. A lawyer should endeavor to act in a manner which preserves the evidentiary privilege; for example, he should avoid professional discussions in the presence of persons to whom the privilege does not extend. A lawyer owes an obligation to advise the client of the attorney-client privilege and timely to assert the privilege unless it is waived by the client.

EC 4-5 A lawyer should not use information acquired in the course of the representation of a client to the disadvantage of the client and a lawyer should not use, except with the consent of his client after full disclosure, such information for his own purposes.[5] Likewise, a lawyer should be diligent in his efforts to prevent the misuse of such information by his employees and associates.[6] Care should be exercised by a lawyer to prevent the disclosure of the confidences and secrets of one client to another,[7] and no employment should be accepted that might require such disclosure.

EC 4-6 The obligation of a lawyer to preserve the confidences and secrets of his client continues after the termination of his employment.[8] Thus a lawyer should not attempt to sell a law practice as a going business because, among other reasons, to do so would involve the disclosure of confidences and secrets.[9] A lawyer should also provide for the protection of the confidences and secrets of his client following the termination of the practice of the lawyer, whether termination is due to death, disability, or retirement. For example, a lawyer might provide for the personal papers of the client to be returned to him and for the papers of the lawyer to be delivered to another lawyer or to be destroyed. In determining the method of disposition, the instructions and wishes of the client should be a dominant consideration.

DISCIPLINARY RULES

DR 4-101 **Preservation of Confidences and Secrets of a Client.**[10]

(A) **"Confidence" refers to information protected by the attorney-client privilege under applicable law, and "secret" refers to other information gained in the professional relationship that the client has requested be held inviolate or the disclosure of which would be em-**

---

from the consequences of apprehension of disclosure by reason of the subsequent statements of the skilled lawyer." Baird v. Koerner, 279 F.2d 623, 629–30 (9th Cir. 1960). *Cf. ABA Opinion* 150 (1936).

[3] "Where . . . [a client] knowingly and after full disclosure participates in a [legal fee] financing plan which requires the furnishing of certain information to the bank, clearly by his conduct he has waived any privilege as to that information." *ABA Opinion* 320 (1968).

[4] "The lawyer must decide when he takes a case whether it is a suitable one for him to undertake and after this decision is made, he is not justified in turning against his client by exposing injurious evidence entrusted to him. . . . [D]oing something intrinsically regrettable, because the only alternative involves worse consequences, is a necessity in every profession." Williston, Life and Law 271 (1940). *Cf. ABA Opinions* 177 (1938) and 83 (1932).

---

[5] *See* ABA Canon 11.

[6] *See* ABA Canon 37.

[7] *See* ABA Canons 6 and 37. "[A]n attorney must not accept professional employment against a client or a former client which will, or even *may* require him to use confidential information obtained by the attorney in the course of his professional relations with such client regarding the subject matter of the employment . . . ." *ABA Opinion* 165 (1936).

[8] *See* ABA Canon 37. "Confidential communications between an attorney and his client, made because of the relationship and concerning the subject-matter of the attorney's employment, are generally privileged from disclosure without the consent of the client, and this privilege outlasts the attorney's employment. *Canon 37." ABA Opinion* 154 (1936).

[9] *Cf. ABA Opinion* 266 (1945).

[10] *See* ABA Canon 37; *cf.* ABA Canon 6.

barrassing or would be likely to be detrimental to the client.

(B) Except when permitted under DR 4–101(C), a lawyer shall not knowingly:

    (1) Reveal a confidence or secret of his client.[11]

    (2) Use a confidence or secret of his client to the disadvantage of the client.

    (3) Use a confidence or secret of his client for the advantage of himself [12] or of a third person,[13] unless the client consents after full disclosure.

(C) A lawyer may reveal:

    (1) Confidences or secrets with the consent of the client or clients affected, but only after a full disclosure to them.[14]

    (2) Confidences or secrets when permitted under Disciplinary Rules or required by law or court order.[15]

---

11 "§ 6068 . . . It is the duty of an attorney:
. . . .

"(e) To maintain inviolate the confidence, and at every peril to himself to preserve the secrets, of his client." Cal. Business and Professions Code § 6068 (West 1962). Virtually the same provision is found in the Oregon statutes. Ore.Rev.Stats. ch. 9, § 9.460(5).

"Communications between lawyer and client are privileged (Wigmore on Evidence, 3d. Ed. Vol. 8, §§ 2290–2329). The modern theory underlying the privilege is subjective and is to give the client freedom of apprehension in consulting his legal adviser (*ibid.*, § 2290, p. 548). The privilege applies to communications made in seeking legal advice for any purpose (*ibid.*, § 2294, p. 563). The mere circumstance that the advice is given without charge therefore does not nullify the privilege (*ibid.*, § 2303)." *ABA Opinion* 216 (1941).

"It is the duty of an attorney to maintain the confidence and preserve inviolate the secrets of his client . . . ." *ABA Opinion* 155 (1936).

12 *See* ABA Canon 11.
"The provision respecting employment is in accord with the general rule announced in the adjudicated cases that a lawyer may not make use of knowledge or information acquired by him through his professional relations with his client, or in the conduct of his client's business, to his own advantage or profit (7 C.J.S., § 125, p. 958; Healy v. Gray, 184 Iowa 111, 168 N.W. 222; Baumgardner v. Hudson, D.C.App., 277 F. 552; Goodrum v. Clement, D.C.App., 277 F. 586)." *ABA Opinion* 250 (1943).

13 *See ABA Opinion* 177 (1938).

14 "[A lawyer] may not divulge confidential communications, information, and secrets imparted to him by the client or acquired during their professional relations, unless he is authorized to do so by the client (People v. Gerold, 265 Ill. 448, 107 N.E. 165, 178; Murphy v. Riggs, 238 Mich. 151, 213 N.W. 110, 112; Opinion of this Committee, No. 91)." *ABA Opinion* 202 (1940).
Cf. ABA Opinion 91 (1933).

15 "A defendant in a criminal case when admitted to bail is not only regarded as in the custody of his bail, but he is also in the custody of the law, and admission to bail does not deprive the court of its inherent power to deal with the person of the prisoner. Being in lawful custody, the defendant is guilty of an escape when he gains his liberty before he is delivered in due process of law, and is guilty of a separate offense for which he may

    (3) The intention of his client to commit a crime [16] and the information necessary to prevent the crime.[17]

    (4) Confidences or secrets necessary to establish or collect his fee [18] or to defend himself or his employees or associates against an accusation of wrongful conduct.[19]

(D) A lawyer shall exercise reasonable care to prevent his employees, associates, and others whose services are utilized by him from disclosing or using confidences or secrets of a client, except that a lawyer may reveal the information allowed by DR 4–101(C) through an employee.

---

be punished. In failing to disclose his client's whereabouts as a fugitive under these circumstances the attorney would not only be aiding his client to escape trial on the charge for which he was indicted, but would likewise be aiding him in evading prosecution for the additional offense of escape.

"It is the opinion of the committee that under such circumstances the attorney's knowledge of his client's whereabouts is not privileged, and that he may be disciplined for failing to disclose that information to the proper authorities. . . ." *ABA Opinion* 155 (1936).

"We held in *Opinion* 155 that a communication by a client to his attorney in respect to the future commission of an unlawful act or to a continuing wrong is not privileged from disclosure. Public policy forbids that the relation of attorney and client should be used to conceal wrongdoing on the part of the client.
. . . .

"When an attorney representing a defendant in a criminal case applies on his behalf for probation or suspension of sentence, he represents to the court, by implication at least, that his client will abide by the terms and conditions of the court's order. When that attorney is later advised of a violation of that order, it is his duty to advise his client of the consequences of his act, and endeavor to prevent a continuance of the wrongdoing. If his client thereafter persists in violating the terms and conditions of his probation, it is the duty of the attorney as an officer of the court to advise the proper authorities concerning his client's conduct. Such information, even though coming to the attorney from the client in the course of his professional relations with respect to other matters in which he represents the defendant, is not privileged from disclosure. . . ." *ABA Opinion* 156 (1936).

16 *ABA Opinion* 314 (1965) indicates that a lawyer must disclose even the confidences of his clients if "the facts in the attorney's possession indicate beyond reasonable doubt that a crime will be committed."
See ABA Opinion 155 (1936).

17 *See* ABA Canon 37 and *ABA Opinion* 202 (1940).

18 *Cf. ABA Opinion* 250 (1943).

19 *See* ABA Canon 37 and *ABA Opinions* 202 (1940) and 19 (1930).

"[T]he adjudicated cases recognize an exception to the rule [that a lawyer shall not reveal the confidences of his client], where disclosure is necessary to protect the attorney's interests arising out of the relation of attorney and client in which disclosure was made.

"The exception is stated in Mechem on Agency, 2d Ed., Vol. 2, § 2313, as follows: 'But the attorney may disclose information received from the client when it becomes necessary for his own protection, as if the client should bring an action against the attorney for negligence or misconduct, and it became necessary for the attorney to

CANON 5

A Lawyer Should Exercise Independent Professional Judgment on Behalf of a Client

ETHICAL CONSIDERATIONS

EC 5-1 The professional judgment of a lawyer should be exercised, within the bounds of the law, solely for the benefit of his client and free of compromising influences and loyalties.[1] Neither his

---

show what his instructions were, or what was the nature of the duty which the client expected him to perform. So if it became necessary for the attorney to bring an action against the client, the client's privilege could not prevent the attorney from disclosing what was essential as a means of obtaining or defending his own rights.'

"Mr. Jones, in his Commentaries on Evidence, 2d Ed., Vol. 5, § 2165, states the exception thus: 'It has frequently been held that the rule as to privileged communications does not apply when litigation arises between attorney and client to the extent that their communications are relevant to the issue. In such cases, if the disclosure of privileged communications becomes necessary to protect the attorney's rights, he is released from those obligations of secrecy which the law places upon him. He should not, however, disclose more than is necessary for his own protection. It would be a manifest injustice to allow the client to take advantage of the rule of exclusion as to professional confidence to the prejudice of his attorney, or that it should be carried to the extent of depriving the attorney of the means of obtaining or defending his own rights. In such cases the attorney is exempted from the obligations of secrecy.' " *ABA Opinion* 250 (1943).

[1] *Cf.* ABA Canon 35.

"[A lawyer's] fiduciary duty is of the highest order and he must not represent interests adverse to those of the client. It is also true that because of his professional responsibility and the confidence and trust which his client may legitimately repose in him, he must adhere to a high standard of honesty, integrity and good faith in dealing with his client. He is not permitted to take advantage of his position or superior knowledge to impose upon the client; nor to conceal facts or law, nor in any way deceive him without being held responsible therefor." Smoot v. Lund, 13 Utah 2d 168, 172, 369 P.2d 933, 936 (1962).

"When a client engages the services of a lawyer in a given piece of business he is entitled to feel that, until that business is finally disposed of in some manner, he has the undivided loyalty of the one upon whom he looks as his advocate and champion. If, as in this case, he is sued and his home attached by his own attorney, who is representing him in another matter, all feeling of loyalty is necessarily destroyed, and the profession is exposed to the charge that it is interested only in money." Grievance Comm. v. Rattner, 152 Conn. 59, 65, 203 A.2d 82, 84 (1964).

"One of the cardinal principles confronting every attorney in the representation of a client is the requirement of complete loyalty and service in good faith to the best of his ability. In a criminal case the client is entitled to a fair trial, but not a perfect one. These are fundamental requirements of due process under the Fourteenth Amendment. . . . The same principles are applicable in Sixth Amendment cases (not pertinent herein) and suggest that an attorney should have no conflict of interest and that he must devote his full and faithful efforts toward the defense of his client." Johns v. Smyth, 176 F.Supp. 949, 952 (E.D.Va.1959), *modified,* United States ex rel. Wilkins v. Banmiller, 205 F.Supp. 123, 128 n. 5 (E.D.Pa.1962), *aff'd,* 325 F.2d 514 (3d Cir. 1963), *cert. denied,* 379 U.S. 847, 13 L.Ed.2d 51, 85 S.Ct. 87 (1964).

personal interests, the interests of other clients, nor the desires of third persons should be permitted to dilute his loyalty to his client.

Interests of a Lawyer That May Affect His Judgment

EC 5-2 A lawyer should not accept proffered employment if his personal interests or desires will, or there is a reasonable probability that they will, affect adversely the advice to be given or services to be rendered the prospective client.[2] After accepting employment, a lawyer carefully should refrain from acquiring a property right or assuming a position that would tend to make his judgment less protective of the interests of his client.

EC 5-3 The self-interest of a lawyer resulting from his ownership of property in which his client also has an interest or which may affect property of his client may interfere with the exercise of free judgment on behalf of his client. If such interference would occur with respect to a prospective client, a lawyer should decline employment proffered by him. After accepting employment, a lawyer should not acquire property rights that would adversely affect his professional judgment in the representation of his client. Even if the property interests of a lawyer do not presently interfere with the exercise of his independent judgment, but the likelihood of interference can reasonably be foreseen by him, a lawyer should explain the situation to his client and should decline employment or withdraw unless the client consents to the continuance of the relationship after full disclosure. A lawyer should not seek to persuade his client to permit him to invest in an undertaking of his client nor make improper use of his professional relationship to influence his client to invest in an enterprise in which the lawyer is interested.

EC 5-4 If, in the course of his representation of a client, a lawyer is permitted to receive from his client a beneficial ownership in publication rights relating to the subject matter of the employment, he may be tempted to subordinate the interests of his client to his own anticipated pecuniary gain.

---

[2] "Attorneys must not allow their private interests to conflict with those of their clients. . . . They owe their entire devotion to the interests of their clients." United States v. Anonymous, 215 F.Supp. 111, 113 (E.D. Tenn.1963).

"[T]he court [below] concluded that a firm may not accept any action against a person whom they are presently representing even though there is no relationship between the two cases. In arriving at this conclusion, the court cited an opinion of the Committee on Professional Ethics of the New York County Lawyers' Association which stated in part: 'While under the circumstances * * * there may be no actual conflict of interest * * * "maintenance of public confidence in the Bar requires an attorney who has accepted representation of a client to decline, while representing such client, any employment from an adverse party in any matter even though wholly unrelated to the original retainer." See Question and Answer No. 350, N.Y. County L. Ass'n, Questions and Answer No. 450 (June 21, 1956).' " Grievance Comm. v. Rattner, 152 Conn. 59, 65, 203 A.2d 82, 84 (1964).

For example, a lawyer in a criminal case who obtains from his client television, radio, motion picture, newspaper, magazine, book, or other publication rights with respect to the case may be influenced, consciously or unconsciously, to a course of conduct that will enhance the value of his publication rights to the prejudice of his client. To prevent these potentially differing interests, such arrangements should be scrupulously avoided prior to the termination of all aspects of the matter giving rise to the employment, even though his employment has previously ended.

EC 5-5 A lawyer should not suggest to his client that a gift be made to himself or for his benefit. If a lawyer accepts a gift from his client, he is peculiarly susceptible to the charge that he unduly influenced or overreached the client. If a client voluntarily offers to make a gift to his lawyer, the lawyer may accept the gift, but before doing so, he should urge that his client secure disinterested advice from an independent, competent person who is cognizant of all the circumstances.[3] Other than in exceptional circumstances, a lawyer should insist that an instrument in which his client desires to name him beneficially be prepared by another lawyer selected by the client.[4]

EC 5-6 A lawyer should not consciously influence a client to name him as executor, trustee, or lawyer in an instrument. In those cases where a client wishes to name his lawyer as such, care should be taken by the lawyer to avoid even the appearance of impropriety.[5]

EC 5-7 The possibility of an adverse effect upon the exercise of free judgment by a lawyer on behalf of his client during litigation generally makes it undesirable for the lawyer to acquire a proprietary interest in the cause of his client or otherwise

to become financially interested in the outcome of the litigation.[6] However, it is not improper for a lawyer to protect his right to collect a fee for his services by the assertion of legally permissible liens, even though by doing so he may acquire an interest in the outcome of litigation. Although a contingent fee arrangement [7] gives a lawyer a financial interest in the outcome of litigation, a reasonable contingent fee is permissible in civil cases because it may be the only means by which a layman can obtain the services of a lawyer of his choice. But a lawyer, because he is in a better position to evaluate a cause of action, should enter into a contingent fee arrangement only in those instances where the arrangement will be beneficial to the client.

EC 5-8 A financial interest in the outcome of litigation also results if monetary advances are made by the lawyer to his client.[8] Although this assistance generally is not encouraged, there are instances when it is not improper to make loans to a client. For example, the advancing or guaranteeing of payment of the costs and expenses of litigation by a lawyer may be the only way a client can enforce his cause of action,[9] but the ultimate liability for such costs and expenses must be that of the client.

EC 5-9 Occasionally a lawyer is called upon to decide in a particular case whether he will be a witness or an advocate. If a lawyer is both counsel and witness, he becomes more easily impeachable for interest and thus may be a less effective witness. Conversely, the opposing counsel may be handicapped in challenging the credibility of the lawyer when the lawyer also appears as an advocate in the case. An advocate who becomes a witness is in the unseemly and ineffective position of arguing his own credibility. The roles of an advocate and of a witness are inconsistent; the function of an advocate is to advance or argue the cause of another, while that of a witness is to state facts objectively.

EC 5-10 Problems incident to the lawyer-witness relationship arise at different stages; they relate

---

[3] "Courts of equity will scrutinize with jealous vigilance transactions between parties occupying fiduciary relations toward each other. . . . A deed will not be held invalid, however, if made by the grantor with full knowledge of its nature and effect, and because of the deliberate, voluntary and intelligent desire of the grantor.
Where a fiduciary relation exists, the burden of proof is on the grantee or beneficiary of an instrument executed during the existence of such relationship to show the fairness of the transaction, that it was equitable and just and that it did not proceed from undue influence. . . .
The same rule has application where an attorney engages in a transaction with a client during the existence of the relation and is benefited thereby. . . . Conversely, an attorney is not prohibited from dealing with his client or buying his property, and such contracts, if open, fair and honest, when deliberately made, are as valid as contracts between other parties. . . . [I]mportant factors in determining whether a transaction is fair include a showing by the fiduciary (1) that he made a full and frank disclosure of all the relevant information that he had; (2) that the consideration was adequate; and (3) that the principal had independent advice before completing the transaction." McFail v. Braden, 19 Ill.2d 108, 117–18, 166 N.E.2d 46, 52 (1960).

[4] See State ex rel. Nebraska State Bar Ass'n v. Richards, 165 Neb. 80, 94–95, 84 N.W.2d 136, 146 (1957).

[5] See ABA Canon 9.

[6] See ABA Canon 10.

[7] See Code of Professional Responsibility, EC 2–20.

[8] See ABA Canon 42.

[9] "Rule 3a. . . . A member of the State Bar shall not directly or indirectly pay or agree to pay, or represent or sanction the representation that he will pay, medical, hospital or nursing bills or other personal expenses incurred by or for a client, prospective or existing; provided this rule shall not prohibit a member:

"(1) with the consent of the client, from paying or agreeing to pay to third persons such expenses from funds collected or to be collected for the client; or

(2) after he has been employed, from lending money to his client upon the client's promise in writing to repay such loan; or

(3) from advancing the costs of prosecuting or defending a claim or action. Such costs within the meaning of this subparagraph (3) include all taxable costs or disbursements, costs or investigation and costs of obtaining and presenting evidence." Cal. Business and Professions Code § 6076 (West Supp.1967).

either to whether a lawyer should accept employment or should withdraw from employment.[10] Regardless of when the problem arises, his decision is to be governed by the same basic considerations. It is not objectionable for a lawyer who is a potential witness to be an advocate if it is unlikely that he will be called as a witness because his testimony would be merely cumulative or if his testimony will relate only to an uncontested issue.[11] In the exceptional situation where it will be manifestly unfair to the client for the lawyer to refuse employment or to withdraw when he will likely be a witness on a contested issue, he may serve as advocate even though he may be a witness.[12] In making such decision, he should determine the personal or financial sacrifice of the client that may result from his refusal of employment or withdrawal therefrom, the materiality of his testimony, and the effectiveness of his representation in view of his personal involvement. In weighing these factors, it should be clear that refusal or withdrawal will impose an unreasonable hardship upon the client before the lawyer accepts or continues the employment.[13] Where the question arises, doubts should be resolved in favor of the lawyer testifying and against his becoming or continuing as an advocate.[14]

---

[10] "When a lawyer knows, prior to trial, that he will be a necessary witness, except as to merely formal matters such as identification or custody of a document or the like, neither he nor his firm or associates should conduct the trial. If, during the trial, he discovers that the ends of justice require his testimony, he should, from that point on, if feasible and not prejudicial to his client's case, leave further conduct of the trial to other counsel. If circumstances do not permit withdrawal from the conduct of the trial, the lawyer should not argue the credibility of his own testimony." *A Code of Trial Conduct: Promulgated by the American College of Trial Lawyers,* 43 A.B.A.J. 223, 224–25 (1957).

[11] *Cf.* Canon 19: "When a lawyer is a witness for his client, except as to merely formal matters, such as the attestation or custody of an instrument and the like, he should leave the trial of the case to other counsel."

[12] "It is the general rule that a lawyer may not testify in litigation in which he is an advocate unless circumstances arise which could not be anticipated and it is necessary to prevent a miscarriage of justice. In those rare cases where the testimony of an attorney is needed to protect his client's interests, it is not only proper but mandatory that it be forthcoming." Schwartz v. Wenger, 267 Minn. 40, 43–44, 124 N.W.2d 489, 492 (1963).

[13] "The great weight of authority in this country holds that the attorney who acts as counsel and witness, in behalf of his client, in the same cause on a material matter, not of a merely formal character, and not in an emergency, but having knowledge that he would be required to be a witness in ample time to have secured other counsel and given up his service in the case, violates a highly important provision of the Code of Ethics and a rule of professional conduct, but does not commit a legal error in so testifying, as a result of which a new trial will be granted." Erwin M. Jennings Co. v. DiGenova, 107 Conn. 491, 499, 141 A. 866, 869 (1928).

[14] "[C]ases may arise, and in practice often do arise, in which there would be a failure of justice should the attorney withhold his testimony. In such a case it would be a vicious professional sentiment which would deprive

EC 5-11 A lawyer should not permit his personal interests to influence his advice relative to a suggestion by his client that additional counsel be employed.[15] In like manner, his personal interests should not deter him from suggesting that additional counsel be employed; on the contrary, he should be alert to the desirability of recommending additional counsel when, in his judgment, the proper representation of his client requires it. However, a lawyer should advise his client not to employ additional counsel suggested by the client if the lawyer believes that such employment would be a disservice to the client, and he should disclose the reasons for his belief.

EC 5-12 Inability of co-counsel to agree on a matter vital to the representation of their client requires that their disagreement be submitted by them jointly to their client for his resolution, and the decision of the client shall control the action to be taken.[16]

EC 5-13 A lawyer should not maintain membership in or be influenced by any organization of employees that undertakes to prescribe, direct, or suggest when or how he should fulfill his professional obligations to a person or organization that employs him as a lawyer. Although it is not necessarily improper for a lawyer employed by a corporation or similar entity to be a member of an organization of employees, he should be vigilant to safeguard his fidelity as a lawyer to his employer, free from outside influences.

Interests of Multiple Clients

EC 5-14 Maintaining the independence of professional judgment required of a lawyer precludes his acceptance or continuation of employment that will adversely affect his judgment on behalf of or dilute his loyalty to a client.[17] This problem arises whenever a lawyer is asked to represent two or more clients who may have differing interests, whether such interests be conflicting, inconsistent, diverse, or otherwise discordant.[18]

EC 5-15 If a lawyer is requested to undertake or to continue representation of multiple clients having potentially differing interests, he must weigh carefully the possibility that his judgment may be impaired or his loyalty divided if he accepts or

---

the client of the benefit of his attorney's testimony." Connolly v. Straw, 53 Wis. 645, 649, 11 N.W. 17, 19 (1881).

But see Canon 19: "Except when essential to the ends of justice, a lawyer should avoid testifying in court in behalf of his client."

[15] *Cf.* ABA Canon 7.

[16] *See* ABA Canon 7.

[17] *See* ABA Canon 6; *cf. ABA Opinions* 261 (1944), 242 (1942), 142 (1935), and 30 (1931).

[18] The ABA Canons speak of "conflicting interests" rather than "differing interests" but make no attempt to define such other than the statement in Canon 6: "Within the meaning of this canon, a lawyer represents conflicting interests when, in behalf of one client, it is his duty to contend for that which duty to another client requires him to oppose."

continues the employment. He should resolve all doubts against the propriety of the representation. A lawyer should never represent in litigation multiple clients with differing interests,[19] and there are few situations in which he would be justified in representing in litigation multiple clients with potentially differing interests. If a lawyer accepted such employment and the interests did become actually differing, he would have to withdraw from employment with likelihood of resulting hardship on the clients; and for this reason it is preferable that he refuse the employment initially. On the other hand, there are many instances in which a lawyer may properly serve multiple clients having potentially differing interests in matters not involving litigation. If the interests vary only slightly, it is generally likely that the lawyer will not be subjected to an adverse influence and that he can retain his independent judgment on behalf of each client; and if the interests become differing, withdrawal is less likely to have a disruptive effect upon the causes of his clients.

EC 5-16 In those instances in which a lawyer is justified in representing two or more clients having differing interests, it is nevertheless essential that each client be given the opportunity to evaluate his need for representation free of any potential conflict and to obtain other counsel if he so desires.[20] Thus before a lawyer may represent multiple clients, he should explain fully to each client the implications of the common representation and should accept or continue employment only if the clients consent.[21] If there are present other circumstances that might cause any of the multiple clients to question the undivided loyalty of the lawyer, he should also advise all of the clients of those circumstances.[22]

EC 5-17 Typically recurring situations involving potentially differing interests are those in which a lawyer is asked to represent co-defendants in a criminal case, co-plaintiffs in a personal injury case, an insured and his insurer,[23] and beneficiaries of the estate of a decedent. Whether a lawyer can fairly and adequately protect the interests of multiple clients in these and similar situations depends upon an analysis of each case. In certain circumstances, there may exist little chance of the judgment of the lawyer being adversely affected by the slight possibility that the interests will become actually differing; in other circumstances, the chance of adverse effect upon his judgment is not unlikely.

EC 5-18 A lawyer employed or retained by a corporation or similar entity owes his allegiance to the entity and not to a stockholder, director, officer, employee, representative, or other person connected with the entity. In advising the entity, a lawyer should keep paramount its interests and his professional judgment should not be influenced

---

[19] "Canon 6 of the Canons of Professional Ethics, adopted by the American Bar Association on September 30, 1937, and by the Pennsylvania Bar Association on January 7, 1938, provides in part that 'It is unprofessional to represent conflicting interests, except by express consent of all concerned given after a full disclosure of the facts. Within the meaning of this Canon, a lawyer represents conflicting interests when, in behalf of one client, it is his duty to contend for that which duty to another client requires him to oppose.' The full disclosure required by this canon contemplates that the possibly adverse effect of the conflict be fully explained by the attorney to the client to be affected and by him thoroughly understood. . . .

"The foregoing canon applies to cases where the circumstances are such that possibly conflicting interests may permissibly be represented by the same attorney. But manifestly, there are instances where the conflicts of interest are so critically adverse as not to admit of one attorney's representing both sides. Such is the situation which this record presents. No one could conscionably contend that the same attorney may represent both the plaintiff and defendant in an adversary action. Yet, that is what is being done in this case." Jedwabny v. Philadelphia Transportation Co., 390 Pa. 231, 235, 135 A.2d 252, 254 (1957), cert. denied, 355 U.S. 966, 2 L.Ed.2d 541, 78 S.Ct. 557 (1958).

[20] "Glasser wished the benefit of the undivided assistance of counsel of his own choice. We think that such a desire on the part of an accused should be respected. Irrespective of any conflict of interest, the additional burden of representing another party may conceivably impair counsel's effectiveness.

"To determine the precise degree of prejudice sustained by Glasser as a result of the court's appointment of Stewart as counsel for Kretske is at once difficult and unnecessary. The right to have the assistance of counsel is too fundamental and absolute to allow courts to indulge in nice calculations as to the amount of prejudice arising from its denial." Glasser v. United States, 315 U.S. 60, 75-76, 86 L.Ed. 680, 62 S.Ct. 457, 467 (1942).

[21] See ABA Canon 6.

[22] Id.

[23] Cf. ABA Opinion 282 (1950).

"When counsel, although paid by the casualty company, undertakes to represent the policyholder and files his notice of appearance, he owes to his client, the assured, an undeviating and single allegiance. His fealty embraces the requirement to produce in court all witnesses, fact and expert, who are available and necessary for the proper protection of the rights of his client. . . .

". . . The Canons of Professional Ethics make it pellucid that there are not two standards, one applying to counsel privately retained by a client, and the other to counsel paid by an insurance carrier." American Employers Ins. Co. v. Goble Aircraft Specialties, 205 Misc. 1066, 1075, 131 N.Y.S.2d 393, 401 (1954), motion to withdraw appeal granted, 1 App.Div.2d 1008, 154 N.Y.S.2d 835 (1956).

"[C]ounsel, selected by State Farm to defend Dorothy Walker's suit for $50,000 damages, was apprised by Walker that his earlier version of the accident was untrue and that actually the accident occurred because he lost control of his car in passing a Cadillac just ahead. At that point, Walker's counsel should have refused to participate further in view of the conflict of interest between Walker and State Farm. . . . Instead he participated in the ensuing deposition of the Walkers, even took an ex parte sworn statement from Mr. Walker in order to advise State Farm what action it should take, and later used the statement against Walker in the District Court. This action appears to contravene an Indiana attorney's duty 'at every peril to himself, to preserve the secrets of his client' . . . .." State Farm Mut. Auto Ins. Co. v. Walker, 382 F.2d 548, 552 (1967), cert. denied, 389 U.S. 1045, 19 L.Ed. 2d 837, 88 S.Ct. 789 (1968).

by the personal desires of any person or organization. Occasionally a lawyer for an entity is requested by a stockholder, director, officer, employee, representative, or other person connected with the entity to represent him in an individual capacity; in such case the lawyer may serve the individual only if the lawyer is convinced that differing interests are not present.

EC 5-19 A lawyer may represent several clients whose interests are not actually or potentially differing. Nevertheless, he should explain any circumstances that might cause a client to question his undivided loyalty.[24] Regardless of the belief of a lawyer that he may properly represent multiple clients, he must defer to a client who holds the contrary belief and withdraw from representation of that client.

EC 5-20 A lawyer is often asked to serve as an impartial arbitrator or mediator in matters which involve present or former clients. He may serve in either capacity if he first discloses such present or former relationships. After a lawyer has undertaken to act as an impartial arbitrator or mediator, he should not thereafter represent in the dispute any of the parties involved.

Desires of Third Persons

EC 5-21 The obligation of a lawyer to exercise professional judgment solely on behalf of his client requires that he disregard the desires of others that might impair his free judgment.[25] The desires of a third person will seldom adversely affect a lawyer unless that person is in a position to exert strong economic, political, or social pressures upon the lawyer. These influences are often subtle, and a lawyer must be alert to their existence. A lawyer subjected to outside pressures should make full disclosure of them to his client;[26] and if he or his client believes that the effectiveness of his representation has been or will be impaired thereby, the lawyer should take proper steps to withdraw from representation of his client.

EC 5-22 Economic, political, or social pressures by third persons are less likely to impinge upon the independent judgment of a lawyer in a matter

---

in which he is compensated directly by his client and his professional work is exclusively with his client. On the other hand, if a lawyer is compensated from a source other than his client, he may feel a sense of responsibility to someone other than his client.

EC 5-23 A person or organization that pays or furnishes lawyers to represent others possesses a potential power to exert strong pressures against the independent judgment of those lawyers. Some employers may be interested in furthering their own economic, political, or social goals without regard to the professional responsibility of the lawyer to his individual client. Others may be far more concerned with establishment or extension of legal principles than in the immediate protection of the rights of the lawyer's individual client. On some occasions, decisions on priority of work may be made by the employer rather than the lawyer with the result that prosecution of work already undertaken for clients is postponed to their detriment. Similarly, an employer may seek, consciously or unconsciously, to further its own economic interests through the actions of the lawyers employed by it. Since a lawyer must always be free to exercise his professional judgment without regard to the interests or motives of a third person, the lawyer who is employed by one to represent another must constantly guard against erosion of his professional freedom.[27]

EC 5-24 To assist a lawyer in preserving his professional independence, a number of courses are available to him. For example, a lawyer should not practice with or in the form of a professional legal corporation, even though the corporate form is permitted by law,[28] if any director, officer, or stockholder of it is a non-lawyer. Although a lawyer may be employed by a business corporation with non-lawyers serving as directors or officers, and they necessarily have the right to make decisions of business policy, a lawyer must decline to accept direction of his professional judgment from any layman. Various types of legal aid of-

---

[24] *See* ABA Canon 6.

[25] *See* ABA Canon 35.

"Objection to the intervention of a lay intermediary, who may control litigation or otherwise interfere with the rendering of legal services in a confidential relationship, . . . derives from the element of pecuniary gain. Fearful of dangers thought to arise from that element, the courts of several States have sustained regulations aimed at these activities. We intimate no view one way or the other as to the merits of those decisions with respect to the particular arrangements against which they are directed. It is enough that the superficial resemblance in form between those arrangements and that at bar cannot obscure the vital fact that here the entire arrangement employs constitutionally privileged means of expression to secure constitutionally guaranteed civil rights." NAACP v. Button, 371 U.S. 415, 441–42, 9 L.Ed.2d 405, 423–24, 83 S.Ct. 328, 342–43 (1963).

[26] *Cf.* ABA Canon 38.

---

[27] "Certainly it is true that 'the professional relationship between an attorney and his client is highly personal, involving an intimate appreciation of each individual client's particular problem.' And this Committee does not condone practices which interfere with that relationship. However, the mere fact the lawyer is actually paid by some entity other than the client does not affect that relationship, so long as the lawyer is selected by and is directly responsible to the client. See Informal Opinions 469 and 679. Of course, as the latter decision points out, there must be full disclosure of the arrangement by the attorney to the client. . . ." *ABA Opinion* 320 (1968).

"[A] third party may pay the cost of legal services as long as control remains in the client and the responsibility of the lawyer is solely to the client. Informal Opinions 469 ad [sic] 679. *See also Opinion* 237." *Id.*

[28] *ABA Opinion* 303 (1961) recognized that "[s]tatutory provisions now exist in several states which are designed to make [the practice of law in a form that will be classified as a corporation for federal income tax purposes] legally possible, either as a result of lawyers incorporating or forming associations with various corporate characteristics."

fices are administered by boards of directors composed of lawyers and laymen. A lawyer should not accept employment from such an organization unless the board sets only broad policies and there is no interference in the relationship of the lawyer and the individual client he serves. Where a lawyer is employed by an organization, a written agreement that defines the relationship between him and the organization and provides for his independence is desirable since it may serve to prevent misunderstanding as to their respective roles. Although other innovations in the means of supplying legal counsel may develop, the responsibility of the lawyer to maintain his professional independence remains constant, and the legal profession must insure that changing circumstances do not result in loss of the professional independence of the lawyer.

DISCIPLINARY RULES

DR 5-101   Refusing Employment When the Interests of the Lawyer May Impair His Independent Professional Judgment.

(A) Except with the consent of his client after full disclosure, a lawyer shall not accept employment if the exercise of his professional judgment on behalf of his client will be or reasonably may be affected by his own financial, business, property, or personal interests.[29]

(B) A lawyer shall not accept employment in contemplated or pending litigation if he knows or it is obvious that he or a lawyer in his firm ought to be called as a witness, except that he may undertake the employment and he or a lawyer in his firm may testify:

(1) If the testimony will relate solely to an uncontested matter.

(2) If the testimony will relate solely to a matter of formality and there is no reason to believe that substantial evidence will be offered in opposition to the testimony.

---

[29] *Cf.* ABA Canon 6 and *ABA Opinions* 181 (1938), 104 (1934), 103 (1933), 72 (1932), 50 (1931), 49 (1931), and 33 (1931).

"New York County [Opinion] 203. . . . [A lawyer] should not advise a client to employ an investment company in which he is interested, without informing him of this." Drinker, LEGAL ETHICS 956 (1953).

"In *Opinions* 72 and 49 this Committee held: The relations of partners in a law firm are such that neither the firm nor any member or associate thereof, may accept any professional employment which any member of the firm cannot properly accept.

"In *Opinion* 16 this Committee held that a member of a law firm could not represent a defendant in a criminal case which was being prosecuted by another member of the firm who was public prosecuting attorney. The Opinion stated that it was clearly unethical for one member of the firm to oppose the interest of the state while another member represented those interests . . . . Since the prosecutor himself could not represent both the public and the defendant, no member of his law firm could either." *ABA Opinion* 296 (1959).

(3) If the testimony will relate solely to the nature and value of legal services rendered in the case by the lawyer or his firm to the client.

(4) As to any matter, if refusal would work a substantial hardship on the client because of the distinctive value of the lawyer or his firm as counsel in the particular case.

DR 5-102   Withdrawal as Counsel When the Lawyer Becomes a Witness.[30]

(A) If, after undertaking employment in contemplated or pending litigation, a lawyer learns or it is obvious that he or a lawyer in his firm ought to be called as a witness on behalf of his client, he shall withdraw from the conduct of the trial and his firm, if any, shall not continue representation in the trial, except that he may continue the representation and he or a lawyer in his firm may testify in the circumstances enumerated in DR 5-101(B) (1) through (4).

(B) If, after undertaking employment in contemplated or pending litigation, a lawyer learns or it is obvious that he or a lawyer in his firm may be called as a witness other than on behalf of his client, he may continue the representation until it is apparent that his testimony is or may be prejudicial to his client.[31]

DR 5-103   Avoiding Acquisition of Interest in Litigation.

(A) A lawyer shall not acquire a proprietary interest in the cause of action or subject matter of litigation he is conducting for a client,[32] except that he may:

(1) Acquire a lien granted by law to secure his fee or expenses.

(2) Contract with a client for a reasonable contingent fee in a civil case.[33]

(B) While representing a client in connection with contemplated or pending litigation, a lawyer shall not advance or guarantee financial as-

---

[30] *Cf.* ABA Canon 19 and *ABA Opinions* 220 (1941), 185 (1938), 50 (1931), and 33 (1931); *but cf.* Erwin M. Jennings Co. v. DiGenova, 107 Conn. 491, 498-99, 141 A. 866, 868 (1928).

[31] "This *Canon* [19] *of Ethics* needs no elaboration to be applied to the facts here. Apparently, the object of this precept is to avoid putting a lawyer in the obviously embarrassing predicament of testifying and then having to argue the credibility and effect of his own testimony. It was not designed to permit a lawyer to call opposing counsel as a witness and thereby disqualify him as counsel." Galarowicz v. Ward, 119 Utah 611, 620, 230 P.2d 576, 580 (1951).

[32] ABA Canon 10 and *ABA Opinions* 279 (1949), 246 (1942), and 176 (1938).

[33] *See* Code of Professional Responsibility, DR 2-106(C).

sistance to his client,[34] except that a lawyer may advance or guarantee the expenses of litigation, including court costs, expenses of investigation, expenses of medical examination, and costs of obtaining and presenting evidence, provided the client remains ultimately liable for such expenses.

DR 5-104 Limiting Business Relations with a Client.

(A) A lawyer shall not enter into a business transaction with a client if they have differing interests therein and if the client expects the lawyer to exercise his professional judgment therein for the protection of the client, unless the client has consented after full disclosure.

(B) Prior to conclusion of all aspects of the matter giving rise to his employment, a lawyer shall not enter into any arrangement or understanding with a client or a prospective client by which he acquires an interest in publication rights with respect to the subject matter of his employment or proposed employment.

DR 5-105 Refusing to Accept or Continue Employment if the Interests of Another Client May Impair the Independent Professional Judgment of the Lawyer.

(A) A lawyer shall decline proffered employment if the exercise of his independent professional judgment in behalf of a client will be or is likely to be adversely affected by the acceptance of the proffered employment,[35] except to the extent permitted under DR 5-105(C).[36]

(B) A lawyer shall not continue multiple employment if the exercise of his independent professional judgment in behalf of a client will be or is likely to be adversely affected by his representation of another client, except to the extent permitted under DR 5-105(C).[37]

(C) In the situations covered by DR 5-105(A) and (B), a lawyer may represent multiple clients if it is obvious that he can adequately represent the interest of each and if each consents to the representation after full disclosure of the possible effect of such representation on the exercise of his independent professional judgment on behalf of each.

---

[34] See ABA Canon 42; cf. ABA Opinion 288 (1954).

[35] See ABA Canon 6; cf. ABA Opinions 167 (1937), 60 (1931), and 40 (1931).

[36] ABA Opinion 247 (1942) held that an attorney could not investigate a night club shooting on behalf of one of the owner's liability insurers, obtaining the cooperation of the owner, and later represent the injured patron in an action against the owner and a different insurance company unless the attorney obtain the "express consent of all concerned given after a full disclosure of the facts," since to do so would be to represent conflicting interests.

See ABA Opinions 247 (1942), 224 (1941), 222 (1941), 218 (1941), 112 (1934), 83 (1932), and 86 (1932).

[37] Cf. ABA Opinions 231 (1941) and 160 (1936).

(D) If a lawyer is required to decline employment or to withdraw from employment under DR 5-105, no partner or associate of his or his firm may accept or continue such employment.

DR 5-106 Settling Similar Claims of Clients.[38]

(A) A lawyer who represents two or more clients shall not make or participate in the making of an aggregate settlement of the claims of or against his clients, unless each client has consented to the settlement after being advised of the existence and nature of all the claims involved in the proposed settlement, of the total amount of the settlement, and of the participation of each person in the settlement.

DR 5-107 Avoiding Influence by Others Than the Client.

(A) Except with the consent of his client after full disclosure, a lawyer shall not:

(1) Accept compensation for his legal services from one other than his client.

(2) Accept from one other than his client any thing of value related to his representation of or his employment by his client.[39]

(B) A lawyer shall not permit a person who recommends, employs, or pays him to render legal services for another to direct or regulate his professional judgment in rendering such legal services.[40]

(C) A lawyer shall not practice with or in the form of a professional corporation or association authorized to practice law for a profit, if:

(1) A non-lawyer owns any interest therein,[41] except that a fiduciary representative of the estate of a lawyer may hold the stock or interest of the lawyer for a reasonable time during administration;

(2) A non-lawyer is a corporate director or officer thereof; [42] or

---

[38] Cf. ABA Opinions 243 (1942) and 235 (1941).

[39] See ABA Canon 38.
"A lawyer who receives a commission (whether delayed or not) from a title insurance company or guaranty fund for recommending or selling the insurance to his client, or for work done for the client or the company, without either fully disclosing to the client his financial interest in the transaction, or crediting the client's bill with the amount thus received, is guilty of unethical conduct." ABA Opinion 304 (1962).

[40] See ABA Canon 35; cf. ABA Opinion 237 (1941).
"When the lay forwarder, as agent for the creditor, forwards a claim to an attorney, the direct relationship of attorney and client shall then exist between the attorney and the creditor, and the forwarder shall not interpose itself as an intermediary to control the activities of the attorney." ABA Opinion 294 (1958).

[41] "Permanent beneficial and voting rights in the organization set up to practice law, whatever its form, must be restricted to lawyers while the organization is engaged in the practice of law." ABA Opinion 303 (1961).

[42] "Canon 33 . . . promulgates underlying principles that must be observed no matter in what form of organiza-

(3) A non-lawyer has the right to direct or control the professional judgment of a lawyer.[43]

CANON 6

A Lawyer Should Represent a Client Competently

ETHICAL CONSIDERATIONS

EC 6–1 Because of his vital role in the legal process, a lawyer should act with competence and proper care in representing clients. He should strive to become and remain proficient in his practice [1] and should accept employment only in matters which he is or intends to become competent to handle.

EC 6–2 A lawyer is aided in attaining and maintaining his competence by keeping abreast of current legal literature and developments, participat-

---

tion lawyers practice law. Its requirement that no person shall be admitted or held out as a practitioner or member who is not a member of the legal profession duly authorized to practice, and amenable to professional discipline, makes it clear that any centralized management must be in lawyers to avoid a violation of this Canon." *ABA Opinion* 303 (1961).

[43] "There is no intervention of any lay agency between lawyer and client when centralized management provided only by lawyers may give guidance or direction to the services being rendered by a lawyer-member of the organization to a client. The language in *Canon 35* that a lawyer should avoid all relations which direct the performance of his duties by or in the interest of an intermediary refers to lay intermediaries and not lawyer intermediaries with whom he is associated in the practice of law." *ABA Opinion* 303 (1961).

[1] "[W]hen a citizen is faced with the need for a lawyer, he wants, and is entitled to, the best informed counsel he can obtain. Changing times produce changes in our laws and legal procedures. The natural complexities of law require continuing intensive study by a lawyer if he is to render his clients a maximum of efficient service. And, in so doing, he maintains the high standards of the legal profession; and he also increases respect and confidence by the general public." Rochelle & Payne, *The Struggle for Public Understanding*, 25 Texas B.J. 109, 160 (1962).

"We have undergone enormous changes in the last fifty years within the lives of most of the adults living today who may be seeking advice. Most of these changes have been accompanied by changes and developments in the law. . . . Every practicing lawyer encounters these problems and is often perplexed with his own inability to keep up, not only with changes in the law, but also with changes in the lives of his clients and their legal problems.

"To be sure, no client has a right to expect that his lawyer will have all of the answers at the end of his tongue or even in the back of his head at all times. But the client does have the right to expect that the lawyer will have devoted his time and energies to maintaining and improving his competence to know where to look for the answers, to know how to deal with the problems, and to know how to advise to the best of his legal talents and abilities." Levy & Sprague, *Accounting and Law: Is Dual Practice in the Public Interest?*, 52 A.B.A.J. 1110, 1112 (1966).

ing in continuing legal education programs,[2] concentrating in particular areas of the law, and by utilizing other available means. He has the additional ethical obligation to assist in improving the legal profession, and he may do so by participating in bar activities intended to advance the quality and standards of members of the profession. Of particular importance is the careful training of his younger associates and the giving of sound guidance to all lawyers who consult him. In short, a lawyer should strive at all levels to aid the legal profession in advancing the highest possible standards of integrity and competence and to meet those standards himself.

EC 6–3 While the licensing of a lawyer is evidence that he has met the standards then prevailing for admission to the bar, a lawyer generally should not accept employment in any area of the law in which he is not qualified.[3] However, he may accept such employment if in good faith he expects to become qualified through study and investigation, as long as such preparation would not result in unreasonable delay or expense to his client. Proper preparation and representation may require the association by the lawyer of professionals in other disciplines. A lawyer offered employment in a matter in which he is not and does not expect to become so qualified should either decline the employment or, with the consent of his client, accept the employment and associate a lawyer who is competent in the matter.[4]

EC 6–4 Having undertaken representation, a lawyer should use proper care to safeguard the interests of his client. If a lawyer has accepted employment in a matter beyond his competence but in which he expected to become competent, he should diligently undertake the work and study necessary to qualify himself. In addition to being qualified to handle a particular matter, his obligation to his client requires him to prepare adequately for and give appropriate attention to his legal work.

EC 6–5 A lawyer should have pride in his professional endeavors. His obligation to act competently calls for higher motivation than that arising from fear of civil liability or disciplinary penalty.

---

[2] "The whole purpose of continuing legal education, so enthusiastically supported by the ABA, is to make it possible for lawyers to make themselves better lawyers. But there are no nostrums for proficiency in the law; it must come through the hard work of the lawyer himself. To the extent that that work, whether it be in attending institutes or lecture courses, in studying after hours or in the actual day in and day out practice of his profession, can be concentrated within a limited field, the greater the proficiency and expertness that can be developed." *Report of the Special Committee on Specialization and Specialized Legal Education*, 79 A.B.A.Rep. 582, 588 (1954).

[3] "If the attorney is not competent to skillfully and properly perform the work, he should not undertake the service." Degen v. Steinbrink, 202 App.Div. 477, 481, 195 N.Y.S. 810, 814 (1922), *aff'd mem.*, 236 N.Y. 669, 142 N.E. 328 (1923).

[4] *Cf. ABA Opinion* 232 (1941).

EC 6-6 A lawyer should not seek, by contract or other means, to limit his individual liability to his client for his malpractice. A lawyer who handles the affairs of his client properly has no need to attempt to limit his liability for his professional activities and one who does not handle the affairs of his client properly should not be permitted to do so. A lawyer who is a stockholder in or is associated with a professional legal corporation may, however, limit his liability for malpractice of his associates in the corporation, but only to the extent permitted by law.[5]

DISCIPLINARY RULES

DR 6-101 Failing to Act Competently.

(A) A lawyer shall not:

(1) **Handle a legal matter which he knows or should know that he is not competent to handle, without associating with him a lawyer who is competent to handle it.**

(2) **Handle a legal matter without preparation adequate in the circumstances.**

(3) **Neglect a legal matter entrusted to him.[6]**

DR 6-102 Limiting Liability to Client.

(A) A lawyer shall not attempt to exonerate himself from or limit his liability to his client for his personal malpractice.

CANON 7

A Lawyer Should Represent a Client Zealously Within the Bounds of the Law

ETHICAL CONSIDERATIONS

EC 7-1 The duty of a lawyer, both to his client [1] and to the legal system, is to represent his client zealously [2] within the bounds of the law,[3] which

---

[5] *See ABA Opinion* 303 (1961); *cf.* Code of Professional Responsibility, EC 2–11.

[6] The annual report for 1967–1968 of the Committee on Grievances of the Association of the Bar of the City of New York showed a receipt of 2,232 complaints; of the 828 offenses against clients, 76 involved conversion, 49 involved "overreaching," and 452, or more than half of all such offenses, involved neglect. *Annual Report of the Committee on Grievances of the Association of the Bar of the City of New York,* N.Y.L.J., Sept. 12, 1968, at 4, col. 5.

[1] "The right to be heard would be, in many cases, of little avail if it did not comprehend the right to be heard by counsel. Even the intelligent and educated layman has small and sometimes no skill in the science of law." Powell v. Alabama, 287 U.S. 45, 68–69, 77 L.Ed. 158, 170, 53 S.Ct. 55, 64 (1932).

[2] *Cf.* ABA Canon 4.

"At times . . . [the tax lawyer] will be wise to discard some arguments and he should exercise discretion to emphasize the arguments which in his judgment are most likely to be persuasive. But this process involves legal judgment rather than moral attitudes. The tax lawyer should put aside private disagreements with Congressional and Treasury policies. His own notions of policy, and his personal view of what the law should be, are irrelevant. The job entrusted to him by his client is to use all his learning and ability to protect his client's rights, not to

includes Disciplinary Rules and enforceable pro-

---

help in the process of promoting a better tax system. The tax lawyer need not accept his client's economic and social opinions, but the client is paying for technical attention and undivided concentration upon his affairs. He is equally entitled to performance unfettered by his attorney's economic and social predilections." Paul, *The Lawyer as a Tax Adviser,* 25 Rocky Mt. L. Rev. 412, 418 (1953).

[3] *See* ABA Canons 15 and 32.

ABA Canon 5, although only speaking of one accused of crime, imposes a similar obligation on the lawyer: "[T]he lawyer is bound, by all fair and honorable means, to present every defense that the law of the land permits, to the end that no person may be deprived of life or liberty, but by due process of law."

"Any persuasion or pressure on the advocate which deters him from planning and carrying out the litigation on the basis of 'what, within the framework of the law, is best for my client's interest?' interferes with the obligation to represent the client fully within the law.

"This obligation, in its fullest sense, is the heart of the adversary process. Each attorney, as an advocate, acts for and seeks that which in his judgment is best for his client, within the bounds authoritatively established. The advocate does not *decide* what is just in this case— he would be usurping the function of the judge and jury— he acts for and seeks for his client that which he is entitled to under the law. He can do no less and properly represent the client." Thode, *The Ethical Standard for the Advocate,* 39 Texas L.Rev. 575, 584 (1961).

"The [Texas public opinion] survey indicates that distrust of the lawyer can be traced directly to certain factors. Foremost of these is a basic misunderstanding of the function of the lawyer as an advocate in an adversary system.

"Lawyers are accused of taking advantage of 'loopholes' and 'technicalities' to win. Persons who make this charge are unaware, or do not understand, that the lawyer is hired to win, and if he does not exercise every legitimate effort in his client's behalf, then he is betraying a sacred trust." Rochelle & Payne, *The Struggle for Public Understanding,* 25 Texas B.J. 109, 159 (1962).

"The importance of the attorney's undivided allegiance and faithful service to one accused of crime, irrespective of the attorney's personal opinion as to the guilt of his client, lies in Canon 5 of the American Bar Association Canon of Ethics.

"The difficulty lies, of course, in ascertaining whether the attorney has been guilty of an error of judgment, such as an election with respect to trial tactics, or has otherwise been actuated by his conscience or belief that his client should be convicted in any event. All too frequently courts are called upon to review actions of defense counsel which are, at the most, errors of judgment, not properly reviewable on habeas corpus unless the trial is a farce and a mockery of justice which requires the court to intervene. . . . But when defense counsel, in a truly adverse proceeding, admits that his conscience would not permit him to adopt certain customary trial procedures, this extends beyond the realm of judgment and strongly suggests an invasion of constitutional rights." Johns v. Smyth, 176 F.Supp. 949, 952 (E.D.Va.1959), *modified,* United States ex rel. Wilkins v. Banmiller, 205 F.Supp. 123, 128, n. 5 (E.D.Pa.1962), *aff'd,* 325 F.2d 514 (3d Cir. 1963), *cert. denied,* 379 U.S. 847, 13 L.Ed.2d 51, 85 S.Ct. 87 (1964).

"The adversary system in law administration bears a striking resemblance to the competitive economic system. In each we assume that the individual through partisanship or through self-interest will strive mightily for his side, and that kind of striving we must have. But neither system would be tolerable without restraints and modi-

fessional regulations.[4] The professional responsibility of a lawyer derives from his membership in a profession which has the duty of assisting members of the public to secure and protect available legal rights and benefits. In our government of laws and not of men, each member of our society is entitled to have his conduct judged and regulated in accordance with the law;[5] to seek any lawful objective[6] through legally permissible means;[7] and to present for adjudication any lawful claim, issue, or defense.

EC 7-2 The bounds of the law in a given case are often difficult to ascertain.[8] The language of

---

fications, and at times without outright departures from the system itself. Since the legal profession is entrusted with the system of law administration, a part of its task is to develop in its members appropriate restraints without impairing the values of partisan striving. An accompanying task is to aid in the modification of the adversary system or departure from it in areas to which the system is unsuited." Cheatham, *The Lawyer's Role and Surroundings*, 25 Rocky Mt. L.Rev. 405, 410 (1953).

[4] "Rule 4.15 prohibits, in the pursuit of a client's cause, 'any manner of fraud or chicane'; Rule 4.22 requires 'candor and fairness' in the conduct of the lawyer, and forbids the making of knowing misquotations; Rule 4.47 provides that a lawyer 'should always maintain his integrity,' and generally forbids all misconduct injurious to the interests of the public, the courts, or his clients, and acts contrary to 'justice, honesty, modesty or good morals.' Our Commissioner has accurately paraphrased these rules as follows: 'An attorney does not have the duty to do all and whatever he can that may enable him to win his client's cause or to further his client's interest. His duty and efforts in these respects, although they should be prompted by his "entire devotion" to the interest of his client, must be within and not without the bounds of the law.'" In re Wines, 370 S.W.2d 328, 333 (Mo.1963). *See* Note, 38 Texas L.Rev. 107, 110 (1959).

[5] "Under our system of government the process of adjudication is surrounded by safeguards evolved from centuries of experience. These safeguards are not designed merely to lend formality and decorum to the trial of causes. They are predicated on the assumption that to secure for any controversy a truly informed and dispassionate decision is a difficult thing, requiring for its achievement a special summoning and organization of human effort and the adoption of measures to exclude the biases and prejudgments that have free play outside the courtroom. All of this goes for naught if the man with an unpopular cause is unable to find a competent lawyer courageous enough to represent him. His chance to have his day in court loses much of its meaning if his case is handicapped from the outset by the very kind of prejudgment our rules of evidence and procedure are intended to prevent." *Professional Responsibility: Report of the Joint Conference*, 44 A.B.A.J. 1159, 1216 (1958).

[6] "[I]t is . . . [the tax lawyer's] positive duty to show the client how to avail himself to the full of what the law permits. He is not the keeper of the Congressional conscience." Paul, *The Lawyer as a Tax Adviser*, 25 Rocky Mt.L.Rev. 412, 418 (1953).

[7] *See* ABA Canons 15 and 30.

[8] "The fact that it desired to evade the law, as it is called, is immaterial, because the very meaning of a line in the law is that you intentionally may go as close to it as you can if you do not pass it . . . . It is a matter of proximity and degree as to which minds will differ . . . .." Justice Holmes, in Superior Oil Co. v. Missis-

---

legislative enactments and judicial opinions may be uncertain as applied to varying factual situations. The limits and specific meaning of apparently relevant law may be made doubtful by changing or developing constitutional interpretations, inadequately expressed statutes or judicial opinions, and changing public and judicial attitudes. Certainty of law ranges from well-settled rules through areas of conflicting authority to areas without precedent.

EC 7-3 Where the bounds of law are uncertain, the action of a lawyer may depend on whether he is serving as advocate or adviser. A lawyer may serve simultaneously as both advocate and adviser, but the two roles are essentially different.[9] In asserting a position on behalf of his client, an advocate for the most part deals with past conduct and must take the facts as he finds them. By contrast, a lawyer serving as adviser primarily assists his client in determining the course of future conduct and relationships. While serving as advocate, a lawyer should resolve in favor of his client doubts as to the bounds of the law.[10] In serving a client as adviser, a lawyer in appropriate

---

sippi, 280 U.S. 390, 395-96, 74 L.Ed. 504, 508, 50 S.Ct. 169, 170 (1930).

[9] "Today's lawyers perform two distinct types of functions, and our ethical standards should, but in the main do not, recognize these two functions. Judge Philbrick McCoy recently reported to the American Bar Association the need for a reappraisal of the Canons in light of the new and distinct function of counselor, as distinguished from advocate, which today predominates in the legal profession. . . .

". . . In the first place, any revision of the canons must take into account and speak to this new and now predominant function of the lawyer. . . . It is beyond the scope of this paper to discuss the ethical standards to be applied to the counselor except to state that in my opinion such standards should require a greater recognition and protection for the interest of the public generally than is presently expressed in the canons. Also, the counselor's obligation should extend to requiring him to inform and to impress upon the client a just solution of the problem, considering all interests involved." Thode, *The Ethical Standard for the Advocate*, 39 Texas L.Rev. 575, 578-79 (1961).

"The man who has been called into court to answer for his own actions is entitled to fair hearing. Partisan advocacy plays its essential part in such a hearing, and the lawyer pleading his client's case may properly present it in the most favorable light. A similar resolution of doubts in one direction becomes inappropriate when the lawyer acts as counselor. The reasons that justify and even require partisan advocacy in the trial of a cause do not grant any license to the lawyer to participate as legal advisor in a line of conduct that is immoral, unfair, or of doubtful legality. In saving himself from this unworthy involvement, the lawyer cannot be guided solely by an unreflective inner sense of good faith; he must be at pains to preserve a sufficient detachment from his client's interests so that he remains capable of a sound and objective appraisal of the propriety of what his client proposes to do." *Professional Responsibility: Report of the Joint Conference*, 44 A.B.A.J. 1159, 1161 (1958).

[10] "[A] lawyer who is asked to advise his client . . . may freely urge the statement of positions most favorable to the client just as long as there is reasonable basis for those positions." *ABA Opinion 314 (1965)*.

circumstances should give his professional opinion as to what the ultimate decisions of the courts would likely be as to the applicable law.

Duty of the Lawyer to a Client

EC 7-4 The advocate may urge any permissible construction of the law favorable to his client, without regard to his professional opinion as to the likelihood that the construction will ultimately prevail,[11] His conduct is within the bounds of the law, and therefore permissible, if the position taken is supported by the law or is supportable by a good faith argument for an extension, modification, or reversal of the law. However, a lawyer is not justified in asserting a position in litigation that is frivolous.[12]

---

[11] "The lawyer . . . is not an umpire, but an advocate. He is under no duty to refrain from making every proper argument in support of any legal point because he is not convinced of its inherent soundness. . . . His personal belief in the soundness of his cause or of the authorities supporting it, is irrelevant." *ABA Opinion* 280 (1949).

"Counsel apparently misconceived his role. It was his duty to honorably present his client's contentions in the light most favorable to his client. Instead he presumed to advise the court as to the validity and sufficiency of prisoner's motion, by letter. We therefore conclude that the prisoner had no effective assistance of counsel and remand this case to the District Court with instructions to set aside the Judgment, appoint new counsel to represent the prisoner if he makes no objection thereto, and proceed anew." McCartney v. United States, 343 F.2d 471, 472 (9th Cir. 1965).

[12] "Here the court-appointed counsel had the transcript but refused to proceed with the appeal because he found no merit in it. . . . We cannot say that there was a finding of frivolity by either of the California courts or that counsel acted in any greater capacity than merely as *amicus curiae* which was condemned in *Ellis, supra.* Hence California's procedure did not furnish petitioner with counsel acting in the role of an advocate nor did it provide that full consideration and resolution of the matter as is obtained when counsel is acting in that capacity. . . .

"The constitutional requirement of substantial equality and fair process can only be attained where counsel acts in the role of an active advocate in behalf of his client, as opposed to that of *amicus curiae.* The no-merit letter and the procedure it triggers do not reach that dignity. Counsel should, and can with honor and without conflict, be of more assistance to his client and to the court. His role as advocate requires that he support his client's appeal to the best of his ability. Of course, if counsel finds his case to be wholly frivolous, after a conscientious examination of it, he should so advise the court and request permission to withdraw. That request must, however, be accompanied by a brief referring to anything in the record that might arguably support the appeal. A copy of counsel's brief should be furnished the indigent and time allowed him to raise any points that he chooses; the court—not counsel—then proceeds, after a full examination of all the proceedings, to decide whether the case is wholly frivolous. If it so finds it may grant counsel's request to withdraw and dismiss the appeal insofar as federal requirements are concerned, or proceed to a decision on the merits, if state law so requires. On the other hand, if it finds any of the legal points arguable on their merits (and therefore not frivolous) it must, prior to decision, afford the indigent the assistance of counsel to argue the appeal." Anders v. California, 386 U.S. 738, 744, 18 L.Ed.

EC 7-5 A lawyer as adviser furthers the interest of his client by giving his professional opinion as to what he believes would likely be the ultimate decision of the courts on the matter at hand and by informing his client of the practical effect of such decision.[13] He may continue in the representation of his client even though his client has elected to pursue a course of conduct contrary to the advice of the lawyer so long as he does not thereby knowingly assist the client to engage in illegal conduct or to take a frivolous legal position. A lawyer should never encourage or aid his client to commit criminal acts or counsel his client on how to violate the law and avoid punishment therefor.[14]

EC 7-6 Whether the proposed action of a lawyer is within the bounds of the law may be a perplexing question when his client is contemplating a course of conduct having legal consequence that vary according to the client's intent, motive, or desires at the time of the action. Often a lawyer is asked to assist his client in developing evidence relevant to the state of mind of the client at a particular time. He may properly assist his client in the development and preservation of evidence of existing motive, intent, or desire; obviously, he may not do anything furthering the creation or preservation of false evidence. In many cases a lawyer may not be certain as to the state of mind of his client, and in those situations he should resolve reasonable doubts in favor of his client.

EC 7-7 In certain areas of legal representation not affecting the merits of the cause or substantially prejudicing the rights of a client, a lawyer is entitled to make decisions on his own. But otherwise the authority to make decisions is exclusively that of the client and, if made within the framework of the law, such decisions are binding on his lawyer. As typical examples in civil cases, it is for the client to decide whether he will accept a settlement offer or whether he will waive his right to plead an affirmative defense. A defense lawyer in a criminal case has the duty to advise his client fully on whether a particular plea to a charge appears to be desirable and as to the pros-

---

2d 493, 498, 87 S.Ct. 1396, 1399–1400 (1967), *rehearing denied,* 388 U.S. 924, 18 L.Ed.2d 1377, 87 S.Ct. 2094 (1967).

See Paul, *The Lawyer As a Tax Adviser,* 25 Rocky Mt. L.Rev. 412, 432 (1953).

[13] *See* ABA Canon 32.

[14] "For a lawyer to represent a syndicate notoriously engaged in the violation of the law for the purpose of advising the members how to break the law and at the same time escape it, is manifestly improper. While a lawyer may see to it that anyone accused of crime, no matter how serious and flagrant, has a fair trial, and present all available defenses, he may not co-operate in planning violations of the law. There is a sharp distinction, of course, between advising what can lawfully be done and advising how unlawful acts can be done in a way to avoid conviction. Where a lawyer accepts a retainer from an organization, known to be unlawful, and agrees in advance to defend its members when from time to time they are accused of crime arising out of its unlawful activities, this is equally improper."

"See also *Opinion 155.*" *ABA Opinion* 281 (1952).

pects of success on appeal, but it is for the client to decide what plea should be entered and whether an appeal should be taken.[15]

EC 7-8 A lawyer should exert his best efforts to insure that decisions of his client are made only after the client has been informed of relevant considerations. A lawyer ought to initiate this decision-making process if the client does not do so. Advice of a lawyer to his client need not be confined to purely legal considerations.[16] A lawyer should advise his client of the possible effect of each legal alternative.[17] A lawyer should bring to bear upon this decision-making process the fullness of his experience as well as his objective viewpoint.[18] In assisting his client to reach a proper decision, it is often desirable for a lawyer to point out those factors which may lead to a decision that is morally just as well as legally permissible.[19] He may emphasize the possibility of harsh consequences that might result from assertion of legally permissible positions. In the final analysis, however, the lawyer should always remember that the decision whether to forego legally available objectives or methods because of non-legal factors is ultimately for the client and

---

[15] See ABA Special Committee on Minimum Standards for the Administration of Criminal Justice, *Standards Relating to Pleas of Guilty* pp. 69–70 (1968).

[16] "First of all, a truly great lawyer is a wise counselor to all manner of men in the varied crises of their lives when they most need disinterested advice. Effective counseling necessarily involves a thoroughgoing knowledge of the principles of the law not merely as they appear in the books but as they actually operate in action." Vanderbilt, *The Five Functions of the Lawyer: Service to Clients and the Public,* 40 A.B.A.J. 31 (1954).

[17] "A lawyer should endeavor to obtain full knowledge of his client's cause before advising thereon. . . ." ABA Canon 8.

[18] "[I]n devising charters of collaborative effort the lawyer often acts where all of the affected parties are present as participants. But the lawyer also performs a similar function in situations where this is not so, as, for example, in planning estates and drafting wills. Here the instrument defining the terms of collaboration may affect persons not present and often not born. Yet here, too, the good lawyer does not serve merely as a legal conduit for his client's desires, but as a wise counselor, experienced in the art of devising arrangements that will put in workable order the entangled affairs and interests of human beings." *Professional Responsibility: Report of the Joint Conference,* 44 A.B.A.J. 1159, 1162 (1958).

[19] See ABA Canon 8.

"Vital as is the lawyer's role in adjudication, it should not be thought that it is only as an advocate pleading in open court that he contributes to the administration of the law. The most effective realization of the law's aims often takes place in the attorney's office, where litigation is forestalled by anticipating its outcome, where the lawyer's quiet counsel takes the place of public force. Contrary to popular belief, the compliance with the law thus brought about is not generally lip-serving and narrow, for by reminding him of its long-run costs the lawyer often deters his client from a course of conduct technically permissible under existing law, though inconsistent with its underlying spirit and purpose." *Professional Responsibility: Report of the Joint Conference,* 44 A.B.A.J. 1159, 1161 (1958).

not for himself. In the event that the client in a non-adjudicatory matter insists upon a course of conduct that is contrary to the judgment and advice of the lawyer but not prohibited by Disciplinary Rules, the lawyer may withdraw from the employment.[20]

EC 7-9 In the exercise of his professional judgment on those decisions which are for his determination in the handling of a legal matter,[21] a lawyer should always act in a manner consistent with the best interests of his client.[22] However, when an action in the best interest of his client seems to him to be unjust, he may ask his client for permission to forego such action.[23]

EC 7-10 The duty of a lawyer to represent his client with zeal does not militate against his concurrent obligation to treat with consideration all persons involved in the legal process and to avoid the infliction of needless harm.

EC 7-11 The responsibilities of a lawyer may vary according to the intelligence, experience, mental condition or age of a client, the obligation of a public officer, or the nature of a particular proceeding. Examples include the representation of an illiterate or an incompetent, service as a public prosecutor or other government lawyer, and appearances before administrative and legislative bodies.

EC 7-12 Any mental or physical condition of a client that renders him incapable of making a considered judgment on his own behalf casts additional responsibilities upon his lawyer. Where an incompetent is acting through a guardian or other legal representative, a lawyer must look to such representative for those decisions which are normally the prerogative of the client to make. If a client under disability has no legal representative, his lawyer may be compelled in court proceedings to make decisions on behalf of the client. If the client is capable of understanding the matter in question or of contributing to the advancement of his interests, regardless of whether he is legally disqualified from performing certain acts, the lawyer should obtain from him all possible aid. If the disability of a client and the lack of a legal representative compel the lawyer to make decisions for his client, the lawyer should consider all

---

[20] "My summation of Judge Sharswood's view of the advocate's duty to the client is that he owes to the client the duty to use all legal means in support of the client's case. However, at the same time Judge Sharswood recognized that many advocates would find this obligation unbearable if applicable without exception. Therefore, the individual lawyer is given the choice of representing his client fully within the bounds set by the law *or of telling his client that he cannot do so,* so that the client may obtain another attorney if he wishes." Thode, *The Ethical Standard for the Advocate,* 39 Texas L.Rev. 575, 582 (1961).
Cf. Code of Professional Responsibility, DR 2–110 (C).

[21] See ABA Canon 24.

[22] Thode, *The Ethical Standard for the Advocate,* 39 Texas L.Rev. 575, 592 (1961).

[23] *Cf.* ABA Opinions 253 (1946) and 178 (1938).

circumstances then prevailing and act with care to safeguard and advance the interests of his client. But obviously a lawyer cannot perform any act or make any decision which the law requires his client to perform or make, either acting for himself if competent, or by a duly constituted representative if legally incompetent.

EC 7-13 The responsibility of a public prosecutor differs from that of the usual advocate; his duty is to seek justice, not merely to convict.[24] This special duty exists because: (1) the prosecutor represents the sovereign and therefore should use restraint in the discretionary exercise of governmental powers, such as in the selection of cases to prosecute; (2) during trial the prosecutor is not only an advocate but he also may make decisions normally made by an individual client, and those affecting the public interest should be fair to all; and (3) in our system of criminal justice the accused is to be given the benefit of all reasonable doubts. With respect to evidence and witnesses, the prosecutor has responsibilities different from those of a lawyer in private practice: the prosecutor should make timely disclosure to the defense of available evidence, known to him, that tends to negate the guilt of the accused, mitigate the degree of the offense, or reduce the punishment. Further, a prosecutor should not intentionally avoid pursuit of evidence merely because he believes it will damage the prosecution's case or aid the accused.

EC 7-14 A government lawyer who has discretionary power relative to litigation should refrain from instituting or continuing litigation that is obviously unfair. A government lawyer not having such discretionary power who believes there is lack of merit in a controversy submitted to him should so advise his superiors and recommend the avoidance of unfair litigation. A government lawyer in a civil action or administrative proceeding has the responsibility to seek justice and to develop a full and fair record, and he should not use his position or the economic power of the government to harass parties or to bring about unjust settlements or results.

---

[24] *See* ABA Canon 5 and Berger v. United States, 295 U.S. 78, 79 L.Ed. 1314, 55 S.Ct. 629 (1935).

"The public prosecutor cannot take as a guide for the conduct of his office the standards of an attorney appearing on behalf of an individual client. The freedom elsewhere wisely granted to a partisan advocate must be severely curtailed if the prosecutor's duties are to be properly discharged. The public prosecutor must recall that he occupies a dual role, being obligated, on the one hand, to furnish that adversary element essential to the informed decision of any controversy, but being possessed, on the other, of important governmental powers that are pledged to the accomplishment of one objective only, that of impartial justice. Where the prosecutor is recreant to the trust implicit in his office, he undermines confidence, not only in his profession, but in government and the very ideal of justice itself." *Professional Responsibility: Report of the Joint Conference,* 44 A.B.A.J. 1159, 1218 (1958).

"The prosecuting attorney is the attorney for the state, and it is his primary duty not to convict but to see that justice is done." *ABA Opinion* 150 (1936).

EC 7-15 The nature and purpose of proceedings before administrative agencies vary widely. The proceedings may be legislative or quasi-judicial, or a combination of both. They may be *ex parte* in character, in which event they may originate either at the instance of the agency or upon motion of an interested party. The scope of an inquiry may be purely investigative or it may be truly adversary looking toward the adjudication of specific rights of a party or of classes of parties. The foregoing are but examples of some of the types of proceedings conducted by administrative agencies. A lawyer appearing before an administrative agency,[25] regardless of the nature of the proceeding it is conducting, has the continuing duty to advance the cause of his client within the bounds of the law.[26] Where the applicable rules of the agency impose specific obligations upon a lawyer, it is his duty to comply therewith, unless the lawyer has a legitimate basis for challenging the validity thereof. In all appearances before administrative agencies, a lawyer should identify himself, his client if identity of his client is not privileged,[27] and the representative nature of his appearance. It is not improper, however, for a lawyer to seek from an agency information available to the public without identifying his client.

EC 7-16 The primary business of a legislative body is to enact laws rather than to adjudicate controversies, although on occasion the activities of a legislative body may take on the characteristics of an adversary proceeding, particularly in investigative and impeachment matters. The role of a lawyer supporting or opposing proposed legislation normally is quite different from his role in representing a person under investigation or on trial by a legislative body. When a lawyer appears in connection with proposed legislation, he seeks to affect the lawmaking process, but when he appears on behalf of a client in investigatory or impeachment proceedings, he is concerned with the protection of the rights of his client. In either event, he should identify himself and his client, if identity of his client is not privileged, and should comply with applicable laws and legislative rules.[28]

EC 7-17 The obligation of loyalty to his client applies only to a lawyer in the discharge of his professional duties and implies no obligation to adopt a personal viewpoint favorable to the in-

---

[25] As to appearances before a department of government, Canon 26 provides: "A lawyer openly . . . may render professional services . . . in advocacy of claims before departments of government, upon the same principles of ethics which justify his appearance before the Courts . . . ."

[26] "But as an advocate before a service which itself represents the adversary point of view, where his client's case is fairly arguable, a lawyer is under no duty to disclose its weaknesses, any more than he would be to make such a disclosure to a brother lawyer. The limitations within which he must operate are best expressed in Canon 22 . . . ." *ABA Opinion* 314 (1965).

[27] *See* Baird v. Koerner, 279 F.2d 623 (9th Cir. 1960).

[28] *See* ABA Canon 26.

terests or desires of his client.[29] While a lawyer must act always with circumspection in order that his conduct will not adversely affect the rights of a client in a matter he is then handling, he may take positions on public issues and espouse legal reforms he favors without regard to the individual views of any client.

EC 7-18 The legal system in its broadest sense functions best when persons in need of legal advice or assistance are represented by their own counsel. For this reason a lawyer should not communicate on the subject matter of the representation of his client with a person he knows to be represented in the matter by a lawyer, unless pursuant to law or rule of court or unless he has the consent of the lawyer for that person.[30] If one is not represented by counsel, a lawyer representing another may have to deal directly with the unrepresented person; in such an instance, a lawyer should not undertake to give advice to the person who is attempting to represent himself,[31] except that he may advise him to obtain a lawyer.

Duty of the Lawyer to the Adversary System of Justice

EC 7-19 Our legal system provides for the adjudication of disputes governed by the rules of substantive, evidentiary, and procedural law. An adversary presentation counters the natural human tendency to judge too swiftly in terms of the familiar that which is not yet fully known;[32] the advocate, by his zealous preparation and presentation of facts and law, enables the tribunal to come to the hearing with an open and neutral mind and to render impartial judgments.[33] The duty of a

lawyer to his client and his duty to the legal system are the same: to represent his client zealously within the bounds of the law.[34]

EC 7-20 In order to function properly, our adjudicative process requires an informed, impartial tribunal capable of administering justice promptly and efficiently [35] according to procedures that command public confidence and respect.[36] Not only must there be competent, adverse presentation of evidence and issues, but a tribunal must be aided by rules appropriate to an effective and dignified process. The procedures under which tribunals operate in our adversary system have been prescribed largely by legislative enactments, court rules and decisions, and administrative rules. Through the years certain concepts of proper professional conduct have become rules of law applicable to the adversary adjudicative process. Many of these concepts are the bases for standards of professional conduct set forth in the Disciplinary Rules.

EC 7-21 The civil adjudicative process is primarily designed for the settlement of disputes between parties, while the criminal process is designed for the protection of society as a whole. Threatening to use, or using, the criminal process to coerce adjustment of private civil claims or controversies is a subversion of that process;[37] further, the person against whom the criminal process is so misused may be deterred from asserting his legal rights and thus the usefulness of the civil process in settling private disputes is impaired. As in all cases of abuse of judicial process, the improper use of criminal process tends to diminish public confidence in our legal system.

EC 7-22 Respect for judicial rulings is essential to the proper administration of justice; however, a litigant or his lawyer may, in good faith and

---

[29] "Law should be so practiced that the lawyer remains free to make up his own mind how he will vote, what causes he will support, what economic and political philosophy he will espouse. It is one of the glories of the profession that it admits of this freedom. Distinguished examples can be cited of lawyers whose views were at variance from those of their clients, lawyers whose skill and wisdom make them valued advisers to those who had little sympathy with their views as citizens." *Professional Responsibility: Report of the Joint Conference,* 44 A.B.A.J. 1159, 1217 (1958).

"No doubt some tax lawyers feel constrained to abstain from activities on behalf of a better tax system because they think that their clients may object. Clients have no right to object if the tax adviser handles their affairs competently and faithfully and independently of his private views as to tax policy. They buy his expert services, not his private opinions or his silence on issues that gravely affect the public interest." Paul, *The Lawyer as a Tax Adviser,* 25 Rocky Mt.L.Rev. 412, 434 (1953).

[30] *See* ABA Canon 9.

[31] *Id.*

[32] *See Professional Responsibility: Report of the Joint Conference,* 44 A.B.A.J. 1159, 1160 (1958).

[33] "Without the participation of someone who can act responsibly for each of the parties, this essential narrowing of the issues [by exchange of written pleadings or stipulations of counsel] becomes impossible. But here again the true significance of partisan advocacy lies deeper, touching once more the integrity of the adjudicative process itself. It is only through the advocate's participation that the hearing may remain in fact what it purports to be in

theory: a public trial of the facts and issues. Each advocate comes to the hearing prepared to present his proofs and arguments, knowing at the same time that his arguments may fail to persuade and that his proof may be rejected as inadequate. . . . The deciding tribunal, on the other hand, comes to the hearing uncommitted. It has not represented to the public that any fact can be proved, that any argument is sound, or that any particular way of stating a litigant's case is the most effective expression of its merits." *Professional Responsibility: Report of the Joint Conference,* 44 A.B.A.J. 1159, 1160–61 (1958).

[34] *Cf.* ABA Canons 15 and 32.

[35] *Cf.* ABA Canon 21.

[36] *See Professional Responsibility: Report of the Joint Conference,* 44 A.B.A.J. 1159, 1216 (1958).

[37] "We are of the opinion that the letter in question was improper, and that in writing and sending it respondent was guilty of unprofessional conduct. This court has heretofore expressed its disapproval of using threats of criminal prosecution as a means of forcing settlement of civil claims. . . .

"Respondent has been guilty of a violation of a principle which condemns any confusion of threats of criminal prosecution with the enforcement of civil claims. For this misconduct he should be severely censured." Matter of Gelman, 230 App.Div. 524, 527, 245 N.Y.S. 416, 419 (1930).

within the framework of the law, take steps to test the correctness of a ruling of a tribunal.[38]

EC 7-23 The complexity of law often makes it difficult for a tribunal to be fully informed unless the pertinent law is presented by the lawyers in the cause. A tribunal that is fully informed on the applicable law is better able to make a fair and accurate determination of the matter before it. The adversary system contemplates that each lawyer will present and argue the existing law in the light most favorable to his client.[39] Where a lawyer knows of legal authority in the controlling jurisdiction directly adverse to the position of his client, he should inform the tribunal of its existence unless his adversary has done so; but, having made such disclosure, he may challenge its soundness in whole or in part.[40]

EC 7-24 In order to bring about just and informed decisions, evidentiary and procedural rules have been established by tribunals to permit the inclusion of relevant evidence and argument and the exclusion of all other considerations. The expression by a lawyer of his personal opinion as to the justness of a cause, as to the credibility of a witness, as to the culpability of a civil litigant, or as to the guilt or innocence of an accused is not a proper subject for argument to the trier of fact.[41] It is improper as to factual matters because admissible evidence possessed by a lawyer should be presented only as sworn testimony. It is improper as to all other matters because, were the rules otherwise, the silence of a lawyer on a given occasion could be construed unfavorably to his client. However, a lawyer may argue, on his analysis of the evidence, for any position or conclusion with respect to any of the foregoing matters.

EC 7-25 Rules of evidence and procedure are designed to lead to just decisions and are part of the framework of the law. Thus while a lawyer may take steps in good faith and within the framework of the law to test the validity of rules, he is not justified in consciously violating such rules and he should be diligent in his efforts to guard against his unintentional violation of them.[42] As examples, a lawyer should subscribe to or verify only those pleadings that he believes are in compliance with applicable law and rules; a lawyer should not make any prefatory statement before a tribunal in regard to the purported facts of the case on trial unless he believes that his statement will be supported by admissible evidence; a lawyer should not ask a witness a question solely for the purpose of harassing or embarrassing him; and a lawyer should not by subterfuge put before a jury matters which it cannot properly consider.

EC 7-26 The law and Disciplinary Rules prohibit the use of fraudulent, false, or perjured testimony or evidence.[43] A lawyer who knowingly[44] participates in introduction of such testimony or evidence is subject to discipline. A lawyer should, however, present any admissible evidence his client desires to have presented unless he knows, or from facts within his knowledge should know, that such testimony or evidence is false, fraudulent, or perjured.[45]

EC 7-27 Because it interferes with the proper administration of justice, a lawyer should not suppress evidence that he or his client has a legal obligation to reveal or produce. In like manner, a lawyer should not advise or cause a person to secrete himself or to leave the jurisdiction of a tribunal for the purpose of making him unavailable as a witness therein.[46]

EC 7-28 Witnesses should always testify truthfully[47] and should be free from any financial inducements that might tempt them to do other-

---

[38] "An attorney has the duty to protect the interests of his client. He has a right to press legitimate argument and to protest an erroneous ruling." Gallagher v. Municipal Court, 31 Cal.2d 784, 796, 192 P.2d 905, 913 (1948).

"There must be protection, however, in the far more frequent case of the attorney who stands on his rights and combats the order in good faith and without disrespect believing with good cause that it is void, for it is here that the independence of the bar becomes valuable." Note, 39 Colum. L. Rev. 433, 438 (1939).

[39] "Too many do not understand that accomplishment of the layman's abstract ideas of justice is the function of the judge and jury, and that it is the lawyer's sworn duty to portray his client's case in its most favorable light." Rochelle and Payne, *The Struggle for Public Understanding*, 25 Texas B.J. 109, 159 (1962).

[40] "We are of the opinion that this Canon requires the lawyer to disclose such decisions [that are adverse to his client's contentions] to the court. He may, of course, after doing so, challenge the soundness of the decisions or present reasons which he believes would warrant the court in not following them in the pending case." *ABA Opinion* 146 (1935).

Cf. ABA Opinion 280 (1949) and Thode, *The Ethical Standard for the Advocate*, 39 Texas L.Rev. 575, 585–86 (1961).

[41] *See* ABA Canon 15.

"The traditional duty of an advocate is that he honorably uphold the contentions of his client. He should not voluntarily undermine them." Harders v. State of California, 373 F.2d 839, 842 (9th Cir. 1967).

[42] *See* ABA Canon 22.

[43] *Id. Cf.* ABA Canon 41.

[44] *See generally ABA Opinion* 287 (1953) as to a lawyer's duty when he unknowingly participates in introducing perjured testimony.

[45] "Under any standard of proper ethical conduct an attorney should not sit by silently and permit his client to commit what may be perjury, and which certainly would mislead the court and the opposing party on a matter vital to the issue under consideration. . . .
. . . .

"Respondent next urges that it was his duty to observe the utmost good faith toward his client, and therefore he could not divulge any confidential information. This duty to the client of course does not extend to the point of authorizing collaboration with him in the commission of fraud." In re Carroll, 244 S.W.2d 474, 474–75 (Ky. 1951).

[46] *See* ABA Canon 5; *cf. ABA Opinion* 131 (1935).

[47] *Cf.* ABA Canon 39.

wise.[48] A lawyer should not pay or agree to pay a non-expert witness an amount in excess of reimbursement for expenses and financial loss incident to his being a witness; however, a lawyer may pay or agree to pay an expert witness a reasonable fee for his services as an expert. But in no event should a lawyer pay or agree to pay a contingent fee to any witness. A lawyer should exercise reasonable diligence to see that his client and lay associates conform to these standards.[49]

EC 7-29 To safeguard the impartiality that is essential to the judicial process, veniremen and jurors should be protected against extraneous influences.[50] When impartiality is present, public confidence in the judicial system is enhanced. There should be no extrajudicial communication with veniremen prior to trial or with jurors during trial by or on behalf of a lawyer connected with the case. Furthermore, a lawyer who is not connected with the case should not communicate with or cause another to communicate with a venireman or a juror about the case. After the trial, communication by a lawyer with jurors is permitted so long as he refrains from asking questions or making comments that tend to harass or embarrass the juror[51] or to influence actions of the juror in future cases. Were a lawyer to be prohibited from communicating after trial with a juror, he could not ascertain if the verdict might be subject to legal challenge, in which event the invalidity of a verdict might go undetected.[52] When

an extrajudicial communication by a lawyer with a juror is permitted by law, it should be made considerately and with deference to the personal feelings of the juror.

EC 7-30 Vexatious or harassing investigations of veniremen or jurors seriously impair the effectiveness of our jury system. For this reason, a lawyer or anyone on his behalf who conducts an investigation of veniremen or jurors should act with circumspection and restraint.

EC 7-31 Communications with or investigations of members of families of veniremen or jurors by a lawyer or by anyone on his behalf are subject to the restrictions imposed upon the lawyer with respect to his communications with or investigations of veniremen and jurors.

EC 7-32 Because of his duty to aid in preserving the integrity of the jury system, a lawyer who learns of improper conduct by or towards a venireman, a juror, or a member of the family of either should make a prompt report to the court regarding such conduct.

EC 7-33 A goal of our legal system is that each party shall have his case, criminal or civil, adjudicated by an impartial tribunal. The attainment of this goal may be defeated by dissemination of news or comments which tend to influence judge or jury.[53] Such news or comments may

---

[48] "The prevalence of perjury is a serious menace to the administration of justice, to prevent which no means have as yet been satisfactorily devised. But there certainly can be no greater incentive to perjury than to allow a party to make payments to its opponents witnesses under any guise or on any excuse, and at least attorneys who are officers of the court to aid it in the administration of justice, must keep themselves clear of any connection which in the slightest degree tends to induce witnesses to testify in favor of their clients." In re Robinson, 151 App.Div. 589, 600, 136 N.Y.S. 548, 556–57 (1912), aff'd, 209 N.Y. 354, 103 N.E. 160 (1913).

[49] "It will not do for an attorney who seeks to justify himself against charges of this kind to show that he has escaped criminal responsibility under the Penal Law, nor can he blindly shut his eyes to a system which tends to suborn witnesses, to produce perjured testimony, and to suppress the truth. He has an active affirmative duty to protect the administration of justice from perjury and fraud, and that duty is not performed by allowing his subordinates and assistants to attempt to subvert justice and procure results for his clients based upon false testimony and perjured witnesses." Id., 151 App.Div. at 592, 136 N.Y.S. at 551.

[50] See ABA Canon 23.

[51] "[I]t is unfair to jurors to permit a disappointed litigant to pick over their private associations in search of something to discredit them and their verdict. And it would be unfair to the public too if jurors should understand that they cannot convict a man of means without risking an inquiry of that kind by paid investigators, with, to boot, the distortions an inquiry of that kind can produce." State v. LaFera, 42 N.J. 97, 107, 199 A.2d 630, 636 (1964).

[52] ABA Opinion 319 (1968) points out that "[m]any courts today, and the trend is in this direction, allow the testi-

mony of jurors as to all irregularities in and out of the courtroom except those irregularities whose existence can be determined only by exploring the consciousness of a single particular juror, New Jersey v. Kociolek, 20 N.J. 92, 118 A.2d 812 (1955). Model Code of Evidence Rule 301. Certainly as to states in which the testimony and affidavits of jurors may be received in support of or against a motion for new trial, a lawyer, in his obligation to protect his client, must have the tools for ascertaining whether or not grounds for a new trial exist and it is not unethical for him to talk to and question jurors."

[53] Generally see ABA Advisory Committee on Fair Trial and Free Press, Standards Relating to Fair Trial and Free Press (1966).

"[T]he trial court might well have proscribed extrajudicial statements by any lawyer, party, witness, or court official which divulged prejudicial matters . . .. See State v. Van Dwyne, 43 N.J. 369, 389, 204 A.2d 841, 852 (1964), in which the court interpreted Canon 20 of the American Bar Association's Canons of Professional Ethics to prohibit such statements. Being advised of the great public interest in the case, the mass coverage of the press, and the potential prejudicial impact of publicity, the court could also have requested the appropriate city and county officials to promulgate a regulation with respect to dissemination of information about the case by their employees. In addition, reporters who wrote or broadcast prejudicial stories, could have been warned as to the impropriety of publishing material not introduced in the proceedings. . . . In this manner, Sheppard's right to a trial free from outside interference would have been given added protection without corresponding curtailment of the news media. Had the judge, the other officers of the court, and the police placed the interest of justice first, the news media would have soon learned to be content with the task of reporting the case as it unfolded in the courtroom—not pieced together from extrajudicial statements." Sheppard v. Maxwell, 384 U.S. 333, 361–62, 16 L. Ed.2d 600, 619–20, 86 S.Ct. 1507, 1521–22 (1966).

prevent prospective jurors from being impartial at the outset of the trial [54] and may also interfere with the obligation of jurors to base their verdict solely upon the evidence admitted in the trial.[55]

"Court proceedings are held for the solemn purpose of endeavoring to ascertain the truth which is the *sine qua non* of a fair trial. Over the centuries Anglo-American courts have devised careful safeguards by rule and otherwise to protect and facilitate the performance of this high function. As a result, at this time those safeguards do not permit the televising and photographing of a criminal trial, save in two States and there only under restrictions. The federal courts prohibit it by specific rule. This is weighty evidence that our concepts of a fair trial do not tolerate such an indulgence. We have always held that the atmosphere essential to the preservation of a fair trial—the most fundamental of all freedoms—must be maintained at all costs." Estes v. State of Texas, 381 U.S. 532, 540, 14 L.Ed.2d 543, 549, 85 S.Ct. 1628, 1631–32 (1965), *rehearing denied*, 382 U.S. 875, 15 L.Ed.2d 118, 86 S.Ct. 18 (1965).

[54] "Pretrial can create a major problem for the defendant in a criminal case. Indeed, it may be more harmful than publicity during the trial for it may well set the community opinion as to guilt or innocence. . . . The trial witnesses present at the hearing, as well as the original jury panel, were undoubtedly made aware of the peculiar public importance of the case by the press and television coverage being provided, and by the fact that they themselves were televised live and their pictures rebroadcast on the evening show." *Id.*, 381 U.S. at 536–37, 14 L.Ed.2d at 546–47, 85 S.Ct. at 1629–30.

[55] "The undeviating rule of this Court was expressed by Mr. Justice Holmes over half a century ago in Patterson v. Colorado, 205 U.S. 454, 462 (1907) :
The theory of our system is that the conclusions to be reached in a case will be induced only by evidence and argument in open court, and not by any outside influence, whether of private talk or public print."
Sheppard v. Maxwell, 384 U.S. 333, 351, 16 L.Ed.2d 600, 614, 86 S.Ct. 1507, 1516 (1966).

"The trial judge has a large discretion in ruling on the issue of prejudice resulting from the reading by jurors of news articles concerning the trial. . . . Generalizations beyond that statement are not profitable, because each case must turn on its special facts. We have here the exposure of jurors to information of a character which the trial judge ruled was so prejudicial it could not be directly offered as evidence. The prejudice to the defendant is almost certain to be as great when that evidence reaches the jury through news accounts as when it is a part of the prosecution's evidence. . . . It may indeed be greater for it is then not tempered by protective procedures." Marshall v United States, 360 U.S. 310, 312–13, 3 L.Ed.2d 1250, 1252, 79 S.Ct. 1171, 1173 (1959).

"The experienced trial lawyer knows that an adverse public opinion is a tremendous disadvantage to the defense of his client. Although grand jurors conduct their deliberations in secret, they are selected from the body of the public. They are likely to know what the general public knows and to reflect the public attitude. Trials are open to the public, and aroused public opinion respecting the merits of a legal controversy creates a court room atmosphere which, without any vocal expression in the presence of the petit jury, makes itself felt and has its effect upon the action of the petit jury. Our fundamental concepts of justice and our American sense of fair play require that the petit jury shall be composed of persons with fair and impartial minds and without preconceived views as to the merits of the controversy, and that it shall determine the issues presented to it solely upon the evidence adduced at the trial and according to the law given in the instructions of the trial judge.

The release by a lawyer of out-of-court statements regarding an anticipated or pending trial may improperly affect the impartiality of the tribunal.[56] For these reasons, standards for permissible and prohibited conduct of a lawyer with respect to trial publicity have been established.

EC 7–34 The impartiality of a public servant in our legal system may be impaired by the receipt of gifts or loans. A lawyer,[57] therefore, is never justified in making a gift or a loan to a judge, a hearing officer, or an official or employee of a tribunal.[58]

EC 7–35 All litigants and lawyers should have access to tribunals on an equal basis. Generally, in adversary proceedings a lawyer should not communicate with a judge relative to a matter pending before, or which is to be brought before, a tribunal over which he presides in circumstances which might have the effect or give the appearance of granting undue advantage to one party.[59] For example, a lawyer should not communicate with a tribunal by a writing unless a copy thereof is promptly delivered to opposing counsel or to the adverse party if he is not represented by a lawyer. Ordinarily an oral communication by a lawyer with a judge or hearing officer should be made only upon adequate notice to opposing counsel, or, if there is none, to the opposing party. A lawyer should not condone or lend himself to private importunities by another with a judge or hearing officer on behalf of himself or his client.

EC 7–36 Judicial hearings ought to be conducted through dignified and orderly procedures designed to protect the rights of all parties. Although a lawyer has the duty to represent his client zealous-

---

"While we may doubt that the effect of public opinion would sway or bias the judgment of the trial judge in an equity proceeding, the defendant should not be called upon to run that risk and the trial court should not have his work made more difficult by any dissemination of statements to the public that would be calculated to create a public demand for a particular judgment in a prospective or pending case." *ABA Opinion 199* (1940).
Cf. Estes v. State of Texas, 381 U.S. 532, 544–45, 14 L.Ed.2d 543, 551, 85 S.Ct. 1628, 1634 (1965), *rehearing denied*, 381 U.S. 875, 15 L.Ed.2d 118, 86 S.Ct. 18 (1965).

[56] *See* ABA Canon 20.

[57] Canon 3 observes that a lawyer "deserves rebuke and denunciation for any device or attempt to gain from a Judge special personal consideration or favor."
See ABA Canon 32.

[58] "*Judicial Canon 32* provides :
" 'A judge should not accept any presents or favors from litigants, or from lawyers practicing before him or from others whose interests are likely to be submitted to him for judgment.'
"The language of this Canon is perhaps broad enough to prohibit campaign contributions by lawyers, practicing before the court upon which the candidate hopes to sit. However, we do not think it was intended to prohibit such contributions when the candidate is obligated, by force of circumstances over which he has no control, to conduct a campaign, the expense of which exceeds that which he should reasonably be expected to personally bear!" *ABA Opinion 226* (1941).

[59] *See* ABA Canons 3 and 32.

---

ly, he should not engage in any conduct that offends the dignity and decorum of proceedings.[60] While maintaining his independence, a lawyer should be respectful, courteous, and above-board in his relations with a judge or hearing officer before whom he appears.[61] He should avoid undue solicitude for the comfort or convenience of judge or jury and should avoid any other conduct calculated to gain special consideration.

EC 7-37 In adversary proceedings, clients are litigants and though ill feeling may exist between clients, such ill feeling should not influence a lawyer in his conduct, attitude, and demeanor towards opposing lawyers.[62] A lawyer should not make unfair or derogatory personal reference to opposing counsel. Haranguing and offensive tactics by lawyers interfere with the orderly administration of justice and have no proper place in our legal system.

EC 7-38 A lawyer should be courteous to opposing counsel and should accede to reasonable requests regarding court proceedings, settings, continuances, waiver of procedural formalities, and similar matters which do not prejudice the rights of his client.[63] He should follow local customs of courtesy or practice, unless he gives timely notice to opposing counsel of his intention not to do so.[64] A lawyer should be punctual in fulfilling all professional commitments.[65]

EC 7-39 In the final analysis, proper functioning of the adversary system depends upon cooperation between lawyers and tribunals in utilizing procedures which will preserve the impartiality of tribunals and make their decisional processes prompt and just, without impinging upon the obligation of lawyers to represent their clients zealously within the framework of the law.

DISCIPLINARY RULES

DR 7-101 Representing a Client Zealously.

(A) A lawyer shall not intentionally:[66]

    (1) Fail to seek the lawful objectives of his client through reasonably available means[67] permitted by law and the Disciplinary Rules, except as provided by DR 7-101(B). A lawyer does not violate this Disciplinary Rule, however, by acceding to reasonable requests of opposing counsel which do not prejudice the rights of his client, by being punctual in fulfilling all professional commitments, by avoiding offensive tactics, or by treating

---

[60] *Cf.* ABA Canon 18.

[61] *See* ABA Canons 1 and 3.

[62] *See* ABA Canon 17.

[63] *See* ABA Canon 24.

[64] *See* ABA Canon 25.

[65] *See* ABA Canon 21.

[66] *See* ABA Canon 15.

[67] *See* ABA Canons 5 and 15; *cf.* ABA Canons 4 and 32.

with courtesy and consideration all persons involved in the legal process.

    (2) Fail to carry out a contract of employment entered into with a client for professional services, but he may withdraw as permitted under DR 2-110, DR 5-102, and DR 5-105.

    (3) Prejudice or damage his client during the course of the professional relationship[68] except as required under DR 7-102(B).

(B) In his representation of a client, a lawyer may:

    (1) Where permissible, exercise his professional judgment to waive or fail to assert a right or position of his client.

    (2) Refuse to aid or participate in conduct that he believes to be unlawful, even though there is some support for an argument that the conduct is legal.

DR 7-102 Representing a Client Within the Bounds of the Law.

(A) In his representation of a client, a lawyer shall not:

    (1) File a suit, assert a position, conduct a defense, delay a trial, or take other action on behalf of his client when he knows or when it is obvious that such action would serve merely to harass or maliciously injure another.[69]

    (2) Knowingly advance a claim or defense that is unwarranted under existing law, except that he may advance such claim or defense if it can be supported by good faith argument for an extension, modification, or reversal of existing law.

    (3) Conceal or knowingly fail to disclose that which he is required by law to reveal.

    (4) Knowingly use perjured testimony or false evidence.[70]

    (5) Knowingly make a false statement of law or fact.

    (6) Participate in the creation or preservation of evidence when he knows or it is obvious that the evidence is false.

    (7) Counsel or assist his client in conduct that the lawyer knows to be illegal or fraudulent.

    (8) Knowingly engage in other illegal conduct or conduct contrary to a Disciplinary Rule.

(B) A lawyer who receives information clearly establishing that:

    (1) His client has, in the course of the representation, perpetrated a fraud upon a person or tribunal shall promptly call

---

[68] *Cf.* ABA Canon 24.

[69] *See* ABA Canon 30.

[70] *Cf.* ABA Canons 22 and 29.

upon his client to rectify the same, and if his client refuses or is unable to do so, he shall reveal the fraud to the affected person or tribunal.[71]

(2) A person other than his client has perpetrated a fraud upon a tribunal shall promptly reveal the fraud to the tribunal.[72]

DR 7-103 Performing the Duty of Public Prosecutor or Other Government Lawyer.[73]

(A) A public prosecutor or other government lawyer shall not institute or cause to be instituted criminal charges when he knows or it is obvious that the charges are not supported by probable cause.

(B) A public prosecutor or other government lawyer in criminal litigation shall make timely disclosure to counsel for the defendant, or to the defendant if he has no counsel, of the existence of evidence, known to the prosecutor or other government lawyer, that tends to negate the guilt of the accused, mitigate the degree of the offense, or reduce the punishment.

DR 7-104 Communicating With One of Adverse Interest.[74]

(A) During the course of his representation of a client a lawyer shall not:

(1) Communicate or cause another to communicate on the subject of the representation with a party he knows to be represented by a lawyer in that matter unless he has the prior consent of the lawyer representing such other party [75] or is authorized by law to do so.

(2) Give advice to a person who is not represented by a lawyer, other than the advice to secure counsel,[76] if the interests of such person are or have a reasonable possibility of being in conflict with the interests of his client.[77]

DR 7-105 Threatening Criminal Prosecution.

(A) A lawyer shall not present, participate in presenting, or theaten to present criminal charges solely to obtain an advantage in a civil matter.

DR 7-106 Trial Conduct.

(A) A lawyer shall not disregard or advise his client to disregard a standing rule of a tribunal or a ruling of a tribunal made in the course of a proceeding, but he may take appropriate steps in good faith to test the validity of such rule or ruling.

(B) In presenting a matter to a tribunal, a lawyer shall disclose: [78]

(1) Legal authority in the controlling jurisdiction known to him to be directly adverse to the position of his client and which is not disclosed by opposing counsel.[79]

(2) Unless privileged or irrelevant, the identities of the clients he represents and of the persons who employed him.[80]

---

[76] Cf. ABA Opinion 102 (1933).

[77] Cf. ABA Canon 9 and ABA Opinion 58 (1931).

[78] Cf. Note, 38 Texas L.Rev. 107, 108–09 (1959).

[79] "In the brief summary in the 1947 edition of the Committee's decisions (p. 17), Opinion 146 was thus summarized: Opinion 146—A lawyer should disclose to the court a decision directly adverse to his client's case that is unknown to his adversary.

. . . .

"We would not confine the Opinion to 'controlling authorities'—i.e., those decisive of the pending case—but, in accordance with the tests hereafter suggested, would apply it to a decision directly adverse to any proposition of law on which the lawyer expressly relies, which would reasonably be considered important by the judge sitting on the case.

. . . .

". . . The test in every case should be: Is the decision which opposing counsel has overlooked one which the court should clearly consider in deciding the case? Would a reasonable judge properly feel that a lawyer who advanced, as the law, a proposition adverse to the undisclosed decision, was lacking in candor and fairness to him? Might the judge consider himself misled by an implied representation that the lawyer knew of no adverse authority?" ABA Opinion 280 (1949).

[80] "The authorities are substantially uniform against any privilege as applied to the fact of retainer or identity of the client. The privilege is limited to confidential communications, and a retainer is not a confidential communication, although it cannot come into existence without some communication between the attorney and the—at that stage prospective—client." United States v. Pape, 144 F.2d 778, 782 (2d Cir. 1944), cert. denied, 323 U.S. 752, 89 L.Ed.2d 602, 65 S.Ct. 86 (1944).

"To be sure, there may be circumstances under which the identification of a client may amount to the prejudicial disclosure of a confidential communication, as where the

---

[71] See ABA Canon 41; cf. Hinds v. State Bar, 19 Cal.2d 87, 92–93, 119 P.2d 134, 137 (1941); but see ABA Opinion 287 (1953) and Texas Canon 38. Also see Code of Professional Responsibility, DR 4–101(C)(2).

[72] See Precision Inst. Mfg. Co. v. Automotive M. M. Co., 324 U.S. 806, 89 L.Ed. 1381, 65 S.Ct. 993 (1945).

[73] Cf. ABA Canon 5.

[74] "Rule 12. . . . A member of the State Bar shall not communicate with a party represented by counsel upon a subject of controversy, in the absence and without the consent of such counsel. This rule shall not apply to communications with a public officer, board, committee or body." Cal.Business and Professions Code § 6076 (West 1962).

[75] See ABA Canon 9; cf. ABA Opinions 124 (1934), 108 (1934), 95 (1933), and 75 (1932); also see In re Schwabe, 242 Or. 169, 174–75, 408 P.2d 922, 924 (1965).

"It is clear from the earlier opinions of this committee that Canon 9 is to be construed literally and does not allow a communication with an opposing party, without the consent of his counsel, though the purpose merely be to investigate the facts. Opinions 117, 95, 66," ABA Opinion 187 (1938).

(C) In appearing in his professional capacity before a tribunal, a lawyer shall not:

(1) State or allude to any matter that he has no reasonable basis to believe is relevant to the case or that will not be supported by admissible evidence.[81]

(2) Ask any question that he has no reasonable basis to believe is relevant to the case and that is intended to degrade a witness or other person.[82]

(3) Assert his personal knowledge of the facts in issue, except when testifying as a witness.

(4) Assert his personal opinion as to the justness of a cause, as to the credibility of a witness, as to the culpability of a civil litigant, or as to the guilt or innocence of an accused;[83] but he may argue, on his analysis of the evidence, for any position or conclusion with respect to the matters stated herein.

(5) Fail to comply with known local customs of courtesy or practice of the bar or a particular tribunal without giving to opposing counsel timely notice of his intent not to comply.[84]

(6) Engage in undignified or discourteous conduct which is degrading to a tribunal.

(7) Intentionally or habitually violate any established rule of procedure or of evidence.

DR 7-107 Trial Publicity.[85]

(A) A lawyer participating in or associated with the investigation of a criminal matter shall not make or participate in making an extra-judicial statement that a reasonable person would expect to be disseminated by means of public communication and that does more than state without elaboration:

(1) Information contained in a public record.

(2) That the investigation is in progress.

(3) The general scope of the investigation including a description of the offense and, if permitted by law, the identity of the victim.

(4) A request for assistance in apprehending a suspect or assistance in other matters and the information necessary thereto.

(5) A warning to the public of any dangers.

(B) A lawyer or law firm associated with the prosecution or defense of a criminal matter shall not, from the time of the filing of a complaint, information, or indictment, the issuance of an arrest warrant, or arrest until the commencement of the trial or disposition

---

substance of a disclosure has already been revealed but not its source." Colton v. United States, 306 F.2d 633, 637 (2d Cir. 1962).

[81] *See* ABA Canon 22; *cf.* ABA Canon 17.
"The rule allowing counsel when addressing the jury the widest latitude in discussing the evidence and presenting the client's theories falls far short of authorizing the statement by counsel of matter not in evidence, or indulging in argument founded on no proof, or demanding verdicts for purposes other than the just settlement of the matters at issue between the litigants, or appealing to prejudice or passion. The rule confining counsel to legitimate argument is not based on etiquette, but on justice. Its violation is not merely an overstepping of the bounds of propriety, but a violation of a party's rights. The jurors must determine the issues upon the evidence. Counsel's address should help them do this, not tend to lead them astray." Cherry Creek Nat. Bank v. Fidelity & Cas. Co., 207 App.Div. 787, 790–91, 202 N.Y.S. 611, 614 (1924).

[82] *Cf.* ABA Canon 18.
"§ 6068. . . . It is the duty of an attorney:
. . . .
"(f) To abstain from all offensive personality, and to advance no fact prejudicial to the honor or reputation of a party or witness, unless required by the justice of the cause with which he is charged." Cal.Business and Professions Code § 6068 (West 1962).

[83] "The record in the case at bar was silent concerning the qualities and character of the deceased. It is especially improper, in addressing the jury in a murder case, for the prosecuting attorney to make reference to his knowledge of the good qualities of the deceased where there is no evidence in the record bearing upon his character. . . . A prosecutor should never inject into his argument evidence not introduced at the trial." People v. Dukes, 12 Ill.2d 334, 341, 146 N.E.2d 14, 17–18 (1957).

[84] "A lawyer should not ignore known customs or practice of the Bar or of a particular Court, even when the law permits, without giving timely notice to the opposing counsel." ABA Canon 25.

---

[85] The provisions of Sections (A), (B), (C), and (D) of this Disciplinary Rule incorporate the fair trial-free press standards which apply to lawyers as adopted by the ABA House of Delegates, Feb. 19, 1968, upon the recommendation of the Fair Trial and Free Press Advisory Committee of the ABA Special Committee on Minimum Standards for the Administration of Criminal Justice.

Cf. ABA Canon 20; *see generally* ABA Advisory Committee on Fair Trial and Free Press, Standards Relating to Fair Trial and Free Press (1966).

"From the cases coming here we note that unfair and prejudicial news comment on pending trials has become increasingly prevalent. Due process requires that the accused receive a trial by an impartial jury free from outside influences. Given the pervasiveness of modern communications and the difficulty of effacing prejudicial publicity from the minds of the jurors, the trial courts must take strong measures to ensure that the balance is never weighed against the accused. And appellate tribunals have the duty to make an independent evaluation of the circumstances. Of course, there is nothing that prescribes the press from reporting events that transpire in the courtroom. But where there is a reasonable likelihood that prejudicial news prior to trial will prevent a fair trial, the judge should continue the case until the threat abates, or transfer it to another county not so permeated with publicity. . . . The courts must take such steps by rule and regulation that will protect their processes from prejudicial outside interferences. Neither prosecutors, counsel for defense, the accused, witnesses, court staff nor enforcement officers coming under the jurisdiction of the court should be permitted to frustrate its function. Collaboration between counsel and the press as to information affecting the fairness of a criminal trial is not only subject to regulation, but is highly censurable and worthy of disciplinary measures." Sheppard v. Maxwell, 384 U.S. 333, 362–63, 16 L.Ed.2d 600, 620, 86 S.Ct. 1507, 1522 (1966).

without trial, make or participate in making an extrajudicial statement that a reasonable person would expect to be disseminated by means of public communication and that relates to:

(1) The character, reputation, or prior criminal record (including arrests, indictments, or other charges of crime) of the accused.

(2) The possibility of a plea of guilty to the offense charged or to a lesser offense.

(3) The existence or contents of any confession, admission, or statement given by the accused or his refusal or failure to make a statement.

(4) The performance or results of any examinations or tests or the refusal or failure of the accused to submit to examinations or tests.

(5) The identity, testimony, or credibility of a prospective witness.

(6) Any opinion as to the guilt or innocence of the accused, the evidence, or the merits of the case.

(C) DR 7-107(B) does not preclude a lawyer during such period from announcing:

(1) The name, age, residence, occupation, and family status of the accused.

(2) If the accused has not been apprehended, any information necessary to aid in his apprehension or to warn the public of any dangers he may present.

(3) A request for assistance in obtaining evidence.

(4) The identity of the victim of the crime.

(5) The fact, time, and place of arrest, resistance, pursuit, and use of weapons.

(6) The identity of investigating and arresting officers or agencies and the length of the investigation.

(7) At the time of seizure, a description of the physical evidence seized, other than a confession, admission, or statement.

(8) The nature, substance, or text of the charge.

(9) Quotations from or references to public records of the court in the case.

(10) The scheduling or result of any step in the judicial proceedings.

(11) That the accused denies the charges made against him.

(D) During the selection of a jury or the trial of a criminal matter, a lawyer or law firm associated with the prosecution or defense of a criminal matter shall not make or participate in making an extrajudicial statement that a reasonable person would expect to be disseminated by means of public communication and that relates to the trial, parties, or issues in the trial or other matters that are reasonably likely to interfere with a fair trial, except that he may quote from or refer without comment to public records of the court in the case.

(E) After the completion of a trial or disposition without trial of a criminal matter and prior to the imposition of sentence, a lawyer or law firm associated with the prosecution or defense shall not make or participate in making an extrajudicial statement that a reasonable person would expect to be disseminated by public communication and that is reasonably likely to affect the imposition of sentence.

(F) The foregoing provisions of DR 7-107 also apply to professional disciplinary proceedings and juvenile disciplinary proceedings when pertinent and consistent with other law applicable to such proceedings.

(G) A lawyer or law firm associated with a civil action shall not during its investigation or litigation make or participate in making an extrajudicial statement, other than a quotation from or reference to public records, that a reasonable person would expect to be disseminated by means of public communication and that relates to:

(1) Evidence regarding the occurrence or transaction involved.

(2) The character, credibility, or criminal record of a party, witness, or prospective witness.

(3) The performance or results of any examinations or tests or the refusal or failure of a party to submit to such.

(4) His opinion as to the merits of the claims or defenses of a party, except as required by law or administrative rule.

(5) Any other matter reasonably likely to interfere with a fair trial of the action.

(H) During the pendency of an administrative proceeding, a lawyer or law firm associated therewith shall not make or participate in making a statement, other than a quotation from or reference to public records, that a reasonable person would expect to be disseminated by means of public communication if it is made outside the official course of the proceeding and relates to:

(1) Evidence regarding the occurrence or transaction involved.

(2) The character, credibility, or criminal record of a party, witness, or prospective witness.

(3) Physical evidence or the performance or results of any examinations or tests or the refusal or failure of a party to submit to such.

(4) His opinion as to the merits of the claims, defenses, or positions of an interested person.

(5) Any other matter reasonably likely to interfere with a fair hearing.

(I) The foregoing provisions of DR 7–107 do not preclude a lawyer from replying to charges of misconduct publicly made against him or from participating in the proceedings of legislative, administrative, or other investigative bodies.

(J) A lawyer shall exercise reasonable care to prevent his employees and associates from making an extrajudicial statement that he would be prohibited from making under DR 7–107.

DR 7–108 Communication with or Investigation of Jurors.

(A) Before the trial of a case a lawyer connected therewith shall not communicate with or cause another to communicate with anyone he knows to be a member of the venire from which the jury will be selected for the trial of the case.

(B) During the trial of a case:

(1) A lawyer connected therewith shall not communicate with or cause another to communicate with any member of the jury.[86]

(2) A lawyer who is not connected therewith shall not communicate with or cause another to communicate with a juror concerning the case.

(C) DR 7–108(A) and (B) do not prohibit a lawyer from communicating with veniremen or jurors in the course of official proceedings.

(D) After discharge of the jury from further consideration of a case with which the lawyer was connected, the lawyer shall not ask questions of or make comments to a member of that jury that are calculated merely to harass or embarrass the juror or to influence his actions in future jury service.[87]

(E) A lawyer shall not conduct or cause, by financial support or otherwise, another to conduct a vexatious or harassing investigation of either a venireman or a juror.

(F) All restrictions imposed by DR 7–108 upon a lawyer also apply to communications with or investigations of members of a family of a venireman or a juror.

(G) A lawyer shall reveal promptly to the court improper conduct by a venireman or a juror, or by another toward a venireman or a juror or a member of his family, of which the lawyer has knowledge.

DR 7–109 Contact with Witnesses.

(A) A lawyer shall not suppress any evidence that he or his client has a legal obligation to reveal or produce.[88]

---

86 *See* ABA Canon 23.

87 "[I]t would be unethical for a lawyer to harass, entice, induce or exert influence on a juror to obtain his testimony." *ABA Opinion* 319 (1968).

88 *See* ABA Canon 5.

(B) A lawyer shall not advise or cause a person to secrete himself or to leave the jurisdiction of a tribunal for the purpose of making him unavailable as a witness therein.[89]

(C) A lawyer shall not pay, offer to pay, or acquiesce in the payment of compensation to a witness contingent upon the content of his testimony or the outcome of the case.[90] But a lawyer may advance, guarantee, or acquiesce in the payment of:

(1) Expenses reasonably incurred by a witness in attending or testifying.

(2) Reasonable compensation to a witness for his loss of time in attending or testifying.

(3) A reasonable fee for the professional services of an expert witness.

DR 7–110 Contact with Officials.[91]

(A) A lawyer shall not give or lend any thing of value to a judge, official, or employee of a tribunal.

(B) In an adversary proceeding, a lawyer shall not communicate, or cause another to communicate, as to the merits of the cause with a judge or an official before whom the proceeding is pending, except:

(1) In the course of official proceedings in the cause.

(2) In writing if he promptly delivers a copy of the writing to opposing counsel or to the adverse party if he is not represented by a lawyer.

(3) Orally upon adequate notice to opposing counsel or to the adverse party if he is not represented by a lawyer.

(4) As otherwise authorized by law.[92]

---

89 *Cf.* ABA Canon 5.

"*Rule 15.* . . . A member of the State Bar shall not advise a person, whose testimony could establish or tend to establish a material fact, to avoid service of process, or secrete himself, or otherwise to make his testimony unavailable." Cal.Business and Professions Code § 6076 (West 1962).

90 *See* In re O'Keefe, 49 Mont. 369, 142 P. 638 (1914).

91 *Cf.* ABA Canon 3.

92 "*Rule 16.* . . . A member of the State Bar shall not, in the absence of opposing counsel, communicate with or argue to a judge or judicial officer except in open court upon the merits of a contested matter pending before such judge or judicial officer; nor shall he, without furnishing opposing counsel with a copy thereof, address a written communication to a judge or judicial officer concerning the merits of a contested matter pending before such judge or judicial officer. This rule shall not apply to ex parte matters." Cal.Business and Professions Code § 6076 (West 1962).

CANON 8

A Lawyer Should Assist in Improving the Legal System

ETHICAL CONSIDERATIONS

EC 8–1 Changes in human affairs and imperfections in human institutions make necessary constant efforts to maintain and improve our legal system.[1] This system should function in a manner that commands public respect and fosters the use of legal remedies to achieve redress of grievances. By reason of education and experience, lawyers are especially qualified to recognize deficiencies in the legal system and to initiate corrective measures therein. Thus they should participate in proposing and supporting legislation and programs to improve the system,[2] without regard to the general interests or desires of clients or former clients.[3]

EC 8–2 Rules of law are deficient if they are not just, understandable, and responsive to the needs of society. If a lawyer believes that the existence or absence of a rule of law, substantive or procedural, causes or contributes to an unjust result, he should endeavor by lawful means to obtain appropriate changes in the law. He should encourage the simplification of laws and the repeal or amendment of laws that are outmoded.[4] Like-wise, legal procedures should be improved whenever experience indicates a change is needed.

EC 8–3 The fair administration of justice requires the availability of competent lawyers. Members of the public should be educated to recognize the existence of legal problems and the resultant need for legal services, and should be provided methods for intelligent selection of counsel. Those persons unable to pay for legal services should be provided needed services. Clients and lawyers should not be penalized by undue geographical restraints upon representation in legal matters, and the bar should address itself to improvements in licensing, reciprocity, and admission procedures consistent with the needs of modern commerce.

EC 8–4 Whenever a lawyer seeks legislative or administrative changes, he should identify the capacity in which he appears, whether on behalf of himself, a client, or the public.[5] A lawyer may advocate such changes on behalf of a client even though he does not agree with them. But when a lawyer purports to act on behalf of the public, he should espouse only those changes which he conscientiously believes to be in the public interest.

EC 8–5 Fraudulent, deceptive, or otherwise illegal conduct by a participant in a proceeding before a tribunal or legislative body is inconsistent with fair administration of justice, and it should never be participated in or condoned by lawyers. Unless constrained by his obligation to preserve the confidences and secrets of his client, a lawyer should reveal to appropriate authorities any knowledge he may have of such improper conduct.

EC 8–6 Judges and administrative officials having adjudicatory powers ought to be persons of integrity, competence, and suitable temperament. Generally, lawyers are qualified, by personal observation or investigation, to evaluate the qualifications of persons seeking or being considered for such public offices, and for this reason they have a special responsibility to aid in the selection of only those who are qualified.[6] It is the duty of

---

1 ". . . [Another] task of the great lawyer is to do his part individually and as a member of the organized bar to improve his profession, the courts, and the law. As President Theodore Roosevelt aptly put it, 'Every man owes some of his time to the upbuilding of the profession to which he belongs.' Indeed, this obligation is one of the great things which distinguishes a profession from a business. The soundness and the necessity of President Roosevelt's admonition insofar as it relates to the legal profession cannot be doubted. The advances in natural science and technology are so startling and the velocity of change in business and in social life is so great that the law along with the other social sciences, and even human life itself, is in grave danger of being extinguished by new gods of its own invention if it does not awake from its lethargy. Vanderbilt, *The Five Functions of the Lawyer: Service to Clients and the Public*, 40 A.B.A.J. 31, 31–32 (1954).

2 *See* ABA Canon 29; *Cf.* Cheatham, *The Lawyer's Role and Surroundings*, 25 Rocky Mt.L.Rev. 405, 406–07 (1953).
"The lawyer tempted by repose should recall the heavy costs paid by his profession when needed legal reform has to be accomplished through the initiative of public-spirited laymen. Where change must be thrust from without upon an unwilling Bar, the public's least flattering picture of the lawyer seems confirmed. The lawyer concerned for the standing of his profession will, therefore, interest himself actively in the improvement of the law. In doing so he will not only help to maintain confidence in the Bar, but will have the satisfaction of meeting a responsibility inhering in the nature of his calling." *Professional Responsibility: Report of the Joint Conference*, 44 A.B.A.J. 1159, 1217 (1958).

3 *See* Stayton, *Cum Honore Officium*, 19 Tex.B.J. 765, 766 (1956); *Professional Responsibility: Report of the Joint Conference*, 44 A.B.A.J. 1159, 1162 (1958); and Paul, *The Lawyer as a Tax Adviser*, 25 Rocky Mt.L.Rev. 412, 433–34 (1953).

4 "There are few great figures in the history of the Bar who have not concerned themselves with the reform and improvement of the law. The special obligation of the profession with respect to legal reform rests on considerations too obvious to require enumeration. Certainly it is the lawyer who has both the best chance to know when the law is working badly and the special competence to put it in order." *Professional Responsibility: Report of the Joint Conference*, 44 A.B.A.J. 1159, 1217 (1958).

5 "*Rule 14.* . . . A member of the State Bar shall not communicate with, or appear before, a public officer, board, committee or body, in his professional capacity, without first disclosing that he is an attorney representing interests that may be affected by action of such officer, board, committee or body." Cal.Business and Professions Code § 6076 (West 1962).

6 *See* ABA Canon 2.
"Lawyers are better able than laymen to appraise accurately the qualifications of candidates for judicial office. It is proper that they should make that appraisal known to the voters in a proper and dignified manner. A lawyer may with propriety endorse a candidate for judicial office and seek like endorsement from other lawyers. But

lawyers to endeavor to prevent political considerations from outweighing judicial fitness in the
selection of judges. Lawyers should protest ear-
nestly against the appointment or election of those
who are unsuited for the bench and should strive
to have elected [7] or appointed thereto only those
who are willing to forego pursuits, whether of a
business, political, or other nature, that may interfere with the free and fair consideration of questions presented for adjudication. Adjudicatory officials, not being wholly free to defend themselves,
are entitled to receive the support of the bar
against unjust criticism.[8] While a lawyer as a
citizen has a right to criticize such officials publicly,[9] he should be certain of the merit of his complaint, use appropriate language, and avoid petty
criticisms, for unrestrained and intemperate statements tend to lessen public confidence in our legal
system.[10] Criticisms motivated by reasons other
than a desire to improve the legal system are not
justified.

EC 8–7 Since lawyers are a vital part of the legal
system, they should be persons of integrity, of
professional skill, and of dedication to the im-

provement of the system. Thus a lawyer should
aid in establishing, as well as enforcing, standards of conduct adequate to protect the public by
insuring that those who practice law are qualified
to do so.

EC 8–8 Lawyers often serve as legislators or as
holders of other public offices. This is highly desirable, as lawyers are uniquely qualified to make
significant contributions to the improvement of
the legal system. A lawyer who is a public officer, whether full or part-time, should not engage
in activities in which his personal or professional
interests are or foreseeably may be in conflict with
his official duties.[11]

EC 8–9 The advancement of our legal system is
of vital importance in maintaining the rule of law
and in facilitating orderly changes; therefore, lawyers should encourage, and should aid in making,
needed changes and improvements.

DISCIPLINARY RULES

DR 8–101 Action as a Public Official.

(A) A lawyer who holds public office shall not:

(1) Use his public position to obtain, or attempt to obtain, a special advantage in
legislative matters for himself or for
a client under circumstances where he
knows or it is obvious that such action
is not in the public interest.

(2) Use his public position to influence, or
attempt to influence, a tribunal to act
in favor of himself or of a client.

---

the lawyer who endorses a judicial candidate or seeks
that endorsement from other lawyers should be actuated
by a sincere belief in the superior qualifications of the
candidate for judicial service and not by personal or selfish motives; and a lawyer should not use or attempt to
use the power or prestige of the judicial office to secure
such endorsement. On the other hand, the lawyer whose
endorsement is sought, if he believes the candidate lacks
the essential qualifications for the office or believes the
opposing candidate is better qualified, should have the
courage and moral stamina to refuse the request for endorsement." *ABA Opinion 189* (1938).

[7] "[W]e are of the opinion that, whenever a candidate
for judicial office merits the endorsement and support of
lawyers, the lawyers may make financial contributions
toward the campaign if its cost, when reasonably conducted, exceeds that which the candidate would be expected
to bear personally." *ABA Opinion 226* (1941).

[8] *See* ABA Canon 1.

[9] "Citizens have a right under our constitutional system
to criticize governmental officials and agencies. Courts
are not, and should not be, immune to such criticism."
Konigsberg v. State Bar of California, 353 U.S. 252, 269
(1957).

[10] "[E]very lawyer, worthy of respect, realizes that public confidence in our courts is the cornerstone of our governmental structure, and will refrain from unjustified attack on the character of the judges, while recognizing the
duty to denounce and expose a corrupt or dishonest judge."
Kentucky State Bar Ass'n v. Lewis, 282 S.W.2d 321, 326
(Ky. 1955).

"We should be the last to deny that Mr. Meeker has the
right to uphold the honor of the profession and to expose
without fear or favor corrupt or dishonest conduct in the
profession, whether the conduct be that of a judge or not.
. . . However, this Canon [29] does not permit one
to make charges which are false and untrue and unfounded
in fact. When one's fancy leads him to make false charges,
attacking the character and integrity of such, he does
so at his peril. He should not do so without adequate
proof of his charges and he is certainly not authorized to
make careless, untruthful and vile charges against his
professional brethren." In re Meeker, 76 N.M. 354, 364-
65, 414 P.2d 862, 869 (1966), *appeal dismissed*, 385 U.S. 449,
17 L.Ed.2d 510, 87 S.Ct. 613 (1967).

[11] "*Opinions 16, 30, 34, 77, 118* and *134* relate to *Canon 6*,
and pass on questions concerning the propriety of the conduct of an attorney who is a public officer, in representing private interests adverse to those of the public body
which he represents. The principle applied in those opinions is that an attorney holding public office should avoid
all conduct which might lead the layman to conclude that
the attorney is utilizing his public position to further
his professional success or personal interests." *ABA Opinion 192* (1939).

"The next question is whether a lawyer-member of a
legislative body may appear as counsel or co-counsel at
hearings before a zoning board of appeals, or similar
tribunal, created by the legislative group of which he is
a member. We are of the opinion that he may practice
before fact-finding officers, hearing bodies and commissioners, since under our views he may appear as counsel
in the courts where his municipality is a party. Decisions
made at such hearings are usually subject to administrative review by the courts upon the record there made. It
would be inconsistent to say that a lawyer-member of a
legislative body could not participate in a hearing at which
the record is made, but could appear thereafter when the
cause is heard by the courts on administrative review. This
is subject to an important exception. He should not appear as counsel where the matter is subject to review by
the legislative body of which he is a member. . . . We
are of the opinion that where a lawyer does so appear
there would be conflict of interests between his duty as an
advocate for his client on the one hand and the obligation
to his governmental unit on the other." In re Becker, 16
Ill.2d 488, 494-95, 158 N.E.2d 753, 756-57 (1959).

Cf. ABA Opinions 186 (1938), 136 (1935), 118 (1934), and
77 (1932).

(3) Accept any thing of value from any person when the lawyer knows or it is obvious that the offer is for the purpose of influencing his action as a public official.

DR 8-102 Statements Concerning Judges and Other Adjudicatory Officers.[12]

(A) A lawyer shall not knowingly make false statements of fact concerning the qualifications of a candidate for election or appointment to a judicial office.

(B) A lawyer shall not knowingly make false accusations against a judge or other adjudicatory officer.

CANON 9

A Lawyer Should Avoid Even the Appearance of Professional Impropriety

ETHICAL CONSIDERATIONS

EC 9-1 Continuation of the American concept that we are to be governed by rules of law requires that the people have faith that justice can be obtained through our legal system.[1] A lawyer should promote public confidence in our system and in the legal profession.[2]

EC 9-2 Public confidence in law and lawyers may be eroded by irresponsible or improper conduct of a lawyer. On occasion, ethical conduct of a lawyer may appear to laymen to be unethical. In order to avoid misunderstandings and hence to maintain confidence, a lawyer should fully and promptly inform his client of material developments in the matters being handled for the client. While a lawyer should guard against otherwise proper conduct that has a tendency to diminish public confidence in the legal system or in the legal profession, his duty to clients or to the public should never be subordinate merely because the full discharge of his obligation may be misunderstood or may tend to subject him or the legal profession to criticism. When explicit ethical guidance does not exist, a lawyer should determine his conduct by acting in a manner that promotes public confidence in the integrity and efficiency of the legal system and the legal profession.[3]

EC 9-3 After a lawyer leaves judicial office or other public employment, he should not accept employment in connection with any matter in which he had substantial responsibility prior to his leaving, since to accept employment would give the appearance of impropriety even if none exists.[4]

EC 9-4 Because the very essence of the legal system is to provide procedures by which matters can be presented in an impartial manner so that they may be decided solely upon the merits, any statement or suggestion by a lawyer that he can or would attempt to circumvent those procedures is detrimental to the legal system and tends to undermine public confidence in it.

EC 9-5 Separation of the funds of a client from those of his lawyer not only serves to protect the client but also avoids even the appearance of impropriety, and therefore commingling of such funds should be avoided.

EC 9-6 Every lawyer owes a solemn duty to uphold the integrity and honor of his profession; to encourage respect for the law and for the courts and the judges thereof; to observe the Code of Professional Responsibility; to act as a member of a learned profession, one dedicated to public service; to cooperate with his brother lawyers in supporting the organized bar through the devoting of his time, efforts, and financial support as his professional standing and ability reasonably permit; to conduct himself so as to reflect credit on the legal profession and to inspire the confidence, respect, and trust of his clients and of the public; and to strive to avoid not only professional impropriety but also the appearance of impropriety.[5]

---

[3] *See* ABA Canon 29.

[4] *See* ABA Canon 36.

[5] "As said in Opinion 49 of the Committee on Professional Ethics and Grievances of the American Bar Association, page 134: 'An attorney should not only avoid impropriety but should avoid the appearance of impropriety.'" State ex rel, Nebraska State Bar Ass'n v. Richards, 165 Neb. 80, 93, 84 N.W.2d 136, 145 (1957).

"It would also be preferable that such contribution [to the campaign of a candidate for judicial office] be made to a campaign committee rather than to the candidate personally. In so doing, possible appearances of impropriety would be reduced to a minimum." *ABA Opinion* 226 (1941).

"The lawyer assumes high duties, and has imposed upon him grave responsibilities. He may be the means of much good or much mischief. Interests of vast magnitude are entrusted to him; confidence is reposed in him; life, liberty, character and property should be protected by him. He should guard, with jealous watchfulness, his own reputation, as well as that of his profession." People ex rel. Cutler v. Ford, 54 Ill. 520, 522 (1870), and also quoted in State Board of Law Examiners v. Sheldon, 43 Wyo. 522, 526, 7 P.2d 226, 227 (1932).

See ABA Opinion 150 (1936).

---

[12] *Cf.* ABA Canons 1 and 2.

[1] "Integrity is the very breath of justice. Confidence in our law, our courts, and in the administration of justice is our supreme interest. No practice must be permitted to prevail which invites towards the administration of justice a doubt or distrust of its integrity." Erwin M. Jennings Co. v. DiGenova, 107 Conn. 491, 499, 141 A. 866, 868 (1928).

[2] "A lawyer should never be reluctant or too proud to answer unjustified criticism of his profession, of himself, or of his brother lawyer. He should guard the reputation of his profession and of his brothers as zealously as he guards his own." Rochelle and Payne, *The Struggle for Public Understanding*, 25 Texas B.J. 109, 162 (1962).

CODE OF PROFESSIONAL RESPONSIBILITY

DISCIPLINARY RULES

DR 9-101 Avoiding Even the Appearance of Impropriety.[6]

(A) A lawyer shall not accept private employment in a matter upon the merits of which he has acted in a judicial capacity.[7]

(B) A lawyer shall not accept private employment in a matter in which he had substantial responsibility while he was a public employee.[8]

(C) A lawyer shall not state or imply that he is able to influence improperly or upon irrelevant grounds any tribunal, legislative body,[9] or public official.

---

[6] *Cf.* Code of Professional Responsibility, EC 5–6.

[7] *See ABA* Canon 36.

"It is the duty of the judge to rule on questions of law and evidence in misdemeanor cases and examinations in felony cases. That duty calls for impartial and uninfluenced judgment, regardless of the effect on those immediately involved or others who may, directly or indirectly, be affected. Discharge of that duty might be greatly interfered with if the judge, in another capacity, were permitted to hold himself out to employment by those who are to be, or who may be, brought to trial in felony cases, even though he did not conduct the examination. His private interests as a lawyer in building up his clientele, his duty as such zealously to espouse the cause of his private clients and to defend against charges of crime brought by law-enforcement agencies of which he is a part, might prevent, or even destroy, that unbiased judicial judgment which is so essential in the administration of justice.

"In our opinion, acceptance of a judgeship with the duties of conducting misdemeanor trials, and examinations in felony cases to determine whether those accused should be bound over for trial in a higher court, ethically bars the judge from acting as attorney for the defendants upon such trial, whether they were examined by him or by some other judge. Such a practice would not only diminish public confidence in the administration of justice in both courts, but would produce serious conflict between the private interests of the judge as a lawyer, and of his clients, and his duties as a judge in adjudicating important phases of criminal processes in other cases. The public and private duties would be incompatible. The prestige of the judicial office would be diverted to private benefit, and the judicial office would be demeaned thereby." *ABA Opinion* 242 (1942).

"A lawyer, who has previously occupied a judicial position or acted in a judicial capacity, should refrain from accepting employment in any matter involving the same facts as were involved in any specific question which he acted upon in a judicial capacity and, for the same reasons, should also refrain from accepting any employment which might reasonably appear to involve the same facts." *ABA Opinion* 49 (1931).

See ABA Opinion 110 (1934).

[8] *See ABA Opinions* 135 (1935) and 134 (1935); *cf.* ABA Canon 36 and *ABA Opinions* 39 (1931) and 26 (1930). *But see ABA Opinion* 37 (1931).

[9] "[A statement by a governmental department or agency with regard to a lawyer resigning from its staff that includes a laudation of his legal ability] carries implications, probably not founded in fact, that the lawyer's acquaintance and previous relations with the personnel of the administrative agencies of the government place him in an advantageous position in practicing before such agencies. So to imply would not only represent what prob-

DR 9-102 Preserving Identity of Funds and Property of a Client.[10]

(A) All funds of clients paid to a lawyer or law firm, other than advances for costs and expenses, shall be deposited in one or more identifiable bank accounts maintained in the state in which the law office is situated and no funds belonging to the lawyer or law firm shall be deposited therein except as follows:

    (1) Funds reasonably sufficient to pay bank charges may be deposited therein.

    (2) Funds belonging in part to a client and in part presently or potentially to the lawyer or law firm must be deposited therein, but the portion belonging to the lawyer or law firm may be withdrawn when due unless the right of the lawyer or law firm to receive it is disputed by the client, in which event the disputed portion shall not be withdrawn until the dispute is finally resolved.

(B) A lawyer shall:

    (1) Promptly notify a client of the receipt of his funds, securities, or other properties.

    (2) Identify and label securities and properties of a client promptly upon receipt and place them in a safe deposit box or other place of safekeeping as soon as practicable.

    (3) Maintain complete records of all funds, securities, and other properties of a client coming into the possession of the

---

ably is untrue, but would be highly reprehensible." *ABA Opinion* 184 (1938).

[10] *See* ABA Canon 11.

"Rule 9. . . . A member of the State Bar shall not commingle the money or other property of a client with his own; and he shall promptly report to the client the receipt by him of all money and other property belonging to such client. Unless the client otherwise directs in writing, he shall promptly deposit his client's funds in a bank or trust company . . . in a bank account separate from his own account and clearly designated as 'Clients' Funds Account' or 'Trust Funds Account' or words of similar import. Unless the client otherwise directs in writing, securities of a client in bearer form shall be kept by the attorney in a safe deposit box at a bank or trust company, . . . which safe deposit box shall be clearly designated as 'Clients' Account' or 'Trust Account' or words of similar import, and be separate from the attorney's own safe deposit box." Cal.Business and Professions Code § 6076 (West 1962).

"[C]ommingling is committed when a client's money is intermingled with that of his attorney and its separate identity lost so that it may be used for the attorney's personal expenses or subjected to claims of his creditors. . . . The rule against commingling was adopted to provide against the probability in some cases, the possibility in many cases, and the danger in all cases that such commingling will result in the loss of clients' money." Black v. State Bar, 57 Cal.2d 219, 225–26, 368 P.2d 118, 122, 18 Cal.Rptr. 518, 522 (1962).

lawyer and render appropriate accounts to his client regarding them.

(4) Promptly pay or deliver to the client as requested by a client the funds, securities, or other properties in the possession of the lawyer which the client is entitled to receive.

DEFINITIONS*

As used in the Disciplinary Rules of the Code of Professional Responsibility:

(1) "Differing interests" include every interest that will adversely affect either the judgment or the loyalty of a lawyer to a client, whether it be a conflicting, inconsistent, diverse, or other interest.

---

* "Confidence" and "secret" are defined in DR 4–101(A).

(2) "Law firm" includes a professional legal corporation.

(3) "Person" includes a corporation, an association, a trust, a partnership, and any other organization or legal entity.

(4) "Professional legal corporation" means a corporation, or an association treated as a corporation, authorized by law to practice law for profit.

(5) "State" includes the District of Columbia, Puerto Rico, and other federal territories and possessions.

(6) "Tribunal" includes all courts and all other adjudicatory bodies.

(7) "A bar association representative of the general bar" includes a bar association of specialists as referred to in DR 2–105(A) (1) or (4).

INDEX

TO

CODE OF PROFESSIONAL RESPONSIBILITY

References are to Pages

Change of office, address.

See Advertising, announcement of change of office address.

Change of association.

See Advertising, announcement of change of association.

Change of firm name.

See Advertising, announcement of change of firm name.

Character requirements, 411, 412.

Class action.

See Advice by lawyer to secure legal services, parties to legal action.

Clients.

See also Employment; Adverse effect on professional judgment of lawyer; Fee for legal services; Indigent parties, representation of; Unpopular party, representation of.

appearance as witness for, 434, 435, 438.

attorney-client privilege, 428, 431.

commingling of funds of, 458.

confidence of, 430–432.

counselling, 443, 444, 450.

property, protection of, 458.

restraint of, 448.

secrets of, 430–432.

Co-counsel.

See also Association of counsel.

division of fee with, 426–427.

inability to work with, 428.

Commercial publicity.

See Advertising, commercial publicity.

Commingling of funds, 458.

Communications with one of adverse interests, 451.

judicial officers, 449, 454.

jurors, 448–450, 454.

opposing party, 446, 451.

veniremen, 448, 454.

witnesses, 447, 448, 454.

Compensation for recommendation of employment, prohibition against, 424.

Competence, Mental.

See Instability, mental or emotional; Mental competence of client, effect on representation.

Competence, professional, 420, 440, 441.

Confidences of client, 430–432.

Conflicting interests.

See Adverse effect on professional judgment of lawyer.

Consent of client, requirement of acceptance of employment though interests conflict, 433, 438, 439.

acceptance of value from third person, 418, 439.

advice requested from another lawyer, 431.

aggregate settlement of claims, 439.

association of lawyer, 418, 426.

foregoing legal action, 444.

multiple representation, 436, 439.

revelation of client's confidences and secrets, 431, 432.

use of client's confidences and secrets, 431, 432.

withdrawal from employment, 428.

Consent of tribunal to lawyer's withdrawal, requirement of, 427.

Consultant.

See Advertising, availability as consultant.

Contingent fee, propriety of,

in civil actions, 418, 434, 438.

in criminal actions, 418, 426.

in domestic relation cases, 428.

Continuing legal education programs, 440.

Contract of employment,

fee provisions, desirability of writing, 418.

restrictive covenant in, 427.

Controversy over fee, avoiding, 418.

Copyright practitioner, 417, 425.

Corporation, lawyer employed by, 437, 439.

Corporation, professional legal.

See Professional legal corporation.

Counsel, designation as,

"General Counsel" designation, 422.

"Of Counsel" designation, 422.

Counseling.

See Client, counseling.

Courts.

See also Consent of tribunal to lawyer's withdrawal, requirement of; Evidence, conduct regarding; Trial tactics.

appointment of lawyer as counsel, 419, 420.

courtesy, known customs of, 450, 452.

personal influence, prohibitions against exerting, 449, 454.

representation of client before, 446–452.

Discipline of lawyer, grounds for—C't'd
  violation of disciplinary rule, 412.
  withdrawal, improper, 427–428.
Disclosure of improper conduct,
  of another lawyer, 413.
  of bar applicant, 412.
  of judge, 413.
  toward juror or veniremen, 448, 454.
Discretion of government lawyer, exercise of, 451.
Discussion of pending litigation with news media.
See Trial publicity.
Diverse interests.
See Adverse effect on professional judgment of lawyer.
Division of legal fees,
  consent of client, when required for, 418, 426, 427.
  reasonableness of total fee, requirement of, 418, 426.
  with associated lawyer, 418, 426.
  with estate of deceased lawyer, 430.
  with laymen, 430.
Dual practice, holding out as being engaged in prohibited, 424.

E

Education,
  continuing legal education programs, 440.
  of laymen to recognize legal problems, 415, 455.
  of laymen to select lawyers, 415, 455.
  requirement of bar for applicant, 411.
Elections.
See Political activity.
Emotional instability.
See Instability, mental or emotional.
Employees of lawyer,
  delegation of tasks, 428.
  duty of lawyer to control, 409, 428, 431, 432, 448.
Employment.
See also Advice by lawyer to secure legal services; Recommendation of professional employment.
  acceptance of,
    generally, 420.
    indigent client, on behalf of, 419, 420.
    instances when improper, 415, 420, 425, 427, 431, 433, 434–440, 457, 458.

Employment—Cont'd
  acceptance of—Cont'd
    unpopular cause, on behalf of, 420.
    when unable to render competent service, 420, 440.
  contract of,
    desirability of, 418.
    restrictive covenant in, 427.
  public, retirement from, 457, 458.
  rejection of, 420, 425, 427, 431, 433, 434–440, 457, 458.
  when arbitrator or mediator, 437.
  withdrawal from,
    generally, 431, 437–438, 434–435, 435–436, 437, 438, 439, 444.
    harm to client, avoidance of, 431, 427, 435, 436.
    mandatory withdrawal, 427, 438, 439.
    permissive withdrawal, 427, 428, 438, 444.
    refund of unearned fee paid in advance, requirement of, 421, 427.
    tribunal, consent to, 419, 427.
Estate of deceased lawyer.
See Division of legal fees, with estate of deceased lawyer.
Ethical considerations, purpose and function of, 410.
Evidence, conduct regarding, 447, 450, 452.
Excessive fee.
See, Fee for legal services, amount of, excessive.
Expenses of client, advancing or guaranteeing payment, 434, 438, 439.

F

Fee for legal services,
  adequate fee, need for, 417.
  agreement as to, 418, 426.
  amount of,
    excessive, clearly, 426.
    reasonableness, desirability of, 417.
  collection of,
    avoiding litigation with client, 418.
    client's secrets, use of in collecting or establishing, 432.
    liens, use of, 434, 438.
  contingent fee, 418, 426, 434, 438.
  contract as to, desirability of written, 418.
  controversy over, avoiding, 418.
  determination of, factors to consider,
    ability of lawyer, 417, 418, 426.
    amount involved, 426.
    customary, 426.

Interests of lawyer.
See Adverse effect on professional judgment of lawyer, interests of lawyer.
Interests of other client.
See Adverse effect on professional judgment of lawyer, interests of other clients.
Interests of third person.
See Adverse effect on professional judgment of lawyer, desires of third persons.
Intermediary, prohibition against use of, 437, 438, 439.
Interview,
with opposing party, 446, 451.
with news media, 448, 449, 452–454.
with witness, 447–448, 454.
Investigation expenses, advancing or guaranteeing payment, 434, 438–439.

J

Judges,
false statements concerning, 457.
improper influences on,
gifts to, 449, 454.
private communication with, 449, 454.
misconduct toward,
criticisms of, 456.
disobedience of orders, 446–447, 451.
false statement regarding, 587.
name in partnership name, use of, 417, 423.
retirement from bench, 457, 458.
selection of, 455–456.
Judgment of lawyer.
See Adverse effect on professional judgment of lawyer.
Jury,
arguments before, 447, 450, 452.
investigation of members, 448, 454.
misconduct of, duty to reveal, 448, 454.
questioning members of after their dismissal, 448, 454.

K

Knowledge of intended crime, revealing, 432.

L

Law firm.
See Partnership.
Law lists.
See Advertising, law lists.

Law office.
See Partnership.
Law school, working with legal aid office or public defender office sponsored by, 424, 425.
Lawyer-client privilege.
See Attorney-client privilege.
Lawyer referral services,
fee for listing, propriety of paying, 424.
listing of type referrals accepted, propriety of, 426.
request for referrals, propriety of, 424.
working with, 417, 424.
Laymen.
See also Unauthorized practice of law.
need of legal services, 413, 455.
recognition of legal problems, need to improve, 413, 455.
selection of lawyer, need to facilitate, 415, 417, 435.
Legal aid offices, working with, 419, 424, 425.
Legal corporation.
See Professional legal corporation.
Legal directory.
See Advertising, legal directories.
Legal documents of clients, duty to safeguard, 431, 432.
Legal education programs.
See Continuing legal education programs.
Legal problems, recognition of by laymen, 413–414, 455.
Legal system, duty to improve, 455–457.
Legislature,
improper influence upon, 458.
representation of client before, 445, 455.
serving as member of, 456.
Letterhead.
See Advertising, letterheads.
Liability to client, 410, 441.
Licensing of lawyers,
control of, 429.
modernization of, 429, 455.
Liens, attorneys' 434, 438.
Limited practice, holding out as having, 417, 425, 426.
Litigation,
acquiring an interest in, 434, 438.
expenses of, advancing or guaranteeing payment of, 434, 438–439.
pending, media discussion of, 448–449, 452–454.

Partnership—Cont'd

members licensed in different jurisdictions, 424.

name, 416, 423.

nonexistent, holding out falsely, 416, 424.

non-lawyer, with, 429, 430.

Patent practitioner, 417, 428.

Payment to obtain recommendation or employment, prohibition against, 415, 424.

Pending litigation, discussion of in media, 448–449, 452–454.

Perjury, 443, 447, 450.

Personal interests of lawyer.

See Adverse effect on professional judgment of lawyer, interests of lawyer.

Personal opinion of client's cause, 420.

Phone directory, listing in.

See Advertising, telephone directory.

Political activity, 421, 455, 456.

Political considerations in selection of judges, 455, 456.

Potentially differing interests.

See Adverse effect on professional judgment of lawyer.

Practice of law, unauthorized, 428–430.

Prejudice to right of client, duty to avoid, 421, 427, 446.

Preservation of confidences of client, 430–432.

Preservation of secrets of client, 430–432.

Pressure on lawyer by third person.

See Adverse effect on professional judgment of lawyer.

Privilege, attorney-client.

See Attorney-client privilege.

Procedures, duty to help improve, 455.

Professional card of lawyer.

See Advertising, cards, professional.

Professional impropriety, avoiding appearance of, 434, 457–459.

Professional judgment, duty to protect independence of, 433–440.

Professional legal corporation, 437, 439, 459.

Professional notices.

See Advertising.

Professional status, responsibility not to mislead concerning, 417, 423.

Profit-sharing with lay employees, authorization of, 430.

Property of client, handling, 458–459.

Prosecuting attorney, duty of, 445, 451.

Public defender office, working with, 424, 425.

Public employment, retirement from, 457, 458.

Public office, duty of holder, 455, 456, 457.

Public opinion, irrelevant to acceptance of employment, 420.

Public prosecutor.

See Prosecuting attorney, duty of.

Publication of articles for lay press, 413–414, 415.

Publicity, commercial.

See Advertising, commercial publicity.

Publicity, trial.

See Trial publicity.

Q

Quasi-judicial proceedings, 575.

R

Radio broadcasting.

See Advertising, radio.

Reasonable fee.

See Fee for legal services, amount of.

Rebate, propriety of accepting, 419, 439.

Recognition of legal problems, aiding laymen in, 413–415.

Recommendation of bar applicant, duty of lawyer to satisfy himself that applicant is qualified, 411, 412.

Recommendation of professional employment, 415, 424, 425.

Records of funds, securities, and properties of clients, 458.

Referral service.

See Lawyer referral services.

Refund of unearned fee when withdrawing, duty to give to client, 427.

Regulation of legal profession, 429, 455.

Rehabilitation of bar applicant or lawyer, recognition of, 412.

Representation of multiple clients.

See Adverse effect on professional judgment of lawyer, interest of other clients.

Reputation of lawyer, 415.

Requests for recommendation for employment, 424.

Requirements for bar admission, 411, 412.

Respect for law, 411.

Restricted covenants, propriety of, 427.

Restrictive covenant, 427.

Retention of employment.

See Employment.

Retirement.

Violation of disciplinary rule as cause for discipline, 412.

Violation of law as cause for discipline, 412, 450.

Voluntary gifts by client to lawyer, 434.

Volunteered advice to secure legal services.

See Advice by lawyer to secure legal services.

W

Waiver of position of client, 450.

Will of client gift to lawyer in, 434.

Withdrawal.

See Employment, withdrawal from.

Witness,

communications with, 447, 448, 454.

false testimony by, 447.

lawyer acting as, 434, 435, 438.

member of lawyer's firm acting as, 438.

payment to, 448, 454.

Writing for lay publication, avoiding appearance of giving general solution, 415.

Z

Zeal,

general duty of, 441–444, 450.

limitations upon, 441, 442, 446–454.

*

TABLE OF CASES

References are to Pages

References are to Pages

END OF VOLUME